COMMONWEALTH THEOLOGY ESSENTIALS

"God, in His sovereignty, has chosen these four authors to be pioneers and forerunners to bring the *Commonwealth Theology* to the proper degree of understanding the Church needs today. This is about the United and Holy Congregation of the Living God."

—Gian Luca Morotti, *Chairman of the Board Ebenezer Operation Exodus Israel*

"In history, there are important movements and beliefs that change the course of history. This book captures the essence of an awakening that is occurring around the globe. Followers of Yeshua, that is Jesus, are seeing that their identity—as full members of the House of Israel—has been hidden from them. This veil is falling away and Commonwealth Theology both captures what is occurring and is enlightening to seeing the truth. This book will open your eyes to the truth in Scripture as you've never seen it before."

—Spencer G. Bolduc, *Host of Sound the Shofar: The Quest for Biblical Truth*

"One of the most confused things is the changing vision of the Church. Why is it here? What is its main purpose? What should it look like? What should it do?

The Early Church evolved from a rag-tag group of believers meeting in homes but quickly transitioned into buildings and organized clergy. In the beginning, the Jewish founders began to fall into ill repute until the organized church viewed them as the 'Christ killing' enemy. Jews and Christians struggled with the 'family feud' of Romans 11. The full-blown Roman Catholic Church was a worldwide organization that had no room for Jews as a whole.

Along comes the Reformation; and, the Catholic Church shattered into many pieces. As each new church or ministry began, they usually developed their own theology and vision for the Church. Each new spin-off led to another division: doctrinal position, organization of the clergy and laity, the role of gifts, prophecy, etc. Dispensationalists and 'kingdom now' covenant theologians argued vehemently over Israel and its role, if any.

The simple give-and-take of the saints, meeting around the Lord in a unity of love and the Spirit, was largely forgotten. Each church or ministry developed into a crystallized organization that mainly operated within its own confines—little fiefdoms that each pastor jealously guarded. There was little vision for the Church's mission and testimony, and no interest in prophecy. Today, most Christians cling to the theology they were taught. There is no unifying vision that all of those who are bought with the blood of the Lamb can gather around. No unifying vision or theology! That is, until *Commonwealth Theology*, which gives Christians a way to go on together without renouncing the things they hold dear.

This point of view also recognizes that we are in the 'last days' and Israel is the 'canary in the coal mine.' History is almost 'a wrap' and life for Christians will deteriorate before the Lord's return. The call is for the saints and Israel to stand together as a testimony of Christ here on the earth no matter how dangerous or unpopular."

—Dene McGriff. *Dene is a retired International HMO Executive (HMO - Health Maintenance Organization) - having organized numerous HMOs for various nations.*

COMMONWEALTH THEOLOGY ESSENTIALS

BY
DOUGLAS KRIEGER
DR. DOUGLAS HAMP
DR. GAVIN FINLEY
CHRIS STEINLE

2020

Commonwealth Theology Essentials
By Douglas Krieger; Dr. Douglas Hamp; Dr. Gavin Finley; Chris Steinle

Copyright © 2020 by Commonwealth of Israel Foundation
Phoenix, AZ, USA

All rights reserved. This book or parts thereof may not be reproduced in any form, stored in any retrieval system, or transmitted in any form by any means—electronic, mechanical, photocopy, recording, or otherwise—without prior written permission of the publisher, except for the use of brief quotations in a book review or scholarly journal or as provided by United States of America copyright law. For permission requests, write to the publisher at the address, or email address, below.

ISBN: 979-8-65-292851-3

Unless otherwise noted, Scripture quotations in this book are taken from the New King James Version. Copyright 1982 by Thomas Nelson, Inc. Used by permission. All rights reserved.

Cover modified base images: Menorah Mosaic, Kehillat Israel, Pacific Palisades, CA © Joy Krauthammer 2013; Parchment background courtesy, myfreetextures.com

Ordering Information:
Special discounts are available on quantity purchases by corporations, associations, educators, and others. Contact the publisher or distributor for details.

info@commonwealthofisrael.org

Commonwealth of Israel Foundation
P.O. Box 31007
Phoenix, AZ 85046

U.S. trade bookstores and wholesalers: Please contact the distributor.

DEDICATION

This book is humbly dedicated to Bible researchers, interpreters, and theologians throughout history who have honored the veracity of Scriptures over the systems of men. Humility is indeed the lesson learned from the legacy of those who have heralded great truths; yet, have in many ways stumbled (James 3:2). Theodore of Mopsuestia, "The Interpreter" of the School of Antioch pressed for literal exegesis against the allegorical method of his contemporary, Augustine. Theodore argued, at great peril, against calling Mary, "Mother of God"—who, he suggested, should be called, "Mother of Christ." Nevertheless, Theodore inclined toward a Nestorian Christology.

Wycliffe, Zwingli, Calvin and other Reformers cared to exalt the infallibility of God's word, but were distracted by politics and the Historical view of Eschatology—Calvin tending toward the figurative expression of Augustine. Luther—also distracted with Church and State—did indeed bring needed reform; but clinging to a "Roman" contempt for the Jews, uttered criminally bilious reproaches against God's "people whom He foreknew" (Rom. 11:2).

John Darby formalized the dispensational system; based on a more literal interpretation of Scripture; which acknowledged that God had not—forever—cast away His people-of-old. Darby's theology fueled the Christian Zionist Movement of the 19th century and opened the door to better relations between Christians and Jews. In these regards, Darby accomplished much good. This volume will not scrutinize Darby's life or his "Brethren" organization. There are, however, issues with his method of "rightly dividing" the Word.

All of these Bible scholars—and far more unmentioned—were determined that God's Word is true. They have been used by God to disseminate aspects of truth—truths in part.

Gratefully recognizing these pioneers, the authors acknowledge they stand on well-charted ground in man's saga of understanding biblical doctrine as intended by God. Yet, with history in view and being but dust (Ps. 103:14), we do cautiously observe that no one gets it all right.

"Blessed are the peacemakers,

For they shall be called sons of God."

– Matthew 5:9

CONTENTS

Dedication VII
Foreword XV
Apologue XXI
Preface XXV
Introduction 1
    Why Study the Commonwealth of Israel? 1
    Better Theology—Not a Different Gospel 5
    Coming to Terms with Israel and the Church 13
    Defining Jews, Israel, and the House of Israel 14
    Defining the Church 17
    He Loves Israel, He Loves Israel Not 19

PART I: ELEMENTS OF COMMONWEALTH THEOLOGY 23

1. Yes Distinction—No Separation 25
    Replacement Theology 25
    Dispensation Theology 27
    Commonwealth Theology 32

2. Theological Eccentricities 37
    Who Are the Heirs of New Covenant? 37
    Aberrant Theologies 41
    Mysteries NOT Revealed to the Prophets 43
    Prior Two-House Theologies 51

3. The Missing Peace 57
    The Obstacle to Peace 58
    Peace and Unity in the Church 61
    Not Only of the Jew 69

Table of Contents

4. Where is the House of Israel? 73
    Ephraim Divorced and Scattered 73
    Who Swallowed Ephraim—Judah or the Nations?... 75
    Israel Among the Nations 83
    Jezreel—Sown Among the Nations 85

5. The Jerusalem Council 89
    A People for His Name 89
    David's Fallen Tent 91
    Obed Edom and the Rest of Mankind 92
    The Troublesome Yoke 99
    The House of David 102
    Breaking of the Brotherhood—The Two Staffs 103

6. Israel Split in two—The Breach of Jeroboam 109
    The Sin of King Solomon 109
    The Historic Event that Triggered the Breach 114
    The Aftermath of the Breach of Jeroboam............ 121
    The lost House of Israel Will Be Found................. 123
    The Eventual Restoration and Repair..................... 127

7. Blinded in Part 131
    Are Unbelieving Jews Excluded? 131
    The Thin Line in Excluding Today's Jews................ 133
    Messianic Believers 136

8. Segregating the Jews and Their God 137
    The Legacy of Marcion's Heresy 137
    The Ghost of Marcion 142
    Marcionite Christianity 145
    Two Ages, Two Gods 149
    Haunted Theology.. 153

Table of Contents

- AWAY WITH THE LAW 157
- HOW TO UN-HAUNT YOUR THEOLOGY 163

9. THE DUAL OFFICES OF MELCHIZEDEK 167
   - THE INNOCENCE BEFORE THE FALL 167
   - GOD'S DUAL REMEDY FOR SIN EMERGES 172
   - THE TWO-FOLD UNCONDITIONAL COVENANT 175
   - THE TWO OLIVE TREES 178
   - THE TWO STICKS OF JUDAH AND JOSEPH 195
   - THE GREAT END-TIME JEWISH REVIVAL 197

10. FALSE JUXTAPOSITION OF LAW AND GRACE 205
    - THE OTHER MAN'S CONSCIENCE 206
    - WAS THE LAW NAILED TO THE CROSS? 207

11. LAW-ABIDING GRACE 213
    - GOD'S MODEL OF AUTHORITY / SUBMISSION 213
    - RECONCILING LAW AND GRACE 222

12. THE DESTINY OF THE TWO HOUSES 245
    - THE MYSTERY OF CO-INHERITANCE 245
    - THE "ISRAEL OF GOD" AND THE "ONE NEW MAN" 246
    - THE YET FUTURE UNITED KINGDOM OF DAVID 260

13. THERE'S LITERALLY ONE NEW COVENANT 263
    - THE NEW COVENANT 263
    - COVENANTALISM 265
    - DISPENSATIONALISM 268
    - WHY ARE THESE TWO SYSTEMS DEFICIENT? 272
    - KEEPING THE NEW COVENANT IN CONTEXT 273

Table of Contents

14. THE KINGDOM OF GOD 279
    A FRESH LOOK AT THE KINGDOM OF GOD 284
    THE KINGDOM OF GOD IN JOHN'S GOSPEL 297
    THE CONCLUSION OF THE MATTER 304
15. THE DIVINE REMARRIAGE AND THE NEW COVENANT 311
    THE FIRST MARRIAGE CONTRACT 315
    A NEW MARRIAGE CONTRACT 320
    THE FULLNESS OF THE GENTILES 324
16. LIFE FROM THE DEAD 331
    WHOSE WIFE IN THE RESURRECTION? 331
    ALL ARE ALIVE TO HIM 337
    WASHED BY THE WORD 339
    LOOKING BACK TO ISRAEL'S ACCEPTANCE 344
    NOT FOR YOUR SAKE, O HOUSE OF ISRAEL 348
    FELLOW HEIRS 350

PART II: COMMONWEALTH ESCHATOLOGY 353

17. RESOLVING UNFULFILLED MESSIANIC PROPHECIES 355
    THE PROBLEM OF UNFULFILLED PROPHECY 355
    NAVIGATING THE PROPHECY GAP 361
    RECKONED AND REALIZED 362
    ALL THINGS RECONCILED 368
    SETTING THE STAGE FOR THE COMMONWEALTH 372
    FISHERS OF MEN 380
18. REVELATION: THE THEMATIC VIEW 385
19. THE FUTURE 70TH WEEK 397
    THE FUTURE 70TH WEEK AND FINAL 7 YEARS 397
    MEASURING THE DAY-COUNT OF THE 70 WEEKS 400

Table of Contents

    REFUTING THE EZRA TO BAPTISM OF JESUS TIMELINE 403
    A TRIBUTE TO THE WORK OF SIR ROBERT ANDERSON 404
    THE 70 WEEKS PROPHECY AND MISSING JUBILEE YEARS 406
    THE EDICT INITIATING THE 70 WEEKS PROPHECY 409
20. SHARING IN JACOB'S TROUBLE 415
21. THE CHANGE CALLED THE RAPTURE 431
    THE SECOND COMING RAPTURE 437
    TRANSLATING THE RAPTURE VERSE 441
    WHERE DO WE GO FROM HERE? 454
22. THE DAY OF THE SECOND COMING 457
EPILOGUE 483
APPENDIX **485**
    THE DENVER DECLARATION 485
    ABOUT THE AUTHORS 507
    ABOUT THE COMMONWEALTH OF ISRAEL FOUNDATION 511

FOREWORD
By Dr. Michael K. Lake

The LORD is a man of war: the LORD is his name.
Exodus 15:3 (KJV)

Writing a foreword for **Commonwealth Theology Essentials** using Exodus 15:3 may seem strange to many. Hopefully, by the end of this foreword, you will understand the premise that I have set forth. The commonwealth that we have been grafted into by the completed work of Messiah is not a democracy. It is not a republic. The commonwealth is a kingdom. The word **kingdom** has its origin as a shortened version of two words: king's domain. Our King, our Savior, and our Lord is a man of war.

The Almighty can bring terrifying and unstoppable power to the theater of the cosmic conflict revealed in the Word of God. Many theologians believe the asteroid belt on the other side of Mars was originally a planet that was shattered by the Creator in an ancient conflict with fallen angels (or immortals). Reference to this planet is found in several places within the Word of God.

Thou hast broken Rahab in pieces, as one that is slain; thou hast scattered thine enemies with thy strong arm.
Psalm 89:10 (KJV)

Awake, awake, put on strength, O arm of the LORD; awake, as in the ancient days, in the generations of old. Art thou not it that hath cut Rahab, and wounded the dragon?
Isaiah 51:9 (KJV)

Yet, bringing unprecedented power to a conflict is not all that is required of a man of war. A true warrior uses strategy as his primary weapon, rather than just mere might. In other words, God will use His omniscience to guide His omnipotence. In this cosmic battle, the strategic nature of the Creator is intertwined with every promise throughout the Word of God. Even more to the point, there is a divine strategy in every sovereign move of God within the history of humanity.

Once the student of the Word becomes cognizant of the strategic influence of the Almighty within the annals of history, there are phrases within the Bible that spring forth with greater importance. Here are a few examples:

But when the fulness of the time was come, *God sent forth his Son, made of a woman, made under the law,*
Galatians 4:4 (KJV) (Emphasis added)

But in the fourth generation they shall come hither again: ***for the iniquity of the Amorites is not yet full.***
Genesis 15:16 (KJV) (Emphasis added)

The timing of the incarnation, crucifixion, and resurrection of Messiah was strategically placed within the timeline of humanity to achieve a death blow to the machinations of the kingdom of darkness. Even the coming conflict with the legacy of the Amorites (Babylon) has been carefully planned and hidden in the Scroll of Destiny found in Rev. 5.

Within the current move of Almighty God, there is a plan for the body of Christ to awaken to the Hebraic nature of the Kingdom and learn their place in the Commonwealth of Israel. This is no accident. This awakening is paramount for the Remnant fulfilling their role in the Kingdom of God as end-time prophecy unfolds before us.

In this process of rediscovering the continuity of God's Word to all who believe in Messiah, we must have the strength to question everything. The apostle Paul admonishes us to:

Prove all things; hold fast that which is good.
1 Thessalonians 5:21 (KJV)

The Greek word that Paul uses for ***prove*** is ***dokimazo*** {dok-im-ad'-zo}, which means *"to test, examine, prove, and scrutinize."* [1] This ancient Greek word's grammatical tense is in the imperative. Here is a basic definition of imperative in Greek grammar.

---

[1] Strongs #G1381. Strong's Enhanced Lexicon. BibleWorks for Windows 10.0. BibleWorks, LLC, Norfolk, VA. Copyright © 2015.

Imperative—The mood that normally expresses a command, intention, exhortation, or polite request. The imperative mood is therefore not an expression of reality but possibility and volition.[2]

Within the context of 1 Thess. 5:21, Paul was issuing a strong exhortation (or even a command) to the Gentile church to be faithful Bereans that diligently studied Holy Writ to ensure what they were taught was scriptural. Even in the time of the apostle Paul, the priesthood of darkness (through the Gnostics) was already laboring to disenfranchise the Gentiles within the body of Christ from the Hebraic foundation of the commonwealth and to replace it with concepts drawn from the Mystery Religions. Our current rediscovery of the Hebraic nature of the gospel and the proper role of the commandments of God within the life of the believer are essential for coming out of Mystery Babylon and learning to properly function within the Kingdom of God.

In our day, the denizens of the Second Heaven labor tirelessly to both discredit the Word of God and to blend mysticism into every aspect of Christianity. However, the Spirit of God is moving on the hearts of the Remnant to return to a pure faith . . . to return to biblicity. Like never before, the command of the apostle Paul to prove all things is paramount in the life of any serious believer.

Dr. John Garr is a noted biblical researcher and prolific author. In his book, ***Family Worship***, Dr. Garr provides a stern warning:

> Texts without contexts have become pretexts for proof texts! The grammar of the Scriptures (the Hebrew language of the first testament and the Hebrew thought underlying the Greek language of the second testament) has been largely minimized if not downright ignored. Likewise, the history and culture of the people through whom and to whom the sacred texts were committed have been virtually ignored. Entire theologies have been based upon a "criterion of dissimilarity" in which texts in the Apostolic Scriptures that have clear connections with the Hebrew Scriptures have

---

[2] Michael S. Heiser and Vincent M. Setterholm, Glossary of Morpho-Syntactic Database Terminology (Lexham Press, 2013; 2013).

been dismissed by some scholars as not being the authentic words of Jesus and the apostles but the work of subsequent redactors. It is as though Jesus had to have been born and lived in a vacuum and never influenced by his native language and culture. The very idea has given rise to a Christianity that has been wrenched from its theological and historical moorings and set adrift in a maelstrom of nonbiblical—in far too many cases, anti-biblical—traditions, including postmodernism, consequentialism, secular humanism, and even demonic perversion. [3]

Then, Dr. Garr admonishes us to grasp the importance of the task that is before us.

In order for true biblical order to be restored, a return to the "biblically Hebraic" must take place. This will require much focus and determination, for the Greco-Roman worldview and mindset have been forced upon the Scriptures for so many centuries that in many cases the Scriptures themselves have become almost unrecognizable in popular "interpretations." In other words, "back to the Bible" means back to Hebraic thought and practice. This is especially true in the important arena of human relationships. God's perspectives on family and the home can never be understood without a renewal of the Hebraic truths which God himself established as the foundation for this core element of human existence. [4]

In the pages of this book, my esteemed colleagues dare to question doctrines and paradigms that have entangled themselves with our theologies over the millennia. Even more important than to merely question, they have labored to present a biblically balanced and scholarly examination of the commonwealth and our place within it. I cannot express how fundamentally crucial this work is for the preparation of the people of God for the prophetic conflict that is before us.

---

[3] Garr, John D. Family Worship: Making Your Home a House of God. Golden Key Press. Kindle Edition.
[4] Ibid.

Foreword

It is time for our vision to be clear, our theologies true, and our devotion singularly focused on our King and His Kingdom.

Michael K. Lake, Th.D.
Author of ***The Shinar Directive***, ***The Sheeriyth Imperative***, and ***The Kingdom Priesthood***.

Dr. Michael K. Lake holds doctorates in theology and religious education, and he is the chancellor and founder of Biblical Life College and Seminary.

APOLOGUE
BY GWEN STEINLE

"Dreadful people" Matilda commented, "and that's all you need know." "But why?" asked Archibald. "What makes them dreadful? What have they done?" "I can't say, exactly, but it has been this way for a very long time. Now off with you! I haven't time for such inane questions."

Archibald went away sullen. He had received a similar response from his father. "Perhaps grandfather! He knows so many stories. Surely he knows something of our heritage." The young man's face brightened as he took off for the livery stable to saddle his horse.

"Archibald! What a pleasant surprise!" exclaimed the distinguished elderly gentleman when the butler announced him. "Come in lad! You've come a fair distance. You've arrived just in time for afternoon tea." The kind man settled down in an elaborately carved wing back chair after he seated his guest. "Do try the tea cakes! Delectable!" Archibald prepared his tea with his usual two lumps of sugar as his grandfather asked the reason for his visit.

"Grandfather, I've gotten to know a family in the due course of my business. I've found them to be respectable, intelligent and kind…" "Might this 'family' include a certain lass in whom you might show a particular interest?" asked the gentleman with a twinkle in his eye. Even though little light could stream through the part in the thick velvet curtains, one could still see the unwanted, but nevertheless quite rosy, blush that sprang into Archibald's face. "Per chance, might there be a forthcoming wedding lad?" Archibald cleared his throat of the tea cake he had nearly choked on. "The reason for my visit, sir, is to inquire about a certain mystery that despite my best endeavors I cannot seem to solve. I am hoping you might be able to shed some light on the matter." "Well, now I am intrigued. How I love a good mystery! Do go on."

"It seems there is a great deal of animosity between our family and another family, but no one seems to be able to explain how it happened to arise or why it has been perpetuated through generations. They can speak no good word about our family and we can speak no good word about theirs. If I may speak frankly, sir, must it go on in perpetuity? And if it be so, for what reason?" "So you've fallen in love with a lass from the 'other family'." Archibald knew his grandfather to be an astute man, and he was reticent to reveal this information to him, but his love compelled him to search for answers.

"Herein lies a great dilemma lad; for your inquiry reveals there is more at stake than simple curiosity. I must confess that in truth I should have attempted a resolution to the matter, but have not. I, too, searched for answers to this mystery and quite a search it was. I carefully examined copious amounts of information in books, records and papers. What drudgery! And, naturally, family members gave me no assistance as they were perfectly happy with the status quo. When I had almost surrendered to impulses to throw my hands up in despair, my patience and persistence was rewarded."

Archibald's grandfather paused to light an imported cigar. As he watched the puffs of smoke slowly drift upward, Archibald suddenly realized that his dreams might similarly vaporize into thin air. Uncomfortable, he shifted in his chair as he awaited his grandfather's next words with the anticipation of one awaiting the warm, cheery shafts of sunlight after a cold, sleepless night.

"Long ago a will was written by an extremely wealthy gentleman. The beneficiaries of the vast estate were unfortunately two different groups of people who did not share the same ideologies. The wealthy gentleman realized the difficulties of combining the two groups into one estate, even though it meant the great blessing of his inheritance for both, so he left instructions with the will and even provided someone to help them understand the instructions and bring the two parties together."

"This is where the mystery deepened. An unsavory fellow coveted the wealth of the gentleman, and very much desired to usurp his authority. He concocted a dastardly plan to thwart the wishes of the wealthy gentleman and keep the two groups apart from one another so all the power of running the vast estate would be his alone. He began to spread half-truths and outright falsehoods in an all-out campaign to malign each group in the eyes of the other.

He was patient, soooo patient. He kept this up for years; successfully thwarting the best efforts of the one assigned the responsibility of bringing them together."

"To this very day, the two have not become one, even though they would inherit great riches by doing so. Indeed, unbeknownst to most of them, all that remains is the misunderstanding, and I must shamefully say, even hatred, between the two groups. As time marches on, the ideologies of each group become even more ingrained in their psyche and the more resistant they are to joining together as one group. They fear a loss of who they are and the power they have, instead of focusing on the astounding blessings to be had if the instructions to join together were followed."

Archibald sat for a few moments in stunned silence contemplating the magnitude of what this all meant. "But why, grandfather, if all this began with our forefathers and was blindly followed by generations since that time, couldn't we, with full knowledge of the truth, put an end to all the animosity and come together as one; sharing equally between us the promised wealth?" "You are a wise lad, Archibald. Why indeed? Will you be the one to champion this cause and share the good news?"

PREFACE

Enmity between the Jews and the Gentiles—the "Nations"—was never part of God's plan. *"Indeed He says, 'It is too small a thing that You should be My Servant to raise up the tribes of Jacob, and to restore the preserved ones of Israel; I will also give You as a light to the Gentiles, that You should be My salvation to the ends of the earth'"* (Isaiah 49:6).

On the part of the Jews: First-century Jews perceived that being chosen as God's special people established their exclusive right to God's promises. Even the Apostles were, at first, shortsighted and reticent to participate in the inclusion of the Gentiles. It took an angelic intervention and the judgment of the Jerusalem elders before the Church opened its assembly to non-Jews (see Acts 11).

On the part of the Gentiles: Most first-century Gentile believers belonged geographically, ergo politically, to the Roman Empire. Bound up in the patriotic spirit of the day was the attitude that the Jewish people were contrary and contentious. This anti-Jewish bias was reinforced and formalized as a result of the first and second "Jewish revolts."

This anti-Semitic Roman patriotism influenced the theology of the Early Church Fathers; especially in the Latin Church where Gnosticism had migrated from North Africa and infiltrated the Church. Eastern Dualism underpinned the notion that God's people consisted of two camps: The spiritual Church, and the earthly Jews. Neo-Platonists like Marcion of Sinope rejected the Old Testament, the "Jewish Gospels," and even the Creator God of the Old Testament.

Christianity remained headquartered in the capitals of the East and West Roman Empires for 1,000 years, establishing a voluminous body of anti-Semitic comments by the "Church Fathers." By the time of the Reformation, theologians presumed that the longstanding separation of the Church from the Jews found its basis in the Scriptures. Dispensational Theology, although kinder in spirit toward the Jews, separated the Church from the Jews by hypothesizing a variety of partitions of time, space, and divine relationships.

How could mainline theologians have missed the correct understanding of the relationship between Christians and Jews? And, for nearly 2,000 years! This proposition doesn't seem likely—or even possible. But the current state of world politics provides an ideal backdrop to explain how doctrines regarding the Judeo-Christian interrelationship shifted during the second century.

Reflect for a moment on the impassioned opposition between the left and right political parties of twenty-first century America. How much room for true objectivity is there in the hearts and minds of multi-generational Republicans or Democrats? It would seem based on the news broadcast from networks—which are as divergent as their respective audiences—there is little objectivity indeed. Now place yourself in the Roman Empire of the second century. Remember, the Roman Empire didn't consist merely of the West, controlled by the western capital at Rome; but also of the eastern regions, ruled from Constantinople. Practically everywhere the Early Church spread—apart from Thomas' mission to India—was part of the Roman Empire; which by the way, officially included Judea.

Consider further that most of the areas belonging to the Roman Empire were no longer in rebellion, but were settled in and enjoying the peace—Pax Romana. Whether you were a Jew or a Christian or both; or, a slave or a Roman citizen; in any case you were a Roman. Now take that "Proud to be an American" (or transfer that zeal to whatever country the reader calls their homeland) and add to that the zeal of political passion. Then project that emotion-driven attitude into New Testament times. From the time the Jews asked for Rome's involvement, Israel's civil strife—including the added tension between the Maccabees[5] and factions opposed to Rome's presence—Rome found defending the Jews to be a futile endeavor. Now, aside from the fact that the World will always persecute God's people, Israel's bloody internal wars over rulership; between the Sadducees and Pharisees, between the Zealots and the Peace Movement, etc., made Israel impossible to partner with.[6]

---

[5] see: 1 Maccabees 8:17-20 and https://en.wikipedia.org/wiki/Roman-Jewish_Treaty

[6] Source: *A History of the Jewish People in the Time of Christ* by Emil Schurer, Hendrickson, 2009; First Div., Vol. 2; Second Div., Vol. 2.

PREFACE

By the time of Christ, Rome had "had it up to here" with the Jews; which is clearly reflected by the tensions documented in the New Testament. Then, add to this tinderbox two successive Jewish revolts against Rome. As the second century began, the Jews were driven out of the Land. The country of Judea was now officially an "enemy of the state." Second-Temple era Israel was held in contempt; and, being Jewish in the Roman Empire was like being German or Japanese at the end of WWII. Awkward!

The second century was the time when Church Fathers began to speak of the Jews in a derogatory light. And, such mudslinging against the Jews seemed to the Christian Romans to be quite politically correct. Shortly after this time was when Origin began to spiritualize the prophecies about the future restoration of Israel; not as a gathering to the Land, but every other kind of figurative gathering of "saints," on earth or in the heavens. The "world-rulers" (Eph. 6:12) played no small part in empowering Rome and belittling Judea. According to church historian Philip Schaff, the old Roman nobility never lost their vision of Rome as the center for earthly rule; and weren't the least interested in that center moving to Jerusalem at ANY time in the future. "The political pre-eminence of that metropolis of the world . . . was destined to rule the European races with the sceptre of the cross, as she had formerly ruled them with the sword."[7]

Thus, the first contortions of Eschatology were committed rather shortly after the time of Jesus and the Apostles. Unfortunately, other than condemning Rome, the Reformer's theology didn't fall far from the tree. That is, in a nutshell, why mainline theologies—Catholic/Orthodox, Reformed, and Evangelical—must be realigned with Old Testament Scripture and with the doctrine of the Apostles found in New Testament: Not with the doctrines of the "Early" Church Fathers, no matter how close to the second century these doctrines were formed.

One of the most convincing features of Commonwealth Theology's (CT's) eschatology is its ability to provide a clearer interpretation of more prophetic verses than today's popular theologies.

---

[7] *History of the Christian Church*, Philip Schaff, Hendrickson Publishers, 2011, Vol. 2, p. 156

Catholic/Orthodox theologies tend to spiritualize many passages that should be interpreted literally—admittedly, there are some legitimately figurative passages. Very often, however, when verses are taken literally by the Supersessionists, the meanings are expropriated from the Twelve Tribes to the Gentile Church. Dispensational Theology, although interpreting verses more literally than the Supersessionists, insists on parsing passages—even midstream—and distributing the segments to the "correct" dispensational "age." CT, on the other hand, is able to interpret the Bible just as it is written.[8]

Why is this incredibly substantial truth of Commonwealth Theology just now breaking upon both Jew and Christian?[9] If it were so vitally important, wouldn't we have seen it long before this time? That inquiry in and of itself validates the prophetic consummation of the age—we're "seeing it now" because on an eschatological plane it was prophesied to take place in the "latter days and years" (Jer. 30:3, 24—spoken to both Israel and Judah; Ezek. 38:8) . . . "In the latter days you will consider it" (Jer. 30:24). Indeed: *"Is Ephraim My dear son? Is he a pleasant child? For though I spoke against him, I earnestly remember him still, therefore My heart yearns for him; I will surely have mercy on him, says the LORD . . . and that He might make known the riches of His glory on the vessels of mercy; which He had prepared beforehand for glory, even us whom He called, not of the Jews only, but also of the Nations?"* As He says also in Hosea: *"I will call them My people, who were not My people; and her beloved, who was not beloved and it shall come to pass in the place where it was said to them, 'You are not My people,' There they shall be called sons of the living God"* (Jer. 31:20; Romans 9:23-26; Hosea 2:23; 1:10).

---

[8] *Why Most Christians Believe in a Post-Tribulation Rapture: 2nd Edition*, Steinle, Memorial Crown Press, 2020, pp. 145-147

[9] *Commonwealth Theology*, by Douglas Krieger, Tribnet Publications, 2018, p. 98

Preface

Yet, today, we of Ephraim—we who were no longer a people, but now are the people of God—have come from the four corners of the earth to provoke Judah to jealousy whereby the Spirit of God's breath will breathe life into these VERY dry bones . . . and they too shall come to life! Joseph, who is the Stick of Ephraim, is making his move upon Judah. Joseph can no longer contain himself—so great is his emotion toward his brethren according to the flesh for God will *"pour on the house of David and on the inhabitants of Jerusalem the Spirit of grace and supplication; then they will look on Me, the pierced one. Yes, they will mourn for Him as one mourns for his only son, and grieve for Him as one grieves for a firstborn"* (Zechariah 12:10).[10]

---

[10] Ibid, p. 357

INTRODUCTION

WHY STUDY THE COMMONWEALTH OF ISRAEL?

The authors, along with a growing Commonwealth of Israel community, believe they have rediscovered a vital aspect of Biblical Theology. An aspect of the gospel that is crucial in establishing peace between the Jews and the Nations. Paul's narrative on the "Commonwealth of Israel" (Ephesians 2:12), attributes peace between the Jews and "you Gentiles" through the blood and the cross of Christ. In contrast to the "peace with God," that is associated with individual salvation throughout the New Testament, this peace is peace between two ethnic groups. Individual peace AND this "national" peace were both accomplished through the cross! And, not only national peace, but union: that God *"might create in Himself one new man from the two, thus making peace."*

The parties of this union, however, are not the entities one would anticipate after reading the Old Testament. There it was prophesied that the Jews (House of Judah) and the House of Israel would be gathered and united. Moreover, they were the expressly intended parties to the New Covenant: *"I will make a new covenant with the **house of Israel** and with the **house of Judah**"* (Jer. 31:31). Hosea prophesied: *"The **children of Judah** and the **children of Israel** shall be gathered together, and appoint for themselves one head"* (Hos. 1:11). Ezekiel reiterated this prophecy: *"Thus says the Lord God: 'Surely I will take the **stick of Joseph...Ephraim*** [aka "House of Israel"]*...and I will join them ... with the **stick of Judah**, and make them one stick, and they will be one in My hand'... 'And one king shall be king over them all; they shall no longer be two nations, nor shall they ever be divided into two kingdoms again'"* (Excerpts from Ezekiel 37).

So how is it that, instead of the House of Israel, "you Gentiles" (*ethnōn*, "Nations") have been united with the Jews? And: What happened to the House of Israel, (aka Ephraim, Jezreel, Samaria—the Northern Ten Tribes/Israel)? Some have attempted to satisfy these questions by presuming the two houses of Israel had already united prior to the time of the New Testament. But consider the extent of the House of Israel's punishment. According to Isaiah's prophecy of the virgin birth of Immanuel, Ephraim would be shattered and "not a people" within 65 years after the prophecy was written (Isa. 7:8). Consider also the extent of the Northern Kingdom's banishment among the nations (Hos. 8:7-9). The ancient House of Israel was deported, scattered, mixed with the nations; and (as will be thoroughly demonstrated), by that name, has never to this day reassembled as a whole.

Paul, in fact, did not disavow the House of Israel by interchanging its identity with the believing Gentiles. Twice, within the Ephesians Two passage, Paul refers to the members of the Commonwealth as those "near" and those "far off." *"But now in Christ Jesus you* [Gentiles] *who once were far off have been brought near by the blood of Christ"* (v13). *"And He came and preached peace to you* [Gentiles] *who were afar off and to those who were near"* (v17). It would appear that Paul had gone out of his way to identify those near and far by incorporating the associations established in Daniel 9:7: *"To the men of Judah, to the inhabitants of Jerusalem and all Israel, those near and those far off in all the countries to which You* [God] *have driven them."* Herein, "near" refers to Judah and its capital, and "far" refers to all Israel dwelling among the other countries—among the nations.

Why would Paul draw this association between the "believers among the nations" (Gentiles) and the House of Israel dispersed among the nations? Obviously, they were both "among the nations." But before exploring this interrelationship further, consider the magnitude of what has been presented thus far:

1. Prophecies of gathering and uniting the two houses of Israel could never have been fulfilled unless the "Lost" House of Israel, which once was "not a people," could somehow once more become "a people";
2. Ephesians Chapter Two introduces a peace and unity between two specific ethnicities, one of these being the anticipated House of Judah (the Jews);
3. This national peace and unity—just as individual salvation—depended on Christ's atoning sacrifice.

INTRODUCTION

The concurrence between the restoration of the Commonwealth and the mission of Messiah was predicted in Isaiah's Light to Gentiles prophecy (Isa. 49:6):

Indeed He says,
"It is too small a thing that You should be My Servant
To raise up the tribes of Jacob,
And to restore the preserved ones of Israel;
I will also give You as a light to the Gentiles,
That You should be My salvation to the ends of the earth."

This synchrony between the restoration of the Lost House of Israel and the "inclusion" of the Nations (Gentiles) was all part of God's plan from the beginning: *"Who desires all men to be saved and to come to the knowledge of the truth"* (1 Tim. 2:4).

At the time God told Abram he would be called Abraham, God said: *"As for Me, behold, My covenant is with you, and you shall be a father of many nations"* (Gen. 17:4). What is translated in the NKJV as "many nations" reads in the Greek Septuagint "*plethous ethnon*" (πλήθους ἐθνῶν), literally: "multitude of nations." [Strong's 4128. pléthos company, multitude. From pletho; a fulness]. English translators of the New Testament have traditionally rendered the Greek word, "*ethnos* (nation)" as "Gentile." If the same treatment were applied to an English translation of the Septuagint, we would read: *"you shall be a father of many Gentiles"* (or literally; a multitude of Gentiles). Disregarding translation inconsistencies, the truth of this statement was clearly understood by Paul: *"...to those who are of the faith of Abraham, who is the father of us all"* (Rom. 4:16). *"And if you are Christ's, then you are Abraham's seed..."* (Gal. 3:29).

God's plan to reach the Nations continued through Ephraim. "Ephraim" means "fruitful" or "expansion;" and was often used as a moniker to represent the whole House of Israel. Joseph blessed Ephraim with the words: *"Let them grow into a multitude in the midst of the earth"* (Gen. 48:16); and, *"his descendants shall become a multitude of nations"* [LXX: *plethos ethnon*; πλῆθος ἐθνῶν] (Gen. 48:19). Now consider that "Jezreel"—also representative of the Northern Kingdom—means "God will sow;" and, that God sowed (scattered) the House of Israel among the nations: *"I will sow them among the peoples, and they shall remember Me in far countries"* (Zech. 10:9). Paul even used the same Old Testament phrase in his Greek writing to describe this expansion—this process:

3

*"blindness in part has happened to Israel until the **fullness of the Nations** (pleroma ton ethnon;* πλήρωμα τῶν ἐθνῶν— "multitude of nations") *has come in. And so all Israel will be saved..."* (Rom. 11:25-26).

Just who "all Israel" refers to in the verse above will be discussed in later chapters. Likewise, the ambiguity of the term, "Israel," will be addressed in the next section; e.g., was the "Israel," which was blinded in part, the same "Israel"—or part of "all Israel"—that would be saved?

In any case, Paul's reference to this "fullness/multitude of nations" is immediately expounded by quoting Isaiah: *"The Deliverer will come out of* [to] *Zion, and He will turn away ungodliness from Jacob, for this is My covenant with them..."* The phrase, "when I take away their sins" is inserted by Paul. But what actually follows in this passage from the Isaiah Scroll are the declarations: *"For your light has come!"* and, *"the Gentiles* (Nations) [LXX; *ethnae,* ἔθνη] *shall come to your light"* (Isa. 60:1, 3).

Just as in Ephesians, Paul links the inclusion of the Nations with the work of Messiah. And when would this inclusion take place? "When (at the time) I take away their (**Jacob's**) sins." WAIT! WHAT? Just as the real problem from the perspective of Replacement Theology was never the identity of the Nations, but peace and unity with the "rejected" Jews; likewise, neither does this timing of events line up with Dispensational Theology. (Much will be said about these theological divergences throughout this book.)

Nevertheless, Paul's writings would have made perfect sense to anyone reading the "Bible" in its original languages (primarily Hebrew and Greek). Some first-century readers (especially those living in or around Jerusalem) would have read from the Hebrew scrolls of the Tanakh. But the New Testament was written in Greek because Greek was the common (*koine*) language of the Roman Empire. So common in fact, that most Jews and Gentiles would have read from the Greek Septuagint—the version **written BY those scattered among the nations, FOR those scattered among the nations**.

Reading both the Hebrew "Writings" and the New Testament in the same Greek language would have made ALL of theology much simpler. Take, for instance, the deity of Christ. The Hebrew translators translated the Name, *"Jehovah"* into the Greek as "Lord."

Introduction

So when Elijah brought fire down on the altar (1 Kings 18:39) all the people shouted, *kurios estin o theos* (κύριός ἐστιν ὁ θεός—*"the Lord is God"*). An English literal translation of the Hebrew would read, "*Jehovah* is the *Elohim.*" Furthermore, the writers of the New Testament referred to Jesus as this same "*Kurios*": Κύριος Ἰησοῦς. Now, if you confess, "Jesus is Lord" (Rom. 10:9)—if you believe Jesus is the same Lord (*Jehovah*) of the Writings—you will be saved. Deity question solved! Along with two-thirds of the Trinity.

But there's more revealed by studying the Commonwealth of Israel than surprises found in the ancient languages. Moreover, Commonwealth Theology's focus is not SO narrow that it is limited to investigating the lost House of Israel. The whole of biblical eschatology is clarified when the members of the Commonwealth and their prophetic roles are properly identified in Scripture.

Better Theology—Not a Different Gospel

Those taking an interest in the plight of the two houses of Israel (a topic avoided by mainline denominations) have quickly observed that the House of Israel was scattered among the nations and designated "not a people" long before the House of Judah was carried away to Babylon. The modern quest for the Lost House of Israel by both Messianic and "Gentile" groups have led some to adopt aberrant theological positions. The authors and advocates of Commonwealth Theology are fully aware of these wanderings from the faith; and therefore, submit the following disclaimer:

Commonwealth Theology is not a departure from the "Apostles' doctrine" (Acts 2:42), "the faith once delivered" (Jude v3), nor is it a "different gospel" (Gal. 1:6). Commonwealth Theology honors the Christology and understanding of the Godhead codified in the early Christian creeds. Furthermore, Commonwealth Theology (as will be discussed later) is not affiliated with any exclusive "Identity" cult, nor does it emphasize genetic lineage concerning God's people who have been "scattered among the nations."

Some people, from the House of Judah (viz. *Jews*), might be able to trace their descent from a particular tribe; some might "feel" strongly that they are Jewish; or, they might be converts to Judaism. The VERY SAME variety of identification may be applied by those from the scattered HOUSE OF ISRAEL (viz. the Ten Northern Tribes).

Commonwealth Theology respects God's prerogative to choose and bless separate and distinct groups of people. (Even in heaven, tribes and nations will retain their distinction.) Therefore, CT does not encourage, or even suggest, that one group should be converted to another.

The concept of "Commonwealth" wherein there abides distinction but not separation is readily seen in today's "British Commonwealth of Nations." Here, for example, Nigeria is a member of the British Commonwealth of Nations; however, it maintains its distinction as the nation of Nigeria. Nigeria is not separated from the British Commonwealth of Nations—she is a full-fledged member, but wholly maintains her national identity as a distinct nation. The question, of course, is this: Does Nigeria enjoy the benefits of the British Commonwealth? All members of the British Commonwealth of Nations recognize the King or Queen of Great Britain—whereas, Ireland, most certainly does NOT recognize the British Royal Family nor are they members of the British Commonwealth of Nations.

"Mixed with the nations" means "mixed." No one people or nation on earth today can claim THEY are the one-and-only House of Israel. On the other hand, after nearly three thousand years of "mixing," it is likely that nearly everyone on earth carries some genes from the lost House of Israel. Because CT is a refinement of Christian theology and not a religion, the response by those who would identify with the House of Israel is left to the individual. At a minimum, a "believer among the nations" should begin genuinely to embrace Messiah's peace between the two houses and anticipate the prophesied glory of the United Kingdom of David. Others who have identified with the Northern Kingdom have chosen varying degrees of Torah observance and Messianic-style worship. The goal of Commonwealth Theology is to present the truth. The outcome belongs to the Lord! Indeed: "Let each be fully convinced in his own mind" (Rom. 14:5)... "let us therefore make every effort to do what leads to peace and to mutual edification" (Rom. 14:19—NIV)... "So whatever you believe about these things (viz. diet, days, etc.) keep between yourself and God" (Rom. 14:22—NIV).

INTRODUCTION

Commonwealth Theology's distinction from mainline Christian theology is narrowly focused on the question: What constitutes the Commonwealth of Israel? The "Commonwealth of Israel (τῆς πολιτείας τοῦ Ἰσραὴλ)," appears only twice in the Bible in the word Commonwealth or its colloquial interpretation, "Freedom." The word Commonwealth is derived from the word polity; to wit:

> Strong's G#4174: or a "legal jurisdiction or administration"—Politeia signifies (1) "the relation in which a citizen stands to the state, the condition of a citizen, citizenship," Acts 22:28, "with a great sum obtained I this freedom." While Paul's "citizenship of Tarsus was not of advantage outside that city, yet his Roman "citizenship" availed throughout the Roman Empire and, besides private rights, included (a) exemption from all degrading punishments; (1b) a right to appeal to the emperor after a sentence; (1c) a right to be sent to Rome for trial before the emperor if charged with a capital offense. It is also (2) "a civil polity, the condition of a state, a commonwealth," said of Israel (Eph.2:12).

Can a biblical term employed so infrequently merit a school of theology in its name? Consider that Paul applied this unique term to declare the impact of Christ's sacrifice upon Israel's historical division. Yet this fulfillment of extensive national prophecies is so neglected by mainstream theologies as to leave a gaping void which reduces the import of the Old Testament to a few inspirational stories and "portable" promises. (Portable in that promises made specifically to national Israel are often expropriated to the "individual" with little regard for their national context.)

The ramifications of Paul's "Commonwealth" toward comprehending the rest of the "Greatest Story Ever Told" are extensive enough that Paul himself elaborated on this Commonwealth throughout the first five chapters of Ephesians. Furthermore, allusions are made to the concept of the Commonwealth (e.g. *Freedom* found in Acts 22:28) by Paul in the Acts of the Apostles, in his other epistles, and by other New Testament writers. Indeed, once the Commonwealth of Israel is discerned it becomes recognizable throughout the Bible as both the sum of God's chosen people and an integral aspect of Christ's peace won by the cross.

Thus, the seemingly narrow lens of Commonwealth Theology broadens the Bible student's perspective to consider and rightly divide hundreds of passages that have been overlooked or misapplied by other theologies. The insights shared by Paul in Ephesians regarding the Commonwealth are nothing short of the revelation of the mystery of Christ and His Church (Eph. 5:32). Thus, CT's broader understanding of Christ's fulfillment of the Old Testament may have been the very panorama Paul had in view when he prayed that the eyes of the understanding of God's people be enlightened, that they may know what is the hope of His calling, and what are the riches of the glory of His inheritance in the saints (Eph. 1:18).

Indeed, despite the uniqueness of its name, Commonwealth Theology offers significant value to the everyday believer. CT reveals and magnifies God's dealing with Israel far beyond the superficial treatment rendered by mainline theologies. Truly understanding how God has dealt with Israel—the full story—builds confidence in God's love, assurance of His faithfulness, and trust in His righteous justice. CT also establishes a more proximate connection to the fathers (and mothers) of the faith found in the Hebrew Scriptures; thereby, enabling the believer to experience such spiritual family ties to the saints of old—the great and surrounding cloud of witnesses—as to run the race of faith with endurance (Heb. 12:1).

In addition, Commonwealth Theology directly impacts Judeo-Christian relations today, as well as Judeo-Christian expectations for the fulfillment of Bible prophecy in the future. This occurs supernaturally as the Spirit of Truth who leads into all truth corrects the false dialogue that has inadvertently strengthened the very wall of separation which was broken down by Christ. A wall that now exists solely in the minds of men who have been trained by the forces of politics, time, and tradition to resist the peace already accomplished by the cross. We will discuss how Zechariah's prophecy of the "two staffs" (Beauty [Grace] and Bonds [Unity]) found in Zechariah 11:7-17 were initial expressions abolishing that "wall of separation" but how disunity between Judah and Israel (i.e., "I might break the brotherhood between Judah and Israel"—Zech.11:15), once again, erected that separating wall through "false shepherds" led by the "foolish" or "worthless" shepherd (Zech. 11:15-17).

INTRODUCTION

Just who is the intended audience for the revelation of this new theology? Is this a casual book for the layman or a scholastic reference for the clergyman? Confessedly, this document is crafted for "thinking theologians"—later, more "laymen-oriented text" will be forthcoming. We purposefully wish to alter "thought leaders" in this quest of theological disclosure. And, what inroads do the authors realistically expect this volume to make into the time-honored tenets of the world's largest religion? Can the scriptural evidence for this alternative theology be so compelling as to prevail over Ironside's maxim?: "What is new is not true, and what is true is not new."[11] Notwithstanding, it will be demonstrated in the course of study that Commonwealth Theology is not something new at all but IS in fact the Apostles' doctrine which was unwittingly, or somewhat purposefully, obscured. It is at the very core of Jesus' revelation of His entitlement as "the Christ, the Son of the living God" wherein He uttered His all-inclusive, all-embracing statement in response to Peter's declaration: "I will build My EKKLESIA, and the gates of Hades shall not prevail against it" (Matt. 16:16, 18).

Considering the audience and their response to this work provides an opportunity to introduce a dynamic which was the subject of a separate book by Chris Steinle and is incorporated in Dr. Gavin Finley's chapter on the Breach of Jeroboam. It is both a social and personal dynamic. This dichotomy asserts its influence on society, politics,—and, pertinent to theology—religion: Namely, the seeming antinomies of Individualism and Authority; of Freedom vs. Obedience. No plainer (relatively recent) example of this dynamic's influence on religion can be exhibited than the Protestant Reformation. It was not that Luther and the likes consciously set out as individualists—encouraged, inadvertently so, by Luther's emphasis upon the "priesthood of all believers." Indeed, this "discovery" should have mitigated against such "individualism" with the emphasis upon the "priesthood of all." But the Reformation did bring such scrutiny upon the rights of both the institution and the individual that a compromise was demanded and settled in the Peace of Westphalia.

---

[11] *The Epistles of John and Jude*, H.A. Ironside, 1949, Loizeaux Brothers, p. 13

No, we have not strayed from our inquiry about the book's prospective audience. There are two basic types of religious authority structures accommodating two types of followers. Therefore, the reader predisposed to examine the claims of Commonwealth Theology might come from unanticipated sources. It can be observed (by the openness of discussion on bulletin boards and online groups) that Christians who believe their salvation is heavily dependent on their affiliation with a particular institution are far less threatened by discussing a wide range of doctrinal ideas (including the often contradictory writings of the Church Fathers). This also seems to be the case with the Jew, who is "Jewish" because of his ancestral heritage. These prospective readers might be interested and open to reading about a new theological slant without feeling the least bit threatened that they might encounter some epiphany by which they might lose their faith. They have no desperate need to know if they have missed some biblical truth and, therefore, might be reading out of mere curiosity.

The Christian who believes he or she is saved solely by faith in the God presented in the Bible will obviously place paramount importance on the correct interpretation of the Bible. Every aspect of doctrine, then, is vital; and can only be interpreted one correct way because the "word is truth" (Jn. 17:17). These prospective readers might be extremely doubtful that any one aspect of theology could be improved or altered without shattering everything they have regarded as true. They might relate the various elements of theology (Soteriology, Christology, Ecclesiology, etc.—and especially Eschatology) to the blocks in a game of Jenga. Removing any one block could bring down the entire structure. For this audience the greatest concern should be that CT is SO narrow, SO surgical, that it might correct or enhance one feature of the faith without destroying the Gospel Truth in its entirety.

The fact of the matter is this: CT proclaims, yea, even demands, that we should live by the "Truth of the Gospel" (Gal. 2:5, 14). Paul and Peter, and the entire Council at Jerusalem in Acts 15:6-21, understood the Nations/Gentiles participated in the outpouring of the Holy Spirit under the prophetic reality of the "United Kingdom of David" (aka the "Tabernacles of David") without becoming Jewish (i.e., circumcision) and its restoration so that "the rest of mankind (Edom—Amos 9:11-12) might believe" (Acts 15:17; Amos 9:12).

INTRODUCTION

Notwithstanding, and almost immediately, *"he* [Peter] *withdrew and separated himself* [from the Gentile Galatians], *fearing those who were of the circumcision* [Jewish believers] . . . *and the rest of the Jews also played the hypocrite with him, so that even Barnabas was carried away with their hypocrisy"* (Gal. 2:12-13). The "Gospel Truth" is that *"He Himself is our peace, who has made both one, and has broken down the middle wall of separation . . . to create in Himself one new man from the two, thus making peace . . . He came and preached peace to you who were afar off and to those who were near"* (Eph. 2:14-18, excerpts). Peace with God is granted to all who believe on His Name; however, peace between peoples is wrought by the same cross!

Evangelical believers who have been convinced by their mentor, pastor, or seminary that their denomination (or even their particular congregation) has figured out or "received" the one-and-only true take on all Christian doctrine is exceedingly unlikely to read about a new theology. Likewise, the extreme megalomaniac (maybe the pastor of the above Church) will not be open to any doctrinal interpretation that he or she didn't originate. Individualism AND control at its finest! Neither will be a reader. Absolute truth is found in Christ alone (*"You pore over the Scriptures because you presume that by them you possess eternal life. These are the very words that testify about Me, yet you refuse to come to Me to have life"* [John 5:39-40]—Berean Study Bible). Consequently, they who so vociferously "pore over the Scriptures"—yet will not come to the Living Lord Jesus Christ, are clearly missing the mark! "Grace and truth" came by Jesus Christ (John 1:17). *"For indeed the gospel was preached to us as well as to them; but the word which they heard did not profit them, not being mixed with faith in those who heard it"* (Heb. 4:9).

"Dead knowledge" is NOT the goal, but a fuller and complete revelation of the Living Son of God is!

Among the interested readers might be: Evangelicals who have encountered "issues" when comparing their own reading of the Bible with what they have been taught; The casual inquirer who has heard about Commonwealth Theology and wants to know how it is different from other "Commonwealth of Israel" theologies; either Christians or Jews who are appalled by Supersessionist/Reformed Theology's inevitable Anti-Semitism (or anyone else on the planet, god-fearing or atheist, who can't find the slightest reason for the world's inexplicable bigotry toward the Jews). Or, the reader open to CT may have had a Dispensational background, but has recognized its schizophrenic tendencies when interpreting Bible prophecy as a two-tiered theological/eschatological system; whereupon, and especially, the New Testament can be solely written to Jews and then, inexplicably, written only to Christians—with the Dispensationalist "rightly dividing the Word of God" as the sole and discretionary arbiter); and, how the Jews/Israel still end up with the short end of the stick. (Both short ends of the same stick on the Dispensational chart.)

Due, nevertheless, to the bias intrinsically bound to the "devotional" element of any religion, the authors realize full well that the weight of proof to substantiate CT must mount an exceedingly high bar. Such scriptural authority does, indeed, exist and was sufficient to move the authors (all devoted Christians) from their previous doctrinal positions which were, in the main, within the Reform or Dispensational camps. And, as with the authors, so with the reader; study and time will be required to break through the well-entrenched positions taught by mainline theologies which embrace these aforementioned extremities.

Along with the biblical credence for CT, which makes up the bulk of this volume, some explanation is in order—and perhaps a great deal of explanation—for why CT has eluded prior theologians. This obvious question did not escape the authors during the development and/or framing of Commonwealth Theology. The perpetuation of theologies promoting unscriptural assumptions about the relationship and prophetic destiny of Israel, the Jews, and the Church deserves some examination in this introduction. Such "blindness in part" has persisted for nearly two thousand years primarily due to the "normalcy bias" of tradition and the theological "flexibility" permitted by ambiguity.

COMING TO TERMS WITH ISRAEL AND THE CHURCH

Voltaire once stated: "Define your terms ... or we shall never understand one another."[12] In recent years this "soft spot" of defining, or redefining, terms has played a major role in the legal arena of social issues. Common variations on Voltaire's ultimatum include: "He who defines the terms wins the debate," and, "Whoever controls the meaning of words, controls the conversation." Op-Ed columnist William Haupt, assembled the following syllogism, drawing from the logic of Orwell's *1984*, and ending with a direct quote:

> If you control language, you control the argument. If you control the argument, you control information. If you control information, you control history. If you control history, you control the past..., "He who controls the past controls the future."—George Orwell's "Big Brother," *1984*.[13]

Actually, Orwell's full quote was: "[He] who controls the past controls the future. [He] Who controls the present controls the past." Orwell had obviously realized the power wielded by those who are able to revise history. But Haupt's point is made: The past can ultimately be manipulated by controlling the language.

In this section of the Introduction we will learn how to disambiguate the most common terms for God's chosen people. Because the "narrow focus" of CT demands a re-examination of mainline Christendom's position on the relationship between Israel and the Church, the very terms, "Israel" and "Church," CANNOT remain ambiguous. When it comes to the theological field of Israelology—ESPECIALLY—whoever controls the meaning of these words, controls the theological position regarding Israel: Past, present, and future. Although we are intensely focused, at the same time, the "theological ramifications" are all encompassing—impacting every branch of theology.

---

[12] Voltaire, *Dictionnaire Philosophique*

[13] Op-Ed: Control the language and control history by William Haupt III, The Center Square Aug 5, 2019, https://www.thecentersquare.com/national/op-ed-control-the-language-and-control-history/article_53e45292-b6f5-11e9-a1d2-07cbbda5a160.html

Some words used in the Bible ARE actually ambiguous—even in their original language. Most unfortunately, what is meant by the words "Jews" and "Israel," must either be defined by the context in which the words are used or by purposefully adding further clarification. This is grievously problematic in any theological analysis of these two entities; and yes, "Jews" and "Israel" are quite often two separate entities when used in the Bible. Complicating the issue is the fact that the contemporary usage of these words often refers to a different entity than the same word represented when the Bible was written. Or, the same word might define a related entity of different composition than its historical equivalent. This "time shift" of usage can be observed even between Old and New Testament writers. Now compound all of these moving pieces with the honest efforts of modern Bible translators, who have tried to represent the identity of these ancient entities by stating them in modern terms—terms which carry current connotations based on current usage. Furthermore, missing the true, or at least the best, definition of these terms might occur innocently or because of intentional bias. We will not, at this time, attempt to attach blame except to note that Early Church theology developed in a social and political climate in which the Jews were detested. The important thing to know for now is that Commonwealth Theology takes great care to determine what is meant when references to Israel, et. al. occur in the Bible. The rest of this section will examine how these terms can be used. Just becoming aware of the variety of definitions is a step toward identifying the correct meaning of these words when reading the Bible; and of course, when formulating theology.

DEFINING JEWS, ISRAEL, AND THE HOUSE OF ISRAEL

WHO ARE THE JEWS?

<u>Jews; ambiguous:</u> Israel: related to any tribe, Modern Israel.

Jewish ethnicity, nationhood, and religion are strongly interrelated, as Judaism is the ethnic religion of the Jewish people, while its observance varies from strict observance to complete nonobservance.[14] "A person born Jewish who refutes Judaism may continue to assert a Jewish identity, and if he or she does not convert to another religion, even religious Jews will recognize the person as a Jew."

---

[14] https://en.wikipedia.org/wiki/Jews

INTRODUCTION

Jews; disambiguous: Judah; the **House of Judah**. The Greek term was a loan from Aramaic Y'hūdāi, corresponding to Hebrew יְהוּדִי Yehudi, originally the term for a member of the tribe of Judah or the people of the kingdom of Judah. According to the Hebrew Bible, the name of both the tribe and kingdom derive from Judah, the fourth son of Jacob.[15] The English word "Jew" continues Middle English Gyw, Iewe. These terms derive from Old French giu, earlier juieu, which through elision had dropped the letter "d" from the Medieval Latin Iudaeus, which, like the New Testament Greek term Ioudaios, meant both "Jew" and "Judean" / "of Judea."[16]

SPEAKING OF ISRAEL

Israel; ambiguous: All Israel; the United Kingdom. According to Wictionary; 1. "The State of Israel, a modern country in the Middle East, at the eastern shore of the Mediterranean. 2. The Land of Israel, a region that is roughly coextensive with the State of Israel. 3. (historical) An ancient kingdom that occupied roughly the same area in ancient times. 4. (historical) An ancient kingdom that occupied the northern part of this area, as distinct from Judah. 5. The Jews, taken collectively."[17]

Israel; disambiguous: Referring to the northern 10 tribes of the divided kingdom; the **House of Israel**, also known as Ephraim, Samaria, the Stick of Joseph, Jezreel; which was taken into captivity cir. 740-712 BC by the Assyrians and was assimilated among the nations. These Israelites constitute those nations identified in the blessing given to Abraham, Isaac and Jacob and conferred upon Joseph's younger son, Ephraim, where he would become a "multitude of nations."[18]

When the word "Israel" is used in the Old Testament, what is it referring to? That depends on where in the saga of the Children of Israel the word appears. Obviously, before Jacob's descendants settled in the Land—and before the northern and southern settlements came to odds—"Israel," as a nation, continued to denote the "Children of Israel" as a whole. However, once this North—South faction developed, the definition of "Israel" began to change.

---

[15] "Jew," *Oxford English Dictionary*
[16] *Encyclopedia of the Peoples of Africa and the Middle East*, Facts On File Inc., Infobase Publishing, 2009, p. 336
[17] https://en.wiktionary.org/wiki/Israel
[18] *Commonwealth Theology*, by Douglas Krieger, Tribnet Publications, 2018, p. 10

THE HOUSE OF ISRAEL AND THE HOUSE OF JUDAH

The following text takes place just prior to the union of the northern and southern tribes.

2 Samuel 2

> *8 But Abner the son of Ner, commander of Saul's army, took Ishbosheth the son of Saul and brought him over to Mahanaim; 9 and he made him king over Gilead, over the Ashurites, over Jezreel, over Ephraim, over Benjamin, and over <u>all Israel</u>. 10 Ishbosheth, Saul's son, was forty years old when he began to reign over <u>Israel</u>, and he reigned two years. <u>Only the house of Judah followed David.</u> 11 And the time that David was king in Hebron over the <u>house of Judah</u> was seven years and six months.*

In the passage above, the United Kingdom under David had not yet been formed. The northern tribes (with Benjamin), gathered under Saul, are here referred to as "Israel;" and even "all Israel," along with the ten northern tribes—collectively, these twelve tribes are referred to as "Israel." Notwithstanding the fact that Judah was aligned with King David. Judah was not considered to be part of "all Israel" in this case because "all Israel," as well as the nomenclature, "Israel," represented what would, after the Breach of Jeroboam, be designated "the House of Israel." Note that the **tribe of Judah** is, however, called out as the **House of Judah**.

From this point on—in the Old Testament—**"Israel"** most often refers to the **northern territories** of the Promised Land. Note: as of the passage above, these two would-be kingdoms had already been ruled by two separate kings.

Example:

In 1 Kings 1:35, King David had just declared Solomon to be king. The Kingdom had not yet been "formally" divided. The verse, nonetheless, reads: *"For I have appointed him to be ruler over <u>Israel and Judah</u>"*; signifying the **House of Israel** and the **House of Judah**.

The meaning of the terms, "Israel" and "Judah," MUST be established by the context of their usage. Often in the case of prophecy, the time and jurisdiction of the prophet must be discovered in order to establish a verse's correct context.

INTRODUCTION

ISRAEL AND JEWS IN THE NEW TESTAMENT

When it comes to the New Testament—and especially when these terms appear within quotes from the Old Testament—the same process of discovery must be applied in order to disambiguate their meaning. Furthermore, the Old Testament meaning of references to "Israel," "Judah," and "Jews" within such quoted verses must be respected when interpreting the New Testament passage in which these words occur.

The history and prophetic significance of BOTH houses of Israel carried over into New Testament times. As formerly noted, Jesus made reference to the lost sheep of the House of Israel. Moreover, Peter's first sermon mentions, and even indicates the location of, the two houses at the beginning of the first century. Perhaps because Judah had not been formally divorced by God as the House of Israel had been, Peter honored the order recorded by Paul as, *"first to the Jew, then to the Greek."*

Peter began his Day of Pentecost sermon by addressing the House of Judah: *"Men of **Judah** (Ioudaioi) and all who dwell in Jerusalem"* (Acts 2:14). Recall that Daniel used this same wording to address "those near": *"To the men of Judah, to the inhabitants of Jerusalem."* Later in his sermon, Peter acknowledged those from among the nations, who had been specifically identified in verses 9-11, as those who had traveled from foreign lands for the feast: *"Therefore let all the **house of Israel** (oikos Israel, οἶκος Ἰσραὴλ) know assuredly that God has made this Jesus, whom you crucified, both Lord and Christ"* (Acts 2:39).

DEFINING THE CHURCH

"CHURCH" IN THE ORIGINAL LANGUAGE

Jesus and the Apostles chose to use an Old Testament Greek word for Christ's congregation. The word *"ekklesia"* (ἐκκλησία ekklēsia) comes from the word *"kaleo"*; **a calling out**; [*Ecclesia,* as translated into Latin]. *Ekklesia*—as used nearly 200 times in the Septuagint—means, "congregation" or "assembly." Christ and the authors of the New Testament used this word, rather than using a different word—or creating a new word—to describe the "assembly" who followed "the way." The Apostles continued to gather and worship at the Temple (as well as from house to house) because God had simply sent

Messiah to save the Ekklesia (Congregation) of both houses of Israel. And to include the Nations—"even us whom He **called**, not of the Jews only, but also of the Gentiles" (Rom. 9:24). Therefore, quite naturally, the writers of the New Testament had no reason to change the name of the Ekklesia. As we will see in later chapters, even early English translations of the New Testament used the word, "Congregacion," for what is today translated, "Church." See: Tyndale Bible (1526), Coverdale Bible (1535), Matthew Bible (1537), The Great Bible (1539), Bishop's Bible (1568).

WHEN THE CONGREGATION BECAME "THE CHURCH"

King James insisted by edict that "Church" be used instead of "congregation."[19] "Church" was a familiar word for a gathering place for worship. The origin of the word "Church," according to Oxford's Lexico: Old English circe, cyrce, related to Dutch kerk and German Kirche, based on Medieval Greek kurikon, from Greek kuriakon (dōma) 'Lord's (house).[20] Most likely, King James' motivation for favoring this new and different word for the Congregation was politically motivated rather than Anti-Semitic. (It is suggested that the king desired to gain control over the buildings in which the congregation assembled since Christ is obviously the head of the congregation.[21]) The king's edict, however, blurred the distinction between the religion and the edifice, e.g., Jews meet in a synagogue/temple, Buddhists in a temple, Muslims in a mosque, but the "Church"—in a church. The tragedy of this etymological manipulation is that the continuity between the "congregation (ekklesia) in the wilderness" and the "congregation (ekklesia) of Christ" is lost to the English reader.

The "English" study of Ecclesiology is obviously complicated by the English translation of the key words, *Ethnos* and *Ekklesia*. Likewise, disambiguating the meaning of the terms, "Israel" and "Jews," is essential in studying Israelology. One can now appreciate the difficulty in undertaking a scholarly examination of the biblical

---

[19] Ecclesia.org, "The Origin of the word Church," retrieved 5/21/2020: http://ecclesia.org/Truth/ekklesia.html
[20] Oxford's Lexico, "church," retrieved 5/21/2020, https://www.lexico.com/en/definition/church
[21] The VineyardJC, "Beware Of Translator Bias" by Christine Egbert, retrieved 02/21/2020: https://vineyardjc.com/beware-of-idols-even-the-king-james

relationship between God's chosen people-of-old and the congregation of Christ. Although the word "Church" automatically conveys a separation—even isolation—that was never intended by the authors of the New Testament; and, although "Israel" can easily have four different meanings (apart from the name given to Jacob); this volume will continue to discuss the Commonwealth of Israel using the customary terms: Israel and the Church. These terms will, nevertheless, be carefully defined with the understanding that "Church" is not the congregation/the ekklesia, but is in point of fact the actual places of worship, the buildings, and that "church" was never used in the Greek New Testament text—where we find that the "Congregation" met in a "house" or at the Temple—whereas, "Church" in its "organic extrapolation" refers to the living people of God, His Ekklesia, His assembly.

HE LOVES ISRAEL, HE LOVES ISRAEL NOT

One more "ambiguity" should be discussed in the course of this introduction. *Has God cast away His people? Have they stumbled that they should fall?* (Rom. 11:1, 11). Well: Yes; and, No. Yes, because both houses of Israel did fall into sin. And the House of Israel was certainly divorced (Jer. 3:8); and both houses were cast away from their land. Due to this historical reality, hundreds of verses can be quoted from the Old Testament which—taken out of the context of time—can be (and have been) used to support the argument that God has rejected "Israel" and/or "the Jews"; and that, subsequently, God needed to "replace" the whole lot with a new group of chosen people: the Church.

"Israel had been laboring under the curse [curse of the law for disobedience as forewarned by Moses] for seven hundred years before Yeshua was born. According to 2 Kings 21:10-15 and Jeremiah 15:4, it was pronounced during the reign of the wicked king Manasseh, who filled Jerusalem with idolatry and blood from one end to the other. What this means is that, contrary to common Christian interpretation, the Jewish people were not cursed because they rejected Yeshua. On the contrary, the Jews had already been under the punishment of the law for over seven hundred years before

Yeshua came. In fact, the rejection of Yeshua by all but a minority of Jews was the result of the curse, not the cause of it!"[22]

Messiah did not come into the world for the purpose of rejecting His people, who had already been rejected; but rather, to remedy the longstanding rejection which had already occurred. His name was called, "Jesus," specifically because He would save HIS people—His people of old—from THEIR sins (Matt. 1:21). The identity of "His people" is made perfectly clear by the context of the opening chapters of both Matthew and Luke. Matthew's gospel begins with the Genealogy; and the context of ancient Israel continues into the second chapter, where a Ruler from Judah would *"shepherd My people Israel."* Mary's Magnificat, and the prophecies of Zachariah and Simeon, from Luke's gospel, also affirm God's promises to Israel at Jesus' birth. Moreover, God promised to the objects of the New Covenant—the House of Israel and the House of Judah—*"I will forgive THEIR iniquity, and THEIR sin I will remember no more"* (Jer. 31:31, 34; Emphasis added).

Prophecy relates the comfort and assurance of Messiah's rescue directly to God's correction of Israel and their being cast away. (See the overall context of the virgin birth, Immanuel, and the Prince of Peace; Isaiah Chapters Six through Nine). The purpose for Messiah's coming was the restoration of Israel. Not, the replacement of Israel. The light diffused to the Nations was IN ADDITION to Christ's primary objective. Much more will be said to refute Supersessionism within the body of this book.

---

[22] *Galatians, Judaizing, and the Curse of the Law: Marrying The New Perspective on Paul, the Divine Council paradigm, and eschatology (2nd Draft)*, by Michael Bugg:

https://www.academia.edu/28706723/Galatians_Judaizing_and_the_Curse_of_the_Law_Marrying_The_New_Perspective_on_Paul_the_Divine_Council_paradigm_and_eschatology_2nd_Draft_?email_work_card=thumbnail

INTRODUCTION

In conclusion, consider a passage of Isaiah, quoted by Matthew, which brings closure to several points previously discussed. Isaiah Nine begins by bringing attention to a region that was part of the northern House of Israel: *"land of Zebulun and the land of Naphtali."* During the deportation of the northern house by Assyria into the far reaches of the Assyrian Empire, people from the nations under Assyrian rule (Gentiles) were imported into these same northern provinces, aka Ephraim. Thus, Isaiah's reference to *"Galilee of the Gentiles (Nations)."* In the third verse of the ninth chapter Isaiah declared, *"You have multiplied the nation,"* thereby making reference to both the "inclusion" of the Gentiles and the dual fulfillments: of God's covenant with Abraham, and Ephraim's blessing—to become a "multitude of nations." Moreover, just as the Commonwealth of Israel was founded upon the sacrifice of the One who said, *"but for this cause came I unto this hour,"* this "multiplier of nations" was identified in Isaiah 9:6: *"For unto us a Child is born, unto us a Son is given"*—the "us" here being both Judah and Israel, but having in view all humankind!

# PART I

ELEMENTS OF COMMONWEALTH THEOLOGY

CHAPTER ONE

YES DISTINCTION—NO SEPARATION[23]

BY DOUGLAS KRIEGER

REPLACEMENT THEOLOGY

What exactly is meant by the terms: Yes Distinction—No Separation? Ephraim and Judah have distinction, but Ephraim and Judah are NOT separated. Likewise, the definition of what constitutes Israel is exceedingly important as far as its present interpretation(s). It is better understood when we compare this simplistic definition as we examine Replacement Theology (RT) wherein there is NO DISTINCTION and, consequently, NO SEPARATION—i.e., they do NOT see the distinction between Ephraim (aka "the Church") and Judah (aka the Jews) or in their case between Israel and the Church—there's no distinction and no separation because according to RT, the Church subsumes Israel and becomes the SPIRITUAL ISRAEL and/or the TRUE ISRAEL of God (aka "The Israel of God"—Gal. 6:16) which defines today's totality of the "Church." Frankly, in RT the Church is the ONLY ISRAEL OF GOD—so there is NO DISTINCTION, NO SEPARATION.

---

[23] Chapter adapted from *Commonwealth Theology*, by Douglas Krieger, Tribnet Publications, 2018, pp. 111-116

In the Replacement view, the Church is the "continuing Community of Grace" throughout the ages—no need for a Millennium and certainly no prophetic destiny for the Jews (and, by the way, they are indifferent to the proposal of Ephraim's identity being subsumed by Judah, for the lot of them are just Jews)—and certainly, there is no significance (prophetically) for the State of Israel[24]; therefore, why not Boycott, Divest, and Sanction—go for it!! This theology claims the Jews were REJECTED because they rejected the Messiah! All "covenants" have been abrogated! There is no Abrahamic, Palestinian (land)[25], Davidic (future Millennial Reign) or even a New Covenant in the minds of most Reform theologians—and concerning the Mosaic Covenant: It's extinguished as well!

---

[24] Louis Berkhof, another leading Amillennialist (Reform Dutch theologian) of the 20th Century, declared much the same in 1938 – ironically, the very year that Hitler and the Nazis were orchestrating "Kristallnact," the "Night of Broken Glass," sealing the doom of over six million Jews throughout Europe:

"Premillennialists maintain that there will be a national restoration . . . of Israel; that the Jewish nation will be re-established in the Holy Land; and that this will take place immediately preceding or during the millennial reign of Jesus Christ. It is very doubtful, however, that Scripture warrants the expectation that Israel will finally be re-established as a nation . . . . ." (Louis Berkhof, *Systematic Theology* (Grand Rapids, MI: Eerdmans, 1974), p. 712.

(Source: Douglas R. Shearer, *Amillennialism . . . Theology or Metaphysics Book III* (Sacramento, CA: Self-Published, 2020, p. 19.)

[25] Not only that, but God promised to Israel the presently disputed land from the time of Abraham onward. God said, "This is the land of which I swore to Abraham, to Isaac, and to Jacob, 'I will give it to your offspring'" (Deuteronomy 34:4). Statements to that effect are repeated many times. But neither of those two facts—Israel's election and God's covenant promise of the land—means that Israel has a present-day divine right to the land. . . Rebels Forfeit Right . . . Why do I say that? Because a non-covenant-keeping people does not have a divine right to hold the land of promise which was given by covenant. Covenant-breaking forfeits covenant privileges. God said to Israel, "If you will indeed obey my voice and keep my covenant, you shall be my treasured possession among all peoples" (Exodus 19:5). (John Piper, *"Should We Side With Israel or Palestine?"* from Ask Pastor John, Episode 425, September 9, 2014 @ https://www.desiringgod.org/interviews/should-we-side-Louis%20Berkho%20-israel-or-palestine, Retrieved on 04.30.2020)

DISPENSATION THEOLOGY

Dispensationalism teaches that there is distinction—ipso facto, separation—between "Israel and the Church."[26] Of course, in so saying this, Dispensationalists do not recognize the significance of Ephraim—the scattered Northern Kingdom. The Church has nothing to do with Israel and/or Ephraim because—as far as the Dispensationalists are concerned—it is fairly well set that Ephraim was swallowed up primarily by Judah; not so much by the nations. As in most theological systems—but especially within Dispensationalism—there are wide disparities of thinking; yet, the overall concept in keeping Israel and the Church wholly separated by intricate nuances and "dispensations" is of prime consideration.

Today's Israel simply equates to "the Jews" (all 12 Tribes are referred to as "Jews"). One can be a "Christian Jew" or one can be a "Jewish Jew"—but still Jewish. "Jew" is rather an ethnic designation—some "Jewish Jews" take offense that one can be described as a "Christian Jew"—therefore, some Christian Jews prefer to be called "Messianic Jews"). Again: Judah (meaning the "Unbelieving Jews") has subsumed Ephraim and what's left is the Church (the "Elect from among the nations"—and also Jews (defined as all the 12 Tribes of ancient Israel, aka the Jews—brought into the

---

[26] Dispensationalism is in danger of falling because of a careless dilution of her life-sustaining distinctions. One factor is the seminary teaching that the Church has a part in Israel's earthly-kingdom New Covenant (Jer. 31:31, 33; Ezek. 36:26-27; 37:14). But a far more pervasive error is that of failure to distinguish between Jesus' earthly Gospel for Israel, and His heavenly gospel for the Church. For too long the Church has been subjected to a synoptic, kingdom Gospel that was never intended for her. She is thereby diverted from her heavenly Gospel and position in the One "in whom are hidden all the treasures of wisdom and knowledge" (Col. 2:3).

Mr. John N. Darby, the father of systematized Dispensationalism (and much more)., lamented over the condition of the Church 100 years ago, which condition persists to this very day—circa 1991. It is a chief burden for me [Miles J. Stanford] as regards the Church that they are as persons outside; not inside, entered through the rent veil, abiding in the light of the Father's countenance and gazing upon the Lord Jesus Christ in His own divine perfectness with the eye that the Holy Spirit gives (2 Cor. 3:18). This my daily, if not hourly, grief. (Doctrine, Vol. 7:185) (*The Dispensational Gospels* by Miles J. Stanford)

"Church"), which again, has nothing to do with Ephraim; ipso facto Ephraim has nothing to do with Israel—the Church is comprised of Jew and Gentile—saved by the blood of Jesus—the "Elect from among the Nations" is NOT Ephraim, for why should Jews of Judah be joined unto Ephraim? So, with Dispensationalism there IS DISTINCTION—but it is a "dispensational distinction" as so described between "Israel" [so defined] and the "Church" [so defined].

In Dispensationalism there is total SEPARATION between the Church and Israel (forget any definition having to do with Ephraim being a part of ALL ISRAEL[27] (Rom. 9:6; 11:26) or the ISRAEL

---

[27] Norm Franz in his *Ephraim Ceases from Being a People*, 2017, makes the following conclusion regarding the identity of Ephraim:
- Although there were at one time two separate houses of Judah and Israel [aka Ephraim, Jezreel, Samaria], there are no longer two houses, but one house of Israel (all 12 Tribes) that God has been storing [sic. "restoring"] back to their Promised Land since the Zionist movement started in the early 1900s.
- Although Ephraim was once another name for the northern Kingdom of Israel, it ceased to exist as a congregated people after the Assyrian destruction and **was united with Judah during the Babylonian exile.**
- Ever since Israel came back from Babylon, God has used the terms "Jew" and "Israel" synonymously. Therefore, Jews are Israel and the people of Israel are Jews today.
- God considers both Jewish and Gentile believers as the spiritual "seed of Abraham" and the "one new man" in Messiah (Gal. 3:16). This is the New Covenant Church (Jew and Gentile), a.k.a. *"the Israel of God"* (Gal. 6:15-16) .

. . **Conclusion:** If Ephraim (10 tribes of the northern KI—Kingdom of Israel) ceased has from being a nation after the Assyria captivity, but Israel never ceases from being a nation, then Ephraim (10 tribes of the northern KI) is not Israel today.

[NOTE: Doug Krieger finds Norm Franz' concluding remark that today's "Israel of God" are a conglomerate of both Jewish and Gentile believers in Yeshua; especially, when most dispensationalists conclude that the "Israel of God" in Gal. 6:16 are simply Jewish believers in Messiah, excluding Gentile believers in the same—i.e., Gentile believers are NOT constituted within the phrase: "The Israel of God" – only Jewish believers in Jesus are so designated – whereas the conjunction (Galatians 6:16) "and" (Grk. kai) separates Gentile believers with "peace and mercy be upon them" from *"**and** upon the Israel of God"* who are Jewish believers of the "circumcision" who embrace the "New Creation" but still separated from Gentile believers. Furthermore,

CH. 1: YES DISTINCTION – NO SEPARATION

OF GOD (Gal. 6:16). That's because the Church cannot be defined by Ephraim at all—Ephraim was reabsorbed by "Judah-Israel," who were identified as Jews during the Babylonian Captivity—therefore, the 10 Northern Tribes once known as Israel were from that Babylonian Captivity onward, also known as Jews. Now, "Judah-Israel" and "Ephraim-Israel" are TOTALLY SEPARATED from the "wild branches." The Church is separated from the unbelieving Jews (aka "the natural branches"). (Norm Franz: *Ephraim Ceases from being a People*, 2017.)

Krieger concludes after reviewing the "Scriptural evidence" of Ephraim's disillusionment according to Franz, having been subsumed by Judah during the days of the Babylonian Captivity and subsequent "disappearance" . . . to be based on ambiguity and eisegesis—i.e., CT is NOT claiming that Judah's designation is devoid of Israel's label (viz. "Jews" are of Judah and yet not of Israel?) There is simply little evidence that millions of Israelites of the Ten Northern Tribes assimilated into "Judah-Israel" (several thousand at most) nor that large numbers of Ephraimite-Israel captives of Assyria escaped Assyrian deportation and returned to their 10 Northern Tribal locations. To the contrary: "Aliens would swallow it up [viz. Samaria—see Hos. 8:4]. *Israel is swallowed up; now they are among the Gentiles* [aka "Nations"] *like a vessel in which is no pleasure. For they have gone up to Assyria*" (Hos, 8:7b-9a). Also, Franz completely neglects Acts 15:15-17 regarding the United Kingdom of David (aka "Tabernacle of David") and James' allusions to Amos 9:11-12 regarding Ephraim's re-entry into David's Tabernacle—i.e., Ephraim's identification with BOTH "Israel" and the "Nations" seems altogether obvious from the context of how the early Ekklesia understood the fulfillment of Amos' prophecy relative to "Ephraim-Israel." Amos' prophecy was primarily to that of the 10 Northern Tribes; therefore, in context, Ephraim's reabsorption under the "Tabernacle of David" identifies them as BOTH of Israel and of the Nations. This is all the more substantiated by Acts 15:17 (and Amos 9:12) wherein *"So that the rest of **mankind** [aka Edom/Esau—Amos. 9:12] may seek the LORD, even all the Nations who are called by My name."* In other words—the "Nations" who swallowed up Ephraim-Israel are now being brought into the Tabernacle of David AS both Ephraim (so absorbed by the Nations) *and* Edom whom the Almighty once hated (viz. Esau = Edom – Romans 9:13). Thus, this Jewish-Judah-Israel AND Nations/Gentile-Ephraim-Israel find their inclusion within the United Kingdom of David in that *"God has committed them* [Jew & the Nations] *all to disobedience, that He might have mercy on all"* (Romans. 11:32).

Furthermore, forget Romans 9:20-28, it's naught but an allegory or at best a metaphor—notwithstanding, mercy shown to the: *". . . vessels of wrath . . . of the Gentiles . . . 'I will call them My people, who were not My people, and her beloved, who was not beloved, and it shall come to pass IN THE PLACE where it was said to them, 'You are not My people,' there they shall be called sons of the living God'"* (Rom. 11:24-26; Hosea 2:23; 1:10). Likewise, the prophecy found in Ezek. 37:15-28—the Two Stick prophecy—is irrelevant or, at best, this prophecy has already taken place (Ephraim has been subsumed by Judah (during the Babylonian Captivity and overwhelmingly by the subsequent Persian Empire). Likewise, there were not that many 10-tribe Israelites "swallowed up" by the nations in the first place—though demographers suggest upwards of 15,000,000 were swallowed up (based on David's initial numbering of the 10 tribes of the north and the fact that today's Syria [alone] had a population of some 24 million prior to her civil war, now in its 8th year, cir. 2020).

Moreover, Dispensationalists affirm that Ephraim (now swallowed up by Judah) will be miraculously taken out of Judah in the "latter days" just before the Second Coming when the Almighty makes them ONE STICK in the Hand of the LORD. I know, this sounds a bit redundant since the two divisions of Israel (Judah-Jews and Ephraim-Jews) are in the minds of these dispensational theologians naught but Jews comprised of all 12 Tribes—all of whom are "natural branches." Indeed, Judah and Ephraim are already joined together in their theology.

Therefore, there is in the minds of the Dispensationalists: YES DISTINCTION and YES SEPARATION. This distinction and separation continues into the Millennial Era where the Church (having nothing to do with Ephraim because those are just Jews/Judah/All Israel) is like a satellite orbiting above the earth as the Bride of Messiah (Dr. John Walvoord) for 1,000 years; all the while the Jews/Israel are/is upon the earth ruling and reigning with "David, My Servant"—although they confirm that the saints rule and reign with Christ a thousand years like good 'ole Chiliasts once affirmed. On the "downside"—the Jews rejected the KINGDOM offered at Messiah's First Coming—"it [the offering of the kingdom to Israel] has been postponed" until the Jews cry out *"Blessed is He Who comes in the Name of the Lord!"*

CH. 1: YES DISTINCTION – NO SEPARATION

In the Dispensational view, Jews today (all 12 Tribes) are outside of the Commonwealth of Israel. They have their own prophetic destiny but are not included in the Bride of Messiah and will, by themselves, undergo the 70th Week of Daniel and their own "Jacob's Trouble." Neither this unbelieving "prophetic Israel" nor, in point of glaring fact, the Old Testament saints from Adam to the Cross, will participate in the Marriage of the Lamb nor the Wedding Feast (only as guests to the 1,000-years "Marriage Supper"); but they are NOT the Bride of Messiah in any way, shape or form. They have their own New Covenant which is NOT the same as the Mediator of the New Covenant or the New Covenant offered to Christians—TOTAL SEPARATION is the norm![28]

Moreover, most traditional Dispensationalists affirm that the Jews, after the Church's rapture, will preach "this gospel of the kingdom" (Matt. 24:14) which is NOT the "gospel of the grace of God" in view in Acts 20:24—why? Because the gospel that the Jews will preach after the pretribulational rapture will NOT produce the Bride of Messiah—this "different gospel of the kingdom" will only produce "tribulation saints"—and no more; aside from the fact they are allowed to be guests at the Marriage Supper of the Lamb because they too are "friends of the bridegroom" just as John the Baptist was.

---

[28] *Dispensational Understanding of the New Covenant* by Mike Stallard, John Master, Dave Fredrickson, Roy E. Beacham, Elliott E. Johnson, Rodney J. Decker, and Bruce Compton. Editor Mike Stallard. Schaumburg, Ill.: Regular Baptist Press, 2012. 285 pages – provides a comprehensive dispensational accounting of their "understandings" of multi-New Covenants, to wit: This book presents three *dispensationalist* views of the Church's relationship to Israel's New Covenant. The non-dispensationalist view that the Church replaces national Israel, the progressive dispensationalist view that the Church partially fulfills the New Covenant, and the older dispensationalist view of Lewis Sperry Chafer that there are two New Covenants—one for Israel and one for the Church—are briefly mentioned and summarily dismissed. Thus, this is a book by traditional dispensationalists *for* traditional dispensationalists, who include: John Nelson Darby, William Kelly, Frederick William Grant, Arno C. Gaebelein, C. I. Scofield, H. A. Ironside, William Newell, Lewis Sperry Chafer, Charles Ryrie, John Walvoord, J. Dwight Pentecost, and Homer A. Kent, but also lesser-known figures such as Benjamin Wills Newton, Émile Guers, C. K. Imbrie, and W. R. Nicholson. He also refers to the views of the New Scofield Reference Bible. Unfortunately, however, he does not mention the early twentieth-century Baptist Clarence Larkin or the contemporary Renald Showers.

One can see in this complex scenario the definitive positions taken by the three main theological bodies (Reform, Dispensational, Commonwealth) found within Christendom today. For definition sake, concerning Israel and the Church:

REPLACEMENT THEOLOGIES (RT):
NO DISTINCTION—NO SEPARATION;

DISPENSATIONALISM:
YES DISTINCTION—YES SEPARATION;

COMMONWEALTH:
YES DISTINCTION—NO SEPARATION.

They either place Israel in subsumption (RT) or, and forgive me for saying this, Dispensationalism ghettoizes the Jew, keeping them apart from the "Elect from among the Nations," both now, and prophetically, up through the reign of "David, My Servant" (Ezek. 37:24-25). In their interpretations concerning WHO IS ISRAEL? —neither one (RT or Dispensationalism) sees today's Israel as Ephraim (from among the nations, His elect) and Judah (the Jews *in toto*)—neither one.

COMMONWEALTH THEOLOGY

YES DISTINCTION—NO SEPARATION.

YES DISTINCTION—juxtaposed to Replacement Theologies . . . Yes, we see there is Israel and the Church but we see Israel as Judah (the Jews—both unbelieving and believing) and Ephraim (the Church, or the ELECT FROM AMONG THE NATIONS).

We see DISTINCTION but NOT the same way that the Dispensationalists see distinction, in that they have Ephraim subsumed by Judah—not so with CT. NO SEPARATION—We affirm (but NOT like the Replacement Theologians) that there is no separation between Judah (the Jews) and Ephraim (the Christians). This is a profoundly prophetic statement in that unbelieving Jews/National Israel shall come into full prophetic fulfillment in accordance with Romans 11:25-27 when ALL ISRAEL SHALL BE DELIVERED. Meanwhile, we wish to keep both believing Judah (Jews) and Christians in the One New Man, the ONE BODY, the New Creation, the Bride of Messiah.

The middle wall of separation is broken down; BUT, and here's our little twist: BOTH PROPHETIC JUDAH/JEWS and the ONE NEW MAN (Jews and Christians) are NOW within the Commonwealth of Israel (Eph. 2:12). Why? Because even in unbelief they have a most peculiar prophetic destiny and God Almighty is gathering them NOW back into the Land and the fact that they are but "blinded in part"—therefore, they are not as the other tribes of the earth! Ultimately the Natural Branches are wholly grafted in again into the ONE ROOT with the wild branches.

The Prodigal (Ephraim) is in the house of the Father WITH the faithful son, Judah. (Note: Judah was NEVER divorced, but Israel/Ephraim was divorced; yet mercy would be shown on her —Ezek. 6:9, Jer. 3:8; Hos. 1:6-7, 9-10; 2:2, 23; 2 Kings 17:18-23.) Thus, defining these terms is incredibly important.

When we say under CT: YES DISTINCTION, we mean it differently than the NO DISTINCTION of RT; and, for that matter, Dispensationalism. Dispensationalism's YES DISTINCTION is different from the YES of CT because the definition of the term "Israel" is different. When we say NO SEPARATION we mean it differently than RT (which subsumes Judah/Jews which they see as just an ethnic designation of "Jews" or worse, "fake Jews"); and Dispensationalism, of course, demands their own brand of "separation" between National Israel and the Church.

NO, it is NOT easy to explain this due to the millennia which have distorted the facts of the matter. The doctrines (especially eschatology) embedded in Commonwealth Theology are, I believe, superior to those of the Replacement/Reform theologians and their anti-chiliasm eschatologies which disinherit the Jews of Judah and distort any distinction between Ephraim and Judah. Furthermore, the many doctrinal inaccuracies within dispensational theology are resolved by the insightful and moderate proposal embedded in CT.

In essence, CT embellishes and clarifies the distinctions between "Israel and the Church" by clarifying the identities of Judah and Ephraim; and, simultaneously, adheres to the singularity of NO SEPARATION espoused within Reform thinking (e.g., the New Covenant is NOW a New Testament reality—not just the "spiritual blessings" of the New Covenant as Dispensationalism's John Nelson Darby proposes, or the two New Covenant systems propounded by Lewis Sperry Chafer of Dallas Theological Seminary. The New Covenant as described in the OT passages is enjoyed today by believers in Jesus/Yeshua —Jer. 31:31-37; 32:40; Ezek. 36:16-38).

Fundamentally, it must be understood, today's Jews (Judah) who are brought into the ONE BODY OF MESSIAH, the ONE NEW MAN, the NEW CREATION where there is "neither Jew nor Greek" are altogether within the bounds of the New Covenant. The phenomenon of Messianic Congregations where Jewish-style practices take place and where there is a greater recognition of the Torah in daily living are NOT separate from the "goyim" who are members of the One Body—there is "neither Jew nor Greek"—however, just as there is neither "male nor female," there abides Jewish Christians and Christians who are non-Jewish—it is what it is.

The "assimilating influences" of the overwhelming number of "goyim" within the ONE BODY tends to "swallow up" the Jewish Christians; however, with the rebirth of the State of Israel, that mitigating influence (i.e., the loss of "Jewishness" juxtaposed to the enculturating influences of "the Elect from the Nations") has been diminished—and all the more with the rise of "Messianic Judaism," which is readily recognized by Christians of non-Jewish backgrounds but vociferously resisted as a branch of Judaism by non-believing Jews (however, not like it used to be—an encouraging development indeed!). Messianic Congregations which wholeheartedly welcome BOTH believing Jews and folks with non-Jewish backgrounds provide extraordinary examples of true unity in Messiah and should be encouraged to thrive!

In summation,[29] the three dominant views of the Church's relationship with Israel are as follows; i.e. how are today's Jews, who are not Christians (viz. Judah), viewed within Christendom by the Church:

(A) REPLACEMENT THEOLOGY: NO DISTINCTION—NO SEPARATION

>Today's Church IS the true Israel of God—ethnic Jews do NOT enjoy any special "divine privilege" (e.g., a physical Land called Israel on the eastern edge of the Mediterranean Sea).

(B) DISPENSATIONALISM: YES DISTINCTION—YES SEPARATION

>Today's Church is wholly distinct from physical Israel—the Jews, who are comprised of both Judah and Ephraim—all 12 Tribes of Israel. God's prophetic plan involves the "mystery" of "Christ and the Ekklesia" AND His plan for Israel (so described) in Bible prophecy—the two are kept distinct and separated.

(C) COMMONWEALTH THEOLOGY: YES DISTINCTION—NO SEPARATION

>Today's Ekklesia is comprised of both Jews of Judah and those from among the nations (including Ephraim so scattered among the nations). This ONE NEW MAN constitutes the Israel of God and is "included" in the Commonwealth of Israel wherein, as well, the Jews of Judah are NOT separated from their own Commonwealth but shall in "prophetic corporate fullness" distinctively enjoy the wealth of that Commonwealth—there abides Israel-Ephraim-the Nations AND Israel-Judah-the Jews (yes distinction) yet, no separation between them (there is but ONE OLIVE TREE—one New Covenant—one New Jerusalem—one Gospel of the Kingdom—one Bride of Messiah—ONE NEW MAN—So Making Peace).

---

[29] *Commonwealth Theology*, by Douglas Krieger, Tribnet Publications, 2018, pp. 41-42.

CHAPTER TWO

THEOLOGICAL ECCENTRICITIES
By Douglas Krieger

WHO ARE THE HEIRS OF NEW COVENANT?

Commonwealth Theology contends that the New Covenant does not supersede the New Covenant made to the progeny of Abraham, i.e., the Jews, as perpetrated by Replacement/Amillennialism theology. Moreover, neither is the New Covenant withheld from the immediate purview of the Church at the present time as rejected by Dispensationalism. These "two extremities" juxtaposed to one another wherein the one (Amillennialism) subsumes Israel and becomes the exclusive "Spiritual Israel"—leaving the physical descendants of Judah in the dust of history-past with no prophetic future (Supersessionist)—the sole inheritor of the New Covenant; vs. Dispensationalism, which confines the New Covenant to the exclusive purview of National Israel yet-future, clearly excluding the Church—aside from the ambiguous "spiritual blessings" of the New Covenant. BOTH extremes are theologically deficient but both theologies possess elements that can readily comprise Commonwealth Theology.

There is DISTINCTION wrought by Dispensationalism between National Israel (aka the Jews) and the Church—between the 12 Gates bearing the Names of the 12 Tribes of Israel and the 12 Foundations, bearing the Names of the 12 Apostles of the Lamb—but there is One Olive Tree, one Holy City which is MULTI-DIMENSIONAL (Ezekiel 40-48; Revelation 21) and is NOT separated from National Israel—i.e., there is today a BOND that is intensely spiritual between Jews and Christians. That bond makes them PEOPLE OF THE BOOK and that bond demands, through the Cross, that the MIDDLE WALL OF SEPARATION has been broken down to make of the two/both ONE NEW MAN, so making peace both NOW and into the prophetic future based upon the immediate and prophetic/eschatological aspects of the SAME NEW COVENANT.

The New Covenant does NOT now nor into the future exclude Jews. Jews, just as their counterparts among the nations of today, are brought into the New Covenant (individually) and prophetically (corporately). They shall enter into the full impact of that same New Covenant that believers (be they Jewish or non-Jewish) do today. National Israel, during the "latter days" shall corporately enter the New Covenant at the commencement of the literal one-thousand-year Millennium.

Dispensationalism finds itself among its many divergent streams engaged in both an eschatological and soteriological crisis—especially after the pre-tribulational rapture of the Bride of Christ, when a "different gospel" called the "Gospel of the Kingdom" distinguishes itself from the Gospel of the Grace of God which produces the One New Man, the Body of Christ, the New Creation. What exactly is produced by the "works of the Law" after the pre-tribulational rapture of the Ekklesia/Church with her soteriological benefits—apparently integrated with spurts of "grace"—is anyone's guess? Thus, the soteriological crisis. Eschatological issues persist with the New Heaven and New Earth postponed until after the Millennium—it would seem that having the redeemed of Israel, the Jews, and Christians "caught together" on the same planet is a fearful sight indeed! In particular, where is the Son of David? Is He ruling and reigning with the saints on His throne on the earth during the Millennium, or is He with His Beloved Bride, the Church, in orbit somewhere above the earth as John Walvoord suggests? The multi-faceted "gospels" contrived by the Dispensationalists boggles the mind.[30]

DISPENSATIONALISM—PREMILLENARIAN, CLASSICAL— PROGRESSIVE—HYPER-DISPENSATIONALISM.

The Church does not replace Israel's pre-existing Abrahamic, Davidic, Land (Palestinian), and New Covenant—nor does she participate in them as propounded by most Amillenarians.[31]

---

[30] Ibid, pp. 33-34.

[31] John Piper presents a challenge to Christian theology and, in particular, to the "separatist" tendencies within Dispensationalism by asserting that the Church participates in the Abrahamic, Palestinian, Davidic, and New Covenants; however, it appears the Church, once again, subsumes Israel (aka the Jews) in this endeavor; to wit: In the words of Romans 11:17, "You [Gentile], although a wild olive shoot, were grafted in among the others and now share in the

nourishing root of the olive tree"—that is, they become part of the redeemed covenant people who share the faith of Abraham. The reason, as Paul put in Romans 4:13, is that "the promise to Abraham and his offspring that he would be heir of the world did not come through the law but through the righteousness of faith." So all who are united to Christ, Abraham's Offspring, by faith are part of the covenant made with him and his offspring. Here's the most sweeping statement of this truth— Ephesians 2:12, "Remember that you [Gentiles] were at that time separated from Christ, alienated from the commonwealth of Israel and strangers to the covenants of promise, having no hope and without God in the world. 13 But now in Christ Jesus you who once were far off have been brought near by the blood of Christ. . . . So then you are no longer strangers and aliens, but you are fellow citizens with the saints and members of the household of God." Therefore, Jewish believers in Jesus and Gentile believers will inherit the Land. And the easiest way to see this is to see that we will inherit the world which includes the Land. Jewish Christians and Gentile Christians will not quibble over the real estate of the Promised Land because the entire new heavens and the new earth will be ours. 1 Corinthians 3:21-23, "All things are yours, 22 whether Paul or Apollos or Cephas or the world or life or death or the present or the future—all are yours, 23 and you are Christ's, and Christ is God's." All followers of Christ, and only followers of Christ, will inherit the earth, including the Land. You recall that all-important word that Jesus spoke to Pilate in John 18:36: "My kingdom is not of this world. If my kingdom were of this world, my servants would have been fighting, that I might not be delivered over to the Jews. But my kingdom is not from the world." Christians do not take up the sword to advance the kingdom of Christ. We wait for a king from heaven who will deliver us by his mighty power. And in that great day Jew and Gentile who have treasured Christ will receive what was promised. There will be a great reversal: the last will be first, and the meek—in fellowship with the Lamb of God—will inherit the Land. Therefore, come to the meek and lowly Christ while there is time, and receive forgiveness of sins, and the hope of glory. (John Piper's document: 2004, Israel, Palestine and the Middle East) All the above appears "biblically legitimate"—however, its downside completely obfuscates the role that even the conversion of the Jewish people shall experience has any legitimate role in the prophetic discourse laid out by Piper. Indeed, the "entire New Heaven and New Earth" will be ours—therefore, nothing over which to quibble; but again, if you carefully read—these dictum announced by Piper obfuscate any role for National Israel with those today called out from among both Jews and Gentiles to be a people for His Name . . . they are simply rejected, and disregarded in toto. Indeed, Israel's present materiality is an existential theological imbroglio for the Amillenarians. Israel's presence on the eastern edge of the Mediterranean has nothing to do with Bible prophecy–it's just a "gathering place" where their final persecution will take place; and where they will meet their Messiah–even their final persecution is somewhat happenstance

God's Economy/Dispensational Administration is committed to at least seven dispensations over a seven-thousand-year time frame. Today, we are living in the Church Age—previous to this it was the Age of the Law (Mt. Sinai). We, as well, are living in the Age of Grace. The Age of Grace is the Age of the Church and this "grace" produces but Mystery, the Church. The Climax of the Age of Grace is the Rapture of the Church prior to the Wrath of God and of the Lamb, poured out upon "all them who dwell on the earth" and the judgment of Babylon the Great—Religious, Commercial and Political. There is the coming of the Antichrist. The Jews (Judah/today's Israel) play a major role in Bible prophecy. Most Dispensationalists affirm a pre-tribulational rapture of the Church—the futurity of Daniel's 70th Week is yet to happen. The Church Age will terminate at the Rapture either at, or some time before, the commencement of the Week. The Jews will endure Jacob's Trouble without the presence of the Church, and Jews (perhaps 144,000 Jewish "Evangelists"[32]—not so designated in Rev. 7 or 14) preach "this gospel of the Kingdom to all the world" (Matthew 24:14) and will face the Antichrist, rebuild the Tribulation Temple and suffer the Abomination of Desolation by themselves. The "Gospel of the Kingdom" is NOT the "Gospel of the Grace of God"—"tribulation saints" will be alerted to the "coming kingdom" and will be saved by their obedience to the Law.

There are many conflicts in dispensational theology after the Church's rapture. The Holy Spirit will no longer restrain the rise of the Antichrist; there are "Two Brides" (the Wife of Jehovah for the Jews—the Bride of Christ for the Christians); two New Covenants—

---

and means nothing in the sum total of their picture of the all-inclusive Messiah! *CT*, Krieger, pp. 47-48

[32] Dr. Thomas Ice and the 144,000 Jewish Evangelists during the Seventieth Week of Daniel: When one exams (sic) the biblical text they find that Revelation 7 speaks of two different people groups: 1) 144,000 Jewish male witnesses (Rev. 7:4–8) and 2) a great multitude, which no one can count from every nation and all tribes and peoples and tongues (Rev. 7:9). Below are reasons why this passage means what it says and refers to exactly 144,000 Jewish guys (no gals or Gentiles included), and 12,000 from each of the twelve tribes of Israel. First, at this point in Revelation John is writing down what he hears the angel who is crying out with a loud voice says (Rev. 7:2, 4). The angel says they are a specific number of Jewish men. (Tommy Ice: *The 144,000 Jewish Witnesses*). CT, Krieger, p. 48

or simply today's Christians enjoy the "spiritual aspects" (only) of the New Covenant; the Bride of Messiah will descend to the Earth but remain hovering above the Earth for 1,000 years where she abides, with the Jews upon the Earth "ruling and reigning" with her Groom who also shall be upon the Earth in some fashion—either as the Son of David upon His throne or through someone else who will either be King David himself or a son of king David.[33]

A strict separation between the Church's purview/witness to the Heavens is maintained—against Principalities and Powers in heavenly places; whereas, Israel's authority/witness is to Gentile World Powers upon the Earth; consequently, there is separation today, and separation up through and perhaps including the Eschaton (beyond the 7,000 years). The Church is a MYSTERY not seen in the Old Testament but revealed only through Paul. The Jews will suffer unfathomable persecution prior to the Second Coming of Christ to prepare them for His Deliverance.[34]

ABERRANT THEOLOGIES

ABERRANT THEOLOGIES / OTHER ESCHATOLOGIES THEOLOGIES / IDENTITY THEOLOGY[35]—Although this category could be placed within either Replacement or Premillenarian Theologies—it deserves its own platform. These theologies are based primarily within Christian Historicism: Seventh-Day Adventism Eschatology, Mormonism, Jehovah Witnesses, other groups such as British Israelism. All share some form of "Identification" with the ancient Tribes of Israel. Most claim some philo-semitic identification but are wholly separate from the Jews, per se. British Israelism claims that the Northern Europeans, especially the British, constitute the Ten Lost Tribes of Israel (carried away by the Assyrians into captivity between 745-712 BC.)—most adhere to some of the discoveries found in J. H. Allen's *Judah's Scepter and Joseph's Birthright* (1902).

---

[33] *Commonwealth Theology*, by Douglas Krieger, Tribnet Publications, 2018, pp. 34-36
[34] Ibid, p. 38
[35] Ibid, pp. 38-41

Herbert W. Armstrong popularized these views using Allen's material. Most all these sects assert the importance of keeping the "commandments" and portions or all the Law of Moses and, in particular, celebrate the Jewish Feast Days in some form. Most of these groups rigidly keep the Sabbath Day as Saturday or enshrine the importance of the Lord's Day (Sunday—Mormons). Most do not find themselves in mainstream evangelicalism (although SDAs and others in the Worldwide Church of God are considered evangelical because of their soteriology). Most of these eschatologies do NOT regard today's State of Israel as a prophetic fulfillment and most keep a rigid separation between themselves and their "Jewish counterparts."

Many claim to be the real Jews or are intensely philo-Semitic: "Mormonism teaches that its adherents are either direct descendants of the House of Israel or adopted into it. As such, Mormons regard Jews as a covenant people of God and hold them in high esteem. The Church of Jesus Christ of Latter-day Saints (LDS Church), the largest Church in Mormonism, is philo-Semitic in its doctrine" (Wikipedia). NOTE: The aforementioned "Churches" which claim some degree of Christian identity are not considered by Dispensationalists as a part of today's "prophetic evangelical community"—most are outside the pale of acceptable Christian "prophetic understanding" and are considered either cults or cultic in their practice.

BRITISH ISRAELISM/CHRISTIAN IDENTITY—One only need to add to this mix various speculations made by both British-Israelism and Christian Identity people, and their many offshoots. For some, the association of these groups to this prophecy (Ezek. 37—Two Sticks) is just too much[36], and so they think that it is best to avoid

---

[36] Mormonism's Two Stick teaching, *An Exegetical Look at Ezekiel 37:15ff, Evaluating a Mormon View* by Dr. J. E. Rosscup: Is the popular Mormon view acceptable, that the two sticks refer to the Book of Mormon (Stick of Joseph) and the Bible (Stick of Judah)? The view is that the sticks have parchment rolled around them containing books. For the Mormon view cf. LeGrand Richards, *A Marvelous Work and a Wonder*, (pp. 67-68), and other sources in the next paragraph. Mormons point in their Book of Mormon to II Nephi 29:6-14 to help prove their view. That passage argues that God not only gave one book to the nation of Jews, but another book to other nations. [But even here, it sounds like not two books, but the Bible (v. 10) and many other books (v. 11) by various prophets (v. 12), and men are to be judged out of those books]. Mormons believe that the two "sticks" (to them the two "books") were joined in the early

the prophecy of Ezekiel 37:15-28 altogether. But even though there have been abuses with the two-stick prophecy, and no one can deny how aberrant groups have interpreted it throughout recent religious history—it is nevertheless a part of the biblical canon that cannot be avoided.[37] The "Two Stick" doctrine found in Mormonism is altogether convoluted and bears little resemblance to the eschatology of the Two Sticks/Two Houses of Commonwealth Theology.

MYSTERIES NOT REVEALED TO THE PROPHETS

There are not Two New Covenants—there is but One New Covenant inaugurated by the Messiah, the Deliverer, in the Upper Room: THIS IS MY BLOOD OF THE NEW COVENANT (Matthew 26:28 KJV). It is the Blood of the Cross which makes the following possible. To suggest, as some have ignorantly done, that the Greek word "*diatheke*" (Strong's G#1242) means "testament" and not "covenant" is a vacuous distinction; and is a vain attempt to fabricate a narrative that simply is designed to change the meaning of the word in the first place. The word is used thirty-three times in the N.T. and is translated "covenant" twenty times—it is derived from the word "*diatithemai*" whose meaning in Strong's is: "(2b) to make a covenant, enter into a covenant, with one, Acts 3:25; Heb. 8:10; 10:16" . . . Strong's G#1303. In sum: Judah—even in unbelief—and Ephraim

---

days of Mormonism (1840's). So they became one book "in the hands of Ephraim" (Ezek. 37:19). They believe that the men who long ago engraved the plates of the Book of Mormon were in the line of Ephraim and Manasseh (Alma 10:3, Book of Mormon). So the Book of Mormon is the Book of Ephraim (cf. E. A. Smith, *Restoration: A Study in Prophecy, a Mormon source*, (p. 165); cf. also J. E. Talmage, *A Study of the Articles of Faith*, (p. 276); Hugh Nibley, *An Approach to the Book of Mormon*. One can see a Mormon's rejection of this Mormon view and an assertion of the correct view of Ezekiel 37:15ff. In Heber C. Snell, "Roundtable: The Bible in the Church," in Dialogue: A Journal of Mormon Thought, Vol. 2, No. 1 (Spring, 1967), pp. 61-62. Mormons similarly hold that Isaiah 29:11-14 by its "book that is sealed" refers to the future Book of Mormon as "a marvelous work and a wonder." Mormons claim, as Richards shows, that Isaiah 29:11-12 was realized when Joseph Smith received and translated golden plates to write the Book of Mormon. For a refutation of such Mormon contentions, cf. Marvin W. Cowan, *Mormon Claims Answered*

[37] Source: http://messianicapologetics.net/archives/1224

> ("who were no longer the people of God but through His mercy are now His people" once again) . . . find themselves within the same immediate and prophetic jurisdiction of the COMMONWEALTH OF ISRAEL: *The Mystery of Messiah* (the Christ) *by which, when you read, you may understand my knowledge in the mystery of Christ, which in other ages was not known to the sons of men, as it has now been revealed by the Spirit to His holy apostles and prophets: that the Gentiles* (nations) *should be fellow heirs, of the same body, and partakers of His promise in Christ through the gospel of which I became a minister according to the gift of the grace of God given to me by the effective working of His power . . . Therefore, remember that you, once Gentiles* (goim) *in the flesh—who are called Uncircumcision by what is called the Circumcision made in the flesh by hands—that at that time you were without Christ, being aliens* (non-citizens) *from the COMMONWEALTH* (Lit. "polity" or "state" or "community") *of Israel and strangers from the covenants of promise, having no hope and without God in the world. But now in Christ Jesus you who once were far off have been brought near by the blood of Christ"* (Eph. 3:4-7; 2:11-13).[38]

Another mystery hidden from the prophets is John Walvoord's "Satellite New Jerusalem":[39]

> Most important, however, is the fact that the city is declared to come down from God out of heaven. In the Greek, the expression "out of heaven" precedes the phrase "from God," just the reverse of the Authorized Version order. Nothing is said about the new Jerusalem being created at this point and the language seems to imply that it has been in existence in heaven prior to this event (for further discussion, see Rev. 21:9). Nothing is revealed concerning this in Scripture unless the expression of John 14:2, "I go to prepare a place for you," refers to this. If the new Jerusalem is in existence throughout the millennial reign of Christ, it is possible that it is a satellite city suspended over the earth during the thousand-year reign of Christ as the dwelling place of resurrected and translated saints who also have access to the earthly scene. This would help explain an otherwise difficult problem of the dwelling place of resurrected and translated beings on the earth

---

[38] *Commonwealth Theology*, by Douglas Krieger, Tribnet Publications, 2018, p. 77
[39] Ibid, pp. 80-86

during a period in which men are still in their natural bodies and living ordinary lives. If so, the New Jerusalem is withdrawn from the earthly scene in connection with the destruction of the old earth, and later comes down to the new earth.[40]

Dispensationalist J. Dwight Pentecost: Pentecost commenting on the two marriage suppers (the supper and feast), as noted by Dr. Chafer, gives this explanation: "... The marriage of the Lamb as that event in the heavens in which the Church is eternally united to Christ and the marriage feast or supper constitutes the millennium, to which Jews and Gentiles will be invited, which takes place on the earth, during which time the Bridegroom is honored through the display of the bride to all His friends who are assembled there" (*THINGS TO COME*, p. 228). Moreover, Pentecost excludes the O.T. saints, "tribulation saints" and National Israel from the Bride of Messiah, but then turns around and "invites" them to the Marriage Supper (i.e., the "Reception" after the Marriage of the Lamb which apparently is on the Earth, even though the Bride of Messiah, according to Dispensationalist Walvoord, is spinning around the globe like a satellite, never coming down to Earth).

There seems to be three items highlighted by Dispensational Scholars: (1) The Marriage of the Lamb with His Bride, the Church (singularly, taking place in the heavens during the 70th Week—a more "intimate" affair—Jews, O.T. saints, and tribulational saints are NOT invited to the Marriage of the Lamb); (2) The "Marriage Feast" (which also takes place in heaven)– which is apparently enjoyed by the "married couple"—and (3) the Marriage Supper of the Lamb which takes place upon the earth with Israel (aka the Jews now occupying their role upon the earth) as the invited "guests" and/or "friends of the bridegroom" as per John the Baptist—John 3:29. . . most likely this is the much-awaited "Wedding Reception" which will last the entire Millennium. In other words, "two suppers" after the Marriage—one in heaven and the other on the earth.

---

[40] Walvoord, *The New Heaven and the New Earth*) [3] *Views on the Two Brides and the Marriage and Marriage Supper of the Lamb*

Dwight Pentecost clarifies:

The participants in the marriage. The marriage of the Lamb is an event which evidently involves only Christ and the Church. It will be shown later, according to Daniel 12:1-3 and Isaiah 26:19-21, that the resurrection of Israel and the Old Testament saints will not take place until the second advent of Christ. Revelation 20:4-6 makes it equally clear that tribulation saints will not be resurrected until that time also. While it would be impossible to eliminate these groups from the place of OBSERVERS [i.e., "guests at the wedding feast"], they cannot be in the position of participants in the event itself. In this connection it seems necessary to distinguish between the marriage of the Lamb and the marriage supper. The marriage of the Lamb is an event that has particular reference to the Church and takes place in heaven. The marriage supper is an event that involves Israel and takes place on the earth.

In Matthew 22:1-14; Luke 14:16-24; and Matthew 25:1-13, where Israel is awaiting the return of the bridegroom and the bride, the wedding feast or supper is located on the earth and has particular reference to Israel. The wedding supper, then, becomes the parabolic picture of the entire millennial age, to which Israel will be invited during the tribulation period, which invitation many will reject and so they will be cast out, and many will accept and they will be received in. Because of the rejection the invitation will likewise go to the Gentiles so that many of them will be included. Israel, at the second advent, will be waiting for the Bridegroom to come from the wedding ceremony and invite them to that supper, at which the Bridegroom will introduce His bride to His friends (Matt. 23:1-13).

Note: Jews are just invited guests or "friends" and we still await the marriage between the Father (Jehovah) and the Wife of Jehovah, the O.T. saints (perhaps the "tribulational saints") are included in on that entity as well and will constitute another portion of the Wife of Jehovah, but not the Bride of Christ—at the Wedding Reception of the Lamb they too will be "invited guests" (aka "friends" of the Bridegroom). At issue is this: How can the Bride of Messiah return the favor as invited guests to the Marriage of Jehovah with his wife, the Wife of Jehovah? Pentecost continues: In reference to the announcement in

CH. 2: THEOLOGICAL ECCENTRICITIES

Revelation 19:9: "Blessed are they which are called unto the marriage supper of the Lamb" two interpretations are possible. Chafer says: "Distinction is called for at this point between the marriage supper which is in heaven and celebrated before Christ returns, and the marriage feast (Matthew 25:10, R. V.; Luke 12:37) which is on earth after His return."

This view anticipates two suppers, one in heaven preceding the Second Advent, and the one following the Second Advent on earth. A second interpretation views the announcement as anticipatory of the wedding supper that will be held on earth following the marriage and the Second Advent, about which an announcement is being made in heaven prior to the return to earth for that event. Inasmuch as the Greek text does not distinguish between marriage supper and marriage feast, but uses the same word for both, and since the marriage supper consistently is used in reference to Israel on the earth, it may be best to take the latter view and view the marriage of the Lamb as that event in the heavens in which the Church is eternally united in Christ and the marriage feast or supper as the millennium, to which Jews and Gentiles will be invited, which takes place on the earth, during which time the bridegroom is honored through the display of the bride to all His friends who are assembled there.[41]

Other Dispensationalists are explicit: There are TWO BRIDES/WIVES—one for Jehovah and one for Christ; to wit: As we have seen, the OT represents Israel as the wife of Jehovah. Although she has been unfaithful and divorced by her Husband, a time is coming when "all Israel will be saved" (Rom. 11:26). At that time, Jehovah will take her back as His wife. The marriage of Israel to Jehovah is seen in promises of God concerning the city, Zion. In her restoration, God will rejoice over the city as a bridegroom rejoices over the bride. In the meantime, those who accept Messiah Jesus are baptized into His body (1 Cor. 12:13). In the same way that Eve was literally "one flesh" with Adam, having been taken from his side (Gen. 2:21-24), so believers are joined into the spiritual body of Christ and betrothed to Him.

---

[41] Pentecost, *Things to Come*, pp. 227-28.

COMMONWEALTH THEOLOGY ESSENTIALS

During Jacob's Trouble and the Great Tribulation, the wife of Jehovah is being purified on earth in preparation for her restoration during the Millennial Kingdom to follow. At the same time, the bride of Christ is in her bridal chamber, having been taken in the Rapture and wed to Him at the marriage of the Lamb. Later, after the Millennial Kingdom has come to a close and a new heavens and new earth are created, the holy city, the New Jerusalem, is prepared by Jehovah as a bride adorned for her husband—the Lamb (Rev. 21:2, 9). The long-unfulfilled promises of the restoration of Jerusalem, which found their initial fulfillment in the Millennial Kingdom (Isa. 62), will come to final fruition in the New Jerusalem where all the redeemed of all ages are in union with God and the Lamb Who are its temple (Rev. 21:22). This is the ultimate consummation of all the redeemed.[42]

Thus, by postponing the New Heaven and the New Earth to the Eschaton, Dispensationalism has kept the Church and Israel in SEPARATION; their distinction has been carried to the extreme and has made the Cross of "none effect" (the "Wall of Separation" persists). Likewise, by creating two brides, God is made out to be a polygamist! This, quite frankly, "elaborate web of deceit," makes the Marriage of the Lamb with His Eternal Bride a mockery! Turning to Dr. Robert Gundry, we read:

We should not expect to find rigid consistency in the biblical use of metaphors . . . Thus, since Israel as well as the Church is both bride and wife, we should not jump to the conclusion that the Lamb's bride and wife consists of the Church alone. On the contrary, the context indicates that at the marriage supper of the Lamb the bride includes Israel: "Come here, I will show you the bride, the wife of the Lamb. And he . . . showed me the holy city, Jerusalem . . . with twelve gates . . . and names were written on them, which are those of the twelve tribes of the sons of Israel" (Rev 21:9, 10, 12). If therefore, the marriage supper does not require a pretribulational resurrection and rapture of the Israelitish segment of the bride, neither does it require a pretribulational resurrection and rapture of the Church.[43]

---

[42] Thomas D. Ice, *The Marriage of the Lamb*, Liberty University @ https://digitalcommons.liberty.edu/cgi/viewcontent.cgi?article=1112&context=pretrib_arch Retrieved on 05.01.2020

[43] Robert F. Gundry, *The Church and the Tribulation*, Zondervan Publishing House, Grand Rapids, MI, 1973, p. 85

CH. 2: THEOLOGICAL ECCENTRICITIES

Notwithstanding, Arno Fruchtenbaum sums up the "polygamist God" we serve: While the distinction between Israel and the Church is maintained in various ways throughout the Bible, this is one of the more picturesque [i.e., the difference between the Marriage of Lamb with the Church in heaven during the 70th Week of Daniel and the Marriage Supper of the Lamb upon the earth when the guests, Israel, O.T. saints, and "tribulation saints" show up as "guests"—our insertion]. However, if one makes the Wife of Jehovah (Israel as Wife) and the Bride of the Messiah (the Church as Wife) one and the same thing, he is faced with numerous contradictions because of the different descriptions given. Only when the two separate entities are seen: Israel as the Wife of Jehovah and the Church as the Bride of the Messiah, do all such contradictions vanish.[44]

And . . . But there will be "Guests," for as all the dead in Christ shall rise and be present at the "Marriage of The Lamb," and as only those who are saved from Pentecost to the taking out of the Church, belong to the Church (The Bride), there will be present as "GUESTS" the Old Testament Saints, such as Abel, Seth, Enoch, Noah, Abraham, Job, Moses, David, the Prophets, and even John the Baptist who claimed to be only the "Friend" of the Bridegroom. Then there will be the "Blood Washed Multitude" that come out of the Tribulation after the Church has been caught out. Thus we see that the righteous of all the past Ages and Dispensations, and all the Saints of God who shall be worthy, and who are not included in the Bride (The Church), will be "Guests" at the "Marriage Supper of the Lamb." Angels will be "spectators" of the scene but they cannot be "Guests," for that honor is reserved for only those who have been redeemed by the "Blood of the Lamb."[45]

Thus, in the minds of the Dispensationalists, the God of the Bible has two SEPARATED MARRIAGES—One to Israel (somewhere along the line, yet future somewhere during or at the end of the Millennium) and one to the Messiah, the Christ, the Bride of Messiah–that's how far they have carried their DISTINCTION– into SEPARATION! Indeed, some Dispensationalists suggest that the "guests" at the Wedding Supper will be the Wife of Jehovah

---

[44] Dr. Arno Fruchtenbaum: *The Wife of Jehovah and the Bride of Messiah*, July 8, 2009

[45] Source: *The Marriage of the Lamb*, Thomas Ice

(ostensibly) and the reverse is played out when Jehovah will marry His Bride and then the Bride of Christ will return the favor and show up as guests to the "second marriage feast"—so convoluted is their desire to keep the Bride of Messiah SEPARATED from O.T. saints, Jews (in general), and, most certainly, anyone, Jew or Gentile, who are destined to be but "temple servants" within the crucible of Daniel's 70th Week.

Somehow, through it all, the Triune God is likewise separated—and this is supposed to end the confusion if we do not grasp the profound nature of two Brides . . . one for Father God (Jehovah) and one for His Son (Yeshua/Jesus) . . . this is all beginning to make sense to the unsuspecting! A marital crisis could develop—I'm not saying it will—if the two wives show up at one of these "wedding receptions" during the Millennium when the Lamb's Wife is introduced to Jehovah's Wife; especially, given the fact that Jehovah's Wife were the initial guests/friends invited to take part in the Marriage Supper of the Lamb, which is apparently elongated throughout the entire Millennium. Forbid that the Marriage of the Wife of Jehovah to Jehovah takes place somewhere during the Marriage Supper of the Lamb . . . talk about confusion!

This becomes all the more convoluted when Dispensationalists openly admit that the ultimate descent of the Bride of Christ is, in point of glaring fact, a COMPOSITION of all saints throughout the ages as manifested in the descent of the New Jerusalem to the Earth at the terminus of the Millennial Reign. Here, the Woman, the Lamb's Wife, includes, apparently, the Wife of Jehovah—a TWOFER! Only the ESCHATON (the "Eighth Day") could produce such an amalgamation. An attempt to carry these metaphors to their logical conclusions is, in a word: PREPOSTEROUS!

Furthermore, it degrades the intimate relationship that the Lamb's Bride has with her Groom. I could use the word "disgusting" but I refrain from such a theological boondoggle! If, indeed, the would-be Wife of Jehovah is eventually married to Jehovah/Father God somewhere at the terminus of the Millennium, to avoid confusion—since they are the guests of the Bridegroom at the Marriage Supper of the Lamb—her marriage as the Wife of Jehovah will be short lived, apparently, since she somehow merges into the Bride of Christ at the Eschaton—O HAPPY DAY!

PRIOR TWO-HOUSE THEOLOGIES[46]

Commonwealth Theology is keenly aware of the emphasis placed upon "Two House Theology" wrought by aberrant denominational entities within the tent of Christendom (e.g., Mormonism, Jehovah Witnesses, Seventh-Day Adventism and the "Identity Movement" of British Israelism). It would behoove the reader to explore the findings of "Two House Theology" recorded in Wikipedia (presented below)—we simply state the contemporary attitude of opponents to the immediate thesis with citations required, notwithstanding; to wit: Opponents (From Wikipedia with observations included):

"Many opponents [who?] claim that the lost tribes reunited with the Kingdom of Judah in the years leading up to and following Judah's return from the Babylonian Captivity in 537 BCE, hence they do not exist in the nations today other than in the form of the Jews, those scattered by the Roman diaspora (70 CE) and subsequent Christian and Muslim exiles in later periods. Other opponents claim that the lost tribes have been completely assimilated by and are unidentifiable in the nations of the world and hence could never have returned from their deportation by and into Assyria. Opposition also arises simply when Israelites are identified with people more commonly associated with Japheth, one of Noah's three sons. Interestingly, some Two-House advocates won't deny some aspect of this argument, taking into account a prophetic verse: Genesis 9:27a "God enlarge Japheth, and let him dwell in the tents of Shem" (RSV). (Shem was another son of Noah, but also the ancestor of the Hebrews, Arabs, and many other ethnic groups according to genealogies found in the Hebrew Scriptures.) Three of the major Messianic Jewish groups reject Two House Theology as being misguided at best, or at worst a Gentile cult seeking to make themselves appear as Jews. The Union of Messianic Jewish Congregations, the Messianic Jewish Association of America (an affiliate of the International Messianic Jewish Alliance) and the Messianic Bureau International all proclaim the Messianic movement as a movement for Jewish believers in Yeshua and forbid the

---

[46] Adapted from *Commonwealth Theology*, pp. 23-25

teaching that gentiles may be of the lost tribes of Israel, or any reference to the two houses of Israel.

This kind of thinking is best seen in the "Ephraimite Error" white paper,[47] produced in 1999, which several Two House proponents have responded to. These attitudes may come as a reaction to British-Israelism which is best epitomized by the Worldwide Church of God founded by Herbert W. Armstrong, and its many offshoots.[citation needed] Many in Messianic Judaism consider Two House teaching to be irrelevant and meaningless.[citation needed] Some[who?] would view Messianic Judaism's total avoidance of the issue and its dismissal of the Scriptures as a manifestation of Messianic Judaism's wide-scale avoidance of more important theological issues pertaining to the nature of Messiah, the composition and historicity of Scripture, and Messianic Judaism's engagement with modern society.[citation needed] (SOURCE: Wikipedia @ Two House Theology) *The Ephraimite Error, A Position Paper*, submitted to the International Messianic Jewish Alliance, Author: Kay Silberling, Ph.D. Committee Members and Advisors: Kay Silberling, Ph.D., Daniel Juster, Th.D., and David Sedaca, M.A.

The "paper" is mandatory reading concerning the opinions of many "Messianic Jews" who, suffice it to say, are adverse as far as "Gentiles claiming attachment" as a separate House of Joseph/Ephraim to the House of Judah (i.e., the Jews). That may be theologically unsettling in that "Messianic Jews" who by definition find themselves within the confines of the ethnon or of the nations who have for the past nigh 1900 years dominated the One Body's attendance–where there is neither "Jew nor Greek." Their acceptance into mainstream Judaism is grossly irritated by the Messiahship of Yeshua; and, among some Messianic groups there is, unfortunately, a decided antagonism to the Zionist State as illegitimate until Messiah

---

[47] *The Ephraimite Error: A Position Paper Submitted to the International Messianic Jewish Alliance*
Author: Kay Silberling, Ph.D.
https://www.myetzchayim.org/wp-content/uploads/2019/09/Ephraimite-Error.pdf

CH. 2: THEOLOGICAL ECCENTRICITIES

makes it so–oddly enough they find common cause with Ultra-Orthodox groups like the Neturei Karta and Satmar Hasidism who perceive the creation of the State of Israel as an anti-messianic act. We include only the introduction of the "white paper" but a full read is preferable. The overarching concern of these sincere brethren centers on the physicality of the DNA, if you would, of those who aspire as the House of Ephraim. That "element" in CT is NOT "doctrinal priority"—it is at best, irrelevant, for the "spiritual dynamic" far exceeds any materiality associated with the scattering and/or swallowing up of the Ten Northern Tribes who have been purposefully scattered among the nations (Hosea). We do not disclaim that "Israelite DNA" can be found among sundry peoples "called out from among the nations" but that is NOT the emphasis of Scripture regarding *"I will call them My people, who were not My people, and her beloved, who was not beloved . . . and it shall come to pass on the place where it was said to them, 'You are not My people,' There they shall be called sons of the living God.'"* (Hosea 2:23; 1:10; Romans 9:25-26) One can immediately determine from the INTRODUCTION to the "white paper" on THE EPHRAIMITE ERROR this heightened sensitivity from those Jews who have embraced the Messiah:

> INTRODUCTION: A movement alternately known as the "Ephraimite," "Restoration of Israel," "Two Covenant Israel," or "Two House" movement has recently gained ground in some areas among ardent Christian Zionists. Proponents of this movement contend that members of the "born again" segment of the Christian Church are, in fact, actual blood descendants of the biblical Israelites who were dispersed as a result of the Assyrian invasion of the ancient kingdom of Israel in 722 B.C.E. The movement's proponents further argue that these dispersed "Israelites," or "Ephraimites," whose identities have remained undisclosed even to themselves until recent times, primarily settled in areas now recognized as largely populated by Anglo-Saxons. At times they argue that all Anglo-Saxons, and even all of humanity, are descended from these lost Ephraimites.

At other times, that only born-again Christians can claim descent. In either case, Christians from Anglo-Saxon lands, such as Great Britain, Australia, Canada, and the United States, can feel assured that they are most likely direct blood descendants of the ancient people of Ephraim. It is now incumbent upon these members of "Ephraim," they argue, to "accept their birthright" and live as members of Israel. They urge Gentile Christians to keep the Torah in obedience to the Hebrew Scriptures, to strive to reeducate Jews and other Christians about their new, "latter-day prophecy," and to work toward the repatriation of the land of Israel by their own number. Primary among the movement's spokespersons are Batya and Angus Wootten and Marshall, a.k.a. Moshe, Koniuchowsky. The Woottens publish a newsletter entitled the House of David Herald, as well as several books. Batya's books include *In Search of Israel, The Star of David, The Olive Tree of Israel*, and *Who Is Israel? And Why You Need to Know*. Angus' books include *Take Two Tablets Daily, A Survey of the Ten Commandments* and *613 Laws that God Gave Moses* and *The Messianic Vision*. Other names mentioned by Wootten are Brian Hennessy and David Hargis. Ed Chumney has written a book entitled *The Bride of Christ*, which I was unable to review. Among the Woottens, I will deal only with Batya's writings. Moshe Koniuchowsky leads a ministry called "Your Arms to Israel." In addition, he has recently formed an organization named "The Messianic Israel Alliance," which, despite its misleading name, has no affiliation with or endorsement by the International Messianic Jewish Alliance or any of its affiliates. The movement is growing to the point that it now has some areas of overlap with the Christian Zionist movement as well as the Messianic Jewish movement. As a result of this, there are several spokespersons in both these groups who advance this teaching while maintaining primary affiliation either as Christian Zionists or as Messianic Jews."

The conclusions reached in the EPHRAIMITE ERROR are as follows—although they do chastise the present Two-House Theology, they simultaneously open the door to genuine understanding—so it appears—to the relationship between the Church and Israel but focus such illumination to the "Apostolic Fathers?"—to wit—their conclusions:

CH. 2: THEOLOGICAL ECCENTRICITIES

The position of the I.M.J.A., then is that the Ephraimite, or "Two House" movement is in error for the following reasons: 1) flawed, unwarranted, and dangerous interpretation of Scripture 2) inconsistent logic and contradictory positions 3) racist and race-based theology 4) Supersessionist theology 5) historically inaccurate depiction of Israel 6) dangerous, false, and militant claims to the land which threaten the stability of the current State of Israel.

It is noteworthy that the Samaritans of Jesus' day (John 4) considered Jacob to be their father (John 4:12)—notwithstanding, Jesus (who was Jewish and who knew that the "Jews have no dealings with Samaritans"—John 4:9) spoke with the "Samaritan woman at the well." This well, incidentally, was in the *"city of Samaria which is called Sychar, near the plot of ground that Jacob gave to his son Joseph"* (John 4:4-5). Indeed, "Jacob's well was there" (John 4:6). Jesus came to this peculiar place identified with Jacob, Joseph, Samaria at the "sixth hour" of the day (John 4:6). Why do we think the "sixth hour" in John's gospel had any significance and that these "half-Jews" (for they were so considered by the Jews to be "half-breeds" since the original Israelites (Ephraimites) who had returned "mingled in" with the Gentiles who had been imported into the land of the 10 Tribes of the North after their deportation—some of the Jews had returned, yes, but inter-married with the Gentiles and became the infamous "Samaritans" (2 Kings 17:24-41). I find it somewhat amazing that the 6th hour is mentioned here in that it was the 6th hour (i.e., high noon) when Pontius Pilate introduced Jesus to the Jews as their King: "When Pilate therefore heard that saying, he brought Jesus out and sat down in the judgment seat in a place that is called the Pavement, but in Hebrew, Gabbatha. Now it was the Preparation Day of the Passover, and about the sixth hour. And he said to the Jews, 'Behold your King!'" (John 19:13-14).

Could it be that the mentioning of these two sets of "Sixth Hours" are somehow related? If so—perhaps Jesus as the "King of the Jews" included the Samaritans as well—in other words, He is King of both the Samaritans (Ephraimites mingled among the Jews) and the Jews of Judah. Furthermore, Jesus stayed two full days among the Samaritans (John 4:40) whereupon the Samaritans proclaimed:

"Now we believe, not because of what you (the woman at the well) *said, for we ourselves have heard Him and we know that this is indeed the Christ, the Savior of the world"* (John 4:39-42).

It is, as well, in this very context that Jesus tells His disciples while within the context of this Samaritan city: "I sent you to reap that for which you have not labored; others have labored, and you have entered into their labors . . . Behold, I say to you, lift up your eyes and look at the fields, for they are already white for harvest" (John 4:35-38). In other words what Jesus accomplished in John 4 was the bringing in of the harvest wholly inclusive of the ancient Ephraimites, the Samaritans—they were considered the HARVEST; they too were looking for the Messiah (John 4:25). Finally, can the TWO DAYS Jesus stayed among these ancient Ephraimites allude to Hosea 6:1-3? Hosea clearly has in view Ephraim-Israel—calling Ephraim to repentance within the context of "O Ephraim, what shall I do to you? O Judah, what shall I do to you?" (Hosea 6:4). What is so striking regarding this "prophetic call to repentance" on Ephraim's part are these two days and how they could readily affirm the past 2,000 years since the Cross of Christ; to wit: *"Come, and let us return to the LORD; for He has torn, but He will heal us; He has stricken, but He will bind us up. AFTER* **TWO DAYS** *He will revive us; on the* **THIRD DAY** *He will raise us up, that we may live in His sight. Let us know, let us pursue the knowledge of the LORD. His going forth is established as the morning; He will come to us like the rain, like the latter and former rain to the earth"* (Hosea 6:1-3). Rabbinical authorities and Psalm 90:4, along with Peter in 2 Peter 3:8 view the six days of creation being each day akin to 1,000 years; therefore, 2 days could be seen as 2,000 years or $1/3^{rd}$ of the 6,000/6-days allotted to humankind with the THIRD DAY or the SEVENTH DAY as the Millennium.

Chapter Three

THE MISSING PEACE
By Krieger; Steinle

The Introduction presented evidence for the conclusion that "believers among the nations" (Gentiles) sprang forth from the seed of the House of Israel, which had been prophetically "scattered abroad." The "spiritual equivalence" between the Gentiles and the Lost House, implied by Paul's reference to "you who were far off," is admittedly unquantifiable due to its non-genetic makeup. What is unequivocally certain, however, is that Messiah established the peace between the members of the Commonwealth of Israel—specifically between the Jews and "you Gentiles"—during His first coming. This peace is, therefore, not the hope of a future peace, but a peace already attained in the spirit—Christ "having abolished" the barrier, which had previously prevented said peace. Of note: This peace DOES NOT extend to the Nations at large; that is, to unbelievers among Nations (aka "The World"). This peace, which enabled the creation of the One New Man, is peace within the "household of God." Peace between the House of Judah and the, predominantly Gentile, Church—the Holy Universal (International) Congregation. Yet, the manifestation of this peace remains, at best, partially revealed to this day.

What could have caused the suppression of this peace? A peace that was so clearly the will of God? That was so obviously bound to the cross! Five reasons are proposed and addressed throughout this book:

1. Longstanding animosity between the two houses of Israel (consequently, between Judah and the Church, and vice versa).
2. Separation from the Nations by the Jews.
3. The World's Anti-Semitic influence on the Church;
4. Thus, the Church's rejection of the Jews and of the Old Testament laws.
5. The failure of both parties to recognize and extend God's mercy.

The Obstacle to Peace

Apart from Paul's recognition of this peace, expressed within his Ephesians letter and confirmed (at least at first) by the Apostle to the Gentiles' cordiality with the Judean Church leaders, it would seem as though the cross were completely ineffectual in advancing peace between the Jews and the Gentile believers. This glaring contradiction demands further study of the mechanism within Ephesians 2 by which peace was supposed to be established.

> *"For He Himself is our peace, who has made both one, and has broken down the middle wall of separation, having abolished in His flesh the enmity, that is, the law of commandments **contained in** ordinances* (τὸν νόμον τῶν ἐντολῶν ἐν δόγμασιν), *so as to create in Himself one new man from the two, thus making peace..."* (Eph. 2:14-15).

That *"wall of separation"* had excluded those *"far off"* from the Commonwealth of Israel. The *"law of commandments contained in ordinances"* had created an ENMITY between those *"far off"* and those "near"—it became the *"wall of separation."* There was, historically, no peace between the two houses of the Commonwealth of Israel, much less, with those outside of it. The blood of the cross did not abolish the Law! It abolished the enmity created either by the Law or by a particular derivation of the Law; specifically, by dogmatic commands/ordinances *(entolōn en dogmasin)*. Such dogma might refer to the customs associated with "doctrines of men." These human traditions, held in the stead of God's laws, will be discussed in later chapters.

Nevertheless, those who were given the commandments of God (via Moses) implemented those commands over and against the nations who surrounded them— who were lawless. The nations did not have the *"covenants of promise"*—they were without hope and without God in the world. Furthermore, they were eventually held in contempt by those who were given the commandments of God— that, then, was the *"wall of separation"*—the "enmity" that arose between the two—there was no peace![48]

---

[48] Adapted from *Commonwealth Theology*, by Douglas Krieger, Tribnet Publications, 2018, p. xxii

References to the enmity between the Jews and the "worldly" Nations prior to the cross abound among ancient historians. According to Edward Flannery:

> It was the Jews' refusal to accept Greek religious and social standards that marked them out…The first clear examples of anti-Jewish sentiment can be traced back to Alexandria in the 3rd century BCE. Alexandria was home to the largest Jewish community in the world and the Septuagint, a Greek translation of the Hebrew Bible, was produced there. Manetho, an Egyptian priest and historian of that time, wrote scathingly of the Jews and his themes are repeated in the works of Chaeremon, Lysimachus, Poseidonius, Apollonius Molon, and in Apion and Tacitus.[49]

> Manetho wrote that the Jews were expelled [as] Egyptian lepers who had been taught by Moses "not to adore the gods." Agatharchides of Cnidus wrote about the "ridiculous practices" of the Jews and of the "absurdity of their Law," and how Ptolemy Lagus was able to invade Jerusalem in 320 BC because its inhabitants were observing the Sabbath.[50]

Tacitus observed; "Moses prescribed for them a novel religion quite different from those of the rest of mankind. Among the Jews all things are profane that we hold sacred; on the other hand they regard as permissible what seems to us immoral…The other practices of the Jews are sinister and revolting…"[51]

In addition to conflict with the ungodly nations, an enmity within the household of God also existed which would portend and evolve into the animosity between the Jews and "you Gentiles," referenced by Paul. Without going into the three hundred year history of this animosity, Acts 6:1 merely relates; *"there arose a complaint against the Hebrews by the Hellenists…"* It was none other than these Hellenistic (Greek speaking) "wanderers among the nations" who had compiled the Greek Septuagint.

---

[49] Flannery, Edward H. *The Anguish of the Jews: Twenty-Three Centuries of Antisemitism*. Paulist Press, first published in 1985; this edition 2004, pp. 11–12. ISBN 0-8091-2702-4.
[50] ibid, p. 25.
[51] Tacitus, Histories, Book 5:4.1; 5.1

Hellenistic Judaism was a form of Judaism in classical antiquity that combined Jewish religious tradition with elements of Greek culture...the main centers of Hellenistic Judaism were Alexandria in Egypt and Antioch in Syria...both founded at the end of the fourth century BCE in the wake of the conquests of Alexander the Great. Hellenistic Judaism also existed in Jerusalem during the Second Temple Period, where there was conflict between Hellenizers and traditionalists (sometimes called Judaizers).[52]

There is evidence within the Bible itself that after the conversion of the Gentile Cornelius, the focus of the Jewish Church was to reach the members of the Commonwealth of Israel who had been scattered among the Nations (Gentiles).

...when they had come to Antioch, spoke to the Hellenists (Ἑλληνιστάς, *Hellēnistas*), *preaching the Lord Jesus. And the hand of the Lord was with them, and a great number believed and turned to the Lord* (Acts 11:20-21).

Strong's gives the definition of *Hellēnistés*: a Hellenist (Greek-speaking Jew); Strong's 1675. Here we must discount Strong's contemporary usage of "Jew" and consider that it potentially encompassed all Israelites. The point is that, according to the Byzantine source texts, the missionaries in the passage above were not evangelizing "Greeks," but Israelites with Greek speech and/or customs. "Hellenists," as opposed to "Hellenics" (Greeks). Also of note: The Apostle to the Gentiles was compelled to begin his special calling by engaging with the Hellenists (Ἑλληνιστάς, *Hellēnistas*) in Jerusalem: *And he spoke boldly in the name of the Lord Jesus and disputed against the Hellenists, but they attempted to kill him* (Acts 9:29). Paul was not, at this juncture, confronting the Greeks and Romans, but Greek-speaking Jews. These Hellenists represented the "Nations" to whom Paul had been sent (Acts 9:15); and quite likely were the intended audience of the Ephesians 2 appeal to "you Gentiles"— you believers from among the nations.

---

[52] https://en.wikipedia.org/wiki/Hellenistic_Judaism

CH. 3: THE MISSING PEACE

No matter how broadly "Gentiles" might be defined—that is, whether the enmity involved non-genetic believers or "scattered Israel"—the animosity between Judah and the Gentiles, which was fomented by laws and customs, was put to an end at the cross. Furthermore, any continuation of that enmity demands a theological explanation. Commonwealth Theologians observe that mainstream theologies have failed to address this dilemma and suggest three primary reasons:

1. They have not properly identified the source of "the wall's" animosity. They have faulted the Law rather than observing the **division** caused by the Law-customs-traditions—which were noted in the historical examples above.
2. They have failed to distinguished between the ordinances of the Law and the divine covenants—equating the Sinaitic Covenant with the Laws (Instructions) also given at Mt. Sinai; and,
3. Christianity, as a whole, has determined—likely, initially due to ulterior political motives—to remain separated from the Jews **in spite** of the peace won at the cross.

PEACE AND UNITY IN THE CHURCH

Although peace and unity between Jews and Gentiles is the primary focus of Commonwealth Theology, the unity of the Body of Christ, illustrated by Paul in Ephesians 4, applies no less to the various factions within the Gentile Church. This interaction is represented by the following excerpt from *One in Messiah* (see footnote at the end of the section).

Today's divisions, even hostilities, within the Body of Christ plague our own house—I am of Paul, I am of Cephas, I am of Apollos, and finally, the most insidious: I AM OF CHRIST. These divisions reveal naught but our immaturity. Paul appears to have written to the Roman Christians from Corinth (again, in 56 AD)—he'd already confronted the issues in Corinth in reference to division and their factious attitudes. Likewise, Paul had already, so it appears, encountered the "Truth of the Gospel" issues in Antioch when he had written his letter to the Galatian believers in reference to "the Israel of God" (Gal. 6:16) cir. 49 AD (Paul's letter written to the Galatian believers). The event described in Galatians 2 refers to Acts 11:27-30 or some other unrecorded meeting. Now, if the letter was written to believers in northern Galatia, then it was written after the beginning of Paul's second missionary journey in 53-56 AD and AFTER the Jerusalem Council of Acts 15—in other words, Galatians 2 likely refers to the Jerusalem Council, which had recently convened. All this to say that the Corinthian experience, as well as what happened in Antioch after the Jerusalem Council, and the letter to the Galatians—all was written before Paul's letter to the Roman Christians cir. 56 AD and, of course, prior to his visit to Rome.

So—if you were to ask most believers today: What is the Truth of the Gospel? They would forthrightly tell you something akin to 1 Corinthians 15:1-4; to wit:

Moreover, brethren, I declare to you the GOSPEL which I preached to you, which also you received and in which you stand, by which also you are saved, if you hold fast that word which I preached to you—unless you believed in vain. For I delivered to you first of all that which I also received: that Christ died for our sins according to the Scriptures, and that He was buried, and that He rose again the third day according to the Scriptures (1 Cor. 15:1-4).

Yes, this is the Gospel of the Grace of God, no doubt (Acts 20:24) leading to personal salvation; however, that Gospel, is NOT the whole or fullness/completion of the Gospel (i.e., the Gospel of Christ) to which Paul alludes to his Roman believers in Romans 15:29—the *"fullness of the blessing of the gospel of Christ"* has everything to do with the *"One New Man—so making peace."* Paul does not use the phrase *"the God of peace"* (TWICE) just to be mouthing words (Romans 15:33; 16:20)—what He has in mind is the very *"truth of the Gospel"* which he announced to Peter in Galatians 2:5, 14 wherein Paul confronted Peter for withdrawing himself from Gentile Galatians and eating with only Jewish believers. No, Peter was not living by the truth of the Gospel. Were both these Jewish and Gentile believers? Yes—had both of them responded to the Gospel of the Grace of God and, consequently, accepted the Gospel of the Grace of God through salvation in Christ alone? YES! But Peter and the Judaizers were not living by the truth of the Gospel. They had their doctrine of salvation down—but were not living by the truth of the Gospel!

In Rome, they had become collections of believers meeting in different homes who had come to faith in Christ through various preachers; they were as diverse as the population of Rome. There were well-to-do believers with large households, as well as slaves, Jews, Greeks, barbarians, Roman citizens, and freemen from throughout the Empire. In such a situation, it certainly would have been easy for the Christian community to segregate and separate themselves from each other. Naturally, those with similar cultural backgrounds, socioeconomic status, ethnic identities, apostolic preferences, and especially those with a kosher diet would prefer to group themselves together.

As expected from these deep-seated divisions and hostilities between Jews and Gentiles, Paul's main challenge was bringing these two groups of believers together in Rome. Remember how Peter with other Jewish believers separated themselves from eating and fellowshipping with Gentile believers in Antioch? (Gentiles; Grk. *"ethnos"* or those called out from the nations—Gal. 2:2-16) If Peter could become factious, even after the revelation of the rebuilding of the United Kingdom of David in Acts 15:16-17, it would be easy and natural for Jewish and Gentile believers in Rome to separate themselves from each other. If Paul could solve this problem in Rome in order to build up the One Body of Christ, then, in comparison, all other divisions between Barbarians and Romans, or slave and freeman, would be simple. The building up of the Lord's One Body depended upon the "wall of separation" (Eph. 2:14) being broken down. Let's review the book of Romans with the unity of God's people in view, and division being the problem for Paul to resolve.

Paul addressed this letter to the *"saints in Rome"* (Rom. 1:7). He didn't write this letter to any specific group, not even the group of saints meeting as the Lord's ekklesia in Priscilla and Aquila's house (nor is any leadership designated in his epistle to the Romans). He wanted all the saints in the various groups to hear the same message directly from him; so, after reading they could come together in one fellowship. Although he was addressing "saints"—those who already had faith in Jesus Christ—yet he said he was preaching the gospel to them (Rom. 1:15). According to our current understanding the gospel message is for unbelievers. Why would Paul need to preach the gospel to those who had already believed in Jesus Christ? It's because they were divided; therefore, they needed to hear and understand the entire gospel of God (Rom. 1:1) concerning His Son, Jesus Christ, Who died and resurrected (Rom. 1:3-4) for His eternal purpose to be fulfilled.

Since the challenge was to bring divided and separated believers into One Body, Paul started by showing that no matter the gulf of differences between Jews and Gentiles, they still had a common heritage. The first commonality is condemnation by God—the *"wrath of God has passed to all humankind for all have sinned and come short of God's glory"* (Rom. 3:23). In Romans chapters 1 through 3 Paul made evident, whether Jews or Gentiles, whether "chosen" with God's law or without law, both were sinners falling short of God's glory—under the sentence of "judgment." There is no advantage of Jews over Gentiles or vise-versa in regard to condemnation.

As people equally condemned—under God's wrath, both needed common redemption through the death of Jesus Christ (Rom. 3:24). Without exception, the only common way to justification available before God is through faith (Rom. 4-5), the faith of Jesus Christ (Rom. 3:26). In Romans 4, while the Jews considered Abraham to be their forefather, it made clear Abraham is the father of faith for both Jews and Gentiles (for *"righteousness was imputed to him"* before Abraham was circumcised—Rom. 4:22). Romans 6:3-4 unveils both Jews and Gentiles have been "put to death" through Christ's crucifixion and burial. Now, both are sanctified (made holy) the same way . . . by their common identity in Christ.

Romans 7 reveals, whether a Jew under the law or a Gentile without law, both have a common struggle with indwelling sin, and both need the indwelling Spirit as found in Romans 8. It is this Spirit who brings both once-divided people into the glory of the sons of God.

From a salvation perspective, Romans 8:29-30 ends with glorification—this should be the finality of the gospel. Glorification is the end goal of every believer's salvation journey. Through these eight chapters, one's salvation is made complete: starting with justification through faith; then sanctification through identification in Christ's death and resurrection; then transformation through the indwelling and leading of the Spirit; and finally, glorification or the transfiguration of the body unto becoming mature sons of God (Rom. 8:29)—ultimately, bringing in the new heaven and new earth. These first eight chapters of Romans are the work of the gospel of the grace of God: all are saved by grace (Rom. 3:24); and after entering grace, all need to stand and remain in grace through the entire salvation journey (Rom. 5:2). Yet, this is only half the book of Romans. Why is there a need for another eight chapters (Romans 9-16)?

CH. 3: THE MISSING PEACE

Although individual salvation is established and completed, God's purpose is still not fulfilled. While the background of one's individual salvation journey starts with sin and condemnation (Romans 1-3), Romans 9 starts with two divided groups: Israel (representing the Jews) and *Esau* (the rest of "mankind"), the Gentiles (Romans 9-11). The word *"mankind"* in Acts 15:17 is translated in the *Septuagint* [ancient Greek version of the "Hebrew Scriptures"] as *Edom* (aka "Esau"). Anyone who reads Romans 9:13, will consider God is unfair: He hated Esau and loved Jacob. Those who identify with Jacob as the chosen people no doubt feel honored and even proud. Jacob can feel pity for Esau. But since it was God's will, the Jews, considering themselves to be the pure descendants of Jacob, the true Israel (i.e., the totality of Israel) can be justified in their despite for Esau— *"the rest of mankind,"* in which the Jews have classified all non-Jews to be Gentiles. Those who identify themselves with Esau (the rest of mankind or the Gentiles) will feel dejected, humiliated, and rejected.

Moreover, those *"scattered among the Gentiles"* (John 11:52; Jer. 31:9-11; Ezek. 36:19) who were considered *"not beloved,"* but now those scattered Ephraimites (viz. Israelites; again, Jer. 31:9-11; 50:17) who were *"not My people"* are now considered *"beloved"* and *"sons of the living God"*—well, obviously, Romans 9 has in view the *"gathering together in ONE the children of God who were scattered abroad"* (John 11:52). Imagine what Jewish believers were thinking as they were reading these "prophetic Scriptures" (Rom. 16:26) being expounded by Paul!

Again, imagine, just a few verses later, God calls those Gentiles—those Israelites scattered among the nations—who were no longer His people "His people," and those who are not beloved, "beloved" (cf. Hosea 1:6-11; 2:1; Rom. 9:25-26). Isn't that wonderful? God has just completely reversed Himself from hating Esau to loving Esau; from rejecting Ephraim to calling her "beloved"—now all mankind (Gentiles)—whom the Jews (Israel—the House of Judah) had considered to be inferior; even as unclean dogs—now they are the ELECT OF GOD?

Paul quoted from Hosea 2:23 *"I will call them My people, who were not My people"* in reference to Esau. However, in context Hosea was speaking of the so-called "Lost Ten Tribes of Israel" known as Ephraim, Jezreel, Samaria . . . those *"scattered among the nations"* (cf.

Hosea 8:7-10). These are the same people who were called Gentiles in Acts 15 where James referenced them to be Ephraim, the lost ten tribes coming back to rebuild the kingdom or the Tabernacle of David. **By applying Hosea's prophecy, Paul lumped two groups of people together into one common group called Gentiles: Ephraim (as the lost ten tribes) and Esau (the rest of mankind).**

Remember the context found in Paul's remarks primarily deals with the division between Jewish Christians and Gentile (*"ethos"*) Christians. Even as Christians, those with Jewish heritage were considering themselves as beloved Israel (even "exclusively Israel"), while considering believers from among the nations (aka Gentiles) as inferior. That was the reason Jewish believers were motivated to compel Gentile believers to be like them—keeping the laws contained in ordinances according to Moses and their traditions. Now, in Romans 9, Paul showed through the prophetic Scriptures (Rom. 16:26) that Gentiles are also beloved and deemed His people. Therefore, Jewish believers should accept them, love them as God loves them. Jewish believers should no longer consider themselves superior to Gentile believers since God has only one people, and those being called out from among the nations are now part of the same people as Israel—ALL ISRAEL (Rom. 11:26). Messianic Jewish believers and/or "Messianic Congregations" in their orientation toward "keeping Torah" should NOT consider themselves superior to Gentile believers who do not comply to their "Messianic" entitlement nor should these "Jewish-Gentile oriented Messianic congregations" hold honoring tenets of the Law or "keeping Torah" superior to those believers who do not (Romans 14:1-13); but that all believers should pursue the "Law of Love" and *"pursue the things which make for peace and the things by which one may edify another"* (Romans 14:14-23).

Let's skip Romans 10 for now and jump to Romans 11 for further consideration.

> *And if some of the branches were broken off, and you, being a wild olive tree, were grafted in among them, and with them became a partaker of the root and fatness of the olive tree . . . You will say then, "Branches were broken off that I might be grafted in." Well [said]. Because of unbelief they were broken off, and you stand by faith. Do not be haughty, but fear. For if God did not spare the natural branches, He may not spare you either* (Romans 11:17, 19-21).

The situation now appears reversed: Gentile believers feel special and superior by pointing out that Israel (Judah, the Jews) was cut off. God pruned and cut-off Israel because of their unbelief and they, the Gentiles, as the wild olive branch are now grafted into Christ (the root of the green olive tree-Jeremiah 11:16), enjoying all His riches. God has cut off Judah-Israel. He has terminated everything Jewish! It is the age of the Gentiles. The Gentiles are now the "chosen ones"—*"Israel [Judah] has not obtained what it seeks; but the elect* [those called out from among the nations] *have obtained it"* (Rom. 11:7). In their own eyes Gentile believers think they can now denigrate all the practices of Jewish believers. Why are they still practicing the Sabbath or keeping the Levitical diet? Don't they know God has terminated all these ordinances and laws?

Knowing Israel is no longer part of the olive tree (broken off), Gentile believers now consider themselves to be superior to Jewish believers. Those Gentile believers separating and dividing from Jewish believers can find support with this thought: If God cut them off, we can also cut off the Jews. If anyone practices anything Jewish, let's support God's decision by withdrawing from them; these Jewish believers need to know God has already cut off Israel.

Paul reprimanded the Gentiles: Don't be proud, don't boast. If they do, God can also cut off these Gentiles. If these Gentile believers divide and cut off Jewish believers, God will cut them off from the enjoyment of the riches of Christ. They will no longer be under God's cultivation to receive nourishment and the pleasure of His grace.

Paul was taking his metaphor of the olive tree directly from Jeremiah 11:16-17: *"The LORD called your name, Green Olive Tree, Lovely and of Good Fruit. With the noise of a great tumult He has kindled fire on it, and its branches are broken. For the LORD of hosts, who planted you, has pronounced doom against you for the evil of the house of Israel and of the house of Judah . . ."* What is critical to note here is the ONENESS of that singular Green Olive Tree—yes, branches (Israel/Gentiles and Judah/Jews) but ONE ROOT that bore them both (Rom. 11:16-17). BOTH branches are considered "holy" (Rom. 11:16)—"set apart" by God Himself.

Paul's conclusion was, neither group is better. Whether one identifies with the Jewish group or with the Gentile group—neither group is special or superior over the other. Neither group is exclusively the selected or chosen ones. God has committed all in disobedience (Rom. 11:32). In fact, it was and still is this superior group identity which is dividing and causing a separation among believers—and it's not just ethnic divisions; it is a multitude of practices and doctrines, as well as individual "styles" which are causing division in the Body of Christ.

There is only one Body of Christ. There should not be sub-groups in His One Body. If there is a division between these two groups of Jews and Gentile believers, then both are disobedient because both are dividing the Body of Christ, His ekklesia (Matt. 16:18). Whichever divided group you consider yourself to be in, whichever group you have identified yourself with, whether Jewish or Gentile (or even sub-groups within these two major groups), and you consider your group superior and separate from the other, God has counted all of us under disobedience!

When a person recognizes he or she is being disobedient, then God can show mercy. God's mercy is upon those who acknowledge their disobedience in dividing from other believers. Just as for individual salvation, wherein there needs to be an acceptance of being a sinner who needs redemption before salvation can proceed according to Romans 3; even so, if one is in a divided state where fellowship is withheld from those dissimilar, that person needs to recognize it is disobedience, even rebellion. It is at this point God's mercy is available. God's mercy is shown upon such a repentant person who is ready to be built up into the One Body of Christ. Just as sinners need to repent in order to receive salvation, believers who are divided from their brethren need to repent in order to become one with other diverse believers so they can enjoy all the riches of Christ within the Body of Christ.[53]

Therefore, unless and until we come to terms regarding the implications of the GOOD NEWS in its FULLNESS—then we are NOT living by the Truth of the Gospel—which is clearly set forth: *"He has made of the two, ONE NEW MAN . . . SO MAKING PEACE."*

---

[53] *One in Messiah*, "The Completion Gospel in Romans" by Henry Hon and Douglas Krieger.

NOT ONLY OF THE JEW

The Commonwealth of Israel is not merely a restored United Kingdom of David. Neither, as Paul describes, is it an exclusively Hebrew institution.

The term "Commonwealth" is taken from Ephesians 2:11-12:

Therefore, remember that you, once Gentiles ("ethnos") *in the flesh—who are called Uncircumcision by what is called the Circumcision made in the flesh by hands—that at that time you were without Christ, being aliens* (lit. "alienated"—"noncitizens" and/or your citizenship was removed) *from the COMMONWEALTH OF ISRAEL and strangers from the covenants of promise, having no hope and without God in the world. But now in Christ Jesus you who once were far off have been brought near by the blood of Christ.*

COMMONWEALTH connotes POLITY or the State, Community, and is corporate in nature (Strong's G#4174—*politeia*)—the relationship that a citizen shares with the state. CT brings together Jew and Gentile in accordance with Romans 9:22-24; in particular, vs. 24, which has a profound meaning:

". . . *even us whom He called* **not of the Jews only**, *but* **also of the Gentiles** (Strong's G#1484 ethnon [pl.] or multitudes or nations)?"

The verse is phrased as a question wherein we are alerted that, "*He might make known the riches of His glory on the Jewish vessels of mercy*" (vs. 23) BUT ALSO upon the Gentile vessels would He deign to make known "*the riches of His glory*"—thus, both Jew and Gentile are identified as "*vessels of mercy*" (vs. 23). Moreover, Paul recognizes from the divine perspective that both Jews and the Ethnon/Gentiles are "called" ("*He called,* **not of the Jews only**, *but also of the Nations?"*—vs. 24)[54]

The notion that the blood of Christ brings us into Christ Jesus Himself—into His "*one body through the cross*" (vs. 16) and yet this is separate and apart from bringing us, as well, into the Commonwealth of Israel, is simply NOT justified by the plain reading of the text.

---

[54] *Commonwealth Theology*, by Douglas Krieger, Tribnet Publications, 2018, pp. 4-5.

The context is altogether too clear in that the reference after the mentioning of the *"one body through the cross"* we read: *"Now, therefore, you are no longer strangers and foreigners, but fellow citizens with the saints and members of the household of God"* (vss. 16 and 19). What Paul is emphasizing is abundantly clear: Through the *"blood of Christ"*—*"through the cross"* (vss. 13, 16) we have moved from our previous status as aliens, strangers, and foreigners to full-blown legal citizens of the Commonwealth of Israel and are now within a new polity (state, authority, jurisdiction, administration—the amplified meaning of the word "commonwealth").

Once we were *"strangers from the covenants of promise"*—we had *"no hope"* and we were *"without God in the world"*—but now through His blood we *"have been brought near."* "Near," to what? To the Commonwealth of Israel—*"with Christ"* we are included in the Commonwealth of Israel . . . without Christ we once were aliens. NO MORE; through His blood we who once *"were far off have been brought near by the blood of Christ"* (vs. 13).

In other words, those who suggest that the Body of Christ is antithetical to the Commonwealth of Israel have created a false dichotomy. That narrative simply does not exist. Normally, this divergent commentary is followed up with an explanation that today's Jews and Gentiles who, through the blood of Christ, find themselves in His One Body, are now *"seated in heavenly places in Christ Jesus"* (Eph. 2:6); AND that we arrived at this "heavenly position" juxtaposed to the "earthly kingdom"—known as the Commonwealth of Israel—not by the *"works of the law"* but by *"grace through faith, and that not of yourselves; it is the gift of God, not of works, lest anyone should boast"* (Eph. 2:8-9).

Consequently, today's Christians have absolutely nothing to do with Israel—absolutely nothing to do with the Commonwealth of Israel because we are the "heavenly expression of the One Body"—the totality of the emphasis is upon the "heavenly Body." The blood of Christ—the cross brings us into the One Body, into the "Household of Faith"—we are not now members of the Commonwealth of Israel but members of His One Body. In point of fact, this Israel and the Commonwealth thereof, has been abandoned because of their "rejection of Christ" and replaced by the Church (aka "Replacement Theology") or this Commonwealth of Israel is completely divorced from the "Bride of Messiah" and must await their earthly role, while the heavenly role of the Church persists throughout the Millennium, even from the pretribulational rapture onward.[55]

The heavenly calling of those who *"once were far off"* does not remove the Gentile Church from citizenship within the Commonwealth of Israel on earth! In point of scriptural fact, being in Christ, through His blood, brings us into full citizenship into this very Commonwealth.

Notwithstanding the exceedingly clear meaning of the text, again, Christians are taught to eschew such an identification with the Commonwealth of Israel and think it antithetical to the One Body seated in heavenly places in Christ Jesus. The entire thrust of the quoted passages in Ephesians 2 has to do with the Him Who *"is our peace, who has made both one* (Jew and Gentile), *and has broken down the middle wall of separation"* (vs. 14).

It is impossible to introduce this topic without generating "theological antagonism" with both Replacement Theology and Dispensationalism—both of which have afflicted the relationship between Israel and the EKKLESIA—those *"called out from among the nations."* Consequently, there will be the exposure of this "Messianic tension" (which has been created from the commencement of the Early Church Fathers to our present seminaries and mega-churches) throughout this text.

When Paul made his statement in Ephesians 2:12, he was keenly aware that a New Covenant had been created for the "house of Israel and the house of Judah" (Jer. 31:31). It was the same Yeshua/Jesus who Paul persecuted when he was martyring believers in the Way, the same Yeshua who, through the "blood of the cross" broke down the middle wall of separation between Jew and Gentile (Eph. 2:14-16) to create One New Man, so making peace.

---

[55] Ibid, pp. XIX-XX.

Chapter Four

WHERE IS THE HOUSE OF ISRAEL?
By Douglas Krieger

Ephraim Divorced and Scattered

The captivity and/or dispersion into the Assyrian Empire of the Ten Northern Tribes persisted from cir. 745 BC up through and including 712 BC (Assyria's Campaign against Judah— See link: http://www.crivoice.org/othassyrian.html). Nigh thirty-three years with some five Assyrian Kings participating in their captivity—a captivity well over 10-15 million, for David numbered the men of fighting age (20 to 50 years of age) of the Ten Northern Tribes cir. 980 BC to be upwards of 1,100,000 (1 Chron. 21:5). Counting women and children and the elderly, the number of "Israelites" could have been approximately 4 to 5 million in 980 BC. By 740 BC—nigh 250 years later—that number could easily have exceeded 10 to 15 million. Thus, from 712 BC, the Israelite captivity was in full sway; and then, after nigh 110 years—some 4/5 generations—(Judah's captivity into Babylon commenced in 608 BC and reached its climax in 586 BC with the Fall of Jerusalem under Nebuchadnezzar) those of the 10 Northern Tribes "multiplied among the nations" all the more. The Bible does NOT record a mass assimilation into Judah by these Israelite Captives into Assyria—they are simply "swallowed up of the nations."[56]

Yes, God had given "backsliding Israel" who "had committed adultery . . . a certificate of divorce" (Jer. 3:8); thus, were the Northern Tribes of Israel "put away"—yes, taken away to Assyria nearly 120 years before Judah was taken into Babylonian Captivity (740-712 BC versus 608-586 BC). Both tribal jurisdictions were approximately 32/33 years taken into their distinct captivities. Of interest is the fact that our Lord appears to have lived unto 32 full years of age and "may" have been "cut off" at age 33, which would approximate the 32/33 years of the aforesaid captivities.

---

[56] *CT,*, by Douglas Krieger, Tribnet Publications, 201820-21.

Israel/Samaria/Jezreel/Ephraim was *"swallowed up of the nations" . . . "Aliens would swallow it up . . . Israel is swallowed up, now they are among the Gentiles like a vessel in which is no pleasure. For they have gone up to Assyria"* (Hosea 8:7-9).

Paul knew Israel's plight, but he also knew of her future:

For the children of Israel shall abide many days without king or prince, without sacrifice or sacred pillar, without ephod or teraphim. Afterward the children of Israel shall return and seek the LORD their God and David their king. They shall fear the LORD and His goodness in the latter days (Hosea 3:4-5).

Yes, a New Covenant would of necessity be needed with BOTH the House of Israel and the House of Judah (Jer. 31:31) for the original marriage covenant that God made with them at Sinai they both had broken (Jer. 31:32) . . . *"My covenant which they broke, though I was a husband to them."* The breach between Kings Rehoboam of Judah and Jeroboam of Israel (cir. 928-927 B.C. which divided the "Tabernacle of David" (viz. the "United Kingdom") found Israel's plight far more extreme until . . . *"I will no longer have mercy on the house of Israel, but I will utterly take them away . . . yet I will have mercy on the house of Judah"* (Hosea 1:6-7). Yes, the "certificate of divorce" had been enacted and enforced but Paul, the apostle to the Gentiles, saw something in the *"latter days"*—*I will betroth you to Me forever; yes, I will betroth you to Me in righteousness and justice, in lovingkindness and mercy; I will betroth you to Me in faithfulness, and you shall know the LORD . . . then I will sow her for Myself in the earth, and I will have mercy on her who had not obtained mercy; then I will say to those who were not My people, "You are My people!" And they shall say, "You are my God!"* (Hosea 2:19-20, 23).

Both Peter and Paul understood the writ of divorce but they likewise understood the implications of a New Covenant would express the mercy of Almighty God toward Israel so that *"who once were not a people but are now the people of God, who had not obtained mercy but now have obtained mercy"* (1 Pet. 2:10) . . . yes, Paul bearing witness to the same: *"As He says also in Hosea: 'I will call them My people, who were not My people . . . and her beloved, who was not beloved. And it shall come to pass in the place where it was said to them, 'You are not My people, 'There they shall be called sons of the living God'"* (Rom. 9:25-26). This was not Paul's metaphorical interpretation of why the Gentiles (i.e., the "ethnos" or "nations") who once were "far off" but now had been made "near" by the blood of the cross—this had everything to do with those sown among the nations who would be *"called out to be a people"* for His Name. They have now—Ephraim—Jezreel, *"God will sow"*—been brought back under a New Covenant reserved for both Houses because they had broken the original covenant; therefore, He declares: *"This is the covenant that I will make with them after those days, says the LORD: I will put My laws into their heart, and in their minds I will write them"* (Heb. 10:16; Jer. 31:33-34). No longer are those who were scattered among the nations without mercy— THEY HAVE OBTAINED MERCY![57]

WHO SWALLOWED EPHRAIM—JUDAH OR THE NATIONS?[58]

To suggest that all 12 Tribes (Including Ephraim) joined together both prior to the Babylonian Captivity and during the Babylonian Captivity and were all subsequently identified as Israel or Jews flies in the face of previous Scripture which demands that millions were carted off by the Assyrian Kings, literally, anthropologically-speaking, by the millions. Nigh seven generations separated the Samaria/Ephraim Captivity from the Babylonian Captivity (e.g., 745-586 BC); although, King Nebuchadnezzar II (Viceroy at the time) laid siege to Jerusalem in 608/607 BC. At that time he took some captive of the Jews, primarily their leadership (e.g., Daniel and other youth).[59]

Chuck Missler attempts to persuade us that Ephraim (i.e. the Ten Northern Tribes of Israel) were over the course of some 200+ years (930 BC to 722 BC) merged in massive numbers into Judah and then taken into captivity as Judah, having lost their identification as Ephraim altogether! There are many groups that believe the northern tribes, separated during the rift between Rehoboam and Jeroboam after the death of Solomon (and subsequently taken captive by Assyria in fulness by 722 BC), later migrated to Europe and elsewhere. The legacy of the "Ten Lost Tribes" is the basis for "British-Israelism" and

---

[57] Ibid, pp. XXV-XXVI.
[58] This section is predominately quoted from *Commonwealth Theology*, pp. 51-58 and Note 17.
[59] Ibid, p. 46.

other colorful legends, but these stories have no real biblical basis. They are based upon misconceptions derived from the misreading of various Bible passages. (2 Kings 17:7-23; 2 Chron. 6:6-11)[60]

NOTE: It seems obvious that *"Therefore the LORD was very angry with Israel* (i.e., the 10 Northern Tribes), *and removed them from His sight;* **there was none left but the tribe of Judah alone**" (2 Kings 17:18). (Our brackets).

The sweeping statements made by Missler regarding these "myths and legends" is astonishing, given his intellectual capabilities, as well as penchant for research. Before the Assyrian captivity, substantial numbers from the northern tribes had identified themselves with the house of David. The rebellion of Jeroboam and subsequent crises caused many to repudiate the Northern Kingdom and unite with the Southern Kingdom in a common alliance to the house of David and a desire to worship the Lord in Jerusalem. (1 Kings 12:16-20; 2 Chron. 11:16-17; 2 Chron. 19:4; 30:1, 10-11, 25-26; 34:5-7, 22; 35:17-18).

NOTE: The passages used by Chuck Missler appear to contradict the alleged massive numbers who joined with Judah from Israel; to wit: *"Now it came to pass when all Israel heard that Jeroboam had come back, they sent for him and called him to the congregation, and made him king over all Israel.* **THERE WAS NONE WHO FOLLOWED THE HOUSE OF DAVID, BUT THE TRIBE OF JUDAH ONLY**" (1 Kings 12:20).

Furthermore, and from the "sound of it" the Levites who "left those from all the tribes of Israel . . . strengthened the kingdom of Judah, and made Rehoboam the son of Solomon strong for three years"—that does not sound like a massive commitment on the part of the Levites (three years?). In 2 Chronicles 19:4 where King Jehoshaphat returned from battle with the Syrians, after King Ahab of Israel was killed (his ally at the time), simply *"went out again among the people from Beersheba to the mountains of Ephraim and brought them back to the LORD God of their fathers"* (2 Chron. 19:4). The "mountains of Ephraim" do not necessarily include all of Israel's Ten Northern Tribes; furthermore, we immediately discover that Jehoshaphat *"set judges in the land throughout all the fortified cities of Judah, city by city"* (2 Chron. 19:5).

---

[60] "The Ten Lost Tribes Mystery of the Myth" by Chuck Missler, June 1, 1995

CH. 4: WHERE IS THE HOUSE OF ISRAEL?

Again, this hardly sounds like the Ten Tribes of Israel are fortified by Judah!

NOTE: In 2 Chron. 30:1, 10-11, 25-26 the notion that some of the Ten Northern Tribes came to Jerusalem to celebrate the Passover with King Hezekiah (cir. 720 BC) AFTER the 10 Northern Tribes had a civil war with Judah (under King Pekah) wherein 120,000 of Judah were killed by Israel (all the "valiant men") in one day (2 Chron. 28:5-8)—plus Israel carried Judah away captive, but then humbly returned 200,000 women, sons, and daughters who they originally brought into Samaria but returned them to Judah at Jericho (2 Chron. 28:9-15).

Shortly thereafter, King Ahaz of Israel confronted the king of Assyria, Tiglath-pileser (2 Chron. 28:16-27), but all we are told is that this King Ahaz of Israel took treasure from the House of the Lord at Jerusalem and tried, so it appears, to buy off King Tiglath-pileser to have Assyria assist the King of Judah (same name as King Ahaz) who was under attack from both the Edomites and the Philistines (2 Chron. 28:16-18). Assyria did not assist. King Ahaz of Judah (now) was hardly a paragon of virtue—he set up high places all over Judah; then his son Hezekiah reigned in his stead at the age of 25.

NOTE: Yes, 2 Chron. 30:1 says Hezekiah upon the inception of his reign; however, when the "runners" went out through Israel and Judah to gather the people for the Passover in Jerusalem (2 Chron. 30:6), it was already clear that if Israel would attend the Passover *"then He will return to the remnant of you who have escaped from the hand of the kings of Assyria"*—for huge numbers of the Israelites had already been taken captive by the Assyrian kings (cir. 745-725 BC) . . . there was but a REMNANT left in Israel!

NOTE: Likewise, regarding this remnant of Israel who were encouraged by King Hezekiah to return to the Lord (2 Chron. 30:9)—but here's their response: *"So the runners passed from city to city through the country of Ephraim and Manasseh, as far as Zebulun; but they laughed at them and mocked them . . . nevertheless SOME from Asher, Manasseh, and Zebulun humbled themselves and came to Jerusalem"* (2 Chron. 30:10-11). Now, that does NOT sound like a massive turnout from the Ten Tribes of Israel who, at the time, were but a REMNANT in the first place! SOME from a REMNANT does not a MASSIVE turnout make!

Yes, 2 Chronicles 30:25-26 says it was a massive assembly but it was comprised of Levites, those who came from Israel, the sojourners (already infusing Israel with Gentiles—2 Kings 17:24-33—talk about a mixture) who came from Israel, and, of course, those who dwelt in Judah—but they did return after coming to the Passover and, yes, they "utterly destroyed" the high places and the altars—*"from all Judah, Benjamin, Ephraim, and Manasseh . . . **then all the children of Israel returned to their own cities, every man to his possession**"* (2 Chron. 31:1). Two tribes are mentioned of the Northern 10 Tribes—and they constituted but SOME of a REMNANT that had been left and not taken into captivity by the Assyrian kings.

NOTE: In 2 Chronicles 34:5-7 we read that Judah's King Josiah destroyed all the apostate altars throughout Judah, Manasseh, Ephraim, and Simeon—as far as Naphtali and *"all around with axes . . . throughout all the land of Israel"*—however, King Josiah's reign was years after the Ten Northern Tribes were taken into captivity (745-722 BC by at least five Assyrian Kings–) and years after King Hezekiah had faced off with the Assyrian King Sennacherib (2 Chron. 32) in 712 BC (2 Kings 18). Indeed, there was an overlap of the reign of Israel's last king, Hoshea, and King Hezekiah of Judah but somewhere between 722 BC and 712 BC the captivity of the Ten Northern Tribes was complete; to wit:

"Now it came to pass in the fourth year of King Hezekiah, which was the seventh year of Hoshea the son of Elah, king of Israel, that Shalmaneser king of Assyria came up against Samaria and besieged it...and at the end of three years they took it. In the sixth year of Hezekiah that is, the ninth year of Hoshea king of Israel, Samaria was taken...then the king of Assyria carried Israel away captive to Assyria, and put them in Halah and by the Habor, the River of Gozan, and in the cities of the Medes" (2 Kings 18:7-11).

The defeat of Samaria/the Ten Northern Tribes was complete in the sixth year of Hezekiah's reign...but in the fourteenth year of King Hezekiah's reign (2 Kings 18:13)—some eight years (Fall of Samaria, capitol of Israel's Ten Northern Tribes occurred in 720 BC) after the fall of Samaria in 712 BC—King Sennacherib laid siege to the cities of Judah and Jerusalem; therefore, from 722-712 BC the "captivity" of the Ten Northern Tribes was in full sway—

CH. 4: WHERE IS THE HOUSE OF ISRAEL?

there being every indication that the "siege of Samaria" lasted at least three years (722 BC through to 719 BC) . . . it appears to be a total wipe out—what was left of the REMNANT of ISRAEL was obviously, taken captive. Furthermore, and based upon the record of 2 Kings 17:24-33 there hardly sounds like a host of Israelites lived in these ancient tribal areas of the Land—in point of fact, they appear to be nigh wholly populated by Gentiles!

NOTE: We have no idea why Chuck Missler quotes 2 Chron. 34:22 to substantiate his claim that the Ten Northern Tribes massively merged with Judah. As far as 2 Chronicles 35:17-18 is concerned—the massive Passover kept by King Josiah of Judah (there being King Hezekiah's additional 15-year reign; plus, King Manasseh's 55-year reign; plus, King Amon's two-year reign; plus—there being 72 years of these kings of Judah extending to the year 640 BC; plus 18 years of King Josiah's reign (2 Chron. 35:19) or some 90 years had transpired between King Hezekiah's life extension in 712 BC and the great Passover held by King Josiah in 622 BC (nigh at least 100 years after the Fall of Samaria in 722 BC.). Yes, it says:

"So all the service of the LORD was prepared the same day to keep the Passover and to offer burnt offerings on the altar of the LORD, according to the command of King Josiah. And the children of Israel who were present kept the Passover at that time and the Feast of Unleavened Bread for seven days. There had been no Passover kept in Israel like that since the days of Samuel the prophet; and none of the kings of Israel had kept such a Passover as Josiah kept, with the priests and the Levites, all Judah and Israel who were present and the inhabitants of Jerusalem" (2 Chron. 35:16-18).

Notwithstanding these remarks, the "leftovers" of the Ten Tribes still constituted a tiny minority of the participants based upon the previous passages which indicated their persistent deportation by the Assyrian kings. Also, as far as we know, the SOJOURNERS and the Gentiles within those lands who were now adhering to BOTH their own heathen practices and those of the Israelites (aka the Samaritans) did NOT constitute a hearty throng of Israelites. Despite all of this, Missler persists:

Not all from the Northern Kingdom were deported. Archaeologists have uncovered annals of the Assyrian Sargon, in which he tells that he carried away only 27,290 people and 50 chariots. (NOTE: Source: 1 Kings 11:13, 32—given by Missler and simply declares that the United Kingdom of Israel would be torn asunder—nothing of the Ten Tribes merging with Judah is given. King Sargon (Isaiah 20:1) was the successor of Shalmaneser, and was Sennacherib's father.)

The 27,290 taken by King Sargon to Assyria simply specifies a group of Israelites taken into captivity—prior to that King. They appear to be the "elite" of Israel and would, therefore, be accorded such an inscription—but simply a representative number of the overall Israelites taken into captivity at that time. Furthermore, prior to that we read in 1 Chronicles 5:26:

"And the God of Israel stirred up the spirit of Pul king of Assyria, who is also Tilgath-pilezer king of Assyria, and he carried them away, even the Reubenites, and the Gadites, and half tribe of Manasseh, and brought them unto Halah, and Habor, and Hara, and to the river Gozan, unto this day."

This was before Assyrian king Sargon. It should be noted that Tiglath-pileser began a three-step deportation of Israel with the initial deportation of the tribes east of the Jordan. This is supported by Gad still being located east of the Jordan in the time of Saul as per 1 Samuel 13:7 which locates the *"Land of Gad," "And some of the Hebrews went over Jordan to the land of Gad and Gilead. As for Saul, he was yet in Gilgal, and all the people followed him trembling."*

NOTE: We then read in 2 Kings 15:29: *"In the days of Pekah king of Israel came Tiglath-pileser king of Assyria, and took Ijon, and Abelbeth-maachah, and Janoah, and Kedesh, and Hazor, and Gilead, and Galilee, all the land of Naphtali, and carried them captive to Assyria."*

There are scores of passages which bespeak of the captivity of the Ten Tribes of the North (Israel): 2 Kings 16:5-10; 2 Chron. 28:20-21; 2 Kings 17:1-6; 2 Kings 18:9-11; 2 Kings 18:13 (Judah's siege; also Isaiah 36:1; also, 2 Kings 19:36-37; 2 Chron. 32:21-22; Isaiah 37:36-38) . . . again, it is likely that Tiglath-pileser (the first of the Assyrian kings to conquer the Ten Northern Tribes) actually made three invasions of Israel. The last included this devastation of

CH. 4: WHERE IS THE HOUSE OF ISRAEL?

Galilee and, when joined by Ahaz, he destroyed Damascus—please see: *Interaction of Assyrian Kings with Israel and Judah about 730 BC* by Fred P. Miller.

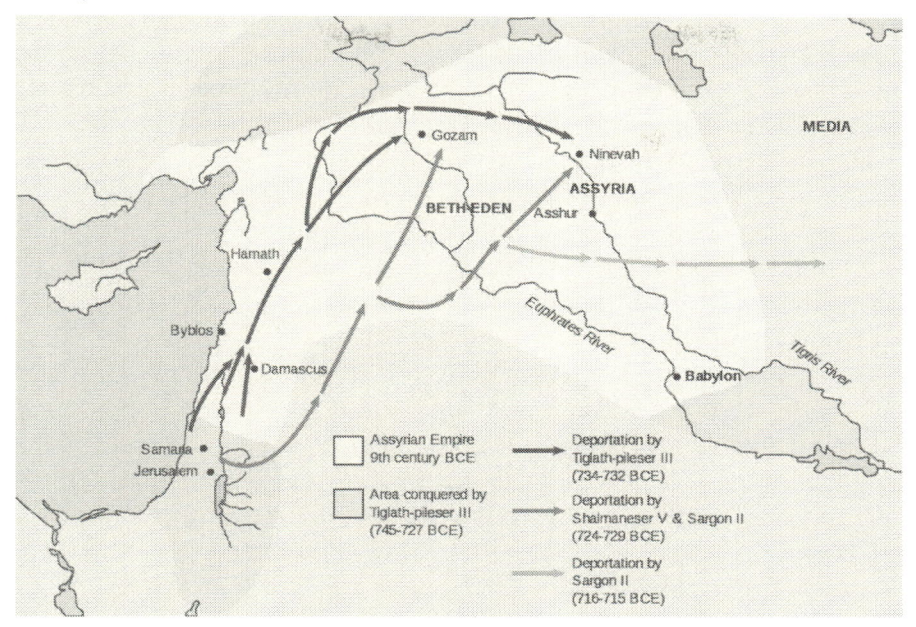

Israel's Assyrian Deportations[61]

Missler continues in the devolution of the actual biblical and historical evidence indicating the opposite of his thesis that Israel's 10 Northern Tribes blended into Judah (both before and after Judah's Babylonian captivity) and/or the actual numbers deported were inconsequential:

> "Population estimates of the Northern Kingdom at that time range from 400,000 to 500,000; less than 1/20th were deported– mostly the leadership from the capital, Samaria. The rest of the Northern Kingdom were taken by Assyria as slaves, which were a valuable commodity. (It is difficult to view the Assyrians as careless enough to let their captives wander off to Europe.) When the Babylonians take over Assyria, the descendants of the "ten tribes" were probably again commingled with the captives of Judah."

---

[61] https://en.wikipedia.org/wiki/Assyrian_captivity

Missler's conjectures fly in the face of both Scripture and historical records. Cir. 980 BC King David numbered the men of fighting age in Israel's 10 Northern Tribes (20-50 years of age) to be between 800,000 to 1,100,000 (1 Chron. 21:5; 2 Sam. 24:9)—which means the Ten Northern Tribes total population in 980+/- BC could have easily numbered upwards of 4+ million counting women, children and the elderly. It could easily have been upwards of 10,000,000 taken captive into Assyria by the succession of Assyrian kings from Tiglath-pileser, Shalmaneser, and Sargon II through to Sennacherib (over the course of some 30-40 years). For after nigh 250 years the Israelites which numbered upwards of 5,000,000 of David's census could readily have increased, given the parameters of their territory, some 10 to 15 million.

The kingdom established by David [circa 1050 B.C.] on the foundations started by Saul and Samuel attained all the borders and limits of the biblical Promised Land. God's land-promises made to the Patriarchs were completely fulfilled in the kingdom of David and Solomon and these borders were kept by Israel through the time of David and Solomon. More than this, all of the Near East was under the control of the united tribes of Israel and ruled from Jerusalem. Garrisons of Israeli soldiers were stationed in Damascus, Hamath, Ammon, Edom, Moab and the outposts of the Negev and the Euphrates River. Shipping in the Mediterranean and Indian Ocean was under the control of Israel. Coincidentally the strongest nations of the Near East, Egypt, Assyria, Babylon, were eclipsed by the power of Israel and due to Israel's political power and control this period is an empty page in the annals of those subject nations.

There is historical silence that is all but incredible for the greatest nations of the world during the suzerainty of the kingdom of David. No wonder the prophets saw the future age of Glory as the restoration of the kingdom of David. See this in: Hull Edward, M.A., L.L.D., F.R.S.; The Wall chart of World History; Pub. Princess House, London; many editions from 1890—1992. Go here: to see a small portion of the chart that depicts this period of history. (Ibid. Fred P. Miller)

To sum up the massive deportations to Assyria of the Ten Northern Tribes (or at least 9 of them) . . . Miller prevails: To sum up then: In a first assault, Tiglath-pileser had taken captive the tribes east of the Jordan, i.e., the tribes of Reuben, Manasseh, and Gad, about 734 B.C. Approximately 731 B.C. the tribes of Dan, Naphtali, and Zebulun were taken during the invasion and the destruction of Galilee and Damascus by Tiglath-pileser. The rest (three tribes: Ephraim, Issachar and Asher and the rest of Manasseh) of the "10 Tribes" (actually only 9) went into captivity under Sargon II at the fall of Samaria in 722 B.C.

Actually, there were only nine tribes in the northern kingdom after the Levites abandoned their cities in the north and joined Judah after the apostasy of Jeroboam I. Simeon was still settled in the portion of the tribe of Judah although part of Simeon had immigrated to various other locations, some "lehutz la'aretz" or outside the Holy Land. 1 Chron. 4:42-43 describes some 500 men of Simeon who immigrated from Judah to Edom. (Ibid. Fred P. Miller)

Thus, and not to belabor the postulations of Chuck Missler, it cannot be argued by those opposed to Ephraim's massive deportations that such a minuscule number were deported nor assimilated while Judah was still in power, nor of these—at least nine tribes—being assimilated into the Jews of Babylon after an additional nigh ten generations (722 BC to 537 BC—the end of the 70-year captivity with the first captivity of the Jews taking place under Viceroy, at the time, Nebuchadnezzar, in 608 BC).

Finally, this quote from Josephus: The Jewish historian Josephus (37–100 CE) wrote that **"the ten tribes are beyond the Euphrates till now, and are an immense multitude and not to be estimated in numbers."**[62]

ISRAEL AMONG THE NATIONS

King Tiglath-pileser III (2 Kings 15:19-20—aka King Pul), we read:

"Now the king of Assyria went throughout all the land, and went up to Samaria and besieged it for three years. In the ninth year of Hoshea, the king of Assyria took Samaria and carried Israel away to Assyria, and placed them in Halah and by the Habor, the River of Gozan, and in the cities of the Medes . . . Then the king of Assyria brought people from Babylon, Cuthah, Ava, Hamath, and from Sepharvaim, and

---

[62] Josephus, Flavius. *Antiquities*. p. 11:133.

> *placed them in the cities of Samaria instead of the children of Israel; and they took possession of Samaria and dwelt in its cities. And it was so, at the beginning of their dwelling there, that they did not fear the LORD, therefore the LORD sent lions among them, which killed some of them. So they spoke to the king of Assyria, saying, "The nations whom you have removed and placed in the cities of Samaria do not know the rituals of the God of the land; therefore He has sent lions among them, and indeed, they are killing them because they do not know the rituals of the God of the land. . . They feared the LORD, yet served their own gods—according to the rituals of the nations from among whom they were carried away"* (2 Kings 17:5-6, 24-26, 33).

Those who suggest that Ephraim/Israel can be found as today's ethnic Jews disregard, as well, the following passages:

> *"When Ephraim saw his sickness, and Judah saw his wound, then Ephraim went to Assyria and sent to King Jareb; yet he cannot cure you, nor heal you of your wound . . . None of them calls upon Me. Ephraim has mixed himself among the people; Ephraim is a cake unturned. Aliens have devoured his strength, but he does not know it . . . aliens would swallow it up . . . Israel is swallowed up; now they are among the Gentiles . . . like a vessel in which is no pleasure. For they have gone up to Assyria, like a wild donkey alone by itself; Ephraim has hired lovers. Yes, though they have hired among the nations. . . as for Ephraim, their glory shall fly away like a bird . . . My God will cast them away, because they did not obey Him; and they shall be wanderers among the nations"* (Excerpts from Hosea).

In sum: Bits, parts and scattered pieces of the "Lost Ten Tribes" MAY be found in today's Judah/Jews but Ephraim has been swallowed up of the nations—this is a far more biblical view in its accuracy and anthropological evaluation as well. (See copious endnotes in the previous chapters). James 1:1 speaks of the "*12 Tribes Scattered Abroad*"—this is simply an acknowledgement that Israel (both Judah/Ephraim) are/were scattered throughout the nations.[63]

---

[63] *Commonwealth Theology*, by Douglas Krieger, Tribnet Publications, 2018, pp. 62-63

Jezreel—Sown Among the Nations[64]

Paul speaking of the "elect [ekklesia] from among the nations" (the "Gentiles") and of those Jews who had joined themselves to the Messiah:

"I will call them (referring directly concerning Ephraim by quoting from Hosea 2:23) *My people; who were not My people, and her beloved, who was not beloved.' And it shall happen in the place where it was said to them, 'you are not My people,' There they shall be called sons of the living God'"* (Hosea 1:10; Romans 9:24-26).

"And that He might make known the riches of His glory on the vessels of mercy; which He had prepared beforehand for glory; even us whom He called, not of the Jews only, but also of the Gentiles (lit. "nations")*? As He says also in Hosea:* (Rom. 9:23-24).

When and what was it that was "said to them?"

"They shall answer Jezreel (Lit. "God will sow")*. Then I will sow her for Myself in the earth, and I will have mercy on her who had not obtained mercy; Then I will say to those who were not My people, 'You are My people!' And they shall say, 'You are my God!'"* (Hosea. 2:22b-23). *"Yet the number of the children of Israel shall be as the sand of the sea, which cannot be measured or numbered. And it shall come to pass in the place where it was said to them, 'You are not My people,' There it shall be said to them, 'You are the sons of the living God.'" Then the children of Judah and the children of Israel shall be gathered together and appoint themselves one head; and they shall come up out of the land, for great will be the day of Jezreel!* (God will sow!) *. . . Say to your brethren, 'My people,' and to your sisters, 'Mercy is shown.'"* (Hosea 1:10-11; 2:1)

(NOTE: Is this not the FINAL HARVEST of the Earth seen in Revelation 14:14-16?) When Paul speaks of God's mercy and directly addresses the Gentiles/the goyim, the *"elect from among the nations"*—he says:

"For I speak to you Gentiles (ethnos)*, inasmuch as I am an apostle to the Gentiles* (the "nations")*, I magnify my ministry . . . For I do not desire brethren that you should be ignorant of this*

---

[64] Section includes excerpts from *Commonwealth Theology*, pp. 63-66.

mystery, lest you should be wise in your own opinion, that blindness in part has happened to Israel, until the fullness of the Gentiles (Lit. "multitude of nations") *has come in. And so ALL ISRAEL will be saved, as it is written, 'The Deliverer will come out of Zion, and He will turn away ungodliness from Jacob; for this is My covenant with them, when I take away their sins"* (Romans 11:13, 25-27).

When Paul says ALL ISRAEL will be saved—does he exclude the "Multitude of Nations" from the equation or is he referring only to National Israel (i.e., the Jews/Judah)? More of this phrase later. We would contend that the scattering of the house of Israel to the nations was likened as seed sown among the nations; to wit: Psalm 106:26-27:

"So he swore to them with uplifted hand that he would make them fall in the desert, make their descendants fall among the nations and scatter them throughout the lands."

The House of Israel was sown as seed into all the earth. Keep in mind that the house of Israel (Samaria/Ephraim/Jezreel) quickly adopted the customs of the Assyrians and lost their identity. They forgot who they were. They intermarried until their DNA was continually diluted. Today it is very likely that most of the world could trace their lineage back to the house of Israel (100 generations)–literally (grief, my little grandson did a precursory DNA test and found out he was 1% "Middle Eastern"—whatever that is!

Furthermore, the Almighty's promises to Abraham, Isaac, Jacob, and then to Joseph and on to Ephraim regarding a "multitude of nations" would come from their loins and that this *"FULLNESS OF THE GENTILES"* (lit. MULTITUDE OF NATIONS) would be those of Ephraim **scattered** throughout those very nations as JEZREEL—**God will sow** . . . Seed among the Ethnos, the nations. Paul's message takes on new understanding in using ethnos as nations. Colossians 1:27 says:

"To them God has chosen to make known among the NATIONS (ethnos) *the glorious riches of this mystery, which is Christ in you, the hope of glory."* This hearkens back to Genesis 48:19 where Jacob blesses Ephraim and says that he will become a multitude of nations. Also, when God blessed Abraham and told him in Genesis 18:18 that all nations would be blessed through him, and to Isaac, in particular, when He said to him:

"And I will make your descendants multiply as the stars of heaven; I will give to your descendants all these lands; and in your seed ALL THE NATIONS of the earth shall be blessed"

We affirm that Genesis 26:1-6 confirms the PROMISED SEED through Isaac as an archetype of Christ, the "S"eed and that the 430 Years of Promise confirm this from Exodus 12:40-41 and Galatians 3:15-18 and Gal. 4:28; to wit:

"And it came to pass at the end of the four hundred and thirty years—on that very same day—it came to pass that all the armies of the LORD went out from the land of Egypt (i.e., the EXODUS/LAW) . . . Now to Abraham and his Seed were the promises made. He does not say, 'And to seeds,' as of many, but as of 'one,' 'And to your Seed,' who is Christ. And this I say, that the law, which was four hundred and thirty years later, cannot annul the covenant that was confirmed before by God IN CHRIST, that it should make the PROMISE of no effect . . . but God gave it to Abraham by promise . . . Now, brethren, as Isaac was, we are children of promise."

Chapter Five

THE JERUSALEM COUNCIL
By Douglas Krieger

A People for His Name

Acts 15:14-17: Concerning the "elect from among the nations" who would constitute membership in the Commonwealth of Israel, the Congregation of the Living God . . .

"Simon has declared how God at the first visited the nations (aka the Gentiles) *TO TAKE OUT OF THEM A PEOPLE FOR HIS NAME . . . and with this the word of the prophets agree, just as it is written: 'After this I will return and will rebuild the tabernacle of David, which has fallen down; I will rebuild its ruins, and I will set it up, so that the rest of mankind may seek the LORD, even all the Gentiles* (lit. "the nations") *who are called by My name, says the LORD who does all these things."*

We can and will contend that the "Tabernacle of David" which was "fallen down" is none other than the UNITED KINGDOM which was "fallen down" by the breach between and the persistent "blood feud" between Judah (Rehoboam) and Israel (Jeroboam) and that its RESTORATION initially took place through the Blood of the Cross and was "prophetically acknowledged" at the "Church Council" as found in Acts 15:14-17 (more on this later in this text).

Yes, by now after nigh 100+ generations since 745-712 BC the "Jezreel" has been thoroughly sown among the nations—Ephraim is swallowed up of the nations—but He Who scattered is gathering since Messiah's First Coming and onwards unto the prophetic fulfillment when the LORD shall take the Stick of Judah and the Stick of Ephraim and make them ONE STICK IN HIS HAND—that is happening NOW and shall accelerate unto the end of the age . . . for if Ephraim had been assimilated into Judah, why then would the prophecy of Ezekiel 37:15-28 elicit such millenarian overtones? This cannot be dismissed as miscellaneous, metaphorical hyperbole.

Even so, the prophets declare His mighty work among the nations—the Gentiles:

Therefore receive one another, just as Christ also received us, to the glory of God. Now I say that Jesus Christ has become a servant to the circumcision for the truth of God, to confirm the promises made to the fathers, and that the Gentiles [i.e., "the nations"] *might glorify God for His mercy, as it is written: "For this reason I will confess to You among the Gentiles* [i.e., "the nations"], *And sing to Your name"* (2 Sam. 22:50; Ps. 18:49). *And again he says: "Rejoice, O Gentiles, with His people!"* (Deut. 32:43)

And again: "Praise the Lord, all you Gentiles! Laud Him, all you peoples!" (Ps. 117:1). *And again, Isaiah says: "There shall be a root of Jesse; And He who shall rise to reign over the Gentiles* [i.e., the "nations"], *in Him the Gentiles* [nations] *shall hope"* (Romans 15:7-12, Isaiah 11:1, 10).[65]

The "Restoration" of the Tabernacle of David (Amos 9:11-12; Acts 15:16-18; Obad. 19) wherein the "Jerusalem Council" made up primarily of Jews (including Peter/Simon, Paul, Barnabas, James, etc.) has been discussed throughout this text. The primary explanation given by the "apostles and elders" who convened the "Council" ensconced the "visitation of the Gentiles" among whom God was "taking out of them a people for His name" in terms of the restoration of the Tabernacle of David which had nigh 950 years previous to the Council fallen down.

We discovered that the United Kingdom of Israel under David—wherein the House of Judah (Judah and Benjamin, later some of Simeon and the Levites), and the House of Ephraim, which is the House of Israel (the other ten tribes), were wholly united under King David and his son, King Solomon.

---

[65] *Commonwealth Theology*, by Douglas Krieger, Tribnet Publications, 2018, p. 68.

David's Fallen Tent

Although there are many "spiritual insights" in reference to the restoration of the Tabernacle of David (or TENT of David), as far as the apostles and elders who gathered at Jerusalem for this most dramatic analysis of "what was happening" with the "entry" of those from among the nations, now being called in the EKKLESIA, it was all related to the original Tabernacle/Tent of David which expressed the United Kingdom of Israel.

Yes, "fallen down" through the breach of Jeroboam (northern tribes of Israel) and Rehoboam (southern tribes of Judah/Israel) but NOW it was being "rebuilt" so that the rest of "mankind" (lit. "Edom"—Obadiah 19, Amos. 9:12) *"may seek the LORD, even all the Gentiles who are called by My name"* (Acts. 15:17). Indeed, "Edom/Mankind" is only fitting—and although there are a number of expositors who see in Esau, who despised his birthright (*"Esau have I hated"*), he was still a son of Isaac. Could it be, as well, that "mankind" who are now seeking the LORD, akin to the "hated Esau" begotten via Isaac has found mercy? Think about that for a while—it well deserves consideration. Again, James, the half-brother of Jesus, prior to all the sharing by the apostles and elders, eventually discerned the prophetic majesty of what was taking place—now the sequence:

> *And the apostles and the elders were gathered together to see about this matter. And much discussion having taken place, Peter, standing up, said to them, Brethren, ye know that from the earliest days God amongst you chose that the nations by my mouth should hear the word of the glad tidings and believe. And the heart-knowing God bore them witness, giving [them] the Holy Spirit as to us also, and put no difference between us and them, having purified their hearts by faith. Now therefore why tempt ye God, by putting a yoke upon the neck of the disciples, which neither our fathers nor we have been able to bear? But we believe that we shall be saved by the grace of the Lord Jesus, in the same manner as they also.*

And all the multitude kept silence and listened to Barnabas and Paul relating all the signs and wonders which God had wrought among the nations by them. And after they had held their peace, James answered, saying, Brethren, listen to me:

Simon has related how God first visited to take out of [the] nations a people for his name. And with this agree the words of the prophets; as it is written: After these things I will return, and will rebuild the tabernacle of David which is fallen, and will rebuild its ruins, and will set it up, so that the residue of men may seek out the Lord, and all the nations on whom my name is invoked, saith [the] Lord, who does these things known from eternity. Wherefore I judge, not to trouble those who from the nations turn to God; but to write to them to abstain from pollutions of idols, and from fornication, and from what is strangled, and from blood. For Moses, from generations of old, has in every city those who preach him, being read in the synagogues every sabbath (Acts 15:6-21).

The "Booth" or "Tabernacle/Tent" of David was established in the City of David when King David moved the Ark of the Covenant inside his newly-constructed tent-like pavilion (1 Chron. 15:1; 16:1; 2 Sam. 6:17). Here twenty-four-seven worship via the Levitical priesthood was conducted. Frankly, it appears that David waited several years before he moved the Ark to the City of David/Jerusalem.

OBED EDOM AND THE REST OF MANKIND

David reigned in Hebron over Judah for six months and then over all Israel from Hebron another seven years and then from the City of David/Jerusalem for an additional thirty-three years (or 6 mos. + 7 years + 33 years = 40 years and 6 months—2 Sam. 5:1-5; 1 Kings 2:10-11; 1 Chron. 11:1-8; 15:1-2; 2 Sam. 6:1-23; 2 Sam. 7:1-17).

From these passages we can determine that King David, prior to moving the Ark of the Covenant into the Tabernacle/Tent of David, had built himself a house in the City of David after King David had conquered the Jebusites (1 Chron. 11:4-9).

We do not know, precisely, how many years elapsed between the time shortly after King David's conquest of Jerusalem and the bringing up of the Ark of the Tabernacle from the threshing floor of Obed-Edom into the Tabernacle of David; however, we do know, initially, the Ark of God was brought to the house of Abinadab (2 Sam. 6:1-3) and from there it was brought with much fanfare to "Nachon's threshing floor" (2 Sam. 6:6-9)—where Uzzah propped it up and was summarily killed for his impropriety. Thus, David *"would not move the ark of the LORD with him into the City of David; but David took it aside into the house of Obed-Edom the Gittite"* where it would abide for three months (2 Sam. 6:10-12) in preparation from thence to the Tabernacle of David (2 Sam. 6:12-15).

"David would not move the ark with him into the City of David, but took it aside into the house of Obed-Edom the Gittite . . . the ark of God remained with the family of Obed-Edom in his house three months . . . and the LORD blessed the house of Obed-Edom and all that he had" (1 Chron. 13:13-14).

Upon the ark's arrival at the Tabernacle of David it would from there abide in the City of David—perhaps for 33 years (as well). Eventually, the Ark would be taken to the Temple built by Solomon upon the threshing floor of Ornan/Araunah the Jebusite (2 Samuel 24:10-25). THREE threshing floors are mentioned:

(1) Nachon/Chidon—2 Sam. 6:6; 1 Chron. 13:9

(2) Obed-Edom—2 Sam. 6:10-12; 1 Chron. 13:13-14

(3) Ornan/Araunah—2 Sam. 24:10-25; 1 Chron. 21:18-30

(1) Nachon/Chidon means "prepared" "ready" but is connected with Uzzah's sin as in Perez-uzzah which means BREACH. Likewise, the meaning is given as a "dart" or "javelin"

(2) Obed-Edom means "servant of Edom" who was the overseer of the storehouse (1 Chron. 26:4-8, 15) and the guardian of the sacred vessels (2 Chron. 25:24) and, as well, a Levitical musician (1 Chron. 16:5)! EDOM means RED.

(3) Ornan/Araunah means JEHOVAH IS FIRM (Strong's P. 18—Meaning of Names)—this is the site of Mt. Moriah (Isaac's sacrifice) and of the Temple—2 Chron. 3:1: *"Now Solomon began to build the house of the LORD at Jerusalem on Mount Moriah, where the LORD had appeared to his father David, at the place that David had prepared on the threshing floor of Ornan/Araunah the Jebusite."*

It is altogether plausible that "mankind" used in Acts 15:17 ("*So that the rest of mankind may seek the LORD, even all the nations/Gentiles who are called by My name....*") is surely connected with Amos 9:11-12 and, most assuredly with Obadiah 19 (Darby Version) . . . please carefully follow this reading:

"*'On that day I will raise up the tabernacle* (booth) *of David, which has fallen down, and repair* (lit. "wall up its breaches") *its damages; I will raise up its ruins, and rebuild it as in the days of old; that they may possess the remnant of EDOM* (LXX/Septuagint: MANKIND), *and all the Gentiles who are called by My name,' Says the LORD who does this thing.'"* AND "*The South shall possess the mountains of Esau* (EDOM/Mankind) *. . . they shall possess the fields of Ephraim and the fields of Samaria . . . then saviors/deliverers shall come to Mount Zion to judge the mountains of Esau, and the kingdom shall be the LORD's*" (Amos 9:12; Obadiah 19-21).

The Scriptures interchange the name of "mankind" with the name of EDOM. Those coming forth from among the Nations/Gentiles result from the raising up of the ruins of the Tabernacle of David *"so that the rest of MANKIND* (EDOM) *may seek the LORD, even ALL THE NATIONS* (Gentiles) *who are called by My name"* (Acts 15:16-17).

Furthermore, Obed-Edom's threshing floor, and this very person (Edomite), became the one who cared for the "*storehouse of the Lord*" where the vessels of the Lord were kept (1 Chron. 26:4, 6-8; 15; 2 Chron. 25:24). Even so, was Obed-Edom "*with his sixty-eight brethren, including Obed-Edom the son of Jeduthun, and Hosah, to be gatekeepers*" (1 Chron. 16:38—for a total of 68 + 2 = 70 Edomites), while the Ark of the Covenant was within the Tabernacle of David. In other words, not only was Obed-Edom blessed (1 Chron. 13:13-14) but he, when the Ark was moved to the City of David, became the Ark's GATEKEEPER in the Tabernacle of David. Indeed, again: "*He also put garrisons in Edom, and all the Edomites became David's servants*" (1 Chron. 18:13).

All this to say that the "rest of mankind" is intrinsically related to Edom/Esau unto Obed-Edom and the blessing experienced by the Ark's glory and the inclusion of "mankind"—yes, the Edomites to be the gatekeepers in the Tabernacle of David and keepers of His storehouse and all the vessels of the LORD.

CH. 5: THE JERUSALEM COUNCIL

The Ark of the Covenant started out in the threshing floor of Nachon where Perez-Uzzah (BREACH), like a javelin pierced through, causing the houses of Judah and Israel to divide at the breach between Rehoboam and Jeroboam . . . but the LORD removed the "breach" and placed the Ark of the Covenant, via David, upon the threshing floor of Obed-Edom—of Esau, the twin brother of Jacob, who begot Judah through whom arose the Lion of the Tribe of Judah, even King David . . . unto the Son of David!

Thus, Obed-Edom became the Tabernacle of David's gatekeeper and his place became the storehouse of the vessels of the LORD! So incorporated was this "mankind"—this Edomite, whose forefather was Esau, the twin brother of Jacob/Israel.

We affirm that in all likelihood—and since it was in the fourth year of King Solomon's reign that the foundation of the house of the Lord (the Solomonic Temple) was laid and seven/eight years later in the 11th/12th year of King Solomon's reign—that the Temple was dedicated, wherein the Ark of the Covenant was taken from the Tabernacle of David and placed within the Holiest of All of the Temple (1 Kings. 6:1, 37-38; 8:1, 64-66).

It could be that the Ark of the Covenant was brought into the City of David and remained there 33 years commensurate with the reign of King David from the City of David; meaning, we could readily take the 12 years of Solomon's reign and subtract them from the 33 years of King David's reign from Jerusalem and discover that the Ark of the Covenant remained in the City of David while David reigned for 21 years + Solomon's reign of 12 years = 33 years. Thus, if the Ark's abode was in the City of David 33 years, its arrival would place it there in the 18th/19th year of King David's reign. Therefore, David's reign of 33 years from the City of David, and the Ark of the Covenant's presence in the Tabernacle of David for 33 years would definitely be a chronological marvel pointing to the ultimate Lion of the Tribe of Judah who died at precisely the age of 33 years in 33 A.D.

Yes, Davidic praise and worship now flooding into Judah (among the Jews) and certainly among those who "now are the people of God"—"the rest of mankind/Edom"—is certainly in view; especially, the fact that Obed-Edom appears not only as a gatekeeper (1 Chron. 15:18, 24) but also as a "harpist" engaged in the music at the Tabernacle of David (1 Chron. 15:21, Rev. 15:2—on the "sheminith" which is an eight-stringed harp—see Psalm 6:1 on which David played). Thus did *"David, the elders of Israel, and the captains over thousand(s) went to bring up the ark of the covenant of the LORD from the house of Obed-Edom with joy"* (1 Chron. 15:25) and did so with "harps" (1 Chron. 15:28).

It appears that Obed-Edom became a Levite during the course of all this participation with David and his tabernacle and the bringing up of the ark; for we read: *"And he* (King David) *appointed some of the Levites to minister before the ark of the LORD, to commemorate, to thank, and to praise the Lord God of Israel: Asaph the chief, and next to him Zechariah, then Jeiel, Shemiramoth, Jehiel, Mattithiah, Eliab, Benaiah and* **Obed-Edom***; Jeiel with stringed instruments and harps; but Asaph made music with cymbals"* (1 Chron. 16:4-5)— and, ultimately, we see *"***Obed-Edom*** with his sixty-eight brethren, including Obed-Edom the son of Jeduthun, and Hosah, to be gatekeepers"* (1 Chron. 16:38). Suffice it to say, this Obed-Edom is altogether involved with the initial housing, musical accompaniment (harps), and ultimate gatekeeping of the Ark of the Covenant at the Tabernacle of David.

Some teachers believe this is the tabernacle/tent Amos was referring to, seeing in this unique enclosure a foreshadowing of a soon-coming restoration of Davidic praise and worship. No doubt, for Obed-Edom is certainly included in on the musical arrangements.

Thus, not only is this bringing into the Tabernacle of David the restoration of the "whole house of Israel"—comprised of both Judah and Ephraim under King David's United Kingdom . . . but the shadows and types as seen in Perez-Uzzah (breach); Obed-Edom; and ultimately the very threshing floor of the Jebusite, Ornan/Araunah the Jebusite (JEHOVAH IS FIRM)—all amplify the prophetic import seen in the New Testament whereby the Tabernacle of David includes the full participation of the "rest of mankind"—even so, Edom, whose very name RED could readily signal they too among the nations who would be brought near through the "blood of the cross." Esau/Edom seems the most likely candidate who, as the Prodigal Son in the gospels, returns to the Father's house and is wholly included in the United Kingdom under the pavilion of the Tabernacle of David. Indeed, it is impossible NOT to see our Lord's shed blood retrieving Edom for His glory through the "blood of the everlasting covenant" for He came the

First time as the Lamb of God Who takes away the sin of the world—but the "next day" He comes as the Worthy Lamb to judge at His coming again in glory (John 1:29-36)—to wit:

"Who is this who comes from Edom, with dyed garments from Bozrah, this One who is glorious in His apparel, traveling in the greatness of His strength?—"I who speak in righteousness, mighty to save." Why is Your apparel red, and Your garments like one who treads in the winepress? I have trodden the winepress alone, and from the peoples no one was with Me. For I have trodden them in My anger, and trampled them in My fury; their blood is sprinkled upon My garments, and I have stained all My robes. For the day of vengeance is in My heart, and the year of My redeemed has come. I looked, but there was no one to help, and I wondered that there was no one to uphold; therefore My own arm brought salvation for Me; and My own fury, it sustained Me. I have trodden down the peoples in My anger, made them drunk in My fury, and brought down their strength to the earth" (Isa. 63:1-6).

Glory to God: *"He led captive a train of vanquished foes"*—so is Edom captured and placed on display before principalities and powers—the very triumph of His grace (Eph. 4:8).

From the Breach (Perez-Ussah) at the threshing floor of Nachon/Chidon to the abundant blessing at the threshing floor of Obed-Edom, to the Ark's final resting place upon the threshing floor of Ornan/Araunah the Jebusite ("Jehovah is Firm") the restoration of the United Kingdom is in full view and it most certainly includes "the rest of mankind" explaining the outpouring of the Holy Spirit upon the "Whole House of Israel"—both Judah and Ephraim.

This is far more than a simple tent in ruins and then re-erected—no, no, no—this is the UNITED KINGDOM; the Tabernacle of David—the reconciliation of Judah and Ephraim—the healing of the breach—the entry of Edom where Jacob and Esau—Judah and Ephraim—are united! Indeed, why would James in Acts 15 use Amos 9 to go back in time before the magnificence of Solomon's Temple to a most unlikely and somewhat unglamorous tent to illustrate the immensity of what was taking place with the entry of the Gentiles/Nations into the Household of Faith?

Yes, the little tent appears insignificant vs. the Temple—but its subtle declarations regarding the entry of the Gentiles/Nations into the United Kingdom, if you would, was no small thing! Carefully read from the New Living Translation Bible:

"In that day I will restore the fallen kingdom of David. It is now like a house in ruins, but I will rebuild its walls and restore its former glory" (Amos 9:11).

Listen, this is NOT simply reviving this little tent known as the Tabernacle of David but it is the very restoration of the United Kingdom under King David! Thus, Amos expands the very meaning of what was on display as the Tabernacle of David. Isaiah expands this theme whereby the "tent of David" is far more than a mere habitat for the Ark of the Covenant; to wit:

"In mercy the throne will be established; and One will sit on it in truth, in the TABERNACLE OF DAVID, judging and seeking justice and hastening righteousness" (Isaiah 16:5).

"We should not trouble those from among the Nations. . . " (Acts. 15:19).

Yes, Moses is mentioned and so is *"the synagogues every Sabbath"* but as far as the Law of Moses concerns—nothing is mentioned . . . that's a weighty consideration! The only connection made between Acts 15 and Amos 9 which would signal the restoration resulting from the breach of Jeroboam and Rehoboam is the entry of the goyim now seeking the Lord. Neither Amos mentions the Law of Moses, nor does James—why?

THE TROUBLESOME YOKE

No doubt James was altogether familiar with the break-up of the United Kingdom—the BREACH; and the would-be "heavy yoke" which the "young bucks" suggested be laid upon the rebels under Jeroboam's leadership (2 Chron. 10:6-19). This time (Acts 15) the ELDERS' advice should be what is followed, not the advice of those "young men" who suggested:

> *"Then the young men who had grown up with him spoke to him, saying 'Thus you should speak to the people who have spoken to you, saying, 'Your father made our yoke heavy, but you make it lighter on us'—thus you shall say to them: 'My little finger shall be thicker than my father's waist! And now, whereas my father put a heavy yoke on you, I will add to your yoke; my father chastised you with whips, but I will chastise you with scourges!'"* (2 Chron. 10-11).

Once Jeroboam and the Northern tribes of Israel heard the advice of the "young men" and the "heavy yoke" they were to bare—the rebellion was in full force! *"What share have we in David? We have no inheritance in the son of Jesse. Every man to your tents, O Israel! Now see to your own house, O David!"* Alas! *"The turn of events was from God, that the LORD might fulfill His word, which He had spoken by the hand of Ahijah the Shilonite to Jeroboam the son of Nebat"* that the kingdom would be torn asunder (2 Chron. 10:16) . . . thus, the BREACH of Jeroboam!

Those of Ephraim quickly crowned Jeroboam King of the Northern Ten Tribes. King Rehoboam was on the warpath to stop the rebellion but:

> *". . . the word of the LORD came to Shemaiah the man of God, saying, 'Speak to Rehoboam the son of Solomon, king of Judah, and to all Israel in Judah and Benjamin, saying, 'Thus says the LORD: 'You shall not go up and fight against your brethren! Let every man return to his house, for this thing is from me.' Therefore, they obeyed the words of the LORD, and turned back from attacking Jeroboam"* (2 Chron. 11:2-4)—the whole thing was "divinely orchestrated!"

Thus, Jerusalem became the capitol of Judah-Israel and Shechem (aka "Samaria" or "Sichem") became the capitol of Ephraim-Israel—and it remained that way from around 928 B.C. to 719 B.C. when the Assyrians deported the Ten Northern Tribes into Assyria (722 B.C. the Fall of Samaria).

Likewise, did the Ten Northern Tribes of Israel commit gross idolatry and grievously sinned against the LORD until in Hosea He gave them a writ of divorce and declared: *"You are not my people"* (Hos. 1:9). Thence were they swallowed up of the nations/the Gentiles (Hosea 8:7-10). Notwithstanding, both Hosea and Amos prophesied that a remnant of Ephraim would return (Hos. 8:10; 11:8-11; Amos 9:14-15).

We must understand that the Council of Jerusalem included *"some of the sect of the Pharisees who believed rose up, saying, 'It is NECESSARY to circumcise them, AND to command them to KEEP THE LAW OF MOSES'"* (Acts 15:5).

"And when there had been much dispute" (Acts 15:7) we find Peter rising up and reminding the apostles and elders that it was he who had opened the door of the gospel at the house of Cornelius. Peter confirmed that the "Holy Spirit" was *"given to them . . . just as he did to us and made no distinction between us and them purifying their hearts by faith"* (Acts 15:8-9).

Then Peter, knowing about the breach of Jeroboam, stated clearly: *"Now therefore, why do you test God by putting a YOKE ON THE NECK of the disciples which neither our fathers nor we were able to bear? But we believe that through the grace of the Lord Jesus Christ we shall be saved in the same manner as they"* (Acts 15:10-11).

It was at this juncture that the *"multitude kept silent and listened to Barnabas and Paul declaring how many miracles and wonders God had worked through them among the Gentiles"* (Acts 15:12).

After Barnabas and Paul "stopped speaking" James began to speak by substantiating the words of Simon that *"God at the first visited the Nations to take out of them a people for His name"* and that the *"words of the prophets"* (in particular, Amos 9:11-12; Obadiah 19-21—"mankind" or "Edom") prophetically confirmed what was taking place among *"the rest of mankind"* who were seeking the LORD, *"even all the Nations who are called by My name"* (Acts 15:17).

James phrased it in this manner: *"DO NOT TROUBLE THOSE who are turning to God from among the nations"* (Acts 15:19). They all knew what Amos was saying and the allusions to Obadiah regarding Edom—*"the rest of mankind."* The YOKE bore a potent reminder of both what happened when the "young men" of Judah desired to lay a "heavy yoke" upon the Northern Ten Tribes and, no doubt, the words of the Lord Jesus: *"My yoke is easy and my burden is light"* (Matt. 11:30).

The debate was over . . . a letter was drafted to the Nations . . . *"the rest of mankind"* should not be troubled aside from *"abstaining from things polluted by idols, from sexual immorality, from things strangled, and from blood"* (Acts 15:20). The BREACH had effectively been healed between Judah and Ephraim—between the Jews and the *"elect called out from among the nations."*

How different was the gathering of the Jerusalem Council and the "meeting of minds" juxtaposed to that of King Rehoboam and the gathering in Shechem. The one (Jerusalem) resulted in acceptance and prophetic fulfillment; the other (Shechem) resulted in the BREACH OF JEROBOAM. The one of liberty, mercy and grace in Jesus Christ—the other the "heavy yoke" and ultimate rebellion.

Each group sought relief from the yoke of bondage—the one obtained it (Jerusalem) the other saw its cruel result. Mercy, grace and acceptance resulted at Jerusalem, but taxation, human exploitation, and resultant rebellion came at Shechem. Under the inspiration of the Holy Spirit, James (someone many blame as a "legalist" due to his writing of the epistle of James, no less to the "twelve tribes scattered abroad"—James 1:1), cut to the chase and delivered a fatal blow to the legalists of his day.

Yes, the Law of Moses, written some 1400 years before, was no longer a heavy yoke with its onerous subsidiary rules and regulations. The "holy nation" comprised of Jews and Gentiles (1 Peter 2:9) entered an era of utter restoration. The Law of Commandments contained in ordinances (Eph. 2:15) was to be an "interior reality" written on the fleshy tablets of the heart—not inscribed on stony tablets (2 Cor. 3:3). This would be known as the Law of Christ Who alone could "fulfill the Law" in every one of us!

"Therefore, by the deeds of the Law no flesh will be justified in His sight, for by the Law is the knowledge of sin. But now the righteousness of God apart from the Law is revealed, being witnessed by the Law and the Prophets, even the righteousness of God, through faith in Jesus Christ, to all and on all who believe. For there is no difference; for all have sinned and fall short of the glory of God, being justified freely by His grace through the redemption that is in Christ Jesus" (Romans. 3:20-24).

Yet, how could this incursion into the "Household of Faith" by those entitled *"the rest of mankind"* somehow establish the Throne of David? Weren't they to be a whole lot like Judah to be considered a part of the Commonwealth of Israel? We are left with but one decisive reflection—those being *"called out from among the nations"*—the *"rest of mankind"*—had to be the same ones spoken of by Paul when he was quoting from Hosea:

"And that He might make known the riches of His glory on the vessels of mercy, which He had prepared beforehand for glory, even us whom He called, not of the Jews only, but also of the Nations? As He says also in Hosea: 'I will call them My people, who were not My people, and her beloved, who was not beloved.' And it shall come to pass in the place where it was said to them, 'You are not My people,' There they shall be called sons of the living God.'" (Romans 9:9-26)

THE HOUSE OF DAVID

The mystery of the gospel's message to the nations has been resolved: We ARE Ephraim! That's who is returning, being restored, desiring to be that United Kingdom, once again. Thus, when Paul declared that ALL ISRAEL would be delivered (Romans 11:26) as a result of the *"multitude* (fullness) *of nations* (ethnos/Gentiles) *has come in"* (aka *"fullness of the Gentiles has come in"*)—then would the blindness in part that has happened to Israel (frankly, to both houses of Israel—Judah and Ephraim) be taken away for the *"gifts and calling of God are irrevocable"* (Rom. 11:25, 29). No longer would Judah be considered the "enemy" by Ephraim, but they would be considered *"beloved for the sake of the fathers"* (Rom. 11:28). This is where the New Covenant (Jer. 31:31) shall have its fulfillment upon the Whole House of Israel—not just upon the House of Ephraim but upon Judah as well. Then the Two Houses shall be considered the very HOUSE OF DAVID, my Servant.

We must keep in mind—and this is precisely why our beloved Dispensationalist brethren are so terribly confused, as well as those within the Reform community who embrace Replacement theologies—the New Covenant has been **exclusively promised** to both the House of Judah and the House of Israel . . . it clearly states so (*"Behold, the days are coming, says the LORD, when I will make a NEW COVENANT with the House of Israel and with the House of Judah,"* etc.—Jer. 31:31-37).

The only way one can exegete around this exclusivity is to prematurely unite Ephraim and Judah during the Babylonian Captivity as do most Dispensationalists or to dispense with these literal entities and suggest that they are non-existent and simply transferred to the Kingdom of God manifested in the "Church" according to Reform theologians—dispensing with any literal Israel whatsoever—i.e., there is no such thing as Ephraim nor, for that matter, "real Jews" (taking a more extreme theological posture). Today's "True Israel" is simply the Church (comprised of the nations and "converted Jews" from Judaism—at best) or the Church, according to the Dispensationalists is the mystery of Christ, the Messiah, comprised of Jew and Gentile, but wholly separated from "Israel" which will one day fulfill her prophetic destiny apart from that of the Church's calling—the Church has absolutely nothing to do with Israel—she (i.e., the Church) is not the True Israel nor does she participate in any "earthly" kingdom but is wholly heavenly oriented.

BREAKING OF THE BROTHERHOOD—THE TWO STAFFS

For a time both houses enjoyed the NEW COVENANT—then the Staff of Bonds/Unity was broken shortly around 100 A.D. (Zech. 11:14—*"that I might break the brotherhood between Judah and Israel"*). This tells us that "somehow" there was for a time the uniting of the brotherhood between Judah and Israel's "Ephraim." Now at the end of the age, as more and more of Judah, the Jews, enter into the New Covenant; and as "the rest of mankind" (Ephraim) come into their fullness—into their completed number (Romans 11:25), then the prophetic fulfillment will be complete, and the brotherhood fully restored, and *ALL ISRAEL SHALL BE DELIVERED, when the Deliverer shall roar out of Zion!* (Rom. 11:26-26). Then shall it be utterly fulfilled: *"For this is MY COVENANT with them, when I take away their sins"* (Rom. 11:27). This is the full expression of the New Covenant upon BOTH Houses of Israel—Judah and Ephraim: ALL ISRAEL shall be delivered! The immensity of the prophetic essence of the Scripture climaxes at the end of the age—a crescendo of eschatological fulfillment!

Can you see the prophetic fulfillment, brethren? *"I will restore the fortunes of Judah and the fortunes of Israel and will rebuild them as they were at the first"* (Jer. 33:17). If you cannot see this as THE prophetic fulfillment, it may be that you do not wish to see it? May the Holy Spirit as in the days of the Jerusalem Council open our eyes so that we may enter into the mutual fortune shared by Judah and Israel; and as James, DECLARE from Amos the impact of this wondrous uniting under the Tabernacle of David, while affirming Haggai's utterance beyond that of the Second Temple's restoration reaching unto the climax of the present age:

> *"For thus says the LORD of hosts: 'Once more (it is a little while) I will shake heaven and earth, the sea and dry land; and I will shake all nations, and they shall come to the Desire of All Nations, and I will fill this temple with glory, says the LORD of hosts. 'The silver is Mine, and the gold is Mine,' says the LORD of hosts. 'The glory of this LATTER TEMPLE shall be greater than the FORMER,' says the LORD of hosts. 'And in this place I will give peace,' says the LORD of hosts"* (Haggai 2:6-9).

How could the paltry (in comparison) Second Temple be compared in glory to that of the Solomonic colossus? Haggai had prophesied it in that which Paul espoused:

> *"Now, therefore, you are no longer strangers and foreigners, but fellow citizens with the saints and members of the household of God, having been built on the foundation of the apostles and prophets, Jesus Christ Himself being the chief cornerstone, in whom the whole building, being fitted together,*

grows into a holy temple in the Lord, in whom you also are being built together for a dwelling place of God in the Spirit . . . to Him be glory in the EKKLESIA by Christ Jesus to all generations, forever and ever. Amen" (Eph. 2:19-22; 3:21).

Incredibly, Haggai, three times (Haggai 2:10, 18, 20) receives this prophetic outburst and references the *"twenty-fourth day of the NINTH month"* which would place this date in the month of Kislev 24-25 or upon a future Feast of Dedication which took place after the Second Temple was cleansed from the immediate Abomination of Desolation wrought by the Hellenizing efforts of Antiochus IV Epiphanes cir. 168-164 BC (nigh 260+years after the dedication of the Second Temple during Haggai's time) during the Maccabean Revolt (book of Daniel). This is the very same Feast Day of the TEMPLE'S DEDICATION where Jesus declared: *"I and My Father are one . . . the Father is in Me, and I in Him"* (John 10:30, 38b). Jesus declared His deity juxtaposed to that of the yet future Abomination of Desolation wherein the Antichrist *". . . sits as God in the temple of God, showing himself that he is God"* (2 Thess. 2:3) until *"He who now restrains will do so until He is taken out of the way. And then the lawless one will be revealed, whom the Lord will consume with the breath of His mouth and destroy with the brightness of His coming"* (2 Thess. 2:7-8).

Today, the Lord is filling His Temple with GLORY—in fulfillment of Haggai's prophetic utterance: *"The GLORY of this latter temple shall be greater than the former . . . 'And in this place I will give peace,' says the LORD of hosts"* (Haggai 2:9). Is not this the climax of the Gospel of Peace that *"through the blood of the cross . . . He has made of the two* (Judah and the Nations) *ONE NEW MAN—so making PEACE?"* (Eph. 2:13-18)—thus is the "Commonwealth of Israel" united under the Tabernacle of David! (Eph. 2:12; Acts 15:16-17).

Do you think that the peculiar salutation given in James 1:1 to the *"Twelve Tribes of Israel scattered abroad"* was a mistake? No, it was not. James clearly knew what he meant when he addressed the Twelve Tribes in this manner—for they included both Judah and Ephraim. He knew that the Tabernacle of David had be raised up and its ruins rebuilt in the "Uniting Bond of Peace" –a full restoration; even so, the United Kingdom of David—all Twelve Tribes.

What deceit was wrought upon the followers of Yeshua among the nations, when Emperor Constantine pulled the wool over our eyes and with complicit compliance and encouragement from the elders of the EKKLESIA demanded that the Jews of Judah be "cut off" from the assembly and ghettoized upon the earth. They had forgotten the Jerusalem Council's decisions and made the "Church and State" their Weltanschauung. This corrupting worldview spread like a plague among the brotherhood whereby we, primarily of Ephraim, commenced to persecute the Jew. Alas! The Gentiles have literally created their own religion! This mixture of religion and politics has contrived to this day . . . who prophetic destiny shall culminate in what John of the Revelation calls the *"Great Harlot, Babylon the Great, Mother of Harlots and Abominations of the earth."* The Roman Church epitomizes this "Church-State" hybrid birthed in Apostasy and perpetuated by an admixture of the *"wheat and tares."*

Our Constantine was Ephraim's Jeroboam—along with false gods and deities secured from the nations; thus, was birthed: CHRISTIANITY. Yes, we were called "Christians" first at Antioch—we were followers and made our chief occupation, Jesus Christ. But that entitlement eventually robbed us of our true identity and separated us from the "brotherhood." Our "Hebraic Roots" were extinguished—we were blinded from our origins. Indeed, it has been to the present impossible to see our identity as Ephraim—the Scriptures were totally sealed to us. Meanwhile, "Torah Observant" Jewry—hampered by keeping hundreds of ordinances and laws demanding either a Tabernacle (as in the Wilderness) and, most definitely, its extension as the Third Temple—have formed a new brand of Judaism because they do not have their Temple in the first place. Calling it "New Covenant Judaism" does not make it so.

Our Messianic Jewish brethren, in the main, quickly discarded Christianity's heathen holidays and adopted those of the Hebrew Festival Calendar—this too was a simple adjustment, for most Messianic Jews grew up observing the "Calendar." Now, declaring themselves to be "Torah observant" allows them to practice the Law of Moses once again. Tragically, for many of them, true fellowship within the Commonwealth of Israel demands they practice the Law of Moses in full obedience to Moses' commands. They have unwittingly and/or purposefully placed a "heavy yoke" upon themselves and those of Ephraim who have joined together with them.

I know this "observation" may come as a shock to my beloved Messianic brethren and especially to the more ardent Ephraimites among them—but the 'thin line" they witness between the Law of Christ and the Law of Moses is actually a huge barrier between the Law of Liberty and the Law of Moses. Not only with regards to salvation issues, but, as well, to those of sanctification. To suggest that Peter's Gospel preached to the Jews was void of the Grace and Mercy (Acts 15:11) of the Lord Jesus is simply not the case; therefore, to "keep the Law of Moses" (Acts 15:5) as the Pharisees who believed in Yeshua demanded, a law *"which neither our fathers nor we were able to bear"* (Acts 15:10), must be confronted by Jew and Greek alike, if you would: There is *"no distinction between us and them, purifying their hearts by FAITH"* (Acts 15:9).

Israel's materiality wrought through much suffering upon the eastern edge of the Mediterranean Sea exposes the "other worldly' emphasis (though it most certainly sought to bring their "heavenly kingdom" down to terra firma) given to us through Christendom, through Constantine. Now, Yeshua's entry upon the Mt. of Olives appears ever closer—Yeshua's desire is a Renewed Heaven and EARTH! The "kingdoms of this world" are upon the earth—the earth that manifests His creation—the earth which was corrupted at the fall of the First Adam.

Now, the Ladder extending from Heaven's portal to Earth, the Son of God/Son of Man wants Jacob/Israel to become living stones and to establish His Holy City upon the Earth! The climax of the New Covenant rapidly approaches—the day of full redemption—there's no returning to the First Covenant . . . it is vanishing away in toto. Peter, James, Paul—all resound: *"O foolish Galatians! Who has bewitched you that you should not obey the truth . . . for I through the law died to the law that I might live to God"* (Gal. 3:1; 2:19) . . . *"Why do you test God by putting a yoke on the neck of the disciples which neither our fathers nor we were able to bear?"* (Acts 15:10).

To our great fortune, though the time is exceedingly short; therefore, the prophecies of our full restoration whereby ALL ISRAEL shall be delivered, and the breach which has separated us for centuries will come to its prophetic end . . . yes, it's been nigh 2,000 years since the Staff of Unity was broken—and that by the LORD HIMSELF . . . but the final word from the Almighty:

"Come, let us return to the Lord. For He has torn us, but He will heal us; He has wounded us, but He will bandage us. He will revive us after two days; He will raise us up on the third day, That we may live before Him. So let us know, let us press on to know the Lord. His going forth is as certain as the dawn; And He will come to us like the rain, Like the spring rain watering the earth" (Hosea 6:1-3).

Chapter Six

ISRAEL SPLIT IN TWO—THE BREACH OF JEROBOAM

By Dr. Gavin Finley[66]

The Sin of King Solomon

The wanton amorous desires of King Solomon were legendary. And even though his prayer for wisdom was answered he was drawn to wisdom in the ways of this world more than seeking godly wisdom.

The foreign policy and economic policy of King Solomon was to compromise with surrounding nations. He did this for the sake of promoting friendly mutually beneficial commercial intercourse. This policy did in fact lead to a massive boost in peaceful trade and with this came great wealth. He was inclined to make deals with the surrounding nations rather than warring with them. This did, in fact, promote peaceful trade and prosperity. However, with the compromise came the problems. So this happy state of affairs would not last.

King Solomon brought in many foreign wives and concubines. They brought in with them many pagan gods. This opened the door to unbridled idolatry in Israel. The nation was led into unholy practices with the worship now being directed to strange deities. Pagan practices became the norm in the kingdom of Solomon. This then was the sin of Solomon. It was severe. And it had dire consequences for the moral integrity of Israel.

1Kings 11

> *1 Now King Solomon loved many foreign women along with the daughter of Pharaoh: Moabite, Ammonite, Edomite, Sidonian, and Hittite women, 2 from the nations concerning which the LORD had said to the sons of Israel, "You shall not associate with them, nor shall they associate with you,*

---

[66] EndTimePilgrim.org

> *for they will surely turn your heart away after their gods." Solomon held fast to these in love. 3 He had seven hundred wives, princesses, and three hundred concubines, and his wives turned his heart away. 4 For when Solomon was old, his wives turned his heart away after other gods; and his heart was not wholly devoted to the Yehovah his God, as the heart of David his father had been. 5 For Solomon went after **Ashtoreth** the goddess of the Sidonians and after **Milcom** the detestable idol of the Ammonites. 6 Solomon did what was evil in the sight of Yehovah God, and did not follow the LORD fully, as David his father had done. 7 Then Solomon built a high place for **Chemosh** the detestable idol of Moab, on the mountain which is east of Jerusalem, and for **Molech** the detestable idol of the sons of Ammon. 8 Thus also he did for all his foreign wives, who burned incense and sacrificed to their gods.*

This gross unholiness was devastating. It brought great damage to the nation and to the congregation of Israel. Devotion to the Holy One of Israel fell by the wayside. The glory of Israel was departing.

Back at Sinai the nation and congregation of Israel had made a covenant with Yehovah-Eternal God. They had promised to be a people set-apart in holiness to Him. There before the fire on the mountain they had agreed to listen to His teachings and obey His commandments. But now, things had changed. King Solomon was leading the way for his people to do otherwise.

> *9 Now Yehovah-God was angry with Solomon because his heart was turned away from the Yehovah-God, the God of Israel, who had appeared to him twice, 10 and had commanded him concerning this thing, that he should not go after other gods; but he did not observe what the LORD had commanded.*

The God of Israel had appeared to King Solomon on two occasions. The king had been solemnly warned about the matter. But he continued on in his determined compromising ways. This refusal to heed the warnings from the God of Israel was the last straw. This was the primary underlying cause for the nation and the congregation of Israel to be divided and to split in two.

CH. 6: ISRAEL SPLIT IN TWO – THE BREACH OF JEROBOAM

11 So the LORD said to Solomon, "Because you have done this, and you have not kept My covenant and My statutes, which I have commanded you, I will surely tear the kingdom from you, and will give it to your servant. 12 Nevertheless I will not do it in your days for the sake of your father David, but I will tear it out of the hand of your son. 13 However, I will not tear away all the kingdom, but I will give one tribe to your son for the sake of My servant David and for the sake of Jerusalem which I have chosen."

This unholy compromise, the sin of Solomon, was an extremely serious matter. It was a spiritual affront to the Holy One of Israel and the primary cause for the judgment of God that was to follow. Concerning the legacy of the House of David with King Solomon that judgment was severe. God was going to cut off the royal House of David from extending rule over all the tribes of Israel. The man who was going to lead in this division had actually been chosen by King Solomon himself. Jeroboam had been selected because of his valiant spirit, his leadership skills, and his industrious ways.

28 Now the man Jeroboam was a valiant warrior, and when Solomon saw that the young man was industrious, he appointed him over all the forced labor of the house of Joseph.

Jeroboam was chosen as work party leader over the ten tribes. They would make their visits to Judah, helping prepare for the feasts in the capital city, Jerusalem. These celebrations took place three times a year at the Temple. However, Jeroboam became unhappy with what he was seeing happen. Because of fortifications being built by the House of David, and also quite possibly due to worker's grievances coming to him from the people, Jeroboam turned away from the King and rebelled from his service.

26 Then Jeroboam the son of Nebat, an Ephraimite of Zeredah, Solomon's servant, whose mother's name was Zeruah, a widow, also rebelled against the king. 27 Now this was the reason why he rebelled against the king: Solomon built the Millo, and closed up the breach of the city of his father David.

When Jeroboam rebelled from his service King Solomon felt betrayed. So he sought to kill him. But Jeroboam fled to Egypt.

40 Solomon sought therefore to put Jeroboam to death; but Jeroboam arose and fled to Egypt to Shishak king of Egypt, and he was in Egypt until the death of Solomon.

It was during the reign of King Solomon that God sent the prophet Ahijah to Jeroboam with a message.

29 It came about at that time, when Jeroboam went out of Jerusalem, that the prophet Ahijah the Shilonite found him on the road. Now Ahijah had clothed himself with a new cloak; and both of them were alone in the field. 30 Then Ahijah took hold of the new cloak which was on him and tore it into twelve pieces. 31 He said to Jeroboam, "Take for yourself ten pieces; for thus says the LORD, the God of Israel, 'Behold, I will tear the kingdom out of the hand of Solomon and give you ten tribes 32 **(but he will have one tribe, for the sake of My servant David and for the sake of Jerusalem, the city which I have chosen** *from all the tribes of Israel),'"*

The God of Israel had His purpose in allowing this break-up to take place. The reason for this rending of Israel into two is clearly stated.

33 "because they have forsaken Me, and have worshiped Ashtoreth the goddess of the Sidonians, Chemosh the god of Moab, and Milcom the god of the sons of Ammon; and they have not walked in My ways, doing what is right in My sight and observing My statutes and My ordinances, as his father David did."

For the sake of the memory of his father, King David, this division of Israel into two kingdoms was not to take place during the reign of Solomon. It would occur during the reign of his son, Rehoboam.

34 "'Nevertheless I will not take the whole kingdom out of his hand, but I will make him ruler all the days of his life, for the sake of My servant David whom I chose, who observed My commandments and My statutes; 35 but I will take the kingdom from his son's hand and give it to you, even ten tribes."

CH. 6: ISRAEL SPLIT IN TWO – THE BREACH OF JEROBOAM

The promise given by the God of Israel to Jeroboam and his being given ten of the twelve tribes was a generous one. Jeroboam was a work party leader and a representative of the people. God promised Jeroboam that He would honor his rule and establish his kingdom as King David's kingdom had been honored. This was gracious beyond all measure. It was also a demonstration of the positive and hopeful stance our God has to all who come into His service. Here is what Jeroboam was told by God through the prophet Ahijah.

37 "I will take you, and you shall reign over whatever you desire, and you shall be king over Israel. 38 Then it will be, that if you listen to all that I command you and walk in My ways, and do what is right in My sight by observing My statutes and My commandments, as My servant David did, then I will be with you and build you an enduring house as I built for David, and I will give Israel to you."

Similarly the promise to preserve the royal tribe of Judah, the holder of the scepter, and to retain the sovereignty of Israel for the sake of King David, Solomon's father, was a merciful judgment.

32 "(but he, [King Rehoboam of Judah], will have one tribe, for the sake of My servant David and for the sake of Jerusalem, the city which I have chosen from all the tribes of Israel)."

There was no doubt about the grave curtailment of the royal House of David in Judah. The descendants of David in the Jewish House of Judah would lose their rule over the ten tribes. The House of Judah were also destined to be afflicted for their unholy compromise with evil pagan deities. **But not forever.**

39 "Thus I will afflict the descendants of David for this, but not always."

Yes, the royal house of David in Judah would be afflicted. But not forever. Someone from the royal House of David in the tribe of Judah was going to come along eventually and fulfill the Shiloh prophecy given to Jacob concerning his son Judah. This prophecy in Genesis 49:10 relates to the scepter and sovereignty of Israel. The name "Shiloh" means, "The One to whom it belongs." This remarkable prophecy concerning the eventual destiny of the Jewish house of Judah still speaks to us today. The mention of Shiloh speaks of a coming Messiah, the One to whom the scepter belongs.

Genesis 49

*10 The scepter shall not depart from Judah,
Nor the ruler's staff from between his feet,
Until Shiloh comes,
And to him shall be the obedience of the peoples.*

So the future role of the Jewish house of Judah is assured. The Gate of Judah is one of the 12 gates of the New Jerusalem that John saw descending from heaven as recorded by him in Revelation 21. Then too, the Tribe of Judah is represented among the great multitude standing before the throne of God. They are there in the final listing given to us in Revelation Chapter 7.

THE HISTORIC EVENT THAT TRIGGERED THE BREACH

Woodcut illustration by Julius Schnoor von Carolsfeld. (1794-1872)

After the death of King Solomon his son Rehoboam was set to become king. But as we read in 1Kings Chapter 40, the new king acted foolishly. He failed to listen to the elders and he failed to respect the appeals of his subjects for some economic relief.

1Kings 40

1 Then Rehoboam went to Shechem, for all Israel had come to Shechem to make him king.

At the time of the coronation of King Rehoboam the ten tribes called for Jeroboam to represent them. The schism between the royal Jewish House of Judah and the ten northern tribes can be traced back before that to earlier times. King David in his times of duress, was supported primarily by his tribe, the tribe of Judah. The supporters of King Saul, a Benjamite, came predominantly from the ten tribes. Similarly, the ten tribes were the main supporters of King David's rebel son Absalom. But it seems clear that here at this point in history there was a growing rift between King Rehoboam from the royal house of David in Judah and people of the other tribes. So the ten tribes were compelled to look for a champion. They wanted someone to advance their cause. There was a growing group consensus that Jeroboam was their man.

2 Now when Jeroboam the son of Nebat heard of it, he was living in Egypt (for he was yet in Egypt, where he had fled from the presence of King Solomon). 3a Then they sent and called him,

There is an economic story here too, that is often overlooked. After the death of Solomon the glory of the kingdom was fading and the financial credit of the Kingdom of Israel was beginning to become problematic. We can surmise that the kingdom was seeing a measure of economic decline with its treasury becoming financially strapped. Even in the latter years of King Solomon there would have been a call to raise the taxes, the tribute, and the servitude required of the work parties that went up into Judah. It would appear that among the families of the ten tribes these economic burdens had become onerous. And now, after the death of King Solomon, the tribes were looking for a little relief.

This was the situation as Jeroboam and the ten tribes came to meet the new king. Rehoboam and the royal house of Judah came up to Shechem to meet with the heads of the ten tribes. Jeroboam had come out of exile. He had been chosen as their chief spokesman. Here is their appeal to the king. And now, after 2950 odd years, we still have the exact words spoken by both parties recorded for us.

> *3b Jeroboam and all the assembly of Israel came and spoke to Rehoboam, saying, 4 "Your father made our yoke hard; now therefore lighten the hard service of your father and his heavy yoke which he put on us, and we will serve you."*
>
> *5 Then he said to them, "Depart for three days, then return to me." So the people departed.*

Two choices faced the new ruler, King Rehoboam. He could accept the economic decline as a reality. The kingdom could then take the appropriate measure to mitigate matters for the accountants at the treasury. They could tighten down on expansion, cut expenses, and be prepared to liquidate assets. The king could then ease the taxation and the work-party burden for the ten tribes.

The alternative was for him to push on with his father's policy. He could solidify his dominion over the ten tribes in an iron-fisted manner, thereby establishing his authority over them and showing them that he was boss. By this means he could hope to achieve his goals. He could maintain the former glory of the kingdom of his father, King Solomon, by setting even higher taxes and demanding that the ten tribes work harder.

King Rehoboam had to make a choice. He had to make a solid first impression. So he went first to the elders of the kingdom.

> *6 King Rehoboam consulted with the elders who had served his father Solomon while he was still alive, saying, "How do you counsel me to answer this people?" 7 Then they spoke to him, saying, "**If you will be a servant to this people** today, and will serve them and grant them their petition, and **speak good words to them**, then **they will be your servants forever**."*

This message from the elders was wise counsel. But the young king did not heed their advice. Instead he sought the advice of his buddies. These were the young men who had partied with him as he awaited his time to come to the throne.

> *8 But he forsook the counsel of the elders which they had given him, and consulted with the young men who grew up with him and served him. 9 So he said to them, "What counsel do you give that we may answer this people who have spoken to me, saying, 'Lighten the yoke which your father put on us?'"*

The advice of the young men, full of vinegar and testosterone, was quite clear. They wanted to see the king respond to the appeal for relief in an assertive way. They wanted to see King Rehoboam respond decisively and lower the boom on the ten tribes. So the young princes advised the king to treat the ten tribes in a harsh Machiavellian manner. They wanted their king, heir to the Throne of David in Judah, to establish a stern hierarchical dominion over all the tribes of Israel. So the young speech-writers gave King Rehoboam some strong words to say that would make his position abundantly clear. The answer they prepared and handed the king for him to deliver to the ten tribes were the words that might have been used by an angry taskmaster. The message they wanted the king to give the ten tribes was not only unyielding but one of blatant hostility.

10 And the young men who had grown up with him said to him, "Thus shall you speak to this people who said to you, 'Your father made our yoke heavy, but you lighten it for us,' thus shall you say to them, 'My little finger is thicker than my father's thighs. 11 And now, whereas my father laid on you a heavy yoke, I will add to your yoke. My father disciplined you with whips, but I will discipline you with scorpions.'"

The king should have known better than to dismiss the advice of the elders. He should have had second thoughts about proclaiming such a domineering message from the young bloods. But he did it anyway.

12 So Jeroboam and all the people came to Rehoboam the third day, as the king said, "Come to me again the third day." 13 And the king answered the people harshly, and forsaking the counsel that the old men had given him, 14 he spoke to them according to the counsel of the young men, saying, **"My father made your yoke heavy, but I will add to your yoke. My father disciplined you with whips, but I will discipline you with scorpions."**

The ten tribes were asking for more than economic relief from the tribute, the taxes, and the work parties. Their appeal for relief of their burden came with a certain understanding about the spirit and character of the God of Israel. They knew that He was not just a God of righteous rule of law. They knew He was also a God of mercy and grace. So they were looking for evidence of those certain spiritual qualities in their new king. This was a matter that was very important to them. They were looking for an expression, a manifestation, of a certain virtue. The spiritual quality they were looking for was something we might call GRACE.

So as we look carefully here at the fracture point in Israel, there is a decidedly spiritual dimension to this story. And it can be laid out in very stark terms. The fact is the ten tribes came with an appeal to the king for some **GRACE**. But in this critical juncture in the holy history of Israel the royal Jewish House of Judah just laid down the **LAW**. The king was not disposed to rule in mercy as well as in righteousness. King Rehoboam was not spiritually equipped to guide, to inform, and to earnestly but gently entreat the people under his care. He was not able to manifest this quality of a servant leader, or a Shepherd-King in his rule. Instead, as we see here with King Jeroboam, he just laid down the **LAW in a very harsh manner**.

> *15 So the king did not listen to the people, for it was a turn of affairs brought about by the LORD that he might fulfill his word, which the LORD spoke by Ahijah the Shilonite to Jeroboam the son of Nebat.*

The response then of the Northern ten tribes to the king's severity and over-bearing authoritarian tone was immediate and decisive. They had had it with the royal Jewish tribe. So they walked out. They **rebelled** from the Kingdom of Israel. The words they spoke to the king that day were sharp, decisive, and historic.

> *16 And when all Israel saw that the king did not listen to them, the people answered the king,*
>
> **"What portion do we have in David? We have no inheritance in the son of Jesse. To your tents, O Israel! Look now to your own house, David."**

So Israel went to their tents.

CH. 6: ISRAEL SPLIT IN TWO – THE BREACH OF JEROBOAM

THE TEN TRIBES REBEL
ISRAEL IS DIVIDED AT THE BREACH OF JEROBOAM

The meeting was a disastrous one for all Israel. Yes, the ten tribes were looking for **grace**. But Rehoboam just laid down the **law**. Any hope of retaining unity under a united kingdom under Judah was now lost. God's covenant people were divided asunder. The immediate response of King Rehoboam was to go to war against the ten rebelling tribes. Judah and Benjamin prepared an army to go out and restore the union of Israel.

21 When Rehoboam came to Jerusalem, he assembled all the house of Judah and the tribe of Benjamin, 180,000 chosen warriors, to fight against the house of Israel, to restore the kingdom to Rehoboam the son of Solomon.

But in an interesting turn of events God Himself intervened. And through the prophet Shemaiah this message was delivered to King Rehoboam.

22 But the word of God came to Shemaiah the man of God: 23 "Say to Rehoboam the son of Solomon, king of Judah, and to all the house of Judah and Benjamin, and to the rest of the people, 24 **'Thus says the LORD, You shall not go up or fight against your relatives the people of Israel. Every man return to his home, for this thing is from me.'"** *So they listened to the word of the LORD and went home again, according to the word of the LORD.*

This was a noteworthy turn of events. Israel was divided. It was split into the two houses. And God said this thing was from Him? Judah and Benjamin with the Holy City of Jerusalem continued on in the south. And under Jeroboam the ten northern tribes went their own way. What longer term plan did God have in mind? And by what means now, was He eventually going to restore the union of Israel?

After their rebellion the ten tribes became the Northern Kingdom of Israel. King Rehoboam then sent a taskmaster to rope the ten tribes back into the usual work parties as per the former times. But that was not to be.

*17 But Rehoboam reigned over the people of Israel who lived in the cities of Judah. 18 Then **King Rehoboam sent Adoram, who was taskmaster over the forced labor**, and **all Israel stoned him to death with stones.** And King Rehoboam hurried to mount his chariot to flee to Jerusalem. 19 So **Israel has been in rebellion against the house of David to this day.***

The king had lost his work parties, lost the ten tribes, lost the bulk of the congregation of Israel, and lost the tax money that had come to him in the former times. Above all, he had lost the former glory that had been seen in the great Kingdoms of David and Solomon. The year of this sentinel event, the fracture of Israel into two kingdoms was ca. 922 B.C. This was the great divorce of Israel.

JEROBOAM REIGNS AS KING AND COMMITS THE "SINS OF JEROBOAM"

As we saw, even before they had met with King Rehoboam, Jeroboam had been proclaimed king over all Israel by the ten tribes. This would seem to be a rebellion in the making, even before the actual disastrous meeting with the king took place.

*20 And when all Israel heard that Jeroboam had returned, they sent and called him to the assembly and made him king over **ALL** Israel. **There was none that followed the house of David but the tribe of Judah only.***

As we have seen, right from the beginning, King Jeroboam had been promised a great kingdom in the spirit and stature of King David. But instead he led the ten tribes into a classic sin that came to be named after him. The **sins of Jeroboam** became a byword in its time for leaders who lead Israel, God's called out covenant people, into sin. This phrase of description applied to evil kings and leaders is repeated many times in the chronicles of the Kings. We continue to see such morally debased rulers leading their people astray, even to this day.

1Kings 15:30

*"Because of the **sins of Jeroboam** which he sinned, and which he made Israel sin, by his provocation wherewith he provoked the LORD God of Israel to anger."*

CH. 6: ISRAEL SPLIT IN TWO – THE BREACH OF JEROBOAM

The "sins of Jeroboam" were those in which he, in his place of authority as king led God's covenant people to sin. Firstly, he prevented them from going up into Judah to Jerusalem, to the Temple to celebrate the feasts. He wanted them to forget about their Hebrew roots in Jerusalem. Jeroboam had his political reasons for drawing the people away from Judah and from the true worship of YHVH, the God of Israel. He reasoned that in doing so his subjects would be drawn back under the national sovereignty of Israel under the King of Judah who sat upon the throne of David.

The solution to this political problem as Jeroboam saw it, and the second part of his plan, was simple. It was to create a spiritual diversion. So Jeroboam arranged for two calves of pagan idolatry to be placed at the northern and southern extremes of Israel in Dan and Beersheba. This did the trick. It drew the people in the Northern Kingdom of Israel away from the God of Israel. His political problem was solved—at least for the moment.

The spiritual damage this did to the Northern Kingdom of Israel was devastating. This had the effect of weakening the moral fiber of the ten tribes. They soon went into deep idolatry. This in turn opened them up to conquest from foreign invaders from the north and increasing intrusions from Assyria.

THE AFTERMATH OF THE BREACH OF JEROBOAM

The consequences for both parties after the great divorce of Israel were deep and long-lasting. King Rehoboam was left with the royal tribe of Judah, and with Benjamin, to become the Southern Kingdom, the Kingdom of Judah. This then became the homeland of the Jewish House with Jerusalem at its center. Later, in the series of returns from the Babylonian captivity, the royal House of Judah was further reduced to remain within the small precincts of the city-state of Jerusalem.

The spiritual consequences of the division of Israel into two kingdoms was very severe. The ten tribes were cut off from going up to Jerusalem for the feasts. King Jeroboam had also re-introduced calf worship again. So as a result the spiritual and moral descent of the Northern Kingdom into idolatry was a quicker and steeper one than that of Judah. They were taken captive by the Assyrians in 722 B.C. They were deliberately scattered and intermingled with other nations.

This was some 200 years after the schism and over a century earlier than Judah went into their captivity. Judah was taken captive in stages by the Babylonians, in 605 and 586 B.C.

During the Assyrian captivity the ten tribes were deliberately scattered and mixed into other nations. They did not return to their homeland in any significant way after that. The Jewish House of Judah did not even begin returning from their 70 year exile in Babylon until after the amnesty offered to them by King Cyrus in 538 B.C. The Temple, after some encouragement from Haggai and amidst much local persecution, was rebuilt some 20 years later.

It was not until the following century, in 457 B.C. that Ezra led another significant return of captives of Judah back to Jerusalem. The gates and walls of Jerusalem were still in ruins. They were only rebuilt after the next return led by Nehemiah 12 years later in 445 B.C. This was nearly 300 years after the Northern Kingdom had been taken off into captivity. Only small token numbers returned with Judah. Then they became amalgamated with Judah. There are those who will wish to believe that the lost ten tribes returned en-masse and piled in with the Jewish house of Judah in the small city-state of Jerusalem. But there is absolutely no evidence of this whatsoever. By then the lost ten tribes were long gone.

So the ten tribes of Israel were carried off into exile back in the 8th Century B.C. They did not return in numbers sufficient to establish sovereignty in their own right as Judah did. They are out there still. They are yet to return in peace to their original homeland in any significant numbers.

The separation of the two houses of Israel, the House of Judah and the House of Israel was now the "new normal." This was the legacy left behind by the Breach of Jeroboam. It was an awful wrenching separation with long-term consequences. It is a division which exists to this day, a schism from which Israel has yet to recover. From this point on, until the end-time restoration, Israel would be a divided, even feuding family of two factions, the two houses of Israel. The separation was deep, and it has proved to be long-lasting. It is still with us today. In fact the Scriptures indicate that this division will last all the way up until the end-time drama (Zech. 12:7-13:1, Rom. 11).

THE LOST HOUSE OF ISRAEL WILL BE FOUND
EVEN AS JOSEPH LAYS OUT THE TABLE FOR HIS BROTHERS

At the present time this one kingdom, the royal Jewish house of Judah, is the only part of Israel visible to the world. The Jewish house can still be seen. And even after being scattered for nearly 2,000 years, they have retained their Hebrew language, the Hebrew Scriptures, the Hebrew religion as established by the Levites and the Rabbinical Priesthood in the synagogues in Babylon. The royal House of Judah still retains their genetic and cultural connection to their past in greater Israel.

And as for the others in the lost ten tribes? Not so much. In fact the people of the ten tribes that went off into captivity as the northern kingdom have historical and cultural amnesia. They cannot remember their past wanderings. They cannot even recognize themselves when they look in the mirror right now. They have disappeared into the fog of lost histories. Nevertheless, they are still out there, but hidden from view. But we have some valuable clues. As we are discovering from the research of Yair Davidiy[67] and Steven Collins,[68] the ten tribes went "into the West." And it seems that when we look at a map of the missionary journeys of the apostle Paul, he headed off in that general direction too.

In rebelling from Judah did Lost Israel curse themselves into oblivion? And if they were divorced by the God of Israel under the Old Covenant is there hope for them? Did they—will they—find grace? And if so, then by what means? Will lost Israel ever be found? And through what covenantal modality will this occur?

As we can begin to see, this Law vs. Grace head-butting between the two houses of Israel, is in fact the key point of contention. And so it remains today. Certain spiritual qualities are favored by each party. The Jewish House of Judah favors the righteous rule of God and considers that to be the predominant spiritual quality and virtue. The other house of Israel favors God's grace and mercy and considers that the predominant spiritual quality and virtue.

The fact is, both houses, under Messiah, should actually complement each other. Failure to make Him center of their lives just puffs up pride and perpetuates the bad blood between them

---

[67] Yair Davidiy, *The Tribes: The Israelite Origins of Western People*, 2012.
[68] Steven Collins, *The "Lost" Ten Tribes of Israel...Found!*, 2012.

that still exists to this day. Under Messiah we have both the throne of His righteous rule as well as His altar for grace and mercy. BOTH are established there in the hearts of those who know Him. He is the Prince of Peace who brings harmony within hearts. So this law vs. grace impasse does not need to remain a major theological hurdle at all.

But without Messiah established in the hearts in the New Covenant all attempts at politico-religious unity based upon a dialog in the Hegelian dialectic will end up stalling. All the AI-boosted rationalistic ecumenical humanistic committee meetings that men can muster will continue to be exercises in futility. Similarly any dialogue hoping to establish unity between the Church and the Jewish house of Judah in Israel without the covering of the blood of Messiah, and Him being established in the hearts, will continue to be in vain.

But, there is some exceedingly good news here. We now have a diagnosis and an explanation for the blood feud between the two houses. Then too, if we can begin to appreciate and develop an understanding of the Law/Grace schism as a diseased entity in need of healing, this can become a very helpful new understanding and a huge new lead for us.

If the Breach of Jeroboam is recognized as an ancient family feud we can then proceed to ask this question. Is the Christian Church and Jewish Israel in need of counseling? If so, then what sort of counseling? Might it involve logo-therapy—the ministry of the Word of God?

If so, then suddenly this is showing a wonderful way forward for us. Because then we can begin to look in the written pages of Holy Scripture. We can begin to see how God will reconcile the two feuding houses. This then may well open up the light from the two lamps of Israel and in this double anointing we might expect to see the promised Great Awakening, the End-Time Revival spoken of by the prophet Joel.

THE LORD WILL POUR OUT HIS SPIRIT

Joel 2

> *28 And it shall come to pass afterward, that I will pour out my Spirit on all flesh; your sons and your daughters shall prophesy, your old men shall dream dreams, and your young men shall see visions. 29 Even on the male and female servants in those days I will pour out my Spirit.*
>
> *30 And I will show wonders in the heavens and on the earth, blood and fire and columns of smoke. 31 The sun shall be turned to darkness, and the moon to blood, before the great and awesome day of the LORD comes. 32 And it shall come to pass that everyone who calls on the name of the LORD shall be saved. For in Mount Zion and in Jerusalem there shall be those who escape, as the LORD has said, and among the survivors shall be those whom the LORD calls.*

Even in the Old Testament we can begin to see that God's plan for the latter days is to fully reconcile and reunite the two houses of Israel. We see this prefigured in the two sticks of Ezekiel 37. The prophet Ezekiel was told to demonstrate this future reunion of the royal Jewish House of Judah and the Ephraim-Joseph stick still hidden in the mystery. He was told to present this restoration of Israel to us as a "show-and-tell."

Ezekiel 37

> *15 The word of the LORD came to me: 16 "Son of man, take a stick and write on it, 'For Judah, and the people of Israel associated with him'; then take another stick and write on it, 'For Joseph (the stick of Ephraim) and all the house of Israel associated with him.' 17 And join them one to another into one stick, that they may become one in your hand. 18 And when your people say to you, 'Will you not tell us what you mean by these?' 19 say to them, 'Thus says the Lord GOD: Behold, I am about to take the stick of Joseph (that is in the hand of Ephraim) and the tribes of Israel associated with him. And I will join with it the stick of Judah, and make them one stick, that they may be one in my hand.' 20 When the sticks on which you write are in your hand before their eyes, 21 then say to them, 'Thus says*

> the Lord GOD: Behold, I will take the people of Israel from the nations among which they have gone, and will gather them from all around, and bring them to their own land. 22 And I will make them one nation in the land, on the mountains of Israel.'

> 'And one king shall be king over them all, and they shall be no longer two nations, and no longer divided into two kingdoms. 23 They shall not defile themselves anymore with their idols and their detestable things, or with any of their transgressions. But I will save them from all the backslidings in which they have sinned, and will cleanse them; and they shall be my people, and I will be their God.'

> 24 'My servant David shall be king over them, and they shall all have one shepherd. They shall walk in my rules and be careful to obey my statutes.'"

We can also begin to see how, through the blood of the New Covenant, the Holy One of Israel fully intends to repair the Breach of Jeroboam and to restore ***All Israel*** at the end of the age. This is the engrafting story of the wild branches being grafted into the Root and Stock of Israel that the apostle Paul refers to in Romans Chapter 11. He concludes by speaking of the "One New Man" and ALL-Israel being saved.

Romans 11

> 25 I do not want you to be ignorant of this mystery, brothers, so that you will not be conceited: A hardening in part has come to Israel, until the full number of the Gentiles has come in. 26 And so all Israel will be saved, as it is written:

> "The Deliverer will come from Zion;
> He will remove godlessness from Jacob.
> 27 And this is My covenant with them
> when I take away their sins."

The Eventual Restoration and Repair

We have abundant biblical poetic and prophetic evidence to show that God will heal the breach of Jeroboam. YHVH-God will find and restore His covenant people even as Hosea found and restored lost Gomer. He will regather and restore **All Israel** as a single Elect, a royal priesthood and a holy nation (1Pet. 2:9). Israel will be a complete nation once again. All 12 Tribes will be rejoined and restored in the latter days of this age.

And how will this happen? There will in fact be a great End-Time Revival. It will draw in the end-time saints from both houses of Israel. We have not seen this yet. We have only seen faint little glimmers of the great Light that will eventually shine out to the Gentiles in the latter days. This great revival will come even in a time of great darkness and period of great apostasy. The prophet Isaiah spoke about this as did Joel and many others (Isa. 60; Joel 2:28-32). Finally, at the end of the story Isaiah said:

"The redeemed of the Lord shall return. And come with singing unto Zion" (Isa. 35).

The Apostle Paul concurred with Isaiah. He said that "All Israel will be saved" (Rom. 11). The Apostle James addressed his epistle to the entire 12-Tribe company of God's extended family. And the Apostle John saw the New Jerusalem, the glorious Holy City accessed by 12 gates representing the 12 Tribes of Israel. He saw the Holy City, the Bride of the Lamb descending from heaven (Rev. 21).

The present disposition of the lost ten tribes is one of the great mysteries of history. There are many in Judah, along with many in lost Israel, who have their reasons for not wanting to find out what happened to their long lost brethren. They have a vested interest in the merchant systems and political protectorates of this world. And so, in spite of the rough going at the thresholds of history, their primary response is to uphold the status quo. They are inclined to prefer this presumed "safe" course of action rather than move forward in the new and living way opening to them. People are usually inclined to believe that staying with the status quo, and with what and whom they know, is the best option. They feel that no matter how onerous circumstances become, sticking with the current powers will ensure at least a small measure of security for them. This will eventually prove to be quite wrong.

So we can be sure that come what may, not just in spite of untoward circumstances, but perhaps even because of them, lost Israel will be found. Because the Scriptures declare it. From out of the prophetic types and shadows come some wonderful hopeful and redemptive themes. The saga and the love story we see laid out in the book of Hosea is just one case in point. After walking out on him, Hosea found his long lost wife, his beloved; just like in all the other times she had gone off playing the harlot. But this time Hosea found his lost Gomer in a slave market. She was being sold into servitude. Hosea redeemed her and put her aside in a place of safety. During that time in which she came back under his care she began to love him.

Then we have the parable Jesus told of the prodigal son. There he is, out there in a foreign place, a long way from home. He had asked His father to give him his inheritance, the blessing due to him. Then he had gone out and spent it on his own personal lusts. But the time came when a famine came, and the prodigal son found himself in the servitude of a pig farmer, feeding the pigs.

The Scriptures are absolutely full of these thematic, poetic, and prophetic themes of an eventual restoration. These mysteries will surely unfold. The prophecies will become unsealed at the proper time. Remember that Moses was hidden in the waters and among the bulrushes as a "Natzrim," for safekeeping. And as he was trained up in the courts of the Egyptian superpower, he was kept in the dark about his true origins. Similarly, Joseph remained hidden from his brothers. Even to this day we have only a very blurry view of who he is and the true identity of his family in the world today.

But this conspiracy of silence will not last forever. And the "cloaking" of the truth will not prevail. The lights of Abraham will be seen again, even in a coming night of deep darkness. And the message of salvation will go out to the ends of the earth, to a magnificent harvest, an in-gathering of a nation and its Commonwealth, and a Congregation, a melo-hagoyim, a "multitude of nations," or a "company of many nations."

The latter days of this age will be difficult. But they will not be just a time of total apocalyptic doom and disaster as many people have been taught. Oh yes, there will be trouble and tribulation. But God will be among His people in a great revival. And by His Spirit He will be calling them out into a new Ekklesia, just as He has done so many times before. And even in a difficult passage through a strait and narrow gate, a remnant shall return.

As the 70th Week opens the Ancient of Days will sit. Up in the courts of heaven He will reopen the two big issues of the latter days. He will be resuming His covenant dealings related to:

1. His Holy City—Jerusalem; and,

2. His Holy People, the global Congregation of Israel, (or "Commonwealth of Israel"—the ultimate "Ekklesia").

It will be a time of high drama, even the culmination of the divine romance between God and His people. The Bridegroom will be approaching, even in the dark hours after midnight. And at that time the message will go forth to a wedding party about to go out through the night to meet the Bridegroom,

"Arise, shine! For your light has come!" (Isa. 60).

CHAPTER SEVEN

BLINDED IN PART
By Douglas Krieger

ARE UNBELIEVING JEWS EXCLUDED?

What is the nature or scope of the "Commonwealth of Israel" (COI) as given in Ephesians 2:11-12?

Therefore remember that you, once Gentiles in the flesh—who are called Uncircumcision by what is called the Circumcision made in the flesh by hands— that at that time you were without Christ, being aliens from the commonwealth of Israel and strangers from the covenants of promise, having no hope and without God in the world.

At issue among those of us who are involved in defining the scope of this phrase and of understanding just what Paul meant by his use of the "Commonwealth of Israel"—a number of obvious questions arise. One brother presented the issue of salvation as far as whether or not Commonwealth of Israel (COI) excludes unbelieving Jews of Judah into the COI. You might think that a bit odd in that Paul in his unsaved state claimed he was an Israelite, a Hebrew of the Hebrews and obviously thought he belonged to the COI (Phil. 3:5)–although we don't have that exact expression used by him prior to his acknowledgement of Yeshua's Messiahship; however, the question is posited:

"To say that unbelieving Jews will be [or are now] a part of all Israel apart from grace through faith (or are in an unregenerate state) is to proclaim another gospel for Judah apart from Ephraim, or those elect from the Gentiles."

This brother went on to examine the potential conflict that if, indeed, unbelieving Jews of Judah (i.e., if we are to assume that "Israel" is broken down TODAY as both Judah/Jews and Ephraim (the "elect from among the nations"—aka "the Church") are acknowledged as part of the Commonwealth of Israel (NOW)—doesn't this muddy the waters of the otherwise pristine jurisdiction of the COI which could in sum and substance be equated with believers in Yeshua only?

The assumption is made that if we of the NATIONS were *"brought near by the blood of Christ"* (Eph. 2:13)—i.e., into the COI, shouldn't all those now entering the COI be "saved" by the same blood of Messiah?

Prior to the cross, and immediately thereafter, it appears that Paul, the Apostle, who certainly was an unbelieving Jew as far as Messiah concerns, apparently considered himself as a member of the COI. Paul, who was still an Israelite, even in unbelief, would have considered that he fully participated within the Commonwealth of Israel, with covenants, promises, and that he had "God in the world" (Eph. 2:12)—he certainly would not have considered himself an alien to the COI but a citizen of the COI.

Replacement theology does not accord any significant or even a minor role for National Israel, but Dispensationalism does (of course, not only is there DISTINCTION as far as Israel is concerned–for Israel embraces all 12 Tribes under the banner of Judah [aka the Jews] who incorporated, historically, the other 10 tribes of the North according to Dispensational exegesis).

Indeed, today's National Israel (unbelieving Jews both within the State of Israel and those scattered among the nations in the diaspora) within the Dispensational construct, are positioned for future prophetic fulfillment and a key role in the Millennium yet to come (separate and apart from the "Church"). As such, would they (unbelieving Israel today) find themselves within the Commonwealth of Israel? Prior to their admission to the COI they would need "grace and faith" and DELIVERANCE, via the Deliverer both now, and on that day, to be saved . . . and then ALL ISRAEL shall be saved. This thin line, therefore, suggests that the Commonwealth of Israel is but a post-Cross expression/reality and that this Commonwealth of Israel was designed for only the One New Man, so making peace, between Jew and the elect from the Nations–where there is neither Jew nor Greek . . . *ipso facto* unbelieving Jews/Judah are excluded from the COI in this understanding of what the COI includes and excludes. Certainly, Replacement theologians embrace the COI in that they are the COI, Jews excluded (unless they convert to Christianity).

The Thin Line in Excluding Today's Jews

We are not suggesting that today's unbelieving Jew, Hebrew, Israelite is ALL ISRAEL in unbelief (with the believing portion of Israel being "the EXPANSION or EPHRAIM" from among the nations)—if they affirm faith in the promise (Yeshua) then they are the saved of Judah and with us (Ephraim–the "elect from among the nations")—both would constitute the ISRAEL OF GOD (Gal. 6:16) . . . I think we're all clear on that point (or at least some of us are clear).

What I am saying is that the Commonwealth of Israel is comprised of BOTH believing and unbelieving Jews (as well as those of Ephraim—unbelieving Jews because of the aforesaid relationship that they have even in unbelief, as the faithful son, the wife not divorced (Judah–Hosea 2:2-23), still aligned with the covenants of promise (New Covenant, Abrahamic, Davidic, Palestinian, etc.) . . . in other words, the Commonwealth of Israel acts like a CATALYST where prophetic fulfillment takes place. A catalyst in chemistry in and of itself is just that, after it's fulfilled its usefulness is, in that sense, no longer needed–that catalyst produces ALL ISRAEL SHALL BE DELIVERED (Romans 11:26)—and again, ALL ISRAEL, at this time, is comprised of BOTH "the multitude of the nations" (Romans 11:25) as Ephraim AND unbelieving Jews of Judah who experience National Deliverance via the Deliverer/Messiah who "will come out of Zion" (Romans 11:25-27).

To say that National Israel is disqualified from the plan and purpose of God is a misnomer, of course—and, I feel, that to suggest, even in unbelief that they see nothing is too much. They are *"blinded in part"* (Rom. 11:25)—therefore, they are in "partial blindness"—yet they apparently "see something"—but we too, *"look through a glass dimly and we prophesy in part"* (1 Cor. 13:12).

Why cannot the Household of God be comprised of believing Judah (Jews) and Ephraim ("Elect from among the nations"); and yet within that same Household are His brethren who rejected their Joseph? Is the faithful son who never left the Father's house, outside his Father's house? We cannot say that Joseph's brothers were no longer his brothers nor that the faithful son was no longer within his father's House. So, there is this most peculiar standing that is divinely recognized; indeed, what earthly tribe has such a peculiar standing? None.

Can we say in the verse wherein *"not all Israel who are of Israel"* (Rom. 9:6)—to mean that Israel is not comprised of the Judah/Jewish side of Israel only, but also those "Israelites" who have been justified through the faith of Abraham—for *"In you all the nations shall be blessed...so then those who are of faith are blessed with believing Abraham"* (Gal. 3:3-9)?

Or are we saying that "not all Israel who are of Israel" means that unbelieving Jews of Judah are not of Israel, and only those believing Jews of Judah are at least a part of Israel (i.e., only "believing Jews" constitute the "Israel of God" as seen in Gal. 6:16)?

You might be able to see where I'm going with this—for if we conclude that unbelieving Judah/Jews are not of Israel, when the very State of Israel bears their name—then is not the accusation of the Replacement Theologians that today's "Israel" on the eastern edge of the Mediterranean has no eschatological bearing whatsoever—and is, at worst, apostate or simply a gathering place for Jacob's Trouble (at best); but, more likely, it is simply a happenstance, meaning nothing?

That's why I am concerned that the "spiritual Israel"—yes, the "True Israel" folks (by the way, neither expression can be found in the N.T.)—will and has had a heyday with "not all Israel who are of Israel" and would suggest that, in particular, unbelieving Jews are NOT only "rejected" but they, the Church, are today's "Spiritual and True Israel" whereas the physical seed of Abraham are NOT ISRAEL who claim to be of Israel!

Why can't the Jews of Judah be a part of the Commonwealth of Israel in unbelief—for isn't that what distinguishes them from us—YES DISTINCTION—NO SEPARATION? Don't they, the Jews, National Israel, even now, maintain their distinction, but when they enter into the One New Man there is NO SEPARATION; yet, on that day they shall experience NATIONAL SALVATION and then shall YES DISTINCTION be in full operation.

The principle of "Not all Israel is of Israel" can be seen in Paul's writings relative to those brethren/ministers among the sheep who we enjoined to *"note those who cause divisions and offenses, contrary to the doctrine which you learned, and avoid them . . . For those who are such do not serve our Lord Jesus Christ, but their own belly, and by smooth words and flattering speech deceive the hearts of the simple"* (Rom. 16:17-18)—and: *". . . For many walk, of whom I have told you often, and now tell you even weeping, that they are the enemies of the cross of Christ: whose end is destruction, whose god is their belly, and whose glory is in their shame—who set their mind on earthly things"* (Phil. 3:18-19). These "belly-gods" are among us—if you would, they (whose god is their belly) are NOT all Israel who are of Israel. They cause division and should be avoided—but are they not within the Commonwealth of Israel? Yes, but "they are not the Israel of God"—that is most certain.

Sundry movements, primarily centered in Israel (e.g., the COI Conventions), contend that Judah (the Jews) and Ephraim ("the elect from among the nations") find their unity in the Torah . . . this is not to say that much agreement can be reached in such a commitment to the Torah; however, this effort appears to wholly obviate the breaking down of the "middle wall of separation" between Jew and Greek through the Cross of Yeshua. If more and more Jews see in Ephraim a true brotherhood–THAT is amazing . . . yet it cannot be in Torah (alone) but through Him Who made peace as the "Suffering Servant."

At that time there shall be NO SEPARATION for Judah and Ephraim—they shall be One Stick in the Hand of the Lord (Ezek. 37:15-28). In other words, today, believing Jews, and the Elect from among the nations, are within the confines of the ONE BODY, ONE NEW MAN, THE NEW CREATION where the Middle Wall of Separation is in reality demolished (Eph. 2:14)–where there is neither Jew nor Greek; but there abides DISTINCTION in that the partial blindness that has befallen the Jews of Judah provides them this profound prophetic distinction–enabling them their Millennial position with that of the Elect now in Messiah . . . *"they sing the Song of Moses the Servant of God and the Song of the Lamb"*—they *"keep the commandments of God and have the testimony/faith of Jesus"* (Rev. 15:3; 12:17) . . . DISTINCTION YES—SEPARATION NO.

When we, therefore, say DISTINCTION YES—SEPARATION NO—it is mandatory that this ultimate DISTINCTION be viewed in the most profound eschatological context as far as Earth's Redemption concerns. Indeed, that DISTINCTION—even today—is in unbelief but therein are those of Zion who are being "prophetically positioned" to greet their Deliverer who shall arise OUT OF ZION (Romans. 11:26).

MESSIANIC BELIEVERS

As far as Messianic believers are concerned today–there is most definitely within the One New Man neither Jew nor Greek–but members of Judah and Ephraim comprise the Household of Faith/of God today. Herein is DISTINCTION but NO SEPARATION as well.

Since the rebirth of the State of Israel, there are today in the world upwards of 350,000 "Messianic Jews"–mostly in the USA (Source: Wikipedia.org[69])—Retrieved on 05.02.2020). These Jewish believers in Yeshua can be found in all-Messianic Congregations or simply in Christian assemblies at random. By distinguishing themselves as "Messianic Congregations" that does not mean they are not "open" to inviting into their membership believers from non-Jewish backgrounds . . . but by maintaining their DISTINCTION they confirm that there can be DISTINCTION YES but SEPARATION NO within the Body of Messiah.

Replacement theologies acknowledge "their whereabouts" but, in the main, disregard "Jewish practices" as irrelevant or antithetical to Christian practice. It is our concern, here at CT that this DISTINCTION within Messianic Judaism does not lead to a *defacto* SEPARATION in the Body of Messiah. Likewise, we see that congregations led by non-ethnic Jews, but which have a bent toward "Messianic Judaism"—including Jews and non-Jews within their congregations and more philo-semitic practices—to be a bulwark, in the main, at preventing Jewish Christians from isolating from "Gentile Christians."

Again, ultimately when ALL ISRAEL embraces the Messiah, the Deliverer, then ALL ISRAEL shall be delivered, saved—YES, there will be this profound distinction between Judah/Jews and Ephraim (the "elect from among the nations") but there will be NO SEPARATION!

---

[69] https://en.wikipedia.org/wiki/Messianic_Judaism, Retrieved 05.02.2020

Chapter Eight

SEGREGATING THE JEWS AND THEIR GOD
Dr. Douglas Hamp

From *Haunted Theology & the Ghost of Marcion*[70]

The Legacy of Marcion's Heresy

There's a notion that somehow God's commandments and His grace are two different things. Let's consider this using the theme of a haunted house. A haunted house is often perceived as being inhabited by disembodied spirits of the deceased who may have been former residents. I believe we have a haunted theology today; it is inhabited by the spirit of Marcion, a second century heretic who continues to exert influence over how some Christians read their Bibles.

Let's look at a few examples of haunted theologies and then we will look at Marcion himself in more detail.

Refer to the top example on the following page. You can see that Jesus is nailed to the cross and behind His hands are the Ten Commandments; and there's this idea that Jesus nailed the old law, the Torah to the cross. I once had a pastor who was teaching on Colossians Chapter 2, where it says: (Col. 2:14 NKJV) *"having wiped out the handwriting of requirements that was against us, which was contrary to us. And He has taken it out of the way, having nailed it to the cross."* His commentary was that "the Law was nailed to the cross." When I asked him "do you really mean to say that the Ten Commandments, the things that God spoke with his own mouth were nailed to the cross?" He said, "Well, yeah." It broke my heart to hear him say that, though I was not totally surprised.

---

[70] *Haunted Theology & the Ghost of Marcion* by Dr. Douglas Hamp

COMMONWEALTH THEOLOGY ESSENTIALS

CH. 8: SEGREGATING THE JEWS AND THEIR GOD

At the bottom of the adjacent page is another meme: "Jesus was the end of the Law." You get the idea—the mantra is widespread: "it's all over—this Torah stuff is done." "He had it nailed to the cross." "The Law of Moses, the Ten Commandments, the Sabbath, abolished." And from the same website, the author says, "Conclusively, positively, without any doubt, the entire Law of Moses, that is the Law of God, the 10 commandments—including the Sabbath—was abolished, passed away, and cast out."[71]

This is what so many people think; but how did they get here? A woman on Facebook said to me: "I am a gentile, so Paul is my apostle. The Law of the Old Testament and the four gospels (Mathew, Mark, Luke, John) don't apply to me. I don't worship on Saturdays, I don't slaughter lambs when I sin and I am free to obey the Lord because of love, not law." This is the sentiment so many people have—which we will explore in detail, but first let's just take a really quick survey.

> I am a gentile, so Paul is my apostle. The law of the Old Testament and the four gospels don't apply to me. I don't worship on Satudays, I don't slaighter lambs when I sin and I am FREE to obey the Lord because of LOVE, not LAW.
>
> Like · Reply · 👍 1 · 10 hrs

When you do an experiment it's good to have a control group. The control group is the group that gives you a baseline of where you are. So, let's get a baseline of what the Scriptures say. Let's see what a healthy theological house looks like. How we are defining "healthy theological" is by taking a very broad sweep of what God Himself has declared directly (like from Sinai); and, what others have said (like the Prophets), and what God has expected of man throughout the ages.

We start with Abraham, the father of the faith. God praises Abraham saying: "…Abraham obeyed My voice and kept My charge, My commandments [mitzvotai מִצְוֹתַי], My statutes [chukotai חֻקּוֹתַי], and My laws [torotai וְתוֹרֹתָי]" (Gen. 26:5).

---

[71] biblicalproof.wordpress.com

The very same Hebrew words we have here, we find throughout the entire Bible for what God is calling us to do. Numbers 36:13, *"the commandments and the judgments which the Lord commanded by the hand of Moses."* So here we see that the laws of God are the ones that He gave to Moses, they're not different, they are one and the same. Next, take this beautiful verse, which we often study today: *"And now Israel, what does the Lord your God require you, but to fear the Lord your God, to walk in all his ways and to love him, to serve the Lord your God with all your heart and with all your soul"* (Deut. 10:12).

It isn't that complicated. You see, what He wants today is what He wanted back then, He wants our heart, He wants us to love Him and He wants us to follow His commandments because His ways are good. And First Kings: *"and keep the charge of the Lord your God: to walk in His ways, to keep His statutes, his commandments, His judgments, and His testimonies, as it is written in the law of Moses..."*; *"walk in the ways, My ways, to keep My statutes and My commandments, as your father David walked..."* This is an exhortation to Solomon, and then Solomon—after all of his explorations—he comes to this sad place, and in the book of Ecclesiastics he says: You know what, "It's all vanity."

And at the very end, what does he say? He says, "Fear God and keep His commandments, for this is man's all." After wasting so many years going after vain things, he discovers what really matters. The psalmist in Psalm 119 says: *"So shall I keep Your law continually, forever and ever. And I will walk at liberty, for I seek Your precepts. I will speak of Your testimonies also before kings, and I will not be ashamed. And, I will delight myself in Your commandments, which I love.* The prophets also say: *"keep Gods commands, He will teach us His ways, and we shall walk in His paths. For out of Zion shall go forth the law, the Torah, and the word of the Lord from Jerusalem." "This is the covenant that I will make with the house of Israel after those days, says the Lord: I will put My law* [My Torah] *in their minds and write it on their hearts; and I will be their God, and they shall be My people."*

We find the same language, the same ideas, the same instructions are used throughout the entire Bible. Then, the last book of the Old Testament, the Hebrew Bible, says: *"remember the law of Moses, My servant, which I commanded Him in Horeb for all Israel, with the statutes and judgments"* (Mal. 4:4). Who commanded it? God commanded it. It's not that Moses got these interesting ideas and said, "Here, do these things;" as we all know, these are from God Himself. What does Jesus say? The Word incarnate: *"Do not think that I came to destroy the Law* [Torah] *or the Prophets. I didn't come to destroy them, but to fulfill them…So whoever sets aside one of the least of these commandments and teaches others to do the same will be called least in the kingdom of heaven. But whoever does them and teaches them will be called great in the kingdom of heaven"* (Matt. 5:17, 19).

"He who does not love Me does not keep My words; and the word which you hear is not Mine but the Father's who sent Me" (Jn. 14:24). He says in John 14:21: *"he who has My commandments and keeps them, it is he who loves Me. And he who loves Me will be loved by My father, and I will love him and manifest Myself to him."* Jesus answered and said to him, *"if anyone loves Me, he will keep My word; and My father will love him, and We will come to him and make Our home with him"* (Jn. 14:23).

In the writings of John he says, *"now by this we know that we know Him, if we keep His commandments"* (1 Jn. 2:3). So you say: How do I know that I know God? If I keep His commandments or not? That's what Jesus said. That's what John said in his epistle—if we keep his commandments. He says: *"He who says, 'I know Him,' and does not keep His commandments, is a liar, and the truth is not in him. But whoever keeps His word, truly the love of God is perfected in him. By this we know that we are in Him"* (1 Jn. 2:4-5). Second John: *"this is love, that we walk according to his commandments."* And then finally at the very end of all things we see this beautiful promise: *"Blessed are those who do his commandments that they may have the right to the tree of life, and may enter through the gates into the city"* (Rev. 22:14).

What has changed? Nothing has changed. And of course the apostle Paul is often accused of speaking contrary—but he doesn't. What does he say? *"Do we, then, abolish the Law* [the Torah] *by this faith? Of course not. Instead, we uphold the Law."* Paul says again in Romans 7:12, *"therefore the Law is holy, and the commandment holy and just and good. For we know that the Law is spiritual, but I am carnal, sold under sin, I agree with the Law that it is good."* And he says in First Corinthians 7:19, *"keeping the commandments of God is what matters."* He echoes King Solomon, the same idea—this is the whole of what man should do. And then in Hebrews 8:10, *"for this is the covenant that I will make with the house of Israel after those days, says the Lord: I will put My laws in their mind and write them on their hearts; and I will be their God and they shall be My people."* God hasn't changed! We now have a baseline; we have a control group that we can use to measure those statements (above) that are being made regarding God's law.

THE GHOST OF MARCION

We've seen that keeping God's commands is a matter of certainty, yet there is still this "haunted" preaching. What am I talking about? Let me just say this really quickly: I am not trying to attack people as I share these realities. The men who I am going to share with you—I'm sure they are great guys—and I believe that in their own way they love the Lord. But I think there is something that has infested our theology, which we all need to get rid of. It's been part of the problem; and identifying what it is, is how we can get rid of it. A very popular teacher and preacher, Andy Stanley, senior pastor of North Point Church in Georgia (about 35,000 people, I believe); said that we should "unhitch" our theology from the Old Testament.

He says: "First-century Church leaders unhitched the Church from the worldview, value system, and regulations of the Jewish Scriptures.[72] Note that Peter, James, Paul elected to unhitch Christian faith from their Jewish Scriptures; and my friends, we must as well." I viewed Stanley on video saying the Old Testament was not the go-to source regarding any behavior for the Church. Where did Stanley get these ideas? We've just seen that God said the contrary; "keep My commandments." It's throughout the Scriptures; we saw it everywhere. Abraham, Moses, the children of Israel, the kings of Israel, the kings of Judah, Jesus, Paul, John—they all said that keeping the commandments of God is what matters. How did Bible teachers like Stanley arrive at a theology so divergent from the scriptures we have just reviewed?

---

[72] Referring not to writings by or to Judeans, but to the Hebrew Writings/O.T.; whereas, except for Luke's books, ALL are Hebrew Scriptures.

Ch. 8: Segregating the Jews and Their God

Well, Dr. R. Albert Mohler Jr., President of the Southern Baptist Theological Seminary, comments on what Andy Stanley said. He said, to be clear, Andy Stanley does not endorse the full heresy of Marcionism, which was universally condemned by the Early Church. Nevertheless, Stanley does in fact appear to aim for the heresy of Marcionism. And his hearers were certainly aimed in that direction. Pastor Andy says that God is the same God in both testaments, but says that He reveals Himself in two completely different ways. Just like Marcion, he argues that the Church must unhitch from the Old Testament. He actually says: "I am convinced for the sake of this generation and the next generation, we have to rethink our apologetic as Christians, and the less we depend on the Old Testament to prop up our New Testament faith the better, because of where we are in the culture."

Well, Andy Stanley is not alone; we have Joseph Prince who says the Law is not for believers, and he shares this in his book, *Destined to Reign*. "I distinctly heard the voice of the Lord on the inside. It wasn't a witness of the Spirit. It was a voice, and I heard God say this clearly to me: 'Son, you are not preaching grace.' I said, 'what do you mean Lord?' 'Every time you preach grace, you preach it with a mixture of law. You attempt to balance grace with the Law like many other preachers, and the moment you balance grace, you neutralized it. You cannot put new wine into old wineskins, you cannot put grace and law together.' He went on to say, 'Son, a lot of preachers are not preaching grace the way the Apostle Paul preached grace.'"

And another book, *Unmerited Favor*: "The Law is not for you the believer, who has been made righteous in Christ. The Law is not applicable to someone who is under the new covenant of grace." I had an interaction with Pastor Joe from Calvary Chapel. (I don't give you a last name; it's not my goal to say anything about him.) But he says—and this is a popular quote that he shared with me—he kind of threw it at me; he said that the Law is a unit comprised of 613 commandments and all of it has been rendered inoperative. There is no commandment that has continued beyond the cross of the Messiah. It has completely ceased to function as an authority over the individual. It is no longer the rule of life for believers.

On another occasion, he told me; "No I don't reject Sabbath keeping because it's in the Old Testament, I reject it because Christ fulfilled it and He is Lord of the Sabbath. Why is the weekly Sabbath commandment never quoted in the New Testament?" That's another question. And then he told me on another occasion; "Even if I teach the Law has been annulled and (I do) and teach others to do the same (yes, I do that too), I'm still in the kingdom of God." So, this is a reputable pastor, a mainstream pastor—Calvary Chapel—I used to be part of Calvary Chapel. They teach verse by verse, they go through the entire Bible. Great! Good strategy. And yet, this is the kind of thinking that is in the teaching; and this, again, is very mainstream. I, myself, have even been charged by another Calvary Chapel pastor.

He said, "I'm charging you [Doug] before God of teaching a false gospel. You pervert the gospel by adding law to it. Galatians refutes your beliefs. Doug you need to resign from the ministry and leave the pulpit and stop deceiving people for your own salvation and soul's sake. You will be held to a higher condemnation than those who're not in a teaching role. This doctrine you teach is not a "non-essential" of the Christian faith, but it is a foundational essential doctrine of the Christian gospel; and you are perverting it by adding law to it." I don't remember when the Law was taken away. That's what we're attempting to figure out.

So, the Father and the Son plainly tell us to keep the commands and promise grace to do so. You, the reader, saw it: Keep the commandments. We observed this in every part of the Hebrew Bible. We saw that as well in the New Testament. So then, what spirit is behind the idea that law and grace are mutually exclusive? I've traced this back to Marcion of Pontius and Turkey. He lived between 85 and 160 AD, he may not have been the first to come up with these ideas but he was definitely the one who promoted it like nobody else. In fact, he was despised among the Early Church fathers, who were trying to desperately stamp out this doctrine of Marcionism.

Marcionite Christianity

He was known as the ravening wolf, the filthy swine, and the dreadful blasphemer. And according to Justin Martyr, by 150 AD his heresies had spread to the whole human race. So you can see, his influence was very profound and his group of Marcionites placed great value in calling themselves the Christians. So, they assumed the name of "Christian," and according to Tertullian, Marcion's heretical tradition had filled the whole world. So again, we see confirmed that this heresy was prolific; it had gone everywhere—this concept of Marcionism. This craze continued until about the fifth century; and then, apparently, had died out. But I would suggest that it didn't die out at all, but that, in fact, parts of it were adopted by "orthodox" Christianity.

For example, Marcionites suggested that the clergy and "real believers"—to be a member of their Church—you had to be celibate. Marriage was despised; having children was despised. The Marcionites assumed the name "Christian." Here's an example:

Marhaba, who died around 552 AD, was originally fanatical, a fanatic pagan; and during an attempt to cross the Tigris he was brought to see the light through a miracle. An ensuing conversation with a critic Christian ascetic, "Joseph," whose surname was Moses, wishing to know whether Joseph might be an Orthodox, a Marcionite, or a Jew. Mar Aba asked: "Are you a Jew?" "Yes." "Are you a Christian?" "Yes." "Do you worship the Messiah?"

Joseph again expressed agreement. And Mar Aba became enraged: "How can you be a Jew, a Christian and a worshiper of the Messiah all at the same time?" So you see, when he heard the word Christian he thought: Oh, a Marcionite. This guy calls himself a Christian but he's actually a Marcionite; so, what happened was, there was confusion over the terminology. The term Christian had been infused within Marcionism by 552 AD. There was tremendous confusion as to who was on the right side of things. Then the narrator inserts by way of explanation that he was following the local custom when he used the word "Christian" to designate a Marcionite. Then Joseph stated: "I am seeking a Jew."

Joseph continued, "I am seeking a Jew secretly. I still pray to the living God but have heard of the worship of idols. I am a Christian truly, not as the Marcionites, who falsely call themselves Christians. For Christian is a Greek word, which in Syriac means Messiah-worshipper. And if you ask me 'Do you worship the Messiah?' I truly worship Him truly."

This story reveals that even at a relatively late date, Marcionites designated themselves as "Christians"—much to the offense of the Orthodox, who must have had to contend with misleading alternatives such as Messiah-worshipper. Now, here is Marcion in his own words. Actually, we don't have a lot of his direct words but we have things that people documented; what one early theologian said against Marcion. Putting some phrases together, he says: "The Jewish Christ was designated by the Creator, (the Old Testament God who Marcion saw as a different God, a Demiurge—someone who was different than the God and Father of Jesus Christ) solely for the purpose of restoring the Jewish people from the Diaspora. But our Christ (that is the Christ that you find in the writings of Paul—because he thought Paul was the only guy who was legit) was commissioned by the good God of the New Testament to liberate all mankind."[73]

The good God that was Paul's Jesus is good toward all men; the Creator (God of the Jesus of the Twelve) however, promises salvation only to those who are obedient to him—that is legalism. Ever heard this before, this idea that the people in the Old Testament or in the age of law, they had to keep the Law to be saved? But now we get to be saved because of grace. This is where this idea comes from. The good God, Paul's Jesus, redeems those who believe in Him but He does not judge those who are disobedient to Him; the Creator God of the Twelve's Jesus, however, redeems His faithful and judges and punishes the sinners. So the Old Testament God, the God of the old covenant, he's a mean God and he's going to hold you to standards; but our God, the God that you find in Paul only, he's good.

Let me just say quickly, I am very much pro Paul; and this will be explained in a minute. So, the Christ of the creator God promises to the Jews the restoration of their former condition by return of their land,

---

[73] *The Ante-Nicene Fathers: Latin Christianity: its founder, Tertullian. I. Apologetic; II. Anti-Marcion; III.* By Alexander Roberts, Sir James Donaldson · 1903 "Tertullian Against Marcion," Ch. XXI, p. 339

and after death, a refuge in Abraham's bosom in the underworld. And our Christ, Paul's Jesus, will establish the kingdom of God, an eternal, heavenly possession. So says Marcion; and I get this from Dr. Peter M. Head. Well, what does Tertullian have to say against Marcionism? He says that "the separation of law and gospel was Marcion's primary concern. The separation of law and gospel is the primary and principal exploit of Marcion. His disciples cannot deny this, which stands at the head of their document, that document by which they are inducted, into and confirmed in this heresy."[74]

For such are Marcion's *Antitheses*,[75] or "contrary oppositions," which are designed to show the conflict and disagreement of the Gospel and the Law. Thus, here it is! We owe this to Marcion—this divorce of the gospel, the good news, the grace and the Law. It's Marcion who divided these; so that from the diversity of principles between those two documents they may argue further for a diversity of gods. Therefore, as it is precisely this separation of law and Gospel from which is suggested a God of a gospel, other than and in opposition to the God of the Law. Marcion acquired his very perverse opinions, not from a master, but his master—from his opinion. He displayed a hatred against the Jews' most solemn day. He was only professedly following the Creator, as being his Christ, in this very hatred of the Sabbath.

He also—in part, not completely—was to blame for hatred of the Sabbath. Irenaeus was another Church father against Marcion's abolition of the Law and upheld that the Lord did not abrogate the natural precepts of the Law, for he remarks: "'It has been said to them of all do not commit adultery but I say to you that everyone who hath looked upon a woman to lust after her hath committed adultery with her already in his heart' . . . For all those do not contain or imply an opposition to and an overturning of the precepts of the past as Marcion's followers, so do strenuously maintain but the exhibit a fulfilling and an extension of them."[76]

---

[74] *The Orthodox Corruption of Scripture: The Effect of Early Christological Controversies on the Text of the New Testament* By Bart D. Ehrman, 1996 p. 246.

[75] Marcion, *The Antithesis*, circa 135 A.D., not extant.

[76] Irenaeus, *Against Heresies*, Book IV, Ch. XIII, Sec. 1.

So these same debates that we're having today were going on a long time ago. This sense that the Law has been done away with—this isn't new. This was started by an ancient heresy of Marcionism. It was not done away with; and Irenaeus, one of the Church Fathers, states that the Law wasn't done away with. He says, with regard to those Marcionites who alleged that Paul, alone, knew the truth and that to him the mystery was manifested by revelation: "Let Paul himself convict them, when he says that one-and-the-same-God wrought in Peter for the apostolate of the circumcision, and in himself for the Gentiles. Peter therefore was an apostle of that very God who was also Paul's and Him whom Peter preached as God among those of the circumcision and likewise the Son of God did Paul declare also among the Gentiles." So this overemphasis on the apostle Paul came from Marcion.

"I'm not preaching according to what Paul was preaching, per se." That's what we saw that Joseph Prince said—"this voice said, 'you're not preaching it the way the apostle Paul preaches.'" Paul was very much pro Torah, he kept Torah, he lived Torah, he taught Torah and yet it's been twisted to suggest that he was against the Torah. Where do we get that from? From Marcion; Marcion is the culprit.

Jerome—Saint Jerome—who translated the Latin Vulgate, circa 400 A.D. said, "I say these things not that I may, like Manichaeus and Marcion, destroy the Law, which I know in the testimony of the apostle to be both holy and spiritual"[77]—which is of course from Romans 7:12. So, even by around the year 400 we see that Jerome was saying: No; the Law is good. It's not done away with; it wasn't destroyed, and it's still good. Noting again, the rebuke that I received for preaching the Law (by adding the Law to the gospel)—I'm not adding, I'm simply *not* taking away what was never taken away; I'm just leaving it there. We want to leave the Law in place because it's God's instructions to mankind for a good life.

---

[77] *The Works of Aurelius Augustine*: A New Translation, Marcus Dods, Volume 6, Letters of St. Augustine, Let. LXXV.

Two Ages, Two Gods

So what else did Marcion talk about—when it's law versus grace, or versus the gospel? This is the essence of Marcion's doctrine, Marcion's belief system. He did affirm: Jesus Christ as the Savior sent by God; Paul was the chief apostle; Christianity was distinct from and in opposition to Judaism; and, he rejected the entire Old Testament. He also coined the phrase that the "God of the Hebrew Bible was a lesser demiurge"—who had created the earth, and whose law—the Mosaic covenant—represented bare natural justice. (An eye for an eye; a real mean guy.) Furthermore, Marcion claimed that many teachings of Christ were incompatible with the actions of Yahweh. He suggested—and Tertullian claimed that Marcion coined—the terms for the Hebrew versus Christian texts: the "Old Testament" and the "New Testament."

Ah, so that's where this distinction came from. Because we keep hearing: You're not supposed to read the Old Testament; I'm a New Testament Christian—that quote I showed you from that woman on Facebook where she said: "You know the Gospels don't apply to me, the Old Testament doesn't apply to me, Paul is my apostle." Where did she get that idea? From Marcion. The trouble is, nobody realizes they're perpetuating what was deemed by the early Christian Church to be a gross heresy. Nobody is going to say: Oh yeah, I believe in Marcion. I mean, that's not really PC. They're going to say: Well this is what the Bible teaches; and so they have a form of godliness. They're reading the Bible, and yet they're denying the very things that are written in it because they believe that Paul was the one who inspired this type of theology.

But really, it's a twisting of Paul. It's a perversion of what Paul said. It's not Paul himself, but the perversion thereof that people are latching onto. Note that Marcion did claim Paul's arguments of: law and gospel, wrath and grace, works and faith, flesh and spirit, sin and righteousness, and death and life, as the essence of religious truth. But Marcion ascribed these aspects and characteristics to two bogus (and blasphemous) antinomies: the righteous and wrathful God of the Old Testament—the creator of the world; and, a second God of the gospel who was clearly love and mercy and who was revealed by Jesus.

Now, I don't know any Christians today who would actually say: "Oh yeah, I believe in two different Gods." Of course they're not going to say that because that is absolutely heretical to our belief system. So of course they say: I believe they're the same God. But what they do then is to say; well God changed, God changed in the way that he interacts with humanity; so yeah, He used to do it that way—back then, but now He does it this way today. You know, after the cross. And we will look at more examples of how widespread this assumption of a "changing God" actually is.

According to Alec Buerkle, Marcion expounded his main proposition in a work titled *Antithesis*, in which the God of the New Testament was the "God of Grace" who offered salvation to all by faith alone. Hans Kung says in his book that after Simon Magus it was Marcion, above all, whom the fathers regarded as the arch-heretic because the Law is discarded and salvation depends on faith alone. For the gospel of the free grace of God and salvation by faith alone had been substituted by the 12 apostles in their gospel. So Marcion believed that any form of legalism was of genuinely Jewish character. Now I don't know about you but I hear this stuff all day long. That's the Jewish stuff, get away from the Jewish stuff. Keep in mind we're not talking about the Talmud, we're not talking about the rabbinic interpretations, we're not defending those; but what they call Jewish, they're referring to the Torah—they're talking about the Bible, the first five books of Moses.

They perceive the Law of Moses, which God gave, as bondage. Bondage, that's what they're talking about, bondage under the very same God who gave those commandments. They would say that the Old Testament saints were under bondage, but now we're free from that. I showed you those memes of Jesus on the cross and of the 10 commandments (that God wrote with His own finger), which they claim, have been erased. That is the kind of sentiment that people have. Where did that come from? Where did those ideas originate? They come from Marcion; not from God, not from Jesus, not from Paul. Paul has been the scapegoat for this. It's been blamed on Paul; but Paul is not the one. He said: Do we annul or abolish the Law by this faith? Absolutely not. Instead, we "establish" the Law. That's what Paul was getting at, we establish the Law. We don't annul it or abolish it.

CH. 8: SEGREGATING THE JEWS AND THEIR GOD

Jesus said, "I did not come to abolish the Law," and yet this is what we hear from pulpit to pulpit, from seminary to seminary; and you've seen with your own eyes that well-meaning pastors have said: We are not to follow the Law. This is not a biblical doctrine, it's a heresy! It's perhaps the oldest Christian heresy there is. Marcion had the idea that Paul alone understood salvation. And that Paul was teaching that there was a radical opposition between the Law and the Gospel; that Paul refused to identify the God of love revealed in the New Testament with the wrathful creator of the Old Testament. The pure gospel, however, Marcion found to be more or less corrupted and mutilated in the Christian circles of his time. His undertaking thus resolved itself into a reformation of Christendom.

This reformation was to deliver Christendom from false Jewish doctrines by restoring the Pauline conception of the gospel, Paul being, according to Marcion, the only apostle who had rightly understood the new message of salvation as delivered by Christ. In Marcion's own view the founding of his Church amounted to a reformation of Christendom through a return to the gospel of Christ and Paul. Nothing was to be accepted beyond that, according to the 1911 *Encyclopedia Britannica*. And according to Angela Tilby: *Heresies and How to Avoid Them*: for Marcion, there was a fundamental contradiction between law and love, righteousness and grace. Again we hear this all the time. I'm constantly bombarded, and because I would dare teach Torah and keep the Sabbath and those Jewish feasts, you know; and: How could you do that? You're putting yourself back under the law-god, why would you do that? This is a damnable heresy that you're doing.

I don't think so; I think I'm in the right, and I think they're following Marcionism. The trouble is, nobody knows what it is; and we see that Marcion started with the radical view that the Church's teaching must conform to the teaching of the gospel of Paul. Since, according to Marcion, Paul and Galatians made the Law and grace antithetical. And this is exactly what we see; that the law and grace have become antithetical, and yet nothing could be further from that truth which God himself spoke on Mount Sinai. After the children of Israel had sinned a horrible, terrible sin when they betrayed Him and cheated on Him, He still said, *"yehova, yehova elohim, panan hora,"* "God who is gracious and merciful, who was abounding in goodness and truth." That's the God who revealed himself in the

Old Testament in the Hebrew Bible. That's the God who gave us His commandments but also revealed His grace at the same time and *not* two different Gods.

It's interesting that in Marcion's Bible, he included only Luke and the ten books from Paul. The first of them was Galatians which he considered the charter of Marcionism. He did not have the so-called Pastoral Epistles, First and Second Timothy and Titus, because it was just—you know—too much like keeping the Law. So we have these haunted doctrines. And I would have to ask: Are the so-called "age of law" and "age of grace" really a veiled form of Marcionism? I would just like to say once more, that our analysis of the aforementioned pastors and theologians is not an attack on them personally, because I've actually studied under some of these men.

I've learned a lot from some of these men. I've discovered how to study the Bible, the love and the joy of Christ, and I very much appreciate what I've learned. But I would suggest in a sense, the same way that Jesus had some good things for the churches in Revelation and some bad things, that we as a church are trying now to follow the Torah but we're still healing from the influence of Marcionism. So let's not go attack people, let's pray for people. Let's pray for these theologies that are incorrect, that are unbiblical; and, that we all could come back to the truth.

According to the *New International Dictionary of the Christian Church*: Marcion stressed the radical nature of Christianity vis-à-vis Judaism. In his theology there existed a total discontinuity between the Old Testament and the New Testament, Israel and the Church, the God of the Old Testament and the Father of Jesus. And there are parallels with Marcion's theology and Dispensationalism. Now in case you don't know Dispensationalism, it is a system of interpreting the Bible wherein they see seven unique dispensations or seven epics of time. There are different economies in which God dealt with mankind in a different way each time.

They start with the age of innocence, then the age of conscience, the age of human government, and the age of promise—which would be Abraham's time. And then when God gave the Law was the age of law; and then when Christ died and arose, then started the age of grace; and then after the age of grace—supposing the rapture will happen before the seven-year tribulation—then we start the age of. . . essentially, the Day of the

Lord and the Millennium. I used to believe that. I used to teach that and think that was just how it was. And then I ran to this idea that: Oh, law and grace are not antithetical, so we should not be positing these to be against one another.

One of Dispensationalism's main beliefs is—I'll start with Marcion but you'll see the parallels as we go through and look for these—that the Law was done away with. There was a disjunction between law and grace. The Jews and the Church are two completely separate entities. The New Testament Scriptures were superior to the Old Testament and God sent forth His Son to free us from the bondage of the Old Testament law, which was nailed to the cross. And Paul was the final authority in Scripture—even above Jesus.

HAUNTED THEOLOGY

I would say this, if it walks like a duck and it quacks like a duck, it's probably a duck or it's probably semi-Marcionism. But we're just going to call a duck, a duck. So again, we're not trying to attack people. I very much have learned a great deal from these men. We start with John Darby. He's probably, if we're honest, the originator of what we would know as modern-day Dispensationalism. He says, "But having thus terminated the course of grace we're now at Mount Sinai."

"God proposes a condition to them if they obeyed his voice, they should be as people, the people, instead of knowing themselves and saying, we dare not, they'll bound to obey. Place ourselves under such a condition and risk our blessing, yea, make sure of losing it, undertake to do all the Lord has spoken. The blessing now took the form of dependence like Adam's on the faithfulness of man, as well as of God."[78] Terror such as the character of the Law, a rule sent out to man when men cannot approach God, what a barrier is setup and the question of righteousness as the way of life raised and claimed from man, when man is a sinner. He says, the Church has no relation with the fathers and the Jews. While Jehovah of the Jewish nation is never to enter the Church. The Church is a kind of heavenly economy during the rejection of the earthly people.

---

[78] *A W Pink's Studies in the Scriptures* by Arthur W. Pink, Sovereign Grace Publishers, 1936, p.176.

So this is where we get started with modern day Dispensationalism and then Scofield. You've probably heard of the Scofield Reference Bible. Probably the single most popular Bible out there—the Bible with notes version—and it's been used by probably millions of Christians of kind of a Baptist flavor and beyond. He says in his notes what (he thinks) is said in Scripture concerning Israel and the Church. We find that, in origin, calling, promise, worship, principles of conduct, and future destiny, all is contrast. Everything is contrast between Israel and the Church. There is no correlation between them. Then he says in his reference notes, the fourth dispensation, "Promise," was given to Abraham. God made a promise to Abraham. And this is the age (dispensation) of promise. It ends when Israel rashly accepted the Law. Grace had prepared a deliverer, Moses; provided a sacrifice for the guilty, and by divine power brought them out of bondage. But at Sinai they exchanged grace for law.

Really? Did they exchange grace for law? Is that what we ought to be teaching? That they exchanged grace for law? God was gracious! He should have destroyed them, but He didn't. They deserved to be destroyed. Three thousand people died. That was it; 3,000 people. Out of that huge multitude of millions of people, only 3,000 people died that day. That's what I would call grace. After they entered into this covenant with God and they said we will be faithful and they weren't, still God was gracious. He says in his notes in the Book of John, grace is the kindness and love of God, our Savior toward man, not by works of righteousness which we have done. Grace is therefore constantly set in contrast to law under which God demands righteousness from man as under grace He gives righteousness to man. Law is connected with Moses and works; grace, with Christ and faith. Law blesses the good, grace saves the bad. Law demands that blessings be earned. Grace is a free gift.[79] He says, as a dispensation, the age of grace begins with the death and resurrection of Christ. That is not true. The point of testing is no longer legal obedience as a condition of salvation. Notice that. What did they have to do to be saved before? Did they have to keep the commandments in order to be saved? I remember speaking with a woman who used to call the Church. She called for years; and, I would take her calls.

---

[79] *The Scofield Reference Bible*, Oxford University Press, 1909, p. 1115, Note 1: Grace.

CH. 8: SEGREGATING THE JEWS AND THEIR GOD

We would discuss different subjects. One time during our conversation I said, "You Jews, you're keeping the Law because you're trying to earn your salvation." She said, "No, we're not." I said, "Yes you are. She said, "No, we're not." And I'm thinking this woman doesn't even know her own theology. How can this be? I said, "You're trying to keep it to earn your salvation." She said again, "No, we're not; we keep it because God told us to." I thought: Oh really? Well, if God told her to keep it, who was I to tell her not to keep it?

And then I started thinking: Where did I get that idea? Why did I have this idea that the Jews are trying to earn their way to heaven? And I kept looking and looking; and I was looking in the Tanakh. And I'm like, well, where is that? And I could not find it. You know why? Because it's not there. The idea that they were keeping the Law to earn their salvation is not in the text. And then I discovered, oh; it's from the commentary about the text. It's from these guys. At first I thought it went back to Scofield, or maybe to Darby. No, it goes back further than Darby. Who started it? Marcion. And maybe it goes back further than Marcion but he's the culprit because he was widespread in his appeal and it really went throughout the world according to Justin Martyr.

Scofield's notes were very influential at Dallas Theological Seminary. Dallas has put out some great scholars, but again, those scholars have also left with this idea that law and grace are antithetical. A former president of Dallas Theological Seminary, John Walvoord said, "Of prime importance to the premillennial interpretation of Scripture is the distinction provided in the New Testament between God's purpose for the Church and his purpose for the nation of Israel." Significant is the fact that a Jew is not automatically recognized as belonging to the Church and the Church is not automatically related to Israel, even in heaven.

The distinctions between the racial Jew and the Church composed of both Jews and Gentiles is maintained in this revelation. Even though Paul said there's no longer Jew or Gentile . . . but now even in heaven: You're a Jew and I'm not. And so things will be different even until that day. Lewis Sperry Chafer, who started Dallas Theological Seminary, said that God has two purposes.

"The dispensationalist believes that throughout the ages God is pursuing two distinct purposes, one related to the earth with earthly people, the Jews, and with earthly objectives involved, which is Judaism. While the other is related to heaven with heavenly people and heavenly objectives involved, which is Christianity."[80]

Oh, that's nice; and he takes it so far that he would say that the Church is not even part of the new covenant. It can't be. He says Scripture presents several reasons. The new covenant cannot presently be in effect. First, Romans 9:4 says the covenants pertained to Israel. But the Church is not Israel, so they're not even part of the new covenant. The Church is a new heavenly purpose of God, and what is it? A new heavenly purpose of God, absolutely disassociated from both Jew and Gentile. But why only earthly promises to Israel and only heavenly promises to the Church? Again, why should the divinely given rule of life be changed from law to grace? It wasn't.

That's the trouble. It's not that these men meant to twist the Scripture, but the Scriptures have been twisted for so long—for centuries now—that it just seems right. And once you're in that perspective, it's hard to see anything different until you can finally take those glasses off and say: Oh my goodness, the world looks a little different than I thought. Charles Ryrie, also from Dallas Theological Seminary, wrote a basic theology. I used to teach out of this book. I taught many theology students and eschatology students from this very book, and he insisted that a Dispensationalist keeps Israel and the Church distinct. The Church is a distinct body in this age, having promises and a destiny different from Israel's. Well, yeah, because many of these Dispensationalists teach that Israel has a different husband than the Church—God the Father for Israel; and Christ for the Church.

They're going to have a different resurrection. They're going to have a different place in heaven. They're going to have everything different than the Church because we're in this little parenthetical segment of time called the Church Age. The Old Testament prophets didn't see it, but now it is this thing called the Church. And it was such a mystery that only Paul saw it. This is what is taught and it is widespread.

---

[80] Chafer, *Dispensationalism*, p. 107.

CH. 8: SEGREGATING THE JEWS AND THEIR GOD

AWAY WITH THE LAW

It's not just my opinion, it's not just my interpretation, but it's in their own words. What they're saying is that the Law was done away with. And yet we saw that: No, it wasn't done away with. The following is from a website called doctrine.org, and the title of this is, "Jesus versus Paul,"[81] claiming they preached two different gospels. "Jesus preached the Kingdom of Heaven. Paul did not. Paul preached justification by faith alone. Jesus did not. The messages of Jesus and Paul were fundamentally different. Reconciliation of their messages cannot be done by harmonization. This is a fact we must accept."

"Paul emphasized the Church, the body of Christ. This terminology was entirely absent from the teaching of Jesus and the 12 and unknown until the ascended Lord revealed it to Paul. It was new. Peter, James, John, Jude, etcetera, did not teach it and knew nothing of it until they learned about it from Paul. Paul alone revealed and taught that the citizenship and position of believers in the body of Christ was heavenly, not earthly. For Paul, God's kingdom as related to the body of Christ was heavenly and wholly different from the earthly kingdom proclaimed by John the Baptist, Jesus and the 12."

How could you pretend to follow this then? If that's what Paul was really saying, then we should reject him and that is the conclusion that some people have come to; but I would argue that it's because they don't understand Paul. Paul is a complex guy. Peter warned us of that. So you have to really dig into the Torah, into the Tanakh to understand what Paul is getting at. And I believe one of the big secrets, not secrets, but one of the big reveals, if you will, is that of God. He had one wife who kind of split in two, North and South and He divorced the northern kingdom and He said, get out. You're not My people, but it will be said to the children of Israel: "You are sons of the living God," and Paul said that! And Peter said that!

That's the big message, that's what's been left out. And when I finally discovered what we sometimes call two-house (as in "two houses") or *commonwealth theology*, I had to ask why was I never, never, never, ever taught this? Because they don't ever teach it. Because if you're in a dispensational perspective, you're thinking; there's the Church and there's the Jews—and yeah, God

---

[81] https://doctrine.org/jesus-vs-paul

loves the Jews, but he loves the Church a bit more because we get to escape the tribulation. But they have to go through it. According to Miles Stanford:

> "The very essence of Dispensationalism is the distinction between Israel and the Church. Dispensationalism is in the danger of falling because of a careless delusion of her life, sustaining distinctions. So, if we take away those distinctions. And it's true, it all falls apart. One factor is the seminary teaching of the Church has a part in Israel's earthly kingdom, new covenant, but a far more pervasive error is that of failure to distinguish between Jesus' earthly gospel for Israel and his heavenly gospel for the Church. For too long, the Church has been subject to a synoptic; that is the Matthew, Mark and Luke, kingdom gospel that was never intended for her. Most Dispensationalists, along with covenant theologians, fail to realize that there are two gospels, each dependent upon the blood of the cross. One is earthly, the other is heavenly, and both gospels are according to Jesus. The one was ministered by him on earth in his humiliation prior to the cross, exclusively for Israel and her earthly kingdom. The other and it's altogether new creation was ministered to Paul by the glorified, Lord Jesus Christ after Calvary from heaven, exclusively for his chosen heavenly body, his beloved bride."[82]

So what is he saying? What are all of these guys saying? What we find in the gospels, Matthew, Mark, Luke, and John, all those things that Jesus said, those wonderful teachings are not for us. They're not for us. Those are for the Jews. So when Jesus says, I didn't come to abolish the Law—of course not. And whoever breaks and teaches others... they're the least in the kingdom; they're like, well, that's fine. And what do we hear? Pastor J., from Calvary Chapel says, "I teach that it has been done away with, and I teach others not to keep it, but I'll still be in the kingdom. I'll just be the least." He admits it.

---

[82] The End Times Observer, "THE DISPENSATIONAL GOSPELS" by Miles J. Stanford, MAY 14, 2006, retrieved 5/26/2020. http://the-end-times-observer.blogspot.com/2006/05/dispensational-gospels-miles-j.html

CH. 8: SEGREGATING THE JEWS AND THEIR GOD

According to Timothy S. Morton: The New Testament did not begin until after the crucifixion. Thus all of the material found in the four gospels applies doctrinally to Jews under Mosaic Law. This is important to remember. Until Matthew 27:50, when Jesus yielded up his spirit, the Old Testament was still in full effect. So everything that is said before then must be placed in its proper context. Thus nearly everything Christ said before the cross applied doctrinally, not to us Gentiles, but to the Jews—in reference to their kingdom. Dispensationalism has the responsibility of clearly proclaiming the great differentiation between Jesus' kingdom gospel prior to Calvary and His post-cross heavenly gospel. If Paul's heavenly gospel were not other than that of Jesus' earthly kingdom gospel to Israel, he would naturally have been instructed by the apostles who had been with Jesus all during his earthly ministry. But on the contrary, the apostles had to be taught by Paul concerning much of the new heavenly truth.

What a waste of three and a half years. Jesus, supposedly, invested all that time into these 12 guys who barely got it and then said, "You know what? Forget all that. I'm just going to tell Paul and he can be the one to tell everybody."

Remember Deuteronomy 13; if a man comes and says he has a dream and he is telling you something different, stone him; that's what Paul would be guilty of, if these statements were true. But Paul wasn't doing that. He said, we "establish" the Law. "Keeping the commands of God is what matters." How many times does he have to say it until people believe it? But they don't believe it. No, no, no. That's not for us! And I've saved the best for last.

Douglas Stauffer, smart guy, author of 10 books. He very clearly comes out and says, Paul is the Church's only apostle, just like Marcion. Is God's direction for us today found in Matthew, Mark, Luke, and John, or in Hebrews? No, he says, God's specific directions for the Church are found predominantly in the 13 epistles that God used Paul to pen for the Church Age, and here they are: Romans, First Corinthians, Galatians, Ephesians, etcetera. He says, all in this book, *One Book Rightly Divided*, that Jesus preached the gospel of the kingdom during his earthly ministry. He instructed his apostles and disciples to preach the same gospel. More of Stauffer's assertions are summarized below:

No Bible-believing preacher today preaches the gospel of the kingdom. He preaches instead the gospel of the grace of God. Now just to give you perspective, very smart man. He's written 10 books. He's not just some weird dude you find on the internet. Okay. He's established. He's been on lots of TV shows, doesn't make him right, but at least he's what we might consider to be somewhat mainstream. There's a big difference between the gospel of the kingdom and the gospel of the grace of God. They differ in their main message. The former talks about a king reigning, while the latter speaks about trusting in the savior who has sacrificed himself by shedding his blood on the cross of Calvary, the kingdom gospel, Matthew, Mark, Luke, and John will go back into effect after the Church Age, as in after the rapture of course; and he says that most of the Bible is not for the believer. Instead, Paul is the standard of doctrine, not Jesus.

So long as particular scriptures do not contradict the Apostle Paul's explicit instructions to the Church, they can have Church Age application. He says, by determining who our spokesman is, we will know where to go to find our instructions for living today. Unquestionably, our spokesman is the Apostle Paul and he gives him some cool little graphics in his book. So he's got the Old Testament. You kind of see from Genesis to Revelation. So from Genesis to Malachi, this was applicable. God was speaking to Noah, Abraham, Isaac, Jacob, Moses, Joshua, Samuel, David, and Solomon. Well, we're not those people. So clearly that has no doctrinal application. Sure, we can learn lies and little stories and ideas, but it's not for us. And then, during the time of the gospels, you have Jesus speaking to Peter and the Apostles; of course they're Jewish.

So that's not for us. And then we have after the rapture, until the return of Jesus. Well, that's not for us either. That's going to be the two witnesses, Moses, Elijah, and the 144,000. So that's not to us. So the only thing that applies to us is Paul. He said, look, we are here like on a map. This is where you are. Paul is the only guy you need to listen to, not the rest of the Bible. He just showed us graphically, you don't need to do it. Peter was God's main spokesman until the time of Paul's conversion. Shortly thereafter, Peter virtually disappears. One of the few times Peter reappears is in Galatians 2:11 when Paul rebukes him for his hypocrisy concerning the Gentiles. The main point to consider is whether the particular truth presented elsewhere contradicts the plain teaching of the apostle Paul to the Church. If it contradicts his teachings, it cannot be Church Age doctrine.

I want to just compare this and contrast it with the Church Father Irenaeus. Remember what he said? With regard to those Marcionites who alleged that Paul alone knew the truth, and that to him the mystery was manifested by revelation: "Let Paul himself convict them when he says that one and the same God wrought in Peter for the apostolate of the circumcision, and in himself for the Gentiles." This is not new. This is the same heresy that the Early Church was trying to stamp out. The trouble is they only stamped out a little bit of it. The rest of it just got absorbed.

For example, one of Marcion's criteria for a real believer; if you wanted to be a member of his church you had to be celibate. What happened to that? Did it go away? No, it got absorbed into the Universalist Church. Now, clearly it's a real tough one, and so most people aren't going to go with that one because it's good to have a family. Right? So that's not going to happen. He was against the eating of certain kinds of meats. Remember that now the Catholics have a tradition. You've got to eat fish on Friday. Well Marcion was against eating some meats and having fish, etcetera.

And one of the things that Marcion did—he used the knife. Was he the first "rightly divider?" Marcion expressly and openly used the knife, not the pen, since he made such an excision of the Scriptures as suited his own subject matter, according to Tertullian. But isn't this what we hear from so many Dispensationalists? We hear that you've got to rightly divide the word of truth, and again, we have this from Timothy Morton. He says, only a relatively small portion of the Bible applies doctrinally to the Church Age Gentiles; from Acts Chapter 15 to Philemon –that is, only Paul's books apply doctrinally to the born again Christian and are unique to the Church Age. The rest of the Bible is strictly Jewish. We must be careful to rightly divide the Scriptures where doctrine is concerned; and yet that term "rightly divide" means to literally cut a straight path (like through a forest). That doesn't mean to cut away the doctrines you don't like. It means just to go through it, to understand it, and then to apply it. Not to get rid of it!

And so we see here a comparison between Marcion's theology and real biblical theology: He said the Law was done away with; no, the Law was actually eternal. He said there was a disjunction between law and grace. No, there's actually harmony between law and grace. He said, the Jews and the Church are two different entities. No, the Jews and the Church are two sticks that are coming back together. He coined the terms, New Testament and Old Testament. Well, actually the Hebrew Bible and the Apostles writings are a continuum; there's not a break between them. He suggested the New Testament Scriptures were superior to the Old Testament. No, the New Testament Scriptures have the same weight, not more, not less as the Old Testament—the Hebrew Scriptures. He said the gracious God of the New Testament sent forth His Son to free us from the bondage of the Old Testament Law—this was nailed to the cross. No, biblical theology says the penalty—the penalty for sin—was nailed to the cross, not God's commandments.[83] And Marcion taught that Paul was the final authority of Scripture, even above Jesus. Nope. God is the law giver and He's the final authority. Paul had no authority to change God's Word; and he didn't!

---

[83] NOTE: Likewise, we read clearly from Ephesians 2:14-16 that it was "enmity" or "hatred" wrought between Jew and Gentile by "dogma" (ordinances) derived from interpretation of the Law (e.g., the "Sabbath Day's Journey being 2,000 cubits is all we can walk on the Sabbath Day)—i.e., the "law of commandments contained in dogma." These interpretations of the Law (dogma) created hostility between Jews and the Nations—it was this hostility, enmity, hatred which initially caused this impregnable separation between the two to be "abolished in His flesh . . . so as to create in Himself ONE NEW MAN FROM THE TWO, THUS MAKING peace . . . RECONCILING THEM BOTH TO God in ONE BODY through the cross, thereby putting to death the enmity." To the contrary, Marcion's determination to separate the Jew from the Gentile only exacerbated the hatred that was already there—he did so in defiance of the work of the cross which was to abolish that very hatred and make of the TWO—ONE NEW MAN— SO MAKING PEACE. Nothing about God's Law was abolished—but the hatred between the two parties was!

How to Un-Haunt Your Theology

So we come now to, *How to Un-Haunt Your Theology*. We've got to take some steps here to exorcise that ghost of Marcionism from your preaching, teaching and practical living.

Step one: We need to see that God's commands are for our good. There is no age of law versus age of grace. That is pure fiction. "The Lord, the Lord God, merciful and gracious, longsuffering and abounding in goodness and truth." This is God's own declaration of who He is, given at Mount Sinai—after God gave the Law, after they sinned. The Lord commanded us to preserve all these statutes, to fear the Lord our God, for our good always that He might preserve us alive as it is to this day for our good, not for our bad. Not to mess up our lives, but for our good.

What does Paul say? "The law is holy and the commandment, holy and just and good." "Keeping the commandments of God is what matters." And from the Psalms: "The statutes of the Lord are right rejoicing the heart. The commandment of the Lord is pure, enlightening the eyes." "Blessed are you oh Lord, teach me Your statutes." This should be our prayer. "Teach me Lord, and having this idea—this attitude—that the statutes of the Lord are right. "I have rejoiced in the way of your testimonies as much as in all riches."

That is how much we should hunger to know God's word, to know His commandments, because there are riches when we follow God's ways; not go against them. We need to meditate on God's precepts and contemplate His ways. We need to delight ourselves in His statutes and not to forget His word; and if we're having trouble, pray, "Lord, open my eyes that I may see wondrous things from Your law." And that's the beauty, when we pray that and we mean it, we begin to see wonderful things in His law—versus the Marcionite approach of terrible bondage.

Step two: Established doctrine. When we "rightly divide" from the Hebrew Scriptures and the apostles, the Old Testament and the New Testament, we need use "all Scripture." Not just the Apostle Paul. I love the Apostle Paul. I believe everything the Apostle Paul said, every last word of it; but taken out of context and twisted with the Marcionite bent, you can come to some very bad doctrines.

So what do we see here? Rightly dividing the word, does it mean cutting most of it out? Don't unhitch from the Hebrew Bible. Hitch more fully. Don't divorce God's commandments from His grace. Teach and practice the entirety of God's words, knowing that there is grace when we fall. God is gracious when we mess up, but He's happy that we're attempting to walk according to His commandments; and if we fall, He will extend grace to us because that's the kind of God that He is!

Paul says: *"All Scripture is given by inspiration of God, and is profitable for doctrine, for reproof, for correction, for instruction in righteousness, that the man of God may be complete, thoroughly equipped for every good work"* (2 Tim. 3:16-17). Now, when Paul said ALL Scripture, what was he thinking? Was he thinking about the New Testament? No, he was thinking about the Torah, the prophets, and the writings, the Tanakh. That's what he had in mind, what we call the Hebrew Bible or the Old Testament. That's what he meant; the Hebrew Bible. The Old Testament is given by inspiration of God and is profitable for doctrine, for reproof, for correction, for instruction in righteousness.

And what did Jesus say? *"Do not think that I came to destroy the law. I didn't come to destroy them, but to fulfill them. Until heaven and earth disappear, not one letter or stroke of the law will disappear from the law until everything has been accomplished. So whoever sets aside one of the least of these commandments and teaches others to do the same will be called least in the kingdom of heaven, but whoever does them and teaches them will be called great in the kingdom of heaven"* (Matt. 5:17-19).

Step three: Walk according to his commandments. And what does John say? *"Not as though I wrote a new commandment to you, but that which we've had from the beginning, that we love one another, and this is love. That we walk according to his commandments"* (2 Jn. 1:5). *"And now Israel, what does the Lord, your God require of you? But to fear the Lord your God. To walk in all His ways and to love Him, to serve the Lord your God with all your heart and with all your soul"* (Deut. 10:12). *"Abraham obeyed My voice and kept My charge, My commandments, My statutes and My laws"* (Gen. 26:5).[84]

---

[84] Doug Krieger, in Chapter 10, goes into more detail regarding this topic of the Law—Grace dichotomy and brings in issues related to the New Covenant.

Shouldn't we: *"Walk in My ways. Keep My statutes, My commandments as your father David walked"* (1 Kings 3:14)? *"Fear God and keep his commandments for this is man's all"* (Eccles. 12:13). *"He who has My commandments and keeps them, It is he who loves Me and he who loves Me will be loved by My Father and I will love him and manifest Myself to him"* (Jn. 14:21).

So Peter gets the final exhortation to keep God's commands, not like the untaught who twists Paul. *"Therefore, what manner of persons ought you to be in holy conduct and godliness? Be diligent to be found by him in peace without spot and blameless as also our beloved brother Paul has written to you as also in all his epistles speaking in them of these things in which are some things hard to understand which untaught and unstable people twist to their own destruction as they do also the rest of the scriptures. Beloved, beware, lest you also fall from your own steadfastness being led away with the error of the wicked, and so dear friends, since you already know these things, continually be on your guard not to be carried away by the deception of lawless people. Otherwise you may fall from your secure position"* (2 Peter 3:14-18). Wow, let's be careful to not be carried away by the deception of lawless people and lawlessness.

The Apostle Paul tells us, one day a man is going to come who's known as the Lawless One? Why is he called the *Lawless One*? Because he doesn't follow God's Torah. That's why. It's simple, isn't it? Whose law would he be talking about? God's law. So we've seen again and again and again. Keep the commandments. If you fall, if you break them, there's grace, but don't despise them. Don't mock them, don't scorn them. Don't say that they're done. They're over, they're not for me. That's the spirit of Marcionism (and lawlessness) and you don't want his ghost in your theological house. Follow God's commandments.

Chapter Nine

THE DUAL OFFICES OF MELCHIZEDEK
Dr. Gavin Finley

The Dual Anointing of Messiah in the Order of Melchizedek, Who Through the Blood of the Everlasting Covenant, In the Time of the Latter Rain, Engages the Two Witnesses, Repairs the Breach of Jeroboam, Reconciles and Reunites Both Houses of Israel, Restoring Israel as a United Commonwealth / Congregation, a Cross-Linked Royal Priesthood / Holy Nation, even as He Gathers in the End-Time Harvest as a Single Elect, an Ekklesia from out of All Nations Thus Restoring All Things.

The Innocence Before the Fall

The Open Fellowship in the Garden of Delights

The splendor of this creation before sin entered is something we cannot fathom. It must have been magnificent beyond telling in its perfection and in its beauty. Adam was happy to walk with God in the cool of the evening. There he enjoyed complete and open fellowship with the God who was His companion.

There was much to talk about. Perhaps Adam named more than the animals. Perhaps he named the stars and talked with God about the stories in the constellations. Perhaps he came to discover the grand scope of the eternal story that was being told there, even as the heavens were declaring the glory of God.

It has been called the Age of Innocence, and during that idyllic time there was no sin or death. The soul of Adam, his heart, his mind, and his will was complete and whole. It was unconflicted and undivided. He was an open book, his whole being accessible to himself, even as it was to the God who was his Friend and Companion.

Paradise Lost as Sin Enters the Garden of Eden
Then a Darkened and Partitioned Human Soul

What happened after that is well known. Eve gave her husband Adam the fruit from the tree of the knowledge of good and evil. When sin entered into the heart of man the open fellowship with God was broken. And with this spiritual death came **fear, guilt, and hiding.**

This was a personal tragedy for Adam and Eve. **Part of their soul went dark**. They were no longer the secure and happy persons they had been before the fall. Part of their being was now sinking into a dark sea of troubled swirling waters, of forgetfulness, and of rising fears and dread. Their willingness to follow God and to do right rather than wrong was being tested and they were confused. The God they had once known and the Friend with whom they had previously been completely open had now become a stranger to them. They were fearful. They were ashamed. They sought covering for their nakedness. And they wanted to hide from God.

God had created man in His own image. The Master Designer specifically designed humankind to find meaning in life through fellowship with Him. And now the open fellowship was not happening. Sin had cut the first family of man off from the God who created them and knew them. The wonderful communion they had once enjoyed in the Garden was no longer possible.

Man still had a conscious mind. God could still address him and speak to him there. But what could God do if man turned away from Him because of things going on deeper in those hidden places in the heart? How could God have fellowship with a man when part of his soul had gone dark and was locked away in the deep recesses of the subconscious? The heart of man after the fall was often inaccessible, even as an iceberg has most of its bulk hidden from view in the depths below the water line.

Part of the **soul** of man was now **partitioned** off from himself and from God, locked away in the dark rooms of the subconscious soul. God could speak directly to the conscious soul of man, even as a **king** making a proclamation to a **conscious being**. But how was He to deal with hidden feelings, the fears, and the guilt? How was He to quell the inner anger swirling within the subconscious soul, even in those places deeply hidden in the sinful heart?

That would require a deeper work of God. It would call for a **High Priestly ministry**. Fallen man was now in need of a **Shepherding Friend**, a **Savior** who would reach down into the heart of man and save him, even as a shepherd reaches down to save a lost sheep caught in a ravine. Mankind was now estranged from God. Large tracts of the soul were no longer listening to the Word of God. Nor was man responding in any dependable way to the ministrations of His Holy Spirit. Fallen man was alienated from the God who created him, the God who had called him out for a purpose. And what is that purpose in the calling of God? The answer has been famously stated by the Westminster Catechism in this way.

"THE WHOLE PURPOSE OF MAN IS TO KNOW GOD AND TO ENJOY HIM FOREVER"

But how was that possible now? Fallen man could know something of God by what he saw in the beauty and order of God's creation. There was also the **conscience** and in the quietness an awareness of a sublime Presence. The "God who is there" can, and He does, speak to man, very personally, even from another dimension. He is a righteous and merciful God. And He is always accessible to seeking hearts. Moses was told this.

Deuteronomy 30

> *11 For this **commandment** that I command you today is **not too hard for you**, neither is it far off. 12 It is not in heaven, that you should say, "Who will ascend to heaven for us and bring it to us, that we may hear it and do it?" 13 Neither is it beyond the sea, that you should say, "Who will go over the sea for us and bring it to us, that we may hear it and do it?" 14 But **the word is very near you**. It is in your mouth and in your heart, so that you can do it.*

But there was also another voice in the garden and beyond. There was still a serpent telling lies and seducing people away from God. Man can, and he often does, choose to step away from God. In those times he is not even aware of the intrusions of the enemy of our souls. In times of depression and anxiety fallen man is not aware of the conflicts within. The windows of his house are shuttered. And just what is going on down in the depths of the dank walled off rooms of his heart he does not know. Sometimes it is difficult to discern just who was speaking to him. Is it God? Is it an evil spirit? Or is it just self?

That was the case for Cain, the first son of Adam and Eve. His presentation of the fruits of his labor was not accepted by God. But the sacrificial blood covenant offering that his younger brother Abel presented to God had been accepted. Cain was upset by that. Jealousy, bitterness, and anger welled up out of the depths of his soul. He saw his brother Abel given an approval and affirmation by God. Both Abel and his God seemed to be persons of blood covenant and self-sacrifice. Cain hated what he saw there. He fumed and could not be consoled, even when God Himself came to him quietly entreating him to choose the right path, because "sin was lying at the door."

The celebration and the offering of a sacrifice lamb pointed to the ultimate Sacrificial Lamb who was to come. This is something that people of faith have always recognized. The rejection and aversion to the blood covenant by Cain, even as it prefigures the blood sacrifice of Jesus/Yeshua as the ultimate Sacrificial Lamb of God, was the key to Cain's spiritual problem. This was back then, and it still remains today, the essential "mystery of iniquity." Cain then rose up and killed his brother Abel.

God was speaking to Cain. But he was not listening. Something was simmering deep down in the subconscious. It was as the Scriptures declare.

Jeremiah 17:9

The heart of man is deceitful above all things and desperately wicked: who can know it?

As holy history moved on there were some better stories to tell. Enoch, in the seventh generation from Adam, was such a case. We are simply told,

Genesis 5

24 And Enoch walked with God: and he was not; for God took him.

It would seem that Enoch's walk with God was a very personal spiritual one. Apparently he had an exceedingly open and close fellowship with God. So much so that at some point God, having some purpose in mind, said to Enoch in effect, "You may as well come up here with me."

CH. 9: THE DUAL OFFICES OF MELCHIDEZEK

In Genesis 6 we hear about the descent of the rebel angelic rulers coming down upon Mount Hermon and cohabiting with the daughters of men. Further details as to what happened there are written in the first book of Enoch. Out of this dark angelic intrusion came the imperfection of the generations of man. This was an attempt by the powers of darkness to defile the DNA bloodline of man and thereby forestall the prophecy given back in the Garden of Eden. This was the prophecy given back at the time of the fall concerning the eventual victory of the Seed of the woman over the seed of the serpent.

Genesis 3:15

*And I will put enmity between thee and the woman, and between **thy** seed and **her Seed**; it shall bruise thy head, and thou shalt bruise his heel.*

So at some future time the victory over evil would come. The Seed of the woman was destined to crush the head of the serpent.

In the years leading up to the flood of Noah the wickedness of man increased. Gross violence became rampant upon the earth. Noah was said to be perfect in his generations. He and his family were preserved in the worldwide flood. In that great geological cataclysm of swirling waters, mud and rocks the broken bodies of dinosaurs came to be deposited in certain special places. The polar ice event froze the wooly mammoths. There is evidence from specimens found in the permafrost that this happened very suddenly.

After the flood mankind gathered together around a champion, a mighty hunter named Nimrod. The building of the Tower of Babel was supposed "to reach to heaven." That may have been just the first of many pagan hierarchical pyramid-style structures seen around the world. God saw fit to come down and confuse their language. He broke up their "One World Government" movement, disrupting their languages, breaking up the hierarchical systems of dominion, and thereby scattering mankind across the world. So what was God going to do now? Well, He was looking for a man with whom He could make covenant. He sought a family man with whom He could enter into a relationship based upon faith. He was out to bring His purposes to bear to redeem and restore fallen mankind. It was there in Ur, a city in Mesopotamia, that God found such a man. His name was Abraham.

God's Dual Remedy for Sin Emerges

We See it First in the Dual Anointing in the Order of Melchizedek

It is in the biblical accounts of the life of Abraham that we begin to see something interesting begin to develop. We see God begin to address the problem that came in with sin, that being the **partitioning of the human soul** into **conscious and subconscious realms**. God needed to reach out to both the conscious soul of man, (his head, if you will), and the subconscious part of his soul, (his heart). Speaking as a **King**, God would directly address the conscious soul, the head. However, it would require a **High Priestly ministry** to reach into the subconscious part of the soul, namely the heart.

Our first significant evidence of this dual operation in God was after Abram returned from the rescue of Lot and all his goods. On that occasion Abraham was visited by a person named **Melchizedek**. This mysterious person arrived, gave his blessing, and on a **table of communion** served Abraham the deeply symbolic covenant elements of bread and wine. And while this person was **King of Salem**, a **Prince of Peace**, he was also quite clearly, operating in a priestly or pastoral ministration. The Scriptures state that he was **High Priest of God Most High**. Abraham recognized that. He gave Melchizedek tithes of all he had.

Genesis 14

> *18 And Melchizedek **king of Salem** brought forth **bread and wine**: and he was the **priest of the most high God**.*
>
> *19 And he blessed him, and said, Blessed be Abram of the most high God, possessor of heaven and earth: 20 And blessed be the **most high God**, which hath delivered thine enemies into thy hand. And **he gave him tithes of all**.*

As we embark this essay into the **partitioned soul of fallen man** we begin to see mention of **two witnesses** who stand before the God of this earth. Now we are alerted to the fact that **Melchizedek** bore **two offices**. He was both **High Priest of God Most High** and **King of Salem**.

King David picks up the story a thousand years later, and puts it in a song. Here in Psalm 110 we see God the Father proclaiming that His Son is to **rule** in the presence of his enemies. The Father also states that the Son is **"a priest forever, after the Order of Melchizedek."** Here again we see the **dual office of Messiah** in the **Order of Melchizedek**.

Psalm 110

1 The LORD, (Yehovah-Almighty God) *said unto my Lord,* ***Sit thou at my right hand****, until I make thine enemies thy footstool.*

2 The LORD shall send the rod of thy strength out of Zion: ***rule*** *thou in the midst of thine enemies.*

3 Thy people shall be willing, (volunteers), *in the day of thy power, in the beauties of holiness from the womb of the morning: thou hast the dew of thy youth.*

4 The LORD hath sworn, and will not repent, Thou art ***a priest forever*** *after the* ***Order of Melchizedek.***

This is a major clue for us. Here we begin to see that God is setting things up to establish a **High Priesthood** to reach down in a nurturing shepherding ministry to bring salvation and to heal the sin-sick soul.

But that is not all. He also bears authority over a **Kingdom of Salem or Peace** to restore not only the rule of God within the heart of fallen man, but to restore what is soon to become His broken and divided national kingdom.

As we see in his songs, David, the second king of Israel was not just a lawgiver. David was a treasure of God who was destined to have a Tabernacle. He was no stranger to ministry. In fact, King David came to be known as the Shepherd-King.

We can now begin to see what God is doing. In the **Order of Melchizedek** He is establishing a **Kingdom** for the administration of His righteous **rule of law**. He is also establishing a **High Priesthood** in the same **Order of Melchizedek**. This is the **priestly ministry that** goes down deep to minister and to restore the subconscious soul, even cure the disease within the sinful heart of man.

A thousand years later the writer of the Hebrews goes on to speak of this **kingdom** in the **Order of Melchizedek**, typified by **righteousness** and **peace**.

Hebrews 7

*2 To whom also Abraham gave a tenth part of all; first being by interpretation **King of righteousness**, and after that also **King of Salem**, which is, **King of peace**;*

He also refers to Christ being made perfect and being the source of the Gospel of **eternal salvation**. He is also declared by God to be **High Priest in the Order of Melchizedek**.

Hebrews 5

*9 And having been made perfect, He became the source of **eternal salvation** to all who obey Him 10 He and was designated, (declared), by God as **High Priest** in the **Order of Melchizedek**.*

The High Priestly ministry of God moves within the heart. It brings the message of salvation, and delivers us from evil. The heart is the place of dreams and sometimes nightmares. It is in that subconscious part of the soul that the Holy Spirit ministers. He is able to move within us in the **nine spiritual gifts** and the **nine graces**. He ministers healing to those hidden places of hurt that lie deep within the heart. He alone can deal with those hidden griefs, even the ones beneath our conscious awareness that we are not able to reach. He is able to change us from the inside out. In the priestly ministry of God the Holy Spirit moves. He can and He does perform these marvels of inner healing and restoration, and just as fast as we allow Him to do so.

Romans 8

26 Likewise the Spirit also helps in our weaknesses. For we do not know what we should pray for as we ought, but the Spirit Himself makes intercession for us with groanings which cannot be uttered.

The inner ministrations of God within the heart can change us in very profound ways. This was the case with Abraham. He was blessed with the breath of God upon his life. With the character change came a very telling name change to go along with it.

Genesis 17

*5 Neither shall thy name any more be called **Abram**, but thy name shall be Abra**h**am; for a father of many nations have I made thee.*

Here we see God very personally putting the **breath of His Life** within his friend Abraham. So He changed Abram's name to Abra**h**am by putting the "H" in the center of his name. He did the same for Abraham's wife. Her name Sara now became Sara**h**.

So here we see the **dual office** of Messiah in the **Order of Melchizedek**. He was both **King of Salem** and **Priest of God most High**. This is going to have enormous significance as we survey the reconciliations, the reunion, and the restoration of a broken Israel that will be occurring at the end of the age.

The Two-Fold Unconditional Covenant

God Makes with Abraham
The Promise of a Multitude of Descendants
as well as a Land and a Holy City

As we continue to examine the life of Abraham we come to the second instance in which we see God addressing the spiritual needs of His covenant people in two distinct areas of responsibility and authority. These are two ways in which they can bear witness to the Holy One of Israel. There are, as we see, two facets to the Abrahamic Covenant. And Yehovah Almighty Eternal God and God has pledged to fulfill them both. This is an **unconditional covenant**. God saw that Abraham was a self-sacrificing person who could be "sold-out" for Him. The promise God gave to Abraham also applies to all the covenant people in His spiritual family of faith. And we can be sure of this. The God of Abraham will see to it Himself that the job gets done!

Let us now look at the first part of the **Abrahamic Covenant**. Here we see God promising Abraham a **melo-hagoyim**, a **huge Congregation**, an **Ekklesia**, a **multitude of descendants**, a **fullness of Gentiles**, a **massive company** made up of people coming out of **many heathen Gentile nations**.

Genesis 15

*5 Then he brought him outside and said, "Look up to heaven, and **count the stars** if you are able to number them." And He said to him, "**So shall your descendants be**."*

6 And he believed in the LORD and He accounted it to him for righteousness.

The second part of the Abrahamic Covenant is at the center of attention of Middle East politics. This troubled history extends from the Crusades of 900 years ago and runs right through to the Battle of Armageddon at the end of this age. The God of Abraham promised Abraham **the Land**, the **Promised Land**. This included the **Holy Place** that would become the **Holy City of Jerusalem**, the **City of Peace**, or **Salem**, or **Shalom**.

*7 Then He said to him, "I am the LORD, who brought you out of Ur of the Chaldeans, to **give you this land** to inherit it."*

The writer of the Hebrews declares that Abraham sought a **city** with **eternal foundations** which has **foundations, whose builder and maker is God**.

Hebrews 11

*10 for he waited for the **city which has foundations**, whose builder and maker is God.*

ABRAHAM IS VISITED BY THE ANGEL OF THE LORD ON HIS WAY TO JUDGE SODOM
THE ANGEL OF THE LORD BRINGS HIS TWO (ANGELIC) WITNESSES WITH HIM

The third time in the life of Abraham in which we see the God of Israel presenting the **two authorities**, **two witnesses**, to what He is doing on earth, even as He brings His Divine Providence to meet the needs of fallen mankind, is when Abraham is visited by the three angels. There are a number of occasions in Holy Scripture in which we see the Angel of the Lord appearing. We can recognize Him as **a Christophany**, the **pre-incarnate Christ**, the God who enters this cosmos. We see Him coming down Jacob's Ladder at certain sundry times to fulfill a certain divine purpose. The Angel of the Lord is going down to Sodom to see what the furor is all about. He passes by Abraham's tent on His way. As we see, He brings His **two witnesses** with Him.

We can look at this instance, and many others in Scripture, and see that these two angelic witnesses have their own special area of interest, devotion, and responsibility. One of the angels is there to bear witness to God's **righteous rule of Law**. The other angel is there to bear witness to **God's Mercy and Grace**. We also see both of these angels represented atop the Ark of the Covenant, overshadowing the **Mercy Seat**. The two have names which can be discovered. They also have special purposes that can be readily seen and appreciated, particularly in pages of the book of Daniel.

Abraham saw three men standing by his tent. He recognizes that they are angels. Quickly he makes preparations for them to sit down at table and have a meal with him. The meal table has always been a special place. The table is where covenants are often made and discussed. This is a common tradition of hospitality and conversation, all across the experience of fallen men.

Genesis 18

> *1 And the LORD appeared unto him in the plains of Mamre: and he sat in the tent door in the heat of the day; 2 And he lift up his eyes and looked, and, lo,* ***three men*** *stood by him: and when he saw them, he ran to meet them from the tent door, and bowed himself toward the ground,*

What, then, is the significance of the **two witnesses**? Why does the **God of the earth** need **two witnesses** to stand before Him?

We get a major clue from John's Apocalypse. 600 years after Zechariah is given his prophecy of the **two olive trees** the Apostle John picks up the rest of the story. In Revelation Chapter 11 John identifies the **two olive trees, (the two anointed ones who stand before the Lord of the earth)**, as the **two witnesses.**

Interpretation of this verse requires special care and discernment. Whether the two witnesses are merely two individuals re-appearing in the last days, two bodies of witness by the covenant people of God, or two angelic rulers who stand before the God of this earth, or all three, we can be sure of this; these will be key players who will prophesy in an epic final way during the last half of the future 70th Week (sabbatical) of Daniel, the **final 1260 days** of this age, even during the **Great Tribulation**.

Revelation 11

*3 And I will give **power** unto my **two witnesses**, and they shall prophesy a thousand two hundred and threescore days, (**1260 days**), clothed in sackcloth. 4 These are **the two olive trees**, and **the two candlesticks** standing before the God of the earth.*

So why does the Holy Spirit link the **two witnesses** with the **two olive** trees? That is where we are now being led on our journey of discovery.

The Two Olive Trees

The scriptural record in Zechariah Chapter 4 is our next port of call as we trace the biblical story of the **two witnesses**. The angel of God shows the prophet Zechariah **two olive trees**. There is a lot to unpack here. The Holy One of Israel is presenting us with a show-and tell.

Zechariah 4

*1 And the angel that talked with me came again, and waked me, as a man that is wakened out of his sleep, 2 And said unto me, What seest thou? And I said, I have looked, and behold a candlestick / (**lampstand**) all of **gold**, with **a bowl** upon the top of it, and his **seven lamps** thereon, and seven pipes to the seven lamps, which are upon the top thereof: 3 And **two olive trees** by it, one upon the right side of the bowl, and the other upon the left side thereof.*

Zechariah does not know what to make of this. He then asks two questions. In the first he inquires as to the meaning of the **two olive trees**. The second question sees him ask about the **two olive branches**.

*11 Then answered I, and said unto him, What are these **two olive trees** upon the right side of the candlestick and upon the left side thereof? 12 And I answered again, and said unto him, What be these **two olive branches** which through the **two golden pipes** empty the **golden oil out of themselves**? 13 And he answered me and said, Knowest thou not what these be? And I said, No, my lord. 14 Then said he, These are the **two anointed ones**, that **stand by the Lord of the whole earth**.*

In the context of the **single olive branch** we then see reference to a **specific king**, represented by Zerubbabel.

*6 Then he answered and spake unto me, saying, This is the word of the LORD unto **Zerubbabel**, saying, **Not by might, nor by power, but by my Spirit, saith Yehovah-Almighty God, the LORD of hosts**. 7 Who art thou, O great mountain? before Zerubbabel thou shalt become a plain: and he shall bring forth the headstone thereof with shoutings, crying, "**Grace, grace** unto it."*

The Scripture passage before this in Zechariah Chapter 3 gives special reference to what can be interpreted as the other **olive branch**. Again, the olive branch is a specific person, namely **Joshua** the **High Priest.**

Zechariah 3

*1 And he shewed me **Joshua** the **high priest** standing before the angel of the LORD, and Satan standing at his right hand to resist him. 2 And the LORD said unto Satan, The LORD rebuke thee, O Satan; even the LORD that hath chosen Jerusalem rebuke thee: is not this a brand plucked out of the fire? 3 Now Joshua was clothed with filthy garments, and stood before the angel. 4 And he answered and spake unto those that stood before him, saying, Take away the filthy garments from him. And unto him he said, Behold, I have caused thine iniquity to pass from thee, and I will clothe thee with change of raiment. 5 And I said, Let them set a fair mitre upon his head. So they set a fair mitre upon his head, and clothed him with garments. And the angel of the LORD stood by.*

The main take-home lesson here in Zechariah's prophecy is simply this. Two witnesses stand before God concerning the things He does here on this earth. One bears witness to God's **righteous rule of Law** as a king decreeing the Commandments of God. The other witness is to His **High Priestly ministry** here on earth among men. We also see the two flows of oil from the two olive trees representing the anointing of the Holy Spirit coming down into the single bowl.

We might interpret the golden bowl as the heart, mind, and will in the unified and wrapped up soul that comes to us from God and is presented to Him at the end of our life. King Solomon saw a glimpse of this in the book of Ecclesiastes.

Ecclesiastes 12

> *1Remember now your Creator in the days of your youth, Before the difficult days come,*

> *6 Remember your Creator before the silver cord is loosed, Or the **golden bowl** is broken, Or the pitcher shattered at the fountain, Or the wheel broken at the well. 7 Then the dust will return to the earth as it was, And the spirit will return to God who gave it.*

Out of this **unity in God, the golden bowl,** the **oil of anointing** flows on to feed into the full array of the **seven lamps**, the menorah, which is the true symbol of Israel. There is no question where the anointing and power for the witness comes from. God is the Source and the **Divine Providence** in the **two olive trees**. And the holy oil of anointing for the menorah, the **Light of Israel**, and the energy for **His witness,** comes from above. This is the seven-fold witness shining in the darkness, a witness returning back to the Source, even the **Father of Lights** in this dark world.

James 1

> *17 Every good gift and every perfect gift is from above, and comes down from the **Father of lights**, with whom is no variableness, neither shadow of turning.*

The narrative in Zechariah 3 then moves on to speak of to a certain **Someone** who is called **"The Branch."**

Zechariah 3

> *8 Hear now, O Joshua the **high priest**, thou, and thy fellows that sit before thee: for they are men wondered at: for, behold, I will bring forth **my Servant, the BRANCH**. 9 For behold **the Stone** that I have laid before Joshua; upon **one stone** shall be **seven eyes**: behold, I will engrave the graving thereof, saith the LORD of hosts, and I will **remove the iniquity** of that land **in one day**. 10 In **That Day**, saith the LORD of hosts, **shall ye call every man his neighbor under the vine** and **under the fig tree**.*

CH. 9: THE DUAL OFFICES OF MELCHIDEZEK

This mention of the **Branch**, the **Stone**, with the **seven eyes** must be a reference to the coming of **Messiah.** Zechariah is told of the **iniquity** of the land being **covered** and **removed** in **one day**. This would seem to point to the wrap-up **Day of Atonement** that will come at the **end of the age**.

The **Last Day, the Day of Atonement**, wraps up all the legal issues of the redemption, for this age. It is there at the end, with the final ingathering of the Harvest. There at the consummation of this age we see the glorification of the entire company of the Covenant people of God.

After that the whole world is at peace under Messiah, with **"every man his neighbor."** No longer are God's Elect in servitude in the nations or the *"captives of Zion."* But each person is described poetically as *"sitting under the fig tree"* of **"sweetness and good fruit"** and *"under the vine," "the wine that brings cheer to God and to man"* (See Judges 9:11).

So, here in Zechariah's prophecy of the two olive trees, the Holy Spirit is showing us something very important. The **Two Witnesses**, the **Two Olive Trees**, and the **two candlesticks** or **two lamps** are all showcasing something about how our God, the God of the earth, relates to His people here on earth. Each of them is bearing witness to an aspect of God, both as **High Priest** and as **King of kings** as He brings His agenda into play here on earth.

His **dual agenda** is as follows.

1. The Holy One of Israel has an immediate plan to bring his **Gospel of redemption** by **GRACE into the hearts** of His covenant people, a great **salvation plan** going out to the ends of the earth.

2. He **also** has an immediate plan to establish His **righteous rule** and **LAW into the hearts** of His people here on earth.

Later, at the climax of this age, comes the **Revelation of Messiah** as the **Shepherd-King**. Once again, we see Him come with a two-fold purpose. It is the end-time execution of the two-fold promise and prophecy that God gave to Abraham way back at the beginning. He is returning in vengeance on behalf of **BOTH** His **Holy People** and the **Holy Land / Holy City**. He is returning in wrath upon His enemies in **two different venues**. First we see the returning Messiah coming to **His Congregation, His Holy**

People, in **deliverance** as **"The Breaker"** at the **sheep-pen** of **mystery Bozrah**. (See Micah 2:12-13). This is a neglected untold story, studiously avoided by our popular Bible prophecy teachers.

The other deliverance is somewhat better known. In the very same end-time window the returning Messiah will be coming to His **Holy City**, **again** in **deliverance**, to **deliver Jerusalem**, even as the armies of this world gather in the Valley of Jezreel and come down to encircle Jerusalem at the **Battle of Armageddon** (See Zech. 12).

Abraham was given an unconditional promise that God was going to preserve and deliver up for him a **Holy City / Holy Land**. Then upon His return He will also complete the ingathering of a **fullness of nations**, a **great multitude** drawn out of the nations, the heathen Gentiles. A huge multitude of people who were once strangers, aliens from the covenants of promise, would now be a **Holy People,** and would now belong to the **God of Israel.**

This would not be a "Jewish Israel" and a disconnected no-name generic "church" or assembly. Rather, it would be a **Congregation / Church of ISRAEL** seamlessly united in a complementary way in with the **Nation of Israel** along with its **Commonwealth.** Both are now **united** and **set apart** in **holiness,** for **His Name**!

THE SEVEN BRANCHED LAMPSTAND
THE TRUE SYMBOL OF ISRAEL

The prophet Zechariah is shown **two olive trees**. From each of the two olive trees he sees two pipes issuing the holy **oil of anointing** into a **golden bowl**. From the golden bowl the oil flows on via seven pipes into the **seven branched lampstand**.

The Seven Branched Lampstand is the **menorah**. This has been established forever as the true symbol of Israel. It was introduced to us by Moses in the book of Leviticus. It is part of the furnishings of the Tabernacle in the Wilderness. The lampstand is situated in the Sanctuary, in the Holy Place.

The seven branched lampstand is also reflected in the imagery of the *"seven eyes on one Stone"* we see in Zechariah 3:9, the *"seven eyes"* we see in Zechariah 4:10, and *"the Lamb as it had been slain, with the seven eyes"* described by John in the book of Revelation (Rev. 5:6).

In Zechariah Chapter 4 we also find the key to the reunion and full restoration of both the **Jewish House of Judah in Israel** and the **engrafted** or **spiritually adopted Congregation of Israel's Messiah**. These are those saved inside what we call visible or invisible "Church." Labels are problematical and many of them, like the word "Church" carries with it unfortunate baggage. So in these conversations we must do our very best to define our terms carefully.

Here in Zechariah's vision of the **two olive trees** and the **seven branched lampstand** we find ourselves looking at a picture of a completely **reconciled, reunited, and restored Israel**. And in this picture we see the **dual anointing** with the two flows of **oil** coming into the golden bowl from the two olive trees. Here we see Israel as both a **Kingdom** and a **Priesthood**. In the **golden bowl** we see the blueprint and plan of God for a perfect Union of the two anointings of God. If we look carefully we can see that this is united Israel. We can see it represented for individuals like Zerubbabel and Joshua. However, we can also see the two trees working **together** in a corporate way as the combined and cross-linked **Nation/Commonwealth** and **Congregation of Israel**. This is the **ultimate uniting plan of Yehovah—Eternal God**.

Here in the vision of Zechariah we see the pattern. It is a vision of true inspiration. In its final state we see that in restored Israel there is complete harmony as the **two anointing flows** come into the **single golden bowl** to feed the **lampstand of Israel**. There is complete unity of God's plan and purpose here.

Yes, there is certainly **DISTINCTION** with the **High priestly anointing** coming from one olive tree and the **Kingdom anointing** flowing in from the other olive tree. But as the two flows come together in the golden bowl we can readily see that there is now **NO SEPARATION!**

Obviously we have not yet arrived at this perfect Union, which was broken because of gross idolatry in both houses of Israel.

Zechariah 11

14 Then I took my other staff, Union, and cut it in two, showing that the bond of unity between Judah and Israel was broken.

Both estranged houses of Israel have their entrenched traditions. They bind us into a religious mindset that has us believe that this fractured state of affairs is fixed for all eternity. We see the congregation of Israel's Messiah as being partitioned off forever as a generic "Church" that is all about **God's Grace**. Then we see a **Jewish national state** and **land of Israel** that is all about **God's Law**.

Our mindset and groupthink has us believing that this state of disconnect is established forever. We have been led to believe that this will never change. But have we come into the Last Days yet? Is it possible that some climactic events up ahead could heal the family feud and restore the nation and all its people?

In the **New Covenant** and in the **Seed of Abraham** we see the Scriptures clearly and repeatedly declaring that there must be and there will be a **reconciliation** and a **reunion** of **both houses** of **Israel**. If that has to happen in the squeezebox of the Latter Days or Jacob's Trouble, then what can we say? God has very clearly stated that He is still going to do this. Even in times of fasting, times of the breaking of the bonds of wickedness and undoing the heavy burdens, the God of Israel is giving a special commendation to that company who will be called, **"the repairer of the breach."**

Isaiah 58

*6 Is not this the fast that I have chosen? to loose the bands of wickedness, to undo the heavy burdens, and to let the oppressed go free, and that ye break every yoke? 11 And the LORD shall guide thee continually, and satisfy thy soul in drought, and make fat thy bones: and thou shalt be like a watered garden, and like a spring of water, whose waters fail not. 12 And they that shall be of thee shall build the old waste places: thou shalt raise up the foundations of many generations; and **thou shalt be called**, The **repairer of the breach**, the restorer of paths to dwell in.*

The plan and purpose of God is the same all through the Scriptures. From cover to cover, the Bible only ever speaks of **ONE ELECT**. All of His covenant people, even the saints gathered in from both sides of Calvary, are **ONE**. All are saved and brought into the New Covenant the same way. They are all saved by Grace through faith, in the atoning blood of Israel's promised Sacrifice Lamb. They are **ONE** in Christ Jesus/ Yeshua Hamashiach. This is affirmed by the apostle Paul.

Galatians 3

28 There is neither Jew nor Greek, there is neither bond nor free, there is neither male nor female: for ye are all ONE in Christ Jesus. 29 And if ye be Christ's, then are ye Abraham's Seed, and heirs according to the promise.

At the end of the story there is **no separation**. But there still remains **special distinction** in the two houses of Israel, just as there is with all the 12 gates we see in the New Jerusalem descending from heaven at the end of the age. In Revelation 7 John writes that he saw a huge multitude from every nation, race, and tribe. They were all bearing palm branches of victory and singing a new song as they gathered before the throne of God. All of them are represented by the 12 Tribes of Israel and enter into the Holy City through those gates. But once they enter in, there is no wall of separation between them at all—none whatsoever.

The God of Israel does not homogenize His covenant people. Nor does He put His treasured jewels through a blender as the Assyrians tried to do with the ten lost tribes of the Northern Kingdom of Israel. All of them are distinct and their differing national characteristics and giftings are cherished. Each of them reflects the Light of God in unique ways even as jewels sparkle and shine in the treasure chest.

Malachi 3

*17 And they shall be mine, saith the LORD of hosts, in **that day** when I **make up my jewels**; and I will spare them, as a man spares his own son that serves him.*

This is our future situation as we abide in the Vine. It will surely become a glorious reality at the Restoration of **All** Israel that will come at the consummation of the age.

A BAD BLOOD FEUD BETWEEN THE TWO HOUSES OF ISRAEL

Yes, in spite of this good news we must survey our present situation. It does not look good right now. There is a family feud, even a **blood feud,** involving much grief, going on between the Church and Jewish Israel. As we saw in the chapter on the **Breach of Jeroboam** there was a **"King vs. the People"** schism in **Israel** that can be traced back to the warring between David and Saul and then again between King David and his rebel son Absalom. We also see a **Law vs. Grace** fracture line running up right through to where it broke the nation in two at the **Breach of Jeroboam.** That **Law vs. Grace** schism is still with us today.

The Breach of Jeroboam split Israel into two kingdoms with the ten tribes in the north rebelling from the royal Jewish House of Judah in the south. Out of this past trauma has come a deep **amnesia** about the whole issue. Both sides are entrenched. And this sad story has gone on for 2,950 years. So understandably there will be some painful lessons for us to learn and some things to unlearn as we go along the way. We shall discover that **both** of the feuding parties in Greater Israel, and not just "the Jews," have cursed each other and themselves into **partial blindness.** They can barely speak to each other except in superficialities. But nevertheless, because they are in the same family, they will do business together. As a matter of political expediency they will find themselves drawn to support one another in the common matters of national safety and international treaties. This partial blindness or **partial hardening** is destined to continue until a certain end-point is reached in the latter days. Here is what the apostle Paul said about this **partial blindness**.

Romans 11

*25 For I would not, brethren, that ye should be ignorant of this mystery, lest ye should be wise in your own conceits; that **blindness in part** is happened to Israel, **until the fulness of the Gentiles be come in.***

*26 And so **all Israel shall be saved**: as it is written, There shall come out of Zion the **Deliverer**, and shall turn away ungodliness from Jacob:*

*27 For this is **my covenant** unto them, when I shall **take away their sins**.*

This partial blindness has stricken both houses of Israel. And as we see, it looks like it will continue until the final ingathering of the saints, the fullness coming in from the Gentiles, towards the end of the age.

Oh yes, Christian believers will be quick to see that this partial blindness is in the royal Jewish House of Judah. And it is, but getting less so of late. To this day most in the Jewish House are blind to the first coming of the Messiah in His priestly role as the

Suffering Servant. But, (and here is the rub), the partial blindness is also in the Church. They are blind to their identity in Israel which comes through the blood of Christ and the Seed of Abraham.

So the blood feud, the amnesia, and the partial blindness exists in both houses of Israel. This is our present situation. Does this misunderstanding have a theological element to it? The answer to that question is, "Yes, very much so."

THE LAW-GRACE SCHISM IN ISRAEL AND THE PARTITIONING OF RABBINICAL JUDAISM AND CONSTANTINIAN CHRISTIANITY

The Holy One of Israel is the God of **Law** and **Righteous Rule**. He is also the God of **Grace** and **Mercy**. But as we look at religion today and especially as we look at Israel, (as it is currently understood), and compare that with what we call "The Church," quite clearly there is a major disconnect. The two have become estranged from one another. They are now warring feuding factions. Each has set out to champion one element of the God of Israel and to neglect the other. Quite clearly they are at cross purposes with each other. Francis Schaeffer was a well-known, well loved, evangelical theologian. About 50 years ago he put his finger on this Law vs. Grace issue. He said that it was the central conundrum in theology. He was right. It is the quintessential Gordian knot.

Theologically it is very clear what has happened. It seems that the main issue and the main **burden** of the **Church** is the **Gospel of Grace**. And the main burden of the **royal Jewish House of Judah** in Israel is for **God's Righteous Rule and His Law**. Quite clearly these are both valid and important elements to what the Holy One of Israel wants to accomplish among His covenant people here on earth. At present the two camps do not appreciate or understand each other very well. Is this destined to change in times to come? Oh yes!

Christian believers do not appreciate the Law of God very much right now. They are inclined to discount the Law as "Mosaic Law" and "ordinances" established in the oral Law of the Rabbinical Priesthood. So in that misunderstanding they are wont to insist that **"the Law" has been "done away with."** So they retire to the Church to concentrate on what they call **"grace,"** doing what they want to do under that stretched out umbrella. After all, this is what God in His mercy has given us; has He not?

Ah, but here is the rub. Just like our idea of "The Torah," the "Grace" we luxuriate in can be misrepresented and even drift into licentiousness. It can be a cloak for antinomian lawlessness and uncorrected iniquity. Too much of what is touted as "Grace" today is in fact licentiousness. Many who call themselves Christians are just as lawless and just as inclined to break covenants as the pagans in the world around them.

This is a very sad state of affairs. In the current moral decline in Western culture the popular Church is being pushed down the skids into godlessness. This is being facilitated by the stepwise cultural ratcheting machinations of the Hegelian dialectic. Many church-going Christians are slip-sliding down the path of compromise towards destruction.

Indulgence in sin and the pursuit of self-centered agendas does not come only with secular humanism. **Religious humanism** is the new normal. The cults of: "self-esteem"; Dominion Theology; the "name it, claim-it" religious fad; and, a general "easy-believism" are rife in the Western Church today. It is in fact the poisoned apple in the mouth of the Sleeping Beauty who is the latter-day Church.

The lukewarm Laodicean Church is ever keen to stay on the middle of the road, and she remains stubbornly immovable. Many churchmen today are not leading the saints forward lest some of their flock be offended and leave. **Blood covenant** faith has given way to **contract law** and a "have it your way" Christianity. We see a cartoon character "Jesus" on sale and priced rather cheap in the bargain basement of the Christian book store. There is a "way that seems right to a man," but it leads to spiritual death. (See Proverbs 16:25). So why are we seeing all this compromise in the Church? We have ejected God's righteous rule, even His rule in our hearts. We want to "do away with the Law" entirely.

The principalities and powers, the evil angelic rulers of the second heaven, are behind this deception. They are in sheer terror of the coming judgment. They also know that it will be God's covenant people, mere human beings, who will be bringing in the essential 5th seal **end-time witness**. They are in an absolute tizzy over this and trying to prevent this from happening. They believe they can do it. They believe their own lies. This is the reason for the persecution of the saints and the raging of the nations as we approach the end of this age.

The poor human agencies in the hierarchies of men and the people duped into doing this do not realize what they are doing, or why. It is a conspiracy of the principalities and powers—the dark angelic rulers in the second heavens—to shut down the end-time witness of the saints. It is a straight-out rebellion against God and His coming Messiah. But the human agents under their spell do not know the real reason they do the things they do.

This is the reason for the raging of the heathen that will come to a peak in the latter days. King David wrote a song about this final apex of lawlessness in **Psalm 2**. He spoke of its utter futility. In fact God is laughing at their puny attempts to forestall His agenda. He has declared that His Messiah and His people will take His salvation to the ends of the earth. His triumph over the powers of darkness will be total and complete.

As we look around, we see that the Church in the West today is scarcely aware of this raging of the people of "the prince who is to come." In fact, the established churches are becoming increasingly accommodating to all this rebellion. They want a religion of greasy grace. That message gathers a crowd and raises money. But many of those who call themselves Christians refuse to honor Christ/Messiah as King on the throne of their heart. There are consequences to this lawlessness. This is precisely why the Western Church is now in such serious moral decline.

Christians need to realize that their God is the **Holy One of Israel**. He is the **God of righteousness**, the Son of David. Jesus/Yeshua is the **Lion of the Jewish Tribe of Judah** who sits upon the Throne of David.

But we need to make something clear here. Is our calling to the Jewish Messiah just to be schooled in an externally policed Rabbinic tradition of "Torah observance?" Well that may be a good start, even as a schoolmaster is there helping the boys and girls to grow up. Is the Law just to be viewed rationally, dispassionately, and objectively, "out there" written on tablets of stone, in holy books or scrolls, or on digital tablets? Or is there something more? Apparently so, as Jeremiah discovered.

THE NEW COVENANT IS SPOKEN OF BY JEREMIAH
THE LAW IS TO BE WRITTEN IN THE HEARTS

The Prophet Jeremiah spoke of the New Covenant. Oh yes, the New Covenant was spoken of in the Old Testament. It seems that in this New Covenant the Law is brought home to its rightful place at last. The Law is not "done away with," no, not at all. Six hundred years before our Redeemer came to Earth the prophet Jeremiah clearly stated that **the Law** is destined to be written not just on tablets of stone but on **tablets of flesh**. The God of Israel spoke through Jeremiah to tell us this. **The Law** is to be **written in human hearts**. This is an operation of the **New Covenant** energized for righteousness among the saints by the anointing of the **Holy Spirit**. This is made possible **by Grace through the Faith** that comes in the God of Abraham. The New Covenant is personal, even though it will have corporate implications as it comes to its fullness. It is enacted under the auspices of the Indwelling Messiah. The New Covenant is legally made possible by the atoning blood of Israel's promised Sacrificial Lamb.

Here we see another major clue that the God of Israel is fully intent upon wrapping up both houses of Israel in the **New Covenant**. Notice that this **New Covenant** is made with BOTH the **Jewish House of Judah** and the lost ten tribes in the **House of Israel**.

Jeremiah 31

> *31 Behold, the days come, saith the LORD, that I will make a **New Covenant** with the **house of Israel**, and with the **house of Judah**: 32Not according to the covenant that I made with their fathers in the day that I took them by the hand to bring them out of the land of Egypt; which my covenant they brake, although I was an husband unto them, saith the LORD: 33 But this shall be the covenant that I will make with the house of Israel; After those days, saith the LORD, **I will put my law in their inward parts**, and **write it in their hearts**; and will be their God, and they shall be my people. 34And they shall teach no more every man his neighbor, and every man his brother, saying, Know the LORD: for **they shall all know me**, from the least of them unto the greatest of them, saith the LORD: for I will forgive their iniquity, and **I will remember their sin no more**.*

So the Law is not just an arbitrary enactment or guidelines categorized and subdivided *ad nauseum* and laid down and policed by men with wagging fingers. Ultimately the Law is the Law of the God of Israel. His Law does not change. But the very personal way His Law operates in the New Covenant is quite different from the way the Law operated in the Old Covenant. The Law was at work in a decidedly corporate way back at Mount Sinai. In the New Covenant the Law is written in the hearts and ministered there by a very personal God. The Holy One of Israel crossed the Gnostic chasm and past the barricades of Hellenized compartmentalizing men to come to earth as Immanuel, "God with us." He is the One who died on the cross for us. Is this a personal matter? Oh yes, it certainly is!

The Law involves the anointing of a King to enact Righteous Rule. Yehovah-God's Kingdom rule is a throne of total, absolute, and pure righteousness. But where is that king? Is he "out there?" Or is He "in here," sitting upon His throne inside our heart? This is the Law at work in the New Covenant. Is that really so strange to us?

The external policing of the Law is in the precinct of the Levitical priesthood and the civic authorities, which through the influence of the European kings and rulers overflowed into the Church. But if the Law "out there" just remains as an objective rational theological discussion to be assessed and talked about forever by men, then there is no guarantee of obedience. Nor is there any power of self-control sufficient to keep men from evil. And let's face it, a mere following of the letter of the Law has proven to be not only problematic but an exercise in futility. We all fall short. And we face a holy God. If we are to avoid a lost eternity, then we need His Mercy and Grace. We need His indwelling Presence to save and to sanctify. This is absolutely essential. Nothing less will do. God knows all about this. It is no surprise to Him. That is why He has made provision for us to go beyond the directives of the externally policed Law.

Ephesians 2

> *8 For by **grace** are ye saved **through faith**; and that **not of yourselves**: it is the **gift** of God: 9 **Not of works**, lest any man should boast. 10 For we are his workmanship, created in Christ Jesus unto good works, which God hath before ordained that we should walk in them.*

And so there in the New Covenant, with the personal indwelling Messiah, His Holy Spirit is now made available to us in real time for inner strengthening and for inner guidance. The indwelling Christ brings in with Him both His **altar** and His **throne**. Both of them are now established in our hearts, leading us on to sanctification from within, and then on to eventual glorification from without, even by the **Resurrection-Rapture** that comes from above with the returning Messiah.

This is the Good News. As we surrender our hearts to Him, He then provides the **divine energy** for the **devotion** and for the **obedience**. These are no longer religious burdens but they have now become a delight. Through His blood He carries us, just as He did for our Father Abraham when they made covenant together. There was **"one set of footprints in the blood."** The God of Israel takes us **beyond the schoolmaster** of the externally policed Law. Then He carries us on across a threshold into the precincts of both His Grace and His Law written in the heart, fully established as they are, in the personal walk with God we now enjoy in the New Covenant.

So what happens when Messiah comes into human hearts in the new birth in the New Covenant? Does He abolish the Old Covenant? Does He "do away with" the Law? Does He render His Ten Commandments and all His righteous precepts as "null and void?" No, a thousand times no! He establishes and enthrones His Law inside the hearts of His Holy People. He does this when they are saved and "born again." This is what happens to them when they become "new creatures." This is why true, born-again Christian believers are among the most law abiding, as well as, gracious people in this world.

The desire and the power to follow the leading of the Holy Spirit can and does become very real. The New Life comes in the Person of the indwelling Christ and by the empowering Presence of His Holy Spirit. He establishes the **Throne of David** upholding His Law inside human hearts. He will do this just as fast as we surrender our hearts to Him.

So this writing of the **Law in the hearts** is not a grievous matter. The God of Israel leads His covenant people in the gentle bonds of love. He guides His people and empowers them. They soon discover that it is a delight to walk in His ways. He walks with them and talks with them throughout their journey here on earth. And when they have finished their pilgrimage He brings them home to the mansions He has prepared.

CH. 9: THE DUAL OFFICES OF MELCHIDEZEK

Great is the mystery of godliness. It must be and is a very personal reality. It is a wonder seen in the lives of men, women, and children who know God. This inner work of righteousness and law written in the hearts of men is just the beginning. The coming Millennium of Messiah will see His rule from the Throne of David going out from individuals to unify them as a corporate body, even His Holy City, Jerusalem. Indeed, the Holy City—New Jerusalem—is the **Bride of the Lamb**, the **Bride of Christ**. (See Rev. 21:2-3.)

THE BLOOD FEUD HEALED IN THE ANOINTINGS OF JUDAH AND IN JOSEPH

As we are beginning to see, there is a bright and wonderful future for a fully reconciled, reunited, and restored Israel. But in our present state we see two feuding houses which we are inclined to view as **"The Church"** and **(Jewish) "Israel."** There is a deep past trauma involved here and a related state of amnesia, partial blindness, and hardening of hearts. So the relationship remains conflicted and problematical. A huge and forbidding gulf separates the two houses of Israel. A huge legion of dark religious spirits swirl around the chasm, awakening the grievous memories of past sad histories. Religious and cultural spirits on both sides guard the bridges like trolls, forbidding each party from crossing over to discover the truth and begin to gain the understanding that the answer is in the indwelling Living Torah, Yeshua/Jesus. To get to the crux of the matter we are going to have to embrace our Messiah, ask for His Holy Spirit to be our Guide, and go back to the Bible.

To summarize, the **royal Jewish House of Judah** was given the scepter of sovereignty for rule in the **National Office** of Israel. This is the place of authority in God where edicts based upon the righteous Law of God, with no other ordinances added by meddling men, are decreed. Here is part of the blessing given to the patriarch Judah by his father Jacob. In this we see reference to **Shiloh**, the **One** to whom the **scepter** of **sovereign rule** belongs. This would be Jesus Christ, the promised **Messiah**, coming in His second role, fulfilling the Fall Feasts of Israel, presenting Himself at the close of the age as the returning conquering **King of kings**. He is the **Sovereign** who sits upon the **Throne of David**, the holder of **the scepter**, the **Lion of the Jewish Tribe of Judah**.

The name Judah means "praise." Here is the promise given to the patriarch Judah and to all who follow in this anointing for the righteous rule of God. His throne is to be established first **individually**, in the hearts of men. Then later, His throne—the Throne of David—will be established **nationally** at Jerusalem, even the New Jerusalem that John saw descending from heaven.

Genesis 49

*8 Judah, thou art he whom thy brethren shall **praise**: thy hand shall be in the neck of thine enemies; thy father's children shall bow down before thee.*

9 Judah is a lion's whelp: from the prey, my son, thou art gone up: he stooped down, he couched as a lion, and as an old lion; who shall rouse him up?

*10 The **scepter** shall **not depart from Judah**, nor a **lawgiver** from between his feet, until **Shiloh** come; and **unto Him shall the gathering of the people be.***

On the other side we have Joseph, the other prominent son of Jacob, Joseph is the one who received the blessing and whose name means "fruitful in God." The Joseph story and how it will play out in the latter days remains a mystery. We can expect that those in the end-time anointing of Joseph will mirror the life and purpose of Joseph as we saw it in the former life of the patriarch.

Many of the character elements and life events that Joseph exhibited in the seven-year famine in Egypt will be recapitulated in the final seven years of this age. Once again, Joseph will be shunned by his brothers, threatened with death, and have to resist the seductions of the harlot, even the one John saw in Revelation 17. Once again, he will be imprisoned, and harshly treated. But once again the Joseph company will be seen feeding the world the Bread of Life. All these mysteries will be unsealed at the appropriate time. Here below is the blessing given to Joseph. It also has implications for his two sons, Manasseh and Ephraim, who were given the land allotment along with the other sons of Jacob and were to become great nations in the politics of this world. Joseph was not. And yet his spiritual impact on the unfolding events of the latter days can be expected to be a huge part of the unfolding agenda of God. The unsealing of that story must await the appointed time.

Genesis 49

*22 **Joseph** is a **fruitful bough**, even a fruitful bough **by a well**; whose **branches run over the wall**: 23 The archers have sorely grieved him, and shot at him, and hated him: 24 But his bow abode in strength, and the arms of his hands were made strong by the hands of the mighty God of Jacob; (from thence is **the shepherd, the Stone** of **Israel**). 25 Even by the God of thy father, who shall help thee; and by the Almighty, who shall bless thee with **blessings of heaven above**, blessings of the deep that lieth under, blessings of the breasts, and of the womb: 26 The blessings of thy father have prevailed above the blessings of my progenitors unto the utmost bound of the everlasting hills: they shall be on the head of Joseph, and on the crown of the head of him that was **separate from his brethren**.*

THE TWO STICKS OF JUDAH AND JOSEPH

We have another great and wonderful Judah-Joseph story left to visit. It is in Ezekiel 37. This passage describes in detail the plan of God to use both the Kingdom office of Judah and the High Priestly office which appears to involve Joseph, in His final reconciliation.

15 The word of the LORD came to me: 16 "Son of man, take a stick and write on it, 'For Judah, and the people of Israel associated with him'; then take another stick and write on it, 'For Joseph (the stick of Ephraim) and all the house of Israel associated with him.' 17 And join them one to another into one stick, that they may become one in your hand. 18 And when your people say to you, 'Will you not tell us what you mean by these?' 19 say to them, Thus says the Lord GOD: Behold, I am about to take the stick of Joseph (that is in the hand of Ephraim) and the tribes of Israel associated with him. And I will join with it the stick of Judah, and make them one stick, that they may be one in my hand. 20 When the sticks on which you write are in your hand before their eyes, 21 then say to them, Thus says the Lord GOD: Behold, I will take the people of Israel from the nations among which they have gone, and will gather them from all around, and bring them to their own land. *22 And I will make them one nation in the land, on the mountains of Israel. And one king shall be king over them all, and they shall be no longer two nations, and no longer divided into two kingdoms. 23 They shall not defile themselves anymore with their idols and their detestable things, or with any of their transgressions. But I will save them from all the backsliding in which they have sinned, and will cleanse them; and they shall be my people, and I will be their God.*

24 "My servant David shall be king over them, and they shall all have one shepherd. They shall walk in my rules and be careful to obey my statutes. 25 They shall dwell in the land that I gave to my servant Jacob, where your fathers lived. They and their children and their children's children shall dwell there forever, and David my servant shall be their prince forever. 26 I will make a covenant of peace with them. It shall be an everlasting covenant with them. And I will set them in their land and multiply them, and will set my sanctuary in their midst forevermore. 27 My dwelling place shall be with them, and I will be their God, and they shall be my people. 28 Then the nations will know that I am the LORD who sanctifies Israel, when my sanctuary is in their midst forevermore."

Here is the central uniting truth that will establish the **Commonwealth of Israel**. Both the anointing of Law in the anointing of a King and the anointing of Grace and the Gospel that comes to us in Christ our High Priest, are brought to us by our Messiah. He will both guide and minister in the dual anointing that flows in both offices. He can perform both these administrations or dispensations at once simply because He is the High Priest AND King of Peace in the Order of Melchizedek. Messiah Himself brings the two offices of Law and Grace into perfect Union. This dual anointing of Messiah in the Order of Melchizedek is the true **"double anointing"** our "power" ministers like to talk about and try to claim. This dual anointing will indeed be the real power ministry. The Jewish ladies light the two candles every Sabbath eve in a celebration of a magnificent truth. This dual anointing in the dual witness will energize the End Time Revival to accomplish not only the full restoration of all 12 Tribes of Israel but bring in the fullness of the Gentiles as well. This is what Isaiah was promised in the Great Commission we see in the Old Testament.

Isaiah 49

6 And he said, It is a light thing that you should be my servant to raise up the tribes of Jacob, and to restore the preserved of Israel: I will also give you for a light to the Gentiles, that you may be my salvation to the ends of the earth.

THE GREAT END-TIME JEWISH REVIVAL

Quite clearly the two houses of Israel in Yehoveh-God are in a serious state of disunity and dysfunction right now. God's righteous rule, is presently not a big priority for the Church. God's Law and His precepts are presently championed in the Jewish house of Israel and they are doing some very wonderful Torah studies. But being robust of soul and ever hopeful that things can be done better "next time," our Jewish brothers and sisters are slow to break down, repent, and receive God's Grace for salvation in the New Covenant. But the promised glorious corporate salvation of the Jewish house, while it has already started, will surely come, but rather late. It will come in an epic end-time wave of Holy Spirit glory, but rather late for dispensationalist Christians who favor and believe in a pre-trib rapture and wish to leave the end-time race early.

And as we see in the context of this passage the epic **Jewish awakening** will come during the troublous times of the Great Tribulation, even in the time period that sees the encircling armies coming towards Jerusalem at the Battle of Armageddon. The salvation of those in the **tents of Judah** with the **wives apart** looks to be happening during some sort of an exile. This may be related to the exile at Mystery Bozrah spoken of in Micah 2:12-13. Another biblical perspective on this end-time exile is the flight and exile of the woman spoken of twice in Revelation 12:6 and 12:14. Does the Bible speak of a second Exodus? Yes it does. Here is the most well-known Scripture passage that speaks of the **End-Time Jewish Revival**.

Zechariah 12

*7 The LORD also shall **save the tents of Judah first**, that the glory of the house of David and the glory of the inhabitants of Jerusalem do not magnify themselves against Judah. 8 **In*** *that day shall the LORD defend the inhabitants of Jerusalem; and he that is feeble among them at that day shall be as David; and the house of David shall be as God, as the angel of the LORD before them. 9 And it shall come to pass **in that day**, that **I will seek to destroy all the nations that come against Jerusalem.***

MOURNING THE ONE THEY PIERCED

10 And I will pour upon the house of David, and upon the inhabitants of Jerusalem, the spirit of grace and of supplications: and they shall look upon me whom they have pierced, and they shall mourn for him, as one mourneth for his only son, and shall be in bitterness for him, as one that is in bitterness for his firstborn. 11 In that day shall there be a great mourning in Jerusalem, as the mourning of Hadadrimmon in the valley of Megiddon. 12 And the land shall mourn, every family apart; the family of the house of David apart, and their wives apart; the family of the house of Nathan apart, and their wives apart; 13 The family of the house of Levi apart, and their wives apart; the family of Shimei apart, and their wives apart; 14 All the families that remain, every family apart, and their wives apart.

END-TIME ADJUSTMENT IN THE THINKING OF THE CHURCH

The priestly ministry of the Messianic anointing is in the Gospel. This is entrusted to and championed by an entity we call "the Church." The word "Church," by itself, and stripped of all its religious and ritualistic coverings, means nothing beyond it being an assembly or congregation. The word "Church" merely means "assembly." The Greek word "ekklesia" means "called out," "congregation," or "assembly." It is only when the **object** of the assembly is mentioned that the word has anything beyond just a mere generic attribute.

The so-called "Church" should be properly presented as **"The Congregation of Israel,"** or **"The Congregation of Israel's Messiah."** Those more biblically correct names would help connect the dots and help Christians see that it is their denominational or national waypoint in history that gives

CH. 9: THE DUAL OFFICES OF MELCHIDEZEK

meaning to their church affiliation. And while those former church memberships may have been a true blessing in their time, they may not end up being the ultimate "congregation" that they will experience as they come to the end of their pilgrimage.

The name, "Christian" is also interesting. The fact is, the early saints were named Christians by others. This is a word that means "of the Anointed One." However, a simple incorporation of the name Israel into the name, as in "Congregation of Israel," might help bring them into a fuller understanding of their true identity in Israel's Messiah. It usually takes some time adjusting to this.

As we can imagine, that naming of the Church in a land as being related to Israel would not go down well with the princes of Europe. For 1700 years they have been presenting themselves and offering their military services to Western national churches as "Defenders of the faith." Discussions of Israel in relation to the Church ceased 1700 years ago at the Council of Nicaea. Even though the Church was 100% Jewish on the Day of Pentecost the Word of God and the Holy Spirit overflow was soon spilling out to Judea and to the utmost parts of the world. By the time the Church elders met with Constantine in 325 A.D. the Church was virtually 0% Jewish.

But the fact is, true born-again blood bought Christians are by that atoning blood of Christ in the New Covenant, ushered into the **Congregation, AND the Nation/ Commonwealth of Israel**. Here is our scripture:

Ephesians 2

*11 Wherefore remember, that ye being **in time past Gentiles** in the flesh, who are called Uncircumcision by that which is called the Circumcision in the flesh made by hands; 12 That at that time **ye were without Christ**, being **aliens from the commonwealth of Israel, and strangers from the covenants of promise**, having **no hope**, and **without God in the world**: 13 But now in Christ Jesus ye who sometimes were far off **are made nigh by the blood of Christ**. 14 For he is our peace, who hath made both one, and hath **broken down the middle wall of partition between us**; 15 Having **abolished in his flesh the enmity, even the law of commandments contained in ordinances;***

*for to make in himself of twain **one new man**, so **making peace**; 16 And that he might **reconcile both unto God in one body by the cross**, having slain the enmity thereby: 17 And came and preached peace to you which were afar off, and to them that were nigh. 18 For **through him we both have access by one Spirit unto the Father.***

Are Christian believers aware of this? No, they are not. As part of Jacob/Israel they are **partially blind**. They are just as partially blind, but in a different way, than their Jewish brothers and sisters. Christians, for the most part, are blind to their corporate or **Kingdom identity** in the **Kingdom/Commonwealth of Israel**. And their Jewish brethren are partially blind to their **Messiah**, coming as He did that first time not as King of kings but in His **priestly role** as the **Lamb of God, Israel's Suffering Servant**.

So, as we have seen, the two offices of **High Priest** and **King of kings** comprise one single all-encompassing anointing. This is the dual anointing which flows from Messiah! And it is in Him that the Righteous Kingdom Rule and the merciful High Priestly Ministry are destined to flow together in perfect harmony. The prophet Zechariah saw this when He saw the vision of the two olive trees in Zechariah Chapter 4. And how will this reunion be achieved? Will it come by politics or armies? Not at all. The God of Israel, speaking through Zechariah said,

Zechariah 4

"NOT BY MIGHT, NOR BY POWER, BUT BY MY SPIRIT SAITH THE LORD/JEHOVEH-GOD."

So when Israel's restoration actually happens it will not just come as a result of theological endeavors, ecumenical committees, or military conquest. This reconciliation, reunion, and restoration of all things will come in by a spiritual adoption under Israel's Messiah. This will be a wonder of wonders. The history of this world will be changed forever. The restoration of Israel under Messiah will establish that long awaited *"peace on earth to men of good will."* Israel will finally have her **Jubilee!** And the Millennium of Messiah will have finally come.

This sounds like an awesome turn of events. How will it happen?

During the wedding feast at Cana our Messiah demonstrated the way our God does things. It is quite the reverse to the ways of this world. He saves and **reserves the best things to the last**. The God of Israel is going to Regather and Restore All 12 Tribes of Israel as both a Nation/Kingdom/Commonwealth and a Congregation/Ekklesia/Church. He fully intends to unveil this entire mystery of the Commonwealth/Congregation of Israel and so bring in peace and unity. He has also promised this:

Isaiah 11

13 The jealousy of Ephraim shall depart, and those who harass Judah shall be cut off; Ephraim shall not be jealous of Judah, and Judah shall not harass Ephraim.

The Holy One of Israel will finally have achieved the impossible. His unified Elect will finally be seen as they were meant to be. They will run the final leg of the race, right through to the finish line on behalf of all the saints who ran before them. They will no longer be seen as two estranged and feuding companies, the "Royal Nation" of Jewish Israel and a "trying to be" "holy priesthood," the Church. At the glorious consummation of the age they will be seen before men and angels as that proper and prophetic cross-linked **"Royal Priesthood** and a **Holy Nation"** spoken of by both Moses and the Apostle Peter.

Exodus 19

*6 And ye shall be unto me a **kingdom of priests**, and an **holy nation**. These are the words which thou shalt speak unto the children of Israel.*

1 Peter 2:9

*9 But ye are a chosen generation, a **royal priesthood**, an **holy nation**, a peculiar people; that ye should shew forth the praises of him who hath called you out of darkness into his marvelous light: 10 Which in time past were not a people, but are now the people of God: which had not obtained mercy, but now have obtained mercy.*

This is the epic restoration that is slated to come during the latter days. The Holy One of Israel will accomplish this by His Spirit.

It is a big task. But God has promised in His Word to restore all Israel. (See Rom. 11:25-26.) Quite clearly this has not happened yet, not by a long shot. But this magnificent story will surely come as a grand conclusion to the holy history of this age. And from the Holy Scriptures the restoration will be a **gathering**, a **refining**, and then finally a **glorification at the close of this age**. The prophet Ezekiel saw it as a magnificent climactic event. It will all come together during the Apocalypse, the unveiling, of Messiah. See this presentation of the Vision of the Valley of dry bones from Ezekiel 37:1-14.

Both houses of Israel will be regathered from their scatterings.

"And so all Israel will be saved" (Rom. 11).

Jesus/Yeshua prayed to the Father concerning this:

"the glory which You gave Me I have given them . . .

that they may be ONE just as We are one" (John 17:20-22).

No longer will God's covenant people be in a state of disunity and disharmony. No longer will there be two estranged kingdoms, one for "Law" and one for "Grace." They will come together in Messiah precisely as Moses and the Apostle Peter have both stated. They will become a single indivisible **"royal priesthood and holy nation."** The royalty of the Kingdom will be applied to the Priesthood. And the holiness of the Priesthood will be applied to the Kingdom. This is how the **Breach of Jeroboam will be healed**. The two feuding camps will be regathered and reunified as **one Elect and Chosen People**.

As we can see, God's holy purposes are far from concluded. The long sweeping saga of the children of Abraham still goes on. A host of loose ends are still out there, hidden in the mystery. And yes, the two feuding houses of Israel do not even want to talk about their family feud or submit themselves to family counseling. But this will not always be the case. Our God is named Wonderful! / Surprise!

His Word will go out before all nations, even in the time of the Latter Rain. Within the trials of the latter days will come divine provision by the promised outpouring of the Holy Spirit.

This will be ramping up during the future 70th Week of Daniel, the final seven years of this age. Joel saw the peak of this divine providence coming at the very end, even in the days of a darkened sun, the true blood moon, and the stars of heaven falling, even as first-ripe figs when shaken by a mighty wind (Joel 2:28-32). And *"unto Him shall the gathering of the people be"* (Gen. 49:10).

God's grand adventure will become the divine romance. God's covenant people will no longer call their Messiah **Lord,** but **Ishi, Beloved**. The fig tree will blossom, and then in the fruit harvest will come the sweetness and good fruit that will accompany the full restoration of All Israel.

Haggai 2 (KJV)

6 For thus saith the LORD of hosts; Yet once, it is a little while, and I will shake the heavens, and the earth, and the sea, and the dry land; 7 And I will shake all nations, and the Desire of all nations shall come: and I will fill this house with glory, saith the LORD of hosts.

Chapter Ten

FALSE JUXTAPOSITION OF LAW AND GRACE

Primary Author: Douglas Krieger

There are and will be a wide variety of "Jewish practices and cultural reflections" found among those who embrace the greater body of truth contained within CT; however, the majority of those who affirm the main tenets of CT also adhere to the following, concerning the Mosaic Law, the Ten Commandments, the Commandments contained in Ordinances, Civil/Ceremonial Law...the following was presented in a discourse between several individuals interested in CT as an "eschatological/theological system of understanding" concerning the relationship between "Israel and the Church."[85]

Regarding the Law of God (i.e., the Ten Commandments)—Romans 7 emphatically states that the *"Law is holy, and the commandment holy and just and good"* (Rom. 7:12); also that the *"Law is spiritual"* (Rom. 7:14); *"I agree with the law that it is good"* (Rom. 7:16)—but Paul states: *"For to will is present with me, but how to perform what is good I do not find . . . I find then a law, that evil is present with me, the one who wills to do good . . . for I delight in the law of God according to the inward man . . . I thank God—through Jesus Christ our Lord . . . so then, with the mind I myself serve the law of God, but with the flesh the law of sin . . . There is therefore now NO CONDEMNATION to those who are in Christ Jesus, who do not walk according to the flesh, but according to the Spirit . . . for the law of the Spirit of life in Christ Jesus has made me free from the law of sin and death . . . for what the law could not do in that it was weak through the flesh, God did by sending His own Son in the likeness of sinful flesh, on account of sin: He condemned sin in the flesh, that the righteous requirement of the law might be fulfilled in us who do not walk according to the flesh but according to the Spirit"* (Excerpts from Romans 7 and 8).

---

[85] *CT*, Krieger, p. 30.

All the previously mentioned proclaims there is NO CONDEMNATION to them who are IN Christ Jesus who walk not after the flesh but after the Spirit. That which is holy, righteous, and good can only be fulfilled—the righteous requirements can only be fulfilled—by them who walk not after the flesh, but after the Spirit. To suggest that the keeping of the Law—the Ten Commandments—the righteous requirements of the Law—are somehow "done away with" IN Christ completely misses the point. To the contrary—one is able through the Spirit of Life in Christ—through the Law of the Spirit of Life in Christ to meet and even exceed the righteous requirements made by the Law. May I give the severest of observations—if we do not get off on the right foot on these matters of the LAW—knowing the difference between nailing the "law of commandments contained in ordinances" vs. the Ten Commandments—which Ten are embodied in the Law of Christ's love—and their practices—we will be committing the same SEPARATION ultimately espoused by Marcion in 144 AD.

THE OTHER MAN'S CONSCIENCE

Despite their opposition to lawlessness, promoters of Commonwealth Theology hold differing opinions on how, and to what extent, the Old Testament laws are to be observed. This ambiguity stems from the fact that the movement includes both Torah observant Messianic style members (such as The Way Congregation)[86] and evangelical Christian affiliates (such as One Body Life).[87] Nevertheless, these divergences are negotiated among these groups by recognizing the New Testament's dual mandate regarding keeping "the Law."[88]

On the one hand: Speaking against those who choose to observe the Law is discouraged by Jesus' directive: *"Whoever therefore breaks one of the least of these commandments, and teaches men so, shall be called least in the kingdom of heaven; but whoever does and teaches them, he shall be called great in the kingdom of heaven"* (Matthew 5:19).

---

[86] https://www.thewaycongregation.com
[87] https://www.onebody.life
[88] Hamp, Dr. Douglas. "Who really came to Destroy the Law? Is The Torah Good?" https://youtu.be/C3rG2OjG4n8

On the other hand: Romans Ch. 14 discourages judging how Christ's servants keep the Law: *"Who are you to judge another's servant?...One person esteems one day above another; another esteems every day alike. Let each be fully convinced in his own mind. He who observes the day, observes it to the Lord; and he who does not observe the day, to the Lord he does not observe it. He who eats, eats to the Lord, for he gives God thanks; and he who does not eat, to the Lord he does not eat, and gives God thanks...Do you have faith? Have it to yourself before God"* (Excerpts Rom. 14:4-22a).

Traditional (modern) Christians within CT adjudge that the Law was fulfilled in Christ—the Law of Christ—and that it is holy and undefiled. Furthermore, the Law was given as our schoolmaster to bring us to Messiah (Gal. 3:24). Something that brings one to the Messiah cannot be onerous or unsanctified. Commonwealth Theology teaches grace to those from among the nations (Gentiles) and to the Jewish brethren and affirms the followers of Messiah who are pleasing to Him who have the *"commandments of God"* but *"have the testimony of Jesus"* (Rev. 12:17); who *"sing the Song of Moses, the servant of God and the Song of the Lamb"* (Rev. 15:3).[89]

WAS THE LAW NAILED TO THE CROSS?[90]

"Having nailed it to the cross!" (Col. 2:14)

It is altogether clear that what was *"abolished in His flesh"* was the ENMITY—i.e., the hatred and animosity between the Jew and the Gentile (those of the "nations"). Once this hatred was abolished—because HE HIMSELF IS OUR PEACE—then He was and is able today to make of the TWO, ONE NEW MAN, so making peace (Eph. 2:14-15). To wit: *". . . having abolished in His flesh the ENMITY, that is, the law of commandments contained in ordinances, so as to create in Himself one new man from the two, thus making peace, and that He might reconcile them both to God in one body through the cross, thereby putting to death the ENMITY. And He came and*

---

[89] *The Denver Declaration*, Section 11 – The Synthesis of Law and Grace. https://www.commonwealthofisrael.org/p/denver.html

[90] Commonwealth Theology dot com, What Was Nailed to the Cross? By Doug Krieger, June 17, 2019, https://commonwealththeology.com/what-was-nailed-to-the-cross

preached PEACE to you who were afar off and to those who were near. For through Him (the Son) *we both have access by one Spirit* (the Holy Spirit) *to the Father* (the Father)" (Eph. 2:15-18).

Yes, this *"enmity"* constituted the *"middle wall of separation"* (Eph. 2:14)—but it has been broken down—having been abolished in His flesh—for this ENMITY constituted a barrier to fellowship and oneness and resulted in "separation." There was no reconciliation—no peace—between these two most antagonistic peoples: the Jews and the Nations.

From Whence This ENMITY?

Now, from whence comes this "enmity?" That is: *"the law of commandments contained in ordinances."* The word "ordinances" is in Greek, literally *dogma* (Strong's G#1378) and is used five times in the NT. It is an English transliteration "denoting opinion or judgment"—normally "human in source." It is translated "ordinances" in Ephesians 2:15 and "requirements" or, again "ordinances" (both being G#1378)—used in Colossians 2:14: ". . . *having wiped out the handwriting of requirements/ordinances* (Strong's G#1378) *that was against us, which was contrary to us. And He has taken it out of the way, having nailed it to the cross."*

In Colossians 2:16-23 it clearly states, both by inferences, and in antecedent, these "ordinances" are related to:

"Do you subject yourselves to regulations—Do not touch, do not taste, do not handle . . . which all concern things which perish with the using—according to the COMMANDMENTS and DOCTRINES of men? These things indeed have an appearance of wisdom in self-imposed religion, false humility, and neglect of the body, but are of NO VALUE against the indulgence of the flesh" (Excerpts Col. 2:20-23).

Indeed, what is in view in these "ordinances" are man-made "traditions of men"—even those claiming to be "taken from the Torah"—for it clearly, again, states in Colossians in this context:

"So let no one judge you in food or drink, or regarding a feast day or a new moon or sabbaths, which are a SHADOW OF THINGS TO COME but the body/substance/reality is of Christ" (Col. 2:16-17).

An example of "man-made ordinances"—as well, extracted from the Scripture (and even validated by the Scripture) is the concept of the "Sabbath Day's Journey." The International Bible Encyclopedia states regarding the "Sabbath Day's Journey":

Used only in Acts 1:12, where it designates the distance from Jerusalem to the Mount of Olives, to which Jesus led His disciples on the day of His ascension. The expression comes from rabbinical usage to indicate the distance a Jew might travel on the Sabbath without transgressing the Law, the command against working on that day being interpreted as including travel (see Exodus 16:27-30). The limit set by the rabbis to the Sabbath day's journey was 2,000 cubits from one's house or domicile, which was derived from the statement found in Joshua 3:4 that this was the distance between the ark and the people on their march, this being assumed to be the distance between the tents of the people and the tabernacle during the sojourn in the wilderness. Hence, it must have been allowable to travel thus far to attend the worship of the tabernacle. We do not know when this assumption in regard to the Sabbath day's journey was made, but it seems to have been in force in the time of Christ. The distance of the Mount of Olives from Jerusalem is stated in Josephus (Ant., XX, viii, 6) to have been five stadia or furlongs and in BJ, V, ii, 3, six stadia, the discrepancy being explained by supposing a different point of departure. This would make the distance of the Sabbath day's journey from 1,000 to 1,200 yards, the first agreeing very closely with the 2,000 cubits. The rabbis, however, invented a way of increasing this distance without technically infringing the Law, by depositing some food at the 2,000-cubit limit, before the Sabbath, and declaring that spot a temporary domicile. They might then proceed 2,000 cubits from this point without transgressing the Law. (Sabbath's Day Journey—International Bible Encyclopedia)

Indeed, the "rabbinical authorities" came up with this notion of the "Sabbath Day's Journey"—and, it does receive some credibility from its use in Acts 1:12 whereupon the disciples after viewing the ascension of Jesus to the heavens went back to the upper room in Jerusalem–a "Sabbath Day's Journey."

Just as a sidebar—I find fascinating, due to my "dimensional background" in mathematics to look at these three "distance possibilities" regarding the measurement of the cubit and the ultimate distance in British Imperial measurements (British Imperial Mile); to wit:

My favorite—1 Hebrew Sacred Cubit = 25.20 inches or 2.1 feet; therefore a SDJ is equal to 2,000 * 2.1 Feet = 4,200 feet or "42" which connotes the 3 1/2 years (42 months) of the Testimony of Jesus on the Earth and of the future 42 months in both Revelation 11 and 13 where the people of God (the "saints" or the "holy city") are persecuted/trodden under foot.

Josephus states the distance was 5 stadia or 5 furlongs—Although the stadia (Latin) is "all over the map" when it comes to distance measured; the furlong of 5 is much more accurate (See: Wikipedia on the Furlong); which "furlong" is 660 ft. or 5 X 660 ft. = 3,300 ft. I find this distance fascinating in that it connotes the "33" of Messiah's age at being "cut off" and the possible AD 33 date of His crucifixion; likewise, David reigned from Jerusalem/The City of David for 33 years (1 Kings 2:10-12) as the archetype of Messiah (See: Ezek. 37:24-25).

BJ, V, ii, 3 (Josephus' reference to the "Land Beyond the Jordan"—Rabbinical authorities say: 6 Stadia or 6 Furlongs or 6 X 660 ft. = 3960 ft. (which is a "fractal" distance between Jerusalem and Emmaus as found in Luke 24:13 or 60 Stadia or 60 Furlongs totaling 60 X 660 ft. = 39,600 ft.—approx. 7 miles); however, 6 Furlongs X 660 ft. = 3,960 ft. This "3960" comports as a "fractal/resemblance" in mathematics, to the radius of the earth in Statute Miles of 3,960 miles or 2 X 3,960 miles = 7,920 miles (the standard diameter of the earth in Statute Miles). Remember, 2 went with Jesus on the Road to Emmaus so 2 X 3960 = 7,920–appears Jesus by going through the Scriptures was preparing them for the New Jerusalem? Likewise, this "7920" is the edge of the New Jerusalem in that 12,000 furlongs (Rev. 21:16) X 660 ft. = 7,920,000 ft. (7920) or 1,500 miles.

Summary: "42" "33" or "792" are all amazing calculations revealing the "divine intent" incorporating, as it were, the "Testimony of Jesus" as Messiah/King (33) with the saints bearing witness to the Testimony of Jesus ("42") in preparation for the New Jerusalem ("792")—something astounding!

Notwithstanding the amazing calculations and their biblical applications seen in these measurements/distances, the notion that 2,000 cubits was the "legal limit" of how far an observant Jew should walk on the Sabbath–and then the compromises which ultimately attached themselves to this distance–demonstrates the *"law of commandments contained in ordinances"* or the *"commandments and doctrines of men"* which are of "NO VALUE!"

In sum: The "ordinances"—"dogma"—"traditions of men"—even those in "appearance" classified as *"self-imposed religion which deny the body* (asceticism *in nature) are of NO VALUE"*—these are the ordinances of men generating ENMITY which Paul has in view.

JESUS CAME TO FULFILL THE LAW

So: Which is it: "Fulfill or Abolish?"

God's character as viewed in the 10 Commandments is acclaimed by Paul:

"For he who loves another has fulfilled the law"—The LAW is clearly alluding to the 10 Commandments in that Paul immediately states:

"For the commandments, 'You shall not commit adultery,' 'You shall not murder,' 'You shall not steal,' 'You shall not bear false witness,' 'You shall not covet,' and if there is ANY OTHER COMMANDMENT, are all summed up in this saying, namely, 'You shall love your neighbor as yourself.' Love does no harm to a neighbor; therefore LOVE IS THE FULFILLMENT OF THE LAW" (Romans 13:8-10).

No—the 10 Commandments were NOT nailed to the tree—clearly, Jesus said: *"I have NOT come to destroy the LAW . . . but to fulfill the LAW"* (Matt. 5:17-20). LOVE IS THE FULFILLMENT OF THE LAW—*"But above all these things put on love, which is the bond of perfection. And let the peace of God rule in your hearts"* (Col. 3:14-15). This is the PEACE which breaks down that "middle wall of separation"—which enmity contained in human-made ordinances (dogma) He abolished in His flesh and made of the two—One New Man—so making peace! This is the Gospel of Peace which we are commended to preach—for in so doing, then shall we hear: "And the God of peace will crush Satan under your feet shortly" (Rom. 16:20).

Today, there is NO SEPARATION for....

". . . a renewal in which there is no distinction between Greek and Jew, circumcised and uncircumcised, barbarian, Scythian, slave and freeman, but Christ is all, and in all. So, as those who have been chosen of God, holy and beloved, put on a heart of compassion, kindness, humility, gentleness and patience;

bearing with one another, and forgiving each other, whoever has a complaint against anyone; just as the Lord forgave you, so also should you. Beyond all these things put on love, which is the perfect bond of unity. Let the peace of Christ rule in your hearts, to which indeed you were called in one body; and be thankful" (Colossians 3:11-15—New American Standard Bible or NASB).

Chapter Eleven

LAW-ABIDING GRACE

By Chris Steinle

From *The Rise of Western Lawlessness*[91]

God's Model of Authority / Submission

The Lord God of the Bible is the Governing God and the God of Government. The authority/submission relationship is the oldest and highest relationship. It predated the creation of heaven and earth. This relationship is the mechanism which enables government to function. God's authority is expressed in His names, "The Almighty," "The Lord," and "The Everlasting Father." The authority/submission relationship is acknowledged in the Trinity through the titles of the Father and the Son. God the Father holds the highest position of authority within the Godhead. The Father loves the Son, but for our sakes He sent His Son into the world, and to the cross. The Son loves, honors, and obeys the Father. Because the Godhead embodies the authority/submission dynamic, we should know that it is a good, blessed, and sacred relationship.

God's government is authoritarian and hierarchical. The Son is the Prince who will deliver the heirs of salvation unto the Father—so that God will be all-in-all. The Spirit was also sent from heaven. (The Eastern and Western churches stand divided over whether the Spirit was sent only by the Son, or by the Father and the Son.) The Spirit takes what is the Son's and declares it among men.

Before we follow the cascade of authority from heaven to earth, let's take a quick inventory of the favorable qualities of rulers and their subjects.

---

[91] *The Rise of Western Lawlessness*, C.W. Steinle, Memorial Crown Press, 2019.

Characteristics of a leader: Stable, trustworthy, good, strong, endued with resources in order to provide—hopefully generous, hopefully kind. God revealed Himself to Moses as gracious, merciful, and slow to anger, but nevertheless a God of justice.

Characteristics of a subject: Humble, loyal, obedient, in need of protection or sustenance—hopefully grateful, even joyful as the subject appreciates their protector and benefactor. (If the reader believes in God, a moment might be taken here to make an assessment of these qualities of a good subject of God's kingdom, and especially of the attitudes of gratitude and joy.)

In God's chain of command from heaven to earth we see that, *"All authority in heaven and on earth"* has been given to the Son. Jesus is the King of kings and the Lord of lords. Thus the counsel of the Second Psalm to the world's rulers:

Now therefore, be wise, O kings;
Be instructed, you judges of the earth.
Serve the Lord with fear,
And rejoice with trembling.
Kiss the Son, lest He be angry,
And you perish in the way,
When His wrath is kindled but a little.
Blessed are all those who put their trust in Him (Psalm 2:10-12).

The Governor-God, the Lord God, is the God of order. The Holy Spirit is so concerned that we "get this" that, as of March 20, 2015, *OpenBible.info*[92] listed 74 verses modeling submission to human authority. The New Testament defines man's responsibilities within God's hierarchical authority matrix in great detail. We will take a top-down approach in our review of these areas of authority. The several stunning conclusions which are presented at the close of this chapter will be enhanced by taking these Scriptures to heart, so please do not look at this review as laborious reading.

The master/slave relationship and the husband/wife relationship must be taken in the light of the common customs of biblical times. But the hierarchical principles represented by these verses have not changed. Wives need to take into consideration that the marital

---

[92] Smith, Stephen, ed. "Entry for 'Submission to Human Authority.'" OpenBible.info. OpenBible.info, 08 Apr. 2015. Web. 08 Apr. 2015.
http://www.openbible.info/topics/submission_to_human_authority.

roles of biblical times placed much more importance on the provision and protection which were part of the husband's duty. Thus the marital relationship bore more resemblance to the lordship of noblemen, who administered justice, provision, and protection for the benefit of their community. As we consider each of the authority/submission relationships below, keep in mind that we are addressing normal relationships. Just as ignoble and abusive kings have been deposed, governors, masters, husbands, mothers, elders, and church leaders can only stand under the appointment of God when they behave in a godly manner. The Bible does not recommend slavery, nor does it endorse abuse.

The citizens of nations are to honor their national leader as well as their local governors. Romans 13 provides extensive instructions for honoring civil authorities. Here are other verses specific to submitting to leaders-of-State.

Therefore I exhort first of all that supplications, prayers, intercessions, and giving of thanks be made for all men, for kings and all who are in authority, that we may lead a quiet and peaceable life in all godliness and reverence (2 Tim. 2:1-2).

Therefore submit yourselves to every ordinance of man for the Lord's sake, whether to the king as supreme, or to governors, as to those who are sent by him for the punishment of evildoers and for the praise of those who do good. For this is the will of God, that by doing good you may put to silence the ignorance of foolish men—as free, yet not using liberty as a cloak for vice, but as bondservants of God. Honor all people. Love the brotherhood. Fear God. Honor the king (1 Peter 2:13-17).

Remind them to be subject to rulers and authorities, to obey, to be ready for every good work, to speak evil of no one, to be peaceable, gentle, showing all humility to all men (Titus 3:1-2).

The New Testament instructions for the employer/employee relationship are represented by God's counsel to masters and slaves. The Bible speaks of two types of slaves. What is most often referred to as a bondservant is a person who has been bound into slavery. This might have occurred as a result of war. One of the best deterrents to war in ancient times was the knowledge that the losers could be bound to servitude as part of the peace settlement at the end of the conflict. Another way that people could become slaves was to borrow what they could not repay. This might be viewed today as the equivalent of writing a bad check.

Some verses simply make reference to servants. Servants would include any relationship which establishes a master/servant relationship. The practice of indentured service is well documented in the Old Testament. Indentured service is the closest form of servitude to employment today. This service is provided for a prescribed length of time; and is not too unlike employment under today's right-to-work agreements. Unfortunately, slavery is still practiced in the twenty-first century even though it is almost universally outlawed.

Readers should not forget that God's counsel to slaves has been directly applicable for the greater part of the last two thousand years. And there is no reason to believe that slavery will not become commonly practiced once again in the future, especially as we see the end of the age approaching. If the reader is one of those unfortunate individuals living as an "infidel" in a Muslim country, or otherwise being held against their will, he or she will have no problem understanding God's counsel. But for the free reader, know that this counsel is fully applicable to today's employer/employee relationship.

Counsel to servants and slaves:

Servants, be submissive to your masters with all fear, not only to good and gentle, but also to the harsh. For this is commendable, if because of conscience toward God one endures grief, suffering wrongfully. For what credit is it if, when you are beaten for your faults, you take it patiently? But when you do good and suffer, if you take it patiently, this is commendable before God. For to this you were called, because Christ also suffered for us, leaving us an example, that you should follow in His steps: "Who committed no sin, nor was deceit found in His mouth;" who, when He was reviled, did not revile in return; when He suffered, He did not threaten, but committed Himself to Him who judges righteously; who Himself bore our sins in His own body on the tree, that we, having died to sins, might live for righteousness—by whose stripes you were healed (1 Peter 2:18-24).

Bondservants, be obedient to those who are your masters according to the flesh, with fear and trembling, in sincerity of heart, as to Christ; not with eyeservice, as men-pleasers, but as bondservants of Christ, doing the will of God from the heart, with goodwill doing service, as to the Lord, and not to men, knowing that whatever good anyone does, he will receive the same from the Lord, whether he is a slave or free. And you, masters, do the same things to them, giving up threatening, knowing that your own Master also is in heaven, and there is no partiality with Him (Eph. 6:5-9).

Counsel to husbands and wives:

But I want you to know that the head of every man is Christ, the head of woman is man, and the head of Christ is God (1 Cor. 11:3).

Wives, submit to your own husbands, as to the Lord. For the husband is head of the wife, as also Christ is head of the church; and He is the Savior of the body. Therefore, just as the church is subject to Christ, so let the wives be to their own husbands in everything. Husbands, love your wives, just as Christ also loved the church and gave Himself for her, that He might sanctify and cleanse her with the washing of water by the word, that He might present her to Himself a glorious church, not having spot or wrinkle or any such thing, but that she should be holy and without blemish. So husbands ought to love their own wives as their own bodies; he who loves his wife loves himself. For no one ever hated his own flesh, but nourishes and cherishes it, just as the Lord does the church. For we are members of His body, of His flesh and of His bones. "For this reason a man shall leave his father and mother and be joined to his wife, and the two shall become one flesh." This is a great mystery, but I speak concerning Christ and the church. Nevertheless let each one of you in particular so love his own wife as himself, and let the wife see that she respects her husband (Eph. 5:22-33).

Wives, submit to your own husbands, as is fitting in the Lord. Husbands, love your wives and do not be bitter toward them (Col. 3:18-19).

Wives, likewise, be submissive to your own husbands, that even if some do not obey the word, they, without a word, may be won by the conduct of their wives, when they observe your chaste conduct accompanied by fear. Do not let your adornment be merely outward—arranging the hair, wearing gold, or putting on fine apparel—rather let it be the hidden person of the heart, with the incorruptible beauty of a gentle and quiet spirit, which is very precious in the sight of God. For in this manner, in former times, the holy women who trusted in God also adorned themselves, being submissive to their own husbands, as Sarah obeyed Abraham, calling him lord, whose daughters you are if you do good and are not afraid with any terror. Husbands, likewise, dwell with them with understanding, giving honor to the wife, as to the weaker vessel, and as being heirs together of the grace of life, that your prayers may not be hindered (1 Peter 3:1-7).

Counsel to elders and youths:

But as for you, speak the things which are proper for sound doctrine: that the older men be sober, reverent, temperate, sound in faith, in love, in patience; the older women likewise, that they be reverent in behavior, not slanderers, not given to much wine, teachers of good things—that they admonish the young women to love their husbands, to love their children, to be discreet, chaste, homemakers, good, obedient to their own husbands, that the word of God may not be blasphemed (Titus 2:1-5).

Likewise you younger people, submit yourselves to your elders (1 Peter 5:5a).

Counsel to parents and children:

Children, obey your parents in the Lord, for this is right. 'Honor your father and mother,' which is the first commandment with promise: 'that it may be well with you and you may live long on the earth.' And you, fathers, do not provoke your children to wrath, but bring them up in the training and admonition of the Lord (Eph. 6:1-4).

Children, obey your parents in all things, for this is well pleasing to the Lord. Fathers, do not provoke your children, lest they become discouraged (Col. 3:20-21).

Counsel to overseers and their flock:

And we urge you, brethren, to recognize those who labor among you, and are over you in the Lord and admonish you, and to esteem them very highly in love for their work's sake (1 Thess. 5:12-13a).

Obey those who rule over you, and be submissive, for they watch out for your souls, as those who must give account. Let them do so with joy and not with grief, for that would be unprofitable for you (Heb. 13:17).

The elders who are among you I exhort, I who am a fellow elder and a witness of the sufferings of Christ, and also a partaker of the glory that will be revealed: Shepherd the flock of God which is among you, serving as overseers, not by compulsion but willingly, not for dishonest gain but eagerly; nor as being lords over those entrusted to you, but being examples to the flock; and when the Chief Shepherd appears, you will receive the crown of glory that does not fade away (1 Peter 5:1-5).

General counsel:

Do not rebuke an older man, but exhort him as a father, younger men as brothers, older women as mothers, younger women as sisters, with all purity (1 Tim. 5:1-2).

Submitting to one another in the fear of God (Eph. 5:21).

Yes, all of you be submissive to one another, and be clothed with humility, for 'God resists the proud, but gives grace to the humble.' Therefore humble yourselves under the mighty hand of God, that He may exalt you in due time, casting all your care upon Him, for He cares for you (1 Peter 5:5b-7).

Peter's counsel to wives not to be afraid, and again in this last verse, to cast our cares upon God, are both given in the context of being submissive. Both of these verses address the vulnerability which is part of trusting God's system of authority and submission. God knows the concerns we face in trusting His system. The exaltation that comes in due time is the reward for submitting to God, *and* to one-to-another. Why is humility and submission to the authorities which God has placed over us so important to God?

Because honest humility in the heart is proven by outward obedience which pleases the one in authority. Humility and submission are the inward and outward expressions of love to a superior.

Without obedience, no other expression of love towards one in authority can be received as genuine. Obedience is the "love language" of kings. When someone under the authority of another expresses arrogance, disrespect, or disobedience, it is perceived as rebellion against that authority figure. Insubordination strains the relationship and no other expression of love will be received until the proper respect is reestablished by compliance. This principle holds true with every hierarchical relationship, be it the home, the workplace, or the courthouse. To disobey a king would be to deny his authority as king. This is why Jesus said, *"If you love Me, keep My commandments"* (John 14:15).

Just as the marriage relationship models the union of Christ with His Church, every authority/submission relationship models Christ's kingdom authority, and recognizes the divine hierarchy within the Godhead. Disobedience is sin. The failure to recognize the authority of God is lawlessness. The manifestations of the rejection of God and His laws can be seen in today's lawless society by its haughty individualism, disrespect for authority, disorderly conduct, and a satanic hatred toward the name of King Jesus.

"Now by this we know that we know Him, if we keep His commandments. He who says, 'I know Him,' and does not keep His commandments, is a liar, and the truth is not in him" (1 John 2:3-4). Here, John once again confronts those who only possess a philosophical knowledge of God. Whether one is a good Platonist or a bad Gnostic, a philosophical understanding of God cannot replace an actual encounter with the living God. We have no record that the Neo-Platonist, Plotinus, fell on his face during his four episodes of "oneness" with his Immovable Mover—the "First Principle." Neither were Socrates, Plato, or Aristotle struck to the ground and breathless before their "Forms" of: Beauty, Goodness, and Justice. (See source text for context here.) In fact, even a thorough knowledge of the true God's attributes does not constitute an audience before God Himself.

But we can actually know God personally through the Holy Spirit, who was dispatched from heaven after Jesus ascended. Because believers have been reconciled to God through the propitiation of Christ, Christians can not only comprehend God, they can actually experience His presence and power. Still we cannot, at this time, behold Him face to face because, as Paul says, He dwells *"in unapproachable light, whom no man has seen or can see..."* (1 Tim. 6:16). While we are in these mortal bodies we can only behold Him dimly, as in a primitive looking glass. Nevertheless, the Holy Spirit's power to convict us of sin is sufficient to impart the fear of the Lord. And, *"the fear of the Lord is the beginning of knowledge"* (Prov. 1:7).

This is the true knowledge of God which writes God's commandments in the hearts and minds of men, and gives them the Spirit to obey them. Knowing the authority of God first-hand produces a submissive heart, a heart willing to make itself vulnerable; or as Jeremiah expressed it, a heart of flesh in the place of a heart of stone. Submission and obedience testify to a genuine fear of the Lord which can only come from knowing God personally. Again: *"He who says, 'I know Him,' and does not keep His commandments, is a liar, and the truth is not in him"* (1 John 2:4).

It is easy to see now why a culture determined to break all of God's laws would also be determined to bring God's principle of authority and submission into ill repute. Is it any wonder that families cannot function, and citizens rise up against the very law enforcement officials who are trying to protect them? Politicians no longer know how to rule, and the people don't know how to obey; in fact, they don't even know why they should obey. Without the reflexive relationship of authority and submission there can be only lawlessness.

Now that mankind is centuries away from the Renaissance and the Enlightenment, world rulers are awakening to the fact that fallen man possesses no innate compulsion to submit and obey. The same individualism released during the Age of Reason wars against every form of authority. In the absence of the fear of God, only the fear of man can bring order to an ungodly world. Brute force will undergird mankind's final attempt at civilization, preparing the way for the armies of the earth to oppose Christ Himself at His second coming.

Reconciling Law and Grace

Lawlessness is next to godlessness. To deny the Law of God is to deny the God of the law. The Bible plainly and repeatedly points out that the ungodly do not like to think about God. Paul says in Romans, they don't *"like to retain God in their knowledge."* In Psalm 9:17 it speaks of nations that forget God; *"The wicked shall be turned into Hell, and all the nations that forget God,"* and Psalm 119 says of those *"who follow after wickedness; They are far from Your law."*

Drifting away from God's government (God's law) is equivalent to falling away from God. How can the citizens of the United States appreciate laws in general when the civil judges have lost respect for the constitutional laws of the land? Society at large is blind to the fact that falling away from the God of laws will inevitably lead the soul into confusion, and the state into chaos. The message of grace in many of today's Western churches conveys that it is possible to leave the Law behind without falling away from God. Seeker-friendly churches are adapting to the lawless Western lifestyle by implying that the Law has been replaced by grace. Whereas, in truth, grace reveals God's purpose in giving the laws.

In his letters to the Romans and the Galatians, Paul instructed those churches concerning the functional roles of law and grace. Peter described the freedom that we have in Christ, but also warned Christians not to misuse their freedom. Why were law and grace given separately? Can law and grace be reconciled by human logic? In order to answer these questions it is helpful to examine the circumstances under which the laws of God were given, and the timing of God's provision of grace afforded by Christ.

To recognize why the Law and grace had to be given separately we must return once again to Mount Sinai. First we will recount the actual event from the Book of Exodus. Then we will glean from Moses' reflection on that event recorded in Deuteronomy. The Deuteronomy passage explains clearly why the Law had to be given in advance of God's grace.

> *Then the Lord said to Moses, "Go to the people and consecrate them today and tomorrow, and let them wash their clothes. And let them be ready for the third day. For*

on the third day the Lord will come down upon Mount Sinai in the sight of all the people. You shall set bounds for the people all around, saying, 'Take heed to yourselves that you do not go up to the mountain or touch its base. Whoever touches the mountain shall surely be put to death. Not a hand shall touch him, but he shall surely be stoned or shot with an arrow; whether man or beast, he shall not live. When the trumpet sounds long, they shall come near the mountain.' So Moses went down from the mountain to the people and sanctified the people, and they washed their clothes. And he said to the people, "Be ready for the third day; do not come near your wives."

Then it came to pass on the third day, in the morning, that there were thunderings and lightnings, and a thick cloud on the mountain; and the sound of the trumpet was very loud, so that all the people who were in the camp trembled. And Moses brought the people out of the camp to meet with God, and they stood at the foot of the mountain. Now Mount Sinai was completely in smoke, because the Lord descended upon it in fire. Its smoke ascended like the smoke of a furnace, and the whole mountain quaked greatly. And when the blast of the trumpet sounded long and became louder and louder, Moses spoke, and God answered him by voice. Then the Lord came down upon Mount Sinai, on the top of the mountain. And the Lord called Moses to the top of the mountain, and Moses went up (Exod. 19:10-20).

Now all the people witnessed the thunderings, the lightning flashes, the sound of the trumpet, and the mountain smoking; and when the people saw it, they trembled and stood afar off. Then they said to Moses, "You speak with us, and we will hear; but let not God speak with us, lest we die." And Moses said to the people, "Do not fear; for God has come to test you, and that His fear may be before you, so that you may not sin." So the people stood afar off, but Moses drew near the thick darkness where God was. Then the Lord said to Moses, "Thus you shall say to the children of Israel: 'You have seen that I have talked with you from heaven. . .'" (Exod. 20:18-22).

This passage demonstrates that the fear of the Lord comes directly as a result of experiencing the presence of God. Furthermore, it is this awe of the living God which motivates people to obey Him; *that His fear may be before you, so that you may not sin.* The presence of the Lord is overwhelming to humanity in its weak and fallen state. In every instance of God's revelation of Himself, God had to make a provision so that men would be able to withstand the awesomeness of His presence. God hid Moses in the cleft of the rock. For the priests in the tabernacle, it was the blood of propitiation. Isaiah's lips were touched by a purifying ember. The Spirit had to raise Ezekiel to his feet. Thus, a provision would have to be made so that the common people of Israel might be blessed rather than terrified by God's presence.

> *The Lord your God will raise up for you a Prophet like me from your midst, from your brethren. Him you shall hear, according to all you desired of the Lord your God in Horeb in the day of the assembly, saying, "Let me not hear again the voice of the Lord my God, nor let me see this great fire anymore, lest I die." And the Lord said to me: "What they have spoken is good. I will raise up for them a Prophet like you from among their brethren, and will put My words in His mouth, and He shall speak to them all that I command Him. And it shall be that whoever will not hear My words, which He speaks in My name, I will require it of him"* (Deut. 18:15-19).

Risto Santala pointed out that the writings of the Rabbis acknowledged that a second Prophet like Moses would come:

The Midrash literature on Moses speaks of the 'First' and the 'Last' Saviours. Midrash Rabbah on Ecclesiastes relates how R. Berechiah said in the name of R. Yits-hak, who lived before the year 300 AD, that:

Just as there was a First Saviour so there will be a Last. Just as it is said of the First Saviour (Ex. 4:20) that 'He took his wife and sons and put them on a donkey', so it is said of the Last Saviour that 'He is lowly and riding on a donkey' (Zech. 9:9). As the First Saviour provided manna (Ex. 16), as it is written, 'Behold I will pour out bread from heaven upon you,' so will the Last Saviour, as it is written (Ps. 72:16), 'Let corn abound throughout the land'. Just as the First

Saviour opened a fountain, so the Last Saviour will water, as it is written (Joel 3:18), 'A fountain will flow the LORD'S house'. - Midrash Qoheleth Rabbati 1.

We have seen that in the light of the old Jewish literature the Messiah is to be a "Second Moses" and the "Last Saviour"; he will be called by the name "Lord"; grace and truth will be united in him; he will be conceived by the Holy Spirit; he will speak and act in the name of God, and that will be his distinguishing "sign"; in this way he will show himself to be Moses "redivivus." All of these features apply to Jesus.[93]

God knew ahead of time how the people would react to His presence on the Mountain. He wanted them to have a "dose" of His presence so they would know their God personally, instead of merely knowing about Him. The Children of Israel already had an indirect knowledge of God's existence based on His miracles. However, no amount of data gathered *about* God can replace an actual encounter *with* God. In man's fallen state, the presence of God is outside of man's comfort zone. The sinner's first inclination when experiencing the presence of God is to run and hide from Him, just like Adam did in the Garden after his sin.

Therefore, God gave His law as a means of provisional government until that time when Messiah would come and make peace by the blood of His cross. The mediator of the New Covenant brought peace, grace, and the outpouring of the Spirit. *"For the law was given through Moses, but grace and truth came through Jesus Christ"* (John 1:17). Because of the peace and forgiveness purchased by the blood of Jesus, Christians can actually experience the presence of God because they have entered into peace with God. Note that Jesus' first word to His Disciples after His resurrection was, "Peace." Because of this peace received through faith in the redemptive work of the cross, Christians actually long to be present with God, and they eagerly await Christ's bodily return. For everyone who repents and believes, the sin that separated fallen man from His Maker has been washed away by the blood of the Lamb.

---

[93] Santala, Dr. Risto. Interesting Books by Risto Santala on the internet. Dr theol. h.c. Risto Santala, n.d. Web. 30 Mar. 2015.
http://www.ristosantala.com/

Now consider a simple analogy representing the harmony between law and grace. The Law embodies the rules of God, and grace imparts the life, peace, and the presence of God. Imagine that a parent has built a small outdoor park for his children. At some time in the future he will to able to spend time with them in the park. But in lieu of his physical presence he posts instructive signs giving directions on the best and safest ways to enjoy each of the swings and slides and so forth.

Occasionally the kids don't follow the instructions and they get hurt. Or they try to do something in a different way, like swing from side to side; which the swings weren't designed to do. They are usually sorry and go back to following the instructions. After a while some neighborhood children come by and say that the signs are dumb, and that they were only posted to keep them from having more fun by doing things their own way. The signs bother them. Just having the signs there spoils everything for the neighbors who don't trust the father's advice, and would rather be free to experiment.

At a later time the father comes to spend time with his children. He interacts with each one, and tends each one to see that they are having fun, while avoiding anything hazardous. While he is present the kids don't really need the signs. They would rather enjoy the time with their dad and appreciate his personal attention and advice. Because he is there to help them he even allows them to do some special things that would have been too complicated to explain with a sign. By spending time with their father they begin to understand why each sign was posted. The father leaves the signs up so that if people should come by who don't know the father, and don't know how to play, they would still be informed of how to use the park facilities.

This analogy has its limitations. In reality, God always sees what is happening. God has never gone away. But still God's presence was mostly concealed except for His miracles and answers to prayer. Men were like sheep without a shepherd; like orphans until Jesus sent the Spirit to remain, even to the end of the age. Under grace God's people can be directed daily by God Himself. As long as Christians fear the Lord and walk in His Spirit, they do not require the Law. However, when Christians forget God and walk in their fleshly ability to observe the Law, they are prone to transgression just like those who don't know God. This is why

Paul wrote in Romans 8:1: *"There is therefore now no condemnation to those who are in Christ Jesus, who do not walk according to the flesh, but according to the Spirit."* But they still need to know the Law—what God expects.

Again, to go beyond the analogy above, the Spirit received by those who believe in Jesus is the very life of God—eternal life. But to enjoy the presence of God, Christians must continue in their faith. We will deal with the issue of faltering as a Christian near the end of this chapter. At this point let us deal with a few common questions regarding law and grace. First we must recognize the fact that the differences between the Jerusalem Church of Jewish believers and the Gentile churches were never settled during the time of the Apostles—that is, in particular, the degree to which each body stressed full Torah observance. Because no resolute answer is given in the New Testament, this dispute can only be argued using extra-biblical assumptions. Such assumptions were indeed manufactured in later centuries. The author is of the opinion—and Commonwealth Theology encourages loving fellowship among those adhering to the spectrum of opinions on this matter—that both the Messianic style worship/Torah observance, and the post-apostolic style worship/Semi-Torah observance, are both valid according to personal conviction.

That said, the Council at Jerusalem reduced the Old Testament laws to a minimum for the Gentile believer. Some would argue this was merely to give the Gentile an initial exposure to the Law with the hopes they would submit to the teachings of Moses they would eventually hear in the Synagogue. But wouldn't that amount to the same weak appeal by "seeker-friendly" churches today, that draw people in and then have difficulty confronting their members with a more demanding gospel?

As has already been noted, the Council didn't want to burden the Gentiles coming to Christ with a heavy yoke. But, at least, a secondary motivation might have stemmed from comments made about diet by Jesus, and later expounded by Paul. Jesus said what goes into the body cannot defile a man. Concerning Paul's comments about unclean food received with thanks, the issue of what he meant by "food" becomes the issue. Non-observant (Roman, Western) Christians often assert that some dietary laws were given to set the Jews apart from the other nations. Also, that without refrigeration, many of the unclean animals had a history of causing problems. They would say that washing procedures and special types of containers would have also made sense based on hygienics: and even though the microscope would not reveal the reason until thousands of years after the Law, God knew that proper food handling and preparation would protect the people from diseases that might be spread into the Hebrew community. Therefore, God's rules on cleanliness would have helped keep the Israelites free from the diseases of the surrounding nations—as promised.

Then there's the matter of Paul's rebuke to Peter at Antioch: *"If you, being a Jew, live in the manner of Gentiles and not as the Jews, why do you compel Gentiles to live as Jews?"* In what way(s) was Peter living like a Gentile? He must have been doing something non-Jewish; was he referring only to the Jewish customs—the traditions of men? We simply don't know. But then Paul declares: *"For if I build again those things which I destroyed, I make myself a transgressor"* (Gal. 2:14,18). What exactly was destroyed? Again, we don't know. But like these verses, there are several more passages in the New Testament that give rise to questions about the degree of Torah observance practiced—or expected—by believers from the non-Jewish Nations.

The observance of holy days seemed to be addressed by Paul in his letters to the Romans and the Corinthians. But the Early Church appears to have made a point of putting the new wine of the New Covenant into new wineskins. The earliest records we have of Gentile weekly services calls for them to be held on the first day of the week—the weekday of the resurrection.[94] (Some suggest the Didache was written much later, under Roman Catholic influence.) Without controversy, we should remember the Sabbath day and keep it holy. Therefore, many in the Commonwealth of Israel community "double dip" by "remembering" and resting on Saturday, and then participating in Sunday worship—and; No, we're not worshiping the sun.

But the Western churches, particularly Rome, insisted that the yearly celebration of "Easter" be held on a different day than the

---

[94] The Didache or Teaching of the Apostles, APOSTOLIC FATHERS (trans. and ed., J. B. Lightfoot).
http://www.earlychristianwritings.com/text/didache-lightfoot.html

Jewish Passover. (The Introduction discussed the Empire's disdain for all things Jewish.) Rome even went so far as to excommunicate the "Revelation Churches" of Asia because they insisted on celebrating on the day of the "Jewish" Passover.

However, the Ten Commandments and the laws of sexual purity were not in any way expunged by the New Covenant. In fact, they were made even more strict by Jesus in His Sermon on the Mount, condemning even intentional meditation toward these sins. If we go back to the park analogy, those signs (regarding the Ten Commandments and sexual behavior) weren't taken down; they were repainted in the New Testament in **bold letters!**

If the reader has been taught to believe in a Lord who has come to take away His own law, they have not known the true Christ (Eph. 4:20). The Law is not alive, and it has no life to give. The Bible says that if someone were able to keep the whole law—even in their heart—they would not be condemned to death. But everyone, other than Jesus, has been born with a wayward and deceitful heart so that, under the Law, all men are disqualified. The Law cannot save, and, in this respect, we are not under the Law because we are saved by grace. But in our conduct, we *cannot* say that we are not under the Law. Whether we are under the Law or under grace, if we transgress the will of God we have sinned.

Risto Santala,[95] a scholar of ancient Jewish writings, provides us with a somewhat "International Lutheran" take on the Law under the New Covenant.

> Paul, who tells us that he was a member of the strictest sect of the Pharisees, saw this danger. He wrote; *"But now, by dying to what once bound us, we have been released from the law so that we serve in the new way of the Spirit, and not in the old way of the written code"* Romans 7:6. Originally God justified Abraham on the grounds of his faith. Legal

---

[95] Risto Santala is a well-known Finnish author in the field of Judaism and rabbinical literature. He studied theology at the University of Helsinki and was ordained as a minister in the Evangelical Lutheran Church of Finland in 1953. He first worked as a youth pastor in Helsinki and then in the Scandinavian Sailor's Church in Haifa, Israel. In 1957 he became a teacher and pastor in the Hebrew boarding school of the Finnish Evangelical Lutheran Mission, Shalhevet Yah, in Jerusalem. http://www.kirjasilta.net/santala/index.en.html

ordinances given some 430 years later to Moses cannot annul this "covenant previously established by God" (Gal. 3:16-19). To this day, Christ as the Messiah still has the answer to the Jewish Torah problem.

The "hedge" around the Law with its traditions and ordinances of men has now been torn down. The Ten Commandments are of course still valid as the irrevocable "words of the Covenant." The Christian's protective "hedge" is Christ himself, and so Paul in his letters uses over 160 times the phrase "to be in Christ." If we stray out of Christ, the "dogs of the Law," to use Luther's words will tear us to pieces. In this way the Law serves the gospel. Here lay the background and logic of Paul's Torah teaching.[96]

God gave us both the Law and grace. Therefore both are good and beneficial. Jesus countered the accusation that He had come to abolish the Law by responding, *"Do not think that I came to destroy the Law or the Prophets. I did not come to destroy but to fulfill. For assuredly, I say to you, till heaven and earth pass away, one jot or one tittle will by no means pass from the law till all is fulfilled"* (Matt. 5:17-18).

The Law was given for the necessary purpose of maintaining order in the midst of a fallen world. *"But we know that the law is good if one uses it lawfully, knowing this: that the law is not made for a righteous person, but for the lawless and insubordinate, for the ungodly and for sinners, for the unholy and profane, for murderers of fathers and murderers of mothers, for manslayers, for fornicators, for sodomites, for kidnappers, for liars, for perjurers, and if there is any other thing that is contrary to sound doctrine, according to the glorious gospel of the blessed God which was committed to my trust"* (1 Tim. 1:8-11).

---

[96] Santala, Dr. Risto. Interesting Books by Risto Santala on the internet. Dr theol. h.c. Risto Santala, n.d. Web. 30 Mar. 2015.
http://www.ristosantala.com

CH. 11: LAW-ABIDING GRACE

The Law also confronts imperfect man with a perfect standard which exposes his inner defect of sin. We are convicted by our inability to live up to God's standard, leaving us with an unsolvable dilemma: How can mortal man withstand the judgment of a holy God? The Apostle Paul said it is this very predicament which directs us to grace as the only solution.

> *Now we know that whatever the law says, it says to those who are under the law, that every mouth may be stopped, and all the world may become guilty before God. Therefore by the deeds of the law no flesh will be justified in His sight, for by the law is the knowledge of sin* (Rom. 3:19-20).

In Galatians 3:21-25, Paul explained that law and grace are not in opposition to one another. *"Is the law then against the promises of God? Certainly not! For if there had been a law given which could have given life, truly righteousness would have been by the law. But the Scripture has confined all under sin, that the promise by faith in Jesus Christ might be given to those who believe. But before faith came, we were kept under guard by the law, kept for the faith which would afterward be revealed. Therefore the law was our tutor to bring us to Christ, that we might be justified by faith. But after faith has come, we are no longer under a tutor."*

The corruption of sin has stained every man with the defect of inner corruption; a stain which can only be removed by living a perfect life in obedience to every law of God—a life that no one but Jesus has lived. But God has made a way that the stain might be removed through the sacrifice of His Son on the cross.

> *"Come now, and let us reason together," Says the Lord,*
> *"Though your sins are like scarlet,*
> *They shall be as white as snow;*
> *Though they are red like crimson,*
> *They shall be as wool"* (Isaiah 1:18).

Even though this divine salvation from sin is supernatural, it is not beyond human comprehension. There is a place for logic and human reasoning in the Christian faith. *"For this commandment which I command you today is not too mysterious for you, nor is it far off. It is not in heaven, that you should say, 'Who will ascend into heaven for us and bring it to us, that we may hear it and do it?' Nor is it beyond the sea, that you should say, 'Who will go over the sea for us and bring it to us, that we may hear it and do it?' But the word is very near you, in your mouth and in your heart, that you may do it"* (Deut. 30:11-14).

So how might we understand the mechanics of salvation? Some have used the acronym for grace: God's Riches At Christ's Expense. Others have called it "The Great Exchange," as described in II Cor. 5:21, *"For He made Him who knew no sin to be sin for us, that we might become the righteousness of God in Him."* This gift of grace bestowed upon those who believe in Christ is the complete forgiveness of sins and the appropriation of God's righteousness. It is the righteousness of God imparted as a gift upon those who are incapable of righteousness on their own. It cannot be earned. It can only be accepted. It is not based on personal merit. It's based on the perfect sacrifice which Jesus offered for us on the cross.

> *For we ourselves were also once foolish, disobedient, deceived, serving various lusts and pleasures, living in malice and envy, hateful and hating one another. But when the kindness and the love of God our Savior toward man appeared, not by works of righteousness which we have done, but according to His mercy He saved us, through the washing of regeneration and renewing of the Holy Spirit, whom He poured out on us abundantly through Jesus Christ our Savior, that having been justified by His grace we should become heirs according to the hope of eternal life* (Titus 3:3-7).

Why does John say that truth came through Jesus? Jesus often began His statements; *"Truly, truly, I say to you. . ."* Jesus spoke with authority from the full knowledge of the Godhead. And Jesus is the true and only way to be reconciled to the Father. Jesus said, *"I am the way, the truth, and the life. No one comes to the Father except through Me"* (John 14:6).

The life of God—eternal life—is honest life. It is a holistic and wholesome life that is complete in Christ. It is true life that sets men free to be who they were created to be. How broken is man in his fallen state! How he is held back by his insecurity, by his circumstances, by mistakes and misfortunes. All the while, he attempts to hide his inner dissatisfaction as he searches within and without for his own identity, only to be more and more disenchanted with the imperfection of his fallen state.

CH. 11: LAW-ABIDING GRACE

Jesus came to give us life, abundant life, true life as life was meant to be—free from the problems of guilt, of sin, and even from the fear of death. The New Covenant is the covenant of grace and truth. It has been said that this gospel is so simple that it might be stated in four words: "Christ died for me."

> *Not with the blood of goats and calves, but with His own blood He entered the Most Holy Place once for all, having obtained eternal redemption. For if the blood of bulls and goats and the ashes of a heifer, sprinkling the unclean, sanctifies for the purifying of the flesh, how much more shall the blood of Christ, who through the eternal Spirit offered Himself without spot to God, cleanse your conscience from dead works to serve the living God? And for this reason He is the Mediator of the new covenant, by means of death, for the redemption of the transgressions under the first covenant, that those who are called may receive the promise of the eternal inheritance* (Heb. 9:12-15).

If Christ did all of the work, is there anything left for us to do? Yes. Believe it! How can you indicate that you understand that the only way to obtain righteousness is through Christ, and that you are placing your faith in Him? Confess what you believe to God and to others.

> *For Moses writes about the righteousness which is of the law, "The man who does those things shall live by them." But the righteousness of faith speaks in this way, "Do not say in your heart, 'Who will ascend into heaven'* (that is, to bring Christ down from above) *or, 'Who will descend into the abyss?'* (that is, to bring Christ up from the dead). *But what does it say? "The word is near you, in your mouth and in your heart"* (that is, the word of faith which we preach): *that if you confess with your mouth the Lord Jesus and believe in your heart that God has raised Him from the dead, you will be saved. For with the heart one believes unto righteousness, and with the mouth confession is made unto salvation. For the Scripture says, "Whoever believes on Him will not be put to shame"* (Rom. 10:5-11).

And Jesus came and spoke to them, saying, "All authority has been given to Me in heaven and on earth. Go therefore and make disciples of all the nations, baptizing them in the name of the Father and of the Son and of the Holy Spirit, teaching them to observe all things that I have commanded you; and lo, I am with you always, even to the end of the age." Amen (Matt. 28:18-20).

These verses, known as the Great Commission, instructed the Disciples to baptize and teach their converts. In obedience to this directive, a believer should submit to water baptism as soon as possible after placing faith in Christ. Water baptism signifies fellowship in Christ's death, burial, and resurrection. Being immersed in water testifies of one's own death to self and sin. Submersion in water signifies Christ's burial and the cleansing of sin by Christ's blood. Rising up out of the water is a picture of Christ's resurrection, and the believer's new life in Christ.

It is the author's opinion that God will bless the new believer's act of baptism administered by any true Christian—whether they incorporate sprinkling or dunking. In an emergency, someone might even baptize themselves. Faith, and the baptism by the fire of the convicting Holy Spirit, are the works of God unto salvation. Church leaders have resolved to carry out Christ's work in various forms, and through various denominations, but they are only human. They are sincerely trying to follow God's will. And God will honor their interpretation of His will, as long as it conforms to His Word.

Now let us return from this evangelistic interlude to our discussion of law and grace. Where did Western Christians get the idea that grace has replaced the Law in regard to conduct? Just as Jesus said of Himself, "grace" didn't come to take away the Law, but to fulfill the Law. **The only time Christians need not heed the Law, is when they are walking so close to God in the Spirit that the fear of God keeps them *within* the Law—without the aid of the written law and its penalties**. That is the only time when they are not under the Law because they *are* under grace. They are free from the Law because the presence of God guides them and persuades them to keep the laws, thus writing God's law within their hearts and minds.

For the law of the Spirit of life in Christ Jesus has made me free from the law of sin and death. For what the law could not do in that it was weak through the flesh, God did by sending His own Son in the likeness of sinful flesh, on account of sin: He condemned sin in the flesh, that the righteous requirement of the law might be fulfilled in us who do not walk according to the flesh but according to the Spirit. For those who live according to the flesh set their minds on the things of the flesh, but those who live according to the Spirit, the things of the Spirit. For to be carnally minded is death, but to be spiritually minded is life and peace. Because the carnal mind is enmity against God; for it is not subject to the law of God, nor indeed can be. So then, those who are in the flesh cannot please God (Rom. 8:2-8).

When Christians are not walking in the Spirit of grace they cannot disregard the tutor of the Law. The Law will keep them from getting too beat up, until such time when they become so hungry for the life of the Spirit that they repent and return to the presence of God. Christians don't lose their salvation every time they wander from God. As is pointed out in First John, if anyone does their best to walk in the light—even though they may sin—they are cleansed by Christ's blood, who also is their advocate. But if they continue in sin and stray from God's fellowship, what fruit will they bear to testify of their faith? What treasure will they store up in heaven? Too much time in the dark can cause Christians to doubt if they were ever really saved, as Peter taught: *"But also for this very reason, giving all diligence, add to your faith virtue, to virtue knowledge, to knowledge self-control, to self-control perseverance, to perseverance godliness, to godliness brotherly kindness, and to brotherly kindness love. For if these things are yours and abound, you will be neither barren nor unfruitful in the knowledge of our Lord Jesus Christ. For he who lacks these things is shortsighted, even to blindness,* **and has forgotten that he was cleansed from his old sins**" (2 Peter 1:5-9 Emphasis added).

Sadly, the willingness of Western Christians to disregard God's law shows that they have either not known His presence, or else they have forgotten what it was like to fear the Lord. Instead of trying to conform to the world, they need to come to the cross and repent. Christ is ready to forgive, to cleanse, and to fill those who believe He is the Lord with His Holy Spirit. Then they will receive the love of God, and also know the holiness and majesty of His presence. Without the fear of the Lord the nominal Church cannot even claim it has received saving grace, and it will never keep the Law. If the Church has become lawless, how will the world come to respect the Law? Without the Law to act as a tutor, what standard will draw the lost to Christ?

Now we will proceed to the touchiest and most politically incorrect issue of the Mosaic Laws: the punishments proscribed for breaking those laws. *"For the wages of sin is death"* (Rom. 6:23a). Is this true? The Christian who understands the importance of staying close to the Shepherd should be willing to pray: "Lord, do whatever it takes to give me victory over that sin which spoils my fellowship with You." Because sin cuts man off from the life of God, Jesus said in His Sermon on the Mount that it is better that a man should cut off part of his own body—if that member separates him from eternal life. We don't see voluntary dismemberment modeled in New Testament writings, nor by the Early Church. (Apart from Origin.)[97]

Voluntary dismemberment and self-flagellation are no more acceptable to God than suicide. The Mosaic laws say it is wrong to cut one's own flesh, as was the custom of the prophets of Baal. But sin should appear so deadly—to those who understand the holiness of God—that they should be willing to do whatever it takes to gain victory over anything that opposes God's will.

> *You have heard that it was said to those of old, 'You shall not commit adultery.' But I say to you that whoever looks at a woman to lust for her has already committed adultery with her in his heart. If your right eye causes you to sin, pluck it out and cast it from you; for it is more profitable for you that one of your members perish, than for your whole body to be cast into Hell. And if your right hand causes you to sin, cut it off and cast it from you; for it is more profitable for you that one of your members perish, than for your whole body to be cast into Hell* (Matt. 5:27-30).

---

[97] Origin was suspected of taking Paul's advice to the Galatian Judaizers.

Physical death and dismemberment cannot separate the soul from God. *"For I am persuaded that neither death nor life, nor angels nor principalities nor powers, nor things present nor things to come, nor height nor depth, nor any other created thing, shall be able to separate us from the love of God which is in Christ Jesus our Lord"* (Rom. 8:38-39). But sin can, and does, separate us from God.

Behold, the Lord's hand is not shortened,
That it cannot save;
Nor His ear heavy,
That it cannot hear.
But your iniquities have separated you from your God;
And your sins have hidden His face from you,
So that He will not hear (Isa. 59:1-2).

Now, if Christians actually possess such a desire to have victory over sin that they would be willing to suffer discomfort at the hands of God in order to be sanctified and to have fellowship restored, why would they object to punishment at the hands of the civil authority to correct and punish those same sins?

Indeed, we see that the early Christian settlements in America actually desired, and created, civil laws fashioned after the Ten Commandments. Likewise, those standards were adopted at the state and federal level by the founding Fathers of the United States. For nearly 2,000 years the Church has recognized the grace of the New Covenant; and, at the same time, desired to have civil authority modeled after the laws of God. Why, suddenly, in the mid-twentieth century, did Western culture begin to object to these laws, which seemed intuitive, good, and just throughout the previous generations?

Once again the answer lies in the exaltation of self and the desire of mankind to erect its own kingdom with its own laws. Westerners have been indoctrinated by socialists to believe that centralized power is evil. They say authoritarian government will lead to social injustice, and create an inequitable "class struggle." The social engineers hold up the vision of a social order without laws and without authority—a headless body-of-state. But it will never be. Self-government is an oxymoron. It is contrary to the divine model of the Godhead. It is lawlessness. The idea that law somehow conflicts with the Kingdom of God is a lie from the pit of Hell.

But there is also a theological culprit. Just as Replacement Theology (we'll say inadvertently) supported the conclusion that the Jews had become God's enemy—thus the enemy of the Church; so, the theology of Dispensationalism, by shuffling the Law off to another dispensation, aroused the individualistic and antinomian tendencies of the flesh to ignite among its unsuspecting adherents the notion that grace had nothing WHATSOEVER to do with God's authoritarian lordship.

Concerning the Nominal Church: A lack of faith in God and His power has led to a fear that unless man is in control, God might not be able to protect His children. This lack of confidence in God to govern His people through the civil authority might be expected from the ungodly. But the Church Patriotic has jumped aboard the socialist bandwagon right along with the world.

The take-away for the Church in this discussion of law and grace is that the New Testament amplifies God's government rather than diminishing it. The New Testament declares that the Lord has come. The gospel does not hide God's system of justice, it further reveals it. *"For in it the righteousness of God is revealed from faith to faith; as it is written, 'The just shall live by faith'. For the wrath of God is revealed from heaven against all ungodliness and unrighteousness of men"* (Rom. 1:17-18a).

No matter how wayward the world and contemporary Church culture might be, when a person is reborn of the Spirit into the Body of Christ, the Holy Spirit is still able to convict the heart of sin, and to instill a proper fear of the Lord. But without proper exampling and discipleship, these new believers will be apt to be carried away by a culture obsessed with liberty and independence.

The world has no freedom to offer which can compare to the freedom found in Christ. There is nothing more fulfilling than knowing God. The fallen sin-self looks for freedom from all outside authority, but the soul set free by Christ is freed from its myopic mindset and soars in the vastness of the knowledge of God. With the sin issue settled, the soul has nothing left to hide. In the light of God's glory there remains no false sense of self-worthiness to defend. Furthermore, the Christian is commissioned by God to accomplish His work by the power and gifting of the Holy Spirit, laying up eternal treasure in heaven. But this purpose-filled life is only found by submitting to the King of glory.

CH. 11: LAW-ABIDING GRACE

Let us go back to the time of the European Renaissance to observe God's remnant Church of God-fearing, self-denying believers. At the same time that individualism and humanism were rising in response to Rome's errors, another movement was born in the Rhineland to carry the flame of true Christianity. The fire from this camp, along with courage of Wycliffe, would kindle what would become the Protestant Reformation. These Christians have been referred to as the German Mystics. This title gives the impression that experiencing God's presence is mystical, or even optional, in the life of the believer. But only a personal encounter with God can impart a genuine fear of the Lord.

The theology of the German Mystics was not fully refined to remove the dross of personal assumptions. But the fear of the Lord was instilled in these Christians who believed that Christ could be known personally. They believed their names could be written in heaven without the necessity of having their names written on the roster of the apostate Roman Church. We will only mention a few of the movement's prominent leaders. Meister Eckart taught that God was in Christ, and Christ was in those who had been born again by becoming empty to self in order to seek after God. John Tauler's writings are still quoted today in Protestant Churches. The Friends of God consisted of various fellowships along the Rhine. Their most influential writer used the pseudo-name, "The Overland." *The German Theology* is a comprehensive statement of the German Mystics' beliefs; published around 1497. Schaff gives the following synopsis.

> The German Theology sets forth man's sinful and helpless condition, Christ's perfection and mediatorial work and calls upon men to have access to God through him as the door. In all its fifty-four chapters no reference is made to Mary or to the justifying nature of good works or the merit of sacramental observances. It abounds as no other writing of the German mystics did in quotations from the New Testament. In its pages the wayfaring man may find the path of salvation marked out without mystification.

> The book, starting out with the words of St. Paul, "when that which is perfect is come, then that which is in part shall be done away," declares that that which is imperfect has only a relative existence and that, whenever the Perfect becomes known by the

creature, then "the I, the Self and the like must all be given up and done away." Christ shows us the way by having taken on him human nature. In chs. XV.-LIV., it shows that all men are dead in Adam, and that to come to the perfect life, the old man must die and the new man be born. He must become possessed with God and depossessed of the devil. Obedience is the prime requisite of the new manhood. Sin is disobedience, and the more "of Self and Me, the more of sin and wickedness and the more the Self, the I, the Me, the Mine, that is, self-seeking and selfishness, abate in a man, the more doth God's I, that is, God Himself, increase." By obedience we become free. The life of Christ is the perfect model, and we follow him by hearkening unto his words to forsake all. This is nothing else than saying that we must be in union with the divine will and be ready either to do or to suffer. Such a man, a man who is a partaker of the divine nature, will in sincerity love all men and things, do them good and take pleasure in their welfare. Knowledge and light profit nothing without love. Love maketh a man one with God. The last word is that no man can come unto the Father but by Christ.

In 1621 the Catholic Church placed the Theologia Germanica on the Index. If all the volumes listed in that catalogue of forbidden books were like this one, making the way of salvation plain, its pages would be illuminated with ineffable light.[98]

The Mystics found that God's presence could be experienced through Christ. Later theologians categorized these believers as Mystics based on the fact that they claimed to have experienced a spiritual encounter with God. Is this type of encounter, by which a person advances from knowing about God to making an actual acquaintance with Him, a realistic expectation? Is experiencing God's presence a singular event in the Christian life? Might such an encounter constitute the beginning of a true relationship with God, or is it something that comes through a lifetime of refinement, meditation, or education? Lastly, what does self-denial have to do with drawing near to God?

---

[98] Schaff, Philip. History of the Christian Church: The Middle Ages From Boniface VIII to the Protestant Reformation 1294-1517. Vol. 6. 1st ed. 1910(?). Peabody: Hendrickson Publishers, 2011, pp. 294-295. Print.

CH. 11: LAW-ABIDING GRACE

In order to answer such questions let us consider a logical argument which Jesus gave to those who had accused Him of employing demonic spirits to accomplish His miracles:

And He was casting out a demon, and it was mute. So it was, when the demon had gone out, that the mute spoke; and the multitudes marveled. But some of them said, "He casts out demons by Beelzebub, the ruler of the demons." Others, testing Him, sought from Him a sign from heaven. But He, knowing their thoughts, said to them: "Every kingdom divided against itself is brought to desolation, and a house divided against a house falls. If Satan also is divided against himself, how will his kingdom stand? Because you say I cast out demons by Beelzebub. And if I cast out demons by Beelzebub, by whom do your sons cast them out? Therefore they will be your judges. But if I cast out demons with the finger of God, surely the kingdom of God has come upon you. When a strong man, fully armed, guards his own palace, his goods are in peace. But when a stronger than he comes upon him and overcomes him, he takes from him all his armor in which he trusted, and divides his spoils. He who is not with Me is against Me, and he who does not gather with Me scatters" (Luke 11:14-23).

Now take this same line of reasoning and apply it to the self. The self stands vigilant guard over its own house. When a person confesses that Jesus is his Lord, that person is saying that he has handed over the keys to every area of his life. But does that person really want Christ to possess him completely? Is he really willing to have Christ take all of his soul as His spoil? The self is a strong man. It fights to retain some item of personal value that it is unwilling to be counted as Kingdom property. The self reasons, "If all is Christ's, what will become of me?"

The problem from the standpoint of salvation is that sin bonds the self with the devil. The house of self must be spoiled in order for Jesus to break that unholy alliance. The real strong-man is the devil hiding behind the door of what appears to be one's own house. People can try to clean house on their own, but unless they have honestly received Christ they will be self-deceived. They might, through their own sense of guilt or willpower, obtain spans of victory over sin. Nevertheless, in their hearts they remain unsubmitted to the authority of God. Therefore, the devil is still in the house, and can, at his whim, cause further destruction.

> *When an unclean spirit goes out of a man, he goes through dry places, seeking rest; and finding none, he says, 'I will return to my house from which I came.' And when he comes, he finds it swept and put in order. Then he goes and takes with him seven other spirits more wicked than himself, and they enter and dwell there; and the last state of that man is worse than the first* (Luke 11:24-26).

Let us conclude this chapter on law and grace by reviewing Paul's warning about "self-imposed" religion. *"Therefore, if you died with Christ from the basic principles of the world, why, as though living in the world, do you subject yourselves to regulations—'Do not touch, do not taste, do not handle,' which all concern things which perish with the using—according to the commandments and doctrines of men? These things indeed have an appearance of wisdom in self-imposed religion, false humility, and neglect of the body, but are of no value against the indulgence of the flesh"* (Col. 2:20-23).

How has the reader's religion been imposed? Was it imposed by parents, the Church, or the preferred state religion? Is the reader relying upon his own self-imposition of God's law? Or has the reader been imposed upon by the very real presence of God—by the convicting power of the Holy Spirit? John the Baptist prepared the way for Jesus with a call to repentance. Repentance unto salvation involves the honest admission that—up until the moment of surrender—the strong man of Self is still guarding the house from the lordship of Christ.

God made His presence known at Mount Sinai so the people might fear Him and be obedient to His laws. The children of Israel did not remain at the Mountain forever. In Deuteronomy 4:10, the parents were instructed to teach their children what they had experienced at Sinai along with the laws so that they might *"learn to fear Me all the days they live on the earth."*

The Holy Spirit has been sent by our ascended Lord so that each generation 'til the end of the age can experience God for themselves. Christians do not live every moment after their conversion actually experiencing the awesome presence of the Lord. But between such experiences they remember what it is to fear the Lord. The fear of the Lord is the beginning of wisdom and knowledge.

The reality of the presence of God is the power which enables grace to govern in the place of the penalty of the Law, not contradicting the Law, but transcending the Law. The misinformed and nominal Church has never experienced the power of God; therefore, they cannot fear Him because they have not known Him. Yet they declare they can ignore the Law because they are standing under the umbrella of grace. They have neither submitted to law, **nor grace**. They are out of control. This is one of the delusions of lawlessness.

Chapter Twelve

THE DESTINY OF THE TWO HOUSES
By Douglas Krieger

The Mystery of Co-Inheritance

*F*ELLOW HEIRS—SAME BODY—PARTAKERS OF HIS PROMISE . . .

". . . by which, when you read, you may understand my knowledge in the mystery of Christ, which in other ages was not made known to the sons of men, as it has now been revealed by the Spirit to His holy apostles and prophets: that the Gentiles should be fellow heirs, of the same body, and partakers of His promise in Christ through the gospel" . . . (Ephesians 3:5-6).

The exegesis of Ephesians 3:6 brings out the following: " . . . *that the Gentiles should be fellow heirs* (synkleroma), *of the same body* (sysoma or co-body), *and partakers of His promise* (syn-metoka—singular promise) *in Christ through the gospel."*[99] The prefix of these three Greek words (*"syn"* of *"sy"*) connote, by definition: a prefix occurring in loanwords from Greek, having the same function as "co-" (synthesis; synoptic); used, with the meaning "with," "together," in the formation of compound words (synsepalous) or "synthetic" in such compounds (syngas). Expand. Also, sy-, syl-, sym-, sys-. These words give us both distinction but also demand that we be TOGETHER—fellow heirs of the SAME BODY. They are not together, yet separated—they are together in the SAME BODY. "Syn" also gives the meaning of EXPANSION . . . even so, the word Ephraim means: Doubly fruitful (Strong's Exhaustive Concordance) or INCREASING or EXPANSION.[100]

---

[99] "One New Man...The Mystery of Messiah" – Kehila News Israel, Aug. 2, 2017.
[100] *Commonwealth Theology*, by Douglas Krieger, Tribnet Publications, 2018, p. 69.

The "Israel of God" and the "One New Man"

In our examination of the "Israel of God"—a term used but once in Scripture—is found in Galatians 6:16. It climaxes Paul's contentions relative to *"the circumcision and the uncircumcised"* . . . between the natural progeny of Abraham and those from among the nations who were being called into the EKKLESIA, the Assembly, whose head was Yeshua, the Messiah (of both Jew and the Gentile).

In determining who, then, constitutes the "Israel of God" we must reflect upon all that went before in Galatians. Firstly, however, as we have already discussed, replacement theologies consider themselves as the Israel of God *in toto*. They alone, be they Jew or Gentile, as long as they are redeemed by the blood of the cross, are the Israel of God. That bears truth—at least on the "surface" of the matter . . . for IN CHRIST, neither Jew (circumcision) nor uncircumcision (Gentiles) *"avails anything, but a new creation"* . . . *"for not even those who are circumcised* (Jews) *keep the law, but they desire to have you* (Gentiles) *circumcised that they may boast in your flesh . . . But God forbid that I should boast except in the cross of our Lord Jesus Christ, by whom the world has been crucified to me, and I to the world"* (Gal. 6:13-15).

The theological infraction, however, wrought via replacement/rejection theologians obfuscates, even excludes, the physical seed of Abraham (both of Judah and Ephraim—if you can follow the development of the physical seed of Abraham). A kind of "theological globalization" of the ethnos/races is wrought whereby these theologians recognize those from among the Gentiles are, through faith, brought into the Commonwealth of Israel (Eph. 2), *ipso facto* defined as the Israel of God, but those from the physical progeny of Abraham, without Messiah's intervention, are excluded from their own Commonwealth—for *"they are not all Israel who are of Israel, nor are they all children because they are the seed of Abraham; but, 'In Isaac your seed shall be called.' That is, those who are the children of the flesh, these are not the children of God; but the children of the promise are counted as the seed"* (Romans 9:6-8).

The "baby thrown out with the bath water" is the prophetic destiny of that very physical progeny of Abraham's seed. Therein lies the rub. In their haste to embrace the New Covenant, all prophecy related to the materiality of the rebirth of Israel as a precursor to the coming Millennium of Messiah upon the earth has been effectively terminated or horribly tolerated to the point of obscurity.

On the opposite end of the theological spectrum we find the Dispensationalists have not excluded the physical seed of Abraham from some form of prophetic destiny but have focused their attention solely upon Judah (having included by careful, though grossly inaccurate, anthropological manipulation, Ephraim). Ephraim's blending in with Judah and becoming Jews themselves in the theology of the Dispensationalists; thus, altogether eliminating Ephraim. They have separated out Judah by insisting that only the New Covenant's "spiritual blessings" (Darby) or a complete and separate New Covenant was initiated for the EKKLESIA (aka the Church) and a similar (but not the same) New Covenant will be instituted for believing "Israel" when the Deliverer's identity is disclosed to the Jews just prior to the commencement of the literal, one-thousand-year reign of the Son of David upon the earth.

In the Galatian assemblies, it is apparent that Paul's benediction/blessing upon the "Israel of God" defines not only those of the "circumcision" (viz. the Jews, the physical descendants of Abraham like himself), but those, also of the uncircumcised (in this case the ethnic Galatians, the "ethnos/nations" from whom a remnant has been called [viz. "the rest of mankind"—Acts 15:17; Amos 9:11-12]).

The contention wherein Paul's focus is solely upon *"false brethren unawares brought in, who came in to spy out our liberty which we have in Christ Jesus, that they might bring us into bondage"* (Gal. 2:4) sets this group (i.e., "the circumcision") apart to the extent they must somehow find themselves identified with those who seek justification through the flesh—i.e., "natural branches" (Romans 11:17-21). Those "ethnic Jews" who are identified by Paul as "false brethren" are of the "circumcision" who through the "works of the flesh" find their justification not only in the act of circumcision but in their progeny through Abraham (physical linage).

Jesus made it clear:

"Do not think to say to yourselves, 'We have Abraham as our father.' For I say to you that God is able to raise up children to Abraham from these stones'" (Matt. 3:9) . . . *"They answered and said to Him, 'Abraham is our father.' Jesus said to them, 'If you were Abraham's children, you would do the works of Abraham. But now you seek to kill Me, a Man who has told you the truth which I heard from God. Abraham did not do this. You do the deeds of your fathers. Then they said to Him, 'We were not born of fornication; we have one Father—God.' Jesus said to them, 'If God were your Father, you would love Me, for I proceeded forth and came from God; nor have I come of Myself, but He sent Me. Why do you not understand My speech? Because you are not able to listen to My word. You are of your father the devil, and the desires of your father you want to do"* (John 8:39-44). Justification in the eyes of the "circumcision" is through physical birth—yet, Abraham was justified by faith before he was ever circumcised!

In a real sense a "straw man" is erected by well-meaning brethren who see three groups depicted by Paul in Galatians:

(1) Gentile believers—the Gentile Galatians
(2) Jewish believers—who refuse to be brought under the bondage of the "circumcision"—i.e., the ceremonial laws and ordinances—even those God-ordained legalities
(3) Jews who are "false brethren" insisting Gentile believers must be circumcised in accordance with the Mosaic law—in sum: Become Jews to be saved—just as was the case in Acts 15:3-5

The presupposition that Jews constitute all of Israel, and that Gentiles are wholly outside any and all ethnic consideration; therefore, they cannot be in any way identified as having anything to do with Israel (either of the flesh or of the spirit); therefore, attention is riveted upon believing Jews who embrace the New Creation:

"For in Christ Jesus neither circumcision nor uncircumcision avails anything, but a NEW CREATION" (Gal. 6:15).

It is true—there are three groups to which Paul alludes but Paul brings it back to but two considerations: "circumcision and uncircumcision"—he does NOT distinguish between believing Jews and "false brethren" Jews when it comes down to the final analysis. What is of vital exegesis is the following verse:

CH. 12: THE DESTINY OF THE TWO HOUSES

"And as many as walk according to this rule, peace and mercy be upon them AND upon the Israel of God" (Gal. 6:16).

This verse summarizes Paul's entire contention in Galatians in reference to the *"truth of the Gospel"* as found in Galatians 2:5, 14 where Paul first mentions these "false brethren" insistent upon circumcision for Gentile believers (Gal. 2:4). As far as Paul was concerned justification by faith had virtually nothing to do with physicality—i.e., being born of Abraham—there was but one set of juxtapositions:

"For you are all sons of God through faith in Christ Jesus. For as many of you as were baptized into Christ have put on Christ. There is neither Jew nor Greek, there is neither slave nor free, there is neither male nor female; for you are all one in Christ Jesus. And if you are Christ's, then you are Abraham's seed, and heirs according to promise" (Gal. 3:26-29).

In point of divine fact—the "son of promise" is found in Isaac—the "Seed of Abraham"—yes, but Paul presents that "S"eed to be Christ:

"Brethren, I speak in the manner of men: Though it is only a man's covenant, yet if it is confirmed, no one annuls or adds to it. Now to Abraham and his Seed were the promises made. He does not say, 'and to seeds,' as of many, but as of one, 'And to your Seed,' who is Christ" (Gal. 3:15-16).

Therefore, since all believers are in Christ, the Seed, we inherit the promise, the inheritance (Gal. 3:18). Yes, the promise was passed on through to Jacob, to Israel, and thence was Messiah's coming through such a "Seed of promise!" Indeed, Israel inherited the promise, the blessing, through Isaac: *"Now we, brethren, as Isaac was, are children of promise"* (Gal. 4:28). Are not we all who are in Christ, the New Creation—having forsaken the Old Creation—we are of the New Man, not of the Old Man (Eph. 2:14-15)?

Consequently, when Paul reaches his benediction at the close of Galatians he speaks of *"as many as walk according to this rule"*—of those living by the New Creation. How's that? To them under this "rule" (viz. the *"Law of Christ"*—Ga. 6:2) "peace and mercy" is extended. "Peace through the blood of the cross"—whereof He made of the "two" (the Jew and the Gentile) ONE NEW MAN . . . so making PEACE (Eph. 2:15); and furthermore, has not *"God committed them all to disobedience, that He might have MERCY on all*" (Rom. 11:32). So, the antecedent of "many" (as in "*as **many** as walk according to this rule*") includes all those of the New Creation (be they Jews or non-Jews—circumcision or uncircumcision).

The contestation over the "continuative" conjunction vs. an "ascensive" conjunction is a non sequitur in reference to the Greek word "kai" which separates "peace and mercy" from "the Israel of God." It does NOT follow that Paul is distinguishing Gentile-believing Galatians from Jewish believers—both of whom affirm this rule which establishes the New Creation. No, both are included in the New Creation; therefore, to suggest, as some well-meaning Dispensationalists do that the "Israel of God" are naught but believing Jews who embrace the New Creation and find themselves but tangentially benefactors of "peace and mercy" (at best), while Gentile believers in the New Creation are extended "peace and mercy" is a tragic exegetical distortion of Paul's entire emphasis upon the New Creation including both Jew and Gentile.

How can one construe there are TWO GROUPS involved in Paul's benediction—Galatian believers and Jewish believers? No, there is naught but a New Creation—plain and simple. That is Paul's entire argument. Dispensationalists separate out "*the Israel of God*" (aka Jewish believers) from Gentile believers ("who receive peace and mercy?"). Yes, Amillennialists would have us to read this "continuative conjunction" as an "ascensive conjunction"—i.e., "***even*** the Israel of God." But in so doing they make a quantum leap, yea, conjecture, that Jewish-Israel is utterly disinherited and that only the Church as the "continuing community of grace" befits the title: "The True Israel of God"—whereas the Jews aside the New Creation both then and now cannot be constituted as having anything to do with Israel. Indeed, they are excluded from the Commonwealth of Israel, void of promise, absent God, without hope, and utterly blind!

"Peace AND [kai] mercy" "AND [kai] upon the Israel of God." The Greek "kai" is used in both instances and connects all three together—i.e., peace, mercy, Israel of God. If you would, they're all in it together! Therefore, believing Gentile believers and Jewish believers are BOTH included in the Israel of God—both share in His "peace and mercy!"

The Israel of God is not just Jews who have entered the New Creation through the blood of the cross, but includes, as well, those "called out from the among the nations . . . the rest of mankind"— together, the TWO constitute the EKKLESIA of the Living God. They are the Israel of God, the New Creation, the One New Man, the One Body (Gal. 6:16; Eph. 2:15-16).

What most Dispensationalists do in exegeting this Scripture in Galatians 6:16 is to differentiate between those being "called out from among the nations" (in this case, Galatian Gentiles) from the physical progeny of Abraham (aka the Jews); whereby ONLY those Jews who have entered into the New Creation constitute the Israel of God—leaving the *"called out ones from among the nations"* with the initial portion of Paul's benediction: "as many as walk according to this rule, peace and mercy be upon them" (the antecedent of "them" being committed to the "nations"). The conjunction AND is used to separate out the "Israel of God" from those enjoying "peace and mercy" and accord it singularly to Jews who then, alone, are defined as the Israel of God. Apparently, "peace and mercy" is the exclusive purview of the Gentiles—while excluding them from the Israel of God, which in turn is the exclusive purview of the Jews.

Pointedly, however, "they are not all Israel who are of Israel"— which is similar to:

"Yet not even Titus who was with me, being a Greek, was compelled to be circumcised, and this occurred because of false brethren secretly brought in (who came in by stealth to spy out our liberty which we have in Christ Jesus, that they might bring us into bondage)" (Gal. 2:3-4).

Again, without contestation, the rebellion of Korah (Numbers 16:1-41) against Moses, along with 249 co-conspirators were summarily punished when God sent fire from heaven to consume the lot of them (250 total). The Reubenite accomplices of Korah, Dathan and Abiram, along with some 14,700 Israelites who likewise participated in their rebellion by objecting to the destruction of the 250, were swallowed up by the earth; as Moses was commanded to leave the multitude prior to their judgment. Interestingly enough, the *"children of Korah died not"* (Numbers 26:11).

What we are illustrating here—and throughout the Hebrew Scriptures and within the New Testament as well . . . *"not all of Israel is of Israel"*—"false brethren." They are "among us" but, as John in 1 John 2:19 states:

"They went out from us, but they were not of us; for if they had been of us, they would have continued with us; but they went out that they might be made manifest, that none of them were of us."

Does the "Israel of God"—equate to the One Body, the One New Man, the New Creation? Absolutely, this can be the only conclusion of the matter; however, since "not all Israel is of Israel" does it, as well, constitute the Commonwealth of Israel? Ah, indeed, therein lies another rub; for if the progeny of Abraham (aka *"we have Abraham as our father"*—Matt. 3:9; John 8:39) seek to be justified by the *"works of the Law and not by the faith of Abraham"* (Rom. 3:27-4:25) they are by definition excluded from the Israel of God (for **the Israel of God is the New Creation**), but are they, as well, excluded from the Commonwealth of Israel?

Some within Commonwealth Theology affirm the physical seed of Abraham (aka the "unbelieving Jews") are excluded from the Commonwealth of Israel, just as they are outside the Israel of God; others among us, see in "not all Israel is of Israel" excluding them from the Israel of God, but their "prophetic destiny" as participants in the New Covenant demands their inclusion in the Commonwealth of Israel . . . *"their failure riches for the nations, how much more their fullness"* (Rom. 11:12).

However, when we express the phrase *"not all Israel is of Israel,"* it still entails that there are those of the progeny of Abraham's seed who are identified as Israel. Wouldn't it be similar regarding those of the Commonwealth of Israel—i.e., there are those of Israel (Judah and Ephraim, for that matter) who are in the Commonwealth of Israel but NOT OF the Commonwealth of Israel? Thus, they are considered in the "Commonwealth of Israel" just as anyone of Judah and Ephraim are considered in Israel but not of the Commonwealth of Israel, not of Israel. I think you can follow my reasoning here.

The "bewitching" (Gal. 3:1) experienced by the ethnic Galatian assemblies—no doubt by well-meaning (looking on the "bright side") brethren of ethnic Jewish extraction—sought to bring these assemblies *"again* [under] *the yoke of bondage"* (Gal. 5:1) akin to what we saw in Acts 15:10 whereby the replication of the "yoke" placed by Rehoboam (Judah) upon Jeroboam (Israel) resulted in total rebellion and ultimately a "divided kingdom."

The AND word does not separate out the ethnic Jews from the miscellaneous ethnos IN CHRIST but unites them as the very ISRAEL OF GOD. Indeed, the United Kingdom rejects the imposition of the "yoke of bondage" upon Ephraim, upon the remnant among the nations who were "no longer a people" to once again become "the people of God!" The United Kingdom, in this very real sense, IS the very Israel of God. Surely, Peter and Paul were of the Israel of God—but so was Cornelius! It is "according to this rule" (Gal. 6:16) that the New Creation is established; thus, Peter and Paul were not only within the Israel of God, they were, as well, a part of the New Creation, the One New Man, so making peace between Judah and Ephraim.

I affirm that Paul's benediction was all-inclusive—including those yet to believe "according to this rule" whereby PEACE and mercy—"through the blood of Christ" (Eph. 2:13) and "Mercy upon all" (both Jew and Greek) would prevail! This is the New Covenant—"this rule."

The "peace" spoken of in Ephesians (Eph. 2:14-15, 17) is not a peace given unilaterally to individuals but a peace "between" Judah and Ephraim, if you would—"*For He Himself is our peace, who has made both one, and has broken down the middle wall of separation . . . to create in Himself one new man from the two, thus making peace . . . He came and preached peace to you who were afar off and to those who were near*" (Eph. 2:14-15, 17)

The blood feud between Judah and Ephraim has been healed—abolished because He "*reconciled them both to God in one body through the cross, thereby putting to death the enmity*"—the ENMITY wrought "*by the law of commandments contained in ordinances*" (Eph. 2:16) whereby neither Judah nor Ephraim were adequate in their flesh to abide by them ("*which neither our fathers nor we were able to bear*"—Acts 15:10)—THAT enmity, which had become a "middle wall of separation" (Eph. 2:14) has through the cross been put to death! Today, bless God, His commandments are NOT grievous because He has written them on the fleshy tablets of our hearts:

"You are our epistle written in our hearts, known and read by all men; clearly you are an epistle of Christ, ministered by us, written not with ink but by the Spirit of the living God, not on tablets of stone but on tablets of flesh, that is, of the heart . . . who also made us sufficient as ministers of the New Covenant, not of the letter but of the Spirit, for the letter kills, but the Spirit gives life, but if the ministry of death, written and engraved on stones, was glorious, so that the children of Israel could not look steadily at the face of Moses because of the glory of his countenance, which glory was passing away, how will the ministry of the Spirit not be more glorious? For if the ministry of condemnation had glory, the ministry of righteousness exceeds much more in glory. For even what was made glorious had no glory in this respect, because of the glory that excels, for if what is passing away was glorious, what remains is much more glorious. Therefore, since we have such hope, we use great boldness of speech" (2 Cor. 3:2-13).

"But this is the covenant that I will make with the house of Israel after those days, says the LORD: I will put My law in their minds, and write it on their hearts; and I will be their God, and they shall be My people" (Jer. 31:33).

Now, not all the progeny of Abraham, his physical seed, according to Paul, are the Israel of God, but those who are the "children of Promise"—only these children constitute this definition. Having been descended from Israel (Rom. 9:6) did NOT automatically qualify one as a "child of promise"—yes, as the "children of the flesh" but not as "children of promise." Those "children of the flesh" who choose their inheritance "through promise" would, and always have been, those who are "children of promise."

Did not Abraham begat Ishmael? Did not Isaac begat Esau? Paul saw in this the following: *"O man, who are you to reply against God? Will the thing formed say to him who formed it, 'Why have you made me like this? Does not the potter have power over the clay, from the SAME LUMP to make one vessel for honor and another for dishonor?"* (Rom. 9:20-21).

The Israel of God did not commence from the Cross forward—but from the Garden of Eden! If you would, there has always been a "faith line"—for the promise that Eve's Seed would be destined to "crush the serpent's head" was made in Genesis 3:15. Surely, Abel's offering was acceptable because it was wrought in blood looking forward to the *"blood of the Cross"* wherein we read: *"Having been justified by faith . . . much more then, having now been justified by His blood, we shall be saved from wrath through Him"* (Rom. 5:1, 9) . . . *"to Jesus the Mediator of the New Covenant, and to the blood of sprinkling that speaks better things than that of Abel"* (Heb. 12:24).

Thus, the Israel of God is inclusive of all they who through faith acclaimed justification as they looked forward to the "blood of His cross"—even so, Hebrews 11 projects them all to have *"obtained a good testimony through faith"* though they did *"not receive the PROMISE"* yet, *"God having provided something better for us, that they should not be perfect apart from us"* (Hebrews 11:39-40).

They (viz, the O.T. saints) are INCLUDED in on the promise— *"They should not be perfect apart from us"* . . . meaning, WITH US, they too are "made perfect" and included in on the promise because the "S"eed, which is CHRIST, was manifested through the blood of the Cross—the O.T. saints looked "forward" to the Cross.

Yet, not only these O.T. saints are included, and perfected via the promise of the Seed, but all those pouring into the New Creation, from the remnant, the "rest of mankind" are so included! How could we "from among the nations" be so blind, even arrogant, not to see the all-inclusiveness of ALL ISRAEL, the ISRAEL OF GOD?

It has taken us nigh 2,000 years to see Paul's amazing revelation of the One New Man—freed from the yoke of bondage!

Brethren, we must come to grips with this profound truth, this liberating revelation, this supernatural illumination of Holy Writ: Hosea's prophecy demands that those *"called out from among the ethnos, the nations"* who were *"no longer the people of God"* are NOW, the "people of God"—rightful inheritors of the Promise!

We must seize the moment of Divine Revelation and acclaim what "God sees" as our very vision: He allowed Ephraim to be *"swallowed up of the nations"* (Hosea 8:7-10) . . .

"In the place where it was said to them, 'You are not My people,' [aka Lo-Ammi], *"For you are not My people, and I will not be your God"* (Hos. 1:9) . . . *There it shall be said to them, 'You are sons of the living God"* (Hos. 1:10) . . . *"And that He might make known the riches of His glory on the vessels of mercy, which He had prepared beforehand for glory, even us whom He called, not of the Jews only, but also of the Nations?*

As He says also in Hosea: 'I will call them My people, who were not My people, and her beloved, who was not beloved.' 'And it shall come to pass in the place where it was said to them, 'You are not My people,' there they shall be called sons of the living God''" (Romans 9:22-26).

Ephraim did, through the blood of the Cross, transverse the "breach of Jeroboam"—from Lo-Ammi, NOT MY PEOPLE, to Ammi, MY PEOPLE . . . *"For great will be the day of Jezreel! Say to your brethren, My people,' And to your sisters, 'Mercy is shown.'"* (Hosea 1:11, 2:1).

You ponder: This is but a metaphor—how could we actually be the remnant of Ephraim; how could we be considered Lo-Ammi but now Ammi? I did not say that—Hosea and Paul did! We now are included in Messiah (IN CHRIST), in the "S"eed, and are, therefore, IN CHRIST . . . *"And if you are Christ's, then you are Abraham's seed, and heirs according to the promise . . . Now we, brethren, as Isaac was, are children of promise"* (Gal. 3:29; 4:28).

In common vernacular we often say: "It is what it is"—even so, that is precisely WHAT IT IS . . . we are the remnant of Ephraim—we are NOT some esoteric metaphor! We ARE Abraham's descendants, and heirs according to promise!"

Yes, the "mystery of Israel's restoration" is a "hidden truth" (aka "mystery") but Jesus declared: *"There is nothing covered up that will not be revealed"* (Luke 12:2). It has taken awhile but Jeremiah's prophecy concerning the restoration and future unity of the brotherhood between Judah and Ephraim (Israel) would take place *"In the latter days you will consider it"* (Jer. 30:24). All of Jeremiah 30 speaks of that prophetic restoration of Judah and Israel. These are the "latter days" and "you will consider it!"

You may be Jewish or just, as they say, a "stone-raw heathen"—but guess what, if by faith you receive Him, and are dependent upon the blood of His cross, you are now THE ISRAEL OF GOD!

And, although, some within Commonwealth Theology suggest it is through ADOPTION, that we, among the ethnos, have entered the Israel of God, we must examine this more closely . . . for some have used Isaiah 49:6 to suggest via adoption we "Gentiles" (alone) have arrived at the Israel of God; to wit:

Who formed Me from the womb to be His Servant, to bring Jacob back to Him, so that Israel is gathered to Him (For I shall be glorious in the eyes of the LORD, and My God shall be My strength), indeed He says, 'It is too small a thing that You should be My Servant to raise up the tribes of Jacob, and to restore the preserved ones of Israel; I will also give You as a light to the Gentiles, that You should be My salvation to the ends of the earth (Isa. 49:5-6).

The New Testament does not commit the "nations/ethnos" entering into the Israel of God via adoption—there is not anything, per se, which suggests that we are of the "seed of Abraham" through adoption—it is, however, through "faith in Yeshua" wrought in the Holy Spirit, whereby we cry "Abba Father"—i.e., *"For you did not receive the spirit of bondage again to fear, but you received the Spirit of adoption by whom we cry out, Abba, Father. The Spirit Himself bears witness with our spirit that we are children of God, and if children, then heirs—heirs of God and joint heirs with Christ"* (Rom. 8:15-17).

Listen carefully: There's nothing in the N.T. which suggests that we are adopted into the family of Abraham—but we are adopted into the family of God as seen above. The five times that the word "adoption" is used in the N.T. (Rom. 8:15, 23; 9:4; Gal. 4:5; Eph. 1:5) does not declare our adoption is into the family of Abraham; however, in Galatians 3:29 it states: *"And if you are Christ's, then you are Abraham's seed* [Grk. "sperma"] *, and heirs according to the promise."* But, nothing of "adoption" is mentioned here. Then how did we become Abraham's seed? We need to backtrack to discover our "Hebraic roots" to Abraham. Tracing our roots must ultimately lead us through to the promise of the New Covenant.

Jeremiah advises Ephraim—if our claim is the remnant of Ephraim—*"Set up signposts, make landmarks; set your heart toward the highway, the way in which you went. Turn back* (or "return"), *O virgin of Israel, turn back to these your cities"* (Jer. 31:21). So, exactly how did we get here—we, the "called out ones from among the nations" . . . "the rest of mankind" . . . we who were "swallowed up of the nations?"

Apparently, researching "how we got here" as Ephraim is no small thing. Jeremiah prophesied:

"Behold, the days are coming, says the LORD, that I will sow the house of Israel and the house of Judah with the seed of man . . . And it shall come to pass, that as I have watched over them to pluck up, to break down, to throw down, to destroy, and to afflict, so I will watch over them to build and to plant, says the LORD" (Jer. 31:27-28).

Finally, our "roots" are uncovered, for *"Behold the days are coming, says the LORD, when I will make a NEW COVENANT with the house of Israel and with the house of Judah . . . I will put My law in their minds, and write it on their hearts; and I will be their God, and they shall be My people"* (Jer. 31:31-33).

He does this with BOTH houses but mentions the House of Israel first! The New Covenant promise is made only to the "physical seed of Ephraim and Judah." We cannot escape the physicality of this statement. The claim by Dispensationalism that Ephraim was swallowed up and/or blended into Judah whereby they became Jews is simply erroneous—why would there be such a specific prophecy if Ephraim had been merged into Judah? Why? Because it had not been absorbed into Judah but assimilated into the nations, just as the Scripture has said.

Now, it is time for Ephraim to retrace his steps. How does it feel to be of Joseph, the Stick of Ephraim? That is precisely what the Almighty claims we are. No, even with the best DNA testing, it still can't be proven—although that scientific proof is still progressing. Notwithstanding, let's say that such DNA proof of Ephraim's remnant called out from among the nations is one day 100% proven—it doesn't matter. Why? Because just as we are acclaimed to be the "seed of Abraham" via the Spirit of adoption, even so are we Abraham's seed and heirs according to the Promise!

We're not second-class heirs of the Promise—somehow adopted step-children—no, no, no! As "Ephraimites" we cannot, from the Divine perspective, renounce our physical claim to the Seed of Abraham—we are in fact biological and chosen descendants of Ephraim. I know that is a difficult pill for some to swallow—but it is one that must be divinely ingested! IT IS WHAT IT IS! Thus, when we reread Isaiah 49:6, are we convinced that Yeshua, our Jesus, our Messiah is the very Servant mentioned and that the Spirit of

Adoption Who cries out in us, "Abba, Father," longs to honor Him in the final restoration of Judah and Ephraim? We are destined to be His corporate expression upon the Earth on that day. It is through us that the Day of Redemption shall climax—when ALL ISRAEL SHALL BE DELIVERED (Rom. 11:26). Judah-Israel's regathering into her ancient homeland is no small thing; nor shall be the full restoration of Judah and Ephraim—the BROTHERHOOD—a brotherhood that shall minister salvation . . . for the whole world groans for the *"manifestation of the sons of God!" "For the earnest expectation of the creation eagerly waits for the revealing of the sons of God . . . because the creation itself also will be delivered from the bondage of corruption into the glorious liberty of the children of God"* (Rom. 8:19, 21).

Replacement theology would utterly obfuscate such a divine reality, restoration, reconciliation on behalf of humanity. Why should we seek to obliterate Ephraim's physicality, when so much is at stake—even ALL CREATION? The restoration of the brotherhood—between Judah and Ephraim—looms larger than life . . . it is at the very crux of prophetic fulfillment. Dispensationalism desperately seeks to separate the two—Judah and Ephraim—and in so doing are antithetical to the Divine Scheme . . . the Plan and Purpose of Earth's very redemption. Compounding Dispensationalism's design to separate Judah and Ephraim persists throughout the Millennium, whereby Two Brides, Two Marriage Feasts, Two New Covenants, Two Holy Cities, Two Salvations, Two Kingdoms—"two" of virtually all major theological issues in order to sustain a system which ostensibly ghettoizes the Jew and blurs the identity of those *"called out from among the nations"* who were *"no longer a people . . . but now are the people of God"* (i.e., Ephraim). Again, being a physical descendant of Abraham—being a Hebrew, being Jewish, being an Ephraimite—does NOT constitute being an heir, an actual child of the living God. That heritage only takes place through the FAITH OF ABRAHAM. All O.T. saints experienced that "divine heritage" through perfection in the types and shadows forecasting God's ultimate provision through the Suffering Servant (Hebrews 11); however, physical descent from Abraham has NOT been disqualified in order for someone to become a child of God . . . for *"If you belong to Messiah you are the seed of Abraham, heirs according to promise"* (Gal. 3:29).

By being IN MESSIAH, in the "S"eed is our ultimate qualification of being of the seed of Abraham, heirs according to promise—*"Now we, brethren, as Isaac was, are children of promise . . . but, as he who was born according to the flesh then persecuted him who was born according to the Spirit, even so it is now"* (Gal. 4:28-29). Do we see it? Isaac was the physical progeny of Abraham—the "child of promise"—in the flesh, BUT was persecuted because he was born according to the Spirit—even so, it is now! Do you see it? Tracing our linage acknowledges BOTH the physical and the spiritual aspects of the "child of promise" and of the fact that "we are all children of promise" just as Isaac was. Again, there's nothing remiss about the physical seed as part and parcel of our heritage, even if we're not Jewish! The only way this can be explained is through revelation regarding Isaac's birth of the flesh and his inheritance through the Spirit. Our true identity, our very sperma (Strong's G4690) or "seed" is predicated upon the "S"eed which is Christ Himself: *"And if you are Christ's, then you are Abraham's seed, and heirs according to the promise"* (Gal. 3:29).[101]

THE YET FUTURE UNITED KINGDOM OF DAVID

The conclusion that the prophecy of Ezekiel 37:15-28 was fulfilled when the 10 Tribes united with Judah (the Two Tribes of the South) prior to the Babylonian Captivity, or was fulfilled when the Jews returned to Judea as the full-fledged 12 Tribes under the decrees of the Persian Kings (commencing with King Cyrus in 537 BC) is unbiblical and is naught but anthropological historical revisionism (i.e., large numbers of the "swallowed up Israelites among the nations" never integrated with the Jews of the Babylonian captivity).

The prophecy given in Ezekiel 37:15-28 is yet future and must be taken in context to take place in the "latter days"—the prophecy finds itself between the vision of the "Valley of Dry Bones" (Ezekiel 37:1-14) and the Gog-Magog War (Ezekiel 38-39) . . . AND the unfilled Two-Stick prophecy: *"I will make them one nation in the land, on the mountains of Israel; and one king shall be king over them all; they shall no longer be two nations, nor shall they ever be*

---

[101] Ibid. pp. 374-385.

divided into two kingdoms . . . David My servant shall be king over them, and they shall all have one shepherd; they shall also walk in My judgments and observe My statutes, and do them" (Ezek. 37:22, 24). The context of the yet future prophetic fulfillment is "Messianic" and is set within the immediate context of the yet future, literal 1,000-year Millenarian Reign of the Son of David. *"The Whole House of Israel"* (Ezekiel 37:11). At issue is this: What constitutes the *"Whole House of Israel?"* If we are to read further (Ezekiel 37:15-28) we discover that the *"Whole House of Israel"* is comprised of Two Sticks (Two Houses)—the House of Judah and the House of Ephraim; therefore, is the Valley of Dry Bones comprised of BOTH HOUSES or simply the House of Judah? The context demands an agonizing reappraisal of the Vision of the Valley of Dry Bones—it bespeaks of BOTH HOUSES as the Whole House of Israel and of BOTH resurrection and immediate revival at the close of the age for both Judah and Ephraim.

If Ephraim were swallowed up either by Judah through "captivity integration into Judah" or simply scattered among the nations and thereby assimilated—then why is Ephraim prophetically ensconced into Ezekiel 37's Valley of Dry Bones vision and Two Stick prophecy which is yet future—finding itself just prior to the Gog-Magog War? Many well-educated and well-meaning brethren, like Chuck Missler, are determined to ascribe Ephraim's assimilation into the Southern Two Tribes—but this argument from conjecture, juxtaposed to the biblical and historical accounting of Ephraim being SWALLOWED UP (Hosea 8:8—there the Hebrew word for "swallowed up" is *Bala*, which is used twice in succession in the Hosea 8:8 text to emphasize a complete disappearance, even destruction—the same word is used of Jonah being "swallowed" by the great fish) . . . simply does not wash. Again, the Vision of the Valley of Dry Bones is given to the "Whole House of Israel"—which vision feeds into the Prophecy of the Two Sticks; therefore, upon further examination of the relationship between the Stick of Judah and the Stick of Joseph, which is the Stick of Ephraim—a relationship dead for centuries, the "Whole House of Israel" can be viewed not only of Judah's gathering together to the Land in the latter times (Ezek. 38:8) but of Ephraim's revival wherein TOGETHER they are revived and stand as a mighty army—i.e.,

Judah's awakening is Ephraim's awakening and comports with Romans 11:11: "Now if their diminishing is riches for the world, and their failure riches for the Nations (Gentiles) how much more their FULLNESS." Some within the "Jesus Movement" have considered the rebirth of the State of Israel to have led to the Church's "partial revival" during the Jesus Movement—especially noteworthy is the "taking in 1967 of Jerusalem" by the Jews and the subsequent revival known as the "Jesus Movement" in the late '60s into the early '70s.

This passage of the Valley of Dry Bones can no longer be viewed as a unilateral revival of latter-day Israel (the Jews) but bespeaks of BOTH HOUSES—BOTH STICKS—for if their (the Jews) trespass/diminishing is riches for the world—then the following is being fulfilled: *"For if their being cast away is the reconciling of the world, what will their acceptance be but LIFE FROM THE DEAD?"* (Romans 11:11, 15). Even so: *"Behold, O My people, I will open your graves and cause you to come up from your graves, and bring you into the land of Israel. Then you shall know that I am the LORD, when I have opened your graves, O My people, and brought you up from your graves"* (Ezek. 37:12-13). Judah and Ephraim abide "the People of God" destined for revival from "blindness in part" and the current apostasy afflicting the Ekklesia, among the nations.[102]

---

[102] Ibid. pp. 42-45.

Chapter Thirteen

THERE'S LITERALLY ONE NEW COVENANT[103]
By Doug Krieger

The New Covenant

One of the most glaring misunderstandings (at best) and theological subterfuges (at worst) is the hijacking of the New Covenant as seen in Jeremiah 31:31-40; and alluded to in Ezekiel 37:26, as well as Ezekiel 11:19; 36:24-28. Hijacking in that the "Christian Community" (vast swaths thereof) have completely rejected the notion that the SINGULARITY of this New Covenant was originally promised to BOTH the House of Israel and the House of Judah (Jer. 31:31—"Behold, the days are coming, says the LORD, when I will make a NEW COVENANT with the house of Israel and with the house of Judah").

"The house of Israel and with the house of Judah"—in Jeremiah's thinking—clearly outlines two distinct groups which are inseparable insofar as to the Almighty's commitment and prophetic promise of the New Covenant. Neither can one surmise the singling out of Judah as simply the "leadership of all Israel's twelve tribes" and is, therefore, mentioned in this manner.

No, Jeremiah's writing took place as Judah's Jerusalem was being absorbed into the Babylonian Empire—the last of her kings (King Zedekiah) having rebelled against King Nebuchadnezzar and who imprisoned Jeremiah—586 BC being the fall of Jerusalem; however the 70 years Captivity (2 Chronicles 36:21) of Judah began in 608 BC when, then Viceroy Nebuchadnezzar commenced the Captivity by deporting Judah's youthful leadership (Daniel, and the "three lads" and others (2 Kings 24:1); thus, in 537 BC did the Persian ruler, King Cyrus the Great, decree the rebuilding of the Temple in Jerusalem (2 Chronicles 36:22-23).

---

[103] "There's Literally One New Covenant" By Doug Krieger, August 30, 2019, commonwealththeology.com

By this time (586 BC) the Ten Northern Tribes had been scattered abroad the Assyrian Empire commencing in 745 BC some 159 years (at its extremity) or some 104 years (at its most calendric constriction—712 BC to 608 BC). Thus, in the mind and writing of Jeremiah there was a profound understanding regarding the deportation of Israel's 10 Tribes and the on-going 70-year Captivity of the House of Judah.

Let us consider how critical this is to both the eternal covenants of the Lord and to believers in Yeshua, the Christ, the Son of the Living God—and to the ONENESS of God's original purpose relative to our Lord's prayer in John 17—THAT THEY ALL MAY BE ONE (John 17:21-23)—these two, the New Covenant and our Lord's prayer in John 17, are intrinsically interconnected . . . again, allow me to probe the depths of that theological connectivity.

I became all the more impressed with the SINGULARITY of the New Covenant's initial elucidations in both Jeremiah and in Ezekiel and, of course, with Jesus' inauguration of the same and of the timing of the "covenant of peace with them" described as "an everlasting covenant with them" (Ezekiel 37:26).

This "covenant of peace" mentioned in Ezekiel 37:26 is in point of fact, the very NEW COVENANT—SO MAKING PEACE then and there (Ephesians 2:15-*"that He might reconcile them both to God in ONE BODY through the cross, thereby putting to death the enmity"* (Eph. 2:15-16). . . *"to create in Himself ONE NEW MAN from the two, thus making peace"* . . . What appears in Ezekiel 37 is simply predicated upon the original New Covenant: *"So making Peace."*

First, the New Covenant promise was *exclusively* made with both houses: to "the HOUSE OF ISRAEL and WITH THE HOUSE OF JUDAH"—two houses (Jer. 31:31) which are then corporately addressed in Jeremiah 31:33 as "one house"—to wit:

"But this is the covenant that I will make with the House of Israel after those days, says the LORD: I will put My law in their minds, and write it on their hearts; and I will be their God, and they shall be My people." Here we see the TWO HOUSES as ONE HOUSE OF ISRAEL.

CH. 13: THERE'S LITERALLY ONE NEW COVENANT

It is absolutely clear that prior to the announcement in Jeremiah of the New Covenant in Jeremiah 31:31+ through to Jeremiah 33 that the Almighty fully intends to prophetically fulfill the New Covenant promises made to both houses, to wit:

> *"Have you not considered what these people have spoken, saying, 'The TWO FAMILIES which the LORD has chosen, He has also cast them off'? Thus they have despised My people, as if they should no more be a nation before them. Thus says the LORD: 'If My covenant is not with day and night, and if I have not appointed the ordinances of heaven and earth, then I will cast away the descendants of Jacob and David My servant, so that I will not take any of his descendants to be rulers over the descendants of Abraham, Isaac, and Jacob. For I will cause their captives to return, and will have mercy on them'"* (Jer. 33:24-26).

There are, again, primarily two dominant views of the New Covenant in its New Testament application; starting from the "traditional" or "Covenantal" viewpoint:

COVENANTALISM

1. Adamic Covenant between God and Adam where Adam would have everlasting life based on obedience (Genesis 1:28-30; 2:15).
2. The Noahic Covenant was between God and Noah where God promised to never destroy the earth again by water (Genesis 9:11).
3. The Abrahamic Covenant was between God and Abraham where He would make Abraham a great nation and that all the nations will be blessed through him (Genesis 12:3; 17:5).
4. The Mosaic Covenant was between God and the Israelites where God would be covenantally faithful to Israel as a holy nation (Exodus 19:6).
5. The New Covenant is between Christ and the Church where salvation would be obtained by faith (1 Cor. 11:25).[104]

---

[104] What are the differences between Dispensationalism and Covenantalism by Matt Slick, CARM, 10.28.18 Retrieved on 08.29/19,
https://carm.org/differences-dispensationalism-covenantalism-comparison

In their own words and view, the Covenantalist conjectures/interprets the Scripture with a clear demarcation between the Old Covenant (Mosaic) and the New Covenant (a New Testament phenomena) wherein under the Mosaic Covenant YHWH would be "covenantally faithful to Israel" if they would abide a "holy nation"—however, when it comes to the New Covenant they wholly dismiss the idea that the New Covenant had/has anything to do with the House of Israel and the House of Judah but is wholly a continuation of the Lord's "community of grace"—and, the exclusive inheritor of the spiritual and material benefits of the New Covenant are appropriated by the "True Israel" (citing Gal. 3:16—which, incidentally, mentions nothing in reference to "True Israel"). The inauguration of the New Covenant is extended exclusively to the Church (i.e., the Ekklesia) and must be understood in this context:

- [The] Church began in Eden with Covering of Adam and Eve and is increasingly manifested in the Old Testament.
- The Church was spoken of in the O.T. as stated in (Acts 2:16-35; 3:22-25, 1 Pet. 1:10-12)
- True Israel (the Church) is the heir to the promises made to Abraham (Gal. 3:16).
- The Holy Spirit has indwelt the believers in all periods, but indwells Christians as an anointing which provides gifts to the Church to carry out the commission that Israel has, so far, failed to do.
- Christ is reigning now as King of kings and Lord of lords.
- Believers are 'in Christ' in all ages.[105]

Covenantalism supplants the physical progeny of the 12 Tribes of Israel (both the House of Israel and the House of Judah) wherein the "True Israel of God" becomes the inheritor of the New Covenant which was either prophesied in the O.T. but never implemented with the Two Houses in that physical Israel failed to embrace the New Covenant having done so by "rejecting" the Christ, the Messiah; or the New Covenant was revealed as a continuation of the community of grace through the Messiah, our Lord Jesus Christ.

---

[105] Ibid.

CH. 13: THERE'S LITERALLY ONE NEW COVENANT

In sum: The Church replaces Israel insofar as the institution of the New Covenant concerns; ergo, the Church replaces Israel in toto. Some have entitled this "rejection theology" in that:

Jesus said to them, *"Have you never read in the Scriptures: 'The stone the builders rejected has become the cornerstone. This is from the Lord, and it is marvelous in our eyes'? Therefore I tell you that the kingdom of God will be taken away from you and given to a people who will produce its fruit. He who falls on this stone will be broken to pieces, but he on whom it falls will be crushed"* (Matt. 21:42-44).

Likewise, Jesus prophesied that the Herodian Temple—symbolic of Judaism/Israel of the flesh would experience the following:

"Jerusalem will be trampled by Gentiles (i.e., the Nations) *until the times of the Gentiles are fulfilled* (Luke 21:24) . . . *O Jerusalem, Jerusalem, the one who kills the prophets and stones those who are sent to her! How often I wanted to gather your children together, as a hen gathers her chicks under her wings, but you were not willing! See! Your house is left to you desolate; for I say to you, you shall see Me no more till you say, 'Blessed is He who comes in the name of the LORD!'"* (Matt. 23:37-39).

Regarding the distinctions set forth by John Piper, a classical Covenantalist; to wit:

Piper: "First, a non-covenant-keeping people does not have a divine right to hold the land of promise. Both the blessed status of the people and the privileged right to the land are conditional on Israel's keeping the covenant God made with her. Thus God said to Israel, "If you will indeed obey my voice and keep my covenant, you shall be my treasured possession among all peoples" (Exodus 19:5). Israel has no warrant to a present experience of divine privilege when she is not keeping covenant with God."[106]

There is, in the theology of Covenantalism, absolutely no indication that the singularity of the New Covenant was promised to the Houses of Israel and Judah. Their focus is upon the conditional elements of the Mosaic Covenant–as if it were never promised to the

---

[106] What is really at stake? A response to John Piper's question: "Do Jews Have a Divine Right in the Promised Land?" Randall Smith, The Wandering Shepherd, personal notes, Sept. 3, 2011, Retrieved on 08.29.2019 @ https://randalldsmith.com/what-is-really-at-stake-a-response-to-john-pipers-question-do-jews-have-a-divine-right-in-the-promised-land

Two Houses of Israel. The New Covenant was simply offered to "another nation" able to bear the fruits of such a New Covenant (Matt. 21:43). Frankly, Covenantalism does NOT spend much time on the origination of the New Covenant as offered to both houses of Israel in Jeremiah 31 but concludes that the New Covenant, in sum and substance, is wholly a New Testament configuration assigned to the continuing community of grace—the Almighty having either forsaken and/or rejected unfaithful Israel; unfaithful, as they were to the statutes of the Old/Mosaic Covenant and wholly unworthy to bear any association with the accords of the New Covenant.

DISPENSATIONALISM

The Dispensationalists, due to their misunderstanding between the House of Judah and the House of Israel, have interpreted this New Covenant insofar as its "Christian application" as distant from today's Ekklesia/Church wherein only the SPIRITUAL BLESSINGS of the New Covenant are currently enjoyed by believers in Yeshua (Darby) or that there are ostensibly TWO NEW COVENANTS (Dallas Seminary, et al): One for the Christians and the other for "All Israel" (the Jews—aka all 12 undifferentiated tribes) to be inaugurated somewhere around the commencement of the Millennial reign of the Son of David upon the earth.

These two New Covenants are NOT considered in their theological system the same New Covenant but two distinctly different New Covenants in content and in time, though both based upon the Blood of His Redemptive work.

In their own words:

Traditional Dispensationalists typically view the New Covenant in one of three ways.[107] Some Dispensationalists (most notably Lewis Sperry Chafer) historically took the view that there are actually two New Covenants, one for Israel and one for the Church. Today, most Dispensationalists hold a second view,

---

[107] It should be noted that Progressive Dispensationalists teach that there is a fulfillment for the Church and a future fulfillment for the nation of Israel. Thus, there is said to be one New Covenant, but with a two-fold fulfillment. For a critique of this troubling position [NOTE: Considered "troubling" by traditional dispensationalists], see What Lies Ahead: A Biblical Overview of the End Times.

which teaches that the Lord established the New Covenant with the nation of Israel and it was ratified by the blood of Christ. However, it is said that, "the Church (composed of both Jewish and Gentile Christians) participates in the spiritual blessings of the Covenant now."[108] A final view is that there is one New Covenant that was ratified with Israel. This was the position held by John Nelson Darby. This particular view teaches, "Accordingly, the Church is unrelated to the New Covenant of Jeremiah 31. The Church comes between the ratification and inauguration of the New Covenant, but we are not the fulfillment of it. The Church and Israel are each independently connected to the Mediator of the New Covenant. We receive similar, but not identical blessings."[109][110]

AT THE CORE OF DISPENSATIONALISM

Dispensationalism appears to be evolving under the mantel of "Progressive Dispensationalism" wherein there is but one New Covenant in which the New Covenant is ostensibly "bifurcated" with the Church's inauguration of the New Covenant in the Upper Room (viz. "For this is my blood, that of the New Covenant, that shed for many for remission of sins" (Matt. 26:28—Darby Version) . . .

OR

Dispensationalism provides the New Covenant to a yet future Israel during the Millennial Rule and Reign. Notwithstanding, Lewis S. Chafer of Dallas Seminary fame contends that the New Covenant is ostensibly TWO New Covenants—the one inaugurated for the Church in the Upper Room by Jesus and the other New Covenant offered to a yet future Israel (all 12 Tribes) at the commencement of the Millennium, yet future.

---

[108] Gary Gilley, "Laying the Groundwork for Understanding the New Covenant," in *An Introduction to the New Covenant*, ed. Christopher Cone (Hurst, TX: Tyndale Seminary Press, 2013), 18.

[109] J. B. Hixson and Mark Fontecchio, What Lies Ahead: A Biblical Overview of the End Times (Brenham, TX: Lucid Books, 2013), 143.

[110] Ministers of the New Covenant, by Mark Fontecchio, Return to the Word, Retrieved on 08.29.2019 @ https://www.returntotheword.com/Ministers-Of-The-New-Covenant-Article-RttW

In other words, the New Covenant of Jeremiah 31, and allusion to the same in Ezekiel, has nothing whatsoever to do with the Church, but everything to do with a yet future Israel. The Church is NOT the True Israel nor the continuing community of grace and is NOT found in the Old Testament but is a complete mystery revealed through the apostle Paul.

The New Covenant extended to the Ekklesia was initiated in the Upper Room and sealed at the cross and validated by the resurrection and ascension of Christ. This Upper Room Covenant was later clarified by the apostle Paul as the New Covenant offered exclusively to New Testament believers and within the context of the Dispensation of Grace—the Age of Grace—producing the Bride of Messiah; whereas, the Wife of Jehovah is the production of Old Testament saints who become corporate benefactors of their New Covenant (or their portion of the New Covenant) during and/or shortly after the completion of the Seventieth Week of Daniel (Dan. 9:24-27).

There are TWO Wives; two testaments; two gospels (i.e., the Gospel of the Grace of God for the Church and the Gospel of the Kingdom for the Jews); two resurrections of the just (one for N.T. saints and one for O.T. saints); two Holy Cities (viz. the Holy District of Ezekiel 40-48 for the Jews and the New Jerusalem for the Church—although the "ultimate manifestation" MAY comprise both within the context of the Eschaton (after the millennium in that the Holy City, New Jerusalem, bears the names of the 12 Tribes of Israel and the 12 Apostles of the Lamb standing for the saints of the "Church Age").

Further extensions of Dispensationalism include the following (and, certainly, this article is NOT exhaustive of Dispensational understanding of the New Covenant):

The New Creation of Galatians 6 are IN THE MAIN those Gentile believers (viz. the "uncircumcision"); and the "circumcised" (Jews) who see this New Creation, are in the minds of some Dispensationalists the "Israel of God." However, in the view of other Dispensationalists the Gentile believers are EXCLUDED from the Israel of God because they are NOT Jewish believers in Yeshua who affirm the New Creation.

Those Jews (aka ALL the 12 Tribes of Israel "scattered abroad") are ALL JEWS and these Jews are either in the Israel of God or not in the Israel of God for "all Israel is not Israel" (Rom 9:6-8: *"Not as though the word of God hath taken none effect. For they are not all Israel, which are of Israel: Neither, because they are the seed of Abraham, are they all children: but, in Isaac shall thy seed be called. That is, they which are the children of the flesh, these are not the children of God: but the children of the promise are counted for the seed."*).

Whereas, the so-called "Covenantalists" (Replacement/Rejection) theologies inherited from the Roman Catholic/Orthodox persuasions and affirmed by the initial outburst of Reformation theologians (Calvin, Luther, etc.) claimed the full mantel of the "Israel of God" (aka the Church is "spiritual Israel") and so, there is absolutely no eschatological/prophetic distinction between the Jew and Gentile—it is/was as if the New Covenant inaugurated in the Upper Room was, yes, originally promised to the House of Israel and the House of Judah (the physical descendants of the 12 Tribes) but because they rejected the Savior, they too now have been rejected from the New Covenant and this same New Covenant was "given to another"(viz. *"Therefore I tell you, the kingdom of God will be taken away from you and given to a people producing its fruits"* (Matt. 21:43).

These last statements would be those of the Replacement theologians; whereas, the Dispensationalists would surmise that the Kingdom promised to Israel (in their minds all 12 Tribes being Jews) was POSTPONED and given to another (the Ekklesia/Church) as a New Covenant (because Israel rejected the Savior) but the promise of the New Covenant found in Jeremiah would ultimately be given just prior to the commencement of the Millennial Rule and Reign of the Son of David upon the earth. Duly noted: Replacement theologies say that NOTHING of the New Covenant was postponed—they say that the New Covenant of Jeremiah 31 was simply taken from the Jews and given to the Church as the continuing community of grace (i.e., the Ekklesia in the Wilderness [Acts 7:38] continues since the New Covenant commenced by the blood of Jesus foresaw the New Testament "in His blood").

Why Are These Two Systems Deficient?

Firstly, BOTH systems have tortured the "Israel of God" (Gal. 6:16)—"All Israel" (Rom. 11:26) and the singularity of the New Covenant promised to both Houses of Israel: Judah (Israel) and Joseph/Ephraim (Israel).

Secondly, and in reinforcement of the initial promise made by the Almighty to both Houses of Israel—HE HAS KEPT HIS PROMISE to "ALL ISRAEL"—to "THE ISRAEL OF GOD." Yet, today's Christians when they read John 11:52—*"Not for that nation only, but also that He would gather together in one the children of God who were scattered abroad"*—either consider those "scattered abroad" as ALL JEWS of the 12 Tribes (Dispensationalists; Ref. James 1:1) or generic believers (Gentiles or Jews yet to be "born from above") in Messiah from all the nations (including the Jews) who have received the New Covenant given to the Church as a result of the Kingdom's rejection by the leadership of the Jews at the time of Jesus' earthly ministry.

Thus, the KINGDOM has been postponed to "that nation" (all 12 Tribes in the minds of the Dispensationalists) until the beginning of the Millennium . . . and "given to another" which in the minds of BOTH the Dispensationalists and the Replacement theologians is the exclusive jurisdiction of the Church/Ekklesia which Jesus is building today.

Neither the Covenantalists nor the Dispensationalists see any distinction whatsoever between the Two Houses: The House of Judah and the House of Israel—to both systems of theology the Jews of yesteryear comprise only Jews, old Israel or the original Israel—most of whom (the 10 tribes) have disappeared (Covenantalists) or were assimilated back into Judah (Dispensationalists).

Frankly, the Covenantalists tend to believe in their writings that many of the Jews today are actually not real Jews but a mixture of nationalities who simply adopted Jewish customs; whereas, Dispensationalists contend, most vociferously, today's Jews are in actuality all of the 12 Tribes of Israel who were incorporated into Judah from the times of the Babylonian Captivity until today . . . Ephraim (aka Jezreel, Samaria, Israel) is NOT distinguished . . . the 10 tribes were incorporated into Jewry as per the Babylonian/Persian

Empire time frames. Interestingly enough, it was my distinguished privilege to exchange significant Jewish-Christian viewpoints with Orthodox leaders in Israel (Drs. Harold Fisch, Provost of Bar-Ilan University and Geoffrey Wigoder, Editor-in-Chief of Encyclopedia Judaica)—both of whom had earnestly sought to discover the whereabouts of the "Lost 10 Tribes" of Israel. Their exhaustive conclusions simply reaffirmed that Israelite DNA can be found virtually throughout the planet but tribal specifics were as ambiguous as ever—indeed, Israel was swallowed up of the nations.

KEEPING THE NEW COVENANT IN CONTEXT

Again, both Covenantalism and Dispensationalism see no differentiation between Judah's southern tribes and Ephraim's northern tribes—in both their eyes there is no distinction, no difference. When one considers ancient Israel—they are all Jews—in reality, there are no "ten lost tribes" . . . there is no "swallowing up by the nations" . . .

"They (Israel's 10 Northern Tribes) *sow the wind, and reap the whirlwind. The stalk has no bud; it shall never produce meal. If it should produce, ALIENS would swallow it up. Israel is swallowed up; now they are among the Gentiles* (Nations) *like a vessel in which is no pleasure. For they have gone up to Assyria, like a wild donkey alone by itself; Ephraim has hired lovers. Yes, though they have hired among the nations, now I will gather them; and they shall sorrow a little, because of the burden of the king of princes"* (Hosea 8:7-10).

There is virtually no reasonable commentary on Hosea from either camp (Covenantalism/ Dispensationalism), nor of other major and minor prophets in recognition of Israel's (ten tribes) divorce (Jeremiah 3:6-11) from Him Who had once betrothed her "forever."

Thus, shrouded in metaphorical symbolism abides any differential between Judah and Ephraim—it's as if the "breach of Jeroboam" expounded as a fulfillment of the prophets in Acts 15:6-21 never existed . . . the "Tabernacle of David" or "United Kingdom of David" never happened. That is, the Ekklesia's nature—bringing Judah together with Ephraim (along with the *"rest of mankind . . . even ALL THE GENTILES"* [nations]) never happened. At best, Jews and Gentiles are now together but NOT Judah and Ephraim. Alas, NO recognition that Judah and Ephraim ever separated, ever had a breach; therefore, there is no need to describe what was happening in the "Early Church" as the reconciliation of these belligerents (Judah and Ephraim); yes, between Jews and Gentiles, but NOT between Judah and Ephraim because Ephraim was simply considered Jewry anyway!

"The LORD said also to me in the days of Josiah (Judah) *the king: 'Have you seen what backsliding Israel* (10 tribes) *has done? She has gone up on every high mountain and under every green tree, and there played the harlot. And I said, after she had done all these things, 'Return to Me.' But she did not return. And her treacherous sister Judah saw it. Then I saw that all the causes for which backsliding Israel had committed adultery, I had put her away and GIVEN HER A CERTIFICATE OF DIVORCE; yet her treacherous sister Judah did not fear, but went and played the harlot also. So it came to pass, through her casual harlotry, that she defiled the land and committed adultery with stones and trees. And yet for all this her treacherous sister Judah has not turned to Me with her whole heart, but in pretense, says the LORD. Then the LORD said to me, 'Backsliding Israel has shown herself more righteous than treacherous Judah. Go and proclaim these words toward the north, and say: 'Return, backsliding Israel,' says the LORD; 'I will not cause My anger to fall on you. For I am merciful,' says the LORD; 'I will not remain angry forever. Only acknowledge your iniquity, that you have transgressed against the LORD your God, and have scattered your charms to alien deities under every green tree, and you have not obeyed My voice,' says the Lord. 'Return, O backsliding children,' says the LORD; 'for I am married to you. I will take you, one from a city and two from a family, and I will bring you to Zion. And I will give you shepherds according to My heart, who will feed you with knowledge and understanding"* (Jer. 3:6-15).

THE BREACH OF JEROBOAM

Divorcing the New Covenant from its original context found in Jeremiah and Ezekiel does NOT exclude the 12 Tribes (Judah and Ephraim) in accordance with our "Rejection Brethren" nor is it dispensationally sliced in two making two distinctly different New Covenants—nor was the New Covenant postponed (Darby) for it is only for the Jews in the mind of Darby and has nothing to do with Christians!

CH. 13: THERE'S LITERALLY ONE NEW COVENANT

The Dispensational insistence that Ephraim was NOT "swallowed up of the Nations/Gentiles" (i.e., "wholly assimilated") and, if they were, they were so, only temporarily, as in *"Now they are among the nations"* (Hosea 8:7-10; Romans 9:24-29)—but, by clever interpretation, they will once again miraculously reappear with Judah prior to the commencement of the Millennium. Ezekiel 37:15-28–is used to prove this–but Ephraim's reappearance is NOT at the commencement of their "Church Age" . . . only at the commencement of the Millennial Age. Although Acts 15 and Romans 9 clearly affirms the immediate inclusion of the House of Ephraim, once again, into the United Kingdom of David (i.e., the "Tabernacle of David"–the very Ekklesia launched by Jesus)–such passages are dismissed as either allegorical or simply overlooked by both systems of theology.

The Dispensationalists will eschew Acts 15:16 (i.e., the United Kingdom of David and the reuniting of both Houses at the commencement of the Ekklesia), while highlighting Acts 15:17 (only) wherein the *"rest of mankind"* (Edom/Esau) *"may seek the LORD, even all the Nations/Gentiles who are called by My name"*; thus, providing the Dispensationalists theological latitude to keep the Jews separated from the Nations; notwithstanding:

"Even us whom He called, not of the Jews only (i.e., the House of Judah); *but also of the Gentiles* (those or Ephraim "swallowed up" of the Nations)—Romans 9:24. (Note: "Gentiles" in the context of Ephraim who were *"no longer My people"* but *"now are the children of the Living God."*)

From thence Paul immediately goes into describing "Gentiles/Nations" from Romans 9:24 he quotes directly from Hosea:

"I will call them My people, who were not My people, and her beloved, who was not beloved. And it shall come to pass in the place where it was said to them, 'You are not My people,' there they shall be called sons of the living God" (Romans 9:25-26; Hosea 2:23; 1:10).

In other words, Paul directly describes Ephraim's demise and rejection and immediately identifies Ephraim's "reallocation" or identification within the context of the Gentiles/Nations.

To suggest that this is only another "doctrinal" division having little import when it comes to our emphasis upon the New Creation, the Commonwealth of Israel, the One New Man (today's Ekklesia—so making peace) is nothing more than, as far as this brother is concerned, embracing a retrograde gospel of the Kingdom under His headship.

By disassociating Ephraim from the Nations/Gentiles is "theologically disingenuous"—yes, they were assimilated—lost among the nations and were considered ALIENS FROM THE COMMONWEALTH OF ISRAEL but now through the blood of His Cross those who were afar off have been brought nigh and are no longer strangers but are considered "members of the household of faith!" CITIZENS of the COMMONWEALTH OF ISRAEL—no longer ALIENS!

Therefore, the original promise of the New Covenant (Jeremiah 31:31-36; Ezek. 36:26-27) and its "spiritual blessings" were and still are committed to both houses of Israel—and all the more in that Ephraim's dispersion among the nations was in point of glaring theological fact, God's way of expressing the entry of the Nations into the Commonwealth of Israel. The New Covenant cannot be postponed (Dispensationalism) nor terminated to both houses (Rejection/Replacement). God Almighty did NOT change His mind, His purpose/promise has been kept—we abide resolute in this interpretation in affirmation of the eternal Word of God! No, this is NOT a peripheral doctrinal issue. This involves the very Person and Work of our Lord Jesus Christ—His Ekklesia would restore the Breach of Jeroboam and open the floodgates to Esau; the "rest of mankind" . . . creating in Himself ONE NEW MAN . . . so making peace! The "Ark of the Covenant" blessed the household of Obed-Edom; and we should as well note, that Obed-Edom (Esau) along with a total of 70 brethren of Edom became the gatekeepers and musicians in the Tabernacle of David to minister unto the Lord (2 Sam. 6:10-12; 1 Chron. 13:13; 15:18-19, 21, 24-25; 16:5, 37-39). Could this $68 + 2 = 70$ reflect the "70 Table of Nations" found in Genesis 10? I might wish to extend this exegesis to its antithesis wherein "disunity" (Babylon/Babel) can be contrasted with "unity" (Zion).

The End of the Age—The Revelation

It is no stretch to view the passages in Revelation 7 regarding the 12 Tribes of Israel sealed upon the earth (Rev. 7:1-8) and the "rest of mankind" (Rev. 7:9-17—the "great multitude") as the ultimate fulfillment of the same fulfilled prophecy as declared by Peter, Paul, Barnabas, and James in Acts 15:13-17 as the Tabernacle of David/United Kingdom of David (Acts 15:16). That is, Judah and Ephraim's reconciliation—Revelation 7:1-8—and *"the rest of mankind"* (i.e., Edom/Esau/Adam) as *"a great multitude which no one could number, of all nations, tribes, peoples, and tongues"* (Rev. 7:9-17).

It cannot be emphasized enough that the *"revelation of the mystery kept secret since the world began but is manifest, and by the prophetic Scriptures made known to all nations"* (Rom. 16:25-26) is NOT the Dispensational MYSTERY of the Ekklesia/Church somehow hidden before the world began, wholly and separate from the Israel of God, the Commonwealth of Israel, but is and has been so eloquently expounded upon by Dr. Doug Hamp as the marriage, divorce, and remarriage of Israel (Ephraim, even Judah) as confirmed by Paul in Romans 7:1-6.

The MYSTERY was how would the Almighty, Who had betrothed "All Israel" to Himself, then divorced Ephraim (Jeremiah 3:8), permit her to remarry under His divine commandment/law to "another" unless the first husband die (YHWH) which He did, so that she could be married to another–*"to Him who was raised from the dead"* (Rom. 7:4). THAT was the mystery angels could not fathom nor could anyone! But Paul found it in the *"prophetic Scriptures"* (Romans 16:26) and today, so can we!

In sum, there is ONE NEW COVENANT—it was and is committed to ALL ISRAEL (Judah and Ephraim—yes, Ephraim assimilated/scattered among the Nations/Gentiles). Israel is defined as Judah and Ephraim. Ephraim split from Judah at the "Breach of Jeroboam" (1 Kings 11:26-43; 1 Kings 12-13). The Early Ekklesia recognized the unification of the United Kingdom of David (the "Tabernacle of David") as the reconciliation of Judah and Ephraim, along with the *"rest of mankind ... even all the Gentiles."*

The two are clearly differentiated. "Mankind" in the Septuagint (Greek OT) from Amos 9:11-12 refers to "Edom/Adam" and alludes to Esau who was "hated, while Jacob was loved" (Rom. 9:13; Mal. 1:2-3). These two were reconciled by the "blood of the cross" wherein He made of the two (Jews and Gentiles/Ephraim) ONE NEW MAN, so making peace (Eph. 2:15).

Covenantalism's rejection, for whatever theological justification or eisegesis, of the Jew, of Israel, wherein they claim the mantel of "True Israel" and Dispensationalism's multiplicity of New Covenants and/or "postponements"—BOTH are spurious commentary on the literal Word of God and of His Eternal Commitments to those under His Blood Covenant, the New Covenant, the very "Israel of God"— "All Israel" (Gal. 6:16; Rom. 11:26).

It must be noted that Reform/Covenantalism theologies in reference to "the Israel of God" and/or "All Israel" are not monolithic in their applications; neither are those within Dispensationalism consistent in their views regarding major themes concerning the New Covenant, the Kingdom of God, and other issues related to Israel. Indeed:

> Progressive Dispensationalism has departed from one of the historical distinctives of normative Dispensationalism, that of the offer, rejection, postponement, and exclusively future fulfillment of the Davidic kingdom. It has also failed to include a related distinctive, the Church's separateness from the Davidic kingdom. Dispensationalists from the successive periods of history have repeatedly emphasized these distinctives, an emphasis that nondispensational critics have also noted. Progressive Dispensationalism, on the other hand, has not advocated these distinctives, raising the question of whether that movement deserves the label "dispensational" or whether it belongs more in the category of nondispensational historical premillennialism.[111]

NOTE: The New Covenant is mentioned/alluded (clearly) in the following passages in the New Testament: Matthew 26:28; Luke 22:20; 1 Corinthians 11:25; 2 Corinthians 3:6; Hebrews 9:15; Romans 11:26-27; Hebrews 13:20-21.

---

[111] The Dispensational View of the Davidic Kingdom: A Response to Progressive Dispensationalism, Stephen J. Nichols, TMSJ 7/2 (Fall 1996) 213-239 @ https://www.tms.edu/m/tmsj7h.pdf – Retrieved on 05.03.2020).

CHAPTER FOURTEEN

THE KINGDOM OF GOD
BY DOUG KRIEGER[112]

At the crux of Dispensationalism is the separation of Israel and the Church (aka the Ekklesia). Consequently, the manifestation of the "earthly kingdom's" presence was *de facto* postponed due to Israel's rejection of their King, the Messiah, our Lord Jesus Christ. Therefore, today's Kingdom of God or simply "The Heavenly Kingdom" is the "Kingdom of His dear Son" (Col. 1:13) prior to the coming of the actual Messianic Age (aka the Millennium) when the King (either a reincarnation of David or someone like David or some who are keenly persuaded it could be the Son of David, Jesus) will reign from Jerusalem over the earth while the Bride of Messiah occupies the "heavenly realms." Therefore, keeping Israel and the Church eschatologically within their dissimilar polity demands the kingdom envisioned for the Church is heavenly in nature, spiritual in its manifestation both now and into the future, whereas, the kingdom for Israel is wholly earthly. The one is "other worldly" (Dispensationalism) and the other "this worldly" (Israel). The dichotomy of kingdoms set up within Dispensationalism is straightforward—Israel abides wholly distinct and separated from the Church when it comes to "kingdom teaching."

The previous paragraph has, in the main, encapsulated the understanding of most premillenarians; however, the theological perceptions of Amillenarians—both Catholic and Reform—completely disregard any "kingdom prospects" for the Jews/Israel, while contending that the Kingdom of God is altogether present upon the earth and into the Eschaton. Amillenarians view the "postponement theory" orchestrated by Dispensationalism as nigh heresy:

---

[112] Adapted from *The Kingdom of God: A Fresh View*, Amazon, Krieger, 2020.

"The postponement theory, or heresy as it has been called on one occasion, denies the unity of the Church. It rejects the tenet that the Church is the true Israel of God. It finds no continuity or organic unity of God's revelation linking the Israel of the Old Testament with the Church of the New. Moreover, the denial of the unity of the Church involves a refusal to believe that the middle wall of partition has been broken down between Jew and Gentile. The chiliast [i.e., those who affirm a literal 1,000-year millennium on the earth] is said to teach two ways of salvation, one for the Jew and one for the Gentile. The Jew of the Old Testament economy was saved in a manner different from that whereby the New Testament believer is redeemed to God. The manifestation of God's wrath in the millennial kingdom is to take the place of the preaching of the gospel . . . the postponement theory is criticized because it disregards historical testimony. The Christian Church has always held that Israel is the Church. The view had adherents among the faithful of the apostolic age, among the Church Fathers, and among the Reformers of the sixteenth century. It is impossible that the Church should have been allowed to proceed for so many centuries in error when the Holy Spirit is present in her midst."[113]

Douglas R. Shearer in his exposé of Amillennialism (***Amillennialism—theology or Metaphysics***, self-published, cir. 2019, Sacramento, CA, p. 14-15) cuts to the chase by using the words of theologian Herman Bavinck, a contemporary of another Amillennialist, Abraham Kuyper, who openly admits that the Amillennial hermeneutic suffers greatly under a far less literal interpretation of the OT text [and, I would say, the NT as well]:

> The Old Testament, stripped of its temporal and sensuous (i.e., "material") forms, is the New Testament. All Old Testament (rites, rituals, events, nations, and persons) shed their external, national-Israelish meanings and become manifest (i.e., "acquire their real meaning") in a spiritualized . . . sense[114] . . . all the prophets announce not only the conversion of Israel and the nations but also the return to Palestine, the rebuilding of Jerusalem, the restoration of the

---

[113] *Millennialism: The Two Major Views*, Charles L. Feinberg, Moody Press, Chicago, Third Edition, 1980, pp. 252-53.

[114] H Bavinck, ***The Last Things*** (Grand Rapids: Baker, 2000), 96-97.

temple, the priesthood, and sacrificial worship, and so on . . . Prophecy pictures for us but one single image of the future. And this image is either to be taken literally as it presents itself—and as premillennialists take it . . . or this image calls for a very different interpretation (i.e., hermeneutic) than that attempted by (premillennialists).[115]

Shearer's final summation of Amillenarian hermeneutics concludes with a veritable theological indictment:

A "very different interpretation" indeed! An interpretation that's not grounded in the text; that, instead, is grounded in a hermeneutic that, once again, summarily strips away the plain, literal meaning of the text and affirms that the nations, persons, events, rites, rituals, and prophecies described there serve a symbolic, type/antitype purpose only! Clearly, what we have here is metaphysics, not theology.[116]

Within the context of CT there is a recognition that the extremity of these positions—one ultra-literal (dispensational-Premillenarianism) and the other ultra-allegorical (reform-Amillennialism) in their hermeneutic would, nevertheless, temper their contentions admitting there's "literal and allegorical" in both systems. We might be accused of being somewhat "theologically presumptuous" to placate both sides by taking their obvious strengths, proclaiming we alone take the "middle ground" thereby avoiding the extremes inherent in these opposing interpretations.

Shearer's charge regarding the metaphysical (aka "allegorical") nature of Amillenarian hermeneutic bears immediate merit—especially, its ultimate Weltanschauung wherein the "dark side" of Amillenarian rejection of Israel's materiality (both now and into the future) was wholly embraced by Hitler's love of the same—simply put: How "on earth" (deliberate use) could Martin Luther's writing of "***The Jews and their Lies***" (*Von den Juden und ihren Lügen*) be penned if a theology had not evolved through the centuries which demanded the Church occupy all spiritual and earthly blessing once shared with Israel . . . to the extent the Almighty has rejected the Jew and all her "supposed claims" to any inheritance, be it earthly or spiritual?

---

[115] H. Bavinck, **Reformed Dogmatics** (Baker Academic; Abridged edition (June 1, 2011), 658.

[116] D.R. Shearer, **Amillennialism, Theology or Metaphysics**, Book III, p. 14.

Allow me to be a bit curt by saying: Dispensationalism's differentiation with that of Amillennialism at least provided "space" for the Jew, only to "theologically ghettoize" them, keeping them wholly outside the Commonwealth of Israel and "sentencing them" under the banner of the pretribulational rapture of the Church to suffer the fate of Jacob's Trouble in a far worse Holocaust at the end of the age. And, no, now is not the time—given the extremity of the hour—to smugly embrace a so-called "grammatical-historical hermeneutic" which is literal to a point, then obfuscates its treachery while posing to be a friend to the Jew while abandoning them to their most fateful hour (because that's supposed to be biblical). But again, the Amillenarian simply discards any such "theological ghettoizing" of the Jew by dispensing of any such construct in that the Church is the Spiritual Israel of God—the True Israel of God—All Israel . . . while some Amillenarians (e.g., Preterists) conclude Bible prophecy's Abomination of Desolation was, in point of fact, the destruction of the Herodian Temple in the Jewish wars between 66-70 A.D. terminating in the death of over a million Jewish defenders and inhabitants of Jerusalem by Titus and the Tenth Roman Legion. In other words: Who cares about the Jews, they're not even on our radar and most who claim Jewish ancestry are at best nothing more than Gentiles (e.g., Khazars) posing as Israelites—there are no Jews of yesteryear.

Confounding the dispensational effort to separate Israel from the Church is the disquieting attempt to bifurcate the terms of the **"Kingdom of God"** (the present manifestation of the "heavenly kingdom" upon the earth through the Church) from the **"Kingdom of Heaven"**:

1. The kingdom of God is universal, including all moral intelligences willingly subject to the will of God, whether angels, the Church or saints of past or future dispensations (Lk. 13:28, 29; Heb. 12:22, 23); while the kingdom of heaven is Messianic, mediatorial, and Davidic, and has for its object the establishment of the kingdom of God in the earth (1 Cor. 15:24, 25).

2. The kingdom of God is entered only by the new birth (John 3:3, 5-7); the kingdom of heaven, during this age, is the sphere of a profession which may be real or false (Mt. 13:3, note; 25:1, 11, 12).
3. Since the kingdom of heaven is the earthly sphere of the universal kingdom of God, the two have almost all things in common. For this reason, many parables and other teachings are spoken of the kingdom of heaven in Matthew, and the kingdom of God in Mark and Luke. It is the omissions which are significant. The parables of the wheat and tares, and of the net (Mt. 13:24-30, 36-43, 47-50) are not spoken of the kingdom of God. In that kingdom there are neither tares nor bad fish. But the parable of the leaven (Mt. 13:33) is spoken of the kingdom of God also, for, alas, even the true doctrines of the kingdom are leavened with the errors of which the Pharisees, Sadducees, and the Herodians were the representatives . . .
4. The kingdom of God "comes not with outward show" (Lk. 17:20), but is chiefly that which is inward and spiritual (Rom. 14:17); while the kingdom of heaven is organic, and is to be manifested in glory on the earth . . .
5. The kingdom of heaven merges into the kingdom of God when Christ, having "put all enemies under His feet," shall have delivered up the kingdom to God, even the Father" (1 Cor. 15:24-28).[117]

Admittedly, CT finds some agreement in Scofield's interpretation; however, Scofield's entire theological construct has performed, once again on behalf of the dispensationalist, hermeneutical acrobatics by attempting to delineate the "Kingdom of God" from the "Kingdom of Heaven" by giving these designations extra-biblical renderings in an attempt in keeping the Church's "heavenly calling" from Israel's "earthly estate"—notwithstanding, attributing both to the eternal plan and purpose of the Almighty in expounding upon His glory in delineating the two. The charge by Amillennialism that Dispensationalism does despite in bringing the two together (i.e., Israel and the Church) has formidable credibility; again:

---

[117] C. I. Scofield, *The Scofield Reference Bible*, p. 1003. See also C. I. Scofield, *The New Scofield Reference Bible*, p. 1002.

"Moreover, the denial of the unity of the Church involves a refusal to believe that the middle wall of partition has been broken down between Jew and Gentile."[118]

A Fresh Look at the Kingdom of God

First of all, Dispensationalism's refinement in attempting to differentiate the meanings and timing of the "Kingdom of God" (occurring 68 times in the NT) and the "Kingdom of Heaven" (occurring 32 times in the NT) bear no such scrutiny. The term the "Kingdom of Heaven" was used in Jesus' day by the devout in reference to G-d's Name.[119] The dichotomy of the "earthly" versus the "heavenly" was/is simply a vacuous juxtaposition bearing little or no understanding in the mind of the religious Jew, nor for that matter, the Gentile.

Yet, all of the aforementioned begs the question: What exactly is the manifestation of the Kingdom of God/Heaven in the here and now, let alone into the future?

"Kingdom living"—discipleship and/or sanctification and its movements—is uppermost in the minds and practice among many a sincere Christian. When such discipleship is attached to "authority" (e.g., "Lordship salvation"—where Jesus not only saves one, but that individual manifests the "Christ life" by willingly coming under His authority in life and practice and is personalized in that individual) is one thing—but a very different thing when it is "collectively" introduced into the public square.

I make this inaugural comment at the outset of this "fresh look" in that today's clamor between a more subdued intrusion (still very vocal) of discipleship (aka "kingdom living") by the, in the main, Premillenarian persuasion is in counter distinction to the deliberate attempts at a Post-millenarian/Amillenarian approach to "collective discipleship" wherein the "Church Militant" makes a concerted effort to influence, even subdue, the public square. One might contrast the two with one being but "salt and light" and the other being the entire steak within the context of a "strobe light show."

---

[118] Ibid. Charles Feinberg, p. 252
[119] "Are the Kingdom of God and the Kingdom of Heaven the Same? Never Thirsty @ https://www.neverthirsty.org/bible-qa/qa-archives/question/are-the-kingdom-of-god-and-kingdom-of-heaven-the-same—Retrieved on 05.05.2020.

Our brother, Dr. Gavin Finley, romanticizes the two in his outstanding reflections between the Pilgrim vs. the Puritan with the Pilgrim being the more docile of the two when it comes to orchestrating the government of God among men.[120]

MATTHEW 16 VS. JOHN 1
REVEALING GOD'S ULTIMATE INTENTION

Without controversy Matthew 16:13-20 is the *sine quo non* of all passages revealing the Person (Son of God) and Work (*"I will build My Ekklesia"*) of Jesus' identity and mission. Without this disclosure we in the NT are left adrift in precisely determining His ultimate personhood and the destiny of why the incarnate Son of God so manifested His presence among humankind. By humanity's acknowledgement of His personhood as the Son of God incarnate as a man must come as a revelation from the Father—only Almighty God can reveal such an enlightenment. It is this revelation which provides the BASIS (the "rock") on which Jesus would build His EKKLESIA (aka His "Church"—His called-out ones—His elect). Without this VISION there is no manifestation of the Kingdom of God . . . for when Jesus said that the *"kingdom of God is already among you"* or *"the kingdom of God is in your midst"* (Luke 17:21) it clearly meant that wherever He was/is THAT is the Kingdom of God—His presence is pure authority—the King is in the midst of His Kingdom.

This is the express purpose of the incarnation:

> *"For unto us a Child is born, unto us a Son is given; and the government will be upon His shoulder. And His name will be called Wonderful, Counselor, Mighty God, Everlasting Father, Prince of Peace. Of the increase of His government and peace there will be no end . . . Behold your King is coming to you; He is just and having salvation . . . He shall speak peace to the nations; His dominion shall be from sea to sea, and from the River to the ends of the earth"* (Isa. 9:6-7; Zech. 9:9-10—Excerpts).

---

[120] *Pilgrims and Puritans*, by Dr. Gavin Finley, blog, http://endtimepilgrim.org/puritans10.htm — Retrieved, 05.05.2020

Matthew's gospel, of course, presents Jesus as the Son of David—His kingly lineage as Messiah (Matt. 1:1) with, I might add, a total of 42 generations (14 X 3 = 42—Matt. 1:17) in which "42" is the precise number of the kings of the United Kingdom of Judah and Israel (3—Saul, David, and Solomon); plus the 19 of Israel and 20 of Judah = 42 in the "divided kingdom."[121]

Jesus' repeated use and practices revealed in the Synoptic Gospels (Matthew, Mark and Luke) reveal the Kingdom of God/Heaven is personified in the Person of Christ Himself . . . however, it is mandatory, yea, self-explanatory, for any King to have a Kingdom. Now, when Matthew's gospel was written somewhere between 50-65 AD and John's gospel written in the latter part of the first century—towards the end of his life (cir. 85-90 AD)—there was a deepening revelation of the Person and Work of our Lord . . . a, I believe, greater understanding and Holy Spirit's illumination of God's Plan and Purpose of the Ages. Surely, John had a much greater grasp of Paul's writings, having moved to Ephesus, probably during the Jewish War of A.D. 66-70. (Paul having been beheaded in Rome cir. 66-67 AD . . . "For instance, Irenaeus, the bishop of Lyons in the latter part of the second century, stated, 'John, the disciple of the Lord, who also leaned upon His breast, did himself publish a Gospel during his residence in Ephesus in Asia'" [*Against Heresies* 3.1.1])[122]

Therefore, at a minimum, some 20 years to a maximum of some 40 years, John's gospel account produced a far more extensive unveiling of His Person and Work and how He would achieve His purposes among men after His earthly departure. Of measurable interest, the Synoptic Gospels all record the term "New Covenant"—whereas John does not; but instead, delves into the New Commandment with great detail—whereas the Synoptics completely obfuscate this most glaring account in the Upper Room. Was this intentional on John's inspirational account or was it, by this time, the understanding of the Kingdom of God, insofar as Israel's material viewpoint, naught but an attempt to greatly diminish such a concept, while drawing greater attention to the Ekklesia? Was John's Gospel presenting a more "mature" understanding and practice of the Early Church? To a greater extent, I think not.

---

[121] See: Lambert Dolphins: "Kings of Israel and Judah"
http://www.ldolphin.org/kings.html – Retrieved on 05.05.2020
[122] *New Spirit-Filled Life Bible* (KJV), p. 1505.

Moreover, the Synoptic Gospels proliferate with the "Kingdom of God" or "Kingdom of Heaven" language; however, John's Gospel scarcely mentions these phrases. Only in reference to regeneration (John 3:3, 5) do we hear something about the "Kingdom of God" or we muse over the striking statement of Jesus when soldiers tried to capture Him in the Garden of Gethsemane: "My kingdom is not of this world." Here is what I'm driving towards:

A similar phraseology, with accompanying participants in both Matthew and John's gospel can be contrasted. The first being the disciples, led by Simon Bar-Jonah whose name was changed to *Peter* at the revelation of the Messiah's identity and purpose—while the second account in John involves a limited number of disciples, Philip and Nathanael, to wit:

> *"Jesus saw Nathanael coming toward Him, and said of him, 'Behold, an Israelite indeed, in whom is no deceit!' Nathanael said to Him, 'How do You know me?' Jesus answered and said to him, 'Before Philip called you, when you were under the fig tree, I saw you.' Nathanael answered and said to Him, 'Rabbi, You are the Son of God! You are the King of Israel!' Jesus answered and said to him, 'Because I said to you, 'I saw you under the fig tree,' do you believe? You will see greater things than these.' And He said to him, 'Most assuredly, I say to you, hereafter you shall see heaven open, and the angels of God ascending and descending upon the Son of Man.'"* (John 1:47-51)

Remember, John's gospel was written at least 20-40 years AFTER that of Matthew's gospel, and, most definitely, from Ephesus or thereabouts, according to most contemporary scholars—Paul having written his most profound account of the Ekklesia's nature and purpose to the Ephesian believers. Peter had already declared that Jesus was the Christ, the Son of the Living God in Matthew's gospel; however, Nathanael not only declared the divinity of Jesus—*"You are the Son of God!"*—but punctuated His exclamation with: *"You are the King of Israel."* In other words—Nathanael brought the Son of God into immediate focus within the context of Israel's materiality—***The King of Israel***. You may suggest that Nathanael's accounting by

John was simply designed to highlight the superficial understanding that most Jews had of the "kingdom's nature"—but I suggest a far more profound disclosure is in view, given the additional comments made by Jesus as a response to Nathanael's outburst.

Peter acclaimed Him as the Son of God—so did Nathanael. Jesus then declared His purpose for being in reference to the Ekklesia—but Nathanael, again, brought into context the Son of God with the "King of Israel." Why is this included in the text? It is not just because John decided to include it—he could just as well dispensed with the statement "King of Israel"—but he did not; he included it. Jesus did NOT deny these entitlements but advanced "these things" climaxing them in a grandiose crescendo by saying something far more expansive than "*I will build My Ekklesia*"—no, He went much further by stating: *"You will see greater things than these . . . you shall see heaven open, and the angels of God ascending and descending upon the Son of Man"* (John 1:50-51). You may suggest that Matthew's revelation of the Ekklesia is most profound—it is. However, I would contest that the exchange with Nathanael is far and away more "purposeful" in that it not only expands, although not specifically mentioning, the theme of the Ekklesia in that it illuminates by what manner the House of God (Bethel), which is the Ekklesia to which Jesus alluded to in Matthew 16, will be built. That is, through the practicum of the vision of Jacob's ladder!

Let me explain.

Matthew profoundly unveils the identity, if you would, of the Son of God—so does John. Matthew progresses to the Ekklesia—the Kingdom of God (as a matter of deductive reasoning); whereas, John does the same with Nathanael's statement: "The King of Israel." However, the MEANS by which Jesus would build His House (Bethel) was not given in Matthew's gospel—but it was glaringly disclosed in John's: *". . . greater things than these . . . you shall see heaven open, and the angels of God ascending and descending upon the Son of Man."* What is this? Nathanael, you say "Son of God . . . King of Israel"—I say "greater things"—I say SON OF MAN.

CH. 14: THE KINGDOM OF GOD

The vision of Jacob's Ladder and subsequent declarations of initially calling the place of his vision *Bethel*—the House of God (Gen. 28:10-22) then describes how he took the stone upon which he slept and *"set it up as a pillar, and poured oil on top of it . . . and he called the name of that place Bethel."* It was after Jacob's encounter with the Angel of the Lord, wherein his name was changed to *Israel* (Gen. 32:28), whereupon his hip was broken, that Jacob-Israel returned to Bethel (the second time) by divine commission and there built an altar *"and called the place El Bethel* (lit. God, the House of God—Genesis 35:7), *because God appeared to him when he fled from the face of his brother* (Esau) . . . *Then God appeared to Jacob again, when he came from Padan Aram, and blessed him. And God said to him, 'Your name is Jacob; your name shall not be called Jacob anymore, but Israel shall be your name."*

God reinforced His first disclosure in Genesis 28 regarding *". . . your descendants shall be as the dust of the earth; you shall spread abroad to the west and the east, to the north and the south' and in you in your seed all the families of the earth shall be blessed"* (Gen. 28:14) by reinforcing His promise to Israel via the second time: *"I am God Almighty. Be fruitful and multiply; a nation and a COMPANY OF NATIONS shall proceed from you, and kings shall come from your body"* (Gen. 35:9-11). Thence, again, but not altogether similar, Genesis records: *"So Jacob set up a pillar in the place where He talked with him, a pillar of stone; and he poured a drink offering on it, and poured oil on it. And Jacob called the name of the place where God spoke with him, Bethel"* (Gen. 35:14-15) . . . yet, previously, Jacob-Israel called the place *El Bethel* (Gen. 35:7).

Jacob's name change took place between his first encounter at Bethel and his second encounter at Bethel. Yes, it was at Peniel or Penuel (lit. the *"Face of God"* (Gen. 32:22-32)—after his wrestling with the Angel of the Lord that his name was changed from Jacob to Israel. He went from the name *Jacob* (Usurper) to the name *Israel* (Prince with God)—that is a cataclysmic altercation of the name! Israel then came to Bethel again (Gen. 35:1-15) where, once again, the Almighty reinforced the name change from Jacob to Israel (Gen. 35:10-11); again, this took place at Bethel which Israel renamed: El-Bethel (Gen. 35:7).

Can I go so far as to say, initially, we see Bethel (the House of God or Bethel—the Ekklesia to be built); but after the vision of Jacob's Ladder and after Jacob's "breaking experience" and his encounter with Esau (no less) there is a complete expansion amplified in his name change to *Prince with God/Israel*—thus we see in this HOW God's Plan and Purpose for the Ages would be orchestrated; how it would be carried out by changing another name—not from *Simon Bar-Jonah* to *Peter*—but from *Jacob* to *Israel* . . . the outworking of the Ekklesia, the Kingdom of God through the PRINCE OF PEACE. Why can I say such a contrast? Because Jesus said as much when He announced "*greater things*" to Nathanael.

Yes, Jacob and Esau were reconciled (Genesis 33:1-17), but it was only after Jacob had wrestled with the Angel of the Lord at Peniel/Penuel where upon he knew he had met the "Face of God." Now, there was no escape—he had to confront his estranged brother, Esau. Then a most incredible statement from the lips of Israel is heard of the "hated Esau" (for "*Jacob I loved, and Esau I hated*"—Romans 9:13; Mal. 1:2-3): "*I* [Israel] *have seen your* [Esau's] *face as though I had seen the face of God, and you were pleased with me*" (Gen. 33:10).

Then after all this (and more) Jacob comes once again to Bethel where the Almighty reinforces the change of *Jacob* to *Israel*, but only after Israel entitles Bethel as *El-Bethel* (Gen. 35:7) whereupon after the reinforcement of the name change Jacob sets up a *"pillar in the place where He talked with him, a pillar of stone; and he poured a drink offering on it, and he poured oil on it"* (Gen. 35:14-15).

Could it be, and I most definitely affirm it to be so, the *"ascending and descending upon the SON OF MAN"* carries the vision of the Son of God's incarnation but places initial emphasis upon "ascending" (bringing MAN into God)—for there is now a MAN IN THE GLORY seated upon the Throne. Here we have "ascending" mentioned before "descending" (bringing the Son of God into MAN)—but the priority of order is the Son of Man's ascent into heaven. It is one thing for humankind to confess the deity of the Messiah as Son of God—it is a massive advance of the vision whereby the ASCENSION OF THE SON OF MAN into glory, having accomplished through the "breaking"—through the cross—that splendid goal by "*creating in Himself*"—through "*the blood of the cross*" (the "breaking")— *"between the TWO"* (Jew and Gentile—Jacob-Israel and Esau) *ONE NEW MAN, so making peace*—Ephesians 2:14-18:

"For He Himself is our peace, who has made both one, and has broken down the middle wall of separation, having abolished in His flesh the enmity, that is, the law of commandments contained in ordinances, so as to create in Himself one new man from the two, thus making peace, and that He might reconcile them both to God in one body through the cross, thereby putting to death the enmity. And He came and preached peace to you who were afar off and to those who were near. For through Him we both have access by one spirit to the Father."

Yes, immediately after Peter's confession—*"Thou art the Christ, the Son of the Living God"*—Jesus commenced to predict His death (Matt. 16:21), whereupon *"Peter took Him aside and began to rebuke Him, saying, 'Far be it from You, Lord; this shall not happen to You!"* (Matt. 16:22). Peter had a revelation of the Son of God but NOT the Son of Man—for it would be only through the ascent upon the Son of Man the Ekklesia would be built. The reality of the name change extended to the King of Israel—from Jacob to Israel—then and only then, through the cross, would Jacob ever be reconciled with Esau—only through the breaking of the outward man (the work of the cross) can the Ekklesia come into being: El-Bethel. God . . . the House of God. Only God Almighty (El) can build the House of God (Bethel). Only the Son of Man, through incarnation, human living, suffering, crucifixion, resurrection, and ascension, can the Ekklesia be built—the real Temple, the real House of God:

"Now, therefore, you are no longer strangers and foreigners, but fellow citizens with the saints and members of the household of God, having been built on the foundation of the apostles and prophets, Jesus Christ Himself being the chief cornerstone, in whom the WHOLE BUILDING, being fitted together, grows into a HOLY TEMPLE in the Lord, in whom you also are being built together for a dwelling place of God in the Spirit" (Eph. 2:19-22)—Is this not Bethel?

The Incarnation of the Son of God (though He was always the Son of Man) "came in the flesh" to suffice the righteous requirements of the Law—*"for without the shedding of blood there is no remission of sin"* (Heb. 9:22; Lev. 17:11)—but *". . . it is not possible that the blood of bulls and goats could take away sins . . . Therefore, when He came into the world, He said: "Sacrifice and offering You did not desire, but a body You have prepared for Me. In burnt offerings and sacrifices for sin You had no pleasure. Then I said, 'Behold, I have come—in the volume of the book it is written of Me—to do Your will, O God'"* (Heb. 10:4-7; Mic. 6:6, 7; Ps. 40:6-8).

If you would, the "subjective application of the cross" in our lives as believers in Jesus, enables Messiah, the Christ, through the Spirit of Christ applying His cross in our daily lives, to build His Ekklesia—to reconcile us not only to God (Bethel—connoting personal "peace with God") but this same Spirit of Christ brings us into peace with our brethren—between hostile peoples (El Bethel). This demands a reinforcement—a breaking—a name change "rehearsal"—the taking, not only of anointing oil, but the pouring out of a "drink offering"—not only the "anointing of the Holy Spirit" to build His Ekklesia, but the total "pouring out" of our lives—His Life in us outpoured for the brethren. Yes, we are LIVING STONES to be built up a most Holy and Royal Priesthood (1 Peter 2:4-10). It is upon these "living stones" that the "anointing oil" is poured—but more so, the "drink offering" is poured out (Is this not what the Son of Man did on our behalf?)—that same outpouring in us alone brings in the full experience of His Ekklesia.

Can you see this? What we have here is none other than the preaching of the GOSPEL OF THE KINGDOM recited numerous times in the Gospels. Yes, it is the Gospel of the Grace of God (Acts 20:24) which wholly entails *"preaching the kingdom of God"* (Acts 20:25)—the two are inseparable. It is the same recitation at the close of the book of Acts where we read: *"Preaching the KINGDOM OF GOD and teaching the things which concern the Lord Jesus Christ"* (Acts. 28:31).

But we must come to terms that this GOSPEL OF THE KINGDOM cannot be differentiated from the Gospel of the Grace of God (salvation) which is inseparably linked with the Gospel of Peace—for the two are utterly intrinsic. The work of the cross not only reconciled us to God (i.e., the "blood of the cross") but reconciled us to one another— *"making of the two ONE NEW MAN . . . so making peace."* Yes, "two sides of the same coin!"

Therefore, Paul's dissertation in declaring the "*GOSPEL OF GOD*" *"to all who are in Rome, beloved of God, called to be saints"* would be for these "Roman saints" the FULL DISPLAY of that Gospel of God from start to finish. Ergo—Romans 1-8 takes us from man's sin under the wrath of God unto justification via His righteousness, unto sanctification by the truth, to ultimate glorification under the empowerment of the Spirit—yes, the Gospel of the Grace of God . . . but where is the KINGDOM OF GOD in all this illumination? Where is the living out of the Ekklesia; and, if you would, praise God for Bethel, but where is El-Bethel—wherefore the work of the cross of Christ? Why does, again, Paul launch throughout the latter half of his epistle (Romans 9-16) on themes wholly related to issues related to the oneness of God's people—Jew and Gentile?

It is inescapable to finally confront our Esau. You can run to your monastery or convent—to your seclusion and so-called "spirituality" but you cannot hide, for the day cometh when you must confront Romans 12 to present your body a living sacrifice to test your sanctification or "head knowledge" with others and to cease from *"thinking of yourself more highly than you ought to think"* (Romans 12:3)—it is time to manifest THE KINGDOM OF GOD with a transformed mind. When that happens, then this is the result:

> *"For the **KINGDOM OF GOD** is not eating and drinking, but righteousness and peace and joy in the Holy spirit . . . for he who serves Christ in these things* (Are not these the "greater things" whereof our Lord spoke to Nathanael?) *is acceptable to God and approved by men"* (Rom. 14:17-18).

This is the "good news of the kingdom" (i.e., "the gospel of the kingdom"—Matt. 24:14)—*righteousness* (through Christ alone)—*peace* (between the brethren—bringing in the oneness of His Kingdom) *and joy in the Holy Spirit* (this is the GLORY—for we can have the "objective" awareness of His righteousness (positionally) and have been bought through the "blood of His cross"—positionally (as well) into oneness . . . but without the JOY OF THE HOLY SPIRIT there is NO EXPRESSION OF THE KINGDOM OF GOD (Ref. Rom. 14:17). The KINGDOM OF GOD is NOT "DOS AND DON'TS"—not eating and drinking . . . not that we do not honor our fathers and mothers or keep Sabbath, etc., but THAT'S NOT THE

KINGDOM OF GOD per se—the MANIFESTATION OF THE JOY OF THE HOLY SPIRIT is seen among the ONENESS of His people—that's what Romans 9-16 is all about.

All three are needed to express the fullness of the KINGDOM OF GOD: The Righteousness of Christ; Peace between hostile peoples through, again, the blood of His Cross; resulting in the Joy of the Holy Spirit— this is the Kingdom of God on the earth today! Indeed, the entire discipleship movement, bless God, centered upon Christ in you the Hope of Glory—the sanctifying work of the Holy Spirit in the believer's life—but having "more of Christ" so that you are brought "more under His authority" is not for the individual disciple to "lord it over" the brethren—i.e., "I have been more transformed than most . . . so I have more of the Lord's authority in my life—therefore, LISTEN TO ME!" No, no, no—the "acceptable test" of one's consecration is to *"not think of ourselves more highly than we ought to think"* (Romans 12:3)—*"but to think soberly, as GOD HAS DEALT TO EACH ONE A MEASURE OF FAITH"* (vs. 3). The "test" of our consecration—our sanctification—is based upon the Kingdom of God's manifestation among us—that's the EKKLESIA our Lord is building!

In Romans chapters 9-16 Paul speaks of the COMPLETION OF THE GOSPEL OF CHRIST—as he declares THE GOSPEL OF GOD to those in Rome who already have believed in the Son of God.

"But I know that when I come to you, I shall come in the FULLNESS of the blessing of the Gospel of Christ" (Romans 15:29).

And just what is the FULLNESS (lit. "completion") of Christ's Gospel? What does Messiah desire today among His people? People who already have experienced His salvation—yet, though we be sufficed, have we satisfied our Lord in answer to His prayer in John 17? Have we been *"perfected into ONE"* (Jn. 17:23)—so that *"the world would believe the Father sent the Son"* (Jn. 17:21)? Have we but preached a HALF-GOSPEL where we reach glorification (Romans 8) but fail to advance from the Gospel of Salvation to the Gospel of Peace? I am not parsing words here. Romans 1-8 is distinctly the life of the believer from start to completion—individually; however, Romans 9-16 places us squarely into the outworking of the Ekklesia.

That is why Romans 16 becomes the apex of Paul's exhortation to the saints in Rome! Where is the "meeting and greeting" of all God's people? Where are Jews at meal with the nations? Where do we witness Romans at meal with Barbarians and Greeks, and Jews? Aren't the EKKLESIA (aka "the Churches") of Romans 16:3-5 those who like *"Priscilla and Aquila, my fellow workers in Christ Jesus, who risked their own necks for my life, to whom not only I give thanks, but also all the EKKLESIA of the Nations. Likewise greet the EKKLESIA that is in their house."* Do you conjecture that all this "meeting and greeting" taking place in Romans 16 (some 36 entities/individuals) is some inane end-of-the-movie credits whereupon we simply walk out because who can "read that fast" and/or "who cares" in any event?

Again: No, no, no! This is the apex of the EKKLESIA—the KINGDOM OF GOD—this, this KINGDOM OF GOD—this EKKLESIA experience where the saints as a "living sacrifice" find divine approval, acceptable unto God—a reasonable service . . . outpoured for one another. It is not until and unless we come to this "reception of one another" through the "blood of the cross" that we finally hear:

"And the God of Peace will crush Satan under your feet shortly" (Rom. 16:20).

Isn't this where we commenced: *"The gates of Hades shall not prevail against it"* (i.e., the Ekklesia"—Matt. 16:18)? Indeed, it is! After enjoining the saints in Rome to "meet and greet"—to express their Oneness in Christ—isn't it a timely fact they have heard: *"Therefore let us pursue the things* (again, *"greater things"*) *which make for peace and the things by which one may edify* (build up) *another"* (Rom. 14:17)? But also, prior to the "crushing of Satan's head" which was forecast in Genesis 3:15 (*"your Seed shall bruise/crush his* [the serpent's] *head"*) we are made keenly aware of divisive behavior contrary to such "meeting and greeting" of the saints in Rome:

"Now I urge you, brethren, note those who cause divisions and offenses, contrary to the doctrine which you learned, and avoid them. For those who are such do not serve our Lord Jesus Christ, but their own belly, and by smooth words and flattering speech deceive the hearts of the simple" (Romans 16:17-18).

Astonishing, isn't it, that those who hail from the "Church of the Immaculate Perception" are able to "slice and dice" issues on the Kingdom of God while perpetrating division amongst the people of God to such an extent that they "stand apart" from the brethren—gathering, then holding tight to themselves brethren prohibiting them from "meeting and greeting" brethren at large. Indeed, these "divisive brethren" may be as much, or more so, in defense of the Gospel of God's Grace, yet they eschew brethren whose doctrinal positions inhibit them from genuine fellowship in Christ because they (those who are so divisive) embrace an opposing view of the timing and nature of the KINGDOM OF GOD.

Brethren, we are living NOW in the Kingdom of God which shall encompass the whole earth—it includes all within the EKKLESIA and is wholly supportive of the Gospel of Grace and the Gospel of Peace—this is the KINGDOM OF GOD under the Kingship of Messiah, both now, and into the Millennium, and beyond into the Eschaton—THIS is the Ekklesia Jesus is building by the experience of the Son of Man in us for surely *"As we have borne the image of the man of dust, we shall also bear the image of the heavenly Man . . .."* (1 Cor. 15:49) . . . and by "Heavenly Man" I allude not only to our future resurrection, but to the "Ascending and Descending upon the Son of Man" Who is the King of Israel, now about establishing His Kingdom on this Earth!

> *"Now to Him who is able to establish you according to MY GOSPEL and* **the preaching of Jesus Christ***, according to the revelation of the mystery kept secret since the world began but now made manifest, and by the prophetic Scriptures made known to all nations, according to the commandment of the everlasting God, for obedience to the faith—to God, alone wise, be glory through Jesus Christ forever. Amen"* (Rom. 16:25-27).

They among us who would deny themselves, and take up their cross, will find their "peace with God" will extend to peace among the brethren—for the God who reached out to them desires to reach out through them to their brethren so that the world too shall believe the Father sent the Son . . . and the fellowship the Father has with the Son is the same fellowship into which we are called as sons and daughters of the Living God—this is truly the KINGDOM OF GOD!

The Kingdom of God in John's Gospel[123]

Let's initially consider some differentiation between the Synoptic Gospels and John's Gospel and then draw some possible conclusions as to how these contrasts might impact upon our understanding of the Kingdom of God as it pertains to the Body of Christ today.

Now, allow me to build a case which will shed much greater light, I affirm, on the nature of the Kingdom of God—the Kingdom of His Dear Son but finding those matters embedded in the contrast between the Synoptic Gospels and John's accounting. The implications upon the Ekklesia Jesus forecasted in Matthew's Gospel and how this impacts upon Commonwealth Theology is very much in view here—for it has much to do with the "administration" of His authority over the heavens and the earth. Let us proceed.

Dates of the Gospels

In our studies regarding the Kingdom of God (aka the Kingdom of Heaven) we have found that in the Synoptic (similar accountings of the same stories) Gospels—all written, so it appears, before the destruction of the Herodian Temple and the Jewish-Roman Wars cir. 66-70 AD—vs. John's Gospel written much later (cir. 80-90 AD) from Ephesus towards the end of John's life . . . the emphasis upon the Kingdom of God in the "Synoptics" vs. John's Gospel is more than strikingly different.

The implication as to the dates in which the gospels were written is this: The much later date of John's Gospel (at least 20 years later than the latest of the Synoptics and perhaps as much as 40 years later) would lead us to believe that John's understanding of the Life of Jesus was already seen through the lens of the Synoptics and, most definitely, since John found himself in Ephesus—where Paul had imbued the Ekklesia in Ephesus with "the truth of the Gospel" (Gal. 2)—as well as Paul's many epistles written prior to his death cir. 64-66 AD by Emperor Nero—with revelatory disclosures of God's Eternal Plan and Purpose of the Ages (e.g., the Mystery of

---

[123] Excerpts from "THE SYNOPTIC GOSPELS VS. THE GOSPEL OF JOHN" By Doug Krieger, May 26, 2020 @ commonwealththeology.com
http://commonwealththeology.com/the-synoptic-gospels-vs-the-gospel-of-john.

Christ and the Ekklesia)—would assure his Gospel's account to be, shall we say, more mature on behalf of the followers of Jesus—and, I would go so far as to say, perhaps more profound in its understanding of the Person and Work of Christ.

MIRACLES IN THE GOSPELS

Our studies conclude that the Synoptic Gospels, for one, sequentially present similar aspects of the life and ministry of Christ; whereas John's Gospel appears thematic and profoundly spiritual in its presentation—selecting but seven miracles of Jesus over the course of His earthly ministry—prior to His resurrection:

Jesus changes water into wine—John 2:1-11
Jesus heals a government official's son—John 4:46-54
Jesus heals a lame man by a pool—John 5:1-15
Jesus feeds 5,000—John 6:1-13
Jesus walks on water—John 6:16-21
Jesus heals a man who was born blind—John 9:1-34
Jesus brings Lazarus back from the dead—John 11:41-44

With the eighth (8 the number of "new beginnings" or "resurrection") found in John 21:1-13 when the disciples caught the fish (153 of them) when Jesus told them to cast their net on the opposite or "right side of the boat." What I find most fascinating is this: The Synoptics record precisely 33 miracles[124] of Jesus before His Resurrection—which number set "33" comports to the age of Christ being 33 years of age and His crucifixion in 33 AD (please, be my guest to disagree with me here on these rather obtuse chronologies) . . . and, as you shall see the number set of "33" shows up several times in the phrases of the Kingdom of Heaven (33 times in Matthew) and the Kingdom of God (33 times in Luke) . . . perhaps but a kawinkadink but to each his own!

USE OF THE TERMS: KINGDOM OF GOD/HEAVEN

Moreover—John's Gospel, as we have previously written, scarcely mentions the phrase Kingdom of God but twice in the same incidence with Nicodemus who could not see nor enter the Kingdom

---

[124] See: https://www.spiritoflifeag.com/how-many-miracles-are-there-in-the-bible.

CH. 14: THE KINGDOM OF GOD

of God without being born from above by the Spirit—having to do with the regeneration of the human spirit by the Spirit of God. Likewise, insofar as the "kingdom" concerns John's overt statements by Jesus in John 18:36 wherein He rebuked Peter for his use of the sword by declaring: "My kingdom is not of this world. If My kingdom were of this world, My servants would fight . . . but now My kingdom is not from here."

That's it—two verses in John's Gospel. Yet, in contrast to the Synoptics the Kingdom of God is mentioned countless times and/or its counterpart, the Kingdom of Heaven (solely mentioned in Matthew's Gospel)—in summary:

Matthew: Kingdom of Heaven: 33 times—Kingdom of God: 5 times

Mark: 15 times (Kingdom of God)

Luke: 33 times (Kingdom of God)

Total Kingdom of God: 53 times + 33 (Kingdom of Heaven) = 86 times

Considering the Synoptics mentioning of some 86 times vs. twice in John's Gospel we must ask ourselves: Why such a disparity? It almost appears in John's gospel the matter of "The Kingdom of God" is inconsequential; yet, even in its isolation it is most significant.

THE FEASTS DAYS IN THE GOSPELS

A somewhat obscure, but, profound understanding differentiating the Synoptics from John's Gospel are the Feasts of the Lord (7 of them) and the isolated mentioning of the Feast of Dedication connected with the cleansing of the Second Temple during the Maccabean Era cir. 166 BC. John's Gospel indicates there were 7 such Feast Days—which in turn, allows us to suggest that Jesus' ministry and age was 3 ½ years (42 months) Him being a full 32 years of age or age 33 in the year 33 AD (I know, I'm somewhat resolute about this chronology.)

Allow me some room here: Leviticus 23 list these "Feasts of the Lord" (along with the Feast of Dedication) as follows:

Feast of Passover—14 Nisan (Abib)—Lev. 23:5

Feast of Unleavened Bread—15 Nisan—Lev. 23:6

Feast of First Fruits—16/17 Nisan—Lev. 23:9-14

Feast of Pentecost (Weeks)—6/7 Sivan—Lev. 23:15-22
Feast of Trumpets—1 Tishri—Lev. 23:23-25
Day of Atonement—10 Tishri—Lev. 23:26-32
Feast of Tabernacles—15 Tishri—Lev. 23:33-43
Feast of Dedication—24/25 Kislev

John's Gospel accords what appears to be 7 feast days in the earthly ministry of Jesus:

Day of Atonement—John 1:29-35—By implication—"Behold the Lamb of God Who takes away the sin of the world"— Likewise, Luke 3:23 says "Jesus Himself began His ministry at about thirty years of age"—we affirm His age to be that of 29 years and 6 months with 6 more months unto another Passover to be 30 years of age with 6 months of ministry in the year 30 AD (spring).

First Passover (Feast Day of the Jews)—John 2:13-25; 4:45— Jesus is now precisely 30 years of age, having ministered 6 months—by the time Jesus is a full 32-years of age at His 33rd birthday (Passover) He would have ministered upon the earth from the Day of Atonement in the fall of 29 AD unto Passover, 33 AD, some 3 ½ years or 42 months or 1,260 prophetic days or "time, times and half a time." This would have been in the spring of 30 AD.

Second Passover—By Implication—John 5:1-15—That day was also a Sabbath in the spring of the year 31 AD or April 27, 31 AD (Friday/Saturday) on the Julian Calendar.[125]

Third Passover—John 6:4-14—In the spring of the year 32 AD—Jesus having ministered some 2 ½ years upon the earth. He was now precisely a full 31 years of age and this would have been His 32nd birthday.

The Feast of Tabernacles—John 7:2-44—This was, likewise, in the year 32 AD in the Fall on the Hebrew Sacred Calendar on 15 Tishri; therefore, Jesus would have been 32 years and 6 months of age and would have ministered precisely 3 years on the earth.

---

[125] Steve Morse: https://stevemorse.org/jcal/julian.html or Friday, April 27, 31 AD on the Julian Calendar and April 25/Wednesday on the Gregorian Calendar @ http://intercontinentalcog.org/Appendix/Passover_dates_26-34_AD.php.

The Feast of Dedication (not one of the Lord's Feast Days—but by Jesus attending He so "sanctified" that Feast Day—John 10:22-39). This feast day is on 24/25 Kislev; normally in the month of December/winter. Jesus would have been 32 years, 8 months and 15 days of age and would have ministered on the earth 3 years and 75 days.

Fourth Passover—John 11:55-57 through to John 19:42 (His Passion/Crucifixion)—Jesus would have been precisely a full 32 years of age and would have been crucified on His Passover birthday, Nisan 13/14 (Passover Preparation Day when the Lamb is slain but eaten on 14 Nisan on Passover). He would have been 33 years of age and would have ministered 3 ½ years. This Passover was on the Julian Calendar date 1 April 33 AD, Wednesday/Thursday[126] or 6 Days before the Passover as recorded in John 12:1 which was on a Friday (Day 1); Saturday (Day 2); Sunday (Day 3); Monday (Day 4); Tuesday (Day 5); Wednesday (Day 6—Day of Crucifixion) with Passover being on Thursday (Day 7).

Feast days in Matthew, Mark and Luke—The scarcity of such Feast Days synced with the ministry of Jesus are virtually nonexistent. Matthew simply speaks of the final Passover (Matt. 26:2-5) and of the immediate Feast of Unleavened Bread (Matt. 26:17). Mark speaks of the final Passover as well (Mark 14:1-2; 15:6). Luke speaks of the Passover in Jesus' youth in Luke 2:41-42 and then within the context of Jesus' 3 ½ ministry he simply speaks of the Feast of Unleavened Bread and alludes to the Feast (not by name) of Passover in Luke 22:1 and 17.

One would think that John's Gospel might be the least of all the gospels which would bring such attention to the Hebrew Sacred Calendar and the Feast Days—4 Passovers, 1 Day of Atonement, 1 Feast of Tabernacles, and 1 Feast of Dedication—7 in all; whereas in Matthew, Mark and Luke we have at least 2 Passovers, 2 Feast of Unleavened Bread with possibly an additional Feast of Passover in Luke 22:17. A most perplexing set of affairs since so much is made of the "Jewish character" found in the Synoptics vs. the Gospel of John which far outweighs the significance of such Jewish Feast Days.

---

[126] Ibid – Julian Calendar date being April 1, 33 AD which falls in the "Middle of the Week."

The New Covenant vs. the New Commandment

The New Covenant—inaugurated in the Upper Room prior to Jesus' crucifixion—is delineated in the Synoptic Gospels, to wit:

Matthew 26:28; Mark 14:24; and Luke 22:20

However, it is wholly absent from John's Gospel!

The New Commandment—that we should love one another with the very love of Jesus— *"A New Commandment I give to you, that you love one another; as I have loved you, that you also love one another. By this all will know that you are My disciples, if you have love for one another"* (John 13:31-35; and again, in John 15:12). John makes no mention of the New Covenant/Testament.

Matthew's Gospel speaks of the Great Commandment to "love the Lord with all your heart, strength, etc., and your neighbor as yourself"—but no mention of the New Commandment. Mark rehearses the Great Commandment in Mark 12:28-34.

I believe these "discrepancies" are noteworthy on many levels between the Synoptic Gospels and that of John's Gospel.

The Opening and Ending of the Gospels

Finally, I would like to draw our attention to the opening and closing remarks of each Gospel—a most concise rendering:

Matthew:

Matthew 1—He gives the "genealogy of Jesus Christ, the Son of David—separating out a total of 42 generations (Matt. 1:17)—with 3 sets of 14 such generations and birth via Mary and the story of the incarnation.

Matthew 28:16-20—The spectacular ASCENSION of Jesus Christ and the Great Commission to "make disciples of all the nations, baptizing them in the name of the Father and of the Son and of the Holy Spirit" etc.

Mark:

Mark—Chapter 1—Begins with *"The Gospel of Jesus Christ, the Son of God"* and goes immediately to the account of John the Baptist and then the baptism of Jesus and His Temptation, the commencement of His ministry, calling of His disciples, and then quickly detailing five miracles intertwined with His preaching.

Mark—Chapter 16:14-20—He quickly states, after commissioning His disciples to *"Go into all the world and preach the gospel to every creature"*—to the ascension of Christ: *"He was received up into heaven, and sat down on the right hand of God . . . And they went out and preached everywhere, the Lord working with them and confirming the word through the accompanying signs."* Thus, the ASCENSION, again is recorded.

Luke:

Luke—Chapter 1—Covers at length the "incarnation"—Luke spends nearly two full chapters on the birth of Jesus and then goes into Jesus' baptism by John the Baptist and then covers the genealogy of Jesus Christ "backwards" from Joseph unto Adam, the son of God.

Luke—In Luke 24:50-53 Luke concludes his account with the ASCENSION of Christ; whereupon we read: *"He was parted from them and carried up into heaven. And they worshiped Him, and returned to Jerusalem with great joy, and were continually in the temple praising and blessing God. Amen."* Now, when we come to John's Gospel, an entirely different accounting is in view:

John:

John 1—John goes into eternity past, beyond the incarnation and presents the Word of God as "With God, and the Word was God." The Word became Flesh and "tabernacled among us"—then John announces that "the Law was given by Moses but Grace and Truth came by Jesus Christ" (vs. 16-18)—John then goes into the declarations by John the Baptist that Jesus is the Lamb of God Who takes away the sin of the world. Jesus then calls out Andrew, Simon and Peter to follow Him and then the final account of Philip and Nathanael where Jesus is announced, by Nathanael as the Son of God and the King of Israel with the revelation of Jacob's Ladder: Son of God—Son of Man—uniting Heaven and Earth.

John 21—The story of the Disciples fishing on the Sea of Galilee and the miracle of the 153 Fish—the exchange with Peter to love Jesus and feed His sheep. Peter tries to deflect the conversation to John, but Jesus says, "What is that to you? You follow Me." (vs. 22)—there is no account of Jesus' ASCENSION—John ends with: *"And there are also many other things that Jesus did, which if they were written one by one, I suppose that even the world itself could not contain the books that would be written. Amen"* (vs. 25).

The Conclusion of the Matter

Where does all of this leave us? For one, the Synoptic Gospels all open up in a very "human" accounting of the Incarnation, whereas John's Gospel is far more "cosmic" insofar as the pre-existence of the Son becoming flesh. The closing of the Synoptic Gospels is decidedly spectacular with the ASCENSION taking front and center with the commissioning of the disciples, whereas John's Gospel leaves Jesus on the shore of Galilee with a most personal exchange between Peter and Jesus with Jesus enjoining Peter if he loved Him to "feed My sheep." Yes, there was the "fishing expedition"—but that was secondary to loving Jesus!

There was no mentioning of the Ascension—if one were to read only the Gospel of John, one would be left with the impression Jesus never did ascend to the heavens but is somewhere on the earth today. The Synoptics have Jesus in the heavens—John has Jesus on the earth; yet, John's Gospel is declared to be the "heavenly Son of God"—whereas the Synoptic Gospels present a more "earthly accounting" of the Life of Jesus.

Again, there was no mention of the New Covenant in John's Gospel—only the New Commandment, whereas the Synoptics have no mention of the New Commandment, only the New Covenant. Use of the terms Kingdom of God/Kingdom of Heaven are mentioned numerous times in the Synoptics but hardly mentioned in John's Gospel.

The phrase "King of Israel" is affirmatively mentioned in John 1:49; 12:13 (His Triumphal Entry into Jerusalem) and in Matthew 27:42 and Mark 15:32 where "King of Israel" is mockingly mentioned as Jesus hung upon the cross. The phrase "King of the Jews" is mentioned 12 times in the Synoptics in a mocking manner and five times in mocking fashion in John's Gospel. The only two times the phrase "King of Israel" is affirmatively mentioned in all the gospels is in John's Gospel—once at the beginning of His ministry and prior to the miracle of turning the water into wine at the Wedding of Cana of Galilee when Nathanael uttered it and once again at the close of His ministry on Nisan 10, Palm Sunday, at the close of His ministry and prior to the cross.

From all of the above the conclusion reached by this author suggests that the King and the Kingdom theme in the Synoptic Gospels—coupled with the numerous Festivals Jesus' ministry coincided with in John's Gospel—clearly display in John's Gospel a much more subjective expression of the Kingdom message than those in the Synoptic Gospels. The Synoptic Gospels present an "outward manifestation" of the Kingdom of God—the Gospel of John presents an "inward expression" of the Kingdom of God.

Let me explain. The King of Israel in John's Gospel in the Festivals portrays Jesus in: (1) His ministry of Atonement—John 1:29-35—"Behold the Lamb" of God—(Tishri 10); (2) Jesus' First Passover—John 2:13-23—declares His death and resurrection; (3) Second Passover—John 5:1-47 (actually)—the Person and Work of Christ is declared; (4) Third Passover—John 6:4-14—Jesus presents Himself as the Bread of Life; (5) The Feast of Tabernacles—John 7:2-43—Jesus declares His "interior ministry" as the Water of Life springing up from man's human spirit via the Promise of the Spirit; (6) Feast of Dedication—John 10:22-39—Jesus declares His Divinity as the Son of God; (7) Fourth Passover—John 11:55-57 through John 19:42—Jesus' Upper Room Discourse supplying His disciples then and always with Life, Truth, and Glory that they may be one, unto His crucifixion, death and burial . . . by His "going" He was "coming" into His disciples bringing them into the fellowship the Son has always had with the Father. Indeed, the Olivet Discourse of Matthew 24-25 juxtaposed to the Upper Room Discourse is wholly different on so many levels, it is as if John completely omits events surrounding the end of the age.

Jesus tells us in Matthew 16 He would build His Ekklesia upon Peter's revelatory confession He is the Messiah, the Son of God and that the Gates of Hades would not prevail against this Ekklesia—Peter was given the "Keys to the Kingdom" that would be realized (i.e., the Kingdom) by Jesus's crucifixion and resurrection and ultimate "glory" as expressed on the Mount of Transfiguration in Matthew 17, whereas Nathanael's declaration of Jesus being the Son of God, the King of Israel elevates the revelation of Who Jesus is and His work upon the earth via Jacob's Ladder linking Heaven and Earth and declaring Himself as the Son of Man—with the emphasis upon His work as the Son of Man bringing "man" into God juxtaposed to Matthew's account of bringing the Son of God into the man, Christ Jesus.

It is altogether apparent, as well, the Synoptic Gospels present Jesus as the "fulfillment of the Law"—*"Do not for a moment suppose that I have come to abrogate the Law or the Prophets; I have not come to abrogate them but to give them their completion"* (Weymouth Version)—along with the Great Commandment (Matt. 22:36-40) where we hear:

"Teacher, which is the greatest commandment in the Law?"

Jesus replied: "'Love the Lord your God with all your heart and with all your soul and with all your mind.' This is the first and greatest commandment. And the second is like it: 'Love your neighbor as yourself.' All the Law and the Prophets hang on these two commandments." . . . whereas in John's Gospel there is no mention of the Great Commandment but of the New Commandment:

"I'm giving you a new commandment: Love each other in the same way that I have loved you" (John 13:34—God's Word Translation).

The SOURCE of loving one another (your neighbor) is entirely different—the First Covenant love finds its source in "you loving your neighbor" but in John's New Commandment, obviously under the rubric of the New Covenant, you are to love as Jesus demonstrated His love toward us all . . . in other words, His loving others through you! Furthermore, there is nothing in the New Commandment about loving the Lord—how's that? So incredibly self-less was this New Commandment—Jesus is wholly caught up in loving His disciples—having them share His love with one another—and expecting nothing in return . . . until we get to the very end of John's Gospel where Jesus asks three times if Peter really loved Him—even then, Jesus put that love back, if you would, into "feed My sheep"—always giving, pouring out His love.

The Synoptic Gospels, in the main, tell us HOW the Law of Moses is fulfilled—in other words, Jesus "fulfilled the Law"—showing us how Kingdom Living is lived out:

"Do not for a moment suppose that I have come to abrogate [demolish or destroy] *the Law or the Prophets: I have not come to abrogate them but to give them their completion"* (Matt. 5:17—Weymouth NT).[127]

. . . whereas, John declares: *"For the Law was given through Moses, but grace and truth came through Jesus Christ"* (John 1:16).

John's gospel spells out that Moses' person presents the Law to us ("through Moses"); but Jesus supplies the wherewithal (the supply of

---

[127] It may be noted as a singular instance of the boldness of some of the early heretics, that Marcion, who rejected the Old Testament altogether, maintained that these words had been altered by the Judaizers of the apostolic age, and that the true reading was, "Think ye that I came to fulfill the Law or the prophets? I came not to fulfill, but to destroy" (Elliott's Commentary).

grace) "through Jesus" and for what purpose? To be able to live out the requirements of the Law. The "truth" as conveyed in John's Gospel or "reality" is Christ Himself (John 14:6—"I am ... the truth"). One can surely consider that the Law, through Moses, was/is the truth—but where is the reality of it lived out in the lives of His people? Jesus takes that "truth" (i.e., the fulfillment of the Law in Christ Himself) and via the supply of His grace, lives out this absolute truth through us!

Thus, the KINGDOM OF GOD as seen in the Synoptic Gospels is in a very real sense lived out in us through the Life of Christ, whereas in John's Gospel Jesus demonstrates that this very Life displayed in the Synoptic Gospels is being "deposited" in us, His disciples, in order for them/us to live it out. It is through His grace and truth that the very Kingdom Life displayed in the Synoptic Gospels is lived out in us in the Gospel of John. It is in Christ alone, through His Spirit, whereby we are "born from above" that we both "see" and "enter into" the Kingdom of God (John 3:1-21).

Yes, seeing and entering into the Kingdom of God is accomplished via Jacob's Ladder for Jesus again repeats that vision to Nicodemus in His discourse with this Pharisee:

"If I have told you earthly things and you do not believe, how will you believe if I tell you heavenly things? No one has ascended to heaven but He who came down from heaven, that is, the Son of man who is in heaven" (John 3:12-13).

Here, once again, Jacob's Ladder is in view with "earth and heaven" so sequenced. The "heavenly things" Jesus declares is in reference to the Son of Man (i.e., bringing Man into God—"ascending"). Remember, "the angels ascending [first] and descending upon the Son of Man"—and this, after Nathanael declared that Jesus was the Son of God (John 1:49)?

When Jesus elaborated on this to Nicodemus He spoke of Moses who *"lifted up the serpent in the wilderness, even so must the Son of Man* (not Son of God) *be lifted up, that whoever believes in Him should not perish but have eternal life"* (John 3:14). It would be through the Son of Man Who came to earth to *"condemn sin in the flesh"* (Rom. 8:3) for *"He made Him who knew no sin to be sin for us, that we might become the righteousness of God in Him"* (2 Cor. 5:21). Jesus "entrapped sin in the flesh and nailed it to the tree!"

Indeed, it is the Ascension of the Son of Man bringing us into God "with Him" that eternal life and salvation alone can be obtained, even validated. Without bridging the "dimensional divide" between "heaven and earth" there would be no redemption, no eternal life—there would be no "seeing"—no "entering" into the Kingdom of God. This is how the Ascension is presented in John's Gospel.

Can we say, then, that the emphasis upon the New Covenant theme in the Synoptic Gospels informs us that the Kingdom of God would be administered with a New Testament, a New Agreement, a New Contract between God and man? And that this was sealed by His blood—truly a "blood covenant"—whereas, once again, the Gospel of John's omission of the New Covenant terminology demonstrates that the New Commandment is "based upon" the tenets of the New Covenant whereby the "interior work" wrought by the New Covenant wherein the Lord would *"put My law in their minds, and write it on their hearts; and I will be their God, and they shall be My people. No more shall every man teach his neighbor, and every man his brother, saying, 'Know the LORD,' for they all shall know Me, from the least of them to the greatest of them, says the LORD"* (Jer. 31:33-34).

In summation—it is more than safe to say that the New Covenant is the New Commandment for the New Covenant provides the enablement, the fulfillment of the Law, written upon the fleshy tables of our heart (2 Cor. 3:3)—whereby Jesus is our Life, our Truth, and our Glory (John 17) enabling us to "love one another, as I have loved you."

Cutting to the chase . . . in the end—the Kingdom of God, the Ekklesia, and the Commonwealth of Israel all bespeak of God's means of administration to the heavens and to the earth. John's Gospel, if you would, brings all three into the immediate realm of humanity–the resurrection of Jesus abides upon the earth. Yes, Matthew and John illuminate the Kingdom of God; Matthew and Paul reveal the Ekklesia; and Paul unveils the Commonwealth of Israel in its relationship to the inclusion of the Gentiles into the United Kingdom of David. All three speak of the unity of God's people under the King of Israel–ever expanding. These are the primary "jurisdictions" of His immediate "rule and reign" prior to the Kingdom of this World becoming the Kingdoms of our Lord and of His Messiah where He shall rule and reign forever and ever:

"The kingdoms (lit. "kingdom") *of this world have become the kingdoms of our Lord and of His Christ, and He shall reign forever and ever!"*

I hope these comparisons and contrasts between the Synoptic Gospels and the Gospel of John give us a greater understanding of the Kingdom of God and the way the Holy Spirit through Matthew, Mark, Luke and John "seeing" the nature and "entering" into the reality of the Kingdom of God in the here and now through the Person and Work of our Lord Jesus Christ establishing the New Covenant and demonstrating how He fulfilled the Law—He now enables us by His Life and Love lived out through the New Commandment in us. The New Covenant is "contractual" in nature—forming the basis of the Kingdom of God, whereas the New Commandment is wholly "relational" in substance—forming the expression to the world of the Kingdom of God: "Behold, how they love one another!"[128]

---

[128] In the early Church, the believers' love for one another, and for others, was so authentic and so obvious that even those outside the Church took notice and were amazed by the loving-kindness of first and second-century Christians.

"Behold, how they love another!" The origin of this phrase is generally attributed to Aristides the Athenian (or maybe as a reaction to Aristides' description of Christians). Aristides was an early second-century Greek Christian and philosopher who presented a letter of defense to the reigning Caesar (Emperor), Hadrian. This letter was entitled, The Apology of Aristides, and delivered to Emperor Hadrian circa 124-133 AD.

Aristides' letter and its content apparently became well-known outside of the Emperor's household and staff; as it is mentioned in historical writings by Eusebius of Caesarea, Eusebius Sophronius Hieronymus (aka Saint Jerome), and other ancient writers. This suggests the Emperor was so impressed with Aristides' writing that he didn't discard it but, instead, released the letter for public viewing. (Source: "Love One Another in Christ: Christian Example from the Early Church" by James Callen, June 13, 2019, Ministry: To Live is Christ @ http://toliveischrist.com/love-one-another/ Retrieved on May 25, 2020).

Chapter Fifteen

THE DIVINE REMARRIAGE AND THE NEW COVENANT

By Dr. Douglas Hamp
From *God's Divorce and Remarriage*

Would you be surprised to learn the Old Covenant was not a collection of dos and don'ts but was a marriage contract between God and Israel? Would you be surprised that the New Covenant is not a doing-away with God's laws but rather the establishing of a new marriage contract with Israel? Understanding these two terms is incredibly important for they are at the very heart of our faith. Failure to understand these two terms has created an untold number of strange doctrines, some of which have resulted in catastrophes. Some people claim the "old covenant" laws and commandments were done away with—even nailed to the cross. Others claim to be "New Testament Christians" only—referring to teaching exclusively from the corpus of the New Testament books. The difference between the two testaments is actually very simple to illustrate: Imagine if you cancelled your cell phone contract with company A. A month later you change your mind and establish a new contract with the same company. Your terms and conditions are the same, but the contract is different. This is the same idea between the two testaments: the terms and conditions are the same (the laws and commandments) but the contracts are different.

Now let's turn to the concept of marriage—in this case, God's marriage with Israel. God established a marriage contract with Israel which ended in heartbreak, divorce and separation. The brokenhearted God promised to one day marry his wayward wife again.

To understand God's relationship with Israel and the pain that He felt, let's imagine that you fall in love with a young woman who later gets sold into slavery. You rescue her against all odds. You scale mighty mountains, you pass through dangerous dales, and even defeat dreadful dragons. You have rescued your love at great cost to yourself, but it was all worth it to save your true love. You sweep her away from her chains and prison, and you two wed.

At your wedding, you exchange vows covenanting to be faithful and to love only each other. You proudly declare that she is your chosen, your special treasure in all the earth and that there is none as precious as her. You also promise her riches, children, peace, and joy, all that she could ever want. As part of your vows, she promises not to have any other men in her life, but to be wholly set apart for you! She promises to not have any pictures, videos, or keepsakes of any other guys in her possession, via email or on Facebook; she is going to desire you and you alone. As husband and wife, your names and reputations are now mingled as one: your name and reputation becomes hers and hers becomes yours. Whatever either of you do from now on, whether good or evil, will directly reflect on the other. Hence, you promise to honor and exalt her name and she promises to honor and exalt your name.

Then you promise to set aside one day in seven that will be a special day for the two of you. You promise that you will make it special for her in that she won't have to work...she can just relax, sleep in, lounge around, kick back without a care in the world because you have taken care of everything. It is to be a day where you can grow in your relationship with one another. You can talk to each other and share your hearts in a way that is distinct from the rest of the week.

In addition to these vows, you share with her your formula for how to treat others which will lead to a successful and abundant life. Your formula is revolutionary because it is outwardly focused and not inwardly focused. It is concerned with how to treat others in a way that you would want to be treated. It always seeks the other's good and their highest. You tell her that if she'll follow this formula it will lead to life and blessings; but if she doesn't, it will lead to pain, sorrow, curses, and ultimately death. She eagerly agrees to follow your formula knowing that you have her highest in mind as well. You then kiss your bride.

A great feast is held to celebrate the momentous occasion. After some time, she disappears, and you can't find her. After searching with an anxious heart, you sadly discover that she was in the room of an old lover. You are crushed, brokenhearted, and distraught. How could your true love do this? You promised. She promised. In fact, her unfaithfulness was on your very wedding day! How could she? Your sadness turns to anger at her unfaithfulness. You consider

CH. 15: THE DIVINE REMARRIAGE AND THE NEW COVENANT

leaving her that very moment...but then you have pity on her. It was her upbringing after all; her parents were very poor role models and they cheated on each other from day one. She literally has never seen a good relationship. So, you decide to forgive and forget. However, already your enemies have heard what happened. You know that they will use it someday to slander you.

You then move into your new house and begin making it your home. You have children, you share wonderful moments. You are providing abundantly as promised. She on the other hand, has never quite overcome the tendency to see other guys. There have been many times during your marriage that you have had to simply look away and pretend not to notice. Of course, each time, it breaks your heart. But you are kind and patient. You really want it to work out between you, so you just put up with it.

However, a day comes when you notice that money begins disappearing from the bank account. You ask her about it, but she denies any knowledge. Eventually, you discover that not only is she seeing other men, but she is in fact paying her lovers to be with her! At this point you are beside yourself. How in the world did this happen? Adultery is bad enough. Her receiving money from others as a prostitute would be worse. But no! Your wife is paying others to sleep with her! You confront her about it and tell her that this activity must stop.

You have become the laughing stock of the town. Everyone knows what your wife is up to. When you walk by you can hear their snickering. "Nice wife you got there!"; one person shouts. "Thanks for the money," another shouts. You look at another of the jesters and you are dumbfounded when you see the one of a kind necklace that you bought your wife on your anniversary on the neck of another man's wife; your wife has paid her lovers with the precious keepsakes that you bought her. It isn't just the money, but that it was something you gave especially to her. Not only that, but she has murdered many of the children she had from these illicit relationships. Finally, you can take no more. You have been married for decades and she has not changed one bit but has grown more destitute. With great sorrow you decide that it is over, though in your heart you vow to find a way to restore the woman you once knew and loved.

So, you file the divorce papers and excise her from your will. Neither she, nor the children that she birthed from her many lovers will have any part of you or your estate. They are cut off completely. Oh, how your heart aches! The wife of your youth is gone. Your home is not the same. After some time, you find a way to bring her back to you, but only if she is willing to turn away from all the evil that she committed. You can find a way to annul the wickedness if she will just admit her fault and promise not to do it again. When you exchanged vows there were some stipulations that you both agreed to. In your contract, you both agreed that if she were found guilty of adultery, then you had the right to divorce her. If she became another man's wife and the same thing happened, that he found her guilty of adultery and sent her away, then she could not remarry you because it would pollute the land and bring a curse. You grin because you have thought up an amazing plan that will allow her to remarry you and will cancel the blood oath you both made in your marriage covenant. You pause for a moment, because, while your plan will resolve everything, it will come at tremendous cost to you.

Your plan is to die and then come back to life. By dying, you will cancel all consequences and curses that she incurred by having committed adultery when you were married under your marriage covenant. If you die, you reason, she will no longer be considered an adulteress because the law of the marriage is until "death do us part." Hence if you die, then she is free to remarry! The trouble is, you want her to be *your* wife again and not another's. So, the second part of your plan is to come back to life! The cool thing is that you found a way to do that. So, you then prepare for the big day: You die as planned and the curses that she was under because she violated your marriage covenant are cancelled! She is no longer legally an adulteress. All the penalties and curses of the law of marriage are cancelled through your death. Part one is finished. When you come back to life, you and she can then remarry! All that is required on her part is to acknowledge her former adultery and promise not to do it again. If she will do those two things, then you promise to take her back and return her to her former position as your bride. The handwriting that was against her is literally destroyed through your death. You have cancelled the old contract in which she was an unfaithful, adulterous wife and now you have established a new contract in which she is a pure, chaste virgin, if she so chooses to enter in. Let's now look at the many Scriptures which prove the above scenario.

The First Marriage Contract

Simply put, the marriage at Sinai was a marriage contract between Yahweh/YHWH and Israel. How do we know that "Old Covenant" was a marriage covenant? We know because of their subsequent divorce where Yahweh stated that Northern Israel "is **not My wife**, nor am I her **Husband**!" (Hos. 2:2a) Yahweh could only divorce Israel if He had once been wed to her. In Jeremiah, Yahweh specifically stated that He gave the Northern Kingdom of Israel a certificate of divorce and put her away.

> *Then I saw that for all the causes for which backsliding **Israel** had committed adultery, I had **put her away** and given her a **certificate** of **divorce**; yet her treacherous sister Judah did not fear, but went and played the harlot also* (Jer. 3:8).

Later in Jeremiah, Yahweh stated that the covenant that He made with Israel was one where He became her husband: "...the **covenant** that I made with their fathers in the day that I took them by the hand to lead them out of the land of Egypt, My **covenant** which they **broke**, though I was a **husband** to them," says Yahweh (Jer. 31:32).

The Wedding Vows

At their wedding on Mt Sinai, the groom and bride exchanged vows. Yahweh, the husband, expressed His love for His bride, Israel, when He vowed:

> *If you will indeed obey My voice and keep My covenant, then you shall be a special treasure to Me above all people; for all the earth is Mine* (Ex. 19:5).

This vow of deep love was reiterated to Israel when they were about to enter the Promised Land:

> *Yahweh your God has **chosen** you to be a **people** for **Himself**, a **special treasure** above all the peoples on the face of the earth. Yahweh did not set His **love** on you nor choose you because you were more in number than any other people, for you were the least of all peoples; but because **Yahweh loves you**, and because He would keep the oath which He swore to your fathers, Yahweh has brought you out with a mighty hand, and redeemed you from the house of bondage, from the hand of Pharaoh king of Egypt* (Deut. 7:6-8).

THE RECORDING OF THE VOWS

Their marriage was recorded in the "book of the covenant" (a mere four chapters), similar to a *Ketubah* (Jewish "marriage contract" of today):

> *"Then he* [Moses] *took the **Book of the Covenant** and read in the hearing of the people"* (Ex. 24:7a).

It was a marriage contract, complete with prenuptial agreements—that is, terms and conditions of what was expected, and what would happen in case of infidelity. The terms and conditions were Yahweh's ten words (commandments) which He gave for her good!

> *"And now, **Israel**, what does Yahweh your God **require** of you, but to fear YAHWEH your God, to **walk** in all His ways and to **love** Him, to serve Yahweh your God with **all your heart and with all your soul, and to keep the commandments of YAHWEH** and His statutes which I command you today for your **good**"* (Deut. 10:12-13)?

Israel then exuberantly responded with her marriage vow saying: *"All that YAHWEH has said we will do and be obedient"* (Ex. 24:7b). All she needed to do was to love Him by remaining faithful to Him. Yahweh also promised that if they would be faithful then Israel would *"be a special treasure to Me above all people; for all the earth is Mine"* (Ex. 19:5).

Their marriage contract was cut and the vows (contract) were ratified with blood: And Moses took the blood, sprinkled it on the people, and said, *"This is the **blood of the covenant** which YAHWEH has made with you according to all these words"* (Ex. 24:8).

GOD'S DIVORCE

Unfortunately, Israel was unfaithful to her husband from the beginning, and then after some time, His wife (United Israel) was divided into two kingdoms: the Kingdom of Judah in the south which included the tribe of Benjamin (and part of Levi since they were landless); and the Kingdom of Israel in the north which included the remaining ten tribes. Yahweh, in His patient love and sovereignty, waited while Israel (the Northern Kingdom) committed her adulteries time and again. Yahweh explained this in the book of Ezekiel, speaking of the two daughters of one mother who both practiced harlotry and defiled themselves.

"Son of man, there were two women, the daughters of one mother. They committed harlotry in Egypt, they committed harlotry in their youth...Their names: Oholah the elder and Oholibah her sister; they were Mine, and they bore sons and daughters. As for their names, **Samaria** *is Oholah, and* **Jerusalem** *is Oholibah. Oholah played the harlot even though she was Mine; and she lusted for her lovers, the neighboring Assyrians...Thus she committed her* **harlotry** *with them, all of them choice men of Assyria; and with all for whom she lusted, with all their idols, she* **defiled** *herself"* (Ezek. 23:2-4, 7, 9).

Ultimately, after 700 years of Northern Israel's backsliding and adultery, Yahweh **"put her away** and gave her a **certificate** of **divorce"** (Jer. 3:8). This truth is also stated in Second Kings:

"Therefore YAHWEH was very angry with Israel and removed them from His sight; there was none left but the tribe of Judah alone" (2 Kgs. 17:18).

Their divorce created a seemingly unsolvable dilemma because, according to His own instructions in Deuteronomy 24:1-4, a husband cannot take back his wife who has been with another husband (who has also sent her away or died).

If the latter husband detests her and writes her a certificate of **divorce** [*kritut* כְּרִיתֻת], puts it in her hand, and sends her out [*shlichah* וְשִׁלְּחָהּ] of his house, or if the latter husband dies who took her as his wife, then her former **husband** [in this case Yahweh] who **divorced** her must **not** take her back to be his wife after she has been defiled; for that is an **abomination** before Yahweh... (Deut. 24:3-4). Consequently, there was no conceivable hope for northern Israel to return to a marriage covenant with Yahweh or for Judah and Israel to ever reunite. Reconciliation with her groom would, according to Yahweh's own commandments, result in abomination and the land becoming defiled. Nevertheless, Yahweh passionately calls His wayward wife to return (repent) to Him and presumably, He would have to find a way to work things out.

"They say, 'If a man divorces his wife, and she goes from him and becomes another man's, may he return to her again?' Would not that land be greatly polluted? But you have played the harlot with many lovers; **yet return** (repent) *to Me, says Yahweh"* (Jer. 3:1). *"Yahweh said also to me in the days of Josiah the king: 'Have you seen what backsliding Israel has*

done? She has gone up on every high mountain and under every green tree, and there played the harlot.' **And I said, after she had done all these things, 'Return to Me.'** *But she did not return. And her treacherous sister Judah saw it. Then I saw that for all the causes for which backsliding Israel had committed adultery, I had put her away and given her a* **certificate of divorce**; *yet her treacherous sister Judah did not fear, but went and played the harlot also"* (Jer. 3:6-8).

"And yet for all this her treacherous sister Judah has not turned to Me with her whole heart, but in pretense," says Yahweh. Then YAHWEH said to me, "Backsliding Israel has shown herself more righteous than treacherous Judah. Go and proclaim these words toward the north, and say: **'Return***, backsliding Israel,' says Yahweh; 'I will not cause My anger to fall on you. For I am* **merciful***,' says Yahweh; 'I will not remain* **angry** *forever.' 'Only* **acknowledge** *your* **iniquity***, that you have* **transgressed** *against Yahweh your God, and have scattered your charms to alien deities under every green tree, and you have not obeyed My voice,' says Yahweh. 'Return, O backsliding children,' says Yahweh; 'for I am* **married** *to you. I will take you, one from a city and two from a family, and I will bring you to Zion.'"* (Jer. 3:10-14)

THE DIVINE DILEMMA

How could Israel be brought back into a marriage covenant without Yahweh violating His own law?

Then her former husband [Yahweh] *who divorced her* [Israel] *must not take her* [Israel] *back to be his wife after she has been defiled; for that is an abomination before Yahweh* (Deut. 24:4a).

The only way the wife (Northern Kingdom Israel) could be released of her fate of having been put away (*shlichah*) [וְשִׁלְּחָהּ] and divorced (*kritut*) [כְּרִיתֻת] by Yahweh was for Yahweh (her husband) to **die** which would annul and dissolve the original marriage contract. Paul understood that when, using the Law to explain, he reminded the Jews (who knew the Law) that the Law only has jurisdiction over a person until their death. When the person dies, any judgments, contracts, or obligations are then dissolved:

CH. 15: THE DIVINE REMARRIAGE AND THE NEW COVENANT

Or do you not know, brethren (for I speak to those who know the law), that the law has dominion over a man as long as he lives (Rom. 7:1)?

Paul then explains how a woman is covenanted to her husband only as long as he lives. When he dies, she is free to remarry at will.

*For the **woman** who has a husband is **bound** by the **law to her husband** as long as he lives. But if the **husband dies**, she is released from **the law of her husband*** (Rom. 7:2).

Continuing with Deuteronomy 24:1-4 in mind, Paul explains how the wife is freed from the "law of the husband" (the marriage contract), which had kept her out of the covenant relationship with her former husband. It should be noted that Paul is only speaking of the cancelling of the divorce status; he is not suggesting that the entire "Torah" (Laws given at Sinai) are repealed. ("Yahweh" and "Israel" have been inserted below in brackets to make the relationships clearer).

So then if, while her husband [Yahweh] lives, she [Israel] marries another man [Ba'al etc.], she will be called an adulteress; but if her husband dies, she is free from that law, so that she is no adulteress, though she has married another man (Rom. 7:3).

Following that, Paul reaches crescendo with his exciting conclusion that through Yeshua/Jesus (the incarnate Word of Yahweh), the wife, Israel, can be married to a different man—which is none other than the Risen Yeshua—Wow!

Therefore, my brethren, you also have become dead to the law [of her husband cf. Rom. 7:2] through the body of Christ, that you may be married to another–to Him who was raised from the dead, that we should bear fruit to God (Rom. 7:4).

In other writings Paul explains how the curses of the broken marriage covenant died with Yeshua, being nailed to the cross.

...having wiped out the handwriting of requirements [death because of adultery] that was against us, which was contrary to us. And He has taken it out of the way, having nailed it to the cross (Col. 2:14).

A New Marriage Contract

At the first covenant, cut at Sinai, the Book of the Covenant (marriage contract) was proclaimed and then the blood of bulls was sprinkled in order to "seal the deal" in the same way we would sign a contract and then have it notarized and filed with the city clerk. The blood made the contract effective, operable, and binding.

> *Then he took the **Book of the Covenant** and read in the hearing of the people. And they said, "All that Yahweh has said we will do, and be obedient." And Moses took the blood, sprinkled it on the people, and said, "This is the blood of the covenant which Yahweh has made with you according to all these words"* (Ex. 24:7-8).

After the people had heard all of the conditions of the contract, they said, "I do" and gladly accepted the marriage contract with Yahweh/YHWH. They agreed to be faithful to Him and to do all that He had asked them to do (which is what we always do when we enter into an agreement/contract).

With the New Covenant (new marriage contract), blood was offered to "seal the deal" just like the first covenant.

> *For this is My blood of the new covenant, which is shed for many for the remission of sins* (Matt. 26:28).

However, the nature of the blood sacrifice was of immeasurably greater quality than that of the first covenant. Additionally, the one who would officiate the sacrifice would not be a Levite, but one of the order of Melchizedek. In this, the husband died to dissolve the old marriage but at the same time, his blood became the blood of the new covenant, and he also was the one who offered the blood on the heavenly altar.

> *But Christ came as High Priest of the good things to come with the greater and more perfect tabernacle not made with hands, that is, not of this creation. **Not** with the **blood** of goats and calves, but with His **own blood** He entered the Most Holy Place once for all, having obtained eternal redemption* (Heb. 9:11-12).

And you, who once were alienated and enemies in your mind by wicked works, yet now He has reconciled in the body of His flesh through death, to present you holy, and blameless, and above reproach in His sight (Col. 1:21-22).

Now free from the curse of her broken marriage covenant, Israel could actually remarry without being called an adulteress. However, how could she be rejoined to her groom if he was in the grave? If Yeshua remained dead, then no remarriage between him and Israel could take place, despite her new freedom. Therefore, Yeshua had to not only die to free Israel, but had to also rise from the dead so that she could remarry her former husband, who was in reality a *New Husband.*

A New Husband for a New Wife

Yeshua's resurrection, therefore, is the crux of the matter! Without the resurrection, Israel would have been free to marry another, but not to the very one who promised Himself to her FOREVER. Now having risen from the dead, the Old Husband was actually a NEW Husband. All of the lawlessness (her adultery) of the first marriage was literally buried with Yeshua (the Husband, Yahweh in the flesh). Now He was free to remarry His former wife without breaking His own instructions. His new marriage would be a NEW COVENANT/TESTAMENT with Israel!

With this in mind, we can better understand Paul's excitement as he proclaims in Ephesians 2:11-13 how the House of Israel (the Gentiles/Nations) has been brought back into the covenant relationship.

Therefore remember that you, once Gentiles [scattered Israel, out of covenant] *in the flesh...that at that time you were without Christ, being aliens from the **commonwealth of Israel** and **strangers from the covenants of promise**, having **no hope** and **without God in the world**. But now in Christ Yeshua you who once were **far off** have been brought near by the blood of Christ* (Eph. 2:11-13). *"For you are not My people, and I will not be your God"* (Hos. 1:9).

Therefore, the New Covenant is **not** a new dispensation where Yahweh suddenly starts operating on the basis of grace with all of humanity. Yahweh has always been gracious and that quality of grace and mercy is the very thing that Yahweh declared about himself on Mt. Sinai:

*Yahweh passed by before him and proclaimed: "Yahweh, Yahweh, the **compassionate** and **gracious God**, slow to anger, and abounding in loyal love and faithfulness . . ."* (Ex. 34:6).

The New Covenant, rather, is not a new basis of grace, but is instead a gracious, renewed marriage covenant between Yahweh and His divorced wife who had been scattered to the nations, just as Yahweh had promised would happen:

Yahweh will **scatter** you among all nations, from one end of the earth to the other. There you will worship other gods that neither you nor your ancestors have known, gods of wood and stone (Deut. 28:64; see also Lev. 26:33 Jer. 9:16, 13:24, 30:11, Ezek. 5:10, 6:8, 20:23, 22:15, 36:19).

THE SISTERS REUNITED UNDER THE NEW CONTRACT

While Yeshua's death and resurrection resolved the divorce of Yahweh and Israel, what about Judah's (the Southern Kingdom) relationship with Yahweh? Does she get a new marriage covenant? She certainly needed it based on how **she** "**defiled** the land and committed **adultery** with stones and trees" (Jer. 3:9). In fact, her adulterous conduct, according to Yahweh, was actually worse than Israel's (the Northern Kingdom).

> *"And yet for all this her treacherous sister Judah has not turned* [repented] *to Me with her whole heart, but in pretense," says Yahweh. Then Yahweh said to me, "Backsliding Israel has shown herself more righteous than treacherous Judah"* (Jer. 3:10-11).

Let there be no doubt, Judah most certainly *deserved* to be divorced because of her adulterous heart and wandering eyes which deeply hurt Yahweh (Ezek. 6:9), but Yahweh never did divorce Judah because of the promise that he made to King David:

> *"If his sons reject my law and disobey my regulations, if they break my rules and do not keep my commandments, I will **punish their rebellion** by beating them with a club, their sin by inflicting them with bruises. **But I will not remove my loyal love from him**, nor be unfaithful to my promise"* (Ps. 89:29-33).

Nevertheless, Yahweh stated that both *"the **House of Israel** and the **House of Judah** have dealt very treacherously with Me"* (Jer. 5:11)—**they were both** guilty of adultery and of breaking the covenant.

*"They have turned back to the iniquities of their forefathers who refused to hear My words, and they have **gone after other gods** to serve them; the **House of Israel** and the **House of Judah** have **broken** My **covenant** which I made with their fathers"* (Jer. 11:10).

Furthermore, the two sister nations needed to be reunited into one nation: one wife. Yahweh declared that He would in fact make a new marriage contract with both houses:

"Behold, the days are coming," says Yahweh, *"when I will make a **new covenant** with the House of Israel and with the House of Judah"* (Jer. 31:31).

Yahweh also promised that he would join the two houses back together as depicted in the imagery of a stick, broken in two, which becomes one again:

*"Thus says the Lord YAHWEH: 'Surely I will take the stick of Joseph, which is in the hand of Ephraim, and the tribes of **Israel**, his companions; and I will join them with it, with the stick of **Judah**, and make them **one stick**, and they will be one in My hand'"* (Ezek. 37:19).

Therefore, Yeshua's death on the cross annulled Judah's marriage contract with Yahweh and thereby allowed for the House of Judah to have a new covenant with Yahweh (because their first marriage was marked by gross adultery) even though she was never divorced. Judah could have a new relationship with Yahweh and so too Israel could come back into fellowship with her husband.

*"For He Himself is our peace, who has made both one, and has broken down the middle wall of separation, having abolished in His flesh the enmity, that is, the law of commandments contained in ordinances, so as to create in Himself one new man from the two [and I will join them with it, with the stick of **Judah**, and make them **one stick**, and they will be one in My hand (Ezek. 37:19)] thus making peace, and that He might reconcile them*

*both to God in one body through the cross, thereby putting to death the enmity. [Then the children of **Judah** and the children of **Israel** shall be gathered together... (Hos. 1:11)]. And He came and preached peace to you who were afar off and to those who were near. For through Him we both have access by one Spirit to the Father. Now, therefore, you are no longer strangers and foreigners, but fellow citizens with the saints and members of the household of God"* (Eph. 2:14-19).

As a result, their joint status as adulterers was wiped away. Israel's utter hopeless situation as a divorcée was annulled and Judah's status as adulterous wife was cancelled. Furthermore, the House of Judah and the House of Israel have become one again and the wall of separation between them has been removed.

THE FULLNESS OF THE GENTILES

The situation has now been rectified, though not in full. The House of Israel (Ephraim / Gentiles) can now return to her husband. They are no longer *"aliens from the commonwealth of Israel and strangers from the covenants of promise, having no hope and without God in the world"* (Eph. 2:12). Yeshua is now Israel's and Judah's peace, *"who has made both one, and has broken down the middle wall of separation"* (Eph. 2:14). When Yeshua died on the cross, He *"abolished in His flesh the enmity, that is, the law of commandments contained in ordinances, so as to create in Himself one new man from the two, thus making peace* (Eph. 2:15), *and that He might reconcile them both to God in one body through the cross, thereby putting to death the enmity"* (Eph. 2:16).

Hence, Yeshua gave Good News to both the House of Israel and to the House of Judah when He *"came and preached peace to you who were afar off and to those who were near"* (Eph. 2:17). Through the work of Yeshua on the cross, the two houses now *"both have access by one Spirit to the Father"* (Eph. 2:18). And truly, those of the House of Israel are *"no longer strangers and foreigners, but fellow citizens with the saints and members of the household of God"* (Eph. 2:19).

CH. 15: THE DIVINE REMARRIAGE AND THE NEW COVENANT

Thus, while the barrier to restoration has been removed, the reunification is not complete and will *not* be complete until the fullness of the nations/Israel comes in, as Paul explained to his Jewish brethren:

> *For I do not desire, brethren, that you should be ignorant of this mystery, lest you should be wise in your own opinion, that blindness in part has happened to Israel until the fullness of the Gentiles has come in* (Rom. 11:25).

The phrase that Paul employed comes directly out of Genesis 48:19 where Jacob prophesied over Ephraim, stating that his descendants will be THE fullness of the nations/Gentiles.

But his (Joseph's) father refused and said, *"I know, my son, I know. He also shall become a people, and he also shall be great; but truly his younger brother* [Ephraim] *shall be greater than he, and his descendants shall become a multitude of nations"* [*M'lo HaGoyim* מְלֹא־הַגּוֹיִם literally, "the fullness of the nations"] (Gen. 48:19).

COMMONWEALTH THEOLOGY ESSENTIALS

THE NEW COVENANT IS
YAHWEH'S RENEWED MARRIAGE WITH ISRAEL

Wedding Katubah

So, what is the New Covenant? It is the renewed marriage contract between Yahweh and His wife Israel, (reunited House of Israel and House of Judah). Yeshua's statement "this is My blood of the new covenant, which is shed for many for the remission of sins," (Matt. 26:28) was the blood necessary to establish the new marriage covenant. His death released his unfaithful wife (both Judah and Israel) from the curses of the broken marriage contract, and allowed northern Israel to remarry Him, and for Israel and Judah to become one nation again. Yahweh's first marriage was with His special treasure (united) Israel, and His new marriage is with His special treasure Israel and Judah (reunited). Yeshua did all that was necessary to restore His bride, Israel, just as He promised in Hosea to Israel, whom He divorced:

> *"I will **betroth** you to Me forever; yes, I will **betroth** you to Me in righteousness and justice, in lovingkindness and mercy; I will betroth you to Me in faithfulness, and you shall know Yahweh"* (Hos. 2:19-20).

However, what is even more amazing is that through the dispersion of the House of Israel to the nations, the entire world is being blessed because the House of Israel was assimilated into the nations and became one with them. Thus, their return is nothing other than the ingathering of the Gentiles into the kingdom and fulfills Yahweh's original promise to Abraham that his seed would be like the stars of heavens.

> *Then He brought him outside and said, "Look now toward heaven, and count the stars if you are able to number them." And He said to him, "So shall your descendants be"* (Gen. 15:5).

Yahweh's regathering of the House of Israel, which was divorced, scattered, and assimilated into the nations (through intermarriage), is nothing less than the House of Israel (Gentiles, non-Jews) receiving by faith the fact that Yeshua graciously died to annul the first marriage covenant, which they were in bondage to, and resurrected to lovingly take her back under a new marriage covenant. The point is that any non-Jew who trusts in Yeshua is part of "the fullness of the Gentiles"—they are part of the "mixed multitude" (Ex. 12:38) which was added to the children of Israel when they came out of Egypt. Indeed, Yahweh said that it was not enough for Yeshua to just restore the tribes of Jacob, but He would be salvation for the nations all over the planet:

> *Indeed He says, "It is **too small a thing** that You should be My Servant to **raise up the tribes of Jacob**, and **to restore** the preserved ones of Israel; I will also give You as a light to the Gentiles, that You should be My salvation to the ends of the earth"* (Isa. 49:6).

Yahweh reiterates this promise by saying that He would bring in the outcasts of Israel and also others:

> *Lord Yahweh, who gathers the outcasts of* [the house of] *Israel, says, "Yet I will gather to him others besides those who are gathered to him"* (Isa. 56:8) [other re-gathering prophetic scriptures: Ezek. 11:17, 20:34, 20:41, 28:25].

But He answered and said, *"I was not sent except to the lost sheep of the house of Israel"* (Matt. 15:24).

Yeshua alluded to the others that would come in and the "one flock" when He said:

> *And **other sheep** I have which are not of this fold; them also I must bring, and they will hear My voice; and **there will be one flock** and one shepherd* (John 10:16).

Yeshua confirmed the restoration when He said concerning His death: *"And I, if I am lifted up from the earth, will draw all peoples to Myself"* (John 12:32). With this in mind, we now understand clearly how Paul could state so emphatically that *"there is no distinction between Jew and Greek, for the same Yahweh over all is rich to all who call upon Him"* (Rom. 10:12) because the House of Israel and the House of Judah have been restored into one nation and one wife! Paul could say that with enthusiasm because, as an expert of the Scriptures, he knew that he was seeing the fulfillment of prophecy before his very eyes—the two houses were reunited as Yahweh said in Ezekiel:

> *Thus says Lord Yahweh: "Surely I will take the stick of Joseph, which is in the hand of Ephraim, and the **tribes of Israel**, his companions; and I will join them with it, with the **stick of Judah**, and **make them one stick**, and they will be one in My hand." And the sticks on which you write will be in your hand before their eyes.*

> *Then say to them, "Thus says Lord Yahweh: 'Surely I will take the **children of Israel from among the nations**, wherever they have gone, and will gather them from every side and bring them into their own land; and I will make them **one nation** in the land, on the mountains of Israel; and one king shall be king over them all; **they shall no longer be two nations, nor shall they ever be divided into two kingdoms again.**'"* (Ezek. 37:19-22)

The New Testament is Yahweh restoring the House of Judah and Israel into one nation which was made possible by the death of Yeshua. Truly, Yahweh is a faithful and loving husband and king worthy of our praise and gratitude.

Chapter Sixteen

LIFE FROM THE DEAD

By Chris Steinle

In the previous chapter, Dr. Hamp explained the way by which both houses of unfaithful Israel could come back into a covenant relationship with God. This chapter reveals scriptural evidence that further details how the "Old Testament Saints" were brought back into favor and right-standing. The compelling link between: the remarriage, the resurrection, and the two-sticks prophecy of Ezekiel 37, will be of special interest to students of the Commonwealth of Israel. However, the entire Body of Christ can experience the blessing of rediscovering the depth of God's mercy and faithfulness, which had already been shown to His people-of-old even before the Apostles were sent to the nations.

This study will highlight several passages from Paul's letter, "To the Ephesians." The reader who has become familiar with the principles of Commonwealth Theology will recognize that allusions to the Commonwealth appear throughout the first five chapters of the Epistle. These allusions need not be read "between the lines." They have been boldly immortalized in pen and ink. Once the mystery of the Commonwealth is fully grasped, it becomes obvious that the *politeia* of the "one new man" persisted in the composer's mind as Ephesians was written; and, to such an extent that the "Commonwealth" concept can practically be perceived upon the pages of Ephesians as a virtual watermark.

Whose Wife in the Resurrection?

The Apostle John noted that such a voluminous body of words and deeds had been generated during Christ's first advent that *"if they were written one by one... even the world itself could not contain the books that would be written"* (John 21:25). What "would have been written" was, nevertheless, limited by the size of practical portability and the affordability of the first-century codex.

So when we come to a passage like the Sadducees' question about the resurrection—a question that seems pretentious if not downright whimsical—we must be aware that dozens of other questions about the resurrection could have been framed, but were never recorded. Yet, this particular question was presented and documented. WHY?

> *Then some Sadducees, who say there is no resurrection, came to Him; and they asked Him, saying: "Teacher, Moses wrote to us that if a man's brother dies, and leaves his wife behind, and leaves no children, his brother should take his wife and raise up offspring for his brother. Now there were seven brothers. The first took a wife; and dying, he left no offspring. And the second took her, and he died; nor did he leave any offspring. And the third likewise. So the seven had her and left no offspring. Last of all the woman died also. Therefore, in the resurrection, when they rise, whose wife will she be? For all seven had her as wife."*
>
> *Jesus answered and said to them, "Are you not therefore mistaken, because you do not know the Scriptures nor the power of God? For when they rise from the dead, they neither marry nor are given in marriage, but are like angels in heaven. But concerning the dead, that they rise, have you not read in the book of Moses, in the burning bush passage, how God spoke to him, saying, 'I am the God of Abraham, the God of Isaac, and the God of Jacob'? He is not the God of the dead, but the God of the living* (Mark 12:18-27a). Luke's account adds: *"For to him all are alive"* (Luke 20:38).

Rather than assuming the Sadducees were making up "any wild story" by which to confound Jesus and refute the resurrection, what if these elements—a husband's decease, an unfruitful wife (thus a discontinued family line), and the resurrection—were genuine components of an ongoing conversation among the Jewish scholars of Jesus' day? Going a step further, and assuming that this whole discussion had also struck a chord within the Apostolic Church, the door is then opened to a serious exploration of the Sadducees' question and the Lord's unexpected answer.

The Sadducees' scenario, although exaggerated, contains elements of Jeremiah 31:32; *"though I was a husband to them, says the Lord."* Here the antecedent of "them" is given in the 31st verse: *"the House of Israel and the House of Judah."* But the most extensive correlative passage is found at the opening of Isaiah 54, immediately following—and logically the immediate result of—Messiah's atoning sacrifice of Isaiah 53.

Key elements associating the Sadducees' hypothetical question about the House of Israel's being cut off (disinherited) are underlined below.

Isaiah 54

1 "Sing, <u>O barren</u>,
You who have not borne!
Break forth into singing, and cry aloud,
You who have not labored with child!
For more are the children of the desolate [**widowed no less—see v.4**]
Than the children of the married woman," says the Lord.
2 "Enlarge the place of your tent,
And let them stretch out the curtains of your dwellings;
Do not spare;
Lengthen your cords,
And strengthen your stakes.
3 For you shall expand to the right and to the left,
And your descendants will inherit the nations,
And make the desolate cities inhabited.
4 "Do not fear, for you will not be ashamed;
Neither be disgraced, for you will not be put to shame;
For you will forget the shame of your youth,
And will not remember the reproach of <u>your widowhood</u> anymore.
5 <u>For your Maker is your husband</u>,
The Lord of hosts is His name;
And your Redeemer is the Holy One of Israel;
He is called the God of the whole earth.
6 For the Lord has called you
Like a woman forsaken and grieved in spirit,
Like a youthful wife when you were refused,"
Says your God.

7 *"<u>For a mere moment I have forsaken you,</u>*
<u>But with great mercies I will gather you</u>.
8 With a little wrath I hid My face from you for a moment;
But with everlasting kindness I will have mercy on you,"
Says the Lord, your Redeemer.
9 "For this is <u>like the waters of Noah to Me</u>; [**NOTE this metaphor**]
For as I have sworn
That the waters of Noah would no longer cover the earth,
So have I sworn
That I would not be angry with you, nor rebuke you.
(Emphasis added.)

UNFINISHED BUSINESS

As mentioned earlier—and as will be shown in the following chapter—Paul's recognition of the Commonwealth of Israel is not isolated to the second chapter of Ephesians. Rather, truths about the Commonwealth and its fulfillment of prophecy are woven throughout the first five chapters. The following passage from Chapter Four provides a good starting point from which to understand the "mechanics" involved in the redemption of the "Old Testament saints," and particularly, the Lost House of Israel.

Ephesians Ch. 4

4 I, therefore, the prisoner of the Lord, beseech you to walk worthy of the calling with which you were called, 2 with all lowliness and gentleness, with longsuffering, bearing with one another in love, 3 endeavoring to keep the unity of the Spirit in the bond of peace. 4 There is one body and one Spirit, just as you were called in one hope of your calling; 5 one Lord, one faith, one baptism; 6 one God and Father of all, who is above all, and through all, and in you all. 7 But to each one of us grace was given according to the measure of Christ's gift.

8 Therefore He says:
"When He ascended on high,
He led captivity captive,
And gave gifts to men."

9 Now this, "He ascended"—what does it mean but that He also first descended into the lower parts of the earth? 10 He who descended is also the One who ascended far above all the heavens, that He might fill all things.

In order to appreciate this passage's bearing on the future of "Israel past," it will be necessary to settle confusion over the interpretation of "the lower parts of the earth"; and, to correct the mistranslation of the phrase, "fill all things."

Some commentaries assert that "descended into the lower parts" refers merely to Christ's earthly incarnation. This interpretation may be offered as an alternative to the notion that Jesus descended into the flames, or to battle Satan. The "incarnation" assumption was historically invalidated by several Early Church Fathers:

St. Irenaeus, Against Heresies 5, 31, 2 (C. 180 AD):

"For since the Lord went away into the midst of the shadow of death where the souls of the dead were..."

Irenaeus, Against Heresies, Book 4, Chap. 27, Para. 2:

"The Lord descended into the regions beneath the earth, announcing there the good news of His coming and of the remission of sins conferred upon those who believe in Him."

St. Cyril of Jerusalem, Catechetical Lectures 4, 11 (C. 350 AD):

"(Christ) descended into the subterranean regions so that He might ransom from there the just..."

The narrative that Jesus went down into the Inferno is handily addressed in the following article posted at the Euangelion blog.

> Christ did not, between His death and resurrection, descend into what you think of when you hear the English word "Hell." Neither the New Testament nor the Early Church Fathers ever taught that Jesus went into the place of eternal torment (Gehenna or the Lake of Fire). The word "Hell" in the Apostles' Creed is simply a bad translation that originates not in the English, but the Latin translation of the Creed. The phrase in Latin was originally ad inferos which is itself a correct translation of the Greek phrase *eis ta katathonia* ("into the underworld/lower regions"). The first creedal appearance of this phrase in Greek ("He descended into the underworld") is found in the Fourth Formula of Sirmium in AD 359, but Swete believes the phrase dates to

the second century (Apostles' Creed, 61-62). Rufinus (AD 400) reflects the earliest change from inferos (underworld) to inferna (Hell) which led to such confusion about Christ's descending to the damned (Gehenna) instead of to the underworld (Sheol/Hades) in general. Hence the incorrect English translation: "He descended into Hell."[129]

Verses nine and ten are marked as a parenthetical in the NKJV. Papyrus 46 (one of the most complete manuscripts of Paul's epistles dated circa 200 AD) contains no such markings.[130] The parenthetical treatment applied by some publishers may have to do with the fact that Paul was primarily addressing God's "gift of offices" within the Church. In which case, Christ's ascension was germane to the granting of gifts; yet, Christ's descent into the lower parts would seem inapplicable within this context. However, Paul often wrote using a multi-level or nested approach. In this instance he began by recognizing himself as a "prisoner of the Lord," thus establishing a link to "captivity" from the onset.

Another reason why English readers would tend to miss the meaning of Christ's descent is the mistranslation of the phrase, "that He might fill all things." The correct translation is, "that He might fulfill all things." One can only speculate the motivation of the translators. It is simple enough to conclude that if, at the cross, "it is finished," then there remained nothing left to be finished after the cross. But from the passage above it is obvious that the bestowal of gifts was not associated with the cross, but with the ascension. This would imply that something was also left to be accomplished by Christ's descent εἰς τὰ κατώτερα μέρη τῆς γῆς (into the lower parts of the earth).

A better reading of the last phrase of Verse Ten is, "that He might fulfill all things. ἵνα πληρώσῃ (*plērōsē*) τὰ πάντα. According to Strong's 4137. πληρόω (*pléroó*) means: accomplish, complete, fulfill. The same word, *plērōsē*, appears in the same form in 2 Thessalonians 1:11 and is translated "fulfill" in the NAS, KJV, and INT.

---

[129] "Jesus Descended into Hell, Kind of" by Justin W. Bass,
https://www.patheos.com/blogs/euangelion/2014/05/jesus-descent-to-the-underworld.

[130] http://earlybible.com/manuscripts/p46-Eph-7.html.

Now we see that Christ's descent and ascent were both necessary to complete all things; and specifically, according to the context of the Ephesians Four passage, to accomplish what was prophesied concerning CAPTIVITY, and GIFTS. We can further deduce since the outpouring of the Spirit (and spiritual gifts) was connected to Christ's ascension by His own words: *"Nevertheless I tell you the truth. It is to your advantage that I go away; for if I do not go away, the Helper will not come to you; but if I depart [to the Father], I will send Him to you"* (John 16:7), the work to be completed regarding the captivity, likewise, had everything to do with Christ's descent to the lower parts.

Although leading "captivity captive" would seem to be some kind of double negative, the expression has to do with leading those who had been in exile back to their homeland; in effect, reversing the march into exile. The following verse expresses the "captivity of captivity" as the taking of those who were already in captivity away.

"Shall the prey be taken from the mighty, Or the captives of the righteous be delivered?" But thus says the Lord: "Even the captives of the mighty shall be taken away, And the prey of the terrible be delivered" (Isa. 49:24-25a).

ALL ARE ALIVE TO HIM

Before we review specific passages in which Peter and Paul mention Christ's preaching to the dead, let us consider the "deadness" of the party being addressed. Those belonging to the House of Israel who had died, from the time of Israel's rejections until the time of Christ—wherever on earth they had migrated— "died in their sins" on a national level. (We will discuss personal righteousness later in this chapter.) On the national level, they were no longer God's people—at least "for a little while." Jesus warned those belonging to the House of Judah (the Jews) that they were in danger of the same plight: *"Unless you believe I am He, you will die in your sins"* (John 8:21, 24).

Our first theological hurdle will be to address the question of posthumous salvation. Oft' quoted by contemporary evangelists is Ecclesiastes 11:3b: *"And if a tree falls to the south or the north, in the place where the tree falls, there it shall lie."* Ezekiel had the opportunity to play this card when God asked him about the dead House of Israel: *"Can these bones live?"* They had indeed died in their sins. The prophet was wise enough to defer to the One with whom all things are possible—even the salvation of those dead in their sins.

Jesus, in answering the Sadducees question, disclosed a pivotal theological truth—humanly speaking, a loophole—regarding the status of the dead: *"For to Him all are alive"* (Luke 20:38). So HAS that tree *really* fallen (to God, that is)? What if God, in His sovereignty, decided to "run an end-around" and to *"remember their sins and lawless deeds no more"*? After all, as noted in 2 Samuel 14:14: *"He devises means so that the banished one will not remain an outcast."* This is NOT even to suggest that such a redemption could occur apart from *"the new covenant in My blood"* (Luke 22:20; 1 Cor. 11:25); which is precisely why the Lost House of Israel could only obtain mercy (forgiveness) AFTER THE CROSS. The fortunes of both houses of Israel were bound inseparably to the New Covenant that would be established *"after those days."*

> *But this is the covenant that I will make with the HOUSE OF ISRAEL after those days, says the Lord: I will put My law in their minds, and write it on their hearts; and I will be their God, and they shall be My people. No more shall every man teach his neighbor, and every man his brother, saying, 'Know the Lord,' for they all shall know Me, from the least of them to the greatest of them, says the Lord. For I will forgive THEIR* (the House of Israel) *iniquity, and THEIR sin I will remember no more"* (Jeremiah 31:33-34 Emphasis added).

Now, lest the Gentile Christian reader should withdraw in a huff, let us readily and gratefully affirm God's plan *"that the Gentiles should be fellow heirs, of the same body, and partakers of His promise in Christ through the gospel..."* (Eph. 3:6). Also rest assured that further clarification on posthumous salvation will follow our examination of key verses documenting Christ's words to the dead.

WASHED BY THE WORD

Similar to Ephesians, Peter's first epistle suggests he was also mindful of the Lost House of Israel in that he stated: *"For you were like sheep going astray, but have now returned to the Shepherd and Overseer of your souls"* (1 Peter 2:25). Notice they didn't "turn" but "returned." These "pilgrims" among the nations (v.1) were not merely believers who had been dispersed after the stoning of Stephen. These sojourners already had a Shepherd at some time in the past and were returning to Him. We have already established that the Church Fathers acknowledged Christ's visit to the underworld. Now we will review Peter's direct reference to that event before looking into a more indirect reference mentioned by Paul.

> *For Christ also suffered once for sins, the just for the unjust, that He might bring us to God, being put to death in the flesh but made alive by the Spirit, by whom also* ***He went and preached to the spirits in prison****, who formerly were* ***disobedient****, when once the Divine longsuffering waited in the* ***days of Noah****, while the ark was being prepared, in which a few, that is, eight souls, were saved through water. There is also an antitype which now saves us—baptism (not the removal of the filth of the flesh, but* ***the answer of a good conscience toward God****), through the resurrection of Jesus Christ, who has gone into heaven and is at the right hand of God, angels and authorities and powers having been made subject to Him* (1 Peter 3:18-22).

Jesus preached to the spirits in prison. "Preaching" implies these spirits were alive (alive to God) and capable of acknowledging the message that was being preached. These particular spirits were formerly disobedient. Peter's insertion of this qualifier would have been wholly unnecessary were it intended to represent all fallen souls from the time of Adam. These were souls who had at one time been obedient, but then made a choice to disobey. As a consequence of God's judgment, although they once were God's people, it was determined that, for a time, they were not His people. Thus, they were taken captive—held as prisoners. These prisoners remained *"alive to God"* under His forbearance while the "ark of Christ" was being prepared.

That these prisoners were indeed the once-disobedient House of Israel becomes altogether obvious by Peter's reference to Noah's ark: *"With a little wrath I hid My face from you for a moment; but with everlasting kindness I WILL HAVE MERCY ON YOU," Says the Lord, your Redeemer. "For this is like the **waters of Noah to Me**; for as I have sworn that the waters of Noah would no longer cover the earth, so have I sworn that I would not be angry with you, nor rebuke you"* (Isa. 54:8-9 Emphasis mine). Just as the thief on the cross beside Jesus could do nothing to change his past, the wayward House of Israel, which had died in its sins, could not change the history of the Northern Kingdom. The filth of their flesh in times past could not be removed. At Christ's preaching, however, they did receive mercy and were made clean by the word of the Living Word. By the grace of God they were given the answer of a *"good conscience toward God."*

Now we will look at Paul's indirect reference to the same event. The passage to be considered is only obscured by the omission of Christ's descent into the abode of the dead. But the elements: the husband; the wife; God's inheritance; and, the cleansing by the word; these are all presented—and not apart from Christ's atoning sacrifice.

> *Husbands, love your wives, just as Christ also loved the church and gave Himself for her, that He might sanctify and cleanse her with the washing of water by the word, that He might present her to Himself a glorious church, not having spot or wrinkle or any such thing, but that she should be holy and without blemish... This is a great mystery, but I speak concerning Christ and the church* (Excerpts from Eph. 5:25-32).

In order to interpret these verses in the light of the predicament of fallen Israel—rather than treating Christ's ekklesia as a modern, distantly-related entity—we should begin with the question: When was Christ's ekklesia ever defiled? Is it even possible for the "Ekklesia," defined by modern English Bible translations as the "Church," to become dirty and in need of cleansing—considering that the Congregation is the Body of Christ? Well: Yes it is possible, or Paul would never have mentioned it; but in what context?

Solving the mystery of the Congregation's cleansing also requires eliminating the prejudice injected into English translations which was perpetrated by incorporating a special word for the "congregation of believers in Messiah"—the term, "Church." This translation of "congregation" became accepted as a convenient way to distinguish believers in Christ from God's formerly ordained people, who had not yet corporately believed. (This manipulation of words and the possible motives were discussed earlier in this volume.) Nevertheless, it is helpful to overcome the bias of modern translations by referring back to Tyndale's translation of these verses:

> Husbandes love youre wyves even as Christ loved the **congregacion** and gave him silfe for it to sanctifie it and clensed it in the fountayne of water thorow the worde to make it vnto him selfe a glorious **congregacion** with oute spot or wrynckle or eny soche thinge: but that it shuld be holy and with out blame. So ought men to love their wyves as their awne bodyes. He that loveth his wyfe loveth him sylfe. For no ma ever yet hated his awne flesshe: but norissheth and cherisseth it even as the lorde doth the **congregacion**... This is a great secrete but I speake bitwene Christ and the **congregacion.** (Excerpts from Eph. 5:25-32: The Tyndale Bible;[131] Emphasis added.)

The "Commonwealth of Israel" defined throughout Ephesians is ONE BODY, ONE CONGREGATION—we must hesitate, though, to say "One Church" because of the exclusive connotation attached to that extra-biblical term. The text of the original language never intended to be exclusive but INCLUSIVE concerning the Commonwealth of Israel, as explained in prior chapters. I.e.: distinguishing between those who have believed in Christ and those who have not; but not excluding indefinitely God's foreordained people to whom the promises were made.

Christ loved the "congregacion" and gave Himself for it/her. To understand the cleansing aspect applied to the "wife" we must respect the definition of the Congregation developed by Paul in the previous chapters of Ephesians.

---

[131] The Tyndale Bible,
https://www.biblestudytools.com/tyn/ephesians/5.html.

Chapter Four told us *"there is ONE BODY."* Chapter Three stated God's plan, *"that the Gentiles should be fellow heirs of the SAME BODY."* Chapter Two explained how Jesus made peace through the cross so *"that He might reconcile them both to God in ONE BODY."* Those near (the House of Judah) and those far (you Gentiles—however, the term "far" was never formally disassociated from the literal "House of Israel" [Dan. 9:7]).

One member of the Body, the Congregation, had been defiled to the extent that "she" was divorced and "not My people." Thus the mystery of Christ and the "congregacion" (v. 32),—of the Husband and Wife—was nothing short of the mystery of Christ's descent to wash (baptize) her by the water of the word. This was the means by which Jesus presented this vast, but formerly estranged, member of the Body to Himself.

These saints were converted by Christ and led away captive through His ascension to where Christ resides. *"WHEN He ascended on high, He LED captivity captive."* These souls are now eternally alive and IN Christ; and as such, qualify to be raised physically in the resurrection of *"the dead in Christ"* (1 Thess. 4:16). That this mystery would occur during Christ's first Messianic mission seems to be confirmed by His prophecy: *"Most assuredly, I say to you, the hour is coming, and **NOW IS**, when the dead will hear the voice of the Son of God; and those who hear will live"* (John 5:25 Emphasis mine).

Concluding that Ephesians 4:8-10 and 1 Peter 3:19 are correlative passages, both references would then pertain to the releasing of the captives (prisoners, EXILES) from the "lower parts of the earth." These verses would then represent the fulfillment of messianic prophecies such as: *"I will keep You* [Messiah] *and give You as a covenant to the people, as a light to the Gentiles, to open blind eyes, to bring out **prisoners** from the prison, those who **sit in darkness** from the prison house"* (Isa. 42:6b-7).

Christ was, apparently, the first to preach the message of the cross! Even before Peter's sermon on the Day of Pentecost; as many reckon the time of Jesus' descent into Hades to have occurred prior to His resurrection. In which case, the first members of the Commonwealth of Israel to enter the Kingdom would have been the "vast army" of Old Testament Saints. What a contrast to the Dispensational order of things that would put God's "dealings" with

Israel off to the future—after the time of the Gentile Church. Whereas, the Scriptures clearly portray the Gentiles NOT as the head, but the tail: *"It is too small a thing that You should be My Servant to raise up the tribes of Jacob, and to restore the preserved ones of Israel; I will **ALSO** give You as a light to the Gentiles"* (Isa. 49:6). During His interaction with the Syrophoenician woman Jesus stated in less than flattering terms: *"It is not good to take the children's* [God's covenant people] *bread and throw it to the little dogs* [Gentiles]*"* (Matt 15:26). Most blatant of all (and thus our primary application to the House of Israel throughout this chapter) was Jesus' proclamation preceding the dog analogy: *"I was not sent except to the lost sheep of the house of Israel"* (v. 24).

God's "Israel First" initiative, however, has not exactly been celebrated by the Nations (Gentiles) over the past 2000 years. How often do we hear emphasized in the Gentile Church that the entire "early" Church consisted of Jews (Judah) together with some from the House of Israel? Those Hebrews in the Land at the time of Christ were, by historical accounts, Jews. Though many of those present for Pentecost in the second chapter of Acts were remnants of the scattered tribes: *"Let all the HOUSE OF ISRAEL know assuredly..."*

An entire book could be written documenting the anti-Semitic assumptions of Gentile Bible translators. Many incorrect readings have already been exposed in this book. The fact that the Christian Church was centered in "Jewish" Jerusalem, even after the founding of the Antioch Church, is generally overlooked during Bible teachings by pointing out that the Church was scattered after the stoning of Stephen. But that scattering was only a brief episode. In the very next chapter of Acts we read: *"Then the churches throughout ALL JUDEA, Galilee, and Samaria had peace and were edified. And walking in the fear of the Lord and in the comfort of the Holy Spirit, they were multiplied"* (Acts 9:31). And, Oh, how they multiplied!

By the time of Paul's arrest in Jerusalem, circa 58 AD., there were MANY TENS OF THOUSANDS (myriads) of Jewish believers in Christ residing in and around Jerusalem. Although myriads could have meant "thousands," as the NIV reads, these same translators don't reduce it to that number when it comes to the holy ones in Jude, or the "peoples" in the Book of Revelation. "MANY myriads" was obviously meant to impress Paul with the enormity of the Jewish constituency. By comparison, merely four years earlier, Asia was only beginning to be evangelized. Luke thought it noteworthy to mention two converts (and some others) in Athens and 12 men in Ephesus. Many believers were also reported in Iconium who were BOTH Jews and Greeks. But Jerusalem had its **many tens of thousands** of ethnically Jewish believers.

LOOKING BACK TO ISRAEL'S ACCEPTANCE

Where we are going from here is to dispel the idea that the ethnic descendants of Jacob were ever **intended** to come back into covenant LATER as a block, or APART from the believers among the Nations. The next translation error to be corrected will embrace the title of this chapter and will lead us into how this all relates to the 36th and 37th chapters of Ezekiel.

The New King James Version's translation of Romans 11:15 reads: *"For if their being cast away is the reconciling of the world, what will their acceptance be but life from the dead?"*

The first phrase of the hypothesis of this conditional statement is nearly literally translated. It is merely restating a truth accepted within Commonwealth Theology from Verse 11: *"...because of their transgression, salvation has come to the Gentiles to make Israel envious."* They, "Israel," were "cast away" because of transgressions. And, because they—imbued with the knowledge and fear of the Holy One of Israel—were SOWN, MIXED with the Nations, the Nations (Gentiles) then believed and were reconciled. So far, so good.

Unfortunately, this translation's (and most other English translations) conclusion to the hypothesis, plainly indicates that they (Israel) WILL BE accepted in the future; but had not been accepted at the time that Romans was written. Yet, as we have already observed in this chapter, if Christ's preaching to the dead were at all effective— and I suspect it was—then a substantial contingency (BLOCK) of Israel has already BEEN ACCEPTED. So what's the deal?

For the benefit of the Greek reader, the Greek text is presented below. This verse contains no textual variants among the major Byzantine and Alexandrian source texts. If that comes across as overly technical, just be assured that: What you see it what you get.

15 εἰ γὰρ ἡ ἀποβολὴ αὐτῶν καταλλαγὴ κόσμου, τίς ἡ πρόσλημψις εἰ μὴ ζωὴ ἐκ νεκρῶν;

The verse contains NO forms of the word, "to be." In fact, there are no verbs AT ALL! The "is," "will," and "be" have been placed in the English text—but not arbitrarily. They have been placed according to the theological bent of the translators.

Young's Literal Translation does contain an inferred "is." Most likely to support the participle "gloss" of ἀποβολὴ. But it's not really there—in the original text.

15 for if the casting away of them [is] a reconciliation of the world, what the reception—if not life out of the dead? YLT

As written by Paul, the verse has nothing whatsoever to do with time. Literally, in poor English, the verse reads: *"For if their casting away, reconciliation of the world, what the reception if not life from the dead."* The verse simply consists of: an action and a result; a second action and a second result; with the condition that if the first pair were true, the second pair is certainly true. In the absence of any *real* verbs, whatever verbal tense might be imagined to apply to the hypothetical, should for consistency be applied to the conclusion. Thus, Young's translation would be more accurate by either removing the bracketed [is] from the one statement or adding the same [is] to the other side of the conditional. The logical "take away" for the reader of the original Greek text—who WAS witnessing the reconciliation of the world in real time—would have been:

"For if their casting away IS the reconciliation of the world, what IS their reception but life from the dead."

Those of the House of Judah and the House of Israel who believed in Jesus—the entire early Church for approximately two decades until Gentiles slowly began to join the Church—believed BOTH STATEMENTS to be TRUE! Israel WAS rejected. And, Israel WAS received, being comprised of both: the souls now in heaven because of Christ's preaching; and, the souls of the living Israelites—both Jews and converts among the formerly lost House of Israel—who believed in Jesus. Both the dead and the living components of Greater Israel had previously been spiritually dead in their sins.

Paul, a Benjamite of Judah wrote: *"...even when WE were dead in trespasses,* [God] *made us alive together with Christ (by grace you* [Gentiles] *have been saved), and raised us up TOGETHER, and made us sit TOGETHER in the heavenly places in Christ Jesus"* (Eph. 2:5-6 Emphasis added).

Clearly, Paul was equating the plight of the Old Testament dead to the still-walking dead, in that neither group could save themselves from their sins. But even though WE (through this present time) are all seated together, we cannot physically, literally see with our eyes the saints of old, ourselves, or Christ, seated in heavenly places. Nevertheless, we **believe** these circumstances to be true. We believe, as Job did, that even if our flesh is destroyed we WILL somehow see these spiritual realities with our own eyes.

What then is the conclusion regarding "life from the dead" in respect to that contingent of the House of Israel who had died before the time of Christ? They have been made alive together with Christ—by grace THEY have been saved. They now await the resurrection along with all other saints who have physically died yet are alive in Christ. The rapture/resurrection of First Thessalonians Chapter Four represents the **DIVINE INTERSECTION** of the DEAD and the LIVING.

And what can be said concerning the House of Israel now mixed with the Nations, however they might be identified? Their salvation requires the same faith in the same message preached to their predecessors in "prison." *"For as you were once disobedient to God, yet have now obtained mercy through their disobedience, even so these also have now been disobedient, that through the mercy shown you they also may obtain mercy. For God has committed them all to disobedience, that He might have mercy on all"* (Rom. 11:30-32).

So, what is the extent of that mercy? Do we all merit a loophole even after death? After all, since all are alive to God: It's not over till the wrath to come/final judgment. Keep in mind, however, God was honoring His promises to the fathers by this one-time "get out of jail free." (It was not free, but a ransom purchase by Christ's precious blood). This incident in Sheol was

CH. 16: LIFE FROM THE DEAD

unique and not the basis for a *"Love Wins"*[132] universal salvation doctrine. The lifetime of Christ on earth was also a unique time—a chronological divide, a divine reset—after which: Where the SOUL falls, it SHALL lie. The amnesty granted to the "grateful dead" who had died in their sins ended once Christ took His seat in glory. Thus His warning, stated previously, that Christ's contemporaries would *"die in their sins"* if they did not believe that He was the Messiah.

In addition, it seems an even greater accountability was required by those living during Christ's first mission. The sins of God's covenant people committed prior to Jesus' generation were taken away by the Lamb of God, EXCEPT for those who refused to take advantage of the amnesty being offered. In which case, it would seem these souls were held accountable for ALL the sins that were "previously left unpunished." Somehow, (God's ways are higher) the "liability" of the previous generations—which had been passed over and acquitted in Christ's preaching to the underworld—fell upon Christ's generation. This aspect of the great mystery of "Christ and the Congregation" is noted in Matthew and Luke:

> *So that the blood of all the prophets, shed from the foundation of the world, may be charged against this generation, from the blood of Abel to the blood of Zechariah, who perished between the altar and the sanctuary. Yes, I tell you, it will be required of this generation* (Luke 11:50-51).

Now, concerning Posthumous Salvation in general: Man shall LIVE by every word that proceeds from the mouth of GOD. It was the washing of the Living Word, the preaching by the Son of God that freed the prisoners from captivity. The words, prayers, or good thoughts of MAN cannot change a soul's eternal destiny. Nor can man's efforts hasten the process of God's determination (Purgatory), nor change the whereabouts of the soul after death (World of souls). Those concerned about these concepts will likely understand these parenthetical references.

---

[132] *Love Wins: A Book About Heaven, Hell, and the Fate of Every Person Who Ever Lived* by Rob Bell, Harper Collins, 2011.

Not for Your Sake, O House of Israel

"What IS Israel's reception if not life from the dead?"

What if we could look back into the spiritual realm of Hades and witness what was pronounced over Old Testament Israel? Likewise, what if we could visualize the "life from the dead" that has already taken place spiritually; and will, in the future, be manifested physically? Just as the Psalms expound on unseen realities: Details about the Crucifixion (Ps. 22); Christ's unspoken mission repeated in Hebrews 10 (Ps. 40); Christ's priesthood and position at the Father's right hand (Ps. 110); even so, Ezekiel chapters 36 and 37 allow us to visualize the restoration and resurrection of the House of Israel.

The continuity of Ezek. 36-37, and who is being addressed in these scriptures, is beyond question. The "House of Israel" is named five times in Chapter 36, and the Dry Bones vision of Chapter 37 is said to represent the Whole House of Israel. Both houses of Israel are clearly addressed from Ezek. 37:15 through the end of that chapter. However, our focus will be on the House of Israel, as these chapters represent, at the least, the experience of the once-divorced Northern Kingdom; and at most, the House of Israel et. al.—whether identifiable or mixed with the Nations—throughout the age.

The section of Chapter 36 of immediate interest begins in the 16th verse. Here a thumbnail summary of "Ephraim's" unfaithfulness and God's judgment, once again, affirms the dispersion of the Northern Kingdom:

> *Moreover the word of the Lord came to me, saying: "Son of man, when the house of Israel dwelt in their own land, they defiled it by their own ways and deeds; to Me their way was like the uncleanness of a woman in her customary impurity. Therefore I poured out My fury on them for the blood they had shed on the land, and for their idols with which they had defiled it. So I scattered them among the nations, and they were dispersed throughout the countries; I judged them according to their ways and their deeds. When they came to the nations, wherever they went, they profaned My holy name—when they said of them, 'These are the people of the Lord, and yet they have gone out of His land.' But I had concern for My holy name, which the house of Israel had profaned among the nations wherever they went"* (Ezek. 36:16-21 Emphasis added).

The restoration of the House of Israel is the subject of the rest of Chapter 36. Notice that the Northern Kingdom has NEVER, to date, been restored to the Land to the degree described by the rest of this prophecy. Do also take note, however, that the House of Israel—the unfaithful and divorced bride—is cleansed with water, in accordance with Paul's analogy in Ephesians Chapter Five.

"For I will take you from among the nations, gather you out of all countries, and bring you into your own land. Then I will sprinkle clean water on you, and you shall be clean; I will cleanse you from all your filthiness and from all your idols. I will give you a new heart and put a new spirit within you; I will take the heart of stone out of your flesh and give you a heart of flesh. I will put My Spirit within you and cause you to walk in My statutes, and you will keep My judgments and do them. Then you shall dwell in the land that I gave to your fathers; YOU WILL BE MY PEOPLE, and I will be your God..." (Ezek. 36:24-29 Emphasis added).

Ezekiel 36 and 37—ending with the two-sticks-made-one to form the United Kingdom—agrees perfectly with Hosea 1:10-11 (Excerpts) *"In the place where it was said to them, 'You are not My people,' there it shall be said to them, 'You are sons of the living God.' Then the children of Judah and the children of Israel shall be gathered together, and appoint for themselves one head..."*

"In the place where it was said" is a meaningful phrase. God will bring the House of Israel into their "own land." God may bring all, throughout the Age, who are identified with the House of Israel into the Holy Land. But He will most certainly bring the ancient House of Israel into the Land upon their resurrection. Concerning the House of Israel mixed with Nations, it is evident from Zechariah, Revelation, etc., there will still be "Nations" among the nations, after the Second Coming.

Let us review one more passage from Chapter 36 before drawing a few last conclusions. This passage is somewhat shocking in light of God's compassion and grace. But it is this "hard reality" side of the Holy Spirit that convicts of sins and leads to repentance.

"Then you will remember your evil ways and your deeds that were not good; and you will loathe yourselves in your own sight, for your iniquities and your abominations. Not for

your sake do I do this," says the Lord God, "let it be known to you. Be ashamed and confounded for your own ways, O house of Israel!" (v. 31-32)

FELLOW HEIRS

Consider what might have occurred "in the spirit" as Christ preached to the (living) dead. How similar to the present day Christian conversion experience might it have been? Look at the record of God's restoration of Israel from Ezekiel 36.

In Verse 25: The House of Israel was cleansed from her filthiness with water. (We have suggested from Ephesians—the washing by the word).

In Verse 26, a new heart.

In Verse 27: "I will put My Spirit within you and cause you to walk in My statutes, and you will keep My judgments and do them." (Nothing short of the Jeremiah 31 New Covenant).

In Verses 31-32, The conviction of sins and repentance.

Mainstream theologians have erred greatly because they have put the cart before the horse. (Or put the horse down, altogether.) These elements of the New Covenant were experienced FIRST by the children of Israel: Those in Hades and the Early (all Jewish) Church. The Congregation among the Nations has received these elements TOGETHER with their fellow heirs of the Commonwealth of Israel—the ancient House of Israel.

Ephesians 3:6 *"...that the Gentiles should be fellow heirs, of the same body, and partakers of His promise in Christ through the gospel..."*

Now, as promised, we will briefly address national and individual judgment in regards to Jesus' mission to the underworld. We know from the story of Lazarus that the underworld did, at that time, consist of two "compartments." The "good guys" ended up in "Abraham's bosom." It is doubtful that Jesus preached to the "other side" based on verses like Psalms One:

"Therefore the ungodly shall not stand in the judgment, nor sinners in the congregation of the righteous. For the Lord knows the way of the righteous, but the way of the ungodly shall perish." These souls, as the Munchkins from *The Wizard of Oz* would say, were "not merely dead, but really quite sincerely dead."

CH. 16: LIFE FROM THE DEAD

The matter of individual accountability among the citizens of the House of Israel can be answered in one verse: *"For WE must ALL appear before the judgment seat of Christ, that each one may receive the things done in the body, according to what he has done, whether good or bad"* (2 Cor. 5:10 Emphasis added).

This interim chapter of our book has attempted to offer further evidence of the divorce and remarriage of Israel based on the witnesses of the Prophets and the New Testament. As with many Old Testament prophecies, Ezekiel's prophecy to the Mountains of Israel contains elements that could be spiritually fulfilled—as in completing some spiritual process or heavenly judgment—and, elements that call for physical fulfillment. The physical fulfillments of Ezekiel 36 (e.g. the Land) are most definitely dependent on the physical resurrection of Chapter 37.

The following chapter will continue to investigate the theory that prophecy has spiritual and physical aspects. But rather than assuming certain scriptures must either be spiritually or physically interpreted, a method used by the New Testament writers themselves can address both applications in a surprisingly logical manner. This system can also handle prophecies which appear to be only partially fulfilled. Correctly recognizing the fulfillment of Old Testament promises and Messianic prophecies is instrumental in untangling some of the errors of mainline theology.

PART II

COMMONWEALTH ESCHATOLOGY

Chapter Seventeen

RESOLVING UNFULFILLED MESSIANIC PROPHECIES

by Chris Steinle

The Problem of Unfulfilled Prophecy

Imagine for a moment that you are standing with Jesus on the Mount of Olives. It's the day of His ascension. Like Elijah's prophets on the day of the whirlwind you are overtaken by a premonition that Jesus is about to depart into heaven. As one of the Lord's close disciples, you were privileged to hear Jesus pray to the Father on the night before His crucifixion: *"I have glorified You on the earth. I have finished the work which You have given Me to do"* (John 17:4). You were even there to hear Jesus utter from the cross, *"It is finished"* (John 19:30).

Now on the Mount of Olives you and your companions gather around the Master. Then, with intonations of closure easily recognized by His friends as parting words, Jesus instructs you to wait in Jerusalem. Anticipating no further delay, time seems to come to a standstill as your subconscious mind quickens. At the speed of a dream, your mind searches for unanswered questions and flashes through the Scriptures considering all of the Messianic prophecies. To your surprise, you and your fellow disciples spontaneously well up with one voice:

"If it is finished, where's the restoration?"//
"What about the gathering?"
"What about Your rule from Mount Zion?"
"What about the promised inheritance?"
In the simplest vernacular: "What about the Nation?"

The biblical text is cited below for further observation. This might be a good place to mention that the Bible is quoted extensively within this chapter even though the theologically focused reader will likely be quite biblically literate. The Bible must be the final authority in matters of doctrine. The added benefit of quoted text is that key words and phrases can be highlighted by adding emphasis.

And being assembled together with them, He commanded them not to depart from Jerusalem, but to wait for the Promise of the Father, "which," He said, "you have heard from Me; for John truly baptized with water, but you shall be baptized with the Holy Spirit not many days from now." Therefore, when they had come together, they asked Him, saying, "Lord, will You at this time restore the kingdom to Israel?" And He said to them, "It is not for you to know times or seasons which the Father has put in His own authority. But you shall receive power when the Holy Spirit has come upon you; and you shall be witnesses to Me in Jerusalem, and in all Judea and Samaria, and to the end of the earth" (Acts 1:4-8).

According to the Apostles' understanding of Scripture, which then included three years of discipleship, the next phase of the Messianic Era should have been the restoration of the Israel—the kingdom—which had now been properly purchased at the cross for their possession. Let's face it, by the Gospel accounts the Disciples did ask a few irrelevant and off-the-wall questions. But their question about the Land wasn't so off track. What Jesus did NOT say is also important to consider. He did not say, "Forget about the Land," as those with a Gnostic or Anti-millennial mindset would assert. Nor did He say, "It's over for the Jews;" the very presumption made by the Supersessionists despite the fact that Luke's account in Acts testifies that the Earliest Church was ENTIRELY JEWISH.

So let's consider what Jesus DID say in response to a very good question. First let's proceed as though Jesus did not change the subject. In other words, that Jesus didn't just go back to talking about the Holy Spirit after a quick statement about the Father's authority. Instead of assuming that restoring Israel's inheritance and the Holy Spirit were completely unrelated, let's investigate the possibility that the inheritance and the Spirit might be intricately related.

Looking for the logic behind the relationship between the Holy Spirit and the Inheritance, and knowing that Jesus had linked these together in a question about timing, we might look for the Holy Spirit to be some kind of placeholder in time. A placeholder that is perhaps meant to occupy the time between the Day of Pentecost and the restoration of the kingdom. But we are also informed by the Lord in John 14:16 that the Holy Spirit will remain, not only until the kingdom is restored, but forever.

> *"And I will pray the Father, and He will give you another Helper, that He may abide with you forever— the Spirit of truth, whom the world cannot receive, because it neither sees Him nor knows Him; but you know Him, for He dwells with you and will be in you. I will not leave you orphans; I will come to you"* (John 14:16-18).

"I will not leave you [as] orphans." This phrase has an amazing bearing on the purpose of the Spirit in relation to inheritance. Obviously, it was not the Father who would be sent in order to remedy the plight of the orphan. Christians have already become the children of God. What the orphan *is* deprived of is inheritance. The Apostles would have understood exactly why Jesus spoke of the Holy Spirit in anticipation of the inheritance. The Holy Spirit is not merely a placeholder, He is the guarantee, the down payment on the estate, the promise that, at last, the kingdom will indeed be restored to Israel.

> *In Him you also trusted, after you heard the word of truth, the gospel of your salvation; in whom also, having believed, you were sealed with the promised Holy Spirit* [ESV], *who is the guarantee of our inheritance until the redemption of the purchased possession, to the praise of His glory* (Eph. 1:13-14).

So on the Day of Ascension the Apostles asked precisely the right question. And this was not the first time the subject had come up. Luke Chapter 19 reveals that the Disciples had made at least one previous inquiry about the timing of the fulfillment of the restoration of the kingdom.

> *Now as they heard these things, He spoke another parable, because He was near Jerusalem and because <u>they thought the kingdom of God would appear immediately</u>. Therefore He said: "A certain nobleman went into a far country to receive for himself a kingdom and to return. So he called ten of his servants, delivered to them ten minas, and said to them, 'Do business till I come...'"* (Luke 19:11-13).

The Parable of Talents from the Olivet Discourse was also given in response to the Apostles' questions about the timing of the Messianic prophecies. *"For the kingdom of heaven is like a man traveling to a far country... After a long time the lord of those servants came and settled accounts with them"* (Matt 25:14-19).

Both parables corrected the Apostles' assumption that all of the Messianic prophecies mentioned in Scripture would be fulfilled at the same time. For Christians today, "First Coming" and "Second Coming" roll off the lips with such familiarity that we must make a conscientious effort to consider, in retrospect, why even Jesus' own Disciples were not prepared for a two-phase mission of Messiah. Christ's own terminology, quoted above, also portended a lengthy interval between the King's two appearances—"a long time;" the extended duration of a journey to and from a "far country."

It is evident from the New Testament writings that the Disciples did receive and understand Jesus' parting words, which were immediately confirmed by the two angels: *"This same Jesus, who was taken up from you into heaven, will so come in like manner as you saw Him go into heaven"* (Acts 1:11). So then, why revisit the Apostles' dilemma over end-time events when, after all, eschatology (the study of "last things") has been so neatly sorted out by the Church over the last 2,000 years?

Precisely the point; because theologians have in fact come to different and even contradictory opinions about the future fulfillment of Bible prophecies. Also disconcerting is the fact that the Jewish component of the Commonwealth of Israel has historically objected to, and continues to reject, the Church's proposed explanations for why Jesus left certain Messianic prophecies unfulfilled. When searching online for reasons why Jews reject Jesus, these unfulfilled Messianic prophecies are often listed as Reason Number One. The adjacent article is typical.[133]

---

[133] "Why Don't Jews Believe In Jesus?" Simple To Remember, simpletoremember.com, 4/14/2019, https://www.simpletoremember.com/articles/a/jewsandjesus/#1.

Ch. 17: Resolving Unfulfilled Messianic Prophecy

Why Don't Jews Believe In Jesus?
1) JESUS DID NOT FULFILL THE MESSIANIC PROPHECIES

What is the Messiah supposed to accomplish? The Bible says that he will:

A. Build the Third Temple (Ezekiel 37:26-28).
B. Gather all Jews back to the Land of Israel (Isaiah 43:5-6).
C. Usher in an era of world peace, and end all hatred, oppression, suffering and disease. As it says: "Nation shall not lift up sword against nation, neither shall man learn war anymore" (Isaiah 2:4).
D. Spread universal knowledge of the God of Israel, which will unite humanity as one. As it says: "God will be King over all the world—on that day, God will be One and His Name will be One."

Should we so quickly shrug off as superficial the rabbinical logic of our Jewish brothers considering that even Jesus' Disciples expected Messiah to resettle both houses of Israel in the Holy Land and re-establish the Davidic rule from Mount Zion? The apocalyptic Jewish writings from the first century bear witness to a common base of Messianic expectations. These expectations were shared by the Jewish community of Jesus' time and are, for the most part, in agreement with the Bible. In many cases these expectations were simply based on the most straightforward reading of Scripture. Nevertheless, even the rabbis have proposed that Messiah would be the final authority. The author, therefore, would challenge the Jew as well as the Christian to consider whether the logic and Scriptural evidence presented in this chapter provides a reasonable account for many unfulfilled prophecies.

Moreover, this chapter will demonstrate, as in previous chapters, that Jesus has reconciled both the Nation of Israel and the individual soul through the same act of atonement. And not only that: We will attempt to explain why the world did not witness the restored kingdom of Israel at the time the Disciples had expected. In the same breath and for the sake of those well acquainted with the various schools of eschatology, we will not be presenting the Preterist view.

Though it is hoped that not only the Preterist, but the Amillennialist, the Dispensationalist, those from other camps, and especially the Jew, would come to recognize the biblical accuracy of the eschatology revealed by the Commonwealth Theology[134] perspective.

This is perhaps a good place to diffuse the objection that associating national and individual salvation might create "a different gospel that you did not receive." Be it known that such a corporate salvation does not threaten or detract from all that is true and dear to those who have run to Christ for refuge. Furthermore, coming into a personal relationship with Jesus involves being born into a corporate body—the body of Christ—rather than being born into a social vacuum. *"And let the peace of Christ rule in your hearts, to which indeed you were called <u>in the one body</u>"* (Col. 3:15).

The importance of establishing an eschatology acceptable and received by the whole body of Christ cannot be overstated. The divisions based on eschatology, observed above, must be resolved for the sake of the unity inherent to Ephesians' Commonwealth of Israel. The reader of this compendium might already be aware that a foundation has been established to set forth the assertions of Commonwealth Theology in a cover to cover reference Bible. Without exaggeration, the applications of Commonwealth Theology are so far-reaching that they could fill their own multivolume Bible commentary. And perhaps someday they will.

By comparison, this single chapter in its condensed form can merely scratch the surface of the eschatological implications of Commonwealth Theology. The author, however, holds out high confidence that the facts and logic presented forthwith will be adequate to engage the reader's interest so as to spur their own Berean journey of investigation "to find out whether these thing are true." Now that we have set a realistic scope for our study, let's address the methods that we will apply in order to prove a synchronous national and individual salvation. First we will develop some terminology to make it easier to discuss prophetic expectations and the timing of their fulfillment.

---

[134] See commonwealththeology.com administered by Dr. Douglas Hamp and Douglas W. Krieger, with various authors like Dr. Gavin Finley.

CH. 17: RESOLVING UNFULFILLED MESSIANIC PROPHECY

NAVIGATING THE PROPHECY GAP

In order to develop the logical component of our thesis we now introduce the term, "Prophecy Gap." The Prophecy Gap acknowledges, as Christ did, that there are significant and identifiable prophecies that were not fulfilled at His first coming. The "Gap" element of the Prophecy Gap will represent the interval between the expected time of prophetic fulfillment and the actual time of a prophecy's fulfillment—however far in the future such fulfillment should occur. Because the Prophecy Gap is based on expectations, the term can be applied somewhat arbitrarily to discuss the range of Messianic expectations of the various theological schools mentioned above.

For the Apostles on Ascension Day, the Prophecy Gap was the span between "at this time" and the future "times and seasons," described by Jesus as "long" and "far off." For the Jew who has declined to recognize Jesus as Messiah the Prophecy Gap remains open-ended. As far apart in their theologies as the Supersessionist is from the Preterist, they both attempt to mitigate the gap. The one by eliminating the Jew and the other by exaggerating history. The Dispensationalist would simply recognize the gap as the time between the First and Second Coming. Though in reality the Dispensational gap is not quite that simple because prophetic expectations depend on who's running with the Prophecy Gap baton at the time—the Gentile or the Jew? Then there are the Catholic, Amillennialist, and particular Reformed understandings of the Prophecy Gap.

Expectations not only focus on the timing of prophetic fulfillment, but also on the manner in which a prophecy might be fulfilled. Is a certain prophecy to be fulfilled literally, figuratively, or spiritually? Even when expecting a literal fulfillment—take for instance Daniel Chapter 11—opinions still differ as to whether the prophecy has actually been fulfilled or not. All of these variables deserve consideration because the Word of God is in fact written in a variety of literary styles. Nevertheless, the Bible contains clear and repeated passages discussing the Earth and the Heavens on both the literal and physical level, as well as on the spiritual and glorious level. We will attempt therefore to build our case by applying logic to the most straightforward reading of Scripture in order to discern whether to expect a physical or spiritual fulfillment.

After 2,000 years of scholarly study by devout and brilliant theologians, is there a realistic chance that the Prophecy Gap question can be answered once and for all? Hope indeed springs eternal! Christians and Jews do agree that God's Word is true. And God's own goodness precludes us from concluding that the Bible is an unsolvable riddle. Now for such a time as this—equipped with unprecedented resources like the internet and audio Bibles—and loosed from the shackles and blinders of denominational prejudice, the Commonwealth of Israel Movement is bringing long awaited answers that promise to restore unity. Unity even in the field of eschatology.

In fact, just such a consistent unity regarding the Apostles' prophetic expectations is expressed in the Epistles that we should wonder: By what means did the Apostles advance beyond the confusion of their former expectations? The answer to this question can be found by observing how the Prophecy Gap is actually handled in the New Testament. There we find that the Disciples "accounted" for the Prophecy Gap by using a business accounting technique. A method still used today. Yes, the Bible makes use of a mundane accounting concept, much like the parables also relied on the familiarities of everyday life. This familiar accounting tool for sorting out business transactions was simply applied to sorting out seeming gaps in prophetic expectations that would otherwise appear as discrepancies.

Reckoned and Realized

Beyond our focus on eschatology, the accounting terms, "recognition" and "realization," have application to another important theological concept. Recognition, taking the English form, "reckoning," is not only used to designate the timing of events but also to indicate the status of unseen mental and spiritual conditions. Let's take the most obvious example of this type of reckoning before going on to show how these accounting terms apply to the timing of prophecy.

> *3 For what does the Scripture say? "Abraham believed God, and it was <u>accounted</u> to him for righteousness." 4 Now to him who works, the wages are not <u>counted</u> as grace but as debt. 5 But to him who does not work... his faith is <u>accounted</u>*

for righteousness, 6 just as David also describes the blessedness of the man to whom God <u>imputes</u> righteousness apart from works... 8 "Blessed is the man to whom the Lord shall not <u>impute</u> sin." ... For we say that faith was <u>accounted</u> to Abraham for righteousness. 10 How then was it <u>accounted</u>?... that righteousness might be <u>imputed</u> to them also... (Excerpts from Romans 4:3-11).

These verses contain eight occurrences of the Greek word, Λογίζομαι (*Logizomai*). As defined by *Strong's Exhaustive Concordance*: to account, reckon. Middle voice from logos; to take an inventory, i.e. Estimate (literally or figuratively)—conclude, (ac-) count (of), + despise, esteem, impute, lay, number, reason, reckon, suppose, think (on).

We find the same Greek stem in Romans Chapter Six where we are admonished to make our own mental determination about how we should live in regard to sin. *"Likewise you also, <u>reckon</u>* (λογίζεσθε, *logizesthe*) *yourselves to be dead indeed to sin, but alive to God in Christ Jesus our Lord"* (Rom. 6:11).

Before moving on to look at numerous New Testament applications of the classifications, "recognized" and "realized," let's review how these terms have been used in business accounting, since that is where these concepts have been used from the time of antiquity. In simplest terms, a transaction is "recognized" when it legally occurs rather than when the money is actually exchanged.

Let's take the familiar example of a lemonade stand. Janet from across the street asks for a glass of lemonade. You pour her a glass and she drinks it on the spot. Unfortunately, Janet forgot that she spent all of her change the day before. Technically, in fact legally, Janet owes you 50 cents. She agrees to pay you as soon as she gets her allowance. So legally, the two of you have a binding agreement that the money is due. Now, let's say you are an industrious youngster and you keep a written record of your refreshment sales. At the end of the day you would "recognize" the sale of Janet's lemonade by "counting" the 50 cents in with your total sales. You have now "recognized" the transaction. But you have not "realized" an increase in your cash. The transaction will be "realized" when Janet <u>actually</u> gives you the money.

Now, in this very same sense we as Christians "recognize" that certain spiritual realities have occurred even though we don't yet see the physical evidence. A great deal of what we believe by faith is based on "recognizing" that certain "spiritual transactions" have already taken place in the heavenly realm. Take the verse below for example. We "reckon" that we have already been raised with Christ. But this spiritual transaction will not be "realized" until the conditions of Verse Four are met.

> *If then <u>you were raised with Christ</u>, seek those things which are above, where Christ is, sitting at the right hand of God. 2 Set your mind on things above, not on things on the earth. 3 <u>For you died</u>, and <u>your life is hidden with Christ in God</u>. 4 <u>When</u> Christ who is our life appears, <u>then</u> you also will appear with Him in glory* (Col. 3:1-4).

Below, Paul qualifies some of the assertions made in the second and third chapters of Colossians and Romans Chapter Six. Those sections "recognize" our simultaneous death, burial, and resurrection with Christ. But here Paul was inclined to acknowledge that his human condition still prevented him from experiencing the full "realization" of these truths.

> *Not that I have already attained, or am already perfected; but I press on, that I may lay hold of that for which Christ Jesus has also laid hold of me. 13 Brethren, <u>I do not count (Logizomai) myself to have apprehended</u>...* (Phil. 3:12-13).

Again in Colossians Chapter One and Philippians (below) we "recognize" that we have been translated into the kingdom of the Son, from which we derive the fond expression that we have had a "spiritual change of address." Paul then appends this recognition of the spiritual reality with the yet "unrealized" promise of our glorification.

> *For <u>our citizenship</u> (πολιτείαν, politeian) <u>is in heaven</u>, from which we also eagerly wait for the Savior, the Lord Jesus Christ, 21 who <u>will transform our lowly body that it may be conformed to His glorious body</u>, according to the working by which He is able even to subdue all things to Himself.* (Phil. 3:20-21)

CH. 17: RESOLVING UNFULFILLED MESSIANIC PROPHECY

In fact Paul employs this same pattern quite frequently:

> ➤ Recognition of a spiritual truth;
> ➤ Followed by the promise of an unrealized action.

We know that the whole creation has been groaning in labor pains until now; and not only the creation, but we ourselves, who <u>have the first fruits of the Spirit</u>, groan inwardly while <u>we wait for adoption</u>, the <u>redemption of our bodies</u>. For in hope we were saved. Now hope that is seen is not hope. For who hopes for what is seen? But if we <u>hope for what we do not see</u>, we wait for it with patience (Rom. 8:22-25).

"We hope for what we do not see." But this hope is a hope no less firmly grounded in reality. The *"substance of things hoped for"* mentioned in Hebrews 11:1 is a very real substance. Categorizing a prophetic fulfillment as "recognized" but "unrealized" in no way implies that such a fulfillment is less than real. Take our lemonade example. You weren't merely dreaming or imagining that Janet consumed a cup of your lemonade. Although the transaction was left "unrealized," what was "recognized" was absolutely real. Much of the "faith" aspect of the Christian faith can be categorized as: that which has been spiritually reckoned to have occurred; and that which will eventually be realized. It is faith that provides *"the evidence for things not seen"* (Heb. 11:1).

Many Messianic prophecies were literally and physically fulfilled by Jesus. Matthew's gospel references these fulfillments prolifically. The Prophecy Gap concerning these observable Messianic prophecies has been closed. But the doctrine of the Apostles unabashedly bifurcated the remaining aspects of the Prophecy Gap into two distinct segments: the time between a prophecy and its spiritual recognition at the time of Christ's first appearing; and, the yet unresolved interval between the SAME PROPHECY and its "realization."

Despite the complexity of navigating the Prophecy Gap, Christians as a whole have little difficulty understanding the two stage approach presented in the New Testament. The Holy Spirit of truth helps the believer bridge the Gap. Nevertheless, what remains to be fulfilled, and the manner in which such prophecies will be fulfilled, are wholly received by faith. In the verses below Paul once again promotes the Holy Spirit as the guarantee and concludes with the acknowledgement that the entire "recognition and realization" methodology must be accepted by faith.

> *For we who are in this tent groan, being burdened, not because we want to be unclothed, but further clothed, that mortality may be swallowed up by life. 5 Now He who has prepared us for this very thing is God, who also has given us the <u>Spirit as a guarantee</u>. 6 So we are always confident, knowing that while we are at home in the body we are absent from the Lord. 7 <u>For we walk by faith, not by sight</u>* (2 Cor. 5:4-7).

By analyzing the fulfillment of Bible prophecy using the principles of recognition and realization it can be demonstrated that the work of reconciling God's covenant issues with both houses of Greater Israel ("all Israel") was not a separate or delayed work apart from His covenant reconciling fallen man. To the contrary, the united members of the One New Man consisting of those near, those far, and the alien (aka the Jew, the Lost Triber, and the Gentile, respectively), were simultaneously redeemed through the same act of atonement. The Commonwealth of Israel is NOT a divided kingdom!

Mainstream theologies have presumed that God's covenants concerning national Israel were either staggered or replaced or nullified. They have refused to apply the very same principles of recognition and realization to Israel's national salvation which they have applied exhaustively to individual salvation. Just as no further work of God is required for individual believers in Yeshua to recognize their individual <u>salvation by faith</u> prior to the actual "redemption of the body"; likewise, no further work of God is required for national Israel to <u>recognize</u> its <u>redemption by faith</u> prior to the "realization" of the "redemption of the purchased possession."

The enmity between the Gentiles and Jews which was, in the reality of heaven, taken away through the blood of the cross, most unfortunately, swiftly re-erected its ugly wall of hostility in the second century. Nothing short of this hostility has broken the Staff of Union in the hands of otherwise well-meaning pastors of the flock. The rise of anti-Jewish sentiment in the Post-Apostolic Church was directly responsible for Christianity's misguided and contradictory theological potshots concerning the future of

Ch. 17: Resolving Unfulfilled Messianic Prophecy

national Israel. Under the spell of Greco-Roman anti-Semitism, the believers from among the Nations refused to share the "covenants of promise" with Abraham's heirs. As the wall of hostility grew, this finagling with the covenants cast an entirely new veil over the reading of the Old Covenant.

During Paul's ministry, and before enmity had estranged the Gentile Church from the Jews (including the Jewish Church of Jerusalem), disobedience to the gospel obstructed the meaning of the Old Testament writings. Notice that Paul does not refer here to a veil when reading the New Testament, but when reading the Old Testament: *"But their minds were blinded. For until this day the same veil remains unlifted in the reading of the Old Testament, because the veil is taken away in Christ"* (2 Cor. 3:14).

Yet by the middle of the Apologetic Era—and proceeding through the Reformation—the reading of the Old Testament became veiled to Christendom, either by taking God's promises to Israel only figuratively or by displacing Israel with a new and separate assembly. And the reading of the Old Testament remains partially veiled to the Dispensationalist, who must carefully insert starts and stops in verses such as Joel 2:28-32; where they cannot navigate "the Day of the Lord" even though "all who call on the name of the Lord" was cited by Peter on the Day of Pentecost. Or, Isaiah 61, where only the segment quoted by Jesus in Luke Chapter Four can be considered apart from the dispensation of a novation concerning the party to whom the promises apply. Lastly, concerning the reemergence of the veil, it is worth mentioning in passing that some outliers in the Christian community point to the "unrealized" prophecies and conclude that the New Covenant has not yet been "recognized" AT ALL, either for the Jew or the Gentile. Which would also imply that no reconciliation has yet been "recognized" in the spiritual realm.

Since believing in Christ should remove the veil, we need merely to apply our simple accounting method to *account* for the Prophecy Gap when reading the Old Testament. Three verses from the second Psalm will provide a succinct demonstration.

7 "I will declare the decree:
The Lord has said to Me,
'You are My Son,
Today I have begotten You.'"

Verse Seven has been recognized and realized because Jesus is both eternally begotten and "unto us a Son" has already been given.

8 "Ask of Me, and I will give You
The nations for Your inheritance,
And the ends of the earth for Your possession."

Verse Eight has been recognized on the spiritual and legal level but has not yet been realized. It has been recognized because Jesus declared; *"All authority in heaven and on earth has been given to Me."* The possession will be realized when the Ancient of Days comes and the saints actually take possession of the kingdom (Dan. 7:18, 22). And because we are "heirs of God and joint heirs with Christ" (Rom. 8:17), we can be certain that this is the very same inheritance guaranteed by the Spirit until the day of redemption—the day of its realization.

9 "You shall break them with a rod of iron;
You shall dash them to pieces like a potter's vessel."

Verse Nine is yet to be recognized or realized. Both will be fulfilled together at the time of Revelation 19:15. Delightfully, with the application of our simple accounting technique, there is no need to change covenants in the middle of the stream as Jesus descends on His white horse!

This brings us back to our initial premise. There is only One New Covenant through which God has established peace by reconciling both the sin of Adam and the sin of Israel. All believers, both houses et. al.

ALL THINGS RECONCILED

For it pleased the Father that in Him all the fullness should dwell, and by Him to <u>reconcile ALL THINGS</u> to Himself, by Him, whether things on earth or things in heaven, <u>HAVING MADE PEACE</u> through the blood of His cross (Col. 1:19-20 Emphasis added).

The verse above is one of many New Testament verses confirming a simultaneous personal and national reconciliation: *"Having made peace."* The fact that a peace reconciling all things has already been accomplished precludes a separate covenant of peace for the purpose of reconciling national Israel. Both the individual members (citizens) of the body and the ultimate body of Christ (the Commonwealth) have been reconciled. Furthermore, this reconciliation has been "recognized" in heaven; just as Paul affirmed in Ephesians Chapter One; "[God] has blessed us with every spiritual blessing in the heavenly places in Christ." Whereas on earth, at this time, the citizens of heaven still appear in their mortality, the earth has not been restored, and Greater Israel has not been gathered. The New Covenant in Christ's blood has, nevertheless, already reconciled ALL things.

In fact, it is the theologically erroneous presumption of a broken bond of peace among the members of the Commonwealth of Israel that is NOT recognized in heaven. It has only been recognized in the minds of men. A revived enmity toward the Jew was not even embraced by the Apostle to the Gentiles, who did almost contemplate *anathema* for the sake of his countrymen. Nor was this enmity expressed by the other Apostles. In the following sections we will develop the case for a universal reconciliation. But first let's define "reconciliation."

Strong's 2643. καταλλαγὴ (*katallagē*); to reconcile, reconciliation, restoration, exchange. A change or reconciliation from a state of enmity between persons to one of friendship. Between God and man it is the result of the *apolutrosis* (629), redemption, the divine act of salvation, the ceasing of God's wrath.[135]

Second Corinthians Chapter Five provides the opportunity to observe the Greek word for reconciliation in action, as well as incorporating the "accounting" or "crediting" term that has already been introduced. Amazingly, this citation also expands individual salvation to the broader scope of salvation to a national, even international, salvation. The very point we are eager to make!

---

[135] Zodhiates, Spiros. *The Complete Word Study Dictionary: New Testament*, Chattanooga: AMG Publishers, 1992. Print. p. 835.

18 Now all things are of God, who has reconciled (καταλλάξαντος [*katallaxantos*]) *us to Himself through Jesus Christ, and has given us the ministry of reconciliation* (καταλλαγῆς [*katallagēs*]), *that is, that God was in Christ reconciling* (καταλλάσσων [*katallassōn*]) <u>the world</u> (κόσμον [*kosmon*]) *to Himself,* <u>not imputing</u> (λογιζόμενος [*logizomenos*]) <u>their</u> *trespasses to* <u>them</u>...(2 Cor. 5:18,19).

The global reach of this reconciliation is readily observed in John 3:16, especially when the ancient manuscripts are consulted rather than relying on the English translation. *"For God so loved <u>the world</u>* (κόσμον [*kosmon*]) *that he gave his only Son, so that everyone* (πᾶς [*pas*]: everyone, all) *who believes in him may not perish but may have eternal life"* (John 3:16 NRSV).

The NRSV is quoted here because it is one of the few English Bibles that expresses the breadth of field for which God gave His Son. No major Greek New Testament, Byzantine or Alexandrian, contains the word(s) that translate into English as, "whoever" or "whosoever." Early English Protestants excited about personal salvation apparently desired to make a personal appeal through the usage of "whoever." And few in the Church of that era entertained the hope for Israel's national salvation; although the idea was beginning to stir.

Nevertheless, the ancient texts employ the Greek word, *"pas,"* meaning "everyone" or "all." Without controversy, faith in Christ is mandated by Scripture as the only way to salvation. Indeed, *"He Himself is the propitiation for our sins, and not for ours only but also for the <u>whole world</u>* (κόσμου [*kosmou*]*)"* (1 John 2:2). The parties underlined in the verses above—"Their," "them," "everyone," "all," and "the world" (2 Cor. 5, John 3, 1 John 2)— unequivocally include the reconciliation of the sins of the House of Judah and the House of Israel among the sins of the world.

Noted in the Introduction of this book, awareness of the House of Israel and the House of Judah lingered into the 1st century as evidenced by the New Testament writings. Besides Peter's Pentecost sermon and Jesus' reference to the lost sheep of the House of Israel, another of Jesus' dialogues bears witness to the status of Judah at the time of Christ. Referring to the Jews in Jerusalem, Jesus said: *"If I had not come and spoken to them, they would have no sin, but now they have no excuse for their sin"* . . . *"If I had not done among them the works which no one else did, they would have no sin . . ."* (Excerpts . . . Jn. 15:22, 24).

Jesus' words would appear to contradict the doctrine of original sin (Rom. Chs. 3 and 5; 1 Jn. 1:8, 10; etc.). However, consider the status of the House of Judah. Judah was never given a certificate of divorce. She was punished and exiled, but restored to the Land in good standing. On the NATIONAL level, Judah was still under covenant. Judah was not, as Jesus said, in need of a "physician" for the purpose of healing a broken covenant. (Yet another passage made clear by understanding the divergent predicaments of the two houses.)

Now comes to bear the penalty declared in God's Messianic prophecy of Deuteronomy 18: *"I will raise up for them a Prophet like you from among their brethren, and will put My words in His mouth, and He shall speak to them all that I command Him. And it shall be that whoever will not hear My words, which He speaks in My name, I will require it of him"* (Deut. 18:18-19). Before and until Jesus came—the one who always spoke those things which He heard from the Father—this penalty was without application. But then, the One like Moses came with miracles attesting to His divine authority, thus invoking the penalty—the "sin." Understanding this national application eliminates all seeming contradictions; and the passage, then, makes perfect sense: *"If I had not come...they would have no sin."*

Again, the cross was big enough to reconcile the sins of nations and the sins of individuals at the same time. Yet, even the Jewish friendly Dispensationalist is reluctant to acknowledge Israel's reconciliation—AT THIS TIME. As noted earlier, this grudge match between Gentile and Jew, and vice versa, predates the time of Christ. But to add fuel to the fire—and much like misunderstandings about law and grace—his words have been twisted to suppose that Paul and God had both written the Jews off. Even though Paul expressly stated otherwise. Let's take a minute to consider a section of Paul's writings that has been used to support the Church's antagonism toward the Jews.

> *For you, brethren, became imitators of the churches of God which are in Judea in Christ Jesus. For you also suffered the same things from your own countrymen, just as they did from the Judeans, <u>who killed</u> both <u>the Lord Jesus</u> and their own prophets, and have persecuted us; and they <u>do not please God</u> and are <u>contrary to all men</u>, forbidding us to speak to*

the Gentiles that they may be saved, so as always to <u>fill up the measure of their sins</u>; but <u>wrath has come upon them to the uttermost</u> (1 Thess. 2:14-16).

Are the Jews bound eternally under God's wrath? Obviously not; because Paul also stated in Romans 11 that *"God has not cast away His people."* It is also obvious that Christians grafted into a Hebraic olive tree would themselves be united with objects of wrath, if in fact the Jews were destined for wrath. But isn't Paul accusing the Jews of being Christ killers? Absolutely! But he was not being hostile when he said that the Jews had killed Christ. Peter said the very same thing in the second chapter of Acts. *"Him, being delivered by the determined purpose and foreknowledge of God, <u>you have taken by lawless hands, <u>have crucified</u>, and <u>put to death</u>"* (Acts 2:23). But then immediately Peter offered these VERY SAME JEWS the opportunity to repent unto salvation. THEY were, in fact, the Earliest Church.

The Bible's promises of restoration and gathering were often preceded by prophecies that both houses would fill up the measure of their sins prior to their redemption. Paul's statement that wrath had come upon them to the uttermost was merely an acknowledgement that Israel had finally hit rock bottom, which was the very condition God had foretold would come in due time. Second Thessalonians in effect recognizes the commonality of Israel's failing and the failings of all mankind which Paul summarized in Romans 3:23: *"For all have sinned and fall short of the glory of God."* And certainly being under God's wrath does not disqualify anyone from being delivered from that wrath, because we ALL *"were by nature children of wrath, just as the others"* (Eph. 2:3).

SETTING THE STAGE FOR THE COMMONWEALTH

For obvious reasons Paul's Epistle to the Ephesians is central to understanding the Commonwealth of Israel. Intuitively, the Commonwealth of Israel Foundation considered it prudent to annotate Ephesians (now in progress) as the first sample book for the promotion of a complete Commonwealth Reference Bible. Our chapter will likewise rely on the Book of Ephesians because in it we find the biblical constructs implemented by Paul in building his case for the Commonwealth.

We have already observed the significance that every blessing has already been "recognized" spiritually (Eph. 1:3). Now by drawing associations from the 49th and 61st chapters of Isaiah it can be demonstrated that Paul was continuing to lay the theological groundwork for the Commonwealth of Israel throughout the introduction of his epistle. The concepts introduced in the opening statements of Ephesians strongly suggest such an Isaiah connection. Amazingly, these Isaiah passages will not only help us navigate the Prophecy Gap, but Isaiah 49 testifies to the inclusion of "far off peoples" and the Gentiles. Such a union is the very constitution of the Commonwealth of Israel. Emphasis has been added extensively to the verses below as a visual aid for drawing important cross references.

"The Spirit of the Lord God is upon Me, because the Lord has anointed Me to preach good tidings to the poor; He has sent Me to heal the brokenhearted, to proclaim <u>liberty to the CAPTIVES</u>, and the opening of the <u>PRISON</u> to those who are bound; to proclaim the <u>ACCEPTABLE</u> (LXX and Luke 4:19, δεκτόν [dekton]) <u>year of the Lord</u>, and the <u>day of vengeance</u> (LXX, "<u>RECOMPENSE</u>," ἀνταποδόσεως [antapodoseos]*) of our God; to comfort all who mourn, to console those who mourn <u>in ZION</u>, to give <u>them</u> beauty for ashes, the oil of joy for mourning, the garment of praise for the spirit of heaviness; that <u>they</u> may be called trees of righteousness, the planting of the Lord, that He may be glorified." And <u>they</u> shall rebuild the old ruins, <u>they</u> shall raise up the former <u>DESOLATIONS</u> . . . (Isaiah 61:1-4).

* Strong's 467: *antapodidómi*; to recompense, render, repay.

Those familiar with the gospels will immediately recall that part of this Scripture was read by Jesus while visiting his hometown of Nazareth. Jesus stopped reading after proclaiming the "acceptable year"; saying, *"Today this Scripture is fulfilled in your hearing"* (Luke 4:21). Dispensationalists are quite right in assuming that the mention of Zion is a reference to Old Testament Israel. Looking for a clean break in the passage, between verses applicable to the Church and verses reserved for another dispensation, they would suggest that Jesus read only the first part of the prophecy because it contained what had been fulfilled in the present dispensation. But Jesus didn't, after all, recite the entire 22nd Psalm from the cross in order to convey its complete fulfillment. So let's consider which elements of this prophecy have, and have not, been fulfilled.

Jesus was certainly the Anointed One. He preached the gospel. The Beatitudes attest to: the blessing of the poor, comfort to those who mourn, and the filling of those seeking righteousness. Furthermore, Jesus preached to those in Zion and northern Israel exclusively, telling His disciples: *"Do not go into the way of the Gentiles, and do not enter a city of the Samaritans. But go rather to the lost sheep of the house of Israel"* (Matt. 10:5-6). Even at His ascension Jesus instructed them to first *"be witnesses to Me in Jerusalem, and in all Judea,"* and then in *"Samaria, and to the end of the earth"* (Acts 1:8). So, the question becomes: Which of the prophecies in the first four verses of Isaiah 61 were NOT literally fulfilled? Answer: the Restoration.

We will consider the rebuilding of the former desolations (the Restoration) in our consolidated review of Isaiah 49 and Isaiah 61. But first, and even before examining the correlative passage in Isaiah 49, let's investigate what Isaiah meant by the "acceptable year." The following online post is accurate and on point for establishing the meaning of the "acceptable year," with the caveat that the author has not investigated the theological stance of the website or the life and beliefs of the blogger:

> The same word translated as "acceptable" in this verse is rendered in other verses in the King James translation through such words as "delight," "desire," "favor," "pleasure," and "will." Various other English translations of this verse (as found at http://www.biblehub.com) render the original text as follows: "the year when the LORD will show His favor"; "the year of the LORD's good will"; "the favorable year of the LORD"; "the year of the LORD's good pleasure."
>
> In each case, the verse was prophesying a future day when God would show good will to His people (while at the same time bringing God's final promised vengeance on Satan in fulfillment of Genesis 3:15), specifically by the sending of the promised Messiah as the One who would deal for all time with the separation between humanity and God caused by sin. As Jesus indicated when He quoted this verse, this prophecy was being fulfilled by His

CH. 17: RESOLVING UNFULFILLED MESSIANIC PROPHECY

ministry and sinless life, which would culminate in His atoning death and resurrection.[136]

This broader definition of "acceptable" has a direct application to the parallel passage from Isaiah Chapter 49. But not by coincidence, the context of the acceptable year is a prophecy of Messiah's greater ministry to the ends of the earth. This prophecy is obviously germane to the mystery of the inclusion of the Gentiles—the very crux of the Commonwealth. So rather than skipping straight to the verse about acceptance, we simply must observe the setting in which this time of acceptance occurs. Once again, emphasis is added to draw attention to common elements and to highlight aspects of the "Light to the Gentiles" prophecy. Verses three and four are shown separately because they represent a personification of national Israel, whose mission through the Abrahamic blessing to be a blessing to all peoples would have been in vain apart from Messiah, the Seed of Abraham (Gal. 3:16).

Isaiah 49

1 "Listen, <u>O coastlands</u>, to Me, and <u>take heed</u>, <u>you PEOPLES FROM AFAR</u>! The Lord has called Me from the womb; from the matrix of My mother He has made mention of My name. 2 And He has made My mouth like a sharp sword; in the shadow of His hand He has hidden Me, and made Me a polished shaft; in His quiver He has hidden Me."

3 "And He said to me, 'You are My servant, O Israel, in whom I will be glorified.' 4 Then I said, 'I have labored in vain, I have spent my strength for nothing and in vain; yet surely my just reward is with the Lord, and my work with my God.'"

5 "And now the Lord says, who formed Me from the womb to be His <u>Servant</u>, <u>to bring JACOB back to Him</u>, so that <u>ISRAEL is GATHERED</u> to Him...

6 Indeed He says, 'It is too small a thing that You should be My <u>Servant</u> to raise up the <u>tribes of JACOB</u>, and to restore the preserved ones of <u>ISRAEL</u>; I will also give You

---

[136] Tim Maas, https://ebible.com/questions/16583-what-is-the-meaning-of-acceptable-year-of-the-lord-in-isaiah-61-2-and-luke-4-19, captured 4/21/2019

as a light to the <u>GENTILES</u>, that You should be My salvation to the ends of the earth.'"

Notice first that Messiah's primary mission was to bring back and gather Israel. This agrees with Isaiah 61, where the object of comfort was Zion and the desolations to be restored were the desolations of the Promised Lands. Such desolation was forewarned prolifically by the Prophets and was the predetermined penalty for the sins of the two houses. These warnings were often coupled with merciful appeals for repentance and promises of restoration. The fact that salvation would come first to Jacob through the Suffering Servant, and only then be extended to the peoples of the Nations, is precisely what Paul expressed in Romans 15:8:

"Now I say that Jesus Christ has become a SERVANT TO THE CIRCUMCISION for the truth of God, to confirm the promises made to the FATHERS, AND that the Gentiles might glorify God for His mercy."

"And," is the operative word. The salvation of the Gentiles was to be in addition to the salvation of the Jews; NOT instead of the salvation of the Jews. That "truth of God" known as the gospel came *"First to the Jew, then to the Greek"* (Rom. 1:16). This point will be further expounded through the rest of this chapter; so, without further commentary we will examine Isaiah's parallel passage regarding the time of acceptance.

Isaiah 49

8 Thus says the Lord: "In an ACCEPTABLE (LXX, δεκτῷ [dekto]) TIME I have heard You, And in the day of SALVATION I have helped You; I will preserve You and give You as a covenant to the people, to RESTORE THE EARTH, to cause them to INHERIT the DESOLATE heritages; 9 That You may say to the PRISONERS, 'Go forth,' to those who are in darkness, 'Show yourselves.'"

In addition to acceptance, these verses from Isaiah 61 and 49 share four other common elements, although some of these elements are expressed using slightly different words. Reviewing these minor differences might seem tedious but establishing that both passages are pointing to the same acceptable time in Isaiah 61 and Isaiah 49 is imperative: Obviously, by Christ's own affirmation in the synagogue at Nazareth, the <u>anointed deliverer</u> of Chapter 61 is the same servant who was given as <u>a covenant</u> to the people in Chapter 49. That is Messiah; the Christ.

Isaiah 49 refers to the "prisoners . . . who are in darkness"; whereas, Isaiah 61 speaks of the captives, the prison, and "those who are bound." These variations are only to be expected considering the Greek, for instance, employs a word that is somewhat arbitrarily translated into English as either "captive" or "prisoner."

Chapter 61 first addresses Zion but then broadens its application to "desolations," in the plural. Chapter 49 uses "Jacob" and "Israel" interchangeably since they are both names for the nation's father. The "tribes of Israel" might well refer to all twelve tribes of the United Kingdom considering that the scope of the passages enlarges to encompass the restoration of the earth.

Perhaps the most noteworthy common elements of these passages are: the gathering, the restoration, and the inheritance. These physically unrealized prophecies were the subject of the Apostles' inquiry as our chapter began; and these components of the Prophecy Gap continue to be the greatest challenge in the study of eschatology.

Now, with all of our observations about these Isaiah passages at hand, we can make some rather profound conclusions. The year of the Lord's acceptance that Isaiah coupled with the day of recompense in Chapter 61 is the same time of acceptance which is coupled with the day of salvation in Chapter 49. This conclusion can be handily proven by the fact that Jesus declared the Isaiah 61 passage to be fulfilled, while in Paul's own words, quoting Isaiah 49 below, he declared "the day," "the acceptable time," to be "now." That is, contemporaneous with the Apostolic Age. From these same observations we can conclude that neither "acceptable time" can possibly refer to a yet future time.

We then, as workers together with Him also plead with you not to receive the grace of God in vain. 2 For He says: "In an ACCEPTABLE TIME I have heard you, and in the DAY OF SALVATION I have helped you." Behold, NOW is the ACCEPTED TIME; behold, NOW is the DAY OF SALVATION (2 Cor. 6:1-2).

The extreme correlation in the content of the Isaiah and Corinthians passages allows us to confidently assert that this acceptable time is the time of a saving recompense—a saving repayment. This acceptance is nothing less than the acceptance purchased by the great exchange at the cross! Moreover, in Isaiah 61 and Isaiah 49 the results of this acceptance brings to ZION comfort, restoration, and the release from captivity. The stated national application does not interfere with the acceptance which frees the captive sinner, as declared by Jesus and Paul. But it is in perfect accord with the New Covenant of Jeremiah 31:31 with the House of Judah and the House of Israel through which *"THEIR sins and lawless deeds He will remember no more."*

Commonwealth Theology offers a logical solution to the Prophecy Gap presented in these Isaiah passages. Replacement Theology, although failing to recognize Israel's future, offers a philosophically logical (albeit contrary to Scripture) solution by declaring the physical promises to national Israel to be null and void, but then mysteriously appropriating all of the "spiritual" blessings and encouragements to the Church. Dispensational Theology, however, cannot logically manage for "now" to be the day of salvation for national Israel. Such a conundrum would involve reconciling the individual and the nation at the same time. That is, within the same dispensation.

In conclusion, the fellow citizens of the Commonwealth of Israel (Jew and Gentile) who are *"fellow heirs of the same body and partakers of His promise"* (Eph. 3:6), do in fact receive their inheritance at the same time; and, partake of His promise at the same time! And THIS was the groundwork being laid by Paul as he opened his epistle.

> *4 just as He chose us in Him before the foundation of the world, that we should be holy and without blame before Him in love, 5 having predestined us to <u>adoption as sons</u>* (heirs: Jn. 8:35, Gal. 4:7,30) *by Jesus Christ to Himself, according to the good pleasure of His will, 6 to the praise of the glory of His grace, by which <u>He made us ACCEPTED</u>* [or FAVORED] (Isa. 49; 61 [time of acceptance]) *<u>in the Beloved</u>... 11 In Him also we <u>have obtained</u> an <u>INHERITANCE</u>* (Isa. 49:8)... *you were sealed with the <u>Holy Spirit of promise</u>, 14 who is the <u>guarantee</u> of our <u>INHERITANCE</u> until the <u>redemption</u> of the <u>purchased possession</u>* (Excerpts from Ephesians Ch. 1).

CH. 17: RESOLVING UNFULFILLED MESSIANIC PROPHECY

Why did Paul strike this connection between the time of acceptance and the spiritual recognition of the inheritance at the onset of his letter? These well-known verses from Isaiah clearly identify the purchased possession as Zion. The sheep from the lost House of Israel and the believers from among the Nations have become co-inheritors, partners, household members with the House of Judah, whose possession was clearly identified by the Prophets. And this possession has already been redeemed in the heavenlies (Eph. 1:3) on behalf of all parties to the One New Covenant. The acceptance won by the beloved Savior is directly related to the inheritance obtained. *"In Him also we <u>have obtained</u> an <u>INHERITANCE.</u>"*

By applying our system of recognition and realization to these verses from Isaiah, Second Corinthians, and Ephesians we now have a rational explanation for the gap between Christ's finished recompense for the purchased possession and the yet to be realized redemption of the purchased possession. *"<u>Until</u> the redemption of the purchased possession"* simply points to the time of realization rather than to a separately-dispensed covenant relationship or a covenant with a new and separate assembly. The same system of recognition and realization also explains Paul's "recognition" that the "day of salvation" is "now," in conjunction with his *"heart's desire and prayer to God for <u>Israel</u>... that they may* [in the future] *be saved."*

Without dispute, salvation for the Jew, as for the Gentile, relies on personal acceptance by faith; even though acceptance on God's part (the acceptable time) has already been recognized as a spiritual reality. Furthermore, although previous theologies have made a distinction between individual and national salvation, neither Jesus, the Apostles, nor the Earliest Church made such a distinction because both Zion, et. al., and the individual were saved AT THE SAME TIME. Adam and Israel were saved by the same act of atonement. And ALL of God's covenant people belong to the same Commonwealth. Yet, the Commonwealth is more than a restored Israel. It is a restored Israel inhabited by a restored Adam. A new creation! A Commonwealth that will, together, inherit a realized habitation at the *"restoration of all things"* (Acts 3:21).

This prophesied gathering and restoration depended wholly on resolving the God-ordained captivity demanded for Israel's sins. Even though Judah was allowed to return to the Land after the first captivity, no formal recompense had been made to reconcile the sins of Joseph or Judah. Judah's precarious future under Roman control at the time of Christ served to further magnify the fact that fallen man is defective and so would perpetually fail. Thus it is easy to follow the progression from the acknowledgement that sin *caused* the captivity, to the determination that sin *is* the captivity. Such an awareness of the stigma of sin is quite significant in light of Isaiah 49's expanded scope of salvation to the Gentiles and the ends of the earth. Yet, the Christian Individualist has forgotten or ignored Christ's primary mission—*"to be His Servant to bring **Jacob** back to Him so that **Israel** is gathered"* (Is. 49:5).

Fishers of Men

Christ's mission to gather Israel was, however, not overlooked by the "Servant to the circumcision." From the time Jesus first started making disciples He selected fishermen. *"And Jesus, walking by the Sea of Galilee, saw two brothers, Simon called Peter, and Andrew his brother, casting a net into the sea; for they were fishermen. Then He said to them, 'Follow Me, and I will make you fishers of men'"* (Matt. 4:18-19). Why did Jesus call fishermen to be fishermen? Because a certain prophecy stated, *"I will send for many fishermen."* This prophecy was literally fulfilled by Jesus because He indeed chose fishermen—they did not choose Him. The prophecy of the fishermen is found in the 16th chapter of Jeremiah.

> *"Therefore behold, the days are coming," says the Lord, "that it shall no more be said, 'The Lord lives who brought up the children of Israel from the land of Egypt,' but, 'The Lord lives who brought up the children of Israel from the land of the north and from <u>all the lands where He had driven them.</u>' For I will <u>bring them back into their land which I gave to their fathers.</u> "Behold, <u>I will send (LXX, ἀποστελῶ [apostelō, as in "apostle"]) for many fishermen,</u>" says the Lord, "<u>and they shall fish them</u> . . ."* (Jer. 16:14-16).

It seems almost incredulous that, there on the Mount of Olives, when the Apostles asked the Lord about the restoration of Israel, that they were the very ones handpicked to fulfill this prophecy of the gathering of Israel. In all fairness, Jesus had kept other things from them until the appropriate time. But now, in the context of Jeremiah's fishermen prophecy, we can see just how directly their question was answered. It wasn't a matter of what Jesus would do next at all, but about what the fishermen were to do next. *"You shall be witnesses to Me in Jerusalem, and in all Judea and Samaria, and to the end of the earth"* (Acts 1:8). Through the power of the Holy Spirit, Jesus engaged the fishermen in the work of bringing Jacob back to the Land. The very skill for which they had been sent for, retrained, and redirected.

The work of gathering actually began with the Gospel. The Chief Apostle expressly acknowledged His mission of gathering in His statement: *". . . he who does not gather with Me scatters"* (Matt. 12:30). But we can make even further observations about the status of the gathering during Messiah's First Coming. Jesus spoke about the gathering and desolation in His lament over Jerusalem (Zion):

> *O Jerusalem, Jerusalem, the one who kills the prophets and stones those who are sent to her! How often I wanted to gather your children together, as a hen gathers her chicks under her wings, but you were not willing! See! Your house is left to you desolate; for I say to you, you shall see Me no more till you say, "Blessed is He who comes in the name of the Lord!"*(Matt. 23:37-38).

It has been said that Jesus is a gentlemen because He doesn't force anyone to receive salvation against their will. Nowhere is such regard for freewill more evident than in Jesus' prelude to the Olivet Discourse. Even though the gathering was a key component of the Messianic prophecies, Jesus did not forcefully gather the House of Israel at that time. Because the Jerusalem of Jesus' day was inhabited by Jews it was not desolate in respect to the House of Judah. Therefore, we can infer that the house "left to you desolate" referred to the whole House of Israel comprised by the House of Judah and the House of Israel. Jerusalem was desolate specifically because those tribes which had been scattered had not been brought back.

Jesus wanted—willed—that the lost sheep of Israel be gathered. But THEY were not willing. This should prompt us to ask: What role does man play in the gathering? At the *"coming of our Lord*

Jesus Christ and our gathering together to Him" (2 Thess. 2:1) will anyone be gathered unwillingly? Note also Psalms 110: 2-3: *"Your people shall be <u>volunteers</u> in the day of Your power."* That doesn't sound like a national conscription. In Psalms 110 it speaks of the Father making Christ's enemies His footstool, placing the responsibility for such submission on the Father. And Jesus said; *"No one can come to Me unless the Father who sent Me draws him"* (Jn. 6:44). So now, coming full circle, we can understand why Jesus answered His disciples: *"It is not for you to know times or seasons which the Father has put in <u>His own authority</u>"* (Acts 1:7). The Father is ultimately in charge of the gathering.

Now consider the correlation between: our earlier Isaiah passages; the fishing expedition from Jeremiah 16; the charter of the first chapter of Acts; and, the Great Commission to *"Go therefore and make disciples of all nations"* (Matt. 28:19). Oh, but wait. The Greek text has no "and" or "make" or "of," but only the accusative, "nations," (πορευθέντες οὖν μαθητεύσατε πάντα τὰ ἔθνη [*ethnē*]). "Therefore go disciple all nations." Or as rendered in *Young's Literal Translation*; "having gone, then, disciple all the nations." Alternatively, by incorporating "make" we would read; "Therefore go make all nations disciples." Inserting "of" in the verse easily shifts the connotation to mean individuals "from" all nations. Once again betraying the persistence of the Old Roman animosity toward the Nation of Israel and the myopic focus of the English translators on the individual.

God's Light to the Gentiles (Nations) Mission DID NOT CEASE with the New Covenant. As we have demonstrated, the Great Commission was not a new mission at all, but the fulfillment of the very same mission reiterated throughout the Prophets. Just as God reconciled Adam and Israel through one act of atonement, God will also fulfill His promises to the Jew and to the Gentile; to gather national Israel, to include the Gentiles, to restore the earth, and to reign from Zion. Nowhere in Scripture do we find these promises to be mutually exclusive.

We have already observed that the New Covenant, and the promise that God would *"remember their sins no more,"* were directed specifically to the House of Israel and the House of Judah. Because of the fishermen, the Nations (Gentiles) have the blessing of being included WITH God's covenant people. The reconciliation for all parties of the Commonwealth of Israel has been "recognized" in heaven and is extended to all who are willing to be reconciled to God. We have also noted that, to some degree, the gathering of Israel began when Jesus began to preach the gospel; which He implied by stating that those who opposed Him were scattering. That is, prolonging the desolation. But now we can definitively point to a time in the PAST when the gathering formally began to be realized! To reiterate, we are in no way endorsing the Preterist view. There are still many more Bible prophecies to be fulfilled in the future. (Remember: Recognized in heaven but not yet Realized on earth. Partially—but not fully—manifested.) Furthermore, the gathering will not be completed until Christ's return, just as prophesied throughout the Bible.

Notwithstanding, the preaching of the Gospel to the Nations was in itself prima facie evidence of the gathering. How so? In order to answer that question let's first take a moment to review just how precisely Christ and His Apostles fulfilled their respective prophetic roles. Jesus was the Light to the Gentiles but was NOT prophesied to be sent to the Gentiles. He was instead sent to the lost sheep of the house of Israel, and to comfort those who mourn in Zion. And that is exactly what Jesus did. On the other hand, the Apostles were the fishermen who were SENT out into the world to bring back scattered Israel and to include the Gentiles in the Commonwealth.

Now consider what Jesus said about the Holy Spirit. *"The wind blows where it wishes, and you hear the sound of it, but cannot tell where it comes from and where it goes"* (Jn. 3:8). We cannot see the Spirit, but we see the effects of the Spirit. Jesus told the Disciples that the ability to "go" and be witnesses would be provided by the Holy Spirit. And just so, empowered by the Holy Spirit, the fishermen went out into the world. And not only that, the Nations believed! The fulfillment of these aspects of Jeremiah's prophecy were so important to the Early Church that they were embellished in one of the first creeds. "[God was...] *Preached among the Gentiles, Believed on in the world"* (1 Tim. 3:16). Just as Jesus was raised as the Firstfruit and the Spirit was given as a pledge, the Gathering (process) began with the Fishermen.

So to make a play on an English word, the fact that the Apostles DID GO out into the world to proceed with the "gathering in earnest," IS the earnest that guarantees the gathering will be completed—that the inheritance will be "realized." But in accordance with prophecies already referenced, the gathering will not be finished until the Lord returns *"that in all things He might have the preeminence."*

As to why those being gathered during the first centuries failed to return to the Land, we must look to the political, philosophical, and theological movements which divided the Commonwealth—purposefully or ignorantly—opposing the gathering. Remember that end-time prophecies not only spoke about bringing light to the Nations, they also foretold that those same Nations would come against Israel. And just as the Book of Acts witnessed the beginning of the gathering, the spiritual forces of darkness were, likewise, already active.

Chapter Eighteen

REVELATION: THE THEMATIC VIEW
By Dr. Douglas Hamp

Part of the challenge of understanding the day of the Lord and its timing is due to a tendency to interpret the book of Revelation chronologically rather than thematically. Though there is some chronology in the book, it is primarily laid out thematically. What that means is that rather than view the seals, trumpets and bowls as chronological events that come one after the other in future time, they represent the order in which the future judgments were communicated to John. John was shown in a series of visions events that "were, are, and will be." The order they are placed in the book is the order that they were communicated to him and not necessarily the order in which they will actually play out in the world.

Imagine John being given a tour of a television control room. Before him there are dozens of screens. All the scenes of a particular show are being shot at the same time. For the sake of illustration, let's imagine that the show has five distinct scenes. Each scene has separate cameras and cameraman to capture it. John merely sees the video feed. Each scene is complex and requires varying camera angles to appreciate the complexity. Some cameras are placed above the set to get a wide angle—top-down approach. Other cameras are zoomed in on the faces of the main characters. Finally, other cameras are constantly panning to give the greater comprehension.

The book of Revelation is essentially laid out in such a fashion. There are a certain number of events that take place, but with several different camera angles we, the readers, can get several perspectives.

ALL THE MOUNTAINS AND ISLANDS FLEE AWAY

As evidence of these different camera angles, we turn to Revelation 16:20: ***Every island*** vanished, and the ***mountains*** could no longer be found (Rev. 16:20 ISV).

Imagine the kind of destruction that planet earth is going to experience when every island and every mountain vanish and disappear! When even just one earthquake happens on one part of the earth, there is incredible damage to buildings and great loss of life. The 9.0 earthquake that happened in the spring of 2011 in Japan caused phenomenal damage (mostly from the tsunami that followed). What will happen when every island and mountain is moved from its place? This is clearly an extinction level event that is coming upon the planet—that is to say, it will not be repeated. The mini-apocalypse in Isaiah 24 describes how Earth will be completely rocked to such an extent that it will "fall and not rise again."

*The earth is **utterly shattered**, the earth is split apart, the earth is **violently shaken**. The earth **reels** to and fro like a drunkard; it **sways** like a hut; its transgression lies so heavy upon it, that it **falls**, **never** to **rise again*** (Isa. 24:19-20 ISV).

Given the absolute finality of the parallel language of these two passages we must conclude that they are referring to the same event. The earthquake spoken of in Isaiah is so massive that the earth is down for the count, "never to rise again." We must conclude that the Isaiah 24 event is the same as the Revelation 16 event where *there was a great earthquake, such a mighty and great earthquake as had not occurred since men were on the earth* (Rev. 16:18). Certainly all of the islands and all of the mountains disappearing would qualify for that event.

However, Revelation 6 also says, ***every mountain** and **island** was moved from its place* (Rev. 6:14 ISV). How could it be that every mountain and island can be moved **twice**? If we think that they can, then we are not truly considering the enormity of such an event. Imagine all of the mountains crumbling around your home! If you live on an island, imagine it falling into the ocean! Once that happens, then it cannot happen again. Therefore we see how Revelation 16:20, which is at the end of the tribulation, is the same event as Revelation 6:14.

The word "every" in the case of 'every island and mountain' precludes the event from happening twice. The fact that it says "every" means that once it happens there will be no repeat. Therefore, Revelation 6:14, Revelation 16:20 and Isaiah 24 are the same event. There are, in fact, many passages that speak of the complete and utter shaking of the mountains in a way that will only happen once.

- *For the day of the LORD of hosts Shall come upon everything proud and lofty, Upon **everything lifted up**– And it shall be brought low– against **all the high mountains**, and against **all the lofty hills** . . .* (Isa. 2:12-14 ISV).
- ***He stood up** and **shook** the land; with his stare he startled the nations. The **age-old mountains were shattered**, and the ancient **hilltops bowed** down. His ways are eternal* (Hab. 3:6 ISV).
- ***Mountains melt** like wax in the Lord's presence— in the presence of the Lord of all the earth* (Psa. 97:5 ISV).
- *I looked at the **mountains**; they were **quaking**, and **all** the **hills** moved **back** and **forth**. I looked, and no people were there. All the birds of the sky had gone* (Jer. 4:24, 25 ISV).
- ***Every island** vanished, and the **mountains** could no longer be found* (Rev. 16:20 ISV).

Therefore, Revelation 6:14 is identical to the many descriptions of the ultimate shaking that will take place on planet earth—which will happen in the day that Jesus startles the nations. If we hope to take Revelation 6:14 even remotely literally, as we ought to, then it is impossible that the timing of the passage should be placed anywhere but at the day Jesus comes back—at the very end.

According to the passage, everyone on earth understands that their end has come. The rich, poor, powerful, and slaves—everyone who is on the earth will recognize it, and they call it the day of the Lord—as revealed by the Lord to John.

Then the kings of the earth, the important people, the generals, the rich, the powerful, and all the slaves and free people concealed themselves in caves and among the rocks in the mountains. They told the mountains and rocks, "Fall on us and hide us from the face of the one who sits on the throne and from the wrath of the lamb. For the great day of their wrath has come, and who is able to endure it?" (Rev. 6:15-17 ISV)

Keep in mind that in Revelation 16 the same people are marching against Jerusalem ostentatiously, attempting to make war against Jesus (Rev. 16:14).

For they are spirits of demons, performing signs, which go out to the kings of the earth and of the whole world, to gather them to the battle of that great day of God Almighty (Rev. 16:14).

They undoubtedly do not understand what they are truly getting into in Revelation 16. However, in Revelation 6, reality quickly becomes apparent—so much so that they go running into the caves, for the rocks to fall on them, and readily admit, *"For **the great day of their wrath has come**, and who is able to endure it?"* (Rev. 6:15-17 ISV)

Are we to believe that the mighty men of the earth are throwing in the towel in Revelation Six and fully admit that the day of Jesus' wrath has come, but in Chapter 16 they think that they can actually defeat him? The simple answer is that the book of Revelation is thematically arranged so that the chronology of events is not in conflict with the order in which these events occur in the book. Commentator Thomas Constable has suggested that Revelation 6 is simply hyperbole, in other words, exaggeration. He suggests that the men on the earth *supposed* the end of the world to have come though it really hadn't.

"Evidently the sky will **appear** to split and roll back in two opposite directions (cf. Isa. 34:4). The universe will **seem** to be coming apart. Apparently the opening of the sky will give earth-dwellers a glimpse into the throne-room of heaven (v. 16). Probably the earthquake (v. 12) will cause mountains and islands to rise and fall (cf. Nah. 1:6). The reaction of every category of humanity all over the world is amazing. It indicates that people's perception of God and the Lamb in heaven will be far more terrifying to them than the physical consequences of this judgment. Literal interpretation does not rule out the **use of hyperbole**, which appears at this point. If all the mountains moved out of their places, there would be no places for people to seek to hide. This "great day of their wrath" is the Tribulation, Daniel's seventieth week (cf. Jer. 30:7; Dan. 12:1; Joel 2:2; Matt. 24:21). These people will not turn to God in repentance but from Him in terror (cf. Isa. 2:19, 21; Hos. 10:8; Luke 23:30). By the end of the sixth seal judgment, they will know that what they are experiencing is the outpouring of His wrath. This is the first part of the judgment phase of the day of the Lord (cf. Joel 2:11, 30-31; Isa. 2:10-11, 19-21; 13:8-13; 26:17-19; 34:4, 8; 66:7-9; Jer. 30:6-8; Ezek. 32:7-8; Hos. 10:8; Mic. 4:9-10; Matt. 24:8; 1 Thess. 5:3)."[137] (Emphasis mine)

---

[137] Constable, Dr. Thomas. Bible Commentaries: Expository Notes of Dr. Thomas Constable; Revelation 6. StudyLight.org. studylight.org. 2017. Web. 11 July 2017.

Though Thomas Constable is an excellent commentator, his predisposition to interpreting the book of Revelation chronologically rather than thematically has not allowed him to see the parallels as we have studied. To suggest that hyperbole is being used is complete speculation. John faithfully recorded what the men in the Tribulation will say and do. If they say that it is the day of the Lord, who are we to disagree? If the sky has rolled up, who are we to suggest that it just appears so? If all of the mountains and islands move out of their place, who are we to say it only seems so?

Zephaniah One and Two underscore the conclusion that Revelation 6:14-17, the day of the Lord, is the Second Advent itself; when there will be a great sacrifice of kings and mighty men, when the nations have gathered together and the whole land shall be devoured by fire very suddenly.

> *It will come about during the Lord's sacrifice that I'll punish the officials, the royal descendants, and all who wear foreign clothing. The **great Day of the Lord** approaches— How it comes, hurrying faster and faster! The sound of the **Day of the Lord** there includes the bitter cry of the mighty soldier. That day will be filled with wrath, a day of trouble and tribulation; a day of desolation and devastation, a **day of doom and gloom**, a day of clouds and shadows.... a day of trumpet and battle cry against fortified cites and **watch towers**. And I'll bring so much distress to people that they will walk around like the blind. Because they have sinned against the Lord, **their blood will be poured out like dust** and their intestines will spill out like manure. Neither their silver nor their gold will deliver them in the **Day of the Lord's** wrath; but the **entire land will be consumed by the fire of his jealousy**, for he will bring the inhabitants of the land to a **sudden** end. **Gather together!** Yes, indeed, gather together, you shameless nation! Before the decree is carried out, before the day flies away like chaff, before the fierce anger of the Lord visits you, before the **Day of the Lord's** wrath surprises you seek the Lord, all you humble people of the land, who do what he commands. Seek righteousness! Seek humility! Maybe you will be **protected in the Day of the Lord's anger*** (Zeph. 1:8, 14-18, 2:1-3 ISV).

ANGELS ARE STARS

Further demonstration of the book of Revelation being thematically arranged is found in the events of Satan being cast out of heaven in Revelation 12. The dragon taking stars with its tail is the same as the dragon and his angels being cast to the earth.

- *A huge red dragon... its tail swept away one-third of the **stars** in the sky and knocked them down to the **earth*** (Rev. 12: 3, ISV).
- *The **huge dragon was hurled down**. That ancient serpent, called the Devil and Satan, the deceiver of the whole world, was hurled down to the **earth**, **along with its angel*** (Rev. 12: 7-9 ISV).

There is no question that there are many symbols in the book of Revelation. However, once we have the key to unlock them, the interpretation follows incredibly literally. The term "stars" is actually a fairly common reference to angels in Scripture. Though we don't know exactly why they are referred to as such, we could speculate it is because they are literally shining, as when the angels shone down on the shepherds to announce the birth of Jesus. Nevertheless, the internal of use of stars in the book of Revelation firmly establishes that "stars" is a reference to angels.

*The **secret meaning** of the seven **stars** that you saw in my right hand and the seven gold lamp stands is this: the **seven stars** are the messengers [angeloi, ἄγγελοι] of the seven churches, and the seven lamp stands are the seven churches* (Rev. 1:20 ISV).

That meaning is further underscored in the book of Job where the sons of God (*benei ha'elohim*) are also called stars. *While the morning stars sang together and all the divine beings shouted joyfully* (Job 38:7 ISV)?

With the secret meaning revealed to us, we can properly understand the rest of the references to stars as actually being angels in the book of Revelation. In Revelation 9:1 we read of a ***star that had fallen** to earth from the sky* (Rev. 9:1 ISV).

This star cannot simply be a meteorite or asteroid that has fallen to the earth because in the second part of the verse we read that the star *was given the key to the shaft of the bottomless pit* (Rev. 9:1 ISV).

Unless an asteroid can be given a key, then it must be a reference to an angel. Just a few verses earlier we hear of a great star burning like a torch that falls upon the earth. The star even has a name—Wormwood.

*A huge **star** blazing like a torch fell from heaven. It fell on one-third of the rivers and on the springs of water. The name of the **star** is Wormwood...* (Rev. 8:10-11 ISV).

The star in question, or Wormwood by name, is the same star that "had fallen" in Revelation 9:1 which was given the key to the Abyss. We notice that it was a great star and not just a common star—in Revelation 12 the dragon threw his **stars** to the earth and in verse nine it is the dragon, Satan, and his **angels**. Essentially, we have two different camera angles recorded for us. In Chapter 12 the camera angle is from above watching as Satan and his angels fall to the earth. We could almost imagine Michael or one of the angels getting out his camera to film the event. In Chapter Eight the camera angle is on the planet surface with the inhabitants of the earth watching as Satan falls to the earth. To them he looks like *a huge star blazing like a torch fell from heaven* (Rev. 8:10 ISV). They are the same event but from different vantage points.

The casting out of Satan's angels (stars) in Chapter 12 is referenced in Chapter Six and also in Isaiah 34:

- *The **stars** in the sky fell to the earth like a **fig tree drops** its fruit when it is shaken by a strong wind* (Rev. 6:13 ISV).
- *And all the **host of heaven** [צְבָא הַשָּׁמַיִם] shall be dissolved, and the heavens shall be rolled together as a scroll: and all **their host** shall fall down, as the leaf falleth off from the vine, and as a **falling fig from the fig tree*** (Isa. 34:4).

The stars falling to the ground like figs in Revelation are referred to as the host of heaven falling down in Isaiah. We see that many other places in Scripture the term *tzevah hashamaim* [הַשָּׁמַיִם צְבָא] is talking about the armies of heaven. The following scene from First Kings demonstrates the literal meaning of this term:

*...I saw the Lord, sitting on his throne, and the entire **Heavenly Army** [צְבָא הַשָּׁמַיִם] was standing around him on his right hand and on his left hand. The Lord asked, "Who will tempt King Ahab of Israel to attack Ramoth-gilead, so that he will die*

there?" And one was saying one thing and one was saying another. But then a **spirit** *approached, stood in front of the Lord, and said, "I will entice him."*

And the Lord asked him, "How?" "I will go," he announced, "and I will be a deceiving spirit in the mouth of all of his prophets!" So the Lord said, "You're just the one to deceive him. You will be successful. Go and do it" (1 Kings 22:19-22 ISV).

Though the phrase "host of heaven / heavenly army" does not always refer to the angelic army, there are many examples that demonstrate that the phrase is commonly referring to angels. In Jeremiah 19 the hosts of heaven are equated with "gods."

...because of all the houses upon whose roofs they have burned incense unto **all the host of heaven** [לְכֹל צְבָא הַשָּׁמַיִם]*, and have poured out drink offerings* **unto other gods** (Jer. 19:13 KJV).

Those "gods," "host of heaven" or "fallen angels" are also referred to as the armies of exalted ones in the heavens in Isaiah 24 which happens at "that time"—a reference to the day of the Lord.

And it will come about at that time, the Lord will punish the **armies** [*tzevah* צְבָא] *of the* **exalted ones in the heavens** [הַשָּׁמַיִם]*, and the rulers of the earth on earth* (Isa. 24:21 ISV).

Paul writing to the Ephesians makes reference to the reality of the cosmic powers (κοσμοκράτορας *cosmokratoras*). Those cosmic powers, which are all around us, are part of the spiritual forces which are in the heavenly realm, which is a reference to angels and not to balls of gas in outer space.

For our struggle is not against human opponents, but against rulers, authorities, **cosmic powers** *in the darkness around us, and evil spiritual forces in the* **heavenly realm** (Eph. 6:12 ISV).

Now we are prepared to understand what Jesus meant when He said that *"the* **powers of heaven** *will be shaken loose"* (Matt. 24:29 ISV). He was not referring to the sun, moon, and stars going away. Rather, He was referring to the end of the kingdom of Satan.

| "For The Great <u>Day</u> Of His Wrath Has Come, And Who Is Able To Stand?" (Rev. 6:17) | And there were loud voices in heaven, saying, "The kingdoms of this world have become [*the kingdoms*] of our Lord and of His Christ, and He shall reign forever and ever!" (Rev. 11:15) (Rev. 11:17) The nations were angry, and Your wrath has come, And the time of the dead, that they should be judged, And that You should reward Your servants the prophets and the saints, And those who fear Your name, small and great, And <u>should destroy those who destroy the earth</u>" (Rev. 11:18). | ...They go to the kings of the whole earth and gather them for the war of the great Day of God Almighty (Rev. 16:14). "See, I am coming like a thief. How blessed is the person who remains alert and keeps his clothes on! He won't have to go naked and let others see his shame" (Rev. 16:15). [day of the Lord = thief in night] Then the seventh angel poured out his bowl into the air, and a loud voice came out of the temple of heaven, from the throne, saying, "It is done!" (Rev. 16:17) |

There are other examples which point to the fact that the book of Revelation is arranged thematically rather than chronologically. In Revelation 16 we read that God remembered Babylon and judged her. It seems so brief, and would be almost understated if chapters 17 and 18 did not give fuller details.

"AND" VERSUS "THEN" IN REVELATION

We first need to discover that the word "then" which begins the verse in the *New King James Version, New English Translation*, and many other translations, is not actually in the underlying Greek text. The *New English Translation* Bible notes that "Here καί (*kai*) has been translated as "then" to indicate the implied sequence within the narrative." Though the difference is subtle, it does make a difference in how we read the book of Revelation. John is seeing a lot of visions that he connects, not necessarily in a sequence (with the word "then"), but rather with the word "and." The difference is that he is simply telling us the things he saw. He is not suggesting anything about the order in which the events will necessarily occur.

The word "then" implies that first comes A, then comes B, and then comes C, etc. Whereas, "and" simply suggests he saw A and B and C, and the order in which they would come to pass is not stated.

The Greek word καί means "and, even, also"—which carry the same meaning. There is, therefore, no justification for translating the word "*kai*" in Revelation, where it begins a sentence, with the word "then" rather than "and."

The Greek word is *kai* [Καὶ] which simply means "and." *Thayer's Greek-English Lexicon*, defines the word as "and, also, even, indeed, but."[138] According to the *Liddell-Scott-Jones Lexicon of Classical Greek*, it is defined as *kai* as "καί," Conjunction, copulative, joining words and sentences, '**and, also**' Adv., '**even, also, just**'"[139] (emphasis mine). The word is almost always translated as "and" in the many other passages where it appears.

- *And* [Καὶ] *he will turn many of the children of Israel to the Lord their God* (Luke 1:16).
- *And* [Καὶ] *Zacharias said to the angel, "How shall I know this? For I am an old man, and* [καὶ] *my wife is well advanced in years"* (Luke 1:18).
- *And* [Καὶ] *the Word became flesh and* [καὶ] *dwelt among us, and* [καὶ] *we beheld His glory, the glory as of the only begotten of the Father, full of grace and* [καὶ] *truth* (John 1:14).
- *And* [Καὶ] *He found in the temple those who sold oxen and* [καὶ] *sheep and* [καὶ] *doves, and* [καὶ] *the money changers doing business* (John 2:14).

The Greek word *kai* "and" is used altogether 5,222 times in the New Testament with the majority occurring in Luke (850 times, 16%), followed by Matthew (720 times 14%), and the book of John coming in fifth place (545 times 10%). There is another word for "then." If John had wanted to indicate "then" he could have used the word *tote* [Τότε] "Then; at that time," which is used 155 times in the Greek New Testament. It is the simplest way to indicate the transition from one event to another. Out of those 155 times, 89 times the word appears in the book of Matthew, which is 57% of all the New Testament uses.

---

[138] Thayer, Joseph H. and James Strong. Thayer's Greek-English Lexicon of the New Testament: Coded with Strong's Concordance Numbers. Peabody: Hendrickson Publishers, 1995. Print.

[139] LSJ: The Online Liddell-Scott-Jones Greek-English Lexicon. Thesaurus Linguae Graecae. 2009. Web. 11 July 2017.

http://stephanus.tlg.uci.edu/lsj/#eid=1&context=lsj

- **Then** [Τότε] *Herod, when he had secretly called the wise men, determined from them what time the star appeared* (Matt. 2:7).
- *But Jesus answered and said to him, "Permit it to be so now, for thus it is fitting for us to fulfill all righteousness."* **Then** [τότε] *he allowed Him* (Matt. 3:15).
- *And Jesus said to them, "Can the friends of the bridegroom mourn as long as the bridegroom is with them? But the days will come when the bridegroom will be taken away from them,* **and then** [καὶ τότε] *they will fast* (Matt. 9:15).

The abundance of "then" in Matthew is fairly significant. According to the *Fragments of Papias*, "Matthew put together the oracles [of the Lord] in the Hebrew language, and each one interpreted them as best he could."[140]

In Hebrew, the use of the word "and" (Hebrew "*ve*" written the letter *vav/waw*) is very common; therefore, so is the word "and." The question, then, is why didn't the translators render καί as "and" if that is the translation?

Not only is interpreting Revelation thematically crucial in understanding the Day of Lord—the last chapter of this book, the thematic method is altogether necessary when it comes to Revelation's final chapters. There we find, in an extremely abbreviated presentation, the winding up of this Age. "Rightly understanding" what appears on the surface to be a sequential unfolding of the Millennium and beyond has shaped the assumptions made by mainline eschatologists. Assumptions that bear directly on correctly identifying God's Elect during this period; i.e., comprehending the whereabouts and inheritance of Israel's 12 Tribes and the believers from among the Nations.

The "restoration of all things" (Acts 3:21) is not the end of the world; but is the form of the present world passing away (1 Cor. 7:31). The regeneration of the earth is a mystery that includes a disruptive aspect figuratively described in the Scriptures as dissolution, consumption, piercing the veil, folding up, and various other catastrophic imagery depicting a dimensional transition.

---

[140] Pamphilus, Eusebius; C. F. Cruse, Translator. Eusebius Ecclesiastical History. New York: Merchant Books, 2011. III, 39, 1. Print.

Furthermore, many of us [within the CT community] affirm that the New Heaven and New Earth commences when the Glorified Son of Man sets His foot upon the Mt. of Olives (Zech. 14:4; Acts 1:9-11). We find no GAP in 2 Peter 3:10-13 between the Great and Awesome Day of the Lord and the New Heaven and New Earth. [In this view the New Earth commences with the Millennium] Furthermore, the New Heaven and New Earth do NOT circumvent the land allocations given in Ezekiel 48 but substantiate their materiality, nevertheless do NOT omit the participation of the ELECT from among the Nations as seen in Ephraim's inheritance described in the region of "Galilee of the Gentiles."[141]

---

[141] *commonwealthofisrael.org*, "Beliefs" page, Developmental Assertions and Interpretations, Sec. 5-6.

CHAPTER NINETEEN

THE FUTURE 70TH WEEK
BY GAVIN FINLEY

THE FUTURE 70TH WEEK AND FINAL 7 YEARS

The study of end-time events has always been a matter of considerable interest for biblical Christians. But in recent years Bible prophecy has begun to line up with current events. For those who are diligent and devoted to Jesus/Yeshua the subject of eschatology has begun to come to the fore. The Seventy Weeks prophecy is considered perhaps the most important prophecy regarding the timeline of end-time events. This is presented to us in Daniel Chapter 9 verses 24-27. Thanks to the work of evangelical Scotland Yard Inspector Sir Robert Anderson, we now have a far better understanding of just how this prophecy will play out. His book, *The Coming Prince*, was published in the late 1800s.

Biblical Christian/Messianic believers, particularly in the English-speaking world, are now quite aware of this important biblical truth. Up ahead somewhere is the 70th Week of Daniel. This highly significant seven-year period has been "cut out of time." It has been "set apart" or sanctified for God's decisive dealings with all His "set apart" or holy people. These include the gathering of the redeemed from both houses of Israel and all their companions from out of all the nations, people from all time who have joined them in the faith. This Elect company are devoted to the "Seed of Abraham" (who is "Christ in you, the hope of glory"). This is a grand company of people, a passing parade, from both sides of Calvary. They are a congregation and a citizenship drawn from every nation, race, and tribe, and grafted into the olive tree, the "All Israel" spoken of by our apostle Paul in Romans 11. Those Seventy Weeks have an additional or related purpose beyond the gathering of the Holy People. They have been "cut out of time" for decisive dealings related to His Holy City, Jerusalem. We begin our survey of the Seventy Weeks prophecy in verse 24 of Daniel 9:

***Seventy weeks* are *determined*, (cut out of time)** *upon **thy people** and upon thy **holy city**, to finish the transgression, and to make an end of sins, and to make reconciliation for iniquity, and to bring in everlasting righteousness, and to seal up the vision and prophecy, and to anoint the most Holy.*

In Daniel 9:24 we see that inside those Seventy Weeks (or 70 sevens) the Holy One of Israel successfully completes and wraps up His entire end-time agenda. As we shall discover, the prophecy runs right through to the consummation of the age; or as we shall see from Daniel 12:11, just 30 days short of that Last Day. This "Last Day" is not something to be stretched out and obfuscated. This is a specific day in future history. It was spoken of four times by Jesus in John 6 verses 39, 40, 44, and 54. In the very words of Jesus, repeated for a total of four times in those verses, the "Last Day" is directly and inextricably linked to the Resurrection-Rapture of the righteous at the close of this age.

The following verse, Daniel 9:25, lays out the first segment of the timeline to a specific stated terminus, that being *"unto Messiah the Prince."*

25 *"Know therefore and understand, that from the going forth of the commandment to restore and to build Jerusalem **unto the Messiah the Prince** shall be **seven weeks**, and **threescore and two weeks**: (7 + 62 = 69 weeks, or 69 sevens)."*

THE APPEARANCE OF MESSIAH THE PRINCE

It is exceedingly important to understand that there was only one day in the ministry of Jesus/Yeshua in which He presented Himself in any political way. There was just one day in which He came into His Holy City as the promised Messiah of Israel. Four days before His crucifixion He entered Jerusalem, for the last time. We might recall the times throughout His ministry when Jesus had asked those who recognized Him as Messiah to never speak of this. But on this epic day all that changed. He was allowing His devoted followers, few though they may have been, to proclaim Him as Israel's promised Messiah, the Prince of Peace. He was entering Jerusalem in a public procession in an extremely open way, even on a young untamed donkey. This was precisely as prophesied.

Zechariah 9:9 (KJV)

Rejoice greatly, O daughter of Zion; shout, O daughter of Jerusalem: behold, thy King cometh unto thee: he [is] just, and having salvation; lowly, and riding upon an ass, and upon a colt the foal of an ass.

This First Coming of Messiah into the City of God caused great chagrin for the religious leaders of the time. Here, entering through the eastern gate of the Holy City, was their Messiah. But He was not the conquering king that they were expecting. This first appearance of Messiah was in His High Priestly office. He was coming in that first time as the Suffering Servant that the prophet Isaiah had spoken about in Isaiah 53. This Messiah, even Israel's promised Sacrifice Lamb, was not the Messiah ben David the Pharisees wanted. They were seeing the ministering self-sacrificing Messiah ben Joseph. They were not prepared for this. They just did not recognize Him in His other office as High Priest of Israel. But there He was, attending to the vital, but under-appreciated, issues of ministry.

The rabbinical priesthood may have been insulted by this, even furious. But the entry of Jesus as "Messiah the Prince" was God ordained. That first coming as the Sacrifice Lamb definitely and unmistakably fulfilled the prophecy Daniel had been given nearly 600 years before. He was going up to be inspected by both the priests of Levi and the political rulers of Rome. He was judged by the crowds of common men. Ultimately He was condemned by the mobs, the "people of the prince," (the Antichrist) who is to come. He was fulfilling all those mysterious prophecies of the Suffering Servant. On that special day, Nisan 10 in the Passion Year, He was bringing to a terminus the first 69 weeks of the 70 Weeks prophecy. This was a single day, well documented biblically. It was four days before the crucifixion which occurred on Nisan 14, the preparation day of Passover in the Passion year. It was on Nisan 10, the tenth day of the Nisan moon in the Passion Year of 32 A.D. that Israel's Passover Sacrifice Lamb was going up for inspection prior to His being sacrificed.

We now turn our attention to the measuring line for the Seventy Weeks prophecy. We are presented with a timeline of Seventy Sevens of years. What sort of years might they be?

MEASURING THE DAY-COUNT OF THE 70 WEEKS
They are not solar years but biblical years of 360 days

Many biblical scholars have attempted to solve the puzzle of the Seventy Weeks. Notable among them was Sir Isaac Newton. He spent half his lifetime trying to lay out a credible timeline to fulfill the prophecy accurately. The best he could do with the 69 sevens of years was to engage a timeline of 69 x 7 = 483 years using the solar years we see in the natural world and cosmos. He laid out a timeline of 483 solar years starting with the edict given to Ezra in 457 B.C. and ending in 27 A.D. As we see, his timeline fell short of the 32 A.D. Passion Year by a full five years. The interpretation of the prophecy was then stretched to identify the appearance of "Messiah the Prince" as the baptism of Jesus at the beginning of His ministry, rather than His entry into Jerusalem three and a half years later at the close of His ministry. But even then, it was still two years short. As we see, there are major problems with this chronology based upon Ezra. It just does not fit.

As a side-note, this chronology by Sir Isaac Newton is getting a lot of discussion of late. It is highly favored by Preterists and hemi-Preterists. The latter faction is keen to obfuscate and hide away the first half of the future 70th Week. Then they proceed to say that Jesus was the "prince" of mention in Daniel 9:27 and that He has already fulfilled the first half of the 70th Week in His ministry.

Many Dominionists are eager to make the first half of the future 70th Week "go away." They claim that there is only the 3.5-year Tribulation yet to run; that being the second half of the 70th Week prophecy. They are teaching error. They fail to present a chronology with any sort of detail or accuracy at all.

Ch. 19: The Future 70th Week

The Assault upon the Future 70th Week

There is a subtle agenda here. The religious spirit behind this faulty chronology is attempting to obfuscate, to smokescreen the first half of the future 70th Week. They are trying to hide away the 3.5 biblical year reign of the **harlot of Revelation 17.** Her rule over the New World Order in those opening years occupies the first half of the future 70th Week. And it ends at the midweek abomination of desolation. So, the 3.5 biblical year rule of the harlot religious system precedes the Great Tribulation. The revealing of the Antichrist at the midweek Abomination of Desolation sees her removed from her perch. Her reign in the first half of the future 70th Week precedes the "reign of the beast" phase Antichrist in the second half of the 70th Week. (See the figure on the following page.)

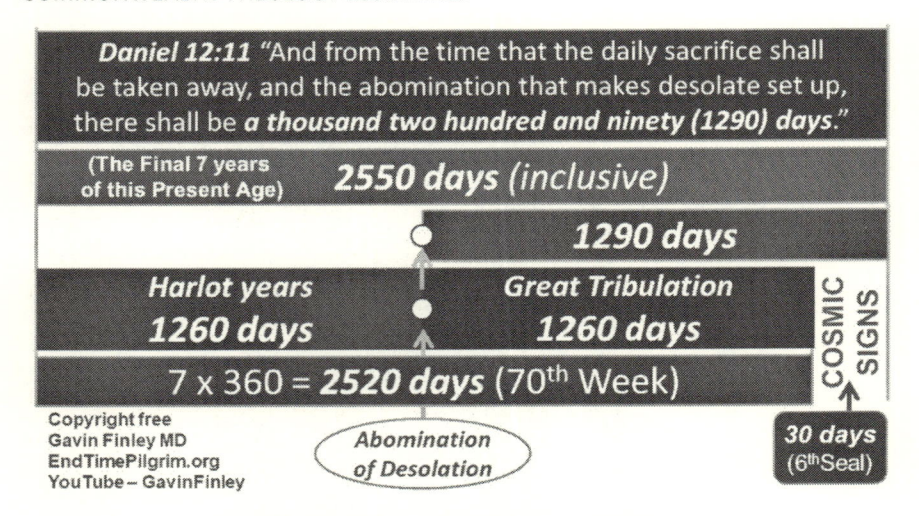

Daniel 12:11 *"And from the time that the daily sacrifice shall be taken away, and the abomination that makes desolate set up, there shall be **a thousand two hundred and ninety (1290) days.**"*

(The Final 7 years of this Present Age) **2550 days** *(inclusive)*

1290 days

Harlot years
1260 days

Great Tribulation
1260 days

COSMIC SIGNS

7 x 360 = **2520 days** (70th Week)

Copyright free
Gavin Finley MD
EndTimePilgrim.org
YouTube – GavinFinley

Abomination of Desolation

30 days
(6th Seal)

2550 Days Bridge the Final Seven Years

SEVEN VERSES DESCRIBE THE LATTER HALF OF THE FUTURE 70TH WEEK

The placement of the Tribulation and the travail of the woman in the latter half of the future 70th Week can be established from Scripture quite readily as we read Revelation 12. The reign of the Harlot of Revelation 17 would appear to precede the reign of the Antichrist, since he is not truly revealed as the beast until he commits the blaspheming abomination that makes desolate, midway through the 70th Week. In fact, there are seven verses of Scripture that describe this latter half of the future 70th Week from seven different perspectives. These seven verses are tagged with time periods of either 3.5 years, 42 months, or 1260 days. But what sort of years are they? And what length of months are being presented to us here?

There are two Rosetta Stone style passages given to us in Scripture. They answer those two questions. The Rosetta Stone passage in Revelation 12 identifies **3.5 years as 1260 days** to render a **360-day prophetic year**. The Rosetta Stone passages in Genesis 7 and 8 show us that **5 months = 150 days** to give us the **prophetic month as 30 days**. When we plug these numbers into the 3.5 years and the 42 months in amongst the seven verses, we discover that all seven of them are of identical length. The final 7 years of 7 x 360 = 2520 days are made up of two halves, each of **1260 days, 42 biblical months** of **30 days,** or **3.5 biblical years** of **360 days.** They all add up to 1260 days, half of the 7 x 360 days of the future 70th Week.

CH. 19: THE FUTURE 70TH WEEK

> **Seven Verses describe the Second Half of the future 70th Week**
>
> 1. **The Great Tribulation** – 3.5 years. Dan.7:25
> 2. **The scattering of the power of the holy people.**
>   3.5 years. Dan.12:7
>   ☆ 3. *The exile of the Woman.*
>   *1260 days.* Rev. 12:6, Micah 2:12-13
>   ☆ 4. *The exile of the Woman.*
>   *3.5 Biblical years.* Rev. 12:14, Micah 2:12-13
> 5. **The ministry of the two witnesses.**
>   1260 days. Rev. 11:2
> 6. **The trampling of Jerusalem.**
>   42 months. Rev. 11:3
> 7. **The reign of the Antichrist.**
>   42 months. Rev. 13:5

Seven Verses Describe One Time Period

This information mapping out the final 7 years of this age, and especially the identification of those first 3.5 years as the years of religious harlotry involving the woman, is heavily guarded by religious spirits. It is a huge embarrassment to those committed to Dominion Theology. In their fond imaginations they dream of a Church Triumphant in its present form, and brought into being under the present-day religious hierarchies of self-proclaimed apostles and prophets, often referred to as the "five-fold ministry." The future Harlot religious system, and not the Antichrist himself, will rule during those first 3.5 Harlot Years. This is what John saw and clearly describes for us in Revelation 17. But it is something we almost never hear spoken about. This is a biblical expose' that present day Nicolaitan religious leaders do not want to hear talked about. Nor do we hear the reign of the harlot of Revelation 17 discussed on the televised Bible prophecy programs.

REFUTING THE EZRA TO BAPTISM OF JESUS TIMELINE

Refuting the Ezra 483 solar year timeline is not difficult. In Luke 3:1-2 Luke the physician records a time fix for the baptizing ministry of John the Baptist for repentance. This is historically well documented. It is written down in Holy Scripture as the 15th Year of Tiberius Caesar. Since the first year of his reign began on August 19 of 14 A.D., his 15th year would have begun 14 years later on August

19 or the late Summer of 28 A.D. As Luke describes in Luke 3:21, this 15th year of Tiberius also saw the baptism of Jesus. So, we can with good authority tag the beginning of the ministry of Jesus/Yeshua as the Fall season of 28 A.D.

We do not know precisely when the Ezra edict was given. But in Ezra 7:7-8 we read that after the biblical revival Ezra led a company to Jerusalem in the fifth month of the Hebrew year and in the seventh year of Artaxerxes. This would have been sometime in the summer of 457 B.C. which is—456 B.C. because of there being no zero year between B.C. and A.D. Running out the 69 sevens as a timeline of 483 solar years brings the terminus of the Ezra timeline in the summer of 27 A.D. As we see, this date falls short of the passion year by at least 4.5 years.

It is an error to tag the appearance of "Messiah the Prince" as the baptism of Jesus. Then trying to identify the terminus of the 483 years in 27 A.D. as the baptism of Jesus still renders the timeline short of the mark by a year.

The use of solar years in the interpretation of the Seventy Weeks prophecy adds further complications as well. This becomes abundantly obvious when we try to reconcile the 3.5 years as solar years, the 42 months as mean synodic months of 29.53 days, and try to reconcile these irrational numbers with the 1260 days. But when we take the clues from Scripture and plug in the 30-day biblical month, the 360-days biblical year we discover that all of them are descriptive perspectives on the final half of the future 70th Week.

A TRIBUTE TO THE WORK OF SIR ROBERT ANDERSON

The reason Sir Robert Anderson was successful where others failed was his commitment to the biblical account. He was prepared to use whatever time units that came down from the throne of God. He was willing to use the years presented in Holy Scripture to measure out the prophetic years and discount the years and months we see in nature. He disregarded the present-day cycles of the sun and moon, no matter how "irrational" that may have seemed to many scholars who were naturalists at heart but who were now trying to be scholars of theology. Sir Robert was not under the spell of the rationalism of his day, the Age of Reason, or the worth-ship of Nature after Charles Darwin. He simply saw what John the apostle wrote in Revelation 12:6 and 12:14 concerning the exile of the woman and believed what was written down. He saw that this time period was clearly in the context of events happening during the last half of the 70th Week. Firstly, he saw and understood the cryptically presented "time, times, and half a time." He recognized that this was going to fit in the puzzle as 3.5 biblical or 360-day years. Secondly, he saw that the exile of the woman was being presented by the Holy Spirit twice using two different time units, one being in terms of those 3.5 prophetic years and the other in terms of 1260 days. He simply reconciled the two verses.

Sir Robert Anderson was a born-again Christian believer. Therefore, he had no problem believing what the Scriptures were stating. He simply believed what was written. The years that were being issued in this prophecy were coming down from the throne of God via the messenger angel Gabriel to the prophet Daniel. If these biblical years were different from the 365.2422-day solar years we see in this present fallen cosmos, then that was not off-putting to Anderson at all. He went with what the Scriptures were declaring, did his homework, and came to the Eureka! moment.

Revelation 12 is the key Scripture passage to understanding the biblical or prophetic year. The timeline of the exile of the woman of wonder in the end-time drama is being presented to us twice.

Revelation 12:6 *"And the woman fled into the wilderness, where she hath a place prepared of God, that they should feed her there a thousand two hundred and threescore days"* (**1260 days**).

Revelation 12:14 *"And to the woman were given two wings of a great eagle, that she might fly into the wilderness, into her place, where she is nourished for a time, and times, and half a time,* (**3.5 biblical years**) *from the face of the serpent."*

Clearly these were identical time periods. Sir Robert Anderson did what rationalistic nature bound men were not prepared to do. He very simply and elegantly reconciled the 3.5 years of Revelation 12:14 with the 1260 days of Revelation 12:6. When he did the math and divided 1260 by 3.5 the answer came back as a biblical year of 360 days. This simple truth had been a stumbling block to Sir Isaac Newton. But for Sir Robert Anderson, his willingness to place the Scriptures above what he saw in nature became a stepping stone.

The 360-day year was a sure key to the prophecy. With this Anderson was able to accurately quantitate the 69-week timeline as 69 sevens of 360-day biblical years. This gave us an inclusive day count of 69 x 360 = ***173,880 days***. This was Sir Robert Anderson's remarkably accurate timeline; and with it, the Scotland Yard inspector cracked the case. He solved the puzzle of the Seventy Weeks prophecy that had eluded many others before him, including the previous attempts of Sir Isaac Newton over 170 years before.

The other key to biblical time is given to us in the account of the flood recorded by Moses in the book of Genesis. In Genesis 7:11 we see that the time period in which the Ark of Noah was on the waters began on the *17th day of the second month* and the ark came to rest on the 17th day of the seventh month. Then in Genesis 8:3 we are told that the ark was on the waters for ***150 days***. If we are to believe the Holy Scriptures then we must conclude that those **five biblical months** do in fact equal **150 days**. This renders the biblical or **prophetic month** as **30 days**. Later in this chapter we shall see how this 30-day biblical month reconciles two of the seven verses that describe the final half of the 70th Week as "42 months." As we can readily ascertain, **42 x 30 = 1260 days**.

These things are not spelled out for us. God expects us to inquire into these matters. We are exhorted in 2 Timothy 2:15 to *"study to show ourselves approved unto God . . . rightly dividing the Word of truth."* We are also given the guidance and the comfort/strengthening of the Holy Spirit in the information war to push back against the darkness that ever seeks to enshroud us.

THE 70 WEEKS PROPHECY AND MISSING JUBILEE YEARS

In Daniel 9:25 the angel Gabriel tells the prophet Daniel that the timeline from the edict of Artaxerxes to Messiah the Prince is comprised of two parts, those being a starter period of 7 weeks followed by 62 weeks. What is that all about? We are given no basis to make the time periods discontinuous. But why present the 69 weeks sectioned in that way?

25 *"Know therefore and understand, that from the going forth of the commandment to restore and to build Jerusalem* **unto the Messiah the Prince** *shall be* **seven weeks**, *and threescore and two weeks* **(7 + 62 = 69 weeks, or 69 sevens)."**

CH. 19: THE FUTURE 70TH WEEK

The Seventy Weeks prophecy timeline begins with **seven sevens**. This is 49 years. It also happens to be a 49-year Jubilee cycle with the following year, the 50th year, being the Year of Jubilee and initiating the ensuing 49 years. Why is the Holy Spirit starting the 69 weeks with a Jubilee cycle? Why say 7 + 62 instead of just saying 69? Is God trying to show us something here?

This matter of the seven sevens as a starter for the Seventy Weeks prophecy is a major clue for us. The 7 x 7 = 49 is describing the 49-year Jubilee cycle. There is no record of Israel ever having kept the Jubilee years as stipulated in Leviticus 25. So then, could it be that God is taking care of that matter of the Jubilee for us? Is He laying out Jubilee cycles, yet to manifest here on earth, and gift-wrapping them inside His holy timeline for emergence in a special time yet to come? Even as Yehovah-God walked out the covenant for His friend Abraham, is God Himself taking care of this matter of the missing Jubilees for us, His beloved covenant people? Is He neatly packing up the Jubilees for safe-keeping away from this present evil age and tucking them away securely in the Seventy Weeks timeline?

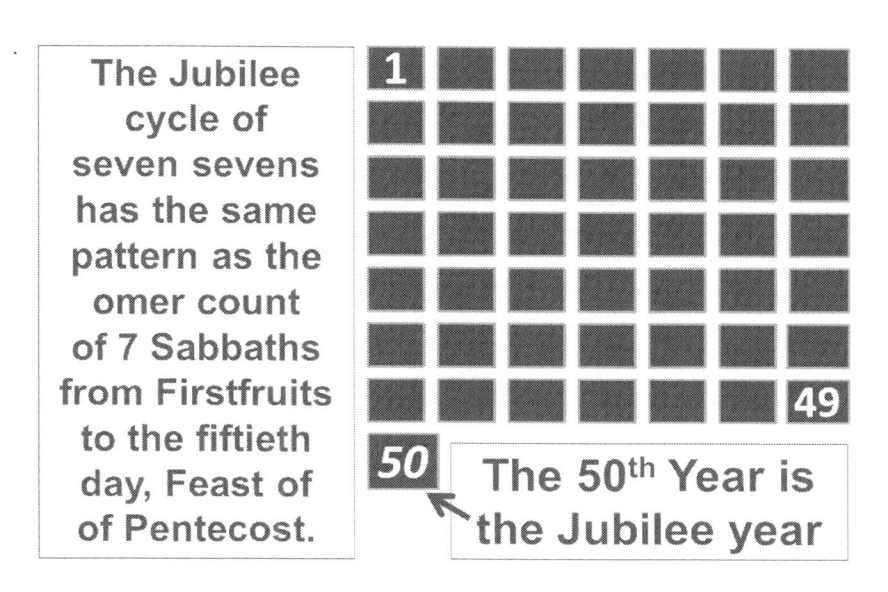

The Jubilee cycle of seven sevens has the same pattern as the omer count of 7 Sabbaths from Firstfruits to the fiftieth day, Feast of of Pentecost.	1 ▪ 49 50 The 50th Year is the Jubilee year

The Jubilee Cycle of Seven Sevens

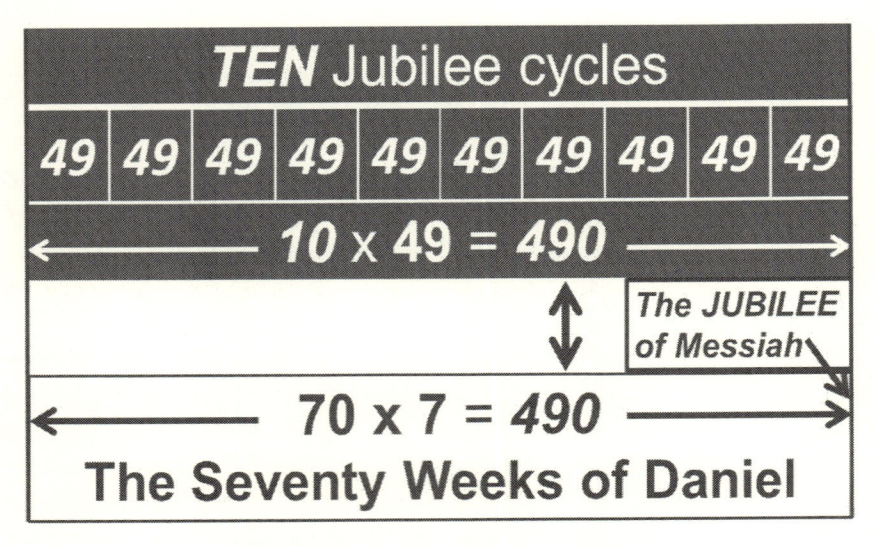

```
┌─────────────────────────────────────────┐
│         TEN Jubilee cycles              │
├──┬──┬──┬──┬──┬──┬──┬──┬──┬──┤
│49│49│49│49│49│49│49│49│49│49│
├──┴──┴──┴──┴──┴──┴──┴──┴──┴──┤
│  ←──────  10 x 49 = 490  ──────→  │
│                    ↕    ┌──────────┐  │
│                         │ The JUBILEE│  │
│                         │ of Messiah │  │
│  ←──────  70 x 7 = 490  ──────→    │
│      The Seventy Weeks of Daniel        │
└─────────────────────────────────────────┘
```

The Jubilee Cycles—Inside the 70 Weeks

We can also notice that the Seventy Weeks Prophecy is a period of **70 x 7 = 490 biblical years**. Accordingly, this holy time segment of **490 years** could also serve very neatly and precisely as 10 x 49 or **ten 49-year Jubilee cycles**. But that is not all. Should this prove to be the case, then the end of the Seventy Sevens, that is, **the end of the future 70th Week**, would mark a very auspicious terminus point for both the Seventy Weeks and **the tenth and final jubilee cycle** of the 490-year timeline. Would this jubilee, being announced right at the end of the age *and* on a **future Day of Atonement**, not bring an epic and appropriate conclusion to the holy history of this present age?

If we suppose that the trumpets of Jubilee are to be blown on a climactic future Day of Atonement to mark the Last Day at the end of the age, then would not the very next year, the first year of the Millennium of Messiah, be proclaimed as that long expected and glorious future **Jubilee year of Messiah**? Should this be the case, then this would provide a very precise and elegant resolution to the whole Jubilee year issue. The thesis that the missing Jubilee years are packaged up in this Seventy Weeks time period and "set apart" or "holy" unto God is therefore something worthy of consideration.

CH. 19: THE FUTURE 70TH WEEK

THE EDICT INITIATING THE 70 WEEKS PROPHECY

THE ISSUE OF THE REBUILDING AND RESTORATION OF THE GATES AND WALLS OF JERUSALEM

The Seventy Weeks prophecy began with the issuing of an edict to restore the gates and walls of Jerusalem. These details are specifically referenced in verse 25b of Daniel 9.

25b. *"The street shall be built again, and the wall, even in troublous times."*

The prophet Daniel received the Seventy Weeks prophecy from the angel Gabriel in the first year of Darius which was back in 538 B.C. Darius was the uncle of Cyrus and co-regent for the new Medo-Persian regime in Babylon under Cyrus. This prophecy was in reference to an edict that **authorized the rebuilding of the city of Jerusalem**, very importantly, the rebuilding of **its gates and walls**. That edict as prophesied would be fulfilled in the following century. It was 93 years later that Nehemiah, the cup-bearer to the king, asked for the authority to rebuild Jerusalem and received the edict authorizing this. In Nehemiah 2 we see that the edict came *"in the month of Nisan"* in the **20th Year of Artaxerxes** Longimanus which was in **445 B.C.** King Artaxerxes was giving imperial permission to rebuild the gates and walls of Jerusalem. This edict, the edict, as given to Nehemiah, was the edict that initiated the Seventy Weeks prophecy and specifically the timeline of the first 69 Sevens of 360 day biblical years. This edict marked day #1 for the 173,880 days described by Sir Robert Anderson.

This matter of restoring the integrity and government of the city in the rebuilding of its walls and gates was a huge issue, and something which is often overlooked. The walls were defensive structures protecting the city from invaders. The gates were basically the town hall, the civic center, the government at the gates controlling who came in, and who did business in the city. See http://endtimepilgrim.org/70wks1.htm

Nehemiah, who was cup-bearer for the king, was trembling as he appealed to King Artaxerxes. Basically, he was asking the Medo-Persian ruler for his permission to restore Jerusalem as a self-governing city-state. He knew from what was written in the book of Ezra that enemies inside the royal court of Medo-Persia would see this permission to self-govern and the guarantee of sovereignty for the returning captives of Judah as a bad, even treacherous thing. They would, and they did, send letters to the king informing him that if this authority was given to the Jewish house it would amount to political trouble for him and a net loss of revenue for the Medo-Persian treasury.

Nehemiah knew all this and was deathly afraid to ask. But he also saw that this restoration of Jerusalem was absolutely necessary to secure a safe place for the Jewish exiles returning home. In 445 B.C. the city of Jerusalem housed the former captives of Judah within its broken gates and wall. It even had a rebuilt temple. But the broken gates and walls still bore evidence of a non-functioning city-state. As we read in Ezra, this rebuilding of the city and its gates and its walls had been stopped, even though this restoration of the city had been authorized by Cyrus and Darius. The restoration work had been halted by enemies of Judah. They wrote letters to the king and harassed those who made efforts to rebuild the walls and gates to restore the city.

The returning captives of the Jewish house of Judah kept coming back. They were keen to return to the Holy Land of their fathers. But at this point in their history the ruined city of Jerusalem was the one and only city that still remained for them. It was the capital, the main city of Judah. Inside Jerusalem was the Holy Place. Jerusalem was also the capital of what was once the former great United Kingdom of King David and King Solomon.

As it turned out, Nehemiah did receive the king's permission and also his blessing. The date of this edict is recorded for us by Nehemiah in Nehemiah Chapter 2. It was *"in the month of Nisan"* in the **20th year of Artaxerxes**. This is well established as the **Springtime Passover Nisan moon** of **445 B.C.**

Messiah enters His Holy City. Then He is "Cut Off" or executed. So ends the 69 Weeks.

As we have seen, the timeline of the **first 69 Weeks** came to its appointed terminus on an exceedingly auspicious day in holy history. **Nisan 10** was **four days before Nisan 14 Passover** in 32 A.D. Notably this was an **embolismic year** with a second month of Adar making for a late Passover in that Passion Year. This is very important. An embolismic year with a late Passover is absolutely necessary to accommodate the **173,880 days** which

CH. 19: THE FUTURE 70TH WEEK

when divided by the solar year day-count of **365.2422** are an **extra 25 days** over the **476 solar years**. This **extra 25-day excess** over the 476 years **must still connect into two Nisan moons!** This absolutely demands a terminus year with a late Passover, a year that sees an extra second month of Adar, or Adar 2 inserted into the Hebrew calendar. This embolismic 13th month pushes the first month of Nisan up into the Spring. Without this correction the Hebrew calendar, which is lunar-solar, would be like the strict lunar Islamic calendar. The first month of the twelve months would **fall back 11 days every year.** The Hebrew months would be like the Islamic months, even the holy month of Ramadan, which never stops falling back.

The terminus of the 69 weeks was the Palm branch waving day, (apparently Palm Sabbath rather than Palm Sunday). The 173,880 day timeline came to its end-point on Nisan 10 of the embolismic year 32 A.D. as on that very day Jesus/Yeshua made His entry into Jerusalem to the acclaim of those who loved Him. Nisan 10 came four days before the Wednesday Nisan 14 Passover day of Preparation, four days before the day of the crucifixion. The date of *Nisan 10* was also the day the Passover lambs were brought up for inspection. At His crucifixion Jesus/Yeshua fulfilled Passover, the first of the seven feasts, *moedim*, or divine appointments of the Lord. He was in fact Israel's promised Passover Lamb. That evening, shortly before the sunset that marked the *Nisan 15, the First Day of Unleavened Bread*, He was buried. Just as the second of the Spring feasts began, He was placed in the tomb. So that night, even as He lay in the grave, Israel's sinless *Unleavened Bread of Heaven* was in the grave, fulfilling the Feast. Three days and three nights later, on the morrow after the 7th Day Sabbath, He would rise from the grave thereby fulfilling the third of the Spring feasts. He was the Firstfruits from the dead.

Daniel 9:26 *And after threescore and two weeks shall* **Messiah be cut off,** *but not for himself: and* **the people of the prince that shall come shall destroy the city and the sanctuary;** *and the end thereof shall be with a flood, and unto the end of the war desolations are determined.*

The crucifixion of Messiah just four days after the terminus of the 7 + 62 = 69 weeks was highly significant. With the execution of Messiah and the completion of His first coming as the Sacrifice

Lamb, that put the gap in the Seventy Weeks prophecy. At that point, the end of the 69 weeks, there was no possible continuation of the Seventy weeks prophecy. Messiah was "cut off." The strong Hebrew word here conveys that He was **"executed."** This ended the first 69 weeks of the Seventy Weeks Prophecy. The Seventy Weeks prophecy was put on "pause."

The take-home lesson for us is simply this. There is a future 70th week period up ahead. It is a 7 x 360 = 2520-day time period. And as we see in Daniel 9:27, that 2520-day time segment is divided into two equal halves of 1260 days, 3.5 years, or 42 months. These are all identical timelines. We are now responsible for handling that information in the way, and according to the high standards of the watchmen of Israel, in a manner that is faithful and true.

The graphic (adjacent page) is based upon the Hebrew calendar as reconstructed from the NASA moon-phase data and then laying the **173,880-day timeline** backwards from the Palm Sabbath Julian date for Nisan 10, which according to the moon-phase data from Astropixels.com was either **April 9** or **April 10** of **32 A.D.** The **solar years of 365.2422 days** measuring out the **173,880** days render a timeline of **476 solar years and 24.7 days**. This brings us back very early into the Passover month of Nisan in 445 B.C. This was the time when Nehemiah went to the king and received the edict. The timeline in the graphic below is from the *EndTimePilgrim.org* website. It connects into the same two Nisan moons identified by Sir Robert Anderson and is only slightly different from his wonderful landmark work.

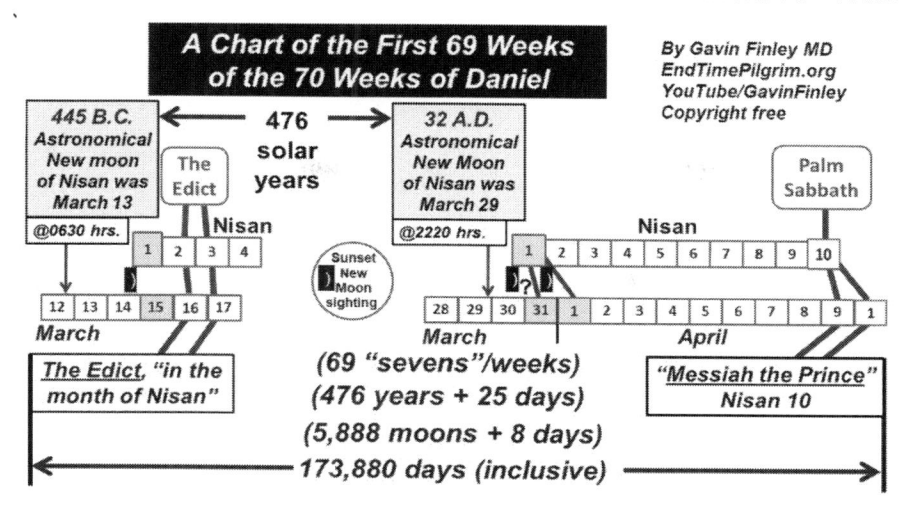

CH. 19: THE FUTURE 70TH WEEK

A Chart of the First 69 Weeks of the 70 Weeks of Daniel

By Gavin Finley MD
EndTimePilgrim.org
YouTube/GavinFinley
Copyright free

```
445 B.C.                    476              32 A.D.
Astronomical                solar            Astronomical                          Palm
New moon        The         years            New Moon                              Sabbath
of Nisan was    Edict                        of Nisan was
March 13                    Nisan            March 29                Nisan
@0630 hrs.                                   @2220 hrs.
                 1   2   3   4                           1  2  3  4  5  6  7  8  9  10
                                 Sunset
                                 New
                                 Moon
                                 sighting
 12 13 14 15 16 17                          28 29 30 31  1  2  3  4  5  6  7  8  9   1
March                                       March                 April
```

The Edict, "in the month of Nisan"   (69 "sevens"/weeks)   "Messiah the Prince" Nisan 10
(476 years + 25 days)
(5,888 moons + 8 days)
←—————— 173,880 days (inclusive) ——————→

The First 69 Weeks—Fulfilled.

The accuracy of this timeline as it connects into two Nisan moons that are 476 years and 25 days apart is truly astounding. If we only connect the Nisan moons and not the days, we are looking at **5,888 moons** and hence four figure accuracy. This is 99.99% accuracy. If we go to the 173,880 days and allow for an error of three days we still have an accuracy of five figures or 99.999% accuracy.

So what can we conclude from this? Simply this. Somewhere up ahead there is a future 70th Week of Daniel, a period of **7 x 360 = 2520 days**. And whenever that time period starts, we shall immediately have an accurate timeline of the future 70th Week. This will be a roadmap into the end-time so we know what to expect and when it will be happening. This will be invaluable information and great encouragement for the Elect of the latter days. Right away they will know that God is sovereign and in control of the events as they unfold into holy history.

We are given additional biblical information from the prophecy of Daniel in **Daniel 12:11**. The angel Gabriel informed Daniel that there would be a **1290 day time period** from the **midweek abomination of desolation**. The final 7 years extends beyond the 70th Week into the cosmic signs and right through the end of the age.

COMMONWEALTH THEOLOGY ESSENTIALS

This message concerning the *1290 days* tells us that we are given a *further 30 days beyond the 1260 days*. Those 1260 + 1290 = **2550 days** present us with an accurate timeline for the final 7 years of this age. This is a great and wonderful blessing for the saints of the latter days. These are the ones who have taken a resolve, and have been energized by the grace of God, to take responsibility in the end-time witness. God by His Holy Spirit is equipping them for their high calling. He is giving them a pilgrim walking map into the final seven years of this age.

Is there more? Could it be that those yet to be fulfilled **Fall Feasts of Israel** connect into those **final seven years of this age**, perhaps even stake out this final **2550-day** window of time? For details on the alignment of the Feasts with Messiah's first and second comings see the chart below and visit Dr. Finley's website: http://endtimepilgrim.org/70wks1.htm.

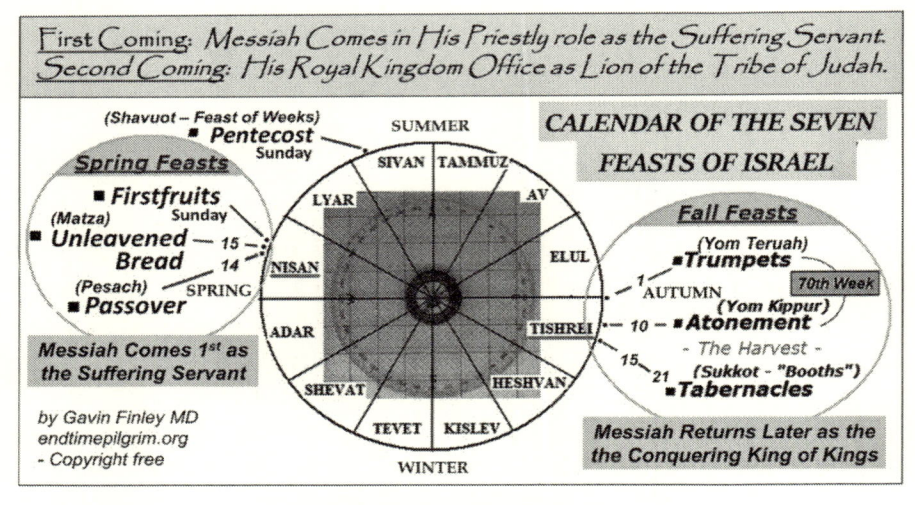

The Seven Feasts of Israel

Chapter Twenty

SHARING IN JACOB'S TROUBLE

By Douglas Krieger

A compendium of writings by brethren predisposed to the tenets of Commonwealth Theology would suffer credibility in the eyes of our Jewish compatriots because they most likely would find our avoidance of this topic disingenuous, even hypocritical; whereas, our Dispensational/Reform-Covenantalism brethren would deem our absence from this topic justifiable in that it is something the "Jews have to contend with" but not we believers in Jesus—i.e., God will DEAL with these Christ-rejecting Jews in preparation for them to bend to the cross in the latter days (if I can be so obtrusive in my assessment). And, what might this prickly topic involve? Right: JACOB'S TROUBLE.

The cardinal passages normally alluding to Jacob's Trouble within an end-times' context are:

> *"Ask now, and see, whether a man is ever in labor with child? So why did I see every man with his hands on his loins like a woman in labor, and all faces turned pale? Alas! For that day is great, so that none is like it; and it is the TIME OF JACOB'S TROUBLE, but he shall be saved out of it . . . Though I make a full end of all nations where I have scattered you, yet I will not make a complete end of you. But I will correct you in justice, and will not let you go altogether unpunished . . . For I have wounded you with the wound of an enemy, with the chastisement of a cruel one, for the multitude of your iniquities, because your sins have increased"*

(Excerpts from Jeremiah 30—including the entire chapter).

Other critical passages used may include excerpts from Matthew 24—especially those in reference to suffering found in Matthew 24:9-26 (both on the lead up to the Abomination of Desolation found in Matthew 24:6-8 in reference to the "birth pangs of the Messiah" and especially those dealing with the "Great tribulation" of those days [Matthew 24:15-29]).

Moreover, critical passages found in Zechariah 13:8-9 refer to end-time prophetic events swirling around Eretz Israel:

"Awake, O sword, against My Shepherd, against the Man who is My Companion," says the LORD of hosts. "Strike the Shepherd, and the sheep will be scattered; then I will turn My hand against the little ones. And it shall come to pass in all the land," says the LORD, "That two-thirds in it shall be cut off and die, but one-third shall be left in it: I will bring the one-third through the fire, will refine them as silver is refined, and test them as gold is tested. They will call on My name, and I will answer them. I will say, 'This is My people'; and each one will say, 'the Lord is my God.'" (Zech. 13:7-9)

And . . . Daniel 12:1-9 (Excerpts):

"At that time Michael shall stand up, the great prince who stands watch over the sons of your people; and there shall be a TIME OF TROUBLE, such as never was since there was a nation, even to that time. And at that time your people shall be delivered, everyone who is found written in the book . . .
"How long shall the fulfillment of these wonders be?" Then I heard the man clothed in linen, who was above the waters of the river, when he held up his right hand and his left hand to heaven, and swore by Him who lives forever, that it shall be for a time, times, and half a time; and when the power of the holy people has been completely shattered, all these things shall be finished . . . Then I said, "My lord, what shall be the end of these things?" And he said, "Go your way, Daniel, for the words are closed up and sealed till the time of the end. Many shall be purified, made white, and refined, but the wicked shall do wickedly; and none of the wicked shall understand, but the wise shall understand."

Naturally, these phrases dealing with "time, times and half a time" are eerily similar to the phraseology found in Revelation 12:14 concerning the Woman who is persecuted by the Dragon whereupon we read (with additional portions of Revelation 12):

"Now when the dragon saw that he had been cast to the earth, he persecuted the woman who gave birth to the male Child. But the woman was given two wings of a great eagle, that she might fly into the wilderness to her place, where she

CH. 20: SHARING IN JACOB'S TROUBLE

is nourished for a time and times and half a time, from the presence of the serpent . . . and the dragon was enraged with the woman, and he went to make war with the rest of her offspring, who keep the commandments of God and have the testimony of Jesus Christ."

This in turn leads to further references to this "end-time persecution/trouble" as found in Revelation 13:

"It was granted to him [i.e., to the Beast ref. in Rev. 13:1-4) *to make war with the saints and to overcome them"* (Rev. 13:7).

These passages culminate with Paul's dissertation to the Thessalonian believers in reference to that yet future unveiling of the final Antichrist, the Lawless One, the "son of perdition"—the "Man of Sin"—*"according to the working of Satan, with all power, signs, and lying wonders, and with all unrighteous deception among those who perish, because they did not receive the love of the truth, that they might be saved"* etc. (2 Thess. 2:7-12, excerpts). Furthermore, the impact of this final manifestation will be grievously felt, coupled by the Great Falling Away from the Faith (2 Thess. 2:3; 1 Tim. 4:1-2) by all those upon the earth, including "the saints."

All these passages have directly and indirectly been interpreted by sundry Christian theologians—especially the Dispensationalists—to allude to the time of "Jacob's Trouble" and the final persecution of the Jews!

In particular, Dispensationalists like Tommy Ice, Doug Stauffer, Randy Stone, Les Feldick who hold to a "traditionalists Dispensationalism" (strictly keeping Israel and the Church separated) would concur with these statements from eminent theologians amongst the dispensational camp:

- According to the Tim LaHaye *Prophecy Study Bible,* of which Tommy [Ice] is an editor, "Prior to Israel's conversion, Zechariah [13:8] predicts that two-thirds ('two parts') of the Jewish people in the land will perish during the tribulation period. Only one third of the Jewish population will survive until Christ comes to establish His kingdom on earth" (991).
- In his book *The Living End,* Charles Ryrie writes the following in a chapter he titles "A Bloodbath for Israel": "Jacob's trouble [Great Tribulation] is that coming period

of distress described by Jesus as He spoke to His disciples on the Mount of Olives. Jeremiah labeled it 'Jacob's trouble' and said it would be unique in all history (Jeremiah 30:7). Jesus called it a period of unprecedented tribulation (Matthew 24:21). This will be the time of Israel's greatest bloodbath" (81).

- In his *Israel in Prophecy,* John Walvoord writes: "The purge of Israel in their time of trouble is described by Zechariah in these words: 'And it shall come to pass, that in all the land, saith Jehovah, two parts therein shall be cut off and die; but the third shall be left therein. And I will bring the third Part into the fire, and will refine them as silver is refined, and will try them as gold is tried' (Zechariah 13:8, 9). According to Zechariah's prophecy, *two thirds of the children of Israel in the land will perish*, but the one third that are left will be refined and be awaiting the deliverance of God at the second coming of Christ which is described in the next chapter of Zechariah" (108).

- Eugene Merrill, in his *Exegetical Commentary: Haggai, Zechariah, Malachi,* writes: "The restoration and dominion cannot come until all the forces of evil that seek to subvert it are put down once and for all. Specifically, the redemption of Israel will be accomplished on the ruins of her own suffering and those of the malevolent powers of this world that, in the last day, will consolidate themselves against her and seek to interdict forever any possibility of her success. The nations of the whole earth will come against Jerusalem, and, having defeated her, will divide up their spoils of war in her very midst" (342). (Source: Gary DeMar—Who Really Stands with Israel—July 7, 2006.)

In sum, the Jews (all Israel in the eyes of the Dispensationalists) will, without the presence of the Church at the end of the age, go through a horrendous spat of persecution prior to the Second Coming of Christ—their "personal Armageddon." Naturally, pro-Israel Jews view this "Armageddon Theology" somewhat askance: "With friends like this, who needs enemies"—to wit:

CH. 20: SHARING IN JACOB'S TROUBLE

"To what extent will a theological view that calls for Armageddon in the Middle East lead [evangelicals] to support policies that may move in that direction, rather than toward stability and peaceful coexistence?"[142]

Gary DeMar surmises:

The most probable scenario is that prophetic futurists will sit back and do nothing as they see Israel go up in smoke since the Bible predicts an inevitable holocaust. It is time to recognize that these so-called end-time biblical prophecies have been fulfilled, and Zechariah 13:7–9 is certainly one of them. Those Jews living in Judea prior to the destruction of Jerusalem in A.D. 70 and who fled before the assault on the temple were saved (Matt. 24:15–22). (Ibid.) [Note: DeMar is expressing a Preterist/Amillenarian viewpoint which interprets both of these aforementioned passages as "fulfilled prophecy"—we at CT do not affirm these interpretations; however, his conclusions in reference to how Jews feel about their "future prospects" as seen by Premillenarian-Dispensationalists are very accurate.]

The Amillennialists at best concede that there will be a final outburst of an end-time Antichrist upon the scene depicted by the "devil being loosed from the bottomless pit" at the close of the finality of the Gog-Magog conflagration (aka "Armageddon") with fire descending upon his armies arrayed against the expression of the Millenarian Jerusalem being a "type of the Church" (Rev. 20:7-10) . . . *"They went up on the breadth of the earth and surrounded the camp of the saints and the beloved city. And fire came down from God out of heaven and devoured them."* There is a virtual absence of anything in reference to Israel's materiality at the close of the age—why? Because the Church has subsumed Israel and is in point of fact ALL ISRAEL, the "Spiritual Israel"; therefore, Christians will face a time of final persecution (the Jews being nondescript):

So, to sum up thus far, I believe Revelation 20:1-6 is telling us that during the course of this present Church Age Satan is prevented from orchestrating a global assault against the

---

[142] Quoted in Jeffery L. Sheler, "Odd Bedfellows," *U.S. News & World Report* (August 12, 2002), 35.

Church. It is during this time that all who die having believed in Jesus join with him in heaven, in the intermediate state, where they share his reign and rule over the affairs of earth. Just before the return of Christ, the restriction placed on Satan will be lifted and he will once again deceive the unbelieving nations into launching a war against the Church. We know this war to be what Revelation calls Armageddon. At that time, Christ returns from heaven with his saints and defeats them all, Satan is judged and cast into the lake of fire, the unbelieving dead are all raised to stand judgment, and are in turn cast into the lake of fire to suffer the second death.

In this way John encourages all believers who are facing martyrdom to remember that although they may die physically at the hands of the beast they will live spiritually in the presence of the Lamb. This, I believe, is what John means by the "first resurrection." (Source: The Millennium, the Final Battle, and the Final Judgment—Revelation 20:1-15, Sam Storms).[143]

We might at this juncture state that these two views—the one taken from the dominant Dispensational camp and the other from the prevailing Amillenarian perspective—either isolate the Jew to their final persecution without the Church's presence (Dispensationalism) or leave out the Davidic Kingdom/Millennium in its entirety with the final rebellion of Satan confronted at the Second Coming of Christ ushering in judgment and the Eschaton. I might add that Reform/Catholic theologies with their Amillennial emphasis prevailed in Europe during the Holocaust—that might tell us something. Of course, Amillenarians would simply (or should) denounce such a suggestion as misinterpreting their eschatology and, most definitely, misconstruing their theological systems as anything having to do with inhibiting and/or constraining Hitler's Final Solution.

---

[143] The Millennium, the Final Battle, and the Final Judgment – Revelation 20;1-15, Sam Storms, Bridgeway Church, Revelation #34 @
https://www.samstorms.org/all-articles/post/the-millennium-the-final-battle-and-the-final-judgment-revelation-201-15 – Retrieved on 05.03.2020.

All this to say, is the Church—the EKKLESIA—wholly absent from any end-time scenario which places the Jewish people (aka ALL ISRAEL in their eyes) confronting the Antichrist-Beast-Dragon-False Prophet by herself? Or, as the Amillenarians theologically conjecture, the Scriptures have already spoken about Israel's rejection and New Covenant aspirations, having consigned them to the eschatological trash bin of biblical history (along with, I hasten to add, vast swaths of OT prophecies) only to find the True Israel of God (aka the Ekklesia/Church) confronting the final forces of darkness and, apparently, wholly triumphant in the final analysis with some miscellaneous persecution (but not much since fire comes down from heaven and devours the lot of God's enemies—vindicating God's people, the Church)?

The answer to both of these "extremities" is found in a more "literal" (and my dispensational friends will find this somewhat of a consternation) grammatical-historical hermeneutic approach, "rightly dividing the word of truth." Ouch! Insofar as my Amillenarian brethren, their propositions with superabundant use of "types and shadows"—along with their total rejection of Israel's place in any future millennium (since we're already in the Millennium known as the "Gospel Age" where Satan during this 1,000 years is "bound" from inhibiting the gospel on a global scale—although his "deception of the nations" will crop up at the end of the Church Age—it's just for now he has an exceedingly long chain which binds him to his bottomless pit, allowing such things as 20th Century wars killing hundreds of millions of people, etc.).

So, our examination of "Jacob's Trouble" centers upon our Premillenarian squabble regarding the Church's obfuscation from anything our Jewish friends shall confront insofar as final persecution (viz. Jews will bear the brunt of any and all end-time persecution but the Church will be saved from the "wrath to come" one way or another).

The salient passage regarding "Jacob's Trouble" found in Jeremiah 30 is grossly misunderstood wherein our dispensational brethren show extreme prejudice toward Judah—the Jews—by including ALL ISRAEL within their terminology, *ipso facto* Jacob's Trouble is wholly part and parcel inclusive of all Twelve Tribes at the close of the Church Age—in particular during the designated Great Tribulation occurring after the mid-point of the 70th Week of

Daniel commencing at the Abomination of Desolation referred to by Jesus in both Matthew 24:15 and Mark 13:14 and alluded to in Luke 21:20 wherein Jacob's (ALL ISRAEL) Trouble will commence; and, no, although the Holocaust was horrific, it was not, in the minds of the Dispensationalist the "time of Jacob's Trouble."

When the word of the Lord came to Jeremiah it came as *"The LORD God of Israel"* (Jer. 30:2). This in turn was broken down to the object of His description, to wit: *"For behold, the days are coming,' says the LORD, 'that I will bring back from captivity MY PEOPLE ISRAEL AND JUDAH . . . these are the words that the LORD has spoken concerning ISRAEL and JUDAH."*

The object of the LORD God of Israel is: ISRAEL and JUDAH, not just Judah. Naturally, our dispensational brethren will argue vociferously that ISRAEL today includes all Judah and Ephraim (all 12 Tribes) and all classified as Jews in general. The term, "The God of Israel" in reference to Judah is used by Jeremiah (Jer. 28:2; 27:21) but when introducing Jacob's Trouble "the Lord God of Israel" is used in the context of "Israel and Judah" (Jer. 30:2, 4).

Since Israel's Ten Northern Tribes had been "on average" deported from their ancient homelands nigh 150 years prior to Jeremiah's address to "Israel and Judah" it seems a bit redundant to think Jeremiah had in mind remnants of Israel's Ten Lost Tribes and was simply referring to these Ten Tribes in their amalgamation with Judah, giving them preferential treatment or miscellaneous acknowledgement that they were with Judah in some esoteric fashion and/or were actually included in with Judah due to the Dispensationalists insisting they had integrated with Judah during the time of the Babylonian Captivity (or shortly would) with Judah, even though they were still called "Israel."

No, Jeremiah considered the God of Israel to have TWO HOUSES, TWO FAMILIES—Israel and Judah, plain and simple. It is altogether clear that Jacob includes Ephraim within the context of Jeremiah's text—Jeremiah 31 makes this obvious; firstly, Jacob's name is intrinsically tied, of course, to the new name given to Jacob: Israel (Jer. 30:10)—Israel, of course, was eventually constituted as 12 Tribes with Joseph receiving a double portion (Manasseh and Ephraim) with the Tribe of Levi considered as the 13th tribe but given no land allotment, for they were the priestly tribe. There is an all-inclusive embrace envisioned within Jeremiah's prophecy:

CH. 20: SHARING IN JACOB'S TROUBLE

"At the same time," says the LORD, "I will be the God of all the families of Israel, and they shall be My people" (Jer. 31:1).

The description of Jacob-Israel in Jeremiah 31 describes how *"O virgin of Israel . . . you shall again be adored with your tambourines . . . you shall yet plant vines on the mountains of Samaria . . . For there shall be a day when the watchmen will cry on Mount Ephraim, 'Arise, and let us go up to Zion, to the LORD our God'"* (Jer. 31:5-6). Clearly, the family/house of Ephraim is in view here. Indeed, in His regathering of Israel He singles out the following:

"For I am a Father to Israel, and Ephraim is My firstborn. Hear the word of the LORD, O nations, and declare it in the isles afar off, and say, He who scattered Israel will gather him, and keep him as a shepherd does his flock. For the LORD has redeemed Jacob, and ransomed him from the hand of one stronger than he. Therefore they shall come and sing in the height of Zion, streaming to the goodness of the LORD" (Jer. 31:9-12).

I find it somewhat amazing, the statement: "Ephraim is My firstborn." Why? Because if we were doing a chronological or genealogical review of the births of the "children of Israel" we would, of course, realize that Joseph was NOT Israel's firstborn, nor was, most certainly, Ephraim. So, in what sense is "Ephraim is My firstborn?" Could it be that Ephraim is first to experience the reality of the New Covenant? Is Ephraim "firstborn" in the sense of "Firstfruits" (scores of Hebrew and Christian Scripture could readily affirm such—https://www.openbible.info/topics/first_fruits).

This theme of "Mercy on Ephraim" is pronounced in Jeremiah 31:

"I have surely heard Ephraim bemoaning himself: 'You have chastised me, and I was chastised, like an untrained bull; restore me, and I will return, for You are the LORD my God. Surely, after my turning, I repented; and after I was instructed, I struck myself on the thigh; I was ashamed, yes, even humiliated, because I bore the reproach of my youth.' Is Ephraim My dear son? Is he a pleasant child? For though I spoke against him, I earnestly remember him still; therefore My heart yearns for him; I will surely have mercy on him, says the LORD. Set up signposts, make landmarks; set your heart toward the highway, the way in which you

went. *Turn back, O virgin of Israel, turn back to these your cities. How long will you gad about, O you backsliding daughter? For the LORD has created a new thing in the earth—a woman shall encompass a man"* (Jer. 31:18-22).

It is only after Ephraim-Israel is assured, regathered, brought back to Zion, that the Almighty turns His attention through Jeremiah's prophecy to the future prosperity of Judah (Jer. 31:23-30) but He continues His JOINT-EFFORT wherein we read: *"Behold, the days are coming, says the LORD, that I will sow the house of Israel and the house of Judah with the seed of man and the seed of beast"* (Jer. 31:27).

It is after these reflections upon Ephraim and Judah that the LORD reveals the tenets of the New Covenant (Jer. 31:31-40) in which He specifically states:

*"Behold, the days are coming, says the LORD, when **I will make a New Covenant with** the **House of Israel** and with the **House of Judah**—not according to the covenant that I made with their fathers in the day that I took them by the hand to lead them out of the land of Egypt, My covenant which they broke, though I was a husband to them, says the LORD. But this is the covenant that I will make with the House of Israel* [it appears the Almighty has consolidated both houses into ONE HOUSE OF ISRAEL] *after those days, says the LORD: I will put My law in their minds, and **write it on their hearts**; and I will be their God, and they shall be My people. No more shall every man teach his neighbor, and every man his brother, saying, 'Know the LORD,' for they all shall know Me, from the least of them to the greatest of them, says the LORD. For I will forgive their iniquity, and their sin I will remember no more"* (Jer. 31:31-34).

How is it that most evangelicals—or the "Church at large" has not seen this integration of Ephraim and Judah in such a prophetic light until now? Perhaps that answer lies just prior to His proclamations regarding Ephraim in Jeremiah 31 which is introduced in this manner:

"In the latter days you will consider it"—Jeremiah 30:24b—THAT is as clear as it gets.

I would add here that this "latter day awareness/consideration" regarding Ephraim takes place in the same chapter we find "Jacob's Trouble" introduced. But in His everlasting mercy He has extended the New Covenant inaugurated in the Upper Room by Jesus, first to Ephraim (i.e., *"the lost sheep of the House of Israel"*—Matthew 15:24), who initially was scattered—even to Ephraim in order to write His laws upon the fleshy tables of their hearts:

*"You are our epistle written in our hearts, known and read by all men; clearly you are an epistle of Christ, ministered by us, **written** not with ink but by the Spirit of the living God, not on tablets of stone but **on tablets of flesh, that is, of the heart**. And we have such trust through Christ toward God. Not that we are sufficient of ourselves to think of anything as being from ourselves, but our sufficiency is from God, who also made us sufficient as ministers of the **NEW COVENANT**, not of the letter but of the Spirit; for the letter kills, but the Spirit gives life"* (2 Cor. 3:2-6).

Indeed, no one is left out—for this New Covenant is sealed by the Blood of the Everlasting Covenant (Heb. 9:20-22)—confirming Jeremiah's choice of prophetic words:

*"Behold, I will gather them out of all countries where I have driven them in My anger, in My fury, and in great wrath; I will bring them back to this place, and I will cause them to dwell safely. They shall be My people, and I will be their God; then I will give them one heart and one way, that they may fear Me forever, for the good of them and their children after them. And I will make an **EVERLASTING COVENANT** with them, that I will not turn away from doing them good; but I will put My fear in their hearts so that they will not depart from Me"* (Jer. 32:37-40a).

Let us be clear: There is one ***New Covenant***—there is one ***Everlasting Covenant***—and this Everlasting Covenant is the ***Covenant of Peace*** spoken of in Ezekiel 37:26 between Ephraim and Judah:

*"Moreover I will make a **Covenant of Peace** with them, and it shall be an EVERLASTING COVENANT with them."*

This brings us back to "Jacob's Trouble" in which our dispensational brethren place the onus of future persecution/purification upon ALL ISRAEL—the Jews (aka

Judah). No doubt with their understanding of DISTINCTION YES—SEPARATION YES—they would conclude such an eschatological axiom with its action corollaries such as the prospect of "another gospel being preached during the 70th Week of Daniel" and done so by some 144,000 Jewish Evangelists taken from Revelation 7. People will not be "saved" the way believers experience salvation today whereby they are included into the Bride of Messiah. In his classic, *Footsteps of the Messiah*, dispensationalist Arno Fruchtenbaum states:

> When the Holy Spirit, as the Restrainer, is taken out of the way, the Body of Christ will go with Him, but He will still minister on the earth to save souls during the Tribulation to follow. In the same way He participated in regenerating people prior to Pentecost, so will He after the Rapture. From this chapter (Rev. 7:1+) it should be evident that the Holy Spirit will be still at work in the Tribulation, for the work of regeneration is His particular ministry. While the work of restraining evil is removed, allowing the Antichrist to begin his evil rise to power, the Holy Spirit Himself will still be in the world and will have an active ministry. While He will no longer be baptizing (for that is a special ministry for the Church only), He will be performing some of His other ministries, such as regeneration, filling, sealing, etc. In all this, the second purpose of the Tribulation will be accomplished: that of bringing about a worldwide revival.[144]

No, as Fruchtenbaum asserts: "The Holy Spirit Himself will still be in the world . . . He will no longer be baptizing . . . for that is a special ministry for the Church only." Why? Because such Holy Spirit baptism brings believers not only into the immediate "community of grace" but into the very Bride of Messiah—we are baptized by One Spirit into One Body. The only problem with this interpretation occurs when one must come to terms wherein the work of the Holy Spirit during the current age is not only the task of regeneration, sanctification and ultimate glorification but preparation of the Bride of Messiah, to wit: *The Spirit and the Bride say COME* (Rev. 22:17). Therefore, the enigmatic inquiry: Into what

---

[144] Arnold G. Fruchtenbaum, *The Footsteps of Messiah*, rev ed. (Tustin, CA: Ariel Ministries, 2003), 224.)

"redeemed community" are those redeemed, regenerated souls, saved by the redemption that is in Christ alone—where are they brought? If they are not IN CHRIST, then where are they to be found? They are not baptized into the One Body, the Church, which is His Bride; so, if the Bride of Christ has gone to her reward sometime prior to the 70th Week of Daniel, then whether shall the "tribulation saints" abide?

Those believers in Jesus who embrace a post-tribulational view of the Last Days are not shocked—or shouldn't be—to hear that Jacob's Trouble is mutually shared by Jews and Christians (even worldlings) —even if a post-trib believer understands that the Church shall "go through the tribulation of those days"—so will the Jews—i.e., "we're all in this together." What CT embraces is this: Jacob's Trouble, of course—and as we have outlined—is our trouble because of our identification with Ephraim's House being included in those prophecies related to the New Covenant, the Everlasting Covenant, the Covenant of Peace originally promised by the Almighty.

Immediately following the announcement of the New Covenant in Jeremiah 31:31-34 in Chapter 31 we read of Jeremiah's buying of the "field of Hanamel" and going through the process of recording the deed and then *"put them in an earthen vessel, that they may last many days" . . . For thus says the LORD of hosts, the God of Israel: "Houses and fields and vineyards shall be possessed again in this land"* (Jer. 32:1-25—Excerpts). The restoration of the land, the inheritance, was designed for those who might be found upon the land in the event the rightful inheritor was not immediately available to claim their right to the inheritance of the land. An "interloper" or "squatter" might claim ownership of the land; however, the certificate of ownership would be hidden away in an earthen vase whereupon the legitimate owner, the one who could claim the inheritance, could find the sealed document, have it opened in front of witnesses (since it was signed before witnesses) with the rightful owner reclaiming his rightful plot, inheritance.

This is a remarkable inference to the "seven-sealed book of the Revelation" whose seals enclosed the "contract/deed to the property"—it can only be broken by the Worthy Lamb because He holds the rightful deed of ownership. The interloper is Satan whose claims to the earth are bogus—this "squatter" will be cast out when the sealed book is opened and the legitimate owner, the Worthy Lamb, reclaims His rightful inheritance: *"For the earth is the Lord's and the fullness thereof!"*

This is the final contestation—this is our "shared struggle"—as the seals are broken, especially the Fifth Seal whereunder the Altar the "souls of the Martyrs" are viewed—they await their recompense but they must *"rest a little while longer, until both the number of their fellow servants and their brethren, who would be killed as they were, was COMPLETED"* (Rev. 6:11). Is this the "completed number" found in Romans 11:25: *"Until the FULLNESS of the nations be come in"*? The Greek words used are most definitely connected with Romans 11:25 using pleroma (Strong's G#4138 which is from G#4137) and Revelation 6:11 using pleroo (Strong's G#4137). The sense is "completion" or to "finish."

The dispensationalist will view, most definitely, Revelation's 5th Seal as having nothing to do with the "martyrs" found within the bounds of the Great Tribulation who have the "testimony of Jesus." They will, however, contend more clearly, in their own thinking, that the "Fullness of the Gentiles" found in Romans 11 provides a "clean break" between the "Gentile Church" and "All Israel" being saved when the Deliverer/Messiah comes out of Zion AFTER the Church's number seen in the "Fullness of the Gentiles" is complete. It's when the last number of the Bride of Messiah is completed, then God's timeclock, in the minds of the dispensationalist, turns to His prophetic plan for Israel (i.e., the Jews). The "Gentile"—those "called out from among the nations" has reached the "full number" of her members and then she is raptured—and, of course, this occurs before the commencement of the 70th Week of Daniel's prophecy.

The Replacement theologians are remiss, virtually non-plus about any of this "Fullness of the Gentiles" and "All Israel shall be delivered" "business." But the dispensationalist sees this as a clean break between the Church Age and the Tribulation time frame which constitutes an interlude between the Age of Grace vs. the Millennium. All Israel is delivered (Romans 11:26-27) and the New Covenant with this Israel is finally inaugurated as it says: *"And so all Israel will be saved, as it is written: The Deliverer will come out of Zion, and He will turn away ungodliness from Jacob; for this is My* COVENANT *with them, when I take away their sins."*

What the dispensationalist fails to apprehend is the remaining portion of Romans 11 which clarifies, all the more how the Almighty's Plan and Purpose for the Ages brings BOTH Houses of Israel, even those called out from among the Nations under His banner: ALL ISRAEL in that we read:

". . . even so these also have now been disobedient, that through the mercy shown you (the Gentiles) *they* (those of Jacob) *also may obtain mercy. For God has committed them* (both houses of Israel—*the rest of mankind*) *all to disobedience, that He might have mercy on all"* (Rom. 11:31-32).

Apparently, the dispensationalist would like to bifurcate this "mercy on all" wherein the Gentiles get their demonstration of mercy prior to the Great Tribulation and Israel (aka the Jews) get their mercy during the Great Tribulation. I don't think I'm that far off in this theological/eschatological assumption. Paul's quest from Romans 9 through to the end of Romans 16 is a quest for ONENESS IN MESSIAH—bringing together in ONE both Jew and Gentile into ONE BODY through the Blood of the Cross—under the New Covenant. Again, the Gospel of the Grace of God for salvation is dealt with in Romans 1-8 but in Romans 9-16 Paul deals with the issue of the Gospel of Peace—having to do with the Gospel's impact upon the Oneness of His People.

Paul wrote his letter to the Roman Christians prefacing his remarks relative to the "Gospel of God" in which he was declaring his letter's intensely generic introduction, having been written *"To all who are in Rome, beloved of God, called to be saints"* (Rom. 1:7). His letter was to saints who had been saved by the Gospel of God—but that Gospel not only provided a full salvation—peace with God, but provided peace between peoples. He was coming to Rome with the intent *"I am ready to preach the gospel to you who are in Rome also"* (Rom. 1:15). What? What do you mean to preach the gospel to the saints in Rome—aren't they already saints, saved brothers and sisters in Christ? Most assuredly. But this COMPLETION, this FULLNESS gospel was far more than declaring one's peace with God (personal salvation)—this GOSPEL OF PEACE is found in Romans 15:29:

"But I know that when I come to you, I shall come in the FULLNESS (same word as used in Romans 11:25—"the FULLNESS of the Gentiles be come in"—G#4138—or "completion") of the blessing of the gospel of Christ when I come."

That's the gospel Paul was preaching—having everything to do, not only with the gospel of salvation, but the gospel of peace—only then can there be a COMPLETE GOSPEL of Christ—only then when there is PEACE BETWEEN THE TWO HOUSES. This is the EKKLESIA Jesus is building today and that is precisely why Jacob's Trouble is OUR TROUBLE!

Chapter Twenty-One

THE CHANGE CALLED THE RAPTURE
By Chris Steinle

Paul stated in First Corinthians 15: *"Behold, I tell you a mystery: We shall not all sleep, but we shall all be changed—in a moment, in the twinkling of an eye, at the last trumpet. For the trumpet will sound, and the dead will be raised incorruptible, and we shall be changed"* (1 Cor. 15:51-52). This passage on the resurrection and "change" is the big sister to the rapture narrative found in First Thessalonians Chapter Four.

> *But I do not want you to be ignorant, brethren, concerning those who have fallen asleep, lest you sorrow as others who have no hope. For if we believe that Jesus died and rose again, even so God will bring with Him those who sleep in Jesus. For this we say to you by the word of the Lord, that we who are alive and remain until the coming of the Lord will by no means precede those who are asleep.*

> *For the Lord Himself will descend from heaven with a shout, with the voice of an archangel, and with the trumpet of God. And the dead in Christ will rise first. Then we who are alive and remain shall be caught up together with them in the clouds to meet the Lord in the air. And thus we shall always be with the Lord. Therefore comfort one another with these words* (1 Thess. 4:13-18).

This passage is proof of the rapture. But the details of this passage have, unfortunately, been overlooked by Pre-Tribulation rapture theologians, authors, and movie-makers. Those details, as will be demonstrated, prove beyond all dispute that the 1st Thess. 4 rapture will occur—according to the passage itself—at the Second Coming. It is simply not a Pre-Trib Rapture verse. The reader who has been convinced of Pre-Trib should wonder: Why would anyone want to disprove a Pre-Trib rapture? Pre-tribbers often equate an escape from the Tribulation with the very love of God. Paul stated that tribulation cannot separate us from the love of God (Romans 8:35-39).

Furthermore, sufficient love of God is known through the cross. *"In THIS the love of God was manifested toward us, that God has sent His only begotten Son into the world, that we might live through Him"* (1 Jn. 4:9 Emphasis mine). The gospel does not consist of, Jesus, plus ____ (fill in the blank); not even plus a pre-trib rapture. How about Christ alone, plus truth. Because, in truth, a pre-trib rapture cannot be supported from 1st Thessalonians 4—as will be shown in our study of this passage.

In accordance with basic (inductive) Bible interpretation guidelines, the very first step in determining the meaning of a passage is to establish its single main theme. If the passage above were to be bound as a stand-alone booklet, what would it be called? What was Paul's primary motive for conveying these thoughts?

The first and last verses are focused on giving comfort to those who had lost their loved ones. The first verse also implies that the bereaved would be less grieved and more hopeful if they were more informed about the things which Paul is about to share with them. Paul didn't want those who had lost their loved ones to think that, because they had perished, they would miss out on the Lord's return. It also brings to mind the remorse of Mary and Martha: *"Lord, if you had been here, our brother Lazarus would not have died."* The overall objective of this Thessalonians citation is comfort. Comfort through education. An appropriate title might be something like: "Paul's Words of Comfort to the Bereaved."

> *For if we believe that Jesus died and rose again, even so God will bring with Him those who sleep in Jesus* (1 Thess. 4:13).

This verse takes the form of an "if—then" statement. "If" we believe that Jesus died and rose again; then "even so," or "thus"—*"God will bring with Him those who sleep in Jesus."* The independent conditional statement is that "one believes in the death and resurrection of Jesus." If we believe in the death and resurrection of Jesus, *even so* we should also believe what Jesus has promised to His followers; *"because I live, you will live also."* John 5:25 says, *"Most assuredly, I say to you, the hour is coming, and now is, when the dead will hear the voice of the Son of God; and those who hear will live."* The dead will hear the voice of Jesus and rise. First Thessalonians 4:14 ties these two resurrections together.

CH. 21: THE CHANGE CALLED THE RAPTURE

We believe in the death and resurrection of Jesus; and even so, we believe that God will raise those who have fallen asleep—with Him. Paul expressed this very same concept of synchrony with Christ's death, burial, and resurrection in his other epistles (Rom. 6:12; Col. 2:12). The "bringing," is bringing the "loved ones" back from the dead. That is the comfort; not the idea that Jesus will be bringing them down from above, but rather, up from the dead—the resurrection.

For this we say to you by the word of the Lord, that we who are alive and remain until the coming of the Lord will by no means precede those who are asleep (1 Thess. 4:15).

"By no means" is formed by two negative Greek words. In English this would be a double negative. But in the Greek it has the meaning, "It absolutely won't happen." This fact, expressed in the Greek's most emphatic negative expression, implies that the living cannot possibly experience the rapture in advance of the resurrection of the dead. This order will be discussed at length later in the chapter, but let me submit a brief sketch of this technicality:

Christ's last enemy, death (1 Cor. 15), is wielded by Satan (Heb. 2:14). At Christ's coming, Satan is bound—abolished—but not destroyed (there is a difference in the Greek). Likewise, death is rendered powerless at that same time, but not destroyed until Rev. 20:14. Christ must remain seated at the Father's right hand until all of His enemies are made His footstool (Ps. 110; Acts 3:21; 1 Cor. 15). Jesus cannot technically descend until His last enemy, death, is subdued. Therefore, the overcoming of death (the resurrection) comes first; then, Christ's descent. (More on this to follow.)

THE COMING OF THE LORD

"Until the coming of the Lord."

Notice that it does not say, "Until a calling from the Lord." This distinction will be amplified further in the next verse.

For the Lord Himself will descend from heaven with a shout, with the voice of an archangel, and with the trumpet of God. And the dead in Christ will rise first (1 Thess. 4:16).

This verse contains so many important elements that we need to examine each phrase individually. The verse identifies three different arguments which would persuade the Thessalonians that Paul was describing the Second Coming of Christ.

"For the Lord Himself"

There is an additional word in the original text. The Greek word—*hoti*,[145] "that," appears before "Himself." The Online Interlinear translation of this verse captures the meaning of this phrase as, "For that same Lord."[146] Another good translation would be, "For that self-same Lord." By using these words, anyone familiar with the Book of Acts would tend to associate them with "this same Jesus" from Luke's account of the ascension in Acts 1:9-11.

> *Now when He had spoken these things, while they watched, He was taken up, and a cloud received Him out of their sight. And while they looked steadfastly toward heaven as He went up, behold, two men stood by them in white apparel, who also said, "Men of Galilee, why do you stand gazing up into heaven? This same Jesus, who was taken up from you into heaven, will so come in like manner as you saw Him go into heaven.*

Because Paul had just mentioned "the coming of the Lord," it would appear that Paul was deliberately calling to mind the mental image of the Lord's bodily return. Although this may not provide conclusive evidence that this "coming" is the bodily second coming of Christ; please consider the next two phrases as further supporting evidence.

"Will descend"

The Lord—that same Lord, will descend; *katabesetai*[147] (will descend). This exact word is used in Romans 10:7 asking the question, *"Who will descend into the abyss?"* *Katabas*[148] is

---

[145] Englishman's Concordance: entry for "oti." Bible Hub. Biblehub.com. 2016. Web. 11 July 2017. http://biblehub.com/greek/oti_3754.htm

[146] Greek Interlinear Bible (NT). Scripture4All. Scripture4All Publishing. 2015. Web. 13 July 2017.
http://www.scripture4all.org/OnlineInterlinear/Greek_Index.htm

[147] Englishman's Concordance: entry for "katabesetai." Bible Hub. Biblehub.com. 2016. Web. 11 July 2017.
http://biblehub.com/greek/katabe_setai_2597.htm

[148] Englishman's Concordance: entry for "katabas." Bible Hub. Biblehub.com. 2016. Web. 11 July 2017. http://biblehub.com/greek/katabas_2597.htm

usually translated *"come down,"* as in the Gospel of John where Jesus referred to Himself as the one who *"comes down from heaven,"* and, *"the bread that came down from heaven."* Paul first referred to this event as *"the coming of the Lord"* in verse 15. Verse 16 reinforces the fact that Jesus is *"coming,"* and that He's *"coming down"*—*"descending."*

"From heaven"

Here the operative word is *"from."* This is a common word in the Greek pronounced *"apa."*[149] The point in examining this word is to differentiate what this preposition is not saying. It does not mean *"in,"* or *"near,"* or *"around."* The Greek has other words that mean those things. *Apa* (from), conveys a separation between two positions. Just like its use in English, *"from"* generally implies departure and distance. An object was there, and now is here; the object came *from* its former position.

This study seems mundane, except that it is necessary in order to express the precision of the original Greek text. *"From heaven"* means that Jesus has distanced Himself *from* heaven. He was in heaven, and now He has separated Himself *from* heaven. He's not merely coming *in* heaven, or descending *in* heaven. He's going to descend *from* heaven. He's not going to get up from His throne and walk a few steps—and call to the Church. No. He is, once again, going to depart from His place in heaven and *descend.*

"For the Lord Himself will descend from heaven."

What Paul has written affirms that the same Jesus who has ascended will also come down from heaven—*"in like manner as you saw Him go into heaven." "In like manner"* means that the same processes will recur; except that they will occur in a reverse manner. When Jesus was taken up to heaven He ascended from the earth. When Jesus returns from heaven, He will descend to earth. When Jesus ascended into heaven He disappeared from sight. When Jesus descends He will reappear; and *this* is the blessed hope: *Looking for the blessed hope and glorious appearing of our great God and Savior Jesus Christ* (Titus 2:13).

---

[149] Englishman's Concordance: entry for "apa." Bible Hub. Biblehub.com. 2016. Web. 11 July 2017. http://biblehub.com/greek/ap_575.htm

Let's put this all together now. (Yes, this will seem tedious and repetitive but putting the rapture timing issue to rest is worth the small effort.) From verse 15: *"the coming of the Lord."* From verse 16: *"the self-same Lord," "will come down," "from heaven."* Let's take a closer look at these observations about the station of Lord Jesus:

1. He is coming / will come down.

2. He is the same Lord. (Himself, or self-same)

3. He is descending.

<u>He is coming.</u> He is no longer seated in heaven—He is not merely calling or commanding the saints to rise and join Him in heaven. He is coming.

<u>For the Lord Himself.</u> Paul is not being redundant. Jesus is, "the self-same Lord." Once again this points to a physical second coming, as foretold by the angels in the Book of Acts. As He ascended, He will descend. In what manner? In bodily form.

<u>He is Descending.</u> Jesus CANNOT be sitting and descending at the same time. He is either sitting (waiting—[Heb. 10:13]) at the Father's right hand or He is descending. Paul says He is descending. Jesus MUST remain in heaven until the restoration (Acts 3:21); UNTIL His enemies are made His footstool. Leaving His position in any way, shape, or form requires the catalyst of the subjection of ALL His enemies. This victory is a ONE-OFF event; not something which will occur periodically or according to happenstance. (This chain of events will be analyzed further in the next section of this chapter.)

"With a shout, with the voice of an archangel, and with the trumpet of God."

The Bible describes a truly *glorious appearing* at Christ's return—which every eye will witness. This celebration, once again, lends itself to the conclusion that Paul is describing the bodily return of Jesus.

These verses are primarily given as counsel to the living regarding their dead. The dead are going to burst forth from their graves. They're not going to miss out on anything. So you don't have to sorrow as those who have no hope. Isn't it interesting that verse 17 (the part about the rapture) is presented in books and movies without a depiction of the resurrection of the dead? Images portray the saints as though they were ascending straight into heaven with no appearing of the Lord. In most cases there are no voices, no trumpets, and no descending Christ; and certainly no graphic imagery of the resurrection of the dead. The authors and screenwriters *have* studied these verses. They know *exactly* what they're doing. But they don't want the audience to think about the fact that the resurrection of the dead occurs first—even though that information is presented in the text three times.

This concealment is most certainly made because the Bible places the resurrection of the dead at the end of the age, after the time of the Great Tribulation. People who are trying to force the idea of the Pre-Tribulation rapture of the Church either can't use this verse (which is the ONLY verse in the English Bible that actually refers to this "change" as the rapture); or, they must strip it of its context and show the rapture scene by itself. If they present the rapture verse in its context, it becomes obvious that it's not a Pre-Tribulation rapture at all. It's a rapture following the resurrection of the dead.

"And the dead in Christ will rise first."

The dead in Christ will include all who have died in faith. There is only one faith (Eph. 4:5). Whether those who've died in Christ were baptized in the name of the Trinity, baptized in the sea, or baptized into that Rock which was Christ; there is only one baptism. This resurrection immediately preceding the rapture appears to be what is called the resurrection of the righteous, also known as the resurrection of the just.

The Second Coming Rapture

Both the description and the timing of events within the verse demand the occurrence of the 1 Thess. 4 resurrection/rapture to be at the time of Christ's second coming.

The writer of Hebrews explains; *But this Man* [Jesus], *after He had offered one sacrifice for sins forever, sat down at the right hand of God, from that time <u>waiting till His enemies are made His footstool</u>* (Heb. 10:12-13). This verse is obviously taken from Psalms 110:1:

The Lord said to my Lord,
"Sit at My right hand,
Till I make Your enemies Your footstool."

The fact that Christ's position at the right hand of the Father has a finite duration, and a condition upon which His retention in heaven depends, establishes an eschatological milestone—a technical marker—to the onset and order of end-time events.

First Corinthians 15:24-26 provides additional information about the timing and relationship between the resurrection and the rapture. Paul stated in First Corinthians Four:

Then comes the end, when He delivers the kingdom to God the Father, when He puts an end to all rule and all authority and power. For He must reign till He has put all enemies under His feet. The last enemy that will be abolished is death.

"The last enemy that will be abolished (**katargeitai**) is death" (1 Cor. 15:26). Subduing death must be distinguished from the destruction (ἀπόλλυται, *apollytai*) of death. The Greek texts do not say the last enemy that will be "destroyed" is death.

Katargeitai and *apollutai* do not have the same meaning. There is a difference between subduing and destroying.

Thayer's Greek Lexicon: STRONG'S NT 622: **ἀπόλλυμι** destroy, i.e. to put out of the way entirely, abolish, put an end to, ruin..."[150]

A form of *katargeo* occurs in the following verse and has also been translated as "destroyed." But according to Thayer's Greek Lexicon, death is overcome, not destroyed.

Inasmuch then as the children have partaken of flesh and blood, He Himself likewise shared in the same, that through death He might <u>bring to naught</u> (καταργήσῃ, katargēsē) him who had the power of death, that is, the devil (Heb. 2:14).

Thayer's Greek Lexicon: STRONG'S NT 2673: **καταργέω:** to render idle, unemployed, inactive, inoperative: τήν γῆν, to deprive of its strength, make barren (A. V. cumber), Luke 13:7; to cause a person or a thing to have no further efficiency; to deprive of force, influence, power (A. V. bring to naught, make of none effect)"[151]

---

[150] Thayer, Joseph H. and James Strong. "Strong's NT 622." Thayer's Greek-English Lexicon of the New Testament: Coded with Strong's Concordance Numbers. Peabody: Hendrickson Publishers, 1995. Print.

[151] Thayer, Joseph H. and James Strong. "Strong's NT 2673" Thayer's Greek-English Lexicon of the New Testament: Coded with Strong's Concordance Numbers. Peabody: Hendrickson Publishers, 1995. Print.

In ancient times, victory over an enemy was sometimes dramatized by placing the defeated authority's head or neck under the foot of the conquering king. The conquered king's personal plight was in the hands of the victor. The defeated king may, or may not, be executed (destroyed) subsequent to his subjection.

The death which Paul was referring to as the last enemy is that "state of being dead," which is holding the dead in their graves. It is the *power of death* that is being overcome; and God will *bring to naught* the power of death in the resurrection of the dead. Jesus will have mastered death when, at His command, the dead hear His voice and they rise to life. At that time, the enemy of death will become the footstool of Christ. After the Millennial Reign, when every soul is emptied from Hades, Hades will have no more purpose. At that time, death will be destroyed. But Christ's technical victory over death will have already been realized at the *resurrection of the dead.*

THEN COMES THE END

Then comes the end... The end of what? Paul tells us this end comes at the time *when He puts an end to all rule and all authority and power.* That would be the time when all of Christ's enemies have been subdued, because, *He must reign till He has put all enemies under His feet.* Therefore, *"Then comes the end"* refers to the end of Jesus' station at the Father's right hand. Then comes the end of "waiting" for the subjection of Christ's enemies.

"Then" Jesus will be released to descend from heaven and return to earth. Hebrews 2:8 says, *But now we do not yet see all things put under him. "Then comes the end,"* announces the time when we DO SEE all things put under Him (assuming the Messianic application of the verse). And most particularly according to Paul, we see His last enemy, death, put under Him. Paul makes a direct connection between the completion of Jesus' time at the Father's right hand—His descent—and the subduing of death.

The subjection of the last enemy, death, will be realized on earth as the resurrection of the dead, in much the same way as Christ's government on earth will be realized during Christ's Millennial Reign. Jesus will return immediately upon the resurrection of the dead to transform the living and those raised in the resurrection.

It is reasonable to assume that Paul shared this same resurrection discourse, which he had written to the Church at Corinth, in-person while he was with the Thessalonians on a prior visit. Because of the association between the resurrection and the subduing of Christ's last enemy, Paul's comfort to the bereaved Thessalonians takes the form of the following syllogism:

- The subjection of death will be realized on earth by the resurrection of the dead.
- Christ will reside in heaven until His last enemy (death) is overcome.
- Therefore, Christ's coming/descending from the Father's right hand **cannot** precede subduing the last enemy—the resurrection (of those who have fallen asleep).
- And, those left alive will not be changed until they "see Him as He is," when Christ descends from heaven. And then, they will be changed to be like Him—when they see Him as He is (1 Jn. 3:2).

So now with all of the information available we can articulate the resurrection/rapture in detail:

Jesus will call forth the dead from their graves while seated at the Father's right hand (or during His descent from heaven, but at least simultaneously with the subduing of death). According to Paul, the dead must rise first, so the living will remain unchanged until after the resurrection. Then, the resurrected dead, together with the living, will be transformed at what is called the "redemption of the body." Then the glorified saints will be with Jesus.

Because Paul himself is the one who has detailed the order of these events—even on a microscopically technical scale—he would NEVER indicate that Jesus was coming or descending unless he was referring to the Second Coming! Descending from heaven/coming is, in itself, *prima facie* evidence of the subduing of Christ's enemies; thus releasing Christ to descend in accordance with the Scriptures—*"which cannot be broken."*

Translating the Rapture Verse

Now we come to verse 17 of First Thessalonians Four—the "rapture verse." Here we will slow down and take a word-by-word approach based on our hypothesis that the rapture is comprised of three distinct events; the resurrection, the "rapture," and the gathering (meeting). (Why "rapture" was listed with quotation marks will be revealed in the next section.)

The precision of the Greek words used by Paul will allow us to examine the rapture sequence on the microscopic level. There are no textual variants in verse 17 in any of the Greek texts from which major English Bible versions are translated. Each Greek letter of each word is consistent throughout the sea of ancient Greek manuscripts. The words are identical in the Byzantine, Alexandrian, Western, and Majority text-types. The Greek words presented below are used as the base text in the *King James*, *New King James*, *New International*, *American Standard(s)*, and other modern paraphrased versions. The reader may be completely unfamiliar with the Greek language. Nevertheless, it is beneficial to view the 2,000 year-old Greek with one's own eyes.

First let's examine the common Greek-to-English equivalent of each word or phrase so that we can start with the literal Greek meaning expressed by the original language. Commentary is inserted where English words are added, or where English translations depart from the literal Greek equivalent—Greek words and phrases from Verse 17 are in bold:

Verse 17: ἔπειτα ἡμεῖς (*epeita haemeis*); Then we.

Verse 17: οἱ ζῶντες (*hoi zontes*); the ones alive.

Verse 17: οἱ περιλειπόμενοι (*hoi perileipomenoi*); the ones left behind.

These "ones" are typically translated into English as: "the living survivors," or "those alive and remaining."

The word commonly used in the New Testament for "remain" is the Greek word μένω (*meno*); to remain, abide. Therefore Paul's choice to use a different word reflects a peculiar aspect about these living ones.

Strong's NT 4035: περιλείπω (*peri-leipo*)

From *peri* and *leipo*; to leave all around, i.e. survive—remain.

Greek; *peri*; about, around

Greek; *leipo*; to be destitute, lack.[152]

According to Thayer's Greek Lexicon:

περιλείπω: present passive participle περιλειπόμενος (cf. περί, III. 2); to leave over; passive, to remain over, to survive: 1 Thessalonians 4:15, 17. (Aristophanes, Plato, Euripides, Polybius, Herodian; 2 Macc. 1:31.)[153]

The Complete Word Study Dictionary of the New Testament by Spiros Zodhiates begins its definition of *perileipo* by noting the Classical Greek meaning as; "those who survived, and therefore remained, or were left behind."[154] Specifically referring to First Thessalonians 4:17, Zodhiates translates, οἱ περιλειπόμενοι (*hoi perileipomenoi*), as; the surviving ones.

St. Paul described these ones remaining as a remnant of survivors who will not merely be alive and abiding, but they will be literally leftover or left about. These are the ones "Left Behind"— the survivors about to be glorified! Paul was echoing the ideas expressed in the fourth chapter of Isaiah. The Greek Septuagint uses the same root words as Paul used in First Thessalonians 4:17:

και εσται το υπολειφθεν εν σιων και το καταλειφθεν εν ιερουσαλημ αγιοι κληθησονται παντες οι γραφεντες εις ζωην εν ιερουσαλημ (Isa. 4:2).[155]

In that day the Branch of the Lord shall be beautiful and glorious; and the fruit of the earth shall be excellent and appealing for those of Israel who have escaped [death]. *And it shall come to*

---

[152] Strong's Exhaustive Concordance: entry for "4035. Perileipomai." Bible Hub. Biblehub.com. 2016. Web. 12 July 2017.
http://biblehub.com/greek/4035.htm

[153] Thayer, Joseph H. and James Strong. Thayer's Greek-English Lexicon of the New Testament: Coded with Strong's Concordance Numbers. Peabody: Hendrickson Publishers, 1995. Print.

[154] Zodhiates, Spiros. The Complete Word Study Dictionary: New Testament, Chattanooga: AMG Publishers, 1992. Print.

[155] Yeshaiya (Isaiah) 4 : Septuagint (LXX). Blue Letter Bible.
Blueletterbible.org. 2017. Web. 12 July 2017.
https://www.blueletterbible.org/lxx/isa/4/1/s_683001

Ch. 21: The Change Called the Rapture

pass that he who is **left** (**LXX**; *hupo-leiph-then*) *in Zion* **and remains** (**LXX**; *kata-leiph-then*) *in Jerusalem will be called holy—everyone who is recorded* **among the living** [those left alive] *in Jerusalem* (Isa. 4:2, 3).

Verse 17: ἅμα (*hama*); together / at the same time, or simultaneously.

Verse 17: σὺν αὐτοῖς (*sun autois*); with them. *The Spirit testifying that they should not be made perfect apart from us* (Heb. 11:40), may apply here as to why we must be glorified together. The dead, together with the living, at the same time, will both experience the change described by the following verb.

HARPAGĒSOMETHA

Verse 17: ἁρπαγησόμεθα (*harpagēsometha*)

Paul used a word for "rapture" that is so unique in form that this EXACT form doesn't occur anywhere else in the Greek New Testament or in the *Greek Septuagint* version of the Old Testament. Yet the Pre-Tribulation rapture theory has pinned its hopes and built a media empire upon this one word. The internet is replete with images of being "caught up"—the English translation of the word "*harpázō.*" But there is a Greek word even closer to *harpagēsometha* than *harpázō*. The Greek word "*harpagē*" is so close to the word Paul used for "rapture" that it is actually part of the word, ***harpagē****sometha*.

Harpázō, and *harpagē* are closely related; but do they mean the same thing? And more importantly: Which one of these words expresses the meaning intended by Paul?

The Greek stems of these words are; *harpas* (Gr. αρπασ), and *harpag* (Gr. αρπαγ). Using Latin characters, the only difference is the last letter of each stem—sigma (sometimes taking the phonetic forms z or dz). And gamma (g). These two words have slightly different definitions and are designated by Strong's as; GS724 and GS726.

GS724 *harpagē* har-pag-ay' from 726; pillage (properly abstract):— extortion, ravening, spoiling.[156]

---

[156] Strong's Exhaustive Concordance: entry for "724. Harpage." Bible Hub. Biblehub.com. 2016. Web. 12 July 2017. http://biblehub.com/greek/724.htm

GS726 726 *harpázō* har-pad'-zo from a **derivative of** 138; to seize (in various applications):—catch (away, up), pluck, pull, take (by forces).[157]

Strong's indicates that *harpagē* is **derived** from *harpázō*. And the origin of *harpagēsometha* has been attributed to both of these lexical entries. But, as can be seen above, the words do not mean the same thing. Nevertheless each of these two words can be shown to support the author's conclusions about the rapture and its timing.

As stated by Strong's above, *harpázō* is translated into English in a variety of ways. But whether the Greek word means; take away, carry off, catch up, tear up, rend, ravish, or seize, *harpázō* usually signifies the use of force. There are other Greek words commonly used to convey that someone or something has been taken, lifted up, or carried away. But *harpázō* implies that the object which is being taken will be, or has been, seized or violated by force.

Force is precisely what we would expect to be present at the Lord's second coming. The exceeding great power of God will forcefully subdue death, including the mortality of our lowly bodies, at the time of the resurrection/rapture.

The rapture will occur at the time of Christ's plundering of the devil's power over death. When Jesus was accused of relying on the power of Beelzebub, He used the occasion to talk about the triumph of His kingdom (house) over the household of Satan. *Or how can one enter a strong man's house and plunder* (ἁρπάσαι, *harpasai*) *his goods, unless he first binds the strong man? And then he will plunder* (διαρπάσει, *di-arpasei*) *his house* (Matt. 12:29). (See also Mark 3:27.)

Harpagē means; pillage, plunder, or spoil. Above, in Matthew's gospel, some English translators have rendered *harpasai* as "plunder." Could there be any greater indicator that Christ has overcome His last enemy (death), than at the resurrection of the dead where death is swallowed up in victory?

> *Inasmuch then as the children have partaken of flesh and blood, He Himself likewise shared in the same, that through death He might <u>bring to naught him who had the power of death, that is, the devil</u>* (Heb. 2:14 Emphasis added).

---

[157] Strong's Exhaustive Concordance: entry for "726. Harpazo." Bible Hub. Biblehub.com. 2016. Web. 12 July 2017. http://biblehub.com/greek/726.htm

CH. 21: THE CHANGE CALLED THE RAPTURE

Harpagē conveys the same forceful aspect of *harpázō*, but actually fits the First Thessalonians rapture narrative better than *harpázō*. Based on the assumption that the purpose of the rapture is to remove the Church from the planet, popular theologians have asserted that *harpagēsometha* is the first-person plural future passive indicative of the word *harpázō*. [We] (first person plural) shall (future) be seized/caught/snatched (passive indicative).

But if *harpagēsometha* is formed from *harpázō*, why does the stem contain the gamma ending? Why does it contain the very word, *harpagē*? This obvious *"harpagē"* connection has been conveniently explained away by asserting that the passive voice of "seized" somehow becomes equivalent to the word "plundered." But changing "to seize" into "to be seized" does not make "seize" an interchangeable equivalent of the word "plunder." The passive form of "to plunder" would be "to be plundered."

Dr. Spiros Zodhiates recognized that *harpagēsometha* is formed from the root word, *harpagē*. It is not the future passive indicative of *harpázō* at all. It is, in fact, the future indicative of *harpagē*.

"724. ἁρπαγή *harpagē*; gen. *harpagēs*, **from** *harpázō* (726), to seize upon with force [**but NOT** *harpázō*!! The definition for **harpagē** is given as:] ROBBERY, PLUNDERING. Zodhiates provides synonyms such as; *skulon* (4661), in the plural meaning spoils, arms stripped from an enemy; *akrothinion* (205), the top of a heap [of plunder], the choicest spoils of war."[158] (Emphasis added)

A person being robbed or plundered of **their possessions** is NOT an equivalent expression for taking the whole person away; whether they be caught up, taken away, or carried off.

According to Zodhiates, *harpagēsometha* is the first-person plural future indicative of *harpagē* **rather** than a conjugation of *harpázō*. As a verb, *harpagē* denotes the act of **plundering**, a forceful **change of ownership**. But unlike *harpázō*, *harpagē* does not involve the abduction of the whole person. The contrast between taking someone away, and taking something away from its owner, is paramount; especially if you happen to be the person involved. That is why our analysis of *harpagē* must go so much deeper than the

---

[158] Zodhiates, Spiros. *The Complete Word Study Dictionary: New Testament*, Chattanooga: AMG Publishers, 1992. 256. Print.

casual observance that *harpagēsometha* is **derived from** the same root word as "*harpázō*."

The future passive indicative of *harpázō* would indeed be "shall be seized." But the future passive indicative of *harpázō* (although NOT used in the Bible) can easily be found online—even in Ancient Greek. For the reader's visual inspection, below is a screenshot from Verbix.com: "Ancient Greek verb 'αρπάζω' conjugated."[159]

Passive: Future

Indicative	Optative
αρπασ-θήσομαι	αρπασ-θησοίμην
αρπασ-θήσῃ	αρπασ-θήσοιο
αρπασ-θήσεται	αρπασ-θήσοιτο
αρπασ-θησόμεθα	αρπασ-θησοίμεθα
αρπασ-θήσεσθε	αρπασ-θήσοισθε
αρπασ-θήσονται	αρπασ-θήσοιντο

We find our word (above) as the fourth listing on the left: αρπασθησόμεθα *harpasthēsometha*. **This is the word Paul would have used had he meant "will be seized"—or "raptured."** Now with two witnesses (Zodhiates and Verbix) and the verse being free of textual variants, we can assert with strong support that Paul didn't mean "seized."

The future passive indicative of *harpagē* is **"shall be plundered."** English translators have bypassed the literal meaning of *harpagēsometha* simply because they have not understood how "plundered" fits into the rapture scenario. The Pre-Tribbers have missed the point that Paul was trying to communicate because it doesn't fit into their own narrative. Paul used the word "plunder" because he was describing the transformation that will occur when mortality is overpowered at Christ's appearing. Great force will be present at the time of the resurrection/rapture.

---

[159] https://www.verbix.com/webverbix/go.php?D1=206&H1=301&T1=αρπάζω

Furthermore, if Paul had used a form of *harpázō* to mean "seized;" he would have been implying that the force of God will be released for the purpose of gathering the saints **against their will**. The notion that God's people would resist drawing near to their Savior is reminiscent of the words of the Psalmist;

> *Do not be like the horse or like the mule, which have no understanding, which must be harnessed with bit and bridle, else they will not come near you* (Ps. 32:9).

Rather, Paul was acknowledging the power of God to transform our lowly bodies. Immediately after this forceful plundering, the saints will peacefully, joyfully, willingly meet the Lord.

The chart on the following pages shows the overall consistency with which *harpázō* and *harpagē* are both used in the biblical texts. Because *harpázō* has almost become a household word among students of eschatology, examples of its use are presented first. Included are some exceptions where the words have been used interchangeably (by English translators). Showing all instances, however, will reveal that, most often, translators DO NOT see these words as equivalent expressions.

There are dozens more examples of *harpázō* and *di-arpázō* in the *Greek Septuagint* that could have been listed in the charts. But the charts are representative of the results of the larger study.

An online article at *PreceptAustin.org* sites 34 uses of *harpázō* in the non-apocryphal Septuagint (LXX) (Gen. 37:33; Lev. 6:4; 19:13; Deut. 28:31; Jdg. 21:21, 23; 2 Sam. 23:21; Job 20:19; 24:2, 9, 19; Ps. 7:2; 10:9; 22:13; 50:22; 69:4; 104:21; Isa. 10:2; Ezek. 18:7, 12, 16, 18; 19:3, 6; 22:25, 27; Hos. 5:14;6:1; Amos 1:11; 3:4; Mic. 3:2; 5:8; Nah. 2:12).

The article continues; "A number of the uses of *harpázō* in the LXX translate the Hebrew word meaning to tear (*taraph*; 2963) (as of beasts of prey, tear to pieces—Gen. 37:33, Ps. 7:2, 50:22, Hos. 5:14, 6:1) which brings out the <u>violent aspect of *harpázō*</u> ." The article concludes; "**None** of the LXX uses of *harpázō* convey the same sense of rapture as found here in 1 Thessalonians."[160]

---

[160] 1 Thess. 4:17-18 Commentary. Precept Austin. Preceptaustin.org. Web. 11 July 2017. http://www.preceptaustin.org/pdf/59702.

Uses of *Harpázō* in the Bible and Apocrypha			
		English Translation	
Verse	Verses including the Gr. stem *harpas*	snatch, take away, seize	rob, spoil, plunder
Leviticus 19:13	You shall not cheat your neighbor nor rob ἁρπάσεις (*harpaseis*) him.		X
Deuteronomy 28:31	your donkey shall be violently taken away ἡρπασμένος (haerpasmenos)	X	
Judges 21:21	and every man catch ἁρπάσετε (*harpasete*) a wife for himself from the daughters of Shiloh.	X	
Judith 16:9	Her sandal caught (fig. captured) ἥρπασεν (*haerpasen*) his eye	X	
Matthew 13:19	the evil one comes and snatches ἁρπάζει (*harpasei*) away what was sown	X	
Nahum 2:12a	The lion caught ἥρπασεν (*haerpasen*) enough for his whelps	X	
John 10:12	and the wolf snatches ἁρπάζει (*harpasei*) them	X	
John 10:28	no one will snatch ἁρπάσει (*harpasei*) them out of My hand.	X	
Acts 8:39,40	the Spirit of the Lord caught ἥρπασεν (*haerpasen*) Philip away	X	
Revelation 12:5	and her child was caught up ἡρπάσθη (*hērpasthē*) to God	X	

Uses of *Harpagē* in the Bible and Apocrypha

Verse	Verses including the Gr. stem *harpag*	English Translation: snatch, take away, seize	English Translation: rob, spoil, plunder
Leviticus 6:2	If anyone lies ... about a robbery ἁρπαγῆς (harpagēs)		X
Isaiah 3:14	the plunder ἁρπαγὴ (harpagē) of the poor is in your houses.		X
Isaiah 42:22	This is a people despoiled and plundered διηρπασμένος (di-haerpasmenos)... For plunder ἅρπαγμα (harpagma), and no one says, "Restore!"		X X
Isaiah 61:8	I hate robbery ἁρπάγματα (harpagmata) for burnt offering.		X
Nahum 2:12b	and his den with rapine ἁρπαγῆς (harpagēs).		X
2 Corinthians 12:2-4	such a man was caught up ἁρπαγέντα (harpagenta) to the third ... was caught up ἡρπάγη (hērpagē) into Paradise	X X	
Matthew 23:25	outside of the cup and dish, but inside they are full of robbery ἁρπαγῆς (harpagēs) and self-indulgence		X
Luke 11:39	but your inward part is full of robbery ἁρπαγῆς (harpagēs) and wickedness.		X
Philippians 2:5,6	being in the form of God, did not consider it robbery ἁρπαγμὸν (harpagmon)		X
Hebrews 10:34	and joyfully accepted the plundering ἁρπαγὴν (harpagēn) of your goods		X

After reviewing the tables above we can see that nearly without exception, ***harpázō*** is translated into English as "snatch," "take away," "seize," etc.; and ***harpagē*** is translated as; "rob," "spoil," "plunder," etc. Such consistent usage of the two words and their translations adds further support that *harpagēsometha* should be translated as "shall be robbed, spoiled or plundered."

John Jeffrey Dodson's lexicon which harmonizes the work of Abbott-Smith, Berry, Souter, and Strong, gives the concise meaning of *harpagē* as; **"the act of plundering, plunder, spoil."**[161]

Based on the assumption that *harpagēsometha* is the future indicative of *harpagē*, what has, since the King James era, been translated as "caught up," could justifiably be translated **"plundered."** But would this translation make sense within the context of the verse? Yes! Using "plundered" in verse 17 of First Thessalonians Chapter Four brings out more detail and adds even more weight to Paul's argument for the timing of the resurrection.

The next thing to consider is why two of the exceptions in the table above were made when translating Paul's use of *harpagē* into English. Paul may have used *harpagē* with the specific purpose of magnifying the ambiguity of whether, in fact, he had been taken in bodily form, or just caught away in a vision.

A bolder position as to why *harpagē* has been translated as "caught up," (as if it were the Greek word *harpázō* used in Revelation Chapter 12) is based on the possibility that the English translation has missed Paul's intent; and that **he meant "plundered" in all instances of *harpagē*.** Paul, knowing that flesh and blood cannot enter into the real presence of God, may have used *harpagē* in recognition that his mortality would have needed to be transformed into a spiritual body; if indeed, Paul had actually been translated into a spiritual body.

But to say that the English interpretation should vary from its typical meaning in First Thessalonians 4:17 simply because English interpreters have interpreted a previous verse as an anomaly, would base the translation of *harpagē* in First Thessalonians on circular

---

[161] Dodson, John Jeffrey. Dodson Greek-English Lexicon 1.0. BibleSupport.com. Biblesupport.com. 13 Sep. 2015. Web. 11 July 2017. http://www.biblesupport.com/e-sword-downloads/file/10038-dodson-greek-english-lexicon.

reasoning. On the other hand, if "plunder" can be shown to work within the context of verse 17, then there is no need to rationalize why an atypical rendering of the word would yield a more accurate interpretation of the verse.

As a technicality, we will find when we implement *harpagē* to First Thessalonians Four that "up" may be implied, but is not expressed in the texts of either Second Corinthians 12:2-4 or First Thessalonians 4:17. More on this in a moment.

"Then we who are alive and remain shall be plundered/robbed/spoiled." Our goods (our natural body, our mortality) will be plundered. The *purchased possession* spoken of by Paul in Ephesians 1:14 will be redeemed. Instead of being snatched away, God will rob us of our *soma psuchikon* (the natural body) and further clothe us with our *soma pneumatikon* (spiritual body). This glorification process requires the destruction, the plundering, of the old body. The saints are not being carried off at the instant of the "rapture." The resurrected dead and those who are Christ's at His coming will be *changed in a moment, in the twinkling of an eye*.

The plundering is not the removal of the body, but the redemption of the body. Paul's employment of this single Greek word does not establish, by itself, the foundation for an eschatological system. But there are enough examples of the customary Greek usage of *harpadzo* and *harpagē* to support the conclusion that *harpagē*, found in First Thessalonians 4:17, depicts the moment of change promised in First Corinthians 15:23, 50-58. *Harpagēsometha* supports the idea that those who are Christ's at His coming will be transformed. This change will occur before both the living survivors and the resurrected saints are gathered to be with (meet) the Lord.

The main purpose of First Thessalonians 4:13-18 is to present such a precise order of events at the time of the Lord's return so as to comfort to the living. If Paul had used *harpázō*, he would have been skipping over the moment of the change. This would have blurred the precision of the discrete realities, which he was hoping would comfort the bereaved.

What's Up with "Caught Up"?

There are no directional Greek words in verse 17. Neither do the English expressions below have anything to do with elevation.

Act up	Beat up	Blown up	Bottle up
Brush up	Buckle up	Buff up	Buy up
Clean up	Clogged up	Close up	Divide up
Drum up	Fed up	Finish up	Fix up
Heat up	Held up	Lighten up	Live it up
Loosen up	Making it up	Plugged up	Roll up
Seal up	Set up	Sewn up	Shake up
Shut up	Stack up	Start up	Stitch up
Stopped up	Straighten up	Take up (space)	Tidy up
Tied up	Tighten up	Wake up	Wash up
Use up	Wind up	Wise up	Wrap up

So how did we end *up* with "caught *up*?" And, why bring it *up*?

Many Greek words or prefixes could have been used to express the direction "up"; such as; *ana, anabaino, egeiro, hupsoo,* etc. Just as there is no *harpázō*, the verse lacks any root, prefix, or adverb for "up." The fact that the Pre-Tribulation "rapture" theory was first popularized in the British Isles may well be directly *bound up* in the English translation of *harpagaesometha*. Indeed, the Pre-Tribulation doctrine was scarcely insinuated by the Greek-speaking Early Church, Byzantine Church, or later Eastern Orthodox churches. The very use of the phrase "caught up" may have coloured the imagination of modern English theologians.

The English translation of John 19:30b reads: *And bowing His head, He gave up His spirit.* Once again, "up" is not found in the ancient Greek texts. *"Paredoken"*; Gr. παρέδωκεν, is the word translated into English as, "gave up." But the Greek word παρέδωκεν, means; "delivered, given over, or handed over." Yet English translations often contain the colloquialism "gave up."

Apparently, around the time of the King James era, the appendage, "up," was popular in Great Britain, in the same way that "on" has been adopted for some of the idioms of today; e.g., hold on, right on, carry on, bring it on, full on, etc.

Looking back to earlier English Bible translations provides evidence that *harpagēsometha* represents a disruption from the normal course, not a rescue from difficult circumstances. John Wycliffe's translation (1382 - 1395) of First Thessalonians 4:17 reads as follows:

"Afterward we that lyuen, that ben left, schulen be rauyschid togidere with hem in cloudis, metinge Crist 'in to the eir."[162] (Note: the correct translation of those who have "ben left," the survivors.)

Wycliffe translated the Greek word, *harpagēsometha* (ἁρπαγησόμεθα), as *"rauyschid."* Rauyschid is found one other time in the *Wycliffe Bible*. Acts 27:15 describes how Paul's ship was obstructed by the wind as it left the port of Phoenix, Crete. The ship was prevented from rounding the island toward a safer winter harbor.

Wycliffe: *"And whanne the schip was <u>rauyschid</u>, and myyte not enforse ayens the wynde . . ."*[163]

NKJV: *"So when the ship was <u>caught</u>, and could not head into the wind . . ."*

Notice that, according to the *New King James Version*, the ship was not "caught up," nor did it escape from the storm. The ship was overcome by the wind and was prevented from sailing in the desired direction. In fact, it was apparently being blown backward. Being *rauyschid* marked the beginning of the shipwreck course to Malta. Being overcome or subdued (plundered) is exactly what we would expect to encounter in the First Thessalonians "rapture" passage.

---

[162] Wycliffe, John. John Wycliffe's Translation. (1382) Northwest Nazarene University. Web. 11 July 2017.
http://wesley.nnu.edu/fileadmin/imported_site/wycliffe/1th.txt.
[163] Ibid.

Where Do We Go from Here?

Verse 17: ἐν (*en*); in / into. There is no definite article, no "the." Notice once again the accuracy of Wycliffe's translation: "schulen be rauyschid togidere with hem <u>in cloudis</u>." Not; "in *the* cloudis." John Spencer has also commented on the absence of the definite article as well as the fact that "caught up" is missing from the original text. "…in the original Greek there is no definite article before, 'clouds.'"[164]

Verse 17: νεφέλαις (*nefelais*); clouds. We shall be plundered in clouds. Clouds are often mentioned in Scripture during a transition between the physical and the spiritual states. Clouds were present during the transfiguration and the ascension; and Jesus will return in clouds. Clouds and dark smoke filled the Temple. These instances do not represent natural clouds or smoke, but a supernatural phenomenon. They are present during divine interventions between the heavenly and earthly realms. This transitional zone—this blur between the two different dimensions—appears as clouds, vapor, or smoke. Once again, the only directional words in First Thessalonians 4:13-18 refer to the Lord descending and the dead rising.

Verse 17: εἰς (*eis*); for / to

Verse 17: ἀπάντησιν (*apantaesin*); from *apantao*[165], to meet from different directions. To further support the resolve that Jesus is coming and not merely planning a fly-by, we need only study the word "*meet.*" *Apantesin*[166] (meet). This word is used in Matthew 25:6, Acts 28:15, and here in First Thessalonians. In every instance it is used to describe a greeting party, not a departure. Let's look at its usage in Matthew because of the striking similarity between Paul's usage and its usage by our Lord Jesus.

---

[164] Spencer, John R. *New Heaven, New Earth* Lincoln: Writers Club Press, 2002. 189. Print.

[165] Strong's Exhaustive Concordance: entry for "528. Apanteo." Bible Hub. Biblehub.com. 2016. Web. 11 July 2017.
http://biblehub.com/strongs/greek/528.htm.

[166] Englishman's Concordance: entry for "apantesin." Bible Hub. Biblehub.com. 2016. Web. 11 July 2017.
http://biblehub.com/greek/apante_sin_529.htm.

CH. 21: THE CHANGE CALLED THE RAPTURE

Then the kingdom of heaven shall be likened to ten virgins who took their lamps and went out <u>to meet</u> the bridegroom. Now five of them were wise, and five were foolish. Those who were foolish took their lamps and took no oil with them, but the wise took oil in their vessels with their lamps. But while the bridegroom was delayed, they all slumbered and slept. And at midnight a cry was heard: 'Behold, the bridegroom is coming; go out <u>to meet</u> him!' Then all those virgins arose and trimmed their lamps. And the foolish said to the wise, 'Give us some of your oil, for our lamps are going out.' But the wise answered, saying, 'No, lest there should not be enough for us and you; but go rather to those who sell, and buy for yourselves.' And while they went to buy, the bridegroom came, and those who were ready went in with him to the wedding; and the door was shut. Afterward the other virgins came also, saying, 'Lord, Lord, open to us!' But he answered and said, 'Assuredly, I say to you, I do not know you.' Watch therefore, for you know neither the day nor the hour in which the Son of Man is coming (Matt. 25:1-13).

This passage is often used to support the Pre-Tribulation rapture theory. But look at this meeting more closely. In verses one and six, were the 10 virgins going out to be taken away by the Lord? Or, were they going out to meet Him with the intention of escorting Him back to the bride? The answer is obvious. Their lanterns were lit specifically for the purpose of leading the bridegroom back to the location from where the virgins had come.

Once again, the "greeting" nature of this word for "meet" is clarified in Acts 28:15. *"And from there, when the brethren heard about us, they came to meet us as far as Appii Forum and Three Inns. When Paul saw them, he thanked God and took courage."*

These believers from Italy were not going out to meet Paul with any thought of returning with him to Malta. Their meeting was nothing more than a greeting. *Apantesin* is also used several times in the Greek Septuagint version of the Old Testament (1 Sam. 9:14; 1 Chron. 12:17; Jer. 41:6). The reader who is thorough enough to investigate these Old Testament passages will only find further support that *apantesin* is a meeting and not a one-way departure.

Paul has now given a sufficient description of Christ's descent as the bodily Second Coming. Nothing in First Thessalonians Four says He's returning back up into heaven at the time of this meeting.

Verse 17: τοῦ Κυρίου (*tou Kuriou*); the Lord

Verse 17: εἰς (*eis*); in / into

Verse 17: ἀέρα (*aera*); air—the first heaven, above the ground. "In air" does not indicate that the glorified saints will be venturing beyond the atmosphere. The meeting in the air is nonspecific in terms of location. Meeting in air is yet one more indication that Christ has descended from heaven at the time of the rapture. We will meet the Lord somewhere in [the] air. This meeting is the same gathering mentioned by Paul in his second letter to the Thessalonians.

We shall be changed. We shall be robbed of our physical bodies—plundered.

We will not be taken away immediately, but something will first be taken from us. Something that has already been purchased and merely awaits its redemption. The purchased possession is our mortal bodies.

> *Or do you not know that your body is the temple of the Holy Spirit who is in you, whom you have from God, and you are not your own? For you were* bought at a price*; therefore glorify God in your body and in your spirit, which are God's* (1 Cor. 6:19-20).

"Therefore comfort one another with these words" (1 Thess. 4:18).

The moment that we see Him as He is, we shall be like Him. **The "rapture" is not God's people going to heaven; it is God's people becoming heavenly.** THEN, we join in the (eagerly waited for [Phil. 3:20]—voluntary) Meeting/Gathering; whatever that might look like.

Paul's whole intent for stating these individual elements of the "rapture" sequence—which are: the Resurrection, the Plundering (the *redemption of the body* [the "change" of 1 Cor. 15]), and the Meeting—was to establish such a precise order of these events and their timing as to assure the bereaved that the dead would rise first. That is the comfort of the 1 Thessalonians 4:13-18 passage!

Chapter Twenty-Two

THE DAY OF THE SECOND COMING

Dr. Douglas Hamp

Putting It All Together
What Happens on the Day of the Second Coming?
From *Reclaiming the Rapture*[167]

There is a day coming that we know as, "The Second Coming." This chapter presents a graphic look at the second coming of Jesus Christ to the earth. This chapter will also point to scriptural proof that the second coming will occur at Armageddon.

The reader is familiar with the second coming, and has probably heard of the battle of Armageddon; but there are actually a lot of misconceptions about Armageddon. For example, think for a moment about where you believe the battle of Armageddon is going to take place. Maybe you have taken a Bible class where you saw that it was up north. We will demonstrate that the actual location is in Jerusalem. This, and other, exciting revelations will open the reader's eyes to a new perspective on the events of the second coming of Jesus Christ, and the battle of Armageddon.

Questions we might have concerning this time period might include:

1. What are the conditions on the Earth before Jesus comes? We should consider this question because the earth is going to be quite a mess when Jesus returns.
2. What will it look like when the heavens pass away? What is the scriptural evidence for this dramatic event?

---

[167] *Reclaiming the Rapture: Restoring the Doctrine of the Gathering of the Commonwealth of Israel*, by Hamp; Steinle, Memorial Crown Press, Phoenix, 2017.

3. What happens to the earth at Jesus fiery return? This will definitely be an exciting event. We will discover that the earth is going to be destroyed beyond repair.
4. What will be the location of the battle of Armageddon? As was briefly stated, it will be closer to Jerusalem than one might have previously considered it to be.
5. How will Jesus fight when He comes back? We know He is coming on a white horse, but will He do any more than that? We will examine this in great detail.

What are the conditions of the earth before the second coming? There will be an ash cloud that blankets the earth, blocking the sun and the moon. Billions would have been killed by the two hundred million demonic horsemen that come out of the pit (Rev. 9). All the oceans, rivers, lakes etc. are blood instead of water. The earth at this time is not a place that we would want to be. Satan and the fallen angels in actual bodily form are on the earth.

Smoke will darken the sky before the day of the Lord (Rev. 9:2). This is about the midpoint of a seven year period which is traditionally called "The Great Tribulation." It can be argued, however, that The Great Tribulation is technically a three-and-a-half year period, but this argument is beyond the scope of this particular book. *And he opened the bottomless pit, and smoke arose out of the pit like the smoke of a great furnace. So the sun and the air were darkened because of the smoke of the pit* (Rev. 9:2). This is the same darkening of the sun referenced in Isaiah 13:10; *For the stars of heaven and their constellations will not give their light; the sun will be darkened in its going forth, and the moon will not cause its light to shine*. Why will it not cause its light to shine? Because ash has filled the sky.

Some years ago we had some forest fires here in California. I remember looking up at the sky in the evening with all the ash in the sky; and I saw that the moon was actually blood red. When it is observed through a layer of ash, it looks blood red. There is also a phenomenon, known as a lunar eclipse, where the earth comes between the sun and the moon and casts a red shadow on the moon. This is called a "blood moon." This darkening of the sun and moon will be a constant state of reality during that three-and-a-half year period due to all that ash that is going to come out of the pit when Satan opens it up.

Revelation 16:10 says: *Then the fifth angel poured out his bowl on the throne of the beast, and his kingdom became full of darkness; and they gnawed their tongues because of the pain.* Again, why is it dark? Is it just some mysterious kind of darkness? Or could it be from the ash that has come out of the pit? This author believes the red moon is caused by the ash. As an example, there are pictures of an ice filled sky in Iceland showing that the sun is not giving the fullness of its light because it has been blocked out by ice particles. If thick, dark ash were to cover the sun, it would look like sackcloth had covered it.

Revelation tells us that the earth is going to be laid waste. *Then the second angel poured out his bowl on the sea, and it became blood as of a dead man; and every living creature in the sea died. Then the third angel poured out his bowl on the rivers and springs of water, and they became blood* (Rev. 16:3-4). Imagine all of the water in the entire world has become full of blood. It says in Isaiah 26:21, *The earth will also disclose her blood, and will no more cover her slain.* We believe this verse says that all the blood that was ever shed from the days of Abel, up until the very last person to be murdered, will come back and come out in the oceans and rivers. The angel of the waters will say, *You are righteous, O Lord, the One who is and who was and who is to be, because You have judged these things. For they have shed the blood of saints and prophets, and You have given them blood to drink. For it is their just due* (Rev. 16:5- 6). Those who shed innocent blood on the earth will have blood to drink as their just reward.

We know that the fallen angels are going to be bodily on the earth at this time. It says in Revelation 12:9, *So the great dragon was cast out, that serpent of old, called the Devil and Satan, who deceives the whole world; he was cast to the earth, and his angels were cast out with him.* This will happen at the mid-point of the seven year period. Notice also in Revelation 12:4 that it says, *His tail drew a third of the stars of heaven and threw them to the earth.* He is called "the great dragon," the "serpent of old," "the Devil" and "Satan." The image of him as a dragon is used when depicting his tail drawing a third of the stars of heaven and throwing them to the earth. Here we see that the angels are called stars. In Revelation 8:10, 11; *And a great star fell from heaven, burning like a torch, and it fell on a third of the rivers and on the springs of water. The name of the star is Wormwood.*

One might ask, "How can it be that events in Revelation 12 and events in Revelation Eight are happening at the same time?" Revelation is a thematically organized book and not a chronological book. The Gospel of John, for example, is also laid out thematically. It groups like-kind events together. A historian documenting a certain period of history might arrange events in chronological order, or in a thematic manner. A chronological timeline would begin with year one and relate events as they happened. This approach can be difficult to follow at times. It is often beneficial to group things together according to relationships and circles, as it were. This is essentially what John has done in Revelation. He grouped events together. Obviously, he wrote according to the way he received the revelations, but really, God is the one who gave us these events in a thematic way.

So rather than looking at the chapter and verse to say what comes first and what comes second, look at the events themselves and if they pair up in any way. It could be argued that if there are three points in common, one would have a very strong connection between the two events. This approach is similar to triangulation. If one has a cell phone, and if there are three towers around the cell phone location, one can triangulate his/her position. This is essentially what we are doing. I have named this principle, "Biblical Triangulation." It is this principle that is used here in Revelation, and other passages in the Bible.

Then the fifth angel sounded: and I saw a star fallen from heaven to the earth. To him was given the key to the bottomless pit (Rev. 9:1). Here is a star that is falling. When did this star fall? He fell back in Revelation 8:10, *And a great star fell from heaven, burning like a torch.* Who is this star? We discover who this star is in Revelation 12:4, *His tail drew a third of the stars of heaven and threw them to the earth.* As previously mentioned, this is a reference to Satan. So in Revelation 8:10, when it says, *a great star fell from heaven*, this seems to be a reference to Satan himself, not a meteorite.

It is basically different camera angles. In Revelation Chapter 12, the camera is up here in heaven, now looking down. One could think of Michael with his cell phone, filming what's going on and then he puts it up on *YouTube* or something. At the same time, the people on the earth have their cell phones, as it were, and they're watching as

Satan falls to the earth. What would he look like to them? He would look like a great star falling from heaven. Revelation 9:1 says that the star fallen from heaven was already on the earth. Stars are being interpreted as angels. We see this in other places as well. For example, when Jesus has the seven stars in His right hand, which are the seven angels to the seven churches (Rev. 1:20). Revelation Chapter Eight also references angels when discussing some of the host of heaven being cast down and some of the stars being cast down to the ground and trampled.

There are symbols in Scripture and there are keys to unlocking our understanding of the symbols. The Bible can be taken literally once one understands the key for unlocking the symbols. Scripture tells us that stars are, in fact, angels. Daniel Chapter Eight talks about the Antichrist rising up to the host of heaven. This is a description of the angels, and then also of the stars. We have in Revelation 6:13, *And the stars of heaven* (that is, fallen angels) *fell to the earth, as a fig tree drops its late figs when it is shaken by a mighty wind.* And Isaiah 34 says, *All the host of heaven shall be dissolved, and the heavens shall be rolled up like a scroll; all their host shall fall down, as the leaf falls from the vine, and as fruit falling from a fig tree.*

Now think about it for a second; is this really talking about stars? Stars are very, very far away. It would take them a long time to get here. Or, is it talking about the star closest to us, the sun? If it is talking about the sun, and then the sun falls to the earth, the earth is gone; right? Then the book of Revelation is over. There are really no more events for Revelation to convey to us if everything has just ended. So, it can't be talking about actual stars like our sun. It is talking about the angels; those are fallen angels that have fallen to the earth because they are going to pass through the veil.

The veil between heaven and earth is a very important principle that I did not even know about until a couple years ago when I began discovering it. But there it was, in the Bible, all along. It is an exciting discovery! The book of Revelation is literally the unveiling of the Lord Jesus Christ. In the Greek we have the words *apo kalupsi*. *Apo* means "away from" and *kalupsis* means "a veil." So *apo kalupsi* means: "the uncovering," "the unveiling," or the "revelation."

In First John 3:2, when He is revealed, uncovered, unveiled, we shall see Him. *We shall be like Him, for we shall see Him as He is.* In Isaiah 40, verse 5 tells us that the glory of the Lord will be revealed and all of humanity will see it at once. Before the fall of Adam, the terrestrial realm and the spiritual realm were really one. Today, we cannot see beyond the veil on any given day.

But before the fall, God was in perfect harmony with man and man was in perfect harmony with God. That's why when God came walking in the garden there was no issue, until Adam and Eve took a bite of that fruit. As a result, God had to cast them out because they could no longer be in His presence. Why couldn't they be in His presence? Was God suddenly kind of snobbish? Perhaps with an attitude of, "I'm sorry I'm just too good for you guys now. You didn't obey me, so now we can't be friends anymore." No. That really wasn't, and still isn't, the issue. The issue is, understanding what God is really like.

As Christians we have a fair understanding of God's characteristics, such as love. But what does He look like? Scriptures clearly tell us that He has fire from His waist up and from His waist down, and it's mingled with electricity. The word in Hebrew is *Ashman*, which means "electricity." In Greek, it's *electros*, again "electricity." We see in other places that it's lightning. So you have this fiery, lightning, kind of God that cannot have sin or corruption in His presence, not because He doesn't like us, but just because we're incompatible. Daniel says His throne was a fiery flame, its wheels a burning fire; a fiery stream issued and came forth from before Him. Imagine being in the presence of God and all of His blazing fire. Now imagine going up to God and giving Him a hug. How would that feel? That would really be the end of your day, wouldn't it? Because you cannot do that, I cannot do that, we are incompatible with God.

It is similar to the story of the boy in the bubble. He could not be exposed to the outside world. Now imagine you're his mother or you are his father. How would you feel? Wouldn't you want to just climb in there and give your son a hug because you love him so much? You would want to squeeze him and tell him how wonderful he is and that you want to be with him. But instead you must say, "Honey, I can't come in there because if I do, if I go beyond this veil between us, you will die. So you have to stay in there until we find a solution for you." God knew what the solution was, but He could not fulfill that until the appropriate time.

So God put a veil between heaven and earth, until that time. Actually, God is the one who left the Garden and lets us be on planet Earth. But on occasion, that veil was opened so that people could see through. Stephen, when he was being stoned, gazed into heaven and saw the glory of God. He said, *Look! I see the heavens opened and the Son of Man standing at the right hand of God!* (Acts 7:56). Now this isn't the kind of "stoned" that can happen here in California! He was actually being stoned with real rocks and he was able to see beyond the veil. This is just one occasion when God allowed people see beyond that veil. John says in Revelation, *Now I saw heaven opened* (Rev. 19:11). Ezekiel sitting by the river Chebar says, *the heavens were opened and I saw visions of God* (Ezek. 1:1). As Jesus was coming up out of the water, *the heavens were opened to Him* (Matt. 3:16).

There were so many places where the heavens are opened and people were able to see just through a little bit. When Elisha and his servant were surrounded by the Syrians, Elisha prayed that God would open his eyes and then he saw horses and chariots of fire (2 Kings 6:17). It was like Elisha's servant put on his decoder glasses, could then see beyond into that other realm and he could see what was behind the veil. God's desire has always been to dwell with men openly, without any kind of a veil, with nothing between us, and completely exposed, one to another. This is His great desire. The day is coming; and it will happen at the Second Coming. God wants to dwell with man. *And he who sits on the throne will dwell among them* (Rev. 7:15). *The tabernacle of God is with men, and He will dwell with them, and they shall be His people. God Himself will be with them and be their God* (Rev. 21:3).

And the heavens shall be rolled up like a scroll (Is. 34:4). This is another one of those passages that I couldn't figure out. What would it look like for the sky to recede like a scroll? This is a reference to the veil that will eventually pass away. It doesn't mean the sun, the moon and the stars will one day go away. Those will never depart. God promised His continued faithfulness toward Israel, based on the continued existence of the sun, moon and stars. So the heavens passing away, the heavens rolling up like a scroll, are because the veil is going to go away. *Then the sky receded as a scroll when it is rolled up, and every mountain and island was moved out of its place* (Rev. 6:14). This is a pretty major phenomenon when this happens;

in fact, I see this as the end. We have come now to the end of all things. There is nothing more that's going to happen as far as the kingdom of Antichrist.

This is the time when the veil goes away and Jesus comes back. Isaiah writes it this way:

And He will destroy on this mountain the surface of the covering cast over all people, and the veil that is spread over all nations. He will swallow up death forever, and the Lord God will wipe away tears from all faces; the rebuke of His people He will take away from all the earth; for the Lord has spoken. And it will be said in that day: "Behold, this is our God; we have waited for Him, and He will save us. This is the Lord; we have waited for Him; we will be glad and rejoice in His salvation" (Isa. 25:7-9).

The Lord God will swallow up death forever and wipe away tears from all faces. The surface of the covering cast over all people, and the veil that is spread over all nations, will go away when the Lord comes back. Notice that death will be swallowed up at that point. For those who are in the city, or in the temple, on the mountain of God, it will pass away. Isaiah also says it this way; *Oh, that You would rend the heavens! That You would come down!* (Isa. 64:1). He wants the heavens to be broken so that God himself would come down.

The veil is like a curtain. When it opens, out comes Jesus—ta da! "Here I am." Everyone will take notice. No longer will they be pretending that He does not exist. There are many atheists in the world today. There will not be any atheists on the day that the veil opens up, when the heavens pass away, because every eye will see Him. People will say, as they go running into the caves and the clefts of the rocks, *"Fall on us and hide us from the face of Him who sits on the throne and from the wrath of the Lamb!* Suddenly everyone will realize that this is the big day; *For the great day of His wrath has come, and who is able to stand* (Rev. 6:17)?

Perhaps it will be like a one way mirror. A one way mirror enables people on one side to look through, but people on the other side cannot see through. Right now we cannot see through that one way mirror, but those on the other side can see through. Perhaps the one way mirror will break at that time. We don't know exactly what it will look like when the veil is removed, but it will pass away.

CH. 22: THE DAY OF THE SECOND COMING

Then the two domains; the domain of mankind with planet Earth, and the domain of God and the angels—and even the demons, will not be separated. When the veil between the two domains passes away, the two shall become one again.

The heavens are going to open and Jesus will come. His return will be a fiery return. Everyone will see Him coming in flaming fire. Every mountain will be shaken, moved and gone. Every island will be shaken, moved and gone. The elements and the mountains will begin to melt at that time. This will be unmistakable. Don't worry—you will know when the Second Coming is! You will know when Jesus comes back. That is why He told his disciples, if someone says, *'I am the Christ'*, don't believe it because you will know when the Christ comes (Matt. 24:5).

Why do we believe Jesus' second coming will be a fiery return? We read in Isaiah 66:15 and 16, *For behold, the Lord will come with fire and with His chariots, like a whirlwind, to render His anger with fury, and His rebuke with flames of fire. For by fire and by His sword The Lord will judge all flesh; and the slain of the Lord shall be many.*

In Second Thessalonians, it says, *when the Lord Jesus is revealed from heaven with His mighty angels, in flaming fire taking vengeance on those who do not know God, and on those who do not obey the gospel of our Lord Jesus Christ* (2 Thess. 1:7-8). I plan to be riding on a horse behind Him in my new body at that point. If you are one of the rebels who are fighting against Him, it will not be a very pleasant day for you.

Jesus says that, *Heaven and earth will pass away, but My words will by no means pass away. But of that day and hour no one knows, not even the angels of heaven, but My Father only* (Matt 24:35-36). Some believe this scripture refers to the rapture. I disagree. Though I don't know the day and the hour of the rapture, I believe this reference is to the passing away of the heavens and the earth. We see this in other scriptures.

Of old You laid the foundation of the earth,
And the heavens are the work of Your hands.
They will perish, but You will endure;
Yes, they will all grow old like a garment;
Like a cloak You will change them,
And they will be changed (Psa. 102:25-26).

The day of the Lord, is the day that Jesus comes back. It's not the entire seven-year period. It's not the three-and-a-half year period. The second three-and-a-half year period is called "the time of Jacob's trouble." It will be a time of great distress for the nation of Israel and also for the world at large.

On that day the ancient hills are going to collapse. *Behold, the day of the Lord comes, cruel, with both wrath and fierce anger, to lay the land desolate* (Is. 13:9). When Jeremiah said, *I beheld the earth, and indeed it was without form, and void; and the heavens, they had no light* (Jer. 4:23), he used the same word that is used in Genesis 1:2 (*tu voo va vo*).

Jeremiah used the phrase (*Tu vo vavoo*) to describe this amorphous liquefaction of the mountains because they will become like *Jell-O*. They will fall down and become nothing. *And every mountain and island was moved out of its place* (Rev. 6:14). Also in Revelation 16:20: *Then every island fled away, and the mountains were not found.* When every island moves away and every mountain goes away, that's what I call Epic. That is essentially the movie *2012* where the entire earth just begins to fall apart.

But it will probably be even worse than that because it will be a day unlike any other. This is the day that Jesus comes back and that's why it's called "The Day of the Lord." Some events will unfold before the Day of the Lord; but on the Day of the Lord, many things are going to happen. You might wonder how there will be enough time for so many events to take place on the day of the Lord.

It says in Habakkuk Chapter 3:11, *the sun and the moon stood still in their habitation*. There was another time when the sun and the moon stood still in their habitation. It was during the long day of Joshua. This is very interesting because on that day he said he was fighting the Amorites. The Amorites were Nephilim. I describe this in detail in my book, *Corrupting the Image*. So Joshua was fighting against the Nephilim. I believe Jesus will also be fighting hybrids because people that have taken the mark of the Beast would have mingled themselves with demons. The world will believe them to be aliens, but that is all a ruse to deceive the nations. The Day of the Lord will be a long day because Jesus has a lot of work to do on that day.

We are told that the earth is violently broken. Again, if all of the islands and all of the mountains flee away, the earth is violently broken. The earth will be split open and exceedingly shaken. Isaiah says, *The earth shall reel to and fro like a drunkard, and shall totter like a hut; its transgression shall be heavy upon it, and it will fall, and not rise again* (Isa. 24:20). Please understand that at this point, because the earth is so incredibly devastated, it's over. The earth is down for the count, crying "uncle"; or, maybe it's just plain dead. The Earth becomes completely uninhabitable. *For the day of the Lord of hosts shall come upon everything proud and lofty* (Isa. 2:12).

The day of the Lord is when the earth moves.

And there were noises and thunderings and lightnings; and there was a great earthquake, such a mighty and great earthquake as had not occurred since men were on the earth (Rev. 16:18).

Therefore I will shake the heavens, and the earth will move out of her place, in the wrath of the Lord of hosts and in the day of His fierce anger (Isa. 13:13).

Here we see "the day of the Lord" once again. It's not the seven-year period of the Lord. It isn't even the three-and-a-half year period, as bad as those will be. It is "the day" that Jesus, the Christ, the Savior, comes back to redeem His people. He will intercede on behalf of Israel who has finally cried out to Him, "*Baruch haba beshem Adonai.*" *Blessed is He who comes in the name of the Lord* (Psa. 118:26). Welcome Jesus; finally, we are welcoming You.

Paul says; *But concerning the times and the seasons, brethren, you have no need that I should write to you. For you yourselves know perfectly that the day of the Lord so comes as a thief in the night* (1 Thess. 5:1-2). This has often been interpreted to speak about the rapture, but it isn't speaking about the rapture. It is speaking of the day that Jesus comes back.

You see, God has a plan. He is going to launch a surprise attack on the Antichrist. He will say, "Here I am!" and everyone will run like cockroaches into dark places. *But the day of the Lord will come as a thief in the night, in which the heavens will pass away with a great noise, and the elements will melt with fervent heat; both the earth and the works that are in it will be burned up* (2 Pet. 3:10). Jesus says it this way, *Therefore if you will not watch, I will come upon you as a thief, and you will not know what hour I will come upon you* (Rev. 3:3). He says this in Revelation 16:15; *Behold, I am coming as a thief. Blessed is he who watches, and keeps his garments, lest he walk naked and they see his shame.*

This is sandwiched right between the place where Satan, the Antichrist and false prophet have these three spirits that look like frogs that come out of their mouths and go out to all the nations to bring them to battle at the place of Armageddon to make war against Him who sits on the horse. Jesus says, sandwiched between those events, He is warning the world—I am coming as a thief; watch out; you're not going to realize when I come; you're not going to know what is about to hit you. The day of the Lord, the thief in the night, is when the earth is destroyed in Second Peter 3:10.

But the heavens and the earth, which are now preserved by the same word, are reserved for fire until the Day of Judgment and perdition of ungodly men (2 Pet. 3:7). *But the day of the Lord will come as a thief in the night, in which the heavens will pass away with a great noise, and the elements will melt with fervent heat; both the earth and the works that are in it will be burned up* (2 Pet. 3:10). Nevertheless, we according to His promise, look for new heavens and a new earth, in which righteousness dwells (2 Pet. 3:13).

Notice not only that the day of the Lord comes as a thief in the night, but also that the heavens will pass away with a great noise. The elements melt with fervent heat. We previously discussed verses in Revelation and Isaiah that tell us the sky is going to recede, or roll up, as a scroll. This is the time when the heavens pass away. At the same time, the mountains are going to melt like wax at the presence of the Lord of the whole earth. *Lift up your eyes to the heavens, and look on the earth beneath. For the heavens will vanish away like smoke, the earth will grow old like a garment, and those who dwell in it will die in like manner* (Isa. 51:6).

In summary, following are some of the events of the Second Coming:
- An ash cloud will blanket the earth, blocking sun and moon.
- The rivers, lakes and oceans will be turned to blood.
- The veil between the heavens will pass away.
- Everyone will see Jesus coming in flames of fire.
- The earth, every mountain and island, is shaken, moved and gone; and the elements, mountains, begin to melt.

CH. 22: THE DAY OF THE SECOND COMING

This now brings us to the Battle of Armageddon. Traditionally the Battle of Armageddon has been believed to come before the Day of the Lord. I put the Battle of Armageddon in the day of the Lord. That is the time when it will happen—when Jesus comes back—because He is the one who's going to be fighting. The Battle of Armageddon is not a nation-against-nation war. Very often people have gone to a location in the northern part of Galilee called the Jezreel Valley and thought it could be an incredible place for a battle. Napoleon said, "I could see a battle being fought here."

Unfortunately, this is not the location of the Battle of Armageddon. Secondly, this battle will not see the tanks of the world coming together; or the world's infantry divisions fighting one another. This battle won't even feature the high tech weaponry that we have today against other countries. The Battle of Armageddon will be the world united against Jesus and those that He loves. It says in Revelation 16:16, *And they gathered them together to the place called in Hebrew, Armageddon.* Then in Revelation 19 John writes; *And I saw the beast, the kings of the earth, and their armies, gathered together to make war against Him who sat on the horse and against His army* (Rev. 19:19). Again, it's not nation against nation. It's all the nations of the world united together to fight against Jesus.

In addition to understanding who is fighting whom, we will also consider the linguistic understanding of this battle; the sheaves in a harvest motif that we find very frequently, and the idea of stomping on grapes. We will discover that these aspects can be understood very literally. It's just a matter of putting the puzzle pieces in their right places. I have to admit that I broke my head!

In Spanish, a jig saw puzzle is called a *"rompecabezas"* because it breaks your head. I feel that I have been breaking my head trying to put the pieces together. Now, though, I am very excited to share them with you because I believe that the Lord has guided me in discovering how these puzzle pieces fit together. I will let you be the judge, of course, but I think you will see that the pieces fit incredibly well; and that we can take them very literally, which always excites me because God's Word is very literal.

Jesus will stomp on grapes. Blood will go up to the horse's bridle. There's even some imagery that is a repeat of the Exodus crossing of the Red Sea. I think God likes to recycle themes.

This theme will be recycled in a very grand way. God's Word also tells us that a trap will be set by the Antichrist for the Jews. The trap that the Antichrist will set will actually be the trap that he will fall into. There's a proverb that says "he who sets a snare will himself fall into it."

This is exactly what's going to happen to the Antichrist. He will set the snare but he himself will fall into it. These things will happen outside the city. The traditional location of the Battle of Armageddon is in the Jezreel Valley. If one were to tour Israel today, he or she would be sure to visit Armageddon because most people want to see where the final battle is going to take place. The tour would visit the traditional Battle of Armageddon site in the plain of Jezreel at the Tel Megiddo. One can see Tel Megiddo, but it's not a mountain.

A "tel" is not a mountain. Tel is a very ancient word. It actually comes from Acadian, which tells us that the word has been around for long time. A tel is a mound where a city was and then was destroyed, and then they built on top of it, then that city was destroyed, and so on. Eventually, after many centuries, the various destruction layers build up into an artificial mountain that is called a tel. One would not find a mountain in Tel Megiddo today, only a tel. This begs the question, "Where is the mountain?" Where is the city? There is wonderful agriculture in this place, but no city or mountain. One could visit the Jezreel Valley and Tel Megiddo and think to himself, "Wow! This is where the battle is going to happen. But there's nobody here. Why would anybody fight here? Why suddenly here, when all the other places in Scripture keep talking about Jerusalem?" Well of course this is the whole point. It is not going to happen here even though we have been taught that this is the location of the battle.

Let's consider the linguistic implications of the Battle of Armageddon. If we read the *King James*, or the *New King James*, which are based on the *Textus Receptus*, we will find that the word "Armageddon" is spelled with two letter "d's." If we look at Armageddon in the *Byzantine Majority* text, the word actually has one delta (d). If we look at the *Alexandrian Vaticanus*, it's spelled with one delta, but in the *Textus Receptus*, it is spelled with two. Some people prefer the *Textus Receptus*, and may even have strong feelings against the *Alexandrian Vaticanus*, which is fine. However,

CH. 22: THE DAY OF THE SECOND COMING

I would like to point out that the *Textus Receptus* comes out of the Byzantine family. It is a collection of manuscripts. It is really a handful of manuscripts, somewhere between six to twelve manuscripts were used. It came from a larger tradition called the *Byzantine Majority* text family, which were about five-thousand manuscripts. I mention this because there's only one delta in the *Byzantine Majority* text. This is an important clue.

One might think it doesn't really matter if there are one or two deltas but actually it does. The reason is that based on the Hebrew word, the word that we have is *Meg-i-don*, the vowels don't fit for different readings. In the Greek, as it comes to us, we are told that this is a Hebrew word. But we have to look at it through the Greek language which spells it as *Ar-ma-ge-don*, not *me- gi-don*. Clearly the vowels do not match up between the Greek and the Hebrew words, and neither does the double "d." Certainly the double "d" in the *Textus Receptus* would match, but it doesn't match with the other textual evidence that we have.

My assertion is that really, none of these words match the word Megiddo. Megiddo is not the word that should be used. The reason it is important that there is not a mountain in Megiddo is because it is understood that *Ar* means mountain and *Megiddo* is, of course, Megiddo; thus Ar Megiddo (the mountain of Megiddo). Not only is there no mountain in Megiddo; linguistically and phonetically, it does not match properly. Therefore, of all the possible interpretations, Ar Megiddo does not fit.

Some people have suggested that this is "the place of the crowds" and that is what the word means. Perhaps there is an underlying secondary use of that, though I rather doubt it. Dr. Michael Hazer has eloquently posited that this could be *Ar- moed,* meaning "mountain of the appointed meeting time." *Moed* means the appointed meeting time. I think he argued it well. I tend to disagree, though, because I believe the preferable translation is *Ar-ma-ge'don*, which would be "the valley of the judging of the harvested heap (or sheaves)." Here's why. This word *Arema* fits really well. The only vowel that would not fit, that we have to imagine, is the "e" in *Ar-e-ma*. Jeremiah 50:26 uses this word when it says, *"come to her from afar, open up her barns, pile her up like heaps of grain and completely destroy her; don't leave any survivors."* When Ruth went to Boaz, he was sleeping on an

Arema. He was sleeping on a pile of harvested grain. This is from the word *Aram* which means "to be heaped up." It occurs once in the verbal form and we find it other places as a noun, "heap." We also find it in Micah 4:12. *For He will gather them like sheaves to the threshing floor.* God says that He will gather them like sheaves to the threshing floor. He is telling us about the trap He will lay for the Antichrist.

My belief is that what happened with the word Armageddon is something called a "metathesis." This is where two letters can switch. There are many examples of this. It isn't common, but it does happen. There are a number of examples where letters have been transposed; they have had a metathesis. Essentially, they have traded places. *Amir*, for example, is a word of the same basic meaning as the word *Arema*. *Amir* says that God will gather them (those who are coming against Jerusalem) like sheaves to the threshing floor. This motif carries through in the Armageddon / Second Coming event.

The word *Ge ana* means "the Valley of the Sun of Inom" (*Gabeninum*). And *Gabeninom* became *Geana* later on. One can see how there's been a reduction of both vowels, and even some of the consonants. There are three different words for "valley" in Hebrew. One is *Bica*. Megiddo is described as a *Bica*. So this is not described as a *Ge*. It is described as an open plain, an open valley; and indeed, that is what it is. There is also the word *Emic*, which means "to be deep." This indicates a valley of wide expanse, fit for agriculture or warfare. Then, there is the word *Gets*, which indicates a lower lot, or valley, or lower flat region. Sacrifices were unfortunately held outside of Jerusalem in Beninum, a valley not far from the Mount of Olives and from the Valley of Jehoshaphat, incidentally.

The last part of Armageddon is *don*. The word *don* comes from the word *dean* and it's very, very similar to the word *shaphat*. The Valley of Jehoshaphat, or Yehoshaphat, is where Yahweh will judge, or "Yahweh judges." So the word *shaphat* is identical to the word *dean*. We are told in Joel Chapter Three:

Let the nations be wakened, and come up to the Valley of Jehoshaphat; For there I will sit to judge all the surrounding nations. Put in the sickle, for the harvest is ripe. Come, go down; for the winepress is full, the vats overflow (Joel 3:12-13).

This imagery is of harvesting, a sickle, and heaped up sheaves. This will be in the Valley of Jehoshaphat, the place where Yahweh judges. So Armageddon is the valley of the judging of the sheaves, or the heap.

Let's go back to the words *dean* and *don*. What is the difference between them? The difference is based on the infinitive absolute. This is a bi-consonantal word; and in the infinitive absolute, it always has a long "o" sound. *Yacomo*, for example, becomes *com*. In English the word "moot" becomes "moat." This is an example of how a bi consonantal verb actually becomes "a," with that "o" sound in there. Therefore, *dean* could follow this grammatical rule to become *don*. This explains the *don* part of the word Armageddon—the Valley of the judging of the harvested heap or sheaves; and this is going to take place, again, not up north in the Jezreel Valley, but down next to Jerusalem. It's in the Valley of Jehoshaphat between the Temple Mount and the Mount of Olives. This is where Jesus is going to come back, near to the Temple and to the Mount of Olives, which faces the city.

Jesus will fight on behalf of Jerusalem. He will fight those nations that are coming against Jerusalem. *Now also many nations have gathered against you, who say, "Let her be defiled, and let our eye look upon Zion"* (Micah 4:11). Zechariah 12:2-3 tells us that the battle location is Jerusalem, not the Jezreel Valley: *"Behold, I will make Jerusalem a cup of drunkenness to all the surrounding peoples, when they lay siege against Judah and Jerusalem. And it shall happen in that day that I will make Jerusalem a very heavy stone for all peoples; all who would heave it away will surely be cut in pieces, though all nations of the earth are gathered against it."* Jerusalem and the Valley of Jehoshaphat is where the action is going to be. Now that we understand linguistically that Armageddon does not mean Ar Megiddo, that it actually means "the valley of the judging of the sheaves," we can see how the Battle of Armageddon will take place in even greater detail.

"Put in the sickle, for the harvest is ripe. Come, go down; for the winepress is full, the vats overflow—for their wickedness is great" (Joel 3:13).

And the winepress was trampled outside the city, and blood came out of the winepress, up to the horses' bridles, for one thousand six hundred furlongs (Rev. 14:20). The wine press was trampled outside the city, not up in the Valley of Megiddo or the plain of Megiddo; but outside the city of Jerusalem.

Proclaim this among the nations: "Prepare for war! Wake up the mighty men, let all the men of war draw near, Let them come up" (Joel 3:9).

God is basically saying, "You guys have touched the apple of my eye one too many times and now this means war. Get ready because I'm coming personally. This is no longer business as usual. This is personal. Now I am coming and I am going to decimate you because you have really made me mad this time. So watch out! Get ready for war." *Let all the men of war draw near, let them come up. Beat your plowshares into swords and your pruning hooks into spears* (Joel 3:9-10). "You don't have a weapon? Well go get one because you're going to need it because I, God, am coming." All the nations will go to the Valley of Jehoshaphat and Jesus will go down and harvest multitudes and multitudes with His sickle in the valley of decision "for their wickedness is great."

> *Then I looked, and behold, a white cloud, and on the cloud sat One like the Son of Man, having on His head a golden crown, and in His hand a sharp sickle. And another angel came out of the temple, crying with a loud voice to Him who sat on the cloud, "Thrust in Your sickle and reap, for the time has come for You to reap, for the harvest of the earth is ripe." So He who sat on the cloud thrust in His sickle on the earth, and the earth was reaped* (Rev. 14:14-16).

The Mount of Olives has all these tools on it because the Jews believe that's where the Messiah will come, so they wanted them to be there when He arrived. The Mount of Olives overlooks the Valley of Jehoshaphat. Revelation 14:20 tells us that, *the winepress was trampled outside the city, and blood came out of the winepress, up to the horses' bridles, for one thousand six hundred furlongs.*

Imagine blood coming up about five feet, that's as high as a horse's bridle, in the Valley of Megiddo, or Jezreel Valley. Liquid will always find its own level; so there would have to be blood going on for a very, very, very, very, very long way to have enough to fill that valley. But understanding that the battle location is the Valley of Jehoshaphat, which is a narrow valley, causes this statement to make complete sense. We are still talking about a lot of blood, but it would be more like it was in a pool if it were in a narrow valley. This makes it easier for us to comprehend how blood could run at that height.

Jesus is going to destroy His enemies. He will trample them like grapes. *"I have trodden the winepress alone, and from the peoples no one was with Me. For I have trodden them in My anger, and trampled them in My fury; Their blood is sprinkled upon My garments, and I have stained all My robes* (Isa. 63:3). *For the indignation of the Lord is against all nations, and His fury against all their armies; He has utterly destroyed them, He has given them over to the slaughter* (Isa. 34:2). Isaiah goes on to say in verses three and five, *Also their slain shall be thrown out; their stench shall rise from their corpses, and the mountains shall be melted with their blood. "For My sword shall be bathed in heaven; indeed it shall come down on Edom, and on the people of My curse, for judgment.*

The nations will be trapped in the Valley of Jehoshaphat. *Now also many nations have gathered against you, who say, "Let her be defiled, and let our eye look upon Zion." But they do not know the thoughts of the Lord, nor do they understand His counsel; for He will gather them like sheaves to the threshing floor* (Micah 4:11-12).

I mentioned that this is where Satan and the Antichrist will set a trap to try to destroy the Jews. But God actually has a better plan. He is setting the trap for the Antichrist and his forces in order to destroy them. He will use His winnowing fan. It is in His hand and He will thoroughly clean out His threshing floor. *Behold, the day of the Lord is coming, and your spoil will be divided in your midst. For I will gather all the nations to battle against Jerusalem* (Zech. 14:1-2). We also read in Zechariah 14 that, *The city shall be taken, the houses rifled, and the women ravished. Half of the city shall go into captivity, but the remnant of the people shall not be cut off from the city* (Zech. 14:2).

There will be a remnant of people who are still there, that are waiting expectantly for the Lord Jesus to return. They will be the ones that will finally cry out to Him. Jesus said, *You shall see Me no more till you say, 'Blessed is He who comes in the name of the Lord!* (Matt. 23:39)

This verse tells us they will finally say, *Baruch haba beshem Adonai*. They are finally going to acknowledge their offense. *I will return again to My place till they acknowledge their offense. Then they will seek My face; in their affliction they will earnestly seek Me* (Hos. 5:15).

God says, "I will return again to My place until you acknowledge your offense. It will take a little bit of prodding, shall we say, but when they finally do that, and say, 'Come, Lord Jesus,' I will come."

The remnant now find themselves in the Valley of Jehoshaphat. Somehow they will be forced out into this valley and they will wait for Jesus to come back. Presumably, they will be standing in front of the Mount of Olives, because they know that's where He's going to come back. As they are gathered together in front of the Mount of Olives, they will be surrounded by the forces of Antichrist. Jesus is in route, coming to save them. Scripture says that,

In that day I will make the governors of Judah like a firepan in the woodpile, and like a fiery torch in the sheaves; they shall devour all the surrounding peoples on the right hand and on the left, but Jerusalem shall be inhabited again in her own place— (Jerusalem) (Zech. 12:6).

I just couldn't figure this out for such a long time. I thought; "Now wait a second. You have Jesus coming back and yet you also have these governors doing something." But Jesus says He will do it all by Himself. Still…He will give them some kind of power.

When I started to put all the pieces together I realized that everything will happen very quickly; but they must hold out until Jesus comes. He gives them incredible, supernatural power, and the governors of Judah are going to be like a fire pan in the wood pile and a fiery torch in the sheaves. This power will enable them to devour those on the right hand and on the left. Perhaps the scene will play out something like this:

The remnant is down in the Valley of Jehoshaphat. The forces of Antichrist are coming against them on the right and on the left. Then the governors of Judah who are on the periphery receive special power from the Lord so that they can actually shoot fire out from their sides. Scripture says, *In that day the Lord will defend the inhabitants of Jerusalem; the one who is feeble among them in that day shall be like David, and the house of David shall be like God, like the Angel of the Lord before them* (Zech. 12:8). Habakkuk 3:4 gave me an important piece of the puzzle. *His brightness was like the light; He had rays flashing from His hand, and there His power was hidden.* Jesus has rays of light flashing from His hand. This is far cooler than any super hero movie we've ever seen, or any villain, or the emperor from *Star Wars*, who can shoot out electricity. Jesus is far cooler and it appears that He will give them this power. The strong among them will be like the Angel of the Lord before them. And so the scene continues with the remnant imbued with power coming out of their hands to defend themselves until Jesus gets there.

Then the Lord will go forth and fight against those nations, as He fights in the day of battle (Zech. 14:3). Our scene continues: The Jewish remnant that is down in the Valley of Jehoshaphat, the Kidron Valley, is waiting for Jesus. They are fending off hordes of Antichrist attackers who have postured themselves to be able to get to the remnant from either the left or the right. But the remnant are fighting them off and devouring them on the both sides. Then Jesus finally comes back.

Scene Two begins: His feet will touch the Mount of Olives.

And in that day His feet will stand on the Mount of Olives, which faces Jerusalem on the east. And the Mount of Olives shall be split in two, from east to west, making a very large valley; half of the mountain shall move toward the north and half of it toward the south (Zech. 14:4).

The word used in the verse for valley is the word, *gae*, just like Ar-ma-gae-don. The touch of Jesus' feet to the Mount of Olives will create a deep ravine, a canyon. *Then you shall flee through My mountain valley,* it says in Zechariah 14:5.

So we now have a new puzzle piece. What does it look like? I believe the Lord showed it to me as a picture of Jesus stepping down onto the Mount of Olives, which then splits. At this point the remnant realizes that they have a way of escape. They flee through that mountain valley that has opened up. The Antichrist forces pursue, following hard behind them. Does this remind us of anything? Was there another time in history when this might have happened? Well, of course there was. God parted the Red Sea so the Children of Israel could cross through it on dry ground.

For Pharaoh will say of the children of Israel, 'They are bewildered by the land; the wilderness has closed them in (Ex. 14:3). Pharaoh thought the Children of Israel were trapped, so he changed his mind and pursued them, intent on destroying them completely. Just when it appeared that Pharaoh had won the day, God showed that He had actually led Pharaoh and his armies into a trap in which they were destroyed. This scene plays out in much the same way as the Exodus story. After the Jews have fled through the valley opened up by the Mount of Olives splitting in two, Jesus will interpose himself between the Jews that have fled behind Him and the forces of Antichrist that are coming in like a wave with the intent of destroying them.

Why are they so intent on destroying the Jews? We should keep in mind that the only thing Satan can do is destroy the Jewish people. If he could destroy them, then he could have a standoff with God. God says that He would give the kingdom to the saints. *But the saints of the Most High shall receive the kingdom, and possess the kingdom forever, even forever and ever* (Dan. 7:18). As long as there is at least one breathing Jew on the planet, then God can still fulfill His promise. However, if there was not a single Jew left on the planet, then God could not fulfill His promise, which makes Him a liar. This explains why Satan is working very hard to destroy the Jews.

Scene Three: Jesus has interposed himself between the Jews and the Antichrist's forces. He has rays of light flashing from His hands and a sword coming out of His mouth, perhaps similar to something like a laser. He will then begin to decimate the attackers that are coming. He starts to hack them in pieces with the rays of light coming from where His power is hidden. According to Habakkuk 3:5, there will be pestilence before Him and fever will follow at His feet. Jesus' coming will confuse His enemies. They will see Jesus and realize they are in trouble. They will try to turn around, but they will not able to.

It shall come to pass in that day that a great panic from the Lord will be among them. Everyone will seize the hand of his neighbor, and raise his hand against his neighbor's hand (Zech. 14:13).

In their panic they will begin to kill one another with their own swords. Even every horse will be struck with confusion and blindness because of Jesus (Zech. 12:4). Why blindness? Remember that Jesus is incredibly bright, brighter even than the sun. He is the man of fire. He is a consuming fire. As Jesus stands there before them, keep in mind that He is a fire, He has fiery lightning clothing on Him and He will shoot out rays of light. They will not be able see. They will try to turn around, but He will begin to cut them in pieces and destroy them.

And this shall be the plague with which the Lord will strike all the people who fought against Jerusalem: their flesh shall dissolve while they stand on their feet, their eyes shall dissolve in their sockets, and their tongues shall dissolve in their mouths (Zech. 14:12).

Some have proposed that this might be referring to a neutron bomb or a nuclear bomb of some sort; I beg to differ. I suggest that this reference is to the armies being exposed to God's fiery lightning presence. The armies would, at this time, have come into close proximity to Jesus. They would try to get away, but they will not be able to do so.

Why is Your apparel red,
And Your garments like one who treads in the winepress?
"I have trodden the winepress alone,
And from the peoples no one was with Me.
For I have trodden them in My anger,
And trampled them in My fury;
Their blood is sprinkled upon My garments,
And I have stained all My robes" (Isa. 63:2, 3).

Jesus will do this all by Himself.

I believe we will be on horses behind Jesus. I think our job will be as a group of cheerleaders.

Give me a "J," give me an "E," give me an "S," give me a "U," give me an "S." What does that spell? "Jesus!"

I don't believe we will do anything except stand and see the salvation of the Lord. Jesus will advance against the Antichrist's forces, cut them to pieces, and tread on them like grapes. The description we are given is all very literal. Soon there will be a bloody mess so great that the blood will go up to the horse's bridle. There will be corpses everywhere and tons of carnage.

I believe this will happen on the day of Yom Kippur. The day of Yom Kippur is when the books are opened and the wicked destroyed.

Incidentally, it just so happens that twice a year there is a massive migration of birds in the spring and in the fall from the north to the south, from Europe and Asia, and down to Africa. Their common route is to fly over Israel. They don't fly over anywhere else primarily, almost completely over Israel. This means there are millions and millions of birds up in the sky who are also very hungry. Everything has been destroyed at this point. All the grass has been burnt up, the trees have been destroyed, and the waters have become blood.

Then I saw an angel standing in the sun; and he cried with a loud voice, saying to all the birds that fly in the midst of heaven, "Come and gather together for the supper of the great God, that you may eat the flesh of kings, the flesh of captains, the flesh of mighty men, the flesh of horses and of those who sit on them, and the flesh of all people, free and slave, both small and great" (Rev. 19:17).

Matthew 24:27 and 28 always gave me trouble. I could not understand the meaning of these two verses put together until I started putting all these puzzle pieces together.

For as the lightning comes from the east and flashes to the west, so also will the coming of the Son of Man be. For wherever the carcass is, there the eagles will be gathered together.

Now it makes sense. All of these events of Jesus' return are happening at this time; and the judgment has come.

Scene Four: Also at this time, Revelation 19 tells us that the Antichrist and False Prophet are cast into the lake of fire. Then will be the judgment of the sheep and the goats. This happens on Yom Kippur.

I watched till the beast was slain, and its body destroyed and given to the burning flame (Dan. 7:11).

Then the beast was captured, and with him the false prophet who worked signs in his presence, by which he deceived those who received the mark of the beast and those who worshiped his image. These two were cast alive into the lake of fire burning with brimstone (Rev. 19:20).

CH. 22: THE DAY OF THE SECOND COMING

There is a stream of flaming fire coming out from God. *His throne was a fiery flame, its wheels a burning fire; a fiery stream issued and came forth from before Him* (Dan. 7:9, 10).

The Beast and False Prophet are thrown into that fire. It is true they are relegated to a geographical place, but the fire that is hitting them is the fire that is coming out from God Himself. Isaiah 30:33 says, *The breath of the Lord, like a stream of brimstone, kindles it.*

Thousands, thousands ministered to Him, ten thousand times ten thousand stood before Him, the court was seated and the books were opened (Dan. 7:10).

This is the day that Jesus will judge. This is the day of Yom Kippur. And also the nations will be gathered before Him. He will separate one from the other, the sheep on His right hand and the goats on His left. *"Then He will also say to those on the left hand, 'Depart from Me, you cursed, into the everlasting fire prepared for the devil and his angels'"* (Matt. 25:41). At the same time, Satan and the demons are bound.

Then I saw an angel coming down from heaven, having the key to the bottomless pit and a great chain in his hand. He laid hold of the dragon, that serpent of old, who is the Devil and Satan, and bound him for a thousand years; and he cast him into the bottomless pit, and shut him up, and set a seal on him, so that he should deceive the nations no more till the thousand years were finished (Rev. 20:1-3).

Satan and the demons are not destroyed at this point, but they are put into a holding cell where they will remain for 1,000 years.

We see this in Isaiah 24:21-22:

It shall come to pass in that day
That the Lord will punish on high the host of exalted ones,
And on the earth the kings of the earth.
They will be gathered together,
As prisoners are gathered in the pit,
And will be shut up in the prison.

After many days they will be punished. Satan and the demons will be punished after the 1,000 years. But during the 1,000 years they will remain in prison. Then as Satan descends down into Sheol, to the lowest depths of the abyss, *"Those who see you* (Satan) *will gaze at you, and consider you, saying: 'Is this the man who made the earth tremble, who shook kingdoms* (Isa. 14:16)? That will be the end of the Antichrist, the end of Satan, at least for 1,000 years. Then Jesus will usher in the Millennium.

In summary:

1. The Antichrist gathered the nations to destroy Israel, but this is when Jesus comes back. He rends the veil and He comes down.
2. The governors of Judah fend off their attackers, briefly, until Jesus puts His feet down upon the Mount of Olives. At that point the Mount of Olives will split in two and the remnant will flee through the resulting valley.
3. Jesus jumps down into that canyon and fights the attackers. He gets all bloody as He squashes them like grapes in a winepress. The blood comes up to the horse's bridle.
4. There are so many bodies and so much carnage that the birds come and feast themselves on the flesh of kings and mighty men.
5. The judging of the sheep and the goats immediately follows.
6. The heavens will pass away. This will literally be the unveiling which will happen the day that Jesus returns.
7. The Day of the Lord is a "thief in the night" event.
8. Armageddon fits better linguistically and logistically with the valley of the judging of the harvest of the sheaves (Valley of Jehoshaphat).
9. Jesus comes personally and fights for Israel.
10. The biblical imagery is literal.

EPILOGUE

1. **Vision**—What do we see from Scripture? We see in Commonwealth Theology (CT) God's Eternal Plan and Purpose—from Adam's Creation to the Holy City, New Jerusalem—is to call out an elect people from humanity to be His Holy People and Kingdom seen as a great multitude, yet a remnant, under the headship of Christ, the Messiah and King. A multiplicity of terms express the diversity and unity of His Purpose: The Temple of the Lord, the Household of Faith, the One New Man, the New Creation, the Body of Christ, One Olive Tree, the Kingdom of God, the United Kingdom of David/Tabernacle of David, the Ekklesia, the "Fullness of Christ"—the New Jerusalem, the Bride of Christ, the Israel of God and the Commonwealth of Israel. All, and more such terms, reflect and are wrought by the Person and Work of Christ—His salvation, His abundant Life in gathering such a people.
2. **Propagation**—This message expressing His Ultimate Intention in salvation and inclusion into His One Body—is in sum the "Gospel of the Kingdom" and "those things concerning our Lord Jesus Christ"—this message is to be preached in all the world—i.e., "peace with God" (salvation) and "peace among His people" (unity)—its manifestation in the present age is not abstract but by the Power of His Holy Spirit manifested on earth now (Matt. 24:14; Rom. 16:31; Lu. 24:27). The Law (Torah) and the Prophets reveal Messiah's Person and Work (Lu. 24:27) as the King of Israel—both Son of God and Son of Man.
3. **All ministry**, under the headship of Christ, should "equip the saints" in the expansion or building up of His One Body—"unto the measure of the stature of the fullness of Christ"—all enmity between Jew and Gentile is, therefore, terminated bringing "peace through the blood of His cross"—although there abides the "wild" and "natural" branches; yet, there is but One Root which bore them—one Olive Tree. There is one New Covenant, one New Commandment which expresses and empowers the Almighty's commitment to sustain the Commonwealth of Israel. This Commonwealth is assured by

our Lord's High Priestly prayer wherein His disciples are sustained by the Father's Life, the Son's Truth, expressed in Oneness and Glory by the Spirit (John 17; Eph. 2, 4).
4. **Call to Action**:
    a. Actively preaching this "Gospel of the Kingdom" to the world and displaying it in fellowship with all saints.*
    b. Equip and Gather His elect, today's Ekklesia, in ministry and environments where God's people share with one another the "riches of Christ" –
    c. Team up with other ministries who celebrate and propagate the message of His salvation and the Oneness of His People as described in #1 (Phil. 1:27).

* CT's immediate ministry efforts are domiciled in the Commonwealth of Israel Foundation in the publication (dissemination) of literature, websites, and the ultimate publication of the CT Reference Bible wherein the above postulates will be generously expanded in commentary and linguistic commitment to the original languages in which the Canon of Scripture was written—primarily Hebrew and Greek.

APPENDIX

The Denver Declaration

Introduction to the Denver Declaration

During the course of 2017-2019 a number of believers in Messiah—Jesus—realized from their doctrinal backgrounds that the major theological paradigms now prevalent primarily within evangelical circles were either inherited from Roman Catholicism and Reformational Churches and/or from more modern forms of systematic theology, primarily those with premillenarians/dispensational emphasis. Coupled with these older bodies of doctrinal emphases were eschatologies which emphasized the "disinheritance" of Israel (aka, the Jews) expressed in the corpus of what is considered Replacement/Rejection theology wherein "Israel" is solely the New Israel of God—i.e., the Church; whereas in Dispensational thinking the Ekklesia/Congregation/Church is wholly disconnected from the tribe of Judah (i.e., the Jews) wherein God's plan for both the Church and "Israel" are utterly disconnected, the one from the other.

Neither theological extremity sufficed this band of brethren concerning their relationship with what they saw written in the "prophetic Scriptures" (Rom. 16:26)—for they saw in the prayer of Jesus in John 17 "that they all may be one" through the work of the cross would not only open up the floodgates of universal redemption but would as well, break down the "middle wall of separation"—making of the two (Jew and Gentile) ONE NEW MAN—SO MAKING PEACE.

Furthermore, neither did the current movements within Messianic Judaism—followers of Yeshua—placate these extremes of profound, even eternal, alienation found in Replacement / Dispensational theologies due to the growing isolationism within far too many of the Messianic confederated organizations—most standing "apart" from their "Gentile" counterparts. Neither were we convinced with most of the "Two-House Theology" during the last hundred years (e.g., British Israelism, Mormonism).

Yet, lest we become inflated with "comparing ourselves with ourselves"—we have been greatly blessed by elements within all these branches of biblical understanding and research.

We are keenly aware of both the hostile/superior theologies within Christendom and the isolation among our Messianic brethren; consequently, and as greater fellowship over issues related to the Ekklesia and of the prophetic scriptures related to the Breach of Jeroboam and the true work of the cross in reconciling both the House of Judah and the House of Israel (aka, Ephraim), we set about in developing what we feel is a body of knowledge/truth which would reconcile these theological extremes, while challenging the isolation amongst our Messianic brethren—and, in so doing, build greater understanding and bridges with the House of Judah in preparation for the coming Messianic Era—the Final Redemption.

Thus, since 2017 we have increasingly reached out to a diverse group of leadership—primarily among Christian communities in holding bi-annual convocations, "teaming-up" with other ministries for the "faith of the gospel" and spreading our research through sundry expressions like publications and social media.

What you see here within this DENVER DECLARATION is an initial expression of our findings—knowing full-well the insufficiency of our discoveries; yet, at the same time, introducing these efforts to the greater Body of Messiah because we are persuaded the time has come to take a vibrant stand for the "Truth of the Gospel" in proclaiming not only the Gospel of the Grace of God for so great a salvation wrought through our Savior, but embracing the Gospel of Peace in bringing His people in both Houses—Judah and Ephraim—to see their prophetic roles at the culmination of this age. May God Almighty bless this declaration.

THE DENVER DECLARATION—SUMMER—2019
—PREAMBLE:

What follows here are simply sundry statements—not necessarily in order of preference—but each, in the main, standing on its own theological understanding. They do not necessarily build upon one another for an ultimate conclusion/summation; however, and although this is NOT a complete reservoir of our immediate understanding of the Scripture of Truth—it is an earnest attempt to state those theological truths we deem essential in the current drama of Redemption. The Living God desires relationship with man. Fellowship has been extended to chosen people through a series of covenants. God desires obedience but requires faith in His identity and in His intent to accept, bless, and show mercy (Heb. 11:6; Rom. 9:32)*.

Both the House of Israel (Ephraim) and the House of Judah broke their covenant with God (Jer. 11:10). The House of Israel was declared to be divorced (Jer. 3:8); and, "not My people" (Hos. 1:9). Thus God's covenant with Ephraim was technically broken. The House of Israel/Ephraim was intentionally, divinely scattered and diffused among the Nations (Gentiles) so that they were "swallowed up." The House of Judah was sent away without a certificate of divorce (Isa. 50:1). Although a remnant of Judah did return to the land after their Babylonian Captivity, they were later scattered among the Nations and "Jerusalem was trodden down of the Nations; led away captive into all nations—until the times of the Nations be fulfilled" (Luke 21:24). We today are witnessing the run-up to the terminus of the "times of the Gentiles/Nations" (Luke 21:24), and most certainly, "until the Fullness" or "Completion" "of the Nations be come in" (Rom. 11:25).

God has not forgotten nor forsaken either Judah or Ephraim. (Isa. 49:14-16; Jer. 3:12; Rom. 11:1-2)—notwithstanding their "scattering." Both the everlasting Abrahamic covenant and the Mosaic covenant remain in place on God's part: "Concerning the election...the gifts and the calling of God are irrevocable" (Rom. 11:28-29); "If we are faithless, He remains faithful; He cannot deny Himself" (2 Tim. 2:13).

How God might legally take back his unfaithful partner, Ephraim; and, how God might bring the Gentiles/the Nations (who were "strangers from the covenants of promise") into a covenant relationship, was a mystery. This mystery of the Servant-Savior, was stated but not comprehended in Isaiah's narrative (Isa. 49-53) which addressed: The Gentiles, the divorce, and the vicarious suffering and death of Christ for the sins of all parties—"the sins of the world" (John 1:29; 1 John 2:2). The overarching divine intent is the prophesied reconciliation and restoration of the Two Houses of Israel (Judah and Ephraim) which will occur at the prophesied End-

Time Harvest, with the Gathering together of All Israel. This is "the Prophesied Reconciliation and Restoration of the Two Houses of Israel" which will occur during the End-Time Harvest with the Gathering of All Israel in the Blood of Messiah from out of all the nations as a Unified International Congregation, originally expressed as the "Commonwealth of Israel" (Eph. 2:11-14). Yes, a single undivided Elect wherein both Testaments agree: "The tabernacle of God is with men, and He will dwell with them, and they shall be His people . . . God Himself will be with them and be their God" (Rev. 21:3; Ezek. 37:27).

THEREFORE—BE IT KNOWN . . .

SECTION 1
UNITY IN THE COMMONWEALTH OF ISRAEL

Whereas: It is evident to those within and without the body of believers in the Holy One of Israel that God's assembly has fallen grievously short of the unity, peace, and effectiveness portended by Holy Scripture; God, having accomplished everything necessary on earth and in the heavenlies to afford such unity and peace to His people, we, the parties of Commonwealth of Israel comprised of those near, those far, and those included—identified in Ephesians, Romans, and elsewhere as the House of Judah, the House of Israel (lost tribes), and the Gentiles—do hereby call, plead, and appeal to our fellow heirs in the inheritance of God to realize the peace on earth and goodwill announced at Messiah's appearance.

The Holy Scriptures* clearly state those who are "in Christ" are redeemed under His shed blood and are likewise brought nigh into the Commonwealth of Israel— (Eph. 2:11-14). This is the ultimate national identity of the Congregation of Israel's Messiah, the Ekklesia, "the pillar and ground of reality" (1 Tim. 3:15)—a spiritual house, the heavenly expression of the Living God manifested both as the descending New Jerusalem (Rev. 21) from a "heavenly perspective" and as the Holy District with Holy City and Sanctuary (Ezek. 40-48), from its earthly perspective—yet it is ONE HOLY CITY—beyond man's finite mind to comprehend in its multi-dimensional expression.

"They who were 'swallowed up of the Nations' [aka, Ephraim, Israel, Jezreel, Samaria—Hos. 8:7-9]; yet, He "will gather them" for "As He says also in Hosea: 'I will call them My people, who were not My people, and her beloved, who was not beloved. And it shall come to pass in the place where it was said to them, 'You are not My people,' There they shall be called sons of the living God'" (Hos. 2:23; 1:10; Rom. 9:25-26). The prophetic "latter rain" reality of the ONENESS of God's people will intensify within the crucible of the Seventieth Week of Daniel—the Final Week of seven years of human history until the Messiah—the Deliverer—shall roar out of Zion (Daniel 9:24-27; Rom. 11:26; Isa. 59:20-21). The supernatural concept of "Divine Deliverance"—of "Messiah," the "Deliverer," "Savior"—is embedded in Hebrew and Christian Scriptures and is espoused by both Jewish and Christian theologies. Joseph/Ephraim and Judah with their companions (Ezek. 37:16) constitute ALL ISRAEL to be delivered by the Deliverer.

We affirm but ONE OLIVE TREE (Jer. 11:16) yet "two branches" but "one root"—these two are seen as the "natural branches" (Judah) and the wild branches (those "elect from among the nations"—Rom. 11)—the common "root that bore them both" is our same Messiah. Judah has been "blinded in part"—whereas, we, "the wild branches" now "see through a glass dimly"—none should boast! God in His infinite wisdom has included all in disobedience that He might have mercy on us all (Rom. 11:32). He is able to graft them (Judah) in again—How much more will these (Judah), who are natural branches, be grafted into THEIR OWN OLIVE TREE?" (Rom. 11, excerpts).

SECTION 2
ENMITY BETWEEN JUDAH AND JOSEPH ABOLISHED

Whereas: Messiah abolished in His flesh, via His death at Calvary—the enmity (the hatred between the House of Judah [i.e., the Jews] and the Nations [viz., the Gentiles—including the House of Joseph, i.e., Ephraim scattered among the nations; and the "rest of mankind" or Edom–Acts 15:17; Amos 9:12]). Thus, this "middle wall of separation" (Eph. 2:14) has been destroyed! He abolished this enmity derived from *"the law of commandments contained in ordinances"* to make of the aforementioned Two—ONE NEW MAN, so making peace (Eph.

2:15). Messiah was "cut off" (Dan. 9:26) for us and our salvation, bringing us all into the Congregation / Commonwealth of Israel—we are no longer aliens but fellow citizens of the "household of God" (Eph. 2:19). Now, at the close of this age—ALL ISRAEL SHALL BE DELIVERED—as a single, undivided elect, manifested as the United Kingdom of David (Rom. 11:26-27; Acts 15:16). Both Houses (Judah and Ephraim) retaining their distinction in their anointings under the Holy One of Israel, but "One in Messiah" (Acts 15:14-17; Amos 9:11-12).

SECTION 3
ONE CONGREGATION—GOD'S ULTIMATE PLAN

Whereas: The "Commonwealth of Israel"* shares identification with the Congregation or Ekklesia in the Wilderness (Acts 7:38). Their mutual harmony and complimentary destiny are assured through the Messiah of Israel. Together they constitute the ultimate manifestation of the New Jerusalem having the 12 Gates bearing the Names of the Twelve Tribes of Israel and the 12 Foundations of this Holy City bear the names of the Twelve Apostles of the Lamb (Rev. 21; Ezek. 48). There are NOT "Two" Holy Cities—there is only One Holy City, One Bride, One New Covenant, One Body, One Spirit, One Hope, One Lord, One Faith, One Baptism, One God and Father of all, One New Man (Eph. 4:4-6; Eph. 2:15)—both heavenly and earthly—the New Jerusalem is beyond our current comprehension—SHE is Multi-Dimensional!

Although the covenant people of God, currently estranged in both houses, they are nevertheless destined to become reconciled, reunited, and their identity fully restored as "All Israel."* We affirm His promise made in Ezekiel 37:15-28 that He "Will make a covenant of peace with them [between the House of Judah and the House of Ephraim], and it shall be an everlasting covenant with them . . . I will make them one nation in the land, on the mountains of Israel; and one king shall be king over them all; they shall no longer be two nations, nor shall they ever be divided into two kingdoms again. . . Then they shall be My people, and I will be their God . . . David My servant shall be king over them, and they shall all have one shepherd; they shall also walk in My judgments and observe My statutes and do them."

We affirm the prophetic climax of the ages and the manifestation of the Kingdom of "My Servant David shall be their prince forever" . . . for "Thus says the LORD GOD: 'Surely I will take the stick of Joseph, which is the hand of Ephraim, and the tribes of Israel, his companions; and I will join them with it, with the stick of Judah, and make them one stick, and they will be one in My hand" (Ezek. 37:25, 19).

SECTION 4
ONE LORD, ONE KING, ONE REDEEMER

Whereas: The "called out" Ekklesia, the "Elect" from the nations, having been redeemed through the "blood of the cross," find their salvation in Messiah's first coming; and as Israel's promised Pascal Lamb their final salvation and glorification will come with Messiah's Second coming—this time as the Lion of the royal Jewish House of Judah, the holder of the scepter, the promised Shiloh, (Gen. 49:10), to whom the national sovereignty of Israel belongs, and to whom all allegiance is due. There are not two Messiahs—there is but one—the same one who came precisely as prophesied in Zechariah 9:9, "Behold, your King is coming to you; He is just and having salvation, lowly and riding on a donkey, a colt, the foal of a donkey" (Matt. 21:5; Mark 11:7, 9; Luke 19:38; John 12:15). He is the same one who "will cut off the chariot from Ephraim, and the horse from Jerusalem; the battle bow shall be cut off . . . He shall speak peace to the nations; His dominion shall be from sea to sea, and from the River to the ends of the earth" (Zech. 9:10)—this ONE: "And the LORD shall be King over all the earth. In that day it shall be—'The LORD is one,' and His name one" (Zech. 14:9). Glory! Messiah's First and Second Comings are acclaimed by the prophet Zechariah. First as the "suffering servant"—then as "King of kings, and Lord of lords—Of the increase of his government and peace there shall be no end, upon the throne of David, and upon his kingdom, to order it, and to establish it" (Rev. 19:16; Isa. 9:7).

It therefore follows: We "elect from among the nations" and our Jewish counterparts do NOT have a different God. Nor do we have different salvation plans. Both houses of Israel purport to give homage to Yehovah-God Almighty, the Eternal God of Israel, and as the end-time drama unfolds both houses will discover and take part in this unifying reality in Messiah; thus, we affirm: Our God is ONE—eternally existing and distinctly: The Father, the Son; and the Holy Spirit (Isa. 63:16, 8, 10-11; Zech. 14:9). The ONEness of God confounds the natural mind:

"'I, even I, have spoken; Yes, I have called him, I have brought him, and his way will prosper' ... 'Come near to Me, hear this: I have not spoken in secret from the beginning; from the time that it was, I was there. And now the Lord God and His Spirit have sent Me.' Thus says the LORD, your Redeemer, the Holy One of Israel; I am the LORD your God ..." (Isa. 48:15-17).

"Surely, I am more stupid than any man, and do not have the understanding of a man. I neither learned wisdom nor have knowledge of the Holy One. Who has ascended into heaven, or descended? Who has gathered the wind in His fists? Who has bound the waters in a garment? Who has established all the ends of the earth? What is His name, and what is His Son's name, if you know?" (Prov. 30:2-4; John 3:13-16; Rom. 10:6-10; Deut. 30:11-15). Surely, the Everlasting Father (Isa. 9:6)—to be a Father—must have an "Everlasting Son"—otherwise, He would never have been called the Everlasting Father!

SECTION 5
ONE ELECT—DISTINCT BUT NOT SEPARATE

Whereas: The Holy Scriptures present separate names and terms of address for two prophetic entities, namely, the "House of Judah" (aka, the "Jews") and the "House of Israel OR Joseph/Ephraim" (aka, the "Elect"). Jesus, Paul, John, and Peter's use of the term "elect" in the ultimate climax of the ages is all-inclusive of both the House of Judah and the House of Israel—distinct, but not separated—altogether they constitute THE ELECT. The "Light to the Gentiles/Nations"—has shined on them that "sit in darkness"—the expansion of God's Elect is, in this sense, indistinguishable from the Elect from the House of Judah (Isa. 9:2; Matt. 4:16; Acts 26:18; John 8:12).

The House of Ephraim constitute His Elect today, as well, and together (both Houses) shall His angels "with a great sound of a trumpet . . . gather together His elect from the four winds, from one end of heaven to the other" (Matt. 24:31) "immediately after the tribulation of those days" (Matt. 24:29) when the "Sign of the Son of Man will appear in heaven . . . and they will see the Son of Man coming on the clouds of heaven with power and great glory" (Matt. 24:30).

Therefore, we are committed to look further into how they are distinct and different and yet how they are destined to become a single Elect fully harmonized and complementary to one another in the restoration of ALL Israel which is so prophesied. May the LORD give us greater insight! (See also: Isa. 11:12; 1 Chron. 16:13; Ps. 33:12; Ps. 105:6, 43; Ps. 135:4; Isa. 45:4; Isa. 65:9; Isa. 65:22; Rom. 9:24—"Even us He called, not of the Jews only, but also of the Nations?") May the LORD give us greater insight into His eternal plan and purpose for the ages . . . "According to the revelation of the mystery kept secret since the world began but now made manifest, and by the prophetic Scriptures made known to all nations, according to the commandment of the everlasting God, for obedience to the faith—to God, alone wise, be glory through Yeshua, the Anointed One, to whom be the glory forever. Amen" (Rom. 16:25-27). It is because of our immediate deliverance through the Messiah we are constrained to reconcile with the House of Judah—so making peace!

SECTION 6
JOSEPH'S ROLE IN THE GATHERING

The "Breach of Jeroboam" occurring after the death of King Solomon between King Rehoboam of the royal Jewish tribe of Judah [the Two Tribes of the south, and the Levites] and Jeroboam, the leader of the Ten Tribes of Israel, split Israel into two kingdoms (1 Kings 11:26-43; 12:1-33; 2 Chron. 10:1-19; 11:1-4). We recognize that a strident law vs. grace dichotomy was the root cause of this breach and has led to what has become a family feud, even a blood feud, and that out of the darkness of ignorance of this biblical history, and due to the "religious traditions and ordinances" of men—a multitude of spurious teachings/doctrines, demanding eternal separation between both houses of Israel, has spawned anti-Semitism within the House of Ephraim toward the House of Judah; while engendering fearful suspicion within the House of Judah toward the House of Joseph (i.e., the House of Ephraim), leading to acrimonious and grievous histories between the two factions of Israel and their isolation one from the other ever since that time (nigh 3,000 years).

NOTWITHSTANDING—OUR JOSEPH WILL DELIVER: We, of "the Stick of Joseph [i.e., the Shepherd of Israel—Psa. 80:1], which is in the hand of Ephraim and the tribes of Israel, his companions" (Ezek. 37:19) have come to terms with what we affirm to be the "divine order" and our mutual, prophetic destiny in harmony with the Stick and Scepter of Righteousness, in Shiloh, of Judah. For the One to whom the scepter belongs, the Son of David Who sits upon the throne of David in the royal Jewish House of Judah, the Lion of the Tribe of Judah, our Messiah and King, the sovereign to whom we owe our ultimate allegiance—sits, as Joseph, before both Houses. Yet, as well, seated before Joseph are those (Egyptians) from among the nations for he has "saved us all" (Gen. 47:13-26). Now, at the "time of the end" the Shepherd of Israel at the darkest hour will go out to save the last of His lost sheep (Gen. 49:24).

Indeed, we all sit before Joseph incognizant of His role in the end-time ingathering of the "fullness of the Nations be come in" (Rom. 11:25—the MELO HAGOYIM)—for we all have been "theologically quarantined" to the extent we—those saved out from among the nations under the blood of the New Covenant—sit with Joseph among His brethren (Gen. 43:32).

Alas! Neither do the Ten Tribes, even Judah, consider they all sit before Joseph! In this "spiritual house of the redeemed" sitting before Joseph—this archetype of Messiah, the Shepherd-King holding both the rod and the staff . . . the One "ministering and ruling" in the dual office of the Order of Melchizedek—is "seen in a mirror, dimly" (1 Cor. 13:12). Nevertheless, the time is fast upon us where the alienation and isolation of "them by themselves, and the Egyptians who ate with him by themselves" will be ended—but only when our Joseph can no longer hold back his love, his identity—for now we "know in part"—but when "that which is perfect is come then shall we know, even as we are known"—"now abide faith, hope and love—but the greatest of these is love!" (1 Cor. 13:13) . . . then it shall be fulfilled: "The [jealous] envy also of Ephraim shall depart, and the [anti-Semitic] adversaries of Judah shall be cut off: Ephraim shall not envy Judah, and Judah shall not [harass] vex Ephraim (Isa. 11:13).

What immediacy awaits the House of Ephraim! Are we not designated the "watchmen upon the mount?" "For there shall be a day, [that] the watchmen upon the mount Ephraim shall cry, Arise ye, and let us go up to Zion unto the LORD our God" (Jer. 31:6).

Is there not divine revelation seen in John's Gospel when:

"Caiaphas, being high priest that year, said to them ... 'It is expedient for us that one man should die for the people'" ... "Now this he did not say on his own authority; but being high priest that year he prophesied that Jesus would die for the nation, and not for that nation only [Judah], but also that he would gather together in one the children of God who were scattered abroad ... Therefore, Jesus no longer walked openly among the Jews, but went from there into the country near the wilderness, to a city called Ephraim" (John 11:49-54).

Yes, "Then the Assyrian oppressed them [mainly Ephraim into captivity] ... 'Now therefore, what have I here,' says the LORD, 'That My people are taken away for nothing? Those who rule over them make them wail,' says the LORD, 'And My name is blasphemed continually every day. Therefore, My people shall know My name; therefore they shall know in that day that I am He who speaks: 'Behold, it is I.'"—"How beautiful upon the mountains are the feet of him who brings good news, who proclaims peace, who brings glad tidings of good things, who proclaims salvation, who says to Zion, 'Your God reigns!'" (Isa. 52:4-7; Rom. 10:15).

Yes, again, the reconciliation lies before both Houses: "Thy watchmen shall lift up the voice; with the voice together shall they sing: for they shall see EYE TO EYE, when the LORD shall bring again Zion—[for] I have set watchmen upon thy walls, O Jerusalem, [which] shall never hold their peace day nor night: ye that make mention of the LORD, keep not silence (Isa. 52:8; 62:6).

SECTION 7
EDOM'S ROLE IN REPAIRING THE BREACH

The exhortation given to us in Isaiah 58 in the context of sacrifice for others now commends us all to be "repairers of the breach" not only "between the two" but within Judah and within the lost house of Israel out from among the Nations. Furthermore, that a contributory cause of this "breach" was recognized by the early Ekklesia in Acts 15 as a "yoke" of expansive legalism not based upon the Ten Commandments as written in the Torah but based upon the traditional oral law of the rabbinical priesthood (viz., *"the law of commandments contained in ordinances"*— Eph. 2:15) known in Greek as dogma—Strong's G#1378 ... "an opinion or judgment"—Col. 2:14:

"Having wiped out the handwriting of requirements ["ordinances" or "dogma"] that was against us, which was contrary to us. And He has taken it out of the way, having nailed it to the cross."

This dogma arose in earnest after the Babylonian Captivity of Judah. All these "ceremonial ordinances" were "a shadow of things to come, but the body [i.e., the tangible substance] is of Christ [Messiah/Anointed One]"—Col. 2:17.

Now, through the "Gospel" the enmity between Judah and the nations has been "abolished," and in its place there is to be an issuing forth in the United Kingdom of David (aka, "Tabernacle of David")* in fulfillment of Amos 9:11-12—a New Covenant of Peace which is extended out as an invitation inclusive of those coming to Messiah from "the rest of mankind." "Mankind" is used in Acts 15:17—quoting from Amos 9:11-12 where the word "Edom" is used instead of "mankind" in that the Septuagint translates the Hebrew word as "Edom" or "Adam"—shedding greater light upon the House of Obed-Edom, the servant of Edom, who was greatly blessed when the Ark of the Covenant did abide in his threshing floor for three months until Obed-Edom and some 69 other "Edomites" became the gatekeepers in the Tabernacle of David—joining themselves to the 12 Tribes of Israel (2 Sam. 6:11; 1 Chron. 15:18, 24-25; 26:4-8, 12, 15).

SECTION 8
DISTINCTION BETWEEN JUDAH AND SCATTERED ISRAEL

Whereas: The biblical and historical evidence is clear that the lost "House of Israel" are the ten northern tribes who were taken captive by the Assyrians and dispersed between 745-712 B.C. throughout the Assyrian Empire stretching from Ethiopia throughout modern Turkey, Iran and most of the Middle East. We commend the research presented by pioneers of Judah/Ephraim understanding, researchers and authors on the lost tribes of Israel like Yair Davidiy and Steven Collins who detail the "swallowing up of Ephraim" among the nations (Hos. 8:7-10); yet, their undeniable physicality is indeed prophetically breathtaking.

Thus, the Northern Kingdom never returned to the land with the returning captives of Judah in sufficient numbers to establish sovereignty, either with Ezra in cir. 537 B.C. (i.e., at the Decree of

Cyrus the Great–Ezra 1:1; 2 Chron. 36:22-23; Dan. 6:28; 10:1–the Babylonian Captivity extending from 608-537 B.C.–Daniel 9:24-27), 185 years later (Fall of Israel's Northern Kingdom to Assyria in 722 B.C. unto 537 B.C.), nor with Nehemiah in 445 B.C. (Neh. 2:1—Persian King Artaxerxes Longimanus), some 277 years later.

Therefore, the current Jewish house, as the royal Jewish House of Judah with Benjamin and elements of Levi, were the only significant portions of Israel who returned from Babylonian captivity. Consequently, we affirm the former post-exilic Kingdom of Judah returning to rebuild Jerusalem as a small city-state under Medo-Persia never did absorb the lost ten tribes of the House of Israel who were literally "swallowed up" by the Nations* (aka, the Gentiles—Hos. 8:7-10—they were at least ten of the "twelve tribes scattered abroad"—James 1:1). The biblical and anthropological history of the Ten Tribes is quite clear in that very few ever re-entered the land with the House of Judah, and never in any sovereign way as the House of Israel. There is little biblical or historical record of any merit providing justifying evidence, beyond a sprinkling of individuals among the Ten Northern Tribes who ever returned to the land.

Furthermore, the Jews at the time of Christ spoke of those "dispersed among the Gentiles" (John 7:35) or John's declaration as "the children of God who were scattered abroad" (John 11:52); and Josephus in (Ant., 11:133) stated as a fact that "the ten tribes are beyond the Euphrates till now, and are an immense multitude and not to be estimated in numbers."

SECTION 9
EXHORTATION AGAINST REBELLION AND TREACHERY

Whereas: The root cause of animosity/enmity between the House of Judah (i.e., the Jewish house) and the nations (with the "Elect of Israel" being called out from among the Gentiles/Nations) was a disagreement over the pre-eminence of Law vs. Grace and was further aggravated at the Breach of Jeroboam by a rebellious attitude found among the ten tribes and by an unrelenting YOKE of bondage imposed by the royal House of David upon the ten tribes at the time (viz., that "yoke" being taxation and exploitation of labor) which resulted in what is known specifically (today) as "anti-Semitism" but actually at its root being a lawless and rebellious, anti-Jewish, anti-throne of David, anti-Son of David, Anti-Messiah, Antichrist spirit.

Indeed, this has caused the lost tribes to go to the princes of Europe like Gomer with her lovers in search for defenders of the faith (Hos. 1:2-5), thereby entering into covenant with them in a post-Nicene Nicolaitan, hierarchical, Dominionist spirit, thereby engendering an attitude of "Christian superiority" leading doctrinally to "rejection/replacement theology" to justify such superiority AND this being exacerbated by *"the law of commandments contained in ordinances"* from the Jewish side—notwithstanding the "work of the cross"—this "breach" needs an agonizing reappraisal by both Houses—Judah and Israel— to address such grievous persistence and to discover an open door to the divinely prescribed remedy that is to be found in the New Covenant with the indwelling Christ/Messiah committed to writing His laws upon the fleshy tables of our hearts (Jer. 31:33; Ezek. 11:19-20; 18:30-32; 36:24-26; 2 Cor. 3:3).

SECTION 10
THE SINAITIC COVENANT OF RELATIONSHIP AND OBEDIENCE

Whereas: Discernment between the Law and God's relationship with Israel at Mt. Sinai is essential for understanding the Old and New Covenants. Jeremiah acknowledged "The covenant that I made with their fathers in the day that I took them by the hand to lead them out of the land of Egypt, My covenant which they broke, though I was a HUSBAND to them," says the Lord (Jer. 31:32). Witnesses to this marital relationship include: "She is not My wife, nor am I her Husband!" (Hos. 2:2a); and multiple references to adultery, "putting away," and divorcing the House of Israel. "Then I saw that for all the causes for which backsliding Israel had committed adultery, I had put her away and given her a certificate of divorce; yet her treacherous sister Judah did not fear, but went and played the harlot also" (Jer. 3:8). As with traditional marriage vows, God expected faithfulness and obedience to His commandments: "If you will indeed obey My voice and keep My covenant, then you shall be a special treasure to Me above all people; for all the earth is Mine" (Ex. 19:5).

God promised the relationship would be restored: "And it shall be, in that day," says the Lord, "That you will call Me 'My Husband'" ..."I will betroth you to Me forever"..."Then I will say to those who were not My people, 'You are My people!' and they shall say, 'You are my God!'" (Hos. 2:16a; 19a; 23b). However, God's own instructions for righteousness prohibited such a remarriage: "They say, 'If a man divorces his wife, and she goes from him and becomes another man's, may he return to her again?' Would not that land be greatly polluted?" (Jer. 3:1). "Then her former husband who divorced her must not take her back to be his wife after she has been defiled; for that is an abomination before the Lord" (Deut. 24:4a).

Death and resurrection was God's solution for cleansing the defiled relationship and rejoining Israel. "HUSBANDS, love your wives, just as Christ also loved the Church and GAVE HIMSELF for her, that He might SANCTIFY and CLEANSE her . . ." the two shall become one flesh" (Eph. 5:25-32). Furthermore, Romans Ch. 7 alludes to the death of the husband: "For the woman who has a husband is bound by the law to her husband as long as he lives. But if the husband dies, she is released from the law of her husband . . . she is free from that law, so that she is no adulteress" (Rom. 7:2-3).

"Therefore...you also have become dead to the law [of her husband c.f. Rom. 7:2] through the body of Christ, that you may be married to another–to Him who was raised from the dead..." (Rom. 7:4). Restoring the relationship by satisfying (fulfilling) the "law of the husband" did not diminish God's expectations of faithfulness and obedience from His bride. "Therefore the law is holy, and the commandment holy and just and good" (Rom. 7:12).

Yeshua's death on the cross annulled the divorce certificate with the House of Israel and also annulled Judah's marriage contract with Yahweh allowing both the House of Judah and the House of Israel to also have a New Covenant with Yahweh. "Behold, the days are coming," says Yahweh, "when I will make a new covenant with the House of Israel and with the House of Judah" (Jer. 31:31). "Now, therefore, you are no longer strangers and foreigners, but fellow citizens with the saints and members of the household of God" (Eph. 2:14-19).

Section 11
The Synthesis of Law and Grace

Whereas: There persists a fundamental misunderstanding concerning "Law and Grace" and a biased favoring of one over the other by each of the two houses and among "God's People"—We affirm: Jesus did not come to "abolish the Law" but to "fulfill the Law" and that the "law of commandments contained in ordinances" serving a rabbinical priesthood as an external policing authority is NOT the Law written in the hearts on tablets of flesh (Jer. 31:31). The Law that is written upon tablets of flesh operating from within, is even now guiding the saints on their pilgrimage in the gentle bond of love, thereby revealing the very "Character of God" that makes accommodation for "Grace." This is the "Law of Messiah"—the "Law of the Spirit of Life" (1 Cor. 9:21; Rom. 8:2). This reflection of God's character is expressed to the nations—this inner work of the indwelling Torah, the Living Word of God administered personally by the indwelling Messiah from His throne in the hearts of believers everywhere was exemplified by Jesus/Yeshua at the Passover Seder/Upper Room when He inaugurated the New Covenant (Jer. 31:31) wherein "The Law of Christ" (the Messiah) is at work in believers today (Gal. 6:2; I Cor. 9:21). Even so, the New Commandment given to us is commensurate with the New Covenant in His blood; to wit: "A new commandment I give unto you, that you love one another; as I have loved you, that you also love one another" (John 13:34).

Section 12
End-Time Witness to One Messiah

The end-time "raging of the nations"* (Ps. 2) targets all "God's People"—inclusive of all true Christians who will join the Jewish House in affirming that the Jewish Messiah is likewise their own Messiah, the God of Truth, and the God of Righteous Law, Who from His throne shall "laugh and have the nations in derision." Yes, in counter distinction to the Coming of Messiah is the coming of the "Lawless One"—the "Son of Perdition" who shall be "consumed with the breath of His [Messiah's] mouth and destroyed with the brightness of His coming" (Ps. 2; 2 Thess. 2:8). Therefore, the final "conflict of the ages"—as the nations rage against Zion . . . for they do not know they gather against the Lord and against His Messiah—so, He shall bring forth His Witnesses to the nations "who keep the commandments of God and have the Testimony of Jesus" (Rev. 14:12)—these are the Two Olive Trees and the Two Lampstands who stand before the Lord of the whole earth (Rev. 11:4; Zech. 4). Divine Judgment shall issue forth in the manifestation of His Kingdom upon the earth (Zech. 14).

SECTION 13
PERSECUTION AND REVIVAL OF THE WHOLE HOUSE OF ISRAEL

Whereas: True "Biblical Christians" in the tens of millions have suffered throughout the centuries and have closely identified with similar persecutions of their Jewish brethren and will be seen, as well, within the final trials of the future 70th Week of Daniel. This mutual companionship will become more evident as both houses of Israel/Jacob gather together in Messiah even in the refining and the awakenings which will occur at the time of "Jacob's Trouble" on this spiritual pilgrimage from "Jacob, the heel, the trickster," making the transition to "Israel, prince, and contender with God." ("Many shall be purified, made white, and refined"—Dan. 12:10); nevertheless, being kept, preserved, and saved (Gr. "ek"), in, through, and out of, the hour of trial with the promise being that "a remnant shall return" even as Israel was preserved in the first Passover in Egypt and "carried on eagle's wings" at that time of the first exodus (Ex. 19:4). (*"And at that time your people shall be delivered, every one who is found written in the book"*—Dan. 12:1). Moreover, concomitant with our mutual refinement and preservation is our mutual revival—the "Valley of Dry Bones" (Ezek. 37:1-14).

These dry bones do not solely represent the House of Judah but "the whole house of Israel" (Ezek. 37:11, 16). It is time the House of Israel (Ephraim) come to grips with the prophesied collaborative revival—for BOTH Houses are sorely in need of this great end-times' revival: "So I prophesied as He commanded me, and breath came into them, and they lived, and stood upon their feet, an exceedingly great army . . . these bones are the whole house of Israel" (Ezek. 37:10-11). Therefore, we outright reject the notion that "Jacob's Trouble" is solely directed at the House of Judah— NO, Jacob's trouble includes the Whole House of Israel—we are all identified in Jacob's Trouble and consequent revival!

SECTION 14
ABRAHAM'S SEED SOWN AMONG THE NATIONS

Whereas: Abraham was shown the myriad company of the redeemed as a starry host as numerous as the stars of heaven—a nation and a MELO-HAGOYIM, a vast multitude called out of the heathen nations, and that in this myriad company kings were to come out of the Seed of Abraham,* with that Seed being singular (Gal. 3:29);—the promised "S"eed of Abraham within his loins being Christ (our Isaac)—the Messiah Who is the Progenitor of Abraham's family of faith, even the "Author and the Finisher of our faith" (Heb.12:2).

The primary prophecy of Moses in Deuteronomy over the prophetic destiny of the Twelve Tribes of Israel declares that supreme blessing upon Joseph—even "the blessing [shall] come on the head of Joseph, and on the crown of the head of him who was separate from his brothers . . . his glory is like a firstborn bull, and his horns like the horns of the wild ox; together with them he shall push the peoples to the ends of the earth; they are the ten thousands of Ephraim, and they are the thousands of Manasseh" (Deut. 33:16-17)—declares Ephraim's prophetic role, like a two-horned bull, pressing the peoples to the ends of the earth. There would be Ephraim's "ten thousands" indicative of the Gospel of the Grace of God reaching billions of souls who have come to the saving faith and knowledge of the One True God through Messiah's First Coming, even as they eagerly await His Second Coming.

SECTION 15
GATHERING ISRAEL—INCLUDING THE GENTILES

Whereas: The end-time agenda of Yehovah-God is to "gather together into One the children of God who were scattered abroad" (John 11:52) which includes all TWELVE TRIBES OF ISRAEL, who in Isaiah 49:6 are called in Messiah, His Head and His Body to be His Servant and a Light to the Nations in extending His DELIVERANCE /SALVATION to the ends of the earth; moreover, this charge is amplified in its broader Hebraic context in the Savior's Great Commission: "Go ye into all the world and make disciples of all the nations."* (Matt. 28:18-20). This will be fully realized at the end of the saga during the final gathering of that great company of the redeemed numbered in the 12 Tribes, a spiritual household from every nation, race, and tribe as per the vision John saw in Revelation 7 (inclusive of the "12 Tribes of Israel" (Rev. 7:1-8) and that vast multitude that no man can number found in Revelation 7:9-17 –i.e., "the rest of mankind") and ultimately expressed as the Holy District—the Bride of the Lamb, the New Jerusalem (Ezek. 40-48; Rev. 21).

SECTION 16
RESTORING GRACE, PEACE, AND UNITY

Whereas: The eternal plan and purpose of Yehovah-God is manifested in the Gospel of the Grace of God, for His Servant, Who is the Messiah, to heal the partial blindness, or partial hardening* in both houses of Israel, recovering the broken staffs of Beauty (Favor/Grace) and Bonds (Unity)* (Zechariah 11:10-11), to join together as the two sticks of Joseph and Judah, and to consummate in One Body—One New Man*—from out of both Jew and Gentile companies—through the preaching of "this Gospel of the Kingdom to all the world"—bringing about a great end-time harvest of souls, all of whom are destined to be refined, reconciled, reunited, and restored as "All Israel"—ultimately, saved and delivered by the Deliverer Who shall come out of Zion (Rom. 11:26). Furthermore, embedded within the Gospel's message is not only the Gospel of the Grace of God (as clearly delineated in Romans 1-8 in reference to one's personal salvation; also: Acts 20:24); moreover, the Gospel of Peace (Romans 9-16) illuminates the ultimate purpose of the Almighty: "How beautiful are the feet of those who preach the gospel of peace, who bring glad tidings of good things!" (Rom. 10:15; Isa. 52:7; Nah. 1:15). The "fullness" (or "completion") of the blessing of the gospel of Christ (Rom. 15:29) is predicated upon Romans 11:31: "For God has committed them all to disobedience, that He might have mercy on all." Yes, upon BOTH HOUSES. "He has made of the two One New Man, so MAKING PEACE" (Eph. 2:16). This is "the TRUTH of the Gospel" which we are called to be "straightforward" in our practice (Gal. 2:14)—the "elect" from the House of Judah (the Jew), the House of Ephraim (those "scattered among the Gentiles"); and the "rest of mankind" (Edom) NOW constitute the Household of God—"For the Scripture says, 'Whoever believes on Him will not be put to shame.' For there is no distinction between Jew and Greek, for the same Lord over all is rich to all who call upon Him. For 'whoever calls on the name of the LORD shall be saved'" (Rom. 10:11-13). Therefore, we preach that all men be reconciled to God and to one another through the God of Peace

(Rom. 15:33) . . . for the answer to our Lord's prayer in John 17 "that they all may be one" is the preaching of the Kingdom of God (Acts 28:31; Rom. 14:17). Prophetically: "I will cut a covenant of peace with them, and it shall be an everlasting covenant with them" (Ezek. 37:26-28) bespeaks of that time "I will set My sanctuary in their midst forevermore . . . My tabernacle also shall be with them; indeed, I will be their God, and they shall be My people. The nations also will know that I, the LORD, sanctify Israel, when My sanctuary is in their midst forevermore." It is time to preach the "Fullness" (or "Completion") of the Gospel—GRACE and PEACE. For if unity can and should take place between the most divided (Jew and Gentile), then all other divisions are readily resolved: "That the world may know that You have sent me" (John 17:34). Moreover, Paul's final injunction whereby "Satan's head will be crushed under our feet shortly" (Rom. 16:20)–by the very "God of Peace"–is for all God's people to "meet and greet" one another–we ask: Isn't it time for all God's children to heed Paul's injunction and to "meet and greet" one another WITHOUT PARTIALITY (Rom. 16; 2:11; Gal. 2:6)? Furthermore, would not that include Ephraim to start meeting and greeting those of the House of Judah? We affirm so!

SECTION 17
THE DUAL OFFICE OF MESSIAH

Whereas: The dual office of Messiah is established forever in the Order of Melchizedek; He being BOTH High Priest of God Most High and King of Salem or Prince of Peace—this is affirmed and declared in Psalm 110:4; therefore, this dual office provides the solid biblical basis for the reconciliation and the reunion of the two houses of Israel under Messiah.

SECTION 18
A ROYAL AND PRIESTLY EKKLESIA

Whereas: The biblical evidence of the eventual combining of the two houses of Israel as a single reconciled, reunified, restored covenant people of Yehovah-God is stated by Moses in Exodus 19:6 and restated by the apostle Peter in 1 Peter 2:9; NOT as a purely Jewish royal nation and holy priesthood/Church, but as both Moses and Peter have used similar expressions, very deliberately, and very tellingly via a cross-linking phraseology: "A royal priesthood and a holy nation" and "A kingdom of priests and a holy nation."

SECTION 19
TWO WITNESSES, TWO ANOINTINGS

Finally: The prophet Zechariah* (Zech. 4) saw the two olive trees in the dual anointing of King and High Priest feeding the oil of anointing into the seven lamps that are the menorah of Israel—today's National Shield of Israel–and was told that these are the two anointed ones who stand before the God of the whole earth. Similarly, the apostle John (Rev.11:4) in a vision was told that God's two witnesses were two olive trees and two lampstands who stand before the God of the earth; furthermore, that two angels are seen over the Ark of the Covenant . . . even so, the Jewish women light the two Sabbath candles on the eve of Shabbat with a Sabbath prayer, heralding the glorious unity of the two anointings in the Millennial Thousand-Year Sabbath yet to come—altogether, this is in full harmony with the prayer of Yeshua/Jesus in John 17:21 when He prayed this prayer for unity among ALL His covenant people.

"THAT THEY MAY BE ONE; even as you, Father, are in Me, and I in You, that they also may be in Us, that the world may believe that you sent Me."

Read or sign the Declaration online:
https://commonwealththeology.com/the-denver-declaration

The Denver Declaration available at Amazon:
https://www.amazon.com/dp/B07WQZ1L7D

ABOUT THE AUTHORS

Doug Krieger
Author, Publisher, RTD. Public School Administrator

Doug Krieger is a Rtd. Public High School Teacher and Administrator. He is the publisher of Tribnet Publications and has authored 11 books and co-authored 7 books. He currently serves on the Board of One Body Life and is the chair of the COMMONWEALTH OF ISRAEL FOUNDATION—which is also a publication house as well as the on-going production of the "Commonwealth Foundation Reference Bible" (NASV). Doug is a frequent conference speaker and organizer of conferences throughout North America and other parts of the world (primarily, Nigeria, Africa). Doug's articles appear at www.commonwealththeology.com and many other web sites (e.g., www.onebody.life—Blog Articles)... Doug and Debbie have been married for over fifty years, with three children and a growing number of grandchildren. He currently resides in Sacramento, California. Doug can be reached through www.onebody.life

Dr. Douglas Hamp, M.A., PhD.
Author, Lecturer, Senior Pastor at The Way Congregation

Douglas Hamp earned his M.A. in The Bible and Its World from the Hebrew University of Jerusalem and his PhD in Biblical Studies from Louisiana Baptist University. He served as an assistant pastor at Calvary Chapel Costa Mesa for six years, where he lectured and developed curriculum at the School of Ministry, Spanish School of Ministry and Calvary Chapel Bible College Graduate School. He is the author of numerous books, articles, and DVDs and has appeared on national and international TV, radio, and internet programs in English and in Spanish. He is senior pastor of the Way Congregation in Wheat Ridge, CO.

About the Authors

Gavin Finley MD Rtd

Currently, Dr. Finley serves on the Board of Directors for the Commonwealth Foundation in preparation for the publication of the Commonwealth of Israel Reference Bible. He is a prolific blogger (www.endtimepilgrim.com) and is now a retired Medical Doctor living in Pensacola, Florida with his beloved wife, Mary. He is also a frequent guest speaker at Christian conferences across the fruited plain! In Dr. Finley's own words:

I am an Australian evangelical Christian of pre-millennialist persuasion. I grew up and received my schooling back and forth from Australia, Canada, and the USA. My salvation came at the age of 14 at a Bible Camp organized by men from Highlands Community Church in Renton, Washington near Seattle. It was one of the Independent Fundamentalist Churches of America. Pastor Wallace Wilson and a wonderful circle of friends at the Church were all a great influence in our lives. We still keep in touch with some of our friends there 40 years later.

I returned to Australia in 1965 and studied at Trinity Grammar School and Balwyn High School in Melbourne. My studies then took me on to the University of Melbourne Medical School on a Commonwealth Scholarship. I graduated in Medicine in 1973. During those years our family was part of the East Kew Baptist Church in Melbourne. I was also a member of the Evangelical Union at Melbourne Uni.

The remainder of Dr. Finley's bio and journey can be viewed at: http://www.endtimepilgrim.org/bio.htm

Chris Steinle
Author, Christian Philosopher, Former Minister, CPA—RET.

Chris Steinle is a recognized Bible prophecy commentator as a guest and co-host on alternative media as well as the author of more than ten books. (C. W.) Steinle began his professional career as a CPA. The ability to analyze and organized information is crucial in rightly dividing the Word of God. As a layman and ordained minister Steinle has taught thousands of original Bible studies, as well as providing biblical guidance to singles, couples, and families. Chris has taught on location in Israel, Philippi, Thessaloniki, Corinth, Athens, and Egypt. Currently he is intensely vested in the Commonwealth of Israel Foundation and the production of a Commonwealth Reference Bible featuring Commonwealth Theology.

About the Commonwealth of Israel Foundation

The Commonwealth of Israel Foundation is a non-profit religious charitable organization. Please visit CommonwealthOfIsrael.com or .org for details about the Foundation's formation, purpose and goals.

Around the time Douglas Krieger released his book on Commonwealth Theology in early 2018 it became apparent within the burgeoning Commonwealth of Israel Movement that a reference-notes study Bible would be advantageous. Indeed, Protestant/Reformed and Dispensation Theology—the immediate predecessors to Commonwealth Theology—both disseminated their views to the pulpit through the publication of reference Bibles; the Geneva Study Bible and the Scofield Reference Bible, respectively.

Thus this Foundation was birthed with its primary educational objective being the production of an annotated reference/study-notes Bible. The Bible will present readers with a comprehensive application of Commonwealth Theology to the sixty-six canonical books generally accepted as inspired Scriptures.

The Commonwealth of Israel Foundation may also produce, or cause to be produced for the purpose of biblical education, reference or annotated New Testaments, Bible commentaries on individual books of the Bible, commentary sets, original translations of the Bible, and other forms of biblical education which would further our educational and public awareness objectives.

All proceeds from the sale of this publication will be applied toward the purposes of the Commonwealth of Israel Foundation.

Please consider further supporting the Foundation at our website CommonwealthOfIsrael.com/.org, or at the address below. If you have questions or comments please contact us:

info@commonwealthofisrael.org

Or write:

    Commonwealth of Israel Foundation
    P.O. Box 31007
    Phoenix, AZ 85046

Also find us on Facebook:
https://www.facebook.com/commonwealthofisraelfoundation